T0145093

Advances in Intelligent Systems and Computing

Volume 710

Series editor

Janusz Kacprzyk, Polish Academy of Sciences, Warsaw, Poland
e-mail: kacprzyk@ibspan.waw.pl

The series "Advances in Intelligent Systems and Computing" contains publications on theory, applications, and design methods of Intelligent Systems and Intelligent Computing. Virtually all disciplines such as engineering, natural sciences, computer and information science, ICT, economics, business, e-commerce, environment, healthcare, life science are covered. The list of topics spans all the areas of modern intelligent systems and computing such as: computational intelligence, soft computing including neural networks, fuzzy systems, evolutionary computing and the fusion of these paradigms, social intelligence, ambient intelligence, computational neuroscience, artificial life, virtual worlds and society, cognitive science and systems, Perception and Vision, DNA and immune based systems, self-organizing and adaptive systems, e-Learning and teaching, human-centered and human-centric computing, recommender systems, intelligent control, robotics and mechatronics including human-machine teaming, knowledge-based paradigms, learning paradigms, machine ethics, intelligent data analysis, knowledge management, intelligent agents, intelligent decision making and support, intelligent network security, trust management, interactive entertainment, Web intelligence and multimedia.

The publications within "Advances in Intelligent Systems and Computing" are primarily proceedings of important conferences, symposia and congresses. They cover significant recent developments in the field, both of a foundational and applicable character. An important characteristic feature of the series is the short publication time and world-wide distribution. This permits a rapid and broad dissemination of research results.

More information about this series at http://www.springer.com/series/11156

Prasant Kumar Pattnaik
Siddharth Swarup Rautaray
Himansu Das · Janmenjoy Nayak
Editors

Progress in Computing, Analytics and Networking

Proceedings of ICCAN 2017

 Springer

Editors
Prasant Kumar Pattnaik
School of Computer Engineering
KIIT University
Bhubaneswar, Odisha
India

Himansu Das
School of Computer Engineering
KIIT University
Bhubaneswar, Odisha
India

Siddharth Swarup Rautaray
School of Computer Engineering
KIIT University
Bhubaneswar, Odisha
India

Janmenjoy Nayak
Department of Computer Science
    and Engineering
Sri Sivani College of Engineering
Srikakulam, Andhra Pradesh
India

ISSN 2194-5357   ISSN 2194-5365   (electronic)
Advances in Intelligent Systems and Computing
ISBN 978-981-10-7870-5   ISBN 978-981-10-7871-2   (eBook)
https://doi.org/10.1007/978-981-10-7871-2

Library of Congress Control Number: 2017963526

Printed on acid-free paper

This Springer imprint is published by the registered company Springer Nature Singapore Pte Ltd. part of Springer Nature
The registered company address is: 152 Beach Road, #21-01/04 Gateway East, Singapore 189721, Singapore

Preface

The International Conference on Computing, Analytics and Networking (ICCAN 2017) is organized by the School of Computer Engineering, KIIT University, Bhubaneswar, India, during December 15–16, 2017. ICCAN focuses on three broad areas of computer science, viz. computing, analytics and networking. The objective of this international conference is to provide a platform for researchers, academicians, industry personals and practitioners to interact and exchange ideas, experience and expertise in the current trends and strategies for computing, analytics and networking.

In response to the call for submissions, ICCAN 2017 received more than 330 papers from authors of different countries. Subsequently, after a rigorous peer review process with the help of program committee members and external reviewers from different countries around the globe, 79 papers are accepted for presentation and publication based on relevance to the conference theme and quality of technical contents with an acceptance ratio of below 25%. We could not also accommodate many promising works as we tried to ensure the highest quality. The articles presented in this volume of the proceedings discuss the cutting-edge technologies and recent advances in the domain of the conference. First and foremost are the authors whose works have made the conference a great success. We wish to thank all the PC members for their hard work, dedication and timely submission of the reviews without which it would have been difficult to maintain the publication schedule.

The technical program also included invited lectures by several distinguished personalities like Sudip Misra (Indian Institute of Technology, Kharagpur, India), Shekhar Verma (Indian Institute of Information Technology, Allahabad) and many more. We express our sincere thanks to all the invited speakers for accepting our invitation to share their expertise.

Our sincere thanks to Achyuta Samanta (Founder of KISS & KIIT University), H. K. Mohanty (Vice Chancellor, KIIT University), Sasmita Samanta (Registrar, KIIT University) and Samaresh Mishra (Dean, School of Computer Engineering, KIIT University) for their excellent support and encouragement in organizing this international event. We are indebted to the Advisory Committee members for their constant guidance and support.

I would like to thank all the program chairs, organizing chairs, session chairs, publicity chairs, publication chairs, track managers, organizing committee, staff of School of Computer Engineering and all members of various committees. Our special thanks to D. N. Dwivedy for his valuable advice and wholehearted involvement in all activities.

We wish to acknowledge and thank all the authors for their scholarly contributions to the conference, which evoked interesting discussions during the technical sessions. Our thanks to all the technical session chairs for managing the sessions effectively. We acknowledge the service rendered by EasyChair for efficient and smooth handling of the activities. We sincerely thank Anil Chandy, Director, and Harmen van Paradijs, Managing Director of Springer, for their cooperation and constant support all through the publication process of this AISC volume.

Last but not least, we thank all the participants and people who directly or indirectly contributed toward making ICCAN 2017 a memorable event.

Bhubaneswar, India   Prasant Kumar Pattnaik
Bhubaneswar, India   Siddharth Swarup Rautaray
Bhubaneswar, India   Himansu Das
Srikakulam, India   Janmenjoy Nayak

Organizing Committee

Advisory Committee

Rajkumar Buyya, FIEEE, The University of Melbourne, Australia
Prasant Mohapatra, FIEEE, University of California, USA
Mohammad S. Obaidat, FIEEE, Fordham University, USA
Vincenzo Piuri, FIEEE, University of Milano, Italy
Carlos A. Coello Coello, FIEEE, CINVESTAV, Mexico
Shekhar Verma, IIIT Allahabad, India
Valentina Emilia Balas, Aurel Vlaicu University of Arad, Romania
Tirthankar Gayen, Jawaharlal Nehru University, India
Dilip Kumar Partihary, IIT Kharagpur, India
Sasmita Samanta, KIIT University, India
Joao Manuel R. S. Tavares, Universidade do Porto, Portugal
Abhaprakash Praharaj, Tata Consultancy Services Limited, Germany
Nilanjan Dey, Techno India College of Technology, India
Sanjeevikumar Padmanaban, University of Johannesburg, South Africa
Ganapati Panda, IIT Bhubaneswar, India
Kenji Suzuki, Illinois Institute of Technology, USA
Pabitra Pal Choudhury, ISI Kolkata, India
Andrey V. Savchenko, National Research University Higher School of Economics, Russia
Rajib Mall, IIT Kharagpur, India
Kuan-Ching Li, Providence University, Taiwan
Bidyut B. Chaudhuri, LFIEEE, Indian Statistical Institute Kolkata, India
Goutam Chakraborty, Iwate Prefectural University, Japan
Pramod Kumar Meher, NTU, Singapore
Ishwar K. Sethi, Oakland University, Rochester, MI
Raj Jain, LFIEEE, Washington University, USA
P. N. Suganthan, NTU, Singapore
Sagar Naik, University of Waterloo, Canada

Ujjwal Maulik, FNAE, Jadavpur University, India
Dhiya AL-Jumeily, Liverpool John Moores University, UK
Anupam Agrawal, IIIT Allahabad, India
Hugo Pedro Proenca, University of Beira Interior, Portugal
L. M. Patnaik, INSA Senior Scientist, IISc Bangalore, India
Hrushikesha Mohanty, KIIT University, India
Tandra Pal, NIT Durgapur, India
Xiao-Zhi Gao, Aalto University, Finland
Prabhat Kumar Mahanti, University of New Brunswick, Canada
Swapan Bhattacharya, Jadavpur University, India
Prashant Pillai, University of Bradford, UK
Arun K. Somani, Iowa State University, Ames, IA
R. V. Rajakumar, Director, IIT Bhubaneswar, India
Ashok Deshpande, University of California, Berkeley, USA
Amitava Chatterjee, Jadavpur University, India
Malay K. Kundu, ISI Kolkata, India
Sushil K. Prasad, Georgia State University, USA
Nabanita Das, ISI Kolkata, India
B. K. Panigrahi, IIT Delhi, India

Program Committee

Wenwu Wang, University of Surrey, UK
Padmalochan Bera, IIT Bhubaneswar, India
Ashutosh Bhatia, BITS Pilani, India
Pierluigi Siano, Universita degli Studi di Salerno, Italy
D. Janakiram, IIT Madras, India
Roberto Caldelli, Universita degli Studi Firenze, Italy
Satchidananda Dehuri, Fakir Mohan University, India
C. W. Chow, National Chiao Tung University, Taiwan
Mohd Helmy Abd Wahab, Universiti Tun Hussein Onn, Malaysia
Kuntal Ghosh, ISI Kolkata, India
Shekhar Verma, IIIT Allahabad, India
Samaresh Mishra, KIIT University, India
Diptendu Sinha Roy, NIT Meghalaya, India
G. C. Deka, Ministry of Skill Development & Entrepreneurship, India
Chinmaya Mahapatra, University of British Columbia, Canada
M. S. Kakkasageri, Basaveshwar Engineering College (Autonomous), India
Y-Chuang Chen, Minghsin University of Science and Technology, Taiwan
Bighnaraj Naik, VSSUT, Burla, India
Prasant Kumar Pattnaik, KIIT University, India
Aniket Mahanti, University of Auckland, New Zealand

M. N. Das, KIIT University, India
Dilip Ranjan Mohanty, Wellington Management, Massachusetts, USA
S. S. Rautaray, KIIT University, India
Qurban A Memon, UAE University
Hajjam El Hassani, Univbersite de Bourgogne Franche Comte, France
Anjali Mathur, Jaipur National University, India
B. K. ROUT, FIE, Birla Institute of Technology & Science, Pilani, India
Bibudhendu Pati, CVRCE, India
Somanath Tripathy, IIT Patna, India
Veena Goswami, KIIT University, India
Gautam K. Das, IIT Guwahati, India
Hemant Kumar Rath, TCS Research & Innovation, Bhubaneswar, India
Janmenjoy Nayak, Sri Sivani College of Engineering, India
Ruggero Donida Labati, Universita' degli Studi di Milano, Italy
Gayadhar Panda, NIT Meghalaya, India
Ala' Aburumman, University of South Australia, Australia
Himansu Das, KIIT University, India
Gunter Fahrnberger, University of Hagen, Germany
Venkata Rao Kasukurthi, Andhra University College of Engineering, India
Pratyay Kuila, NIT Sikkim, India
Babita Majhi, Central University, Bilaspur, India
Durga Prasad Mohapatra, NIT Rourkela, India
Chandal Nahak, IIT Kharagpur, India
Gyanendra Kr. Verma, NIT Kurukshetra, India
Pradheepkumar Singaravelu, NEC India Pvt Ltd, India
Marco Mussetta, Politechico Di Milano, Italy
Indrajit Saha, NITTTR, Kolkata, India
Vasanth Iyer, Florida International University, Warrensburg, MO
Felix Albu, Valahia University of Targoviste, Romania
K. Hemant Reddy, NIST, India
Mohamed Amine Ferrag, Guelma University, Algeria
Neha Sharma, ZIBACAR, India
Monish Chatterjee, Asansol Engineering College, India
Biswajit Sahoo, KIIT University, India
Angelo Genovese, Universita degli Studi di Milano, Italy
S. N. Mohanty, KIIT University, India
Pankaj Kumar Sa, NIT Rourkela, India
Carlo Vallati, University of Pisa, Italy
Santosh Pani, KIIT University, India
Radu-Emil Precup, SMIEEE, Politehnica University of Timisoara, Romania
Bernd E. Wolfinger, University of Hamburg, Germany
R. N. Satpathy, TAT, India
Biswa Ranjan Swain, TAT, India
Meenakshi D'Souza, IIIT Bangalore, India
P. G. Sapna, Coimbatore Institute of Technology, India

Neeraj Kumar, Thapar University Patiala, India
Natarajan Meghanathan, Jackson State University, USA
J. Mohanty, KIIT University, India
Manjusha Pandey, KIIT University, India
Ajay Kumar Jena, KIIT University, India
Malka Halgamuge, The University of Melbourne, Australia
Sarangapani Jagannathan, Missouri University of Science and Technology, USA
Alok kumar Jagadev, KIIT University, India
Subhankar Dhar, San Jose State University, USA
Santi Maity, IIEST, India
B. S. P. Mishra, KIIT University, India
S. K. Swain, KIIT University, India
Minakhi Rout, KIIT University, India
Sipra DasBit, IIEST, India
Kiran K., UVCE, India
Dariusz Jacek Jakobczak, Koszalin University of Technology, Poland
Mithileysh Sathiyanarayanan, City, University of London, UK
Shikha Mehta, Jaypee Institute of Information Technology, Noida, India
Chittaranjan Pradhan, KIIT University, India
Jagannath Singh, KIIT University, India

Contents

About the Editors

Prasant Kumar Pattnaik Ph.D. (Computer Science), Fellow IETE, Senior Member IEEE, is a Professor at the School of Computer Engineering, KIIT University, Bhubaneswar, India. He has more than a decade of teaching and research experience. He has published numbers of research papers in peer-reviewed international journals and conferences. His areas of specialization are mobile computing, cloud computing, brain–computer interface and privacy preservation. He has been editor of some published volumes with Springer and IGI Global.

Siddharth Swarup Rautaray Ph.D. (Information Technology), Member IET, IEEE, ACM, is an Assistant Professor at the School of Computer Engineering, KIIT University, Bhubaneswar, India. His research interest includes big data analytics, human–computer interaction and image processing. He has published research papers in various international journals and conferences. He has been organizing chair/committee member of different international conferences, workshops and symposiums. He has also been a reviewer for different reputed journals and conferences.

Himansu Das is working as an as Assistant Professor at the School of Computer Engineering, KIIT University, Bhubaneswar, Odisha, India. He has received his B.Tech and M.Tech from Biju Pattnaik University of Technology (BPUT), Odisha, India. He has published several research papers in various international journals and conferences. He has also edited several books of international repute. He is associated with different international bodies as editorial/reviewer board member of various journals and conferences. He is proficient in the field of Computer Science and Engineering and served as an organizing chair, publicity chair and act as member of program committees of many national and international conferences. He is also associated with various educational and research societies such as IACSIT, ISTE, UACEE, CSI, IET, IAENG, ISCA. He has 10 years of teaching and research experience in different engineering colleges. His research interest includes grid computing, cloud computing and machine learning.

Janmenjoy Nayak is working as an Associate Professor at Sri Sivani College of Engineering, Srikakulam, Andhra Pradesh, India. He has been awarded INSPIRE Research Fellowship from Department of Science and Technology, Government of India (both as JRF and as SRF levels) for doing his Doctoral Research in the Department of CSE, Veer Surendra Sai University of Technology, Burla, Odisha, India. He completed his M.Tech. (gold medalist and topper of the batch) in Computer Science from Fakir Mohan University, Balasore, Odisha, India, and M.Sc. (gold medalist and topper of the batch) in Computer Science from Ravenshaw University, Cuttack, Odisha, India. He has published more than 50 research papers in various reputed, peer-reviewed international conferences, refereed journals and chapters. He has also authored one textbook on "Formal Languages and Automata Theory" in Vikash Publishing House Pvt. Ltd, which has been widely acclaimed throughout the country and abroad by the students of all levels. He is the recipient of Young Faculty in Engineering-2017 Award by Venus International Foundation, Chennai. He has been serving as an active member of reviewer committee of various reputed, peer-reviewed journals such as IET Intelligent Transport Systems, Elsevier, Springer, Inderscience and IGI Global. He is the life member of some of the reputed societies like CSI, India, OITS, OMS and IAENG (Hong Kong). His area of interest includes data mining, nature-inspired algorithms and soft computing.

Location-Independent Key Distribution for Sensor Network Using Regular Graph

Monjul Saikia and Md. Anwar Hussain

Abstract Regular graph is the type of graph whose degree of all vertices are same, and this property makes it very useful in design of key distribution algorithm. Keys in wireless sensor node need to be evenly distributed for efficient storage and good connectivity. In the past various methods have been proposed to overcome the problem of key predistribution for wireless sensor network. Among these, the balanced incomplete block design technique from the theory of combinatorics provides a meaningful enhancement in key predistribution. Also various improvements have been done over this technique for especial arrangement of sensor network. Here, we use Paley graph a class of regular graph to model our key distribution in a location-independent sensor environment, where locations of sensor nodes are assumed to be unknown prior to deployment or key distribution. Experiments were performed and presented here.

Keywords Location-independent KPS · Wireless sensor network · Graph
Strongly regular graph

1 Introduction

The process of distributing a shared key among nodes in a sensor network prior to deployment is called key predistribution scheme. Due to high vulnerability of sensor network towards attack, it is very much essential to use robust security mechanism to protect sensitive data. As sensor nodes are battery operated and very low computation capable, there for high complexity algorithm cannot run by them. Therefore, it is essential to use low complexity yet efficient algorithm to solve the purpose.

M. Saikia (✉)
Department of CSE, North Eastern Regional Institute of Science
and Technology, Nurjuli 791109, Arunachal Pradesh, India
e-mail: monjuls@gmail.com

Md. A. Hussain
Department of ECE, North Eastern Regional Institute of Science
and Technology, Nurjuli 791109, Arunachal Pradesh, India
e-mail: ah@nerist.ac.in

© Springer Nature Singapore Pte Ltd. 2018
P. K. Pattnaik et al. (eds.), *Progress in Computing, Analytics and Networking*,
Advances in Intelligent Systems and Computing 710,
https://doi.org/10.1007/978-981-10-7871-2_1

Various key predistribution schemes have been proposed early. Special care needs to be given during key distribution phase. Sensor nodes forward data packet through its neighbour nodes to base station. Symmetric key encryption algorithm is used by repeated encrypting and decrypting in each transmission and provides an efficient security suitable to use in practice. In a random key predistribution scheme, keys are picked from a large key pool and shuffled among nodes. Although it is simple and easy to implement, it gives a very fair chance to share at least one key among each node in the network [1]. Xiao et al. [2] in their paper give a survey with details of key management schemes applicable for wireless sensor networks. Lin et al. [3] propose an efficient predeployment key scheme to transmit data securely in a wireless sensor networks using Lagrange interpolation polynomial. Martin et al. [1] gave a key establishment scheme for an application-oriented framework for wireless sensor network. Blom [4] gave an optimal class of symmetric key generation systems for wireless sensor network. Camtepe et al. [5] discuss the use of combinatorial design theory for key distribution mechanisms for wireless sensor networks. Chakrabarti et al. [6] propose a hybrid design of key predistribution scheme for wireless sensor networks to improve connectivity and resilience. Chan et al. [7] gave a new random key predistribution schemes for sensor networks. Kendall and Martin [8] introduced a graph-theoretic design and analysis of key predistribution schemes. Saikia and Hussain [9] discuss the performance analysis of expander graph-based key predistribution scheme in wireless sensor network. Klonowski and Syga [10] propose an enhancement for privacy of ad hoc systems with key predistribution. Zhao [11] gives an analysis of connectivity of heterogeneous, secure sensor networks in their work.

1.1 Organization of the Paper

A brief overview and work done by the researchers in the past were discussed in Sect. 1. The remaining of the paper is organized as follows: Section 2 discusses the properties of a regular graph an Paley graph, and Sect. 3 discusses the conversion idea of graph to KPS and the proposed model. Section 4 gives simulation and experimental results, and Sect. 5 concludes the paper.

2 Properties of Regular Graph

Simply a graph is defined as an ordered pair denoted as $G = (V, E)$ comprising of a set vertices V or called nodes with a set of edges E. Graph has a numerous applications in computer science. A strongly regular graph is a type of graph having some spacial properties as defined below.

Let V be a set of with v number of vertices, then graph $G = (V, E)$ is a regular graph if degree of each vertices is k where the degree of a graph vertex v of a graph

G is the number of edges which touches v. On the other hand, G is said to be strongly regular if there exist integers λ and μ such that following two conditions hold:

- There is λ common neighbours for every two adjacent vertices and
- There is μ common neighbours for every two non-adjacent vertices.

In short a strongly regular graph is represented with 4-tuple $srg(v, k, \lambda, \mu)$, where v indicates number of vertices, k indicates degree of vertices, λ indicates number of common neighbours of adjacent vertices and μ is number of common neighbours of non-adjacent vertices. Raj Chandra Bose first introduced this strongly regular graphs in 1963 [12].

For a strongly regular graph, the complement is also strongly regular. For an $srg(v, k, \lambda, \mu)$, its complement $srg(v, v - k - 1, v - 2 - 2, k + \mu, v - 2k + \lambda)$ is also regular. The four parameters in v, k, λ and μ of an strongly regular graph are not independent and must satisfy the relation $(v - k - 1)\mu = k(k - \lambda - 1)$.

Paley graphs: Paley graphs are dense, undirected graphs. These are constructed from the elements collecting from a suitable finite field and by connecting pairs of elements. The elements are deferred by quadratic residue. Interesting properties of Paley graphs make it useful in graph theory experiments and can be applied in many applications. These graphs are named after the inventor Raymond Paley. These graph are also closely related to construction of Hadamard matrices [13]. The Paley graph of order q is a graph on q nodes, where q is a prime power and having degree k.

Definition: Let q be a prime power satisfying $q = 1(mod)4$, i.e. a prime congruent to $1 mod 4$. Let set of vertices be $V = F_q$ and set of edges be $E = \{\{a, b\} : a - b \in (F_q)^2\}$. If a pair $\{a, b\}$ is included in E, it is included under each of two elements. For, $a - b = -(b - a)$, and -1 is a square, from which it ensures that $(a - b)$ is a square if and only if $(b - a)$ is a square. By definition $G = (V, E)$ is said to be Paley graph of order q.

For $q = 4t + 1$, the parameters are $v = 4t + 1, k = 2t, \lambda = t1, \mu = t$. Simple Paley graphs therefore exist for orders $5, 9, 13, 17, 25, 29, 37, 41, 49, 53, 61, 73, 81, 89, 97,$ $101, 109, 113, 121, 125, 137, 149, 157, 169, \ldots$. Figure 1a, b shows two examples of Paley graph with $q = 5$ and $q = 9$.

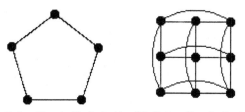

(a) Paley Graph (5, 2, 0, 1)   (b) Paley Graph (9, 4, 1, 2)

Fig. 1 Examples of Paley graph

3 Conversion of Graph to KPS Idea

Following assumptions were made prior to deployment of the network:

- N number of sensor nodes need to be distributed in a target area.
- Expected location of the sensor nodes is not known prior.
- k number of keys can be stored in each sensor node.
- A key pool containing random symmetric keys with identifier is computed earlier.

The idea of conversion of a regular graph to KPS is to assign a unique pairwise key to every edge of G; i.e. preload each node with the set of keys which correspond to its set of edges.

4 Simulation and Experimental Results

In our experiments, we have taken various possible combinations of Paley graph as discussed in previous section. Some of the simulation results are as shown here.

Example 1: A Paley graph (13, 6, 2, 3) as in Fig. 2a used for distributing keys among 13 nodes. The random placement of these nodes and their key graph is shown in Fig. 3a.

Example 2: A Paley graph (17, 8, 3, 4) as in Fig. 2b used for distributing keys among 17 nodes. The random placement of these nodes and their key graph is shown in Fig. 3b.

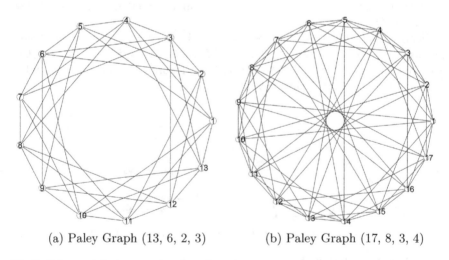

(a) Paley Graph (13, 6, 2, 3)   (b) Paley Graph (17, 8, 3, 4)

Fig. 2 Paley graph for two experiments performed

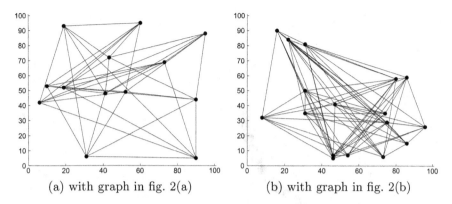

(a) with graph in fig. 2(a)   (b) with graph in fig. 2(b)

Fig. 3 Actual node placement with graph in two experiments

Key Ring Formation: Example 1: The key ring formation for an experiment with Paley graph (13, 6, 2, 3) is as given below. Here, thirteen nodes store six keys each and each node has degree six.

$$\{1, 2, 3, 4, 5, 6\}$$
$$\{1, 7, 8, 9, 10, 11\}$$
$$\{7, 12, 13, 14, 15, 16\}$$
$$\{2, 12, 17, 18, 19, 20\}$$
$$\{3, 8, 17, 21, 22, 23\}$$
$$\{9, 13, 21, 24, 25, 26\}$$
$$\{14, 18, 24, 27, 28, 29\}$$
$$\{19, 22, 27, 30, 31, 32\}$$
$$\{23, 25, 30, 33, 34, 35\}$$
$$\{4, 2628, 33, 36, 37\}$$
$$\{5, 10, 29, 31, 36, 38\}$$
$$\{11, 15, 32, 34, 38, 39\}$$
$$\{6, 16, 20, 35, 37, 39\}$$

Example 2: KPS with Paley graph (17, 8, 3, 4)—the key ring formation is as follows, where seventeen nodes store eight keys each:

$$\{1, 2, 3, 4, 5, 6, 7, 8\}$$
$$\{1, 9, 10, 11, 12, 13, 14, 15\}$$
$$\{2, 9, 16, 17, 18, 19, 20, 21\}$$
$$\{10, 16, 22, 23, 24, 25, 26, 27\}$$
$$\{3, 17, 22, 28, 29, 30, 31, 32\}$$
$$\{11, 23, 28, 33, 34, 35, 36, 37\}$$
$$\{18, 29, 33, 38, 39, 40, 41, 42\}$$

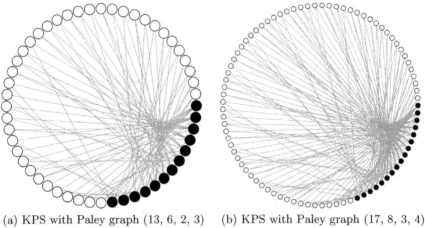

(a) KPS with Paley graph (13, 6, 2, 3)   (b) KPS with Paley graph (17, 8, 3, 4)

Fig. 4 Incidence graph for KPS with Paley graph

$$\{24, 34, 38, 43, 44, 45, 46, 47\}$$
$$\{4, 30, 39, 43, 48, 49, 50, 51\}$$
$$\{5, 12, 35, 44, 48, 52, 53, 54\}$$
$$\{13, 19, 40, 49, 52, 55, 56, 57\}$$
$$\{20, 25, 45, 53, 55, 58, 59, 60\}$$
$$\{26, 31, 50, 56, 58, 61, 62, 63\}$$
$$\{6, 32, 36, 54, 59, 61, 64, 65\}$$
$$\{14, 37, 41, 57, 62, 64, 66, 67\}$$
$$\{7, 21, 42, 46, 60, 65, 66, 68\}$$
$$\{8, 15, 27, 47, 5163, 67, 68\}$$

Incidence graph for KPS with Paley graph (13, 6, 2, 3) is as shown in Fig. 4a where black vertices indicated sensor nodes and white indicated a key. Incidence graph for KPS with Paley graph (17, 8, 3, 4) is as shown in Fig. 4b.

Table 1 shows experiments for required number of total nodes, respective key ring size and total possible key-pair, total actual key-pair after KPS, probability of connectivity, maximum hop count, average hop count, average affected nodes if one node is compromised and resilience of the network.

5 Conclusion

Paley graph is a strongly regular graph and gives advantages for special distribution of keys in a sensor network. Thus, connectivity among nodes after deployment is found to be very high. As in Paley graph, the number of vertices that can be picked is restricted over finite prime field that limits in the options of number of nodes to

Table 1 Simulation Results: (a) total number of nodes (b) ring size (c) deployment area in metre (d) total possible pair (e) total key-pair (f) probability of connectivity (g) maximum hop count (h) average hop count (i) average affected nodes if one node is compromised and (j) resilience

(a)	(b)	(c)	(d)	(e)	(f)	(g)	(h)	(i)	(j)
13	6	100	78	39	0.5	2	1.5	3	0.7692
17	8	100	136	68	0.5	2	1.5	4	0.7647
25	10	100	300	125	0.5	2	1.5	5	0.8000
29	14	100	406	203	0.5	2	1.5	7	0.7586
37	18	100	666	333	0.5	2	1.5	9	0.7567
41	20	100	820	410	0.5	2	1.5	10	0.7560
53	26	100	1378	689	0.5	2	1.5	13	0.7547
61	30	100	1830	915	0.5	2	1.5	15	0.7540
73	36	100	2628	1314	0.5	2	1.5	18	0.7534
89	44	100	3916	1958	0.5	2	1.5	22	0.7528
97	48	100	4656	2328	0.5	2	1.5	24	0.7525
101	50	100	5050	2525	0.5	2	1.5	25	0.7524
109	54	100	5886	2943	0.5	2	1.5	27	0.7522
113	56	100	6328	3164	0.5	2	1.5	28	0.7522
125	52	100	7750	3250	0.5	2	1.5	26	0.7920
137	68	100	9316	4658	0.5	2	1.5	34	0.7518
149	74	100	11026	5513	0.5	2	1.5	37	0.7516
157	78	100	12246	6123	0.5	2	1.5	39	0.7515
169	78	100	14196	6591	0.5	2	1.5	39	0.7692

be deployed over network. Connectivity, resilience and key storage requirement is found to be very efficient. Various experiments were performed to evaluate these matrices and presented here.

Acknowledgements We acknowledge all faculty members from Department of ECE, NERIST who provided insight and expertise that greatly assisted the research and greatly improved the manuscript. We also acknowledge the suggestions in improving the manuscript from faculty members of Computer Science Department, NERIST.

References

1. Martin, K. M., & Paterson, M. (2008). An application-oriented framework for wireless sensor network key establishment. Electronic Notes in Theoretical Computer Science, 192(2), 31–41.
2. Xiao, Y., Rayi, V. K., Sun, B., Du, X., Hu, F., & Galloway, M. (2007). A survey of key management schemes in wireless sensor networks. Computer communications, 30(11), 2314–2341.
3. Lin, H. Y., Pan, D. J., Zhao, X. X., & Qiu, Z. R. (2008, April). A rapid and efficient predeployment key scheme for secure data transmissions in sensor networks using Lagrange inter-

polation polynomial. In Information Security and Assurance, 2008. ISA 2008. International Conference on (pp. 261–265). IEEE.

4. Blom, R. (1984, April). An optimal class of symmetric key generation systems. In Workshop on the Theory and Application of Cryptographic Techniques (pp. 335–338). Springer Berlin Heidelberg.
5. Camtepe, S. A., & Yener, B. (2007). Combinatorial design of key distribution mechanisms for wireless sensor networks. IEEE/ACM Transactions on networking, 15(2), 346–358.
6. Chakrabarti, D., Maitra, S., & Roy, B. (2005, December). A hybrid design of key predistribution scheme for wireless sensor networks. In International Conference on Information Systems Security (pp. 228–238). Springer Berlin Heidelberg.
7. Chan, H., Perrig, A., & Song, D. (2003, May). Random key predistribution schemes for sensor networks. In Security and Privacy, 2003. Proceedings. 2003 Symposium on (pp. 197–213). IEEE.
8. Kendall, M., & Martin, K. M. (2016). Graph-theoretic design and analysis of key predistribution schemes. Designs, Codes and Cryptography, 81(1), 11–34.
9. Saikia, M., & Hussain, M. A. (2016, August). Performance Analysis of Expander Graph Based Key Predistribution Scheme in WSN. In International Conference on Smart Trends for Information Technology and Computer Communications (pp. 724–732). Springer, Singapore.
10. Klonowski, M., & Syga, P. (2017). Enhancing Privacy for Ad Hoc Systems with Predeployment Key Distribution. Ad Hoc Networks.
11. Zhao, J. (2016). Analyzing Connectivity of Heterogeneous Secure Sensor Networks. IEEE Transactions on Control of Network Systems.
12. Bose, R. (1963). Strongly regular graphs, partial geometries and partially balanced designs. Pacific Journal of Mathematics, 13(2), 389–419.
13. Paley, R. E. (1933). On orthogonal matrices. Studies in Applied Mathematics, 12(1–4), 311–320.
14. Baker, R. D., Ebert, G. L., Hemmeter, J., & Woldar, A. (1996). Maximal cliques in the Paley graph of square order. Journal of statistical planning and inference, 56(1), 33–38.
15. Godsil, C., & Royle, G. (2001). Algebraic graph theory, volume 207 of Graduate Texts in Mathematics.
16. Sloane, N. J. (2007). The on-line encyclopedia of integer sequences. In Towards Mechanized Mathematical Assistants (pp. 130–130). Springer Berlin Heidelberg.

A Trust-Based Technique for Secure Spectrum Access in Cognitive Radio Networks

Sumit Kar, Srinivas Sethi and Ramesh Kumar Sahoo

Abstract *Cognitive radio networks (CRNs)* are becoming an important part of wireless communications, which can improve the utilization of the limited and scarce spectrum resources. However, the flexibility and the unique characteristics of CRN make it vulnerable to varied types of attack. Moreover, security is a key requirement at every step of its functionality (spectrum sensing, spectrum analysis, spectrum decision and spectrum act). Numerous researches have mainly focused on to provide security at the cognition capability (spectrum sensing, spectrum analysis and spectrum decision) of CRN for detecting the appropriate spectrum holes. However, after obtaining access to the spectrum hole (Spectrum Act), a *Cognitive Radio (CR)* may behave maliciously to achieve own benefits or for some other reasons. Such maliciousness can severely affect the normal activities of the whole network. Therefore, there is a need to track and record the behaviour during the spectrum access of a CR user, which can encourage the CR users to obey the opportunistic spectrum access policy. In this paper, we construct a trust-based approach for secure spectrum access in CRN. The CR nodes trust value is determined from its past activities, and based on which, it is decided whether the CR node will get access the primary users free spectrum or not.

Keywords Cognitive radio networks · Trust · Secure spectrum access
Malicious node detection

S. Kar (✉) · S. Sethi · R. K. Sahoo
Department of Computer Science Engineering and Application,
IGIT, Sarang 759146, Odisha, India
e-mail: sumittalk2u@gmail.com

S. Sethi
e-mail: srinivas_sethi@igitsarang.ac.in

R. K. Sahoo
e-mail: ramesh0986@gmail.com

© Springer Nature Singapore Pte Ltd. 2018
P. K. Pattnaik et al. (eds.), *Progress in Computing, Analytics and Networking*,
Advances in Intelligent Systems and Computing 710,
https://doi.org/10.1007/978-981-10-7871-2_2

1 Introduction

The growth of wireless applications has led to an increasing interest in CRN in recent years. In conventional spectrum management (static) policy, most of the spectrum is allocated to licensed users for their exclusive use. A survey made by *Federal Communications Commission (FCC)* has found that spectrum utilization varies from 15 to 85% with wide variance in time and space [1]. It concludes that most of the licensed spectrum is largely underutilized and the spectrum shortage problem can be solved up to some extent by efficient utilization of the fellow licensed band. Over the last decade, *cognitive radio (CR)* has been evolved as a promising wireless communication paradigm to meet the spectrum demands of the increasing wireless applications by efficient utilization of the limited radio spectrum [2].

In CRN, users can be divided into two categories: primary users (PUs) or incumbent users, which hold license to use a particular portion of a spectrum and secondary users (SUs) or cognitive users, which are unlicensed users. In CRN, the SUs (unlicensed users) can use the PUs (licensed user) free spectrum or spectrum white space on a non-interface basis to it [2]. For which, the SU has to truthfully perform out-of-bound sensing to find the spectrum holes and also in-band sensing to detect the arrival of the concerned PU that has been occupied by the SU [3]. Thus, when a SU detects the return signal of the PU in its operating channel, it has to quit the channel immediately and search for new spectrum holes nearby to avoid any interface. However, some malicious or compromised node might disobey this basic spectrum access policy intentionally. This leads to the violation of the basic spectrum sharing regulations and agreements of this novel technology [4]. To ensuring proper security from the malicious spectrum usage in CRN, the objective of this paper is to build a trust-based mechanism. As a result, the spectrum being allocated to malicious users can be avoided. In addition to encourage fair user, a highly trusted user gets priority to access spectrum band.

The rest of this paper is organized as follows. Section 2 gives an overview of related works. In Sect. 3, we define the system model of CRN. Section 4 highlights the motivation and the major contribution of our work. The proposed trust-based spectrum allocation is described in Sect. 5. Then in Sect. 6, performance analysis and functionality evaluation of our proposed method are given. Section 7 concludes this paper.

2 Related Work

In addition to improve the system performance and operational technology of CRN, ensuring proper security is particularly an important problem that needs to be addressed. As CRN operates in wireless media, in addition to all the traditional wireless communication security threats, CRN introduces significant new class of threats due to its unique characteristics and functioning techniques [5].

Studies in [5–7] show the details analysis of the major possible security vulnerabilities in CRN paradigm. While the set of security challenges in CRNs are diverse, we focus on to ensure secure spectrum access in this paper. So that, spectrum can only be assigned to the proper authenticated users as per their requirements and the spectrum allocation to malicious node can be restricted. Recently, trust establishment scheme has been proposed for a wide range of applications in *wireless sensor networks (WSNs)* [8, 9] peer-to-peer networks, ad hoc networks [10] and e-commerce for network defence and security. In [11], the trustworthiness of each SU in CRN is evaluated using its sensing reputation and etiquette reputation. The sensing reputation reflects the sensing report correctness of a SU during the spectrum sensing stage. Whereas, the etiquette reputation shows how fairly a SU has obeyed the spectrum opportunistic usage regulations during its past spectrum use. Finally, both the reputation values are considered during channel allocation among the SUs. The authors [4] proposed a principal agent-based joint spectrum sensing and access mechanism to nullify the effect of both the rational and irrational intelligent malicious users. A conjoint trust assessment mechanism has been proposed in [12], for secure communication in CRN. In the proposed method, before allocating the spectrum to a SU, its trust value from both the Primary User Network (PUN) and Secondary User Network (SUN) are obtained and combined. Based on the combined trust value, the spectrum allocation decision to the requesting SU is taken by the PUBS. A new trust value-based spectrum allocation algorithm for cognitive wireless sensor networks that uses the last diminisher algorithm has been proposed in [13]. The authors in [14] proposed a trust-based authentication mechanism for secure communication in CRN. The mechanism also includes trust update procedure when a new node joins or leaves the network. Finally, the trust value is used as a measure during the spectrum allocation.

3   System Model

CRNs can be deployed in three different types of architectures: infrastructure-based (like IEEE 802.22), infrastructure-less (ad hoc) and mesh architecture [15]. In this work, we focus on the infrastructure-based CRN architecture. Referring to Fig. 1, in infrastructure-based architecture all the SUs are connected to the *secondary user base station (SUBS)* or *fusion centre (FC)* and all the PUs are connected to the *primary user base station (PUBS)*. The SUs can only communicate between themselves through the SUBS. However, the PUBS and SUBS can able to communicate among themselves. It is assumed that except the SUS, the PUs, PUBS and SUBS are trustworthy entities. Thus, in the system model, two networks exist, i.e. *secondary user network (SUN)* and *primary user network (PUN)* as illustrated in Fig. 1. In order to use the spectrum opportunistically, first the SUs need to sense the white spaces. If the system relies on cooperative spectrum sensing, each SU conducts their sensing process individually and sends their local sensing observations to the SUBS. The SUBS takes the final decision by integrating the individual sensing observations received from all the SUs and allocates channels to SUs. However, to access the PU's free

Fig. 1 CRN architecture

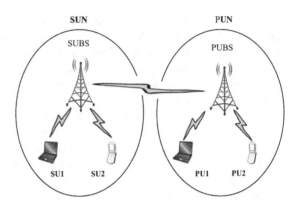

spectrum, a SU needs the PU's authorization. As reported in [12], a SU's authorization can also be checked by calculating its trustworthiness. Further, after getting permission to access, the SUs should obey the opportunistic spectrum access policy and avoid causing harmful interference to the PU during their communication. So, when the PU resumes transmission, the concerned SU has to quit the occupied band immediately and search for new spectrum holes nearby.

4 Motivation and Contribution

Security techniques like cryptography and authentication are typically insufficient to protect the network from the compromised internal members [9]. Because after authenticated, a compromised internal member may use its privilege to achieve its desired goal. Also, due to the limited resources and other unique characteristics of CRN, the implementation of cryptographic mechanisms becomes more difficult. In contrast, trust management-based mechanism can be a viable solution to identify such malicious and compromised nodes which have been authenticated [9]. In view of the above facts, the motivations of our work are to address the following objectives:

- To use the licensed spectrum opportunistically, a SU needs the authorization and trust from the original owner, i.e. the concerned PU [16]. Also after spectrum allocation, the SU has to obey certain rules and regulations.
- To ensure secure communication in CRN and to reduce the probability of allocating the channels to malicious nodes, it is essential to detect the malicious nodes that violate the opportunistic access policy.
- The history of earned trust during its previous spectrum usage can be an efficient measure for the current and future spectrum allocation. Also as an incentive for the fairness, the SU with highest trust shall get priority to access the available spectrum.

Motivated by the above challenges, this paper makes the following main contributions:

- We calculate the feedback trust value of the requesting SU in a PUN. If the calculated trust value is above or equal to 0.8, then the fellow spectrum band is assigned to the requesting SU. If the trust value is less than 0.6, the requesting SU is marked as a malicious one and is debarred from accessing the spectrum. Otherwise, the PUN asks for the recommended trust from the SUBS, following the next points.
- For calculating the recommended trust value, we first calculate the direct trust value of a SU with SUN, and secondly, we calculate the indirect trust value given by the other neighbouring nodes of the concern SU.
- We combine both the direct and indirect trust values to get the recommended trust value of the requesting SU. If the computed recommended trust value is above certain threshold, then the SUBS recommends to assigning the spectrum to the SU. Otherwise, the SUBS recommends the PUBS, not to assign the spectrum.

5 Proposed Approach

In this section, we present our proposed trust-based secure spectrum access procedure in detail. When a SU requests to access a PU free spectrum after completing the sensing process, the concern PU needs to check its authorization. In the proposed model, the authorization of a SU can be verified by calculation of its trustworthiness by evaluating the past behaviour and the recommendations given by other neighbouring nodes. Based on the above concept, the proposed model consists of the following two phases, i.e. trust calculation and spectrum allocation.

5.1 Trust Calculation

The trust calculation of a SU consists of the following two steps, i.e. feedback trust calculation and recommended trust calculation

Step-I: Feedback trust calculation is based on the previous interaction history of the concerned SU with the PUs of the PUN. Here the feedback in terms trust value express how truthfully the SU has obeyed the opportunistic spectrum usage policy in past. Consider a centralized collaborative CRN with K number of PUs and N SUs. Let U= $\{u_1, u_2, \ldots, u_n\}$ denote the set of N SUs in the network. When a SU requests to access any PU's free band, the PUBS asks all the PUs with which the SU has already interacted before to send its feedback trust value. Accordingly, each SU owns a feedback table and it is kept and updated by the PUBS. Let till current time t, there are n number of previous interactions has been completed between PU_j and SU_i. Based on this, each PU_j makes a feedback trust evaluation of SU_i denoted by $FT(i,j)$, such that $[0 \leq FT(i,j) \leq 1]$. The calculation of $FT(i,j)$ applies beta-function method [17] based on the previously obtained positive and negative feedback of SU_i by PU_j is defined as:

$$FT(i,j) = \frac{i_p + 1}{i_p + i_n + 2} \tag{1}$$

where i_p denotes the number of positive feedback and i_n denotes the negative feedback obtained. For example, let $i_p = 8$ and $i_n = 2$, then $FT(i,j) = 0.75$. After getting all the feedbacks for SU_i, the PUBS calculates the final feedback trust using the following equation

$$FT_i = \frac{\sum_{j=1}^{k} FT(i,j)}{p} \tag{2}$$

where P = number of PUs that give the feedback. Based on the calculated feedback trust value, the trustworthiness of the node is predicted as listed in Table 1. If the trust level gets a place in label 1, then the SU is directly given permission to access the free spectrum band. But if a trust level maps to level 3, then the SU is blacklisted and is debarred from accessing the network in near future. However, if it is placed in level 2 or if there is no previous interaction history, then the PUBS asks the recommendation from the SUBS.

Step-II: Recommended trust calculation involves two kinds of trust, i.e. direct trust and indirect trust. The direct trust is established between the SU and the SUBS, and the indirect trust is established between the SU and its neighbours.

Direct trust calculation refers to the behaviour/performance of a SU after its association with the SUN. In our model, the direct trust value is determined by two different attributes based on certain context, i.e. (i) normal joining or normal leaving the CRN and (ii) the calculated sensing trust during the spectrum sensing stage. For the first context, a SUs reputation is set to zero at the beginning. After authentication if a SU joins to the network normally, its trust value is incremented by d and for abnormal joining it is decremented by d. Similarly for each normal leaving the network, the trust value increases by d and for each abnormal leaving it is decremented by d. Here, d is a predefined time quantum. Thus, the first attribute T_{Ai}, i.e. the trust value of SU_i based on the first context, can be computed as follows:

$$T_{Ai} = \begin{cases} T_{Ai} + d & \text{for each normal joining and leaving} \\ T_{Ai} - d & \text{for each abnormal joining and abnormal leaving} \end{cases} \tag{3}$$

Table 1 Trust table

Level	Trust range	Meaning
1	0.8–1	Trusted
2	0.6–0.79	Suspicious
3	0–0.59	Malicious

The second attribute T_{Bi} can be the trust calculated based on the sensing accuracy during the spectrum sensing state. In this paper, we have collected the sensing trust T_{Bi} of different SUs by referring our previous work [18]. Finally, the direct trust DT_i of SU_i can be calculated as

$$DT_i = a.T_{Ai} + b.T_{Bi} \tag{4}$$

where a and b are the attribute weights for T_{Ai} and T_{Bi}, respectively, such that $a + b = 1$.

Indirect trust calculation involves the trust exists between the concern SU and one-hop neighbours of it. For which, the SUBS asks all the one-hop neighbouring nodes to send the trust value of the concerned SU. To prevent the malicious or intentional recommendations, the SUBS only considers the recommendation from SUs, whose recorded direct trust value is above certain threshold μ. The indirect trust value of node SU_i by node SU_j at time t is measured as follows:

$$T_i(j) = \frac{a_{ij}}{a_{ij} + b_{ij}} \tag{5}$$

where a_{ij} and b_{ij} are the number of instances of good behaviour and bad behaviour of node i with node j within the $\varDelta$ time interval. The SUBS collects all the recommendations from the neighbours and calculates the average of it to get the indirect trust IT_i of the concerned SU_i as given below [14]:

$$IT_i = \begin{cases} 0.5 \text{ if } |j| < R \\ \frac{\sum_{j \in N} T_j(i)}{|j|} \end{cases} \tag{6}$$

where N = total SUs in the network, R = threshold of the minimum number of required recommendations and $|j|$ = total number of recommendations received. Finally, the SUBS combines both the DT_i and IT_i to obtain the final recommended trust value RT_i for the requesting SU_i using the following equation and send it to the PUBS.

$$RT_i = w1.DT_i + w2.IT_i \tag{7}$$

where w1 and w2 are the weights given to the direct trust and the indirect trust, respectively.

5.2 Spectrum Allocation

After getting the value of the RTi, the PUBS compares it with a specific threshold λ. If it is greater than or equal to λ, then the requesting SU will give permission to access the PUs free spectrum band defined as follows:

$RT_i \geq \lambda$ the request is approved

$RT_i < \lambda$ the request is denied

However, if more than one SU applies to obtain access a particular PU, then the SU having highest feedback trust FT_i gets the priority to access the PU spectrum.

6 Experimental Results and Observations

In this section, we show the simulation result of our proposed approach using MATLAB as simulation tool. We consider 5 PUs in the PUN and 40 SUs in the SUN. The simulation parameters are listed in Table 2.

First, we obtained the feedback trust of all the 40 SUs in the network as illustrated in Fig. 2. It is observed from Fig. 2 that SU_4 and SU_{17} are detected as malicious and debarred from accessing the network. Similarly SU_{20}, SU_{22}, SU_{23}, SU_{27} and SU_{35} are detected as trusted user and can access the free spectrum. However, the remaining users are detected as suspicious and need the further verification by calculating their recommended trust. Secondly, we calculate the recommended trust for the detected suspicious users as shown in Fig. 3. From Fig. 3, we can see that SU_1, SU_2, SU_3, SU_5, SU_6, SU_7, SU_8, SU_9, SU_{10}, SU_{11}, SU_{12}, SU_{13}, SU_{14}, SU_{15}, SU_{16}, SU_{18}, SU_{19}, SU_{34} are detected as malicious and their request to access the PU's free spectrum is not approved, whereas SU_{21}, SU_{24}, SU_{25}, SU_{26}, SU_{28}, SU_{29}, SU_{30}, SU_{31}, SU_{32}, SU_{33}, SU_{36}, SU_{37}, SU_{38}, SU_{39} and SU_{40} are finally detected as trusted and their request to access the PU's free spectrum is approved. However, if more than one SU applies to obtain access a particular PU at the same time, then the SU having highest feedback trust FT_i gets the priority to access the PU spectrum.

Table 2 Simulation parameters

Parameter	Value
Number of PUs (K)	5
Number of SUs (N)	40
Weight factor a and b	0.5 each
d	1
R	2
Weight factor w1	0.6
Weight factor w2	0.4
λ	0.8

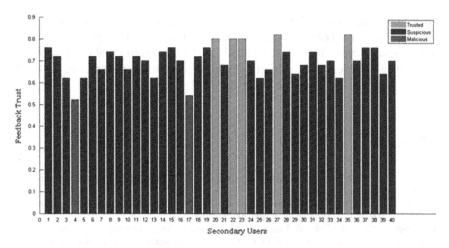

Fig. 2 Feedback trust

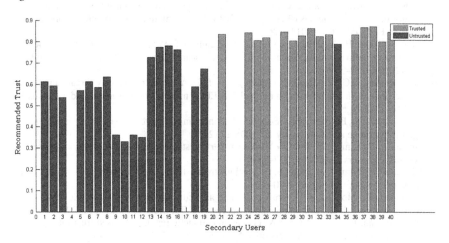

Fig. 3 Recommended trust

7 Conclusions

In CRN, some malicious SU may violate the opportunistic spectrum access regulations by creating interface with PUs. Such selfishness and malicious activities can seriously damage the normal operation of this novel technology. To encourage the CR users to obey the opportunistic spectrum access policy and to combat malicious behaviour, trust management is an essential tool. This article proposes a trust-based approach for secure spectrum access in CRN, where feedback trust from PUN and recommended trust from SUN are used to measure the trustworthiness of SUs. Moreover, the sensing trust also has been included during the recommended trust calculation to encourage SUs to perform faithful and positive spectrum sensing. This work thus tracks the behaviour and measures the trustworthiness of the SUs in the entire cognitive cycle. The theoretical and simulation experimental results demonstrate the effectiveness and feasibility of our proposed scheme. In future, our work will focus on cross-layer defence model for CRN.

References

1. Force, S.P.T.: Spectrum policy task force report. Technical Report 02-135, Federal Communications Commission (2002)
2. Haykin, S.: Cognitive radio: brain-empowered wireless communications. IEEE Journal on Selected Areas in Communications **23** (2005) 201–220
3. Bansal, T., Chen, B., Sinha, P.: Fastprobe: Malicious user detection in cognitive radio networks through active transmissions. In: IEEE Conference on Computer Communications, INFOCOM 2014, Toronto, Canada (2014) 2517–2525
4. Wang, W., Chen, L., Shin, K.G., Duan, L.: Secure cooperative spectrum sensing and access against intelligent malicious behaviors. In: 2014 IEEE Conference on Computer Communications, INFOCOM 2014. (2014) 1267–1275
5. Attar, A., Tang, H., Vasilakos, A.V., Yu, F.R., Leung, V.C.M.: A survey of security challenges in cognitive radio networks: Solutions and future research directions. Proceedings of the IEEE **100** (2012) 3172–3186
6. Fragkiadakis, A.G., Tragos, E.Z., Askoxylakis, I.G.: A survey on security threats and detection techniques in cognitive radio networks. IEEE Communications Surveys and Tutorials **15** (2013) 428–445
7. Kar, S., Sethi, S., Bhuyan, M.K.: Security challenges in cognitive radio network and defending against byzantine attack: a survey. IJCNDS **17** (2016) 120–146
8. Ishmanov, F., Kim, S.W., Nam, S.Y.: A secure trust establishment scheme for wireless sensor networks. Sensors **14** (2014) 1877–1897
9. Ishmanov, F., Kim, S.W., Nam, S.Y.: A robust trust establishment scheme for wireless sensor networks. Sensors **15** (2015) 7040–7061
10. Govindan, K., Mohapatra, P.: Trust computations and trust dynamics in mobile ad-hoc networks: A survey. IEEE Communications Surveys and Tutorials **14** (2012) 279–298
11. Pei, Q., Yuan, B., Li, L., Li, H.: A sensing and etiquette reputation-based trust management for centralized cognitive radio networks. Neurocomputing **101** (2013) 129–138
12. Parvin, S., Hussain, F.K., Hussain, O.K.: Conjoint trust assessment for secure communication in cognitive radio networks. Mathematical and Computer Modelling **58** (2013) 1340–1350
13. Pei, Q., Li, Z., Ma, L.: A trust value-based spectrum allocation algorithm in CWSNs. IJDSN **9** (2013)
14. Parvin, S., Han, S., Tian, B., Hussain, F.K.: Trust-based authentication for secure communication in cognitive radio networks. In: IEEE/IFIP 8th International Conference on Embedded and Ubiquitous Computing. (2010) 589–596
15. Chen, K.C., Peng, Y.J., Prasad, N., Liang, Y.C., Sun, S.: Cognitive radio network architecture: Part I—General structure. In: Proceedings of the 2nd international conference on ubiquitous information management and communication, ACM (2008) 114–119
16. Chen, R., Park, J.M., Hou, Y., J.H. Reed: Toward secure distributed spectrum sensing in cognitive radio networks. Communications Magazine, IEEE **46** (2008) 50–55
17. He, D., Chen, C., Chan, S., Bu, J., Vasilakos, A.V.: Retrust: Attack-resistant and lightweight trust management for medical sensor networks. IEEE Trans. Information Technology in Biomedicine **16** (2012) 623–632
18. Kar, S., Sethi, S., Sahoo, R.K.: A multi-factor trust management scheme for secure spectrum sensing in cognitive radio networks. Wireless Personal Communications **97** (2017) 2523–2540

Flow Aggregator Module for Analysing Network Traffic

Nour Moustafa, Gideon Creech and Jill Slay

Abstract Network flow aggregation is a significant task for network analysis, which summarises the flows and improves the performance of intrusion detection systems (IDSs). Although there are some well-known flow analysis tools in the industry, such as NetFlow, sFlow and IPFIX, they can only aggregate one attribute at a time which increases networks' overheads while running network analysis. In this paper, to address this challenge, we propose a new flow aggregator module which provides promising results compared with the existing tools using the UNSW-NB15 data set.

Keywords Network flow aggregation · Intrusion detection system (IDS)
Sampling techniques · Association rule mining (ARM)

1 Introduction

With the large sizes and high speeds of current networks, flow aggregation has become necessary for various applications, such as network planning and monitoring, and security management [8]. Capturing and processing network data in terms of 'volume', 'velocity' and 'variety' which are increasing considerably is called the phenomenon of 'big data' [13].

Network applications, in particular IDSs and flow aggregation tools (FATs), cannot deal directly with raw packets due to the difficulty of extracting relevant features from them. IDSs monitor network traffic to identify suspicious activities [12], while FATs collect similar network events to effectively facilitate investigating user

N. Moustafa (✉) · G. Creech · J. Slay
The Australian Centre for Cyber Security, University of New South Wales,
Canberra, Australia
e-mail: nour.moustafa@unsw.edu.au

G. Creech
e-mail: G.Creech@adfa.edu.au

J. Slay
e-mail: j.slay@adfa.edu.au

© Springer Nature Singapore Pte Ltd. 2018
P. K. Pattnaik et al. (eds.), *Progress in Computing, Analytics and Networking*,
Advances in Intelligent Systems and Computing 710,
https://doi.org/10.1007/978-981-10-7871-2_3

and network activities [3]. These applications have to include features for success-fully executing their potential procedures. These features consist of a set of network observations that should not be duplicated and reflect user and network behaviours to improve the performances of the network applications deployed.

In an ordinary case, network flows are collected at the chokepoints, such as ingress router and switch devices, to decrease network's overheads. These devices have lim-ited buffers and simple methods for aggregating flows which can collect flows by only one attribute for a particular time, for example source/destination IP addresses or protocols [1].

Aggregating flows using many attributes, however, could identify patterns of sev-eral attack types and security malware, such as DoS, DDoS and flash crowds. Since these types generate massive numbers of flows that demand careful analysis to group similar ones using some flow identifiers (i.e. source/destination IPs and ports, and protocols), IDSs cannot efficiently summarise and recognise abnormal instances by aggregating a single attribute [15].

In this paper, we design a new aggregator module based on the theory of flow-level analysis to reduce the computational resources required and address the above limitations of existing flow tools. It consists of four main tasks: sniffing network data; collecting them; analysing them using approaches of big data analysis; and sending them to an IDS or FAT. The experimental analysis of this module is conducted on the UNSW-NB15 data set[1] [11] which is the latest data set for analysing network data and involves a wide variety of legitimate and suspicious instances.

The rest of this paper is organised as follows: Sect. 2 explains the background and related work, the flow aggregator module is presented in Sect. 3, Sect. 4 describes and discusses the experimental results and Sect. 5 concludes the paper.

2 Background and Related Work

Network flow analysis is a means of obtaining important information from raw pack-ets using statistical and machine-learning algorithms [15]. Its procedures include capturing, collecting, logging and aggregating network data for query and analysis to produce significant features which help an IDS and FAT to summarise these data and identify abnormal events, respectively.

There are two types of network data analysis: deep packet inspection and flow-level analysis [8]. The first requires analysing the packet payload but takes a long processing time and faces the data encryption problem. The second extracts sta-tistical information from packets without analysing their actual data and takes less processing time. Therefore, it is significant to apply a flow analysis while building network monitoring and security applications. Popular tools for flow aggregation are NetFlow [7], sFlow [5] and IPFIX [8] which extract flows and aggregate them using

---

[1]The UNSW-NB15 dataset, https://www.unsw.adfa.edu.au/australian-centre-for-cyber-security/cybersecurity/ADFA-NB15-Datasets/, February 2017.

only one feature, but this study presents a new aggregator module for accumulating more than one attribute for each specific time, identifying collaborative attacks such as DoS and DDoS.

The most common techniques for aggregating flows are sampling ones, which provide dynamic perceptions of network activities by inspecting packet headers. They group packet information using diverse metrics in order to design some clusters with data that are significant for identifying particular network problems. While the accuracy of packet sampling depends on the sampling rate as well as the application and periodicity of the measured criteria, some important packets are often dropped [6]. Specifically, these techniques have a problem of data distortion as they sometimes omit relevant instances that would assist in generating patterns included in the data collected.

To address this problem, Carela-Español et al. [2] analysed the impact of sampling on the accuracy of network classification using machine-learning algorithms. Zhang et al. [17] developed two methods for classifying high-rate flows that should have short processing times, with low memory and CPU costs. Shirali-Shahreza et al. [16] proposed a simple random sampling technique that dynamically accumulates similar flows and relies on counting any received packets.

However, these techniques, especially simple random sampling, are only effective for summarising network data but not for IDSs because they often omit observations which might be malicious. In our aggregator module, we use a simple random sampling technique to summarise the network data and the association rule mining (ARM) approach [9, 10] which efficiently correlates the most repeated observations without losing any observations.

3   Flow Aggregator Module

The huge numbers of flows in current networks require an aggregator module that begins by sniffing packets and then collects them in a data source to summarise network patterns and establish an effective IDS. We suggest a new one based on the concept of flow analysis that decreases the computational time to be a real-time processing and tackles the above limitations of existing flow tools. Figure 1 shows the four main components of this proposed module. Firstly, a data collector gathers raw packets at the chokepoints of a network which are logged in a MySQL database and can easily be used at any platform to handle structured big data.

Secondly, network flows are collected using the MySQL's functions[2] to cluster the data with more than one feature of the flow identifiers which addresses the limits of existing tools for flow aggregation. These flow features can accumulate more information about legitimate and suspicious activities, thereby improving the performances of an IDS and summarisation techniques. If the data of the source and

---

[2]MySQL aggregation functions, http://dev.mysql.com/doc/refman/5.7/en/group-by-functions. html, January 2017.

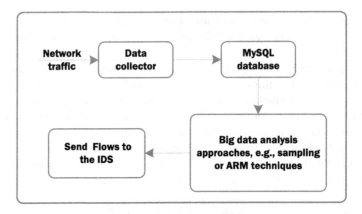

Fig. 1 New flow aggregator module

destination IP addresses are clustered, this will provide a better indication of the number of flows occurring between the two hosts rather than on only each side. We use the 'count' aggregate functions to collect all possible combinations of the flow identifiers to extract the important features which have the characteristics of normal and suspicious flows as follows:

- *Select COUNT(*) as flows, srcip, dstip from network_data group by srcip, dstip;*
- *Select COUNT(*) as flows, srcip, srcport from network_data group by srcip, src-port; and*
- *Select COUNT(*) as flows, dstip, dsport from network_data group by dstip, dsport, srcport.*

In the above queries, *flows* refer to the number of flows occurring between any two features, *srcip* the source IP address, *dstip* the destination IP address, *srcport* the source port address, *dsport* the destination port address and proto the protocol type. Each query retrieves the number of flows occurring between the attributes. Ensuring a set of distinct flows is difficult since many factors should be considered, for example the fields of the datagram header, counters and timers of flows. However, developing a dynamic aggregator module for defining distinct flows is crucial for tracking the non-stationary properties of IP addresses.

Thirdly, the simple random sampling and ARM techniques used to select the important network flows are discussed below. It is worth mentioning that improving the performance of an IDS demands aggregated flows without duplicating and missing values while processing in a real network. Finally, these flows will be sent to the IDS which can differentiate between suspicious and normal observations.

3.1 Simple Random Sampling (SRS) Technique

This technique randomly selects a sample of a given size in which no instances are included more than once, with all subsets of the instances given an equal probability. Furthermore, any given pair of values has the same probability of selection as any other, which decreases data bias and simplifies the data inspection of samples selected from N instances [6], with each network packet having an equal probability of being chosen. This technique randomly selects n dissimilar numbers in the range of 1 to N and then chooses all packets with locations equal to one of these numbers.

Selecting only relevant flows is very significant for establishing an effective IDS and precisely summarising network data, so we apply the simple random sampling technique due to its merits [4]. Firstly, it can reduce data bias which simplifies its analysis because, when choosing a subset of a data source, the variance between instances in this subset is a reflection of the variances in the entire data source. Secondly, it can decrease the processing time by selecting only a partition of the data source that could have a wide variety of patterns. However, it is difficult to specify the number of instances inspected per time which is called a sample size.

We set the sample size of this mechanism according to the online or offline mode/processing for monitoring a network. In the online mode, we use the sliding window method [14] which chooses the number of flows of network traffic in each specified time period and the aggregator module collects and analyses network flows every 1 or 2 min. In the offline mode, we choose a particular number of instances from a data source to be inspected at a time and the aggregator module sequentially analyses each 100 instances.

3.2 Association Rule Mining (ARM) Technique

This is a data mining technique used to measure the correlation between two or more attributes in a data source which determines the strongest rules governing their attributes [9]. We propose processing large numbers of network flows based on this technique to accumulate all possible flows, thereby tackling the problem of data distortion that occurs in sampling techniques.

To explain the ARM technique, let $r = \{f_1, f_2, \ldots, f_N\}$ be a set of features and D a data source involving T transactions $(t_1, t_2, \ldots, t_N)$. Each transaction has a correlation between attributes of $t_j \subseteq r$. The association rule $(f_1$ (i.e. antecedent) $\Rightarrow f_2$ (i.e. precedent)) is subject to the constraints of $(1) \exists t_j, f_1, f_2 \in t_j$ $(2) f_1 \subseteq r, f_2 \subseteq r$ (3) $f_1 \cap f_2 = \Phi$.

For its application to a data source, ARM has two measures, *support (sup)* and *confidence (conf)*, which compute the strongest association rules that have several patterns in the data source. The first estimates the frequency of the feature values which is the proportion of the association of each rule, as in Eq. (1). The second measures the frequency of a precedent if the antecedent has already occurred, as in Eq. (2).

$$sup(f_1 \Rightarrow f_2) = \frac{|\#t_j|f_1,f_2 \in t_j|}{N} \qquad (1)$$

$$conf(f_1 \Rightarrow f_2) = \frac{|\#t_j|f_1,f_2 \in t_j|}{|\#t_j|f_1 \in t_j|} \qquad (2)$$

The ARM technique determines all the repeated item sets and generates their strongest rules, with the strongest in a data source (D) declared as follows: (1) the estimated support of a rule is greater than a user-specified minimum one (i.e. $sup \geq minsup$) and (2) the estimated confidence of a rule is greater than a minimum confidence threshold (i.e. $conf \geq minconf$).

Likewise, in the sampling technique, we choose the sample size analysed using the ARM technique according to the online or offline mode of network data processing. In the online mode, we apply the sliding window to select the number of flows over network data for each particular time period. In the offline mode, we select a certain number of instances from a data source to be processed each time.

4   Experimental Results and Discussion

As current networks send and receive huge numbers of flows, the aggregator module is significant for building an online IDS and summarising network data. Each sequence of flows in a network is often generated from separate activities, for example retrieving a web page or chatting and as, while monitoring network traffic, an IDS and summarisation techniques cannot oversee all flows, several missing packets could have suspicious activities. Therefore, we suggest choosing observations which do not have duplicates or missing activities. We use the simple random sampling and ARM techniques to select those relevant observations and demonstrate their influence on the design of an effective IDS.

Table 1 presents examples of data samples taken from the UNSW-NB15 data set for applying the two techniques. It shows information of the flow identifiers (i.e. srcip, sport, dstip, dsport and proto) and the class labels for the observations which clarify the impacts of these techniques. There are 10 instances, 5 normal (i.e. 0) and 5 attack (i.e. 1). We apply both techniques to demonstrate how relevant flows can be selected.

In the SRS technique, we select half the instances that could have suitable information about network flows, as listed in Table 2. By selecting them, important information, including some malicious observations, is deleted. However, with large numbers of flows, selecting only distinct ones will enhance the performance of an IDS because the statistical properties of the entire data source and selected samples are quite similar, as evidenced in Figs. 2 and 3, respectively.

Table 1 Examples of data samples for applying simple random sampling and ARM techniques

No.	Srcip	Sport	Dstip	Dsport	Proto	Label
1	149.171.126.14	179	175.45.176.3	33159	Tcp	0
2	175.45.176.3	22592	149.171.126.16	143	Tcp	0
3	175.45.176.2	61809	149.171.126.19	161	Udp	0
4	175.45.176.0	45235	149.171.126.16	21	Tcp	0
5	175.45.176.0	15816	149.171.126.10	5060	Udp	0
6	175.45.176.0	3716	149.171.126.15	80	Tcp	1
7	175.45.176.2	7434	149.171.126.16	80	Tcp	1
8	175.45.176.0	16495	149.171.126.10	80	Tcp	1
9	175.45.176.2	9710	149.171.126.15	32780	Udp	1
10	175.45.176.1	15982	149.171.126.14	5060	Udp	1

Table 2 Samples selected using simple random sampling technique

Srcip	Sport	Dstip	Dsport	Proto	Label
175.45.176.0	16495	149.171.126.10	80	Tcp	1
175.45.176.2	61809	149.171.126.19	161	Udp	0
175.45.176.1	15982	149.171.126.14	5060	Udp	0
149.171.126.14	179	175.45.176.3	33159	Tcp	0
175.45.176.0	3716	149.171.126.15	80	Tcp	1

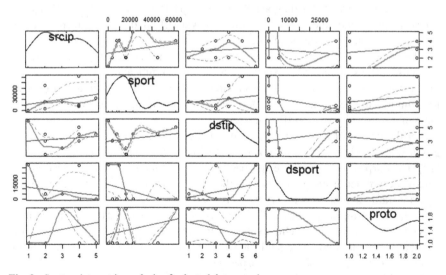

Fig. 2 Scatterplot matrix analysis of selected data samples

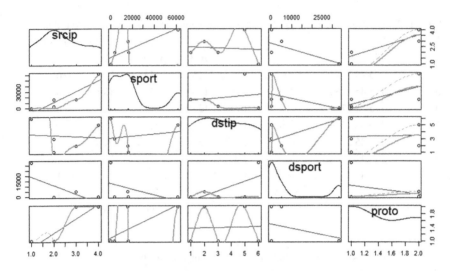

Fig. 3 Scatterplot matrix analysis of parts of selected samples

The scatterplot matrices presented in these two figures illustrate the statistical characteristics of the samples and their selected parts using the simple random sampling technique. They indicate if there are linear correlations between multiple features which help to identify analytical features that could have the same relationships. The features are provided in diagonal lines from top left to bottom right and then each is drawn against the others. The plots on the lower left-hand side are mirror images of those on the upper right-hand side.

There are slight differences between the features in the two figures. However, when using the simple random sampling technique, significant flows with information about suspicious instances are sometimes removed. This technique is effective for summarising network data to determine their patterns and active protocols, services and source/destination IP addresses.

For the design of an effective IDS, it is better to use correlation approaches to gather relevant observations from networks without omitting any distinct instances [12]. The purpose of using these approaches is to accumulate all the proper flows in a network without dropping any among the chokepoints to ensure a full analysis of network traffic in relatively less processing time.

Using flow sampling, a subset of all received packets is selected to identify anomalous events. However, this technique results in an inaccurate traffic analysis as some suspicious instances could be neglected, and it makes protocol analysis difficult to execute as not all protocols can be inspected.

To tackle the problem of missing flows, we use the ARM technique to select all instances with duplicated pair values of more than one. Table 3 shows the entire item sets appearing more than once in Table 1, and as selecting any of them reduces the processing time of an IDS for the same activities taking place between the same two endpoints, we use only those instances while running the IDS. This method performs

Table 3 Examples using ARM technique to select important observations

Item sets	No.
dstip =149.171.126.16, proto = tcp	2, 7
dsport = 80, proto = tcp	6, 7, 8
dsport = 5060, proto = udp	5, 10
srcip = 175.45.176.0, proto = tcp	4, 6, 8
srcip = 175.45.176.0, dstip = 149.171.126.10	5, 9
srcip = 175.45.176.2, proto = udp	3, 9

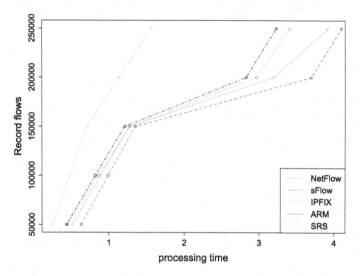

Fig. 4 Comparison of flow aggregator techniques

better than other approaches in terms of collecting instances for each specified time as it relies on instances with frequent values. If these values are similar for consecutive observations, only one is selected in order to improve the processing time of the IDS.

The ARM and SRS techniques are compared with the NetFlow, sFlow and IPFIX tools in terms of processing time and extracting distinct records using the CSV files of the UNSW-NB15 data sets to demonstrate the capability of our aggregator module. The experimental results show that our module can generate the majority of relevant flows with a low processing time as shown in Fig. 4.

This is because our module is designed to aggregate the flows using the five flow identifiers but the other techniques can only aggregate via one attribute. Moreover, we use the MySQL database to keep these flows in order to easily process by the IDS. To conclude, we recommend using the ARM technique if we identify abnormal instances, hence ensuring analysing all observed records. Conversely, if we monitor the network activities such as network capacity and user events, it is better to use the sampling technique.

5 Conclusion

This paper discussed a proposed flow aggregator module for collecting significant observations that occur in networks. It consists of the functions of sniffing network traffic data, collecting them in a data source for handling and aggregating similar data flows using the two techniques of simple random sampling and ARM for detection purposes. This module shows that, although the sampling technique is effective for summarisation and takes less processing time, the ARM approach is better for detection as, unlike the sampling technique, it does not lose any flow. In future, we plan to use this module as a first step in improving the performance of an IDS.

References

1. Ahmed, M., Mahmood, A.N., Maher, M.J.: A novel approach for network traffic summarization. In: International Conference on Scalable Information Systems, pp. 51–60. Springer (2014)
2. Carela-Español, V., Barlet-Ros, P., Cabellos-Aparicio, A., Solé-Pareta, J.: Analysis of the impact of sampling on netflow traffic classification. Computer Networks 55(5), 1083–1099 (2011)
3. Cecil, A.: A summary of network traffic monitoring and analysis techniques. In: Conference on Instruction & Technology (CIT), pp. 10–25 (2012)
4. Cochran, W.G.: Sampling techniques. John Wiley & Sons (2007)
5. Duffield, N.: Sampling for passive internet measurement: A review. Statistical Science pp. 472–498 (2004)
6. Hulboj, M.M., Jurga, R.E.: Packet sampling and network monitoring (2007)
7. Kerr, D.R., Bruins, B.L.: Network flow switching and flow data export (2009). US Patent 7,475,156
8. Li, B., Springer, J., Bebis, G., Gunes, M.H.: A survey of network flow applications. Journal of Network and Computer Applications 36(2), 567–581 (2013)
9. Moustafa, N., Slay, J.: A hybrid feature selection for network intrusion detection systems: Central points (2015)
10. Moustafa, N., Slay, J.: The significant features of the UNSW-NB15 and the KDD99 data sets for network intrusion detection systems. In: Building Analysis Datasets and Gathering Experience Returns for Security (BADGERS), 2015 4th International Workshop on, pp. 25–31. IEEE (2015)
11. Moustafa, N., Slay, J.: UNSW-NB15: a comprehensive data set for network intrusion detection systems (UNSW-NB15 network data set). In: Military Communications and Information Systems Conference (MilCIS), 2015, pp. 1–6. IEEE (2015)
12. Moustafa, N., Slay, J.: The evaluation of network anomaly detection systems: Statistical analysis of the UNSW-NB15 data set and the comparison with the KDD99 data set. Information Security Journal: A Global Perspective 25(1–3), 18–31 (2016)
13. Moustafa, N., Slay, J., Creech, G.: Novel geometric area analysis technique for anomaly detection using trapezoidal area estimation on large-scale networks. IEEE Transactions on Big Data 99, 1–1 (2017). https://doi.org/10.1109/TBDATA.2017.2715166
14. Nikolai, J., Wang, Y.: Hypervisor-based cloud intrusion detection system. In: Computing, Networking and Communications (ICNC), 2014 International Conference on, pp. 989–993. IEEE (2014)
15. Rieke, M., Dennis, J.S., Thorson, S.R.: Systems and methods for network data flow aggregation (2015). US Patent App. 14/974,378

16. Shirali-Shahreza, S., Ganjali, Y.: Flexam: flexible sampling extension for monitoring and security applications in openflow. In: Proceedings of the second ACM SIGCOMM workshop on Hot topics in software defined networking, pp. 167–168. ACM (2013)
17. Zhang, Y., Binxing, F., Hao, L.: Identifying high-rate flows based on sequential sampling. IEICE TRANSACTIONS on Information and Systems **93**(5), 1162–1174 (2010)

Chaos-based Modified Morphological Genetic Algorithm for Software Development Cost Estimation

Saurabh Bilgaiyan, Kunwar Aditya, Samaresh Mishra and Madhabananda Das

Abstract We have proposed a morphological approach based on an evolutionary learning for software development cost estimation (SDCE). The dilation–erosion perceptron (DEP) method which is a hybrid artificial neuron is built on mathematical morphology (MM) framework. This method has its roots in the complete lattice theory. The proposed work also presents an evolutionary learning procedure, i.e., a chaotic modified genetic algorithm (CMGA) to construct the DEP (CMGA) model overcoming the drawbacks arising in the morphological operator's gradient estimation in the classical learning procedure of DEP. The experimental analysis was conducted on estimation of five different SDCE problems and then analyzed using three performance measurement metrics.

Keywords Dilation–Erosion perceptron · Evolutionary learning · Genetic algorithms · Performance measurement metrics and SDCE

1 Introduction

Software engineering is the field of study that encompasses the various phases of software development starting from its inception phase right upto its testing, deployment, and maintenance [1]. Software Project Management (SPM) is the process of efficiently managing the entire project development stages such as planning,

S. Bilgaiyan (✉) · K. Aditya · S. Mishra · M. Das
School of Computer Engineering, KIIT, Deemed to be University,
Bhubaneswar 751024, Odisha, India
e-mail: saurabh.bilgaiyanfcs@kiit.ac.in

K. Aditya
e-mail: 1421019@kiit.ac.in

S. Mishra
e-mail: smishrafcs@kiit.ac.in

M. Das
e-mail: mndas_prof@kiit.ac.in

© Springer Nature Singapore Pte Ltd. 2018   31
P. K. Pattnaik et al. (eds.), *Progress in Computing, Analytics and Networking*,
Advances in Intelligent Systems and Computing 710,
https://doi.org/10.1007/978-981-10-7871-2_4

integrating, and controlling. Planning is done even before the actual project's development is started and includes gathering of requirements and resources. Integrating basically corresponds to combining all the ideas and proposals made during the planning phase to be executed for the development of the software. Controlling the various phases to ensure their timely completion is done throughout the development process [2, 3].

Estimation of the total software development cost is an important task to be performed in the planning phase. Cost estimation is basically a prediction of finance, time, and manpower that is to be incurred in the development of software. In the initial phases of the development, the accurate prediction of the above said parameters is difficult because of inaccurate and incomplete presence of data and also because of its dynamic nature [2, 4].

An accurate prediction of costs in the development of the software is an important task. According to the Chaos Report of the Standish Group in 1994, around 16.2% of the software was delivered on time whereas in 2012, the number went up to 39%, because of the use of various software cost estimation techniques. The techniques used can further be improved to get an even higher success rate [5, 6].

The hybrid perceptron which is also known as DEP uses the fundamental operators from MM on complete lattice theory. DEP has proved that it is very useful and produces better results while solving the prediction problems [6].

In order to solve the SDCE problem, this paper presents an evolutionary morphological approach which uses the DEP with a chaotically modified evolutionary learning procedure, i.e., DEP (CMGA). To conduct an experimental analysis, datasets of KotenGray, Kemerer, COCOMO, Albrecht, and Desharnais were used. In order to assess the performance, an evaluation function (EF) and two performance metrics, i.e., Prediction (PRED(x)) and Mean Magnitude of Relative Error (MMRE), were used. Finally, the results were compared to best existing methods present in the literature.

2   Dilation–Erosion Perceptron

The dilation–erosion perceptron also known as DEP, proposed by R. de A. Arajo et al. [6], is composed of a convex collaboration of dilation and erosion operators from the domain of MM with the foundation in complete lattice theory.

Let q be the output of the DEP model corresponding to the input $p = (p_1, p_2 ... p_n)$ $\epsilon \mathbb{R}^n$ where p represents a real-valued input signal within a n-point moving window. The local signal transformation rule p $\rightarrow$ q represents a translation invariant morphological system given by Eqs. (1, 2 and 3):

$$q = \lambda\alpha + (1 - \lambda)\beta, \lambda\epsilon[0, 1] \qquad (1)$$

$$\alpha = \delta_a(x) = \bigvee_{j=1}^{n}(x_j + a_j) \qquad (2)$$

$$\beta = \varepsilon_b(x) = \bigwedge_{j=1}^{n}(x_j + b_j) \qquad (3)$$

where a, b ϵ $\mathbb{R}^n$ and λ ϵ $\mathbb{R}^n$ and n represents the input signal dimension. The terms a and b represent the structuring elements dilation and erosion operators from the domain of MM.

3　Proposed CMGA Algorithm for Estimating Cost of Traditional Software Development

This proposed work presents a CMGA-based morphological learning process to accurately estimate the cost incurred in the development process. The proposed approach focuses on a mathematical morphological (MM) framework-based hybrid artificial neuron (also called dilation–erosion perceptron or DEP) with algebraic foundations in complete lattice theory. The proposed CMPSO-DEP model was tested on five well-known datasets of software projects with three popular performance metrics, and the results were compared with the best existing models available in the literature.

3.1　Population Initialization Using Chaotic Opposition-based Learning Method

Random initialization is mostly done if no information is available about the solution. The population initialization has been done using chaotic maps owing to its randomness and sensitivity dependence on initial condition, which is further used to extract search space information and to increase the population diversity [7, 8].

Better initial solution can be obtained by replacing randomly initialized population with opposition-based population initialization, which also accelerates convergence speed [9]. The following steps are followed for the initialization process:

Here, x_{minq} and x_{maxq} represent the minimum and maximum possible positions of the solution (system boundary). In this method, we selected sinusoidal iterator, given by:

$$cho_{(l+1)} = \sin(\pi cho_l), cho_l \epsilon [0, 1], l = 0, 1, 2...Max_l \qquad (4)$$

where l represents the iteration counter, and Max_l represents preset maximum number of chaotic iterations.

Algorithm 1: Steps for Chaotic Opposition Based Population Initialization Algorithm (COPI)

---

begin
  (COPI) [7];
  Data: Number of chaotic itereations $Max_I = 300$
  Population size=N
  Result: Initial population
  for $p=1$ *to* N **do**
    for $q=1$ *to* E **do**
      Randomly initialize variable $cho_{0q} \epsilon [0, 1]$;
      for $r=1$ *to* Max_I **do**
        | $cho_{rq} = \sin(\pi cho_{r-1,q})$
      end
      $x_{pq} = x_{minq} + cho_{rq}(x_{maxq} - x_{minq})$
    end
  end
  (—Start Opposition Based Method—);
  for $p=1$ *to* N **do**
    for $q=1$ *to* E **do**
      | $opx_{pq} = x_{minq} + x_{maxq} - x_{pq}$
    end
  end
  Select N fittest individuals from $(X(N) \cup OPX(N))$ as initial population;
end

3.2 Proposed Evolutionary Learning Algorithm

The training process used the weight vector w = (a, b, λ) where the parameters of vector w correspond to the parameters of the DEP model. The parameters of weight vector (for DEP model) are adjusted according to the error criterion, and this process is continued until the CMGA converges to its final state [10]. Each ith individual from gth generation of the population shows a candidate solution corresponding to a weight vector, denoted by $w_i^{(g)}$ for the DEP model. We define a fitness function $ff(w_i^{(g)})$ for adjusting the parameters of weight vector, given by:

$$ff(w_i^{(g)}) = \frac{1}{I} \sum_{r=1}^{I} e^2(r) \tag{5}$$

where I represents the number of input patterns, and e(r) represents the instantaneous error which is given by:

$$e(r) = d(r) - q(r) \tag{6}$$

where the desired output signal is represented by d(r), and the actual model output signal is represented by q(r) for the sample r.

The process of CMGA (as given in Algorithm 2) starts with a random initialization of the population. Then the process selects two parents for performing crossover and mutation operator depending upon the defined criteria. This process will generate the new offspring for the next population until the termination criteria is reached. Finally, best individual (candidate solution) from the final population is chosen as a solution for problem domain area. In the simulation, the size of population consists

---

Algorithm 2: Steps for DEP(CMGA) Algorithm

---

begin
   DEP(MGA);
   Data: Chaotically Initialize Population according to COPI algorithm
   Result: Predicted Value
   initialization of CMGA parameters;
   initialization of stopping criteria;
   g=0;
   while *Termination criteria is not satisfied* **do**
     g=g+1;
     for *i=1 to pop* **do**
       initialization of DEP parameters taking values from $w_i^{(g)}$;
       for all input patterns, calculate the value of q and the instantaneous error;
       use Eq. 5 to assess the individual fitness $ff(w_i^{(g)})$;
     end
     from the population, select the parents ($w_{p1}^{(g)}$ and $w_{p2}^{(g)}$)
     for *i=1 to 4* **do**
       initialization of DEP parameters taking values from oc_i;
       for all input patterns, calculate the value of q and the instantaneous error;
       use Eq. 5 to assess the individual fitness $ff(oc_i)$;
     end
     oc_{best} denotes the best evaluated offspring
     for *i=1 to 3* **do**
       initialization of DEP parameters taking values from ocm_i;
       for all input patterns, calculate the value of q and the instantaneous error;
       use Eq. 5 to assess the individual fitness $ff(ocm_i)$;
     end
     $w_{worse}^{(g)}$ is replaced by oc_{best};
     if *random number $\leq PM_s$* **then**
       then $w_{worse}^{(g)}$ is replaced with the one having the smallest fitness among ocm_1, ocm_2 and ocm_3;
     else
       for *i=1 to 3* **do**
         if $ff(ocm_i) \leq ff(w_{worse}^{(g)})$ **then**
           then $w_{worse}^{(g)}$ is replaced by ocm_i
         end
       end
     end
   end
end

---

of ten individuals, i.e., Pop=10 and the maximum iterations are 10000 (stopping criteria).

A Roulette wheel approach was used to obtain a selection of two parents (i.e., vector $w_{p1}^{(g)}$ and $w_{p2}^{(g)}$ $\epsilon\mathbb{R}^n$ where p1 and p2 represent integer indexes having range within [1, pop]) that was used for crossover operation, for exchanging information.

Here, h ϵ [0, 1] denotes the crossover weight (in this work, the value of h is taken as 0.9). As the value of h tends to 1, the greater contribution from parents is observed. $max(w_{p1}^{(g)}, w_{p2}^{(g)})$ and $min(w_{p1}^{(g)}, w_{p2}^{(g)})$ vectors represent the element-wise maximum and minimum of $w_{p1}^{(g)}$ and $w_{p2}^{(g)}$. The maximum possible gene value and minimum possible gene value are represented by w_{max}, w_{min} $\epsilon\mathbb{R}^n$. Out of the four generated offspring, the one displaying the smallest fitness value is selected as oc_{best} $\epsilon\mathbb{R}^n$ which will replace the individual having the greatest fitness value in the population, i.e., $w_{worse}^{(g)}$ with worse ϵ [1, pop].

After the end of crossover process, with the mutation probability of 0.2, three new mutated offspring (ocm_1, ocm_2, ocm_3 $\epsilon\mathbb{R}^n$) are generated from oc_{best} given by [10]:

$$ocm_i = oc_{best} + u_i v_i, i = 1, 2, 3. \tag{7}$$

Here, u_i must satisfy the inequality $w_{min} \leq oc_{best} + u_i \leq w_{max}$. Vector v_i is in-between [0, 1] and satisfies the conditions: Vector v_1 has randomly selected nonzero entry, v_2 is randomly selected binary vector, and v_3 is constant vector 1. After generating the three mutated offspring, we will generate a random number within [0, 1] interval. If this is smaller than probability of mutation selection, i.e., PM_s, then $w_{worse}^{(g)}$ is replaced by the mutated offspring having the minimum fitness value; otherwise, if the fitness value of ocm_i is less than that of $w_{worse}^{(g)}$, then we replace the latter with ocm_i.

4 Performance Measures

For prediction evaluation, out of the many performance criteria available in the literature, only one performance criterion is usually employed. The mean squared error (MSE) can be used to provide directions to the prediction model (while training process), but it cannot be considered as a good measure for comparing different models of prediction [11].

The first metric MMRE identifies model deviation given by Eq. 8:

$$MMRE = \frac{1}{N} \sum_{i=1}^{N} \frac{|Actual_i - Predicted_i|}{Actual_i} \tag{8}$$

Here, N represents the number of input patterns, $Actual_i$ represents desired output, and $Predicted_i$ represents the predicted value.

PRED(x) represents the second metric which is the percentage of prediction value falling within the range of actual value given by Eqs. 9 and 10 [6].

$$PRED(x) = \frac{100}{N} \sum_{i=1}^{N} P_i \qquad (9)$$

where,

$$P_i = \begin{cases} 1, & if(MMRE_i) < \frac{x}{100} \\ 0, & Otherwise \end{cases} \qquad (10)$$

where x = 25.

Further, the EF which is a combination of MMRE and PRED is used to provide a more vigorous prediction model given by Eq. 11 [6].

$$Eval_f = \frac{PRED(25)}{1 + MMRE} \qquad (11)$$

5 Simulations and Conclusive Studies

The proposed DEP (CMGA) algorithm was tested through MATLAB on five complex real-world software development cost estimation (SDCE) problems (COCOMO, Kemerer, Albrecht, Desharnais, and KotenGray [6]). Datasets were normalized to lie within [0,1]. The parameters of DEP, a, b (lies within [−1,1]) and λ (lies within [0,1]), were initialized randomly. Tables 1, 2, 3, 4, and 5 show that proposed model has consistent global performance having an averaged improvement of around 3.1648% regarding MRLHD and 1.9302% regarding the DEP (BP).

Table 1 Predicted result values for Albrecht dataset

Type of model	PRED(25)	MMRE	$Eval_f$
SVR with linear kernel [12]	58.33	0.6719	34.8884
SVR-RBF kernel [12]	66.66	0.5072	44.2277
Bagging [13]	70.83	0.4178	49.9577
SVR-RBF using GA [12]	70.42	0.4465	48.6830
SVR-linear using GA [12]	56.25	0.6628	33.8285
MRL [14]	70.83	0.4087	50.2804
MRLHD [14]	75.00	0.3810	54.3085
DEP (BP) [15]	75.00	0.3699	54.7485
DEP (CMGA)	77.08	0.3492	57.1301

Table 2 Predicted result values for Kemerer dataset

Type of model	PRED(25)	MMRE	$Eval_f$
SVR with linear kernel [12]	60.00	0.4608	41.0734
SVR-RBF kernel [12]	60.00	0.4439	41.5541
Bagging [13]	60.00	0.4297	41.9668
SVR-RBF using GA [12]	66.67	0.3695	48.6820
SVR-linear using GA [12]	60.00	0.4373	41.7449
MRL [14]	66.67	0.3014	51.2294
MRLHD [14]	73.33	0.2779	57.3832
DEP (BP) [15]	73.33	0.2619	58.1108
DEP (CMGA)	74.89	0.2478	60.0176

Table 3 Predicted result values for KotenGray dataset

Model of type	PRED(25)	MMRE	$Eval_f$
SVR with linear kernel [12]	88.24	0.1133	79.2599
SVR-RBF kernel [12]	88.24	0.1108	79.4382
Bagging [13]	94.12	0.1001	85.5559
SVR-RBF using GA [12]	94.12	0.0947	85.9779
SVR-linear using GA [12]	94.12	0.0895	86.3883
MRL [14]	94.12	0.0710	87.8805
MRLHD [14]	94.12	0.0689	88.0531
DEP (BP) [15]	94.12	0.0572	89.0276
DEP (CMGA)	94.33	0.0509	89.7611

Table 4 Predicted result values for COCOMO dataset

Type of model	PRED(25)	MMRE	$Eval_f$
SVR with linear kernel [12]	81.82	0.1573	70.6990
SVR-RBF kernel [12]	72.73	0.1802	61.6251
Bagging [13]	72.73	0.1754	61.8768
SVR-RBF using GA [12]	72.73	0.1729	62.0087
SVR-linear using GA [12]	81.82	0.1481	71.2656
MRL [14]	81.82	0.1436	71.5460
MRLHD [14]	90.90	0.1298	80.4567
DEP (BP) [15]	90.90	0.1127	81.6932
DEP (CMGA)	91.00	0.1033	82.4798

Table 5 Predicted result values for Desharnais dataset

Type of model	PRED(25)	MMRE	$Eval_f$
SVR with linear kernel [12]	55.00	0.4829	37.0895
SVR-RBF kernel [12]	60.00	0.4543	41.2570
Bagging [13]	65.00	0.4076	46.1779
SVR-RBF using GA [12]	80.00	0.3302	60.1413
SVR-linear using GA [12]	80.00	0.3154	61.8180
MRL [14]	85.00	0.1509	73.8552
MRLHD [14]	90.00	0.0981	81.9597
DEP (BP) [15]	90.00	0.0835	83.0641
DEP (CMGA)	90.00	0.0809	83.2639

6 Conclusion

This paper presented an evolutionary learning process based on MM to solve the SDCE problem. Proposed model's performance was measured using performance metrics such as PRED(25) and MMRE. Also, an EF was used to generate a global indicator of the performance. Five databases such as Albrecht, Desharnais, Kemerer, COCOMO, and KotenGray were used to carry out experimental validation of the proposed model, to check its robustness by comparing with results previously found in the literature. The proposed model has shown consistent global performance with an averaged improvement of around 3.1648% regarding MRLHD and 1.9302% regarding the DEP (BP). As future work, we shall implement the proposed model to other datasets and in other software engineering problems.

References

1. Bilgaiyan, S., Mishra, S., Das, M.: A Review of Software Cost Estimation in Agile Software Development using Soft Computing Techniques, 2nd International Conference on Computational Intelligence and Networks, IEEE, pp. 112–117 (2016).
2. Demir, K. A.: 3PR Framework for Software Project Management: People, Process, Product, and Risk. Software Project Management for Distributed Computing, Springer, pp. 143–170 (2017).
3. Singh, J., Sahoo, B.: Software Effort Estimation with Different Artificial Neural Network. 2nd National Conference on Computing, Communication and Sensor Network, Vol. 4, No. 3, pp. 13–17 (2011).
4. Jorgensen, M., Shepperd, M.: A Systematic Review of Software Development Cost Estimation Studies. IEEE Transactions on Software Engineering, Vol. 33, No. 1, pp. 33–53 (2007).
5. The Standish Group. CHAOS Manifesto. Availaible on: https://larlet.fr/static/david/stream/ ChaosManifesto2013.pdf, 2013.
6. Arajo, R de A., et al.: An Evolutionary Morphological Approach for Software Development Cost Estimation. Neural Networks, Elsevier, Vol. 32, pp. 285–291 (2012).

7. Gao, W-f, et al.: Particle Swarm Optimization with Chaotic Opposition-based population Initialization and Stochastic Search Technique. Communications in Nonlinear Science and Numerical Simulation, Elsevier, Vol. 17, No. 4, pp. 4316–4327 (2012).

8. Liu, B., Wang, L., et al.: Improved particle Swarm Optimization Combined with Chaos. Chaos, Solitons and Fractals, Vol. 25, No. 1, pp. 1261–1271 (2005).

9. Rahnamayan, S., et al.: Opposition-Based Differential Evolution. IEEE Transactions on Evolutionary Computation, Vol. 12, No. 1, pp. 64–79 (2008).

10. Leung, F. H. F., Lam, H. K., Ling, S. H., Tam, P. K. S.: Tuning of the Structure and Parameters of the Neural Network using an Improved Genetic Algorithm. IEEE Transactions on Neural Networks, Vol. 14, No. 1, pp. 79–88 (2003).

11. Clements, M. P., Hendry, D. F.: On The Limitations of Comparing Mean Square Forecast Errors. Journals of Forecasting, Vol. 12, No. 8, pp. 617–637 (1993).

12. Oliveira, A. L. I., Braga, P. L., Lima, R. M., Cornelio, M. L.: GA-based Method for Feature Selection and Parameters Optimization for Machine Learning Regression Applied to Software Effort Estimation. Information and Software Technology, Elsevier, Vol. 52, No. 1, pp. 6129–6139 (2010).

13. Braga, P. L., et al.: Software Effort Estimation using Machine learning Techniques with Robust Confidence Intervals. IEEE International Conference on Tools with Artificial Intelligence, No. 8, pp. 1595–1600 (2007).

14. Arajo, R. de A., de Oliveira, A. L. I., Soares, S. C. B., Meira, S. R. de L.: Gradient based Morphological Approach for Software Development Cost Estimation. IEEE International Joint Conference on Neural Networks, pp. 588–594 (2011).

15. Arajo, R. de A.: A class of Hybrid Morphological Perceptrons with Application in Time Series Forecasting. Knowledge-Based Systems, Elsevier, Vol. 24, No. 4, pp. 513–529 (2011).

An Efficient Block Phase Correlation Approach for CMFD System

Badal Soni, Pradip K. Das and Dalton Meitei Thounaojam

Abstract Copy–move forgery is the most basic technique to alter an image. In this method, one region of an image is copied and pasted into another location of the same image, with an attempt to cover a potentially important feature or duplicate some features. As the copied part resides in the same image, its important properties, such as noise, brightness, texture, are compatible with rest of the image making its detection very difficult. The existing techniques for detecting copy–move forgery suffer from the computational time problem. In this paper, an efficient block-based copy–move forgery detection algorithm is present that reduces the processing time in identifying the duplicated regions in an image. Proposed method is tested on CoMoFoD dataset. Experimental results show the ability of the proposed method to accurately detect the tampered regions as well as reducing the time complexity.

Keywords Copy–move · Forgery · Phase correlation · DFT

1 Introduction

The most extensive way to circulate a message in today's world is through digital image. Images can be used as proof against various crimes and as evidence for various other purposes. But with the advancement of computer technology, various image-editing software tools have been developed with the help of which an image can be easily tampered to change the information carried by it. Hence, it is very essential to protect the authenticity of an image. As forgers develop more

B. Soni (✉) · D. M. Thounaojam
National Institute of Technology, Silchar, India
e-mail: soni.badal88@gmail.com

D. M. Thounaojam
e-mail: dalton.meitei@gmail.com

P. K. Das
Indian Institute of Technology, Guwahati, India
e-mail: pkdas@iitg.ernet.in

© Springer Nature Singapore Pte Ltd. 2018   41
P. K. Pattnaik et al. (eds.), *Progress in Computing, Analytics and Networking*,
Advances in Intelligent Systems and Computing 710,
https://doi.org/10.1007/978-981-10-7871-2_5

sophisticated forgeries, researchers must keep up to design more advanced ways of detecting these forgeries. Copy–move forgery is an potential tampering technique.

In [1], a method for CMFD, based on principle component analysis (PCA), is given. The fixed size overlapping blocks division is performed on image after that PCA of these blocks is calculated to yield a reduced dimensional representation. In [2], a SVD-based method to detect the tempered regions is given. In this, singular value features of the image are extracted using SVD and sort using lexicographic sorting. For block similarity matching, the features are first transformed into a kd-tree and then similar blocks are found using Euclidean distance. In [3], a block-based copy–move forgery detection technique based upon discrete cosine transform (DCT) is given. In this paper, forgery detection is performed by shift vectors analysis of the sorted DCT coefficients. In [4], a method which is an improved version of DCT method is given. This method removes the limitations of DCT-based block matching algorithm by changing the structure of matching algorithm. In similarity matching, all the feature row vectors are not considered instead the characteristics of DCT coefficients are utilized to set a more stronger criterion to establish similarity. In [5] for efficient detection, robust features are extracted from the circular blocks. For each block, four features are extracted and used for finding similar blocks. Feature vectors' dimension is low which means that the method has a low computational complexity. Paper [6] proposed a method that increases the efficiency of DCT method for detection of copy–move forgery in complex and smooth image. Images are divided into two categories: complex and smooth. For smooth images, small size block is considered. While for complex images, large block size is considered. This method can detect forgery in compressed JPEG formats, blur Gaussian, and additive white Gaussian noises. However, it is not robust to geometrical operations. In [7], discrete wavelet transform-based copy–move forgery detection technique is given. In this technique, 2-D DWT is initially applied on the tampered image and block division is performed by using approximate coefficients of DWT. Matching is performed by calculating distance between all block pairs. It seems that the given algorithm is not suitable for forgery detection in case of geometric transformation attacks. In [8], dyadic wavelet transform (DyWT) is used. In this method, image blocks are sorted and matching between block pairs is performed. Decision of forgery depends upon the matching threshold which is obtained experimentally. DyWT is shift invariant therefore leads to optimal results as compared to DWT. Key point-based methods are divided into two categories. They are SIFT [9] and SURF based. A generalized 2NN procedure for SIFT descriptors matching is proposed in [10] for CMFD. In [11], SURF descriptors are extracted from image and extracted SURF descriptors are matched for forgery detection. In [12], image is divided into blocks and Gabor feature descriptor of each block is calculated. These Gabor descriptors are used for matching of blocks and forgery decision. It is reported that proposed method underperformed when the forged region has undergone by different geometric transformations.

In this paper, an efficient copy–move forgery detection approach is given. In this approach, tampered image is first divided into fixed size overlapping blocks after that low contrast blocks are eliminated for the further processing. Phase correlation is computed between the sorted blocks for deciding the forgery present in the image. The paper is organized as Sect. 1 address existing work. Proposed methodology is given in Sect. 2. Experimental results and discussions of proposed method are given in Sect. 3. Conclusions and future scope are given in Sect. 4.

2 Proposed Methodology

Block diagram of proposed method is given in Fig. 1. Proposed method consists of following step:

2.1 RGB to Grayscale Conversion

The proposed method is applied on gray images. So the tampered colored image is converted to gray scale in the preprocessing step.

2.2 Overlapping Blocks Division

In this algorithm, tampered image is divided into overlapping blocks. The block size is used in 8×8 and 16×16. Overlapping blocks are created by sliding over the

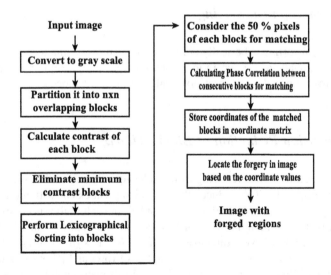

Fig. 1 Flowchart of proposed algorithm

original image one pixel at a time across the rows and columns. The number of overlapping blocks obtained for an image of $m \times n$ dimensions is $(m - b + 1) \times (n - b + 1)$ where size of the block is $b \times b$. All the overlapping created blocks are stored in a matrix for further processing.

2.3 Eliminating Low Contrast Blocks

Contrast may be defined as a ratio between the darkest spots and the brightest spots of an image. In the proposed method, the overlapped blocks which are low in contrast are excluded. This is because in a given image, forgery is mainly performed on portions of high contrast region like a human character or an object with respect to the background where the contrast is typically high. Low contrast regions include uniform regions like sky, water, and any other object where the color is uniformly distributed. By excluding the low contrast blocks, the number of blocks are reduced drastically. In the proposed method, the Michelson contrast is used since we are looking for uniform regions. The threshold value is set to 0.5. The Michelson contrast is given in Eq. 1

$$W_m = \frac{L_{max} - L_{min}}{L_{max} + L_{min}} \tag{1}$$

where L_{max} and L_{min} represent highest and lowest pixel values. It is used mainly when both the dark and the bright features are equivalent.

2.4 Lexicographical Sorting

Lexicographical sorting is basically defined as the natural sorting technique or sorting based on alphabetical order. In the proposed algorithm, lexicographical sorting enables us to sort based on the first-pixel value of the $b \times b$ block.

2.5 Dimension Reduction of Blocks Matrix

Blocks matrix dimension is reducing by considering only half of the columns in the given matching blocks. This reduces the time by a great extent without decreasing the accuracy as it can be assumed that the first half of each of the successive blocks is a match then the remaining half of blocks will also match. Thus, if the overlapping blocks matrix have a dimension of $[(m - b + 1) \times (n - b + 1)] \times [(b \times b)]$, where $[(m - b + 1) \times (n - b + 1)]$ is the number of rows and $[(b \times b)]$ is the number of columns. The dimension of the modified blocks matrix will be $[(m - b + 1) \times (n - b + 1)] \times [(b^2/2)]$.

2.6 Block Matching using Phase Correlation

Phase correlation analysis is used for blocks matching in the given forged image. There are various other ways for matching like the most popular one is the similarity matching using Euclidean distance. Phase correlation provides a simple and clear evaluation of matching for two blocks or images. The correlation between the two images produces an image with top intensities at locations where the two images match the most. Correlation is done by gliding one image over the other and taking the outcome of the products of the corresponding samples at each point. The idea behind correlation is that the resulting image will have the greatest value at the point where the images of hills and bottoms match up. Phase correlation (PC) is performed in frequency domain using the fast Fourier transform. The ratio PC between two blocks $B1$ and $B2$ is calculated by using Eq. 2

$$PC = \frac{FT(B1) * conj(FT(B2))}{||FT(B1) * conj(FT(B2))||} \tag{2}$$

Here FT is the fast Fourier transform and conj is the complex conjugate. Fourier transform is given in Eq. 3 and Inverse Fourier transform is given in Eq. 4. The maximum phase correlation is the maximum value of all the values of PC.

$$X[k] = \sum_{n=0}^{n-1} x[n] e^{-\frac{2\pi njk}{N}} \tag{3}$$

$$x[n] = \frac{1}{N} \sum_{k=0}^{N-1} X[k] e^{\frac{2\pi njk}{N}} \tag{4}$$

In the proposed method, the phase correlation for the block corresponding to the row i with the block corresponding to $i + 1$ rows is calculated. If the calculated maximum phase correlation value exceeds a predefined threshold value χ, then store the coordinates of the corresponding ith block and the $(i + 1)$th block in a coordinate record cell.

2.7 Storing of Match Blocks Coordinate

Matching is performed using phase correlation of the coordinates of the two successive blocks $B1$ and $B2$. If matching is found between the successive blocks, then blocks coordinate are stored in an array for further processing.

2.8 Display Forgery

The coordinates obtained from the previous step are the match block coordinates. Using these coordinates, forgery is localized in the tampered image by coloring the match region of image.

Algorithm 1 CMFD based on Block Phase correlation

 1: **procedure** START(Input tampered image)
 2:    Convert image to gray scale
 3:    *Parameters:* Blocksize, Contrast threshhold
 4:    $A \leftarrow$ Overlapping blocks
 5:    $B \leftarrow$ x,y coordinates of overlapping blocks
 6:    $C \leftarrow$ Exclude Low Contrast (A)
 7:    $A\_sort \leftarrow$ Sort matrix C lexicographically
 8:    $D \leftarrow A\_sort/2$
 9:    **for** $i = 1$ *to size of D* **do**
10:
11:        $PC \leftarrow \frac{FT(D(i)) \times conj(FT(D(i+1)))}{||FT(D(i)) \times conj(FT(D(i+1)))||}$
12:   ▷ using Equation 2
13:        $P \leftarrow$ IFFT(PC)
14:        **if** $max(P) >= \chi$ **then**
15:            $CoorRec \leftarrow$ coordinates of matched rows
16:            $i \leftarrow i + 1$
17:        **for** $i = 1$ *to size of CoorRec* **do**
18:            $ImgOut \leftarrow$ Forged regions using CoorRec
19:        **end for**
20:    **end for**
21:    *Localized the forgery in Image by coloring the match regions*
22: **end procedure**

---

3 Experimental Results and Discussions

The proposed methodology is improved the accuracy as well as reduced the time complexity. In implementation, we used a HP laptop, Intel Core i5-3230M (2.60 GHz), Memory 4 GB. The dataset used for the testing purpose is CoMoFoD [13]. CoMoFoD is the standard image dataset used for forgery detection purpose. It has 260 image sets, in which 200 sets for small size 512×512 images and 60 sets for large size 3000×2000 images. Both small and large image categories consist of images undergone through translation, rotation, and scaling transformations. Performance analysis of proposed forgery detection technique is done by calculating detection error rates at image level. False positive rate (FPR), is the number of original images detected as forged. True positive rate (TPR) is the number of images correctly detected as forged. Figure 2 shows the input forged images from CoMoFoD dataset and corresponding forged regions. Table 1 shows the processing time of different images with block size 8×8 and 16×16.

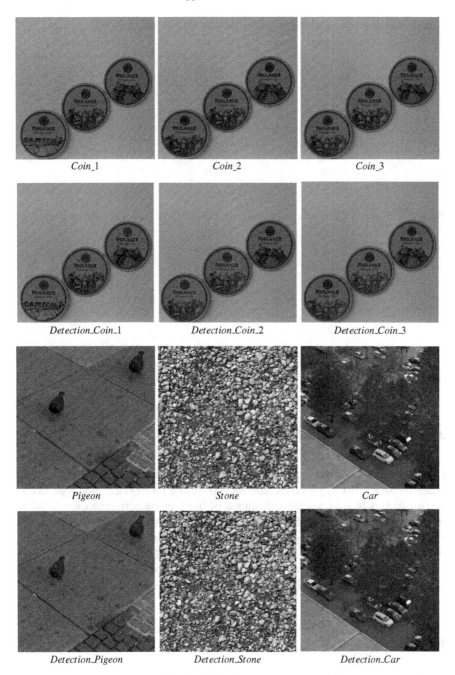

Fig. 2 Tampered images from CoMoFoD dataset and corresponding forgery detection results

Table 1　Processing time of proposed system in CoMoFoD dataset images

Sl. no.	Image	Average processing time (in sec) for block size 8 × 8	Average processing time (in sec) for block size 16 × 16
1	Coin_1	18.869	13.243
2	Coin_2	24.385	15.139
3	Coin_3	28.889	26.735
4	Pigeon	11.743	11.341
5	Stone	20.217	17.691
6	Car	16.969	14.399

Table 2　TPR and FPR of the proposed system for CoMoFoD database with different block size

Sl. no.	Block size	TPR (%)	FPR (%)
1	4 × 4	94.8	6.4
2	8 × 8	97.8	8.4
3	12 × 12	98.6	12.6
4	16 × 16	99.4	18.2

Experimental results show that system is achieving high TPR and FPR for large block size (Table 2). For our experiment, we consider the block size 8 × 8.

4　Conclusions and Future Work

Copy–move forgery detection is one of the emerging problems in the field of digital image forensics. In this paper, an efficient copy–move forgery detection approach is given which is based upon the calculation of block phase correlation for deciding the forgery present in the image. It is observed from experimental results that the proposed algorithm achieves improvement in terms of computation time. The results of the proposed method are based upon the block size and matching thresholds value. The proposed model works well for almost all dimension of images. It can also be extended to detect multiple forgery presents in images.

References

1. Popescu, A. C., and Farid, H.: 'Exposing digital forgeries by detecting traces of resampling', IEEE Transactions on Signal Processing, 2005, 53, (2), pp. 758–767.
2. Ting, Z., and Rang-Ding, W. : 'Copy-move forgery detection based on SVD in digital image'. Proceedings in International Congress on Image and Signal Processing (CISP), October 2009, pp. 1–5.

3. Fridrich, J., Soukal, D., and Lukas, J.: 'Detection of copy-move forgery in digital images'. Proceedings of Digital Forensic Research Workshop, 2003.
4. Sunil Kumar, Jagannath Desai, Shaktidev Mukherjee, "A Fast DCT Based Method for Copy Move Forgery Detection", Proceeding of the 2013 IEEE Second International Conference of Image Information Processing (ICIIP-2013).
5. Cao, Y. Gao, T. Fan, L. Yang, Q. (2012), "A Robust Detection Algorithm For Copy-Move Forgery in Digital Images", Forensic Science International, vol. 214, No. 13, pp. 33–43.
6. Elhem Mohebbian, Mahdi Hariri, "Increase the efficiency of DCT method for detection of Copy-Move Forgery in complex and smooth images", International Conference on Knowledge Based Engineering & Innovation(KBEI) Nov 5–6, 2015.
7. J. Zhang, Z. Feng and Y. Su, A new approach for detecting copy-move forgery in digital images, 11th IEEE Singapore International Conference on the Communication Systems, ICCS, 2008.
8. Muhammad, G., Hussain, M., Khawaji, K., and Bebis, G.: 'Blind copy-move image forgery detection using dyadic undecimated wavelet transform'. Proceedings of the international conference on Digital Signal Processing (DSP), July 2011.
9. D. G. Lowe, Distinctive image features from scale-invariant keypoints, International Journal of Computer Vision, vol. 60, no. 2, pp. 91–110, 2004.
10. Amerini, I., Ballan, L., Caldelli, R., Bimbo, A.D., and Serra, G.: "A SIFT-based forensic method for copymove attack detection and transformation recovery", IEEE Transactions on Information Forensics and Security, 2011, 6, (3), pp. 1099–1110.
11. Xu Bo, Wang Junwen, Liu Guangjie and Dai Yuewei, "Image Copy-move Forgery Detection Based on SURF", 2010 International Conference on Multimedia Information Networking and Security.
12. Hsu, H. and Wang, M. (2012), "Detection of Copy-Move Forgery Image Using Gabor Descriptor", in Proceedings of the International Conference on Anti-Counterfeiting, Security and Identification (ASID 12), IEEE, August 2012, pp. 1–4.
13. Tralic D., Zupancic I., Grgic S., Grgic M., "CoMoFoD—New Database for Copy-Move Forgery Detection", in Proc. 55th International Symposium ELMAR-2013, pp. 49–54, September 2013.

Automated Validation of DNSSEC

Kollapalli Ramesh Babu and Vineet Padmanabhan

Abstract Nowadays, the usage of Internet and network-based services has become common. Some of the services are very critical and require robust security to avoid intolerable consequences. As we all know, to provide such services, a robust cryptographic technique-based security protocol must be used. The designing of such a secure protocol is always a challenging task. The complexity of security protocols is getting high day by day, due to their functionalities and type of services that they provide to protect the resources from unauthorized accesses. As the complexity grows, it becomes very difficult and tedious task to verify its correctness manually. Therefore, we need some automatic mechanism to verify and validate the correctness of a given security protocol. The problem that we addressed in this paper is validation of the security protocol DNSSEC using automated verification tool called AVISPA.

Keywords Cryptographic techniques · DNSSEC · AVISPA

1 Introduction

Nowadays, the usage of online services specifically e-commerce services, online banking, online trading, online payments, etc., is getting more and more. In order to provide such services in a smooth and fair manner, one should use a highly sophisticated security protocols. The designing of highly secure protocols is always daunting, because the past experience with the usage of security protocols clearly shows that a large number of *logical flaws* are present in published or deployed security protocols.

K. Ramesh Babu (✉) · V. Padmanabhan
School of Computer & Information Science, University of Hyderabad,
Hyderabad 500046, India
e-mail: krubabu@gmail.com

V. Padmanabhan
e-mail: vineetcs@uohyd.ernet.in

© Springer Nature Singapore Pte Ltd. 2018
P. K. Pattnaik et al. (eds.), *Progress in Computing, Analytics and Networking*,
Advances in Intelligent Systems and Computing 710,
https://doi.org/10.1007/978-981-10-7871-2_6

One simple example is the well-known protocol called Needham–Schroeder [1] that was proved as correct by using BAN logic [2]. But after seventeen years, G. Lowe detected a flaw by using Casper/FDR [3] tool. The same flaw was not detected in the original proof by using BAN logic because of wrong assumptions on the intruder model. However, missing of detection/identification of a flaw clearly indicates that we should never underestimate the complexity of protocol analysis. This example illustrates the importance of an automatic verification tool in assessing the security of such cryptographic protocols.

The main objective of applying automated validation tools to security protocols is to detect the *logical flaws* which are subtle and hard to find. And also to detect a strategy or technique by which the protocol can be attacked.

Rest of the paper is organized as follows: In Sect. 2, we have discussed briefly about DNS and DNSEC protocols. In Sect. 3, we have discussed AVISPA architecture and its specification language HLPSL. In Sect. 4, we have discussed overview of DNSSEC protocol specification process. In Sect. 5, we have discussed validation of DNSSEC using AVISPA. In Sect. 6, we have presented the results. In Sect. 7, we have provided conclusion.

2 DNS and DNSSEC

Every system that is connected to computer network, specifically Internet, is assigned with a unique address called Internet Protocol Address (IP address), to identify and access it. These addresses are numericals, as a human being we feel easy to remember names instead of numericals. To overcome the difficulty and to make it convenient for accessing of any system connected to network, a service is provided by the Internet and name of that service is Domain Name System (DNS) [4, 5]. DNS maps a given domain name to an IP address and vice versa.

When DNS service is not functioning according to expectations, then it leads to very serious unwanted consequences, depending on the types of failures. Some consequences are simple and typical like making a service unaccessible such as a Web site is not reachable, and some are very dangerous like redirecting to wrong Web site, which may collect our confidential data such as passwords, credit/debit pin numbers, and bank account details that may lead to huge financial loss.

In order to avoid such situations, Domain Name System Security Extensions (DNSSEC) [6, 7] was designed. DNSSEC protocol provides two types of security services: One is *data integrity* and another is *data authentication*. Data integrity means ensuring of received data is the same as that of the sent one. Data authentication means ensuring of the genuinity of a sender server.

DNSSEC protects DNS by adding four records and using *chain of trust* technique [7]. The four records that are added by DNSSEC are namely DNS Public Key (DNSKEY) record that holds signing public key of a zone, Resource Record Signature (RRSIG) record that holds digital signatures of DNS replies, Delegation Signer (DS) record that holds the hash value of a child zone's DNSKEY, and Next Secure

(NSEC) record that holds next valid name in the zone file and also it used to provide proof of nonexistence of a given name within a zone.

DNS basically works in client–server scenario and send/receive data in the form of Resource Records (RRs) [8]. DNS server creates public key and private key pair and publishes the public key in the zone. A client that is DNSSEC-enabled can get a zone's public key. Once client learns/aware zone's public key, then it can authenticate that zone's signed data. DNSSEC-enabled client authenticates zone information by forming an authentication chain (*chain of trust*) from a newly learned public key back to a previously known authentication public key, which in turn must have been learned and verified previously. An alternating sequence of DNS public key (DNSKEY) RRsets and Delegation Signer (DS) RRsets forms a chain of trust [8].

In next section, we discuss AVISPA and its specification language HLPSL.

3 AVISPA and HLPSL

Automated Validation of Internet Security Protocols and Applications (AVISPA) [9, 10] is an automatic formal validation tool used to verify correctness of security properties of Internet security protocols. AVISPA uses a high-level protocol specification language (HLPSL) [11, 12] to write a protocol specification. HLPSL is a simple, expressive, and intuitive language to model a protocol for AVISPA. The general structure of HLPSL specification is shown below.

Structure of a HLPSL specification.

BasicRole_definition+
CompositionRole_definition?
EnvironmentRole_definition?
Goal_declaration?

HLPSL is basically a role-based language, which means each participant in a security protocol is represented as one role in HLPSL specification, including the environment in which the protocol is going to execute. In general, any HLPSL specification of a protocol consists of one more basic role definitions, followed by the definition of composite role where we combine one or more basic roles together so that they get executed together, usually parallel. Followed by the definition of environment role where we instantiate composition role to create one or more sessions. Finally, we specify security parameters as goals that we want to verify by the tool.

Now, we discuss the architecture of AVISPA tool which is shown in Fig. 1.

AVISPA tool accepts input specification in HLPSL and translates HLPSL specifications into Intermediate Format (IF). IF is an intermediate step where the rules are rewritten such that it will be more comfortable/convenient to further processing

Fig. 1 Architecture of
AVISPA tool

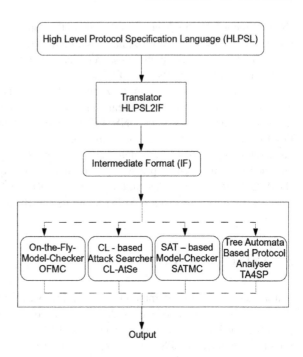

it by back-end analyzers. The IF of a protocol is executed over finite number of times or entirely if no loop exist. Finally, the execution may end up with either an identification of an attack on a given protocol or the protocol is proved as safe over a given number of sessions. AVISPA currently supports four back-end analyzers called On-the-Fly Model-Checker (OFMC), SAT-based Model-Checker (SATMC), Constraint-Logic-based Attack Searcher (CL-AtSe) and Tree Automata based on Automatic Approximations for the Analysis of Security Protocols (TA4SP) to check the correctness of the given protocol. AVISPA uses Dolev-Yao (DY) channels for sending and receiving of messages between the participants of security protocol, where the presence of intruder is also considered to account. AVISPA tool is aimed at countering two types of attacks—one is the *man-in-the-middle* attack and the other one is *replay* attack.

Before writing actual DNSSEC protocol specification using HLPSL to verify with the AVISPA tool, it is always suggested to represent the protocol using Alice - Bob (A - B) notion. Representation of a protocol using (A - B) notion will help us in getting clarity and better understanding of a protocol in terms of representation of messages exchanged between principles. Therefore in next section, we discuss (A - B) notion of DNSSEC protocol.

4   An Overview of DNSSEC Specification Process

The DNSSEC protocol representation using (A - B) notion is as shown below.

```
Alice - Bob (A - B) Notation:
1. C  ->  S:  DNS_req
2. S  ->  C:  DNS_res, RRSIG, DNSKEY(S)
3. C "verify" if  H(DNS_res) == {RRSIG}_DNSKY then
       go to Step 4.
       else discard DNS_res and exit.
4. C  ->  R:  DS_req
5. R  ->  C:  DS_res, RRSIG, DNSKEY(R)
6. C "verify" if  H(DS_res) == {RRSIG}_DNSKEY then
       go to step 7.
       else discard DS_res and exit
7. C "verify" if H(DNSKEY(S)) == (DS_res) then
   accept DNS_res.
   else discard DNS_res and exit.
```

In the above representation, we have used the following notion: Client(C), Server(S), and Root(R). Here in step 1, client sends DNS request (DNS_{req}) to the server. In step 2, after receiving DNS request from client (here we are not showing the receiving of the message, which we are assuming it as implicit, because server will send a response only after receiving a request from client), server sends DNS response (DNS_{res}) signature of the response (RRSIG) and public key of the server (DNSKEY) to client. In step 3, after receiving these three $(DNS_{res}$, RRSIG, and DNSKEY(S)) records, client verifies integrity of DNS_{res} (i.e., checking whether the DNS response gets modified during transit or not). Here, integrity checking is carried out by computing hash value for DNS_{res} and compared it with decrypted RRSIG value using public key of server (DNSKEY(S)). If both match, then client believes that DNS_{res} did not get modified during transit, therefore the client accepts the DNS_{res} and continues with step 4. Else, DNS_{res} gets modified during transit, therefore the client discards DNS_{res} and exits the process.

In step 4, client sends DS request (DS_{req}) to root server. In step 5, after receiving DS_{req} from client, server at root sends DS response (DS_{res}), signature of the response (RRSIG), and public key (DNSKEY) of root server to client. In step 6, after receiving these three $(DS_{res}$, RRSIG, and DNSKEY(R)) records, client verifies the integrity of DS_{res}. Here, integrity checking process is similar to step 3. If DS_{res} did not get modified during transit, then client accepts the DNS_{res} and continues to step 7. Else, client discards DS_{res} and exits the process. In step 7, we verify the public key sent by the server (DNSKEY(S)) and the hash value of the public key of server (DS_{res}) sent by the root. If both match, then client accepts and trusts DNS_{res} sent by the server else client discards the DNS_{res} and exits the process. Every client believes root, therefore no need to verify data sent by root.

In steps 3 and 6, we verified *data integrity* property, and in step 7, we verified *data origin authentication* property of DNSSEC protocol.

After understanding of DNSSEC protocol clearly, in next section, we discuss HLPSL specification of DNSSEC protocol.

5   Validating DNSSEC Using AVISPA

Each participant in DNSSEC protocol is represented as one role in HLPSL. Here, we have defined one role for client, one for server, and one for root. After defining the basic roles, then we defined the composition role to combine the client, server, and root together and execute parallelly. After that we define the environment role to start the session between the roles combined in composition role and also to start execution of a program. Finally, we define the goals of the protocol that we want to validate using AVISPA tool.

DNSSEC Protocol Specification in HLPSL
Role of Client

```
role client( C, S, R : agent,
Kc, Kr, Ks : public_key,
     DNS_req, DNS_res,
     DS_req,  DS_res : text,
     SND, RCV : channel(dy))
played_by C def=
local
State : nat,
  H : hash_func,
    Ns, Nr : text,
R1, R2 : text,
    RRSIG1, RRSIG : text,
DNSKeyMap : (agent.public_key) set

init
State:=0 /\ DNSKeyMap:={(C.Kc),(R.Kr)}

transition
1. State = 0 /\ RCV(start) =|>
     State':=1 /\ SND(S.DNS_req)

2. State = 1 /\ RCV(C.DNS_res) /\ RCV(C.Ks)
                /\ RCV(C.{H(DNS_res)}_inv(Ks))
            =|> State':=2 /\ SND(R.DS_req)
```

```
                    /\ request(C,S,c_s_ks,inv(Ks))

   3. State = 2 /\ RCV(C.DS_res)   /\ RCV(C.Kr)
                    /\ RCV(C.{H(DS_res)}_inv(Kr))
                    =|> State':=3   /\ request(C,R,c_r_kr,inv(Kr))
   end role
```

Similarly, server, root, environment, and composition roles are defined. Finally, we have defined goal section as shown below.

Goal Section

```
goal

authentication_on  c_r_kr
authentication_on  c_s_ks

end  goal
environment()
```

6   Results

We have obtained the following results, when the DNSSEC protocol specification is validated using AVISPA tool. Here, we are displaying few of them.

Results of DNSSEC Protocol with On-the-Fly Model-Checker (OFMC) as Back-End Analyzer

Figure 2 shows execution summary of OFMC. It is clear from figure that the given specification is SAFE (it means no attack is possible under specified constraints) and specified goals are fulfilled. We can also see the execution statistics like parse time, search time, number of nodes visited, and depth.

Figure 3a shows sequence of interactions between client, server, and root. First, client sends DNS request to server. Server sends a DNS response to client. In order to authenticate DNS response, client sends DS request to root. Root sends DS response to client. Now, client make uses DS response to authenticate DNS response from server.

Figure 3b is similar to Fig. 3a, except that communication between client and server, client and root will pass through intruder. Result shows that even in the presence of intruder, communication did not get disturbed and we got the same results.

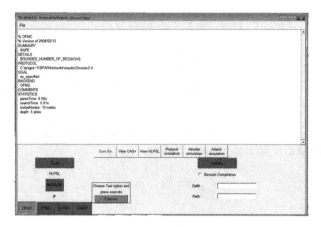

Fig. 2 OFMC summary analysis of DNSSEC protocol with single session

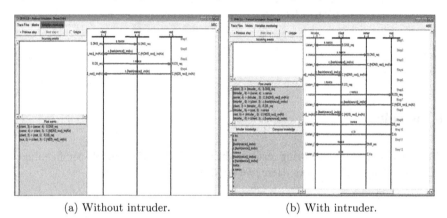

(a) Without intruder.   (b) With intruder.

Fig. 3 OFMC analysis of DNSSEC protocol with single session

7 Conclusion

The complexity of designing and implementing the security protocols is becoming a challenge day to day. As the complexity grows, the manual verification of correctness of a security protocol becomes too difficult. Therefore, we need automation tools to check whether all specified security goals are fulfilled or not and also to verify the existence of vulnerabilities which can be further exploited to breach the security goals. In this paper, we presented the usage of an automation tool called AVISPA to validate the DNSSEC protocol.

References

1. Roger M. Needham and Michael D. Schroeder. Using encryption for authentication in large networks of computers. Communications of the ACM, 21(12): 993–999, 1978.
2. Michael Burrows, Martin Abadi, and Roger M. Needham. A logic of authentication. ACM Transactions on Computer Systems, 8(1): 1836, 1990.
3. Gavin Lowe. An attack on the Needham-Schroeder public-key authentication protocol. Information Processing Letters, 56(3): 131–133, 1995.
4. P. Mockapetris. Domain Names: Concepts and Facilities. Request for Comments 1034, Nov. 1987.
5. P. Mockapetris and K. Dunlop. Development of the Domain Name System. In Proc. of ACM SIGCOMM, Stanford, CA, 1988.
6. R. Arends, R. Austein, M. Larson, D. Massey, and S. Rose, Dns security introduction and requirements, RFC 4033, Internet Engineering Task Force, 1, March, 2005.
7. R. Arends, R. Austein, M. Larson, D. Massey, and S. Rose, Resource records for the dns security extensions, RFC 4034, Internet Engineering Task Force, 1, March, 2005.
8. Kollapalli Ramesh Babu, Vineet Padmanabhan, Wilson Naik Bhukya: Reasoning about DNSSEC. MIWAI 2011: 75–86.
9. The AVISPA team, AVISPA v1.1 User Manual, 2006.
10. A. Armando, D. Basin, Y. Boichut, Y. Chevalier, L. Compagna, J. Cuellar, P. Hankes Drielsma, P. C. Heam, O. Kouchnarenko, J. Mantovani, S. Modersheim, D. von Oheimb, M. Rusinowitch, J. Santiago, M. Turuani, L. Vigan'o, and L. Vigneron. The avispa tool for the automated validation of internet security protocols and applications, pp. 281–285, Springer Berlin Heidelberg, Berlin, Heidelberg, 2005.
11. The AVISPA team, HLPSL Tutorial, 2006.
12. Chevalier, Y., Compagna, L., Cuellar, J., Hankes Drielsma, P., Mantovani, J., Mdersheim, S., Vigneron, L.: A High Level Protocol Specification Language for Industrial Security-Sensitive Protocols. In: Proc. SAPS 2004. Austrian Computer Society, 2004.

Optimal Clustering in Weibull Distributed WSNs Based on Realistic Energy Dissipation Model

Vinay Kumar, Sadanand Yadav, Vishal Kumar, Joydeep Sengupta, Rajeev Tripathi and Sudarshan Tiwari

Abstract In this paper, a realistic energy consumption model of sensor node has been provided by considering eleven key energy consumption sources, some of which are ignored by contemporary energy consumption models. Clustering is a technique by which we can reduce energy consumption of networks. Optimizing the number of clusters improves the scalability of system, reduces the system collisions and delays. To this end, we proposed a realistic energy consumption model of a sensor node, by using that, provided an analytical expression for finding the optimal number of clusters in a Weibull distributed WSNs.

Keywords Energy efficiency · Wireless sensor networks · Optimal cluster size Weibull distribution

1 Introduction

The development of power efficient and inexpensive multi-functional sensors has gained a global-level attention in recent years. The high density of sensor nodes

V. Kumar (✉) · S. Yadav · V. Kumar · J. Sengupta
Visvesvaraya National Institute of Technology, Nagpur 440010, India
e-mail: vk@ece.vnit.ac.in

S. Yadav
e-mail: sadanand.0501@gmail.com

V. Kumar
e-mail: vishalk212@yahoo.com

J. Sengupta
e-mail: jsengupta@ece.vnit.ac.in

R. Tripathi · S. Tiwari
Motilal Nehru National Institute of Technology, Allahabad 211004, India
e-mail: director@mnnit.ac.in

S. Tiwari
e-mail: stiwari@mnnit.ac.in

© Springer Nature Singapore Pte Ltd. 2018
P. K. Pattnaik et al. (eds.), *Progress in Computing, Analytics and Networking*,
Advances in Intelligent Systems and Computing 710,
https://doi.org/10.1007/978-981-10-7871-2_7

provides better coverage and connectivity and increases the probability of packet collision and overheads. As a consequence, scalability became a challenging problem in WSNs' design as the node density increases. To support high scalability, bandwidth reuse and betterment of data aggregation, nodes are often grouped into sparsely coinciding subsets called clusters. Optimal clustering is a method of forming clusters such that the total energy consumption needed to gather network information is minimized as compared with the other existing clustering patterns. Forming optimal number of clusters in sensing field improves energy efficiency, latency, network lifetime, and scalability. In this paper, we are using classical sensing model for BS to analyze the system purpose [1, 2].

1.1 Motivation and Contributions

Halgamuge et al. [3] proposed an energy dissipation model for sensor node. Authors have included possible sources of energy consumption that are excluded in previous energy models, i.e., transmit energy, sensor logging, sensor sensing, and actuation. In [4], Navid et al. provided an analytical expression for optimal number of clusters that minimizes the total energy expenditure in network. In this, sensor node follows the uniform and random distribution. Vinay kumar et al. [2] proposed a model in which nodes follow random and uniform distribution. In this, BS follows tunable Elfes sensing model. Energy consumption model of node considered only transmitter and receiver energies. Vinay kumar et al. [1] have proposed a model in which nodes follow Gaussian random distribution. In this, BS follows classical sensing model and energy consumption of nodes only considered transmitter and receiver energy. Main contribution of this paper is to develop realistic energy dissipation model of sensor node. Moreover, we have also provided analytical expression for optimal number of cluster using Weibull distribution when BS at center. In Sect. 2, proposed model has been describe. In Sect. 3, analytical formulation of optimal cluster based on realistic energy dissipation model of sensor node has been derived. Sect. 4 discusses the performance evaluation. Section 5 presents the conclusion of the work.

2 Proposed Realistic Energy Dissipation Model and Optimal Clustering Using Weibull Distribution

In this section, we have described the realistic energy dissipation model of sensor node and derived the analytical models for optimal clustering using Weibull distributed WSNs. Precise prediction of sensor network lifetime calls for a realistic energy consumption model of sensor node. Various attempts have been made to model the energy consumption of sensor node. We list out several energy models and point out the energy consumption sources that were not considered in those models which are shown in Table 1. Figure 1a shows energy consumption model of sensor nodes, and Fig. 1b shows taxonomy of components which consume energy in sensor node.

Table 1 Energy consumption sources considered by various energy models

Energy source		Heinzelman et al. [6]	Millie et al. [7]	Zhu et al. [8]	Halgamuge et al. [3]	Proposed model
Communication	Transmitter	Yes	Yes	Yes	Yes	Yes
	Receiver	Yes	Yes	Yes	Yes	Yes
	Coding	No	No	No	No	Yes
Processing	Logging	No	Yes	Yes	Yes	Yes
	Micro-controller	No	Yes	Yes	Yes	Yes
	Data compression	No	No	No	No	Yes
Sensing	Transducer (Passive)	No	No	No	No	Yes
	Signal conditioning	No	No	Yes	Yes	Yes
	A/D converter	No	No	Yes	Yes	Yes
Actuation		No	No	No	Yes	Yes
Transient		No	Yes	No	Yes	Yes

2.1 Energy Consumption in Sensing Unit

Sensor sensing consumes power during conversion of non-electrical signals to electrical signals by transducer, signal conditioning, and analog-to-digital conversion (ADC) process. An active transducer either generates or amplifies an electrical signal directly in response to the physical parameter and it does not need for its operation any external power source; hence the power consumed by the active transducer is zero [5]. A passive transducer on contrary to the above requires an external power source for its operation. The energy consumed by a passive transducer is given by Eq. (1) [5].

$$E_{PT} = i_{ext}^2 Z_{equ} T = E_{transduc} \tag{1}$$

where i_{ext} is the current supplied by the external source, Z_{equ} is the equivalent impedance of the transducer circuit, and T is the time taken by the whole process.

2.1.1 Energy Consumption in Signal Conditioning and Analog-to-Digital (A/D) Conversion

In the signal conditioning stage, noises are removed and filtering is done and it is carried by operational amplifiers (op-amps) [9]. Op-amps are used for the amplification of the signal. So energy required by the signal conditioning unit is given by Eq. (2)

$$E_{SCE} = V_{out}^2 Z_{equi} T \tag{2}$$

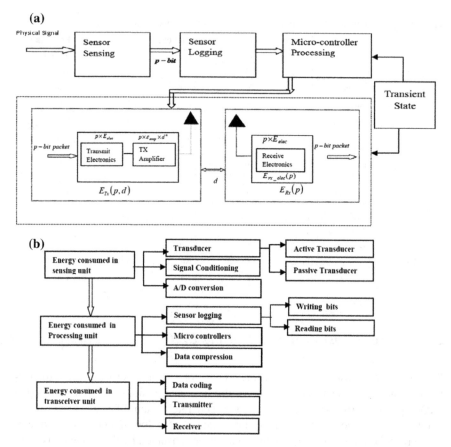

Fig. 1 **a** Realistic energy dissipation model of a sensor node. **b** Taxonomy of components which consumes energy in a sensor node

where $V_{out} = A_V V_{In}$, V_{In} is I/P voltage, $A_V = (\frac{-R_2}{R_1})$ is voltage gain of the operational amplifier (op-amp) in inverting mode and in non-inverting mode voltage gain is $A_V = (1 + \frac{R_2}{R_1})$ and R_2 is the feedback resistance, R_1 is the input resistance, $Z_e qui$ is the total output impedance of the op-amp, T is the time taken by the whole process.

An ADC requires a sampling circuit which samples the analog signal and converts it into a digital signal. Energy consumed by ADC for a given resolution (N), for a time duration T, can be written as $E_{ADC} = 24NT2^{2N}$ [5]. So the total energy consumed by the sensing unit is given by Eq. (3)

$$E_{sensen} = E_{tranduc} + E_{SCE} + E_{ADC} \times p \tag{3}$$

where 'p' is the number of bits.

2.2 Energy Consumed in Processing of Signal

In this subsection, we discuss energy consumed by a node during logging, micro-controller processing, and data compression.

2.2.1 Sensor Logging

Sources of sensor power consumption for reading p bit data packet, and writing this data in memory energy consumption of sensor logging of a sensor node per round is given by Eq. (4) [3].

$$E_{loggn}(p) = E_{write} + E_{read} = \frac{pV}{8}(I_{write} + I_{read}) \tag{4}$$

where E_{write}, E_{read} are energy consumed to write data and to read p bit packet data, I_{write} and I_{read} are currents to write and read l byte data.

2.2.2 Micro-Controllers Processing

In micro-controller, the energy is majorly consumed by aggregation and processing operations. It is attributed by two factors: Energy lost in switching (denoted by E_{switch}) and energy lost due to leakage currents (denoted by E_{leak}). Total energy consumed by the sensor node for data processing/data aggregation of p bit packet, per round is given as follows [3]:

$$E_{pro}(p, C_L) = pC_L C_{avg} V^2 + pV(I_0 e^{\frac{V}{n_p V_t}})(\frac{C_L}{f}) \tag{5}$$

where C_L is the clock cycle count per task, C_{avg} is the switched average capacitance per cycle, I_0 is the leakage current, n_p is a processor dependant constant, V_t is thermal voltage, f is sensor frequency, and V is the supply voltage to sensor.

2.2.3 Data Compression

The energy consumption in data compression unit [10] for p bits is given by equation, $E_{comp} = R\left(\frac{R}{r}\right)^{\alpha} E_b^{comp} \times p$, where R data rate measured in bits per second, r is compression ratio, E_b^{comp} is an energy cost to compress one unit of sensed data by the data compressor, α is a constant and it is algorithm dependent. The total energy consumed by processing unit is given by equation $E_{process} = E_{loggn} \times p + E_{pro}(p, C_L) + E_{comp}(p)$.

2.2.4   Transient Energy

Processing and transceiver unit supports active, sleep, and ideal modes of operation. Transition between different operating modes takes significant energy consumption. Upon reading a busy tone of the channel, a wakes up for a duration of T_A and then sleeps for T_S (assuming $T_S \geqslant T_A$). The duty cycle of the sensor node, c_N can be written as, $c_N = \frac{T_{tranON} + T_A + T_{tranOFF}}{T_{tranON} + T_A + T_{tranOFF} + T_S}$ [3], where T_{tranON} and $T_{tranOFF}$ are the respective time durations required for sleep to ideal and ideal to sleep transitions. The total energy dissipated from the sensor node per round is calculated by Eq. (6)

$$E_{transn} = T_A V_{sup}(c_N I_A + I_S(1 - c_N)) \tag{6}$$

where I_S and I_A are currents for sleep and active modes, respectively, and V_{sup} is the supply voltage.

2.3   Energy Consumed by Processing Unit

In this section, we discuss energy consumed by coding process and energy consumed during data transmission and reception. The energy required for coding of data is approximately proportional to the coding bit rate R_c [11]. The energy consumption of encoding in one frame is given as below:

$$E_f = E_0 + E_r R_c + E_c \tag{7}$$

where E_0 is miscellaneous energy overheads, E_r is linear factor constant, and E_c is energy consumption of parametric coding.

2.3.1   Radio Transmission and Receiving

Energy consumption of radio is the sum of transmitter and receiver energy and given by Eq. (8)

$$E_c = E_{Tx}(p, d) + E_{Rx}(p) \tag{8}$$

$$E_{Tx}(p, d) = p E_{elec} + p \epsilon_{amp} d^n \tag{9}$$

$$E_{Rx}(p) = p E_{elec} \tag{10}$$

Equations (9) and (10) represent the energy spent to run the transmitter or the receiver circuitry to transmit or receive a data packet of one bit, and ϵ_{amp} is the energy dissipated the transmission amplifier to convey one bit of data packet to the receiver node at a distance of 1 m, d is inter-distance of transmitter and receiver nodes, and n is path loss exponent. Values of n is 2 for free space model and n is 4 for multi-path model. Total energy consumed in a sensor node during one round is given by the Eq. (11).

$$E_{TN} = E_{PN} + E_{SCE} + E_{ADC}(p) + E_{logg}(p) + E_{Pro}(p, C_L) + E_{Comp}(p) + E_{cpo}$$
$$+ E_{Trans} + E_c + + E_{Tx}(p, d) + E_{Rx}(p) \tag{11}$$

3   Analytical Formulation of Optimal Cluster Based on Realistic Energy Dissipation Model of Sensor Node

In this section, we try to find the energy consumption according to the proposed energy model. Consider that N number of sensor nodes are distributed in $M \times M$ region. Network is divided into h number of clusters. Each cluster has $\frac{N}{h}$ sensors. Hence, there will be one cluster head and $(\frac{N}{h} - 1)$ nodes in each cluster. The sensor nodes transmit data to their respective CH. Then CH will forward the data to the sink node. Here, we assume that cluster nodes do not perform data processing, data compression, and coding. These processes are performed only by CH. Hence, total energy consumption of a sensor node i in cluster j per round is given by Eq. (12)

$$E_{i,j} = p(E_{sensen} + E_{loggn} + E_{transn}(p) + E_{elec}(p) + E_{amp}d_{toCH}^n \tag{12}$$

where d_{toch}^n is distance between ith node and cluster head in cluster, E_{sensen} is the sensing energy, E_{loggn} is logging energy, E_{transn} is transient energy, E_{elec} is the electronics energy. In the same manner, the total energy consumption of cluster head CH_j per round is by Eq. (13)

$$E_{CH}(j) = p(E_{sensech} + E_{loggch} + E_{proch} + E_{comp} + E_f + E_{transch}(p) + E_{elec}+$$
$$E_{amp}d_{toBS}^4 \tag{13}$$

The total energy consumption of jth cluster CH_j per round is given by Eq. (14)

$$E_{tot} = E_{CH}(j) + \sum_{i=1}^{h} [E(i,j)] \tag{14}$$

Total energy consumed in a cluster head for transmission between cluster head and sink consider multi-path fading, i.e., $n = 4$ and $E_{amp} = E_{mp}$

$$E_{head}(j) = p(E_{sensech} + E_{loggch} + E_{proch} + E_{comp} + E_f + E_{transch}(p) + E_{elec}+$$
$$E_{amp}d_{toBS}^4 \tag{15}$$

Total Energy consumption in a sensor node for transmission between cluster head and node consider free space fading, i.e., $n = 2$ and $E_{amp} = E_{fs}$

$$E_{node} = p(E_{sensech} + E_{loggch} + E_{transsn}(p) + E_{elec} + E_{fa}\frac{M^2}{6h} \tag{16}$$

Energy consumption in a cluster (Table 2)

$$E_{cluster} = E_{head} + \left(\frac{N}{h} - 1\right)E_{node} \approx E_{head} + \left(\frac{N}{h}\right)E_{node} \tag{17}$$

Total energy consumption in network

$$E_{total} = hE_{cluster} \tag{18}$$

To find optimum value of h for which energy is minimum put derivative of energy with respect to h equal to zero. Optimum value of h is given by Eq. (19)

$$h_{opt} = \sqrt{\frac{N}{6}}M\sqrt{\frac{E_{fs}}{D_a}} \tag{19}$$

where $D_a = \left(E_{sensech} + E_{loggch} + E_{transsn} + E_{amp}d^4\right)$

3.1 Optimal Cluster for Weibull Distributed Sensor Network

The sensor node distribution has a wide range of shapes and scales among various deployment environments. In this paper, the classical Weibull distribution is used to model the sensor node lifetime. In this model, we take the sensing field as a circular-shaped (radius R = M). In our model, we put the BS considered to be at the center of the sensing field. In this case, the probability density function is given by Eq. (20) [15].

$$f(x) = \begin{cases} \frac{\beta}{\alpha}\left(\frac{x}{a}\right)^{\beta-1}e^{\left(-\frac{x}{a}\right)^{\beta}} & \text{for} \quad 0 \leq x \leq \frac{M}{2} \\ 0 & \text{Otherwise} \end{cases} \tag{20}$$

3.1.1 Calculation of Expected Value of d^2_{toBS} and d^4_{toBS}

To evaluate the expected distance d^2_{toBS} from the center to the overall area of the sensing field, we integrate $d^2_{toBS} = x^2 + y^2$ to pdf $f(x)$ in the interval of $[-\frac{M}{2}, \frac{M}{2}]$ and

Table 2 Simulation parameters [3, 7, 12–14]

C avg	Average capacitance switched per cycle	22 pF	CL	Clock cycle count per task	0.97×10^6
np	Processor dependant constant	21.26	V	Sensor supply voltage	2.7 V
E_{elec}	Energy dissipation: electronics	50 nJ/bit	f	Sensor frequency	191.42 MHz
E_{mp}	Energy dissipation multi-path fading	0.0013 pJ/bit/m4	I_0	Leakage current	1.196 mA
T_{tranON}	Time duration sleep idle	2450 μs	V_t	Thermal voltage	0.2 V
$T_{tranOFF}$	Time duration idle sleep	250 μs	p	Transmit packet size	1 kb
T_{sens}	Time duration sensor node sensing	0.5 mS	I_A	Current in wakeup mode	8 mA
I_{sens}	Current sensing activity	25 mA	I_S	Current in sleeping mode	1 μA
I_{write}	Current flash writing 1 byte data	18.4 mA	T_A	Active time	1 ms
I_{read}	Current flash reading 1 byte data	6.2 mA	T_S	Sleeping time	299 ms
T_{write}	Time duration flash writing	12.9 ms	M	Dimension of sensing field	100 m
T_{read}	Time duration flash reading	565 μS	E_f	Energy consumed in coding	3.5 pJ/bit
E_{fs}	Energy dissipation free space fading	7 nJ/bit/m2	N	Number of nodes	100
E_{comp}	Energy consumed in compression	2.181835×10^{-4}/bit			

Table 3 Average value of d_{toBS}^2, d_{toBS}^4 for Weibull distributed WSNs

Average value of d_{toBS}^2

(β/α)	150	160	170	180	190	200	210	220	230	240	250
1	$0.114M^3$	$0.106M^3$	$0.100\,M^3$	$0.942M^3$	$0.891M^3$	$0.845M^3$	$0.804M^3$	$0.766M^3$	$0.732M^3$	$0.701M^3$	$0.672M^3$
3	$0.172M^3$	$0.142M^3$	$0.118M^3$	$0.100M^3$	$0.850M^3$	$0.729M^3$	$0.629M^3$	$0.547M^3$	$0.479M^3$	$0.421M^3$	$0.373M^3$
5	$0.215M^3$	$0.156M^3$	$0.115M^3$	$0.086M^3$	$0.066M^3$	$0.051M^3$	$0.040M^3$	$0.031M^3$	$0.025\,M^3$	$0.020\,M^3$	$0.016M^3$

Average value of d_{toBS}^4

(β/α)	150	160	170	180	190	200	210	220	230	240	250
1	$2.67M^4$	$2.49M^4$	$2.34M^4$	$2.20M^4$	$2.08M^4$	$1.97M^4$	$1.88M^4$	$1.79M^4$	$1.71M^4$	$1.63M^4$	$1.57M^4$
3	$0.476M^4$	$0.392M^4$	$0.327M^4$	$0.275M^4$	$0.234M^4$	$0.200M^4$	$0.173M^4$	$0.150M^4$	$1.32M^4$	$1.16M^4$	$1.02M^4$
5	$0.063M^4$	$0.045M^4$	$0.033M^4$	$0.025M^4$	$0.019M^4$	$0.015M^4$	$0.011M^4$	$0.009M^4$	$0.007M^4$	$0.006M^4$	$0.004M^4$

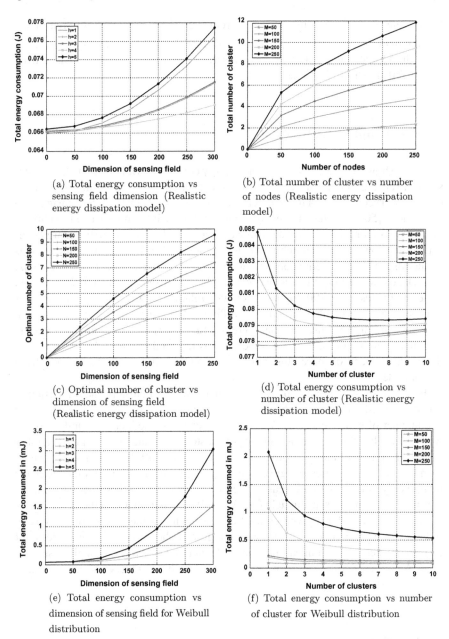

(a) Total energy consumption vs sensing field dimension (Realistic energy dissipation model)

(b) Total number of cluster vs number of nodes (Realistic energy dissipation model)

(c) Optimal number of cluster vs dimension of sensing field (Realistic energy dissipation model)

(d) Total energy consumption vs number of cluster (Realistic energy dissipation model)

(e) Total energy consumption vs dimension of sensing field for Weibull distribution

(f) Total energy consumption vs number of cluster for Weibull distribution

Fig. 2 Total energy consumption and optimal number of cluster plot for realistic energy dissipation model and Weibull distribution

to evaluate the expected distance d^4_{toBS} from the center to the overall area of the sensing field, we integrate $d^4_{toBS} = (x^2 + y^2)^4$ to pdf $f(x)$ in the interval of $[-\frac{M}{2}, \frac{M}{2}]$. The values for all combination of α which varies from 1 to 5 and β which varies from 150 to 250 are shown in Table 3.

4 Performance Evaluation

Figure 2a shows the variation of the total energy consumed with respect to the dimensions of sensing field for different values of cluster count. From the above figure, it can be observed that when the number of clusters varies from 1 to 5 for sensing field dimensions [50–300], then the energy consumption will be more when the number of clusters is more than 5. When sensing dimension is less than 100, the energy consumption is lowest for the number of clusters equal to 2. When the area dimension is greater than 100, the energy consumption is lowest for the number of clusters equal to 4. Hence, we can say that the optimal number of clusters is equal to 2 when area dimension is less than 100. Figure 2b shows a relation between the optimal number of clusters and the number of nodes for different dimensions of sensing field. From the above graph, it is observed that there is a linear variation in number of clusters with total number of nodes. This is because as the total number of nodes increase there will be need of more cluster heads to collect and process data locally from sensor nodes.

Figure 2c shows a relation between optimal number of clusters and dimension of sensing field for different number of sensor node. As the dimension of sensing field and number of nodes increases, the number of clusters also increases uniformly. So we can say that the maximum number of clusters is obtained for a given number of sensor nodes with a dimension of sensing field of 250. From Fig. 2d, it can be seen that for a given area of sensing field, as the number of clusters increases the total energy consumption decreases. Figure 2e shows graphs between total energy consumed and area of sensing field for a Weibull distribution. From the above graph, it can be seen that for a given optimal cluster count, as the dimension of sensing field increases more energy is consumed. Figure 2f shows an exponential decay of consumed energy with a linear increase of the number of clusters in a given sensing field. A list of values of all the parameters used in the current work can be seen in Table 2.

5 Conclusion

In this paper, we proposed a new and realistic energy dissipation model for sensor nodes. With the help of the proposed model, the lifetime of wireless sensor network can be measured more accurately as compared with a simple energy consumption model. We also analyzed the performance of Weibull distribution of sensor nodes in terms of total energy consumption of network. Moreover, we showed that the optimal number of clusters is a very crucial parameter to measure the performance of network.

References

1. Kumar, V., Dhok, S. B., Tripathi, R. and Tiwari, S.: Cluster size optimization in gaussian distributed wireless sensor networks, International Journal of Engineering and Technology (IJET), vol. 6, no. 3, pp. 1581–1592, (2014).
2. Kumar, V., Dhok, S. B., Tripathi, R. and Tiwari, S.: Cluster size optimisation with tunable elfes sensing model for single and multi-hop wireless sensor networks, International Journal of Electronics, vol. 104, no. 2, pp. 312–327, (2017).
3. Halgamuge, M. N., Zukerman, M., Ramamohanarao, K., and Vu, H. L.: An estimation of sensor energy consumption, Progress In Electromagnetics Research B, (2009).
4. Amini, N., Vahdatpour, A., Xu, W., Gerla, M., and Sarrafzadeh, M.: Cluster size optimization in sensor networks with decentralized cluster-based protocols, Computer communications, vol. 35, no. 2, pp. 207–220, (2012).
5. Matsuzawa, A.: Energy efficient adc design with low voltage operation, in ASIC (ASICON), 2011 IEEE 9th International Conference on. IEEE, pp. 508–511, (2011).
6. Heinzelman, W. B., Chandrakasan, A. P., and Balakrishnan, H.: An application specific protocol architecture for wireless microsensor networks, IEEE Transactions on wireless communications, vol. 1, no. 4, pp. 660–670, (2002).
7. Miller, M. J., and Vaidya, N. H.: A mac protocol to reduce sensor network energy consumption using a wakeup radio, IEEE Transactions on mobile Computing, vol. 4, no. 3, pp. 228–242, (2005).
8. Zhu J., and Papavassiliou, S.: On the energy-efficient organization and the lifetime of multi-hop sensor networks, IEEE Communications letters, vol. 7, no. 11, pp. 537–539, (2003).
9. Sindhu, P. and Udaykumar, M. S.: Optimized power controller for residential energy consumption, International Journal for trends in Engineering Technology, vol. 1, pp. 11–24, (2014).
10. Yang, M. Chen, L. and Xiong, W.: Compression/transmission power allocation in multimedia wireless sensor networks, in International Conference on Computing, Networking and Communications (ICNC), IEEE, pp. 1103–1107, (2014).
11. Shah, H. T., Ilyas, S. I. A. and Mouftah, M.: Pervasive communications handbook. CRC Press, (2011).
12. Wang, A., and Chandrakasan, A.: Energy-efficient dsps for wireless sensor networks, IEEE Signal Processing Magazine, vol. 19, no. 4, pp. 68–78, (2002).
13. Shnayder, V., Hempstead, M., Chen, B. R., Allen, G. W., and Welsh, M.: Simulating the power consumption of large-scale sensor network applications, in Proceedings of the 2nd international conference on Embedded networked sensor systems. ACM, pp. 188–200, (2004).
14. Rahimi, M., Shah, H. Sukhatme, G. S., Heideman, J., and Estrin, D.: Studying the feasibility of energy harvesting in a mobile sensor network, in IEEE International Conference on Robotics and Automation, vol. 1. IEEE, pp. 19–24, (2003).
15. Lee, J. J., Krishnamachari, B. and Kuo, C. C. J., Impact of energy depletion and reliability on wireless sensor network connectivity, in Defense and Security. International Society for Optics and Photonics, pp. 169–180, (2004).

An Empirical Analysis of Articles on Sentiment Analysis

Vishal Vyas and V. Uma

Abstract Expression of a thought is not only important for an individual but there is a necessity for an automated system to get an opinion from it. Sentiment analysis (SA) or opinion mining (OM) is used to identify the sentiment/opinion of the speaker. Web 2.0 provides us various platforms such as Twitter, Facebook where we comment or post to express our happiness, anger, disbelief, sadness, etc. For SA of text, computationally it is required to know the concepts and technologies being used in the field of SA. This article gives brief knowledge about the techniques used in SA by categorizing various articles over the past four years. This article also explains the preprocessing steps, various application programmable interface (API), and available datasets for a better understanding of SA. This article is concluded with a future work which needs a separate attention of researchers to improve the performance of sentiment analysis.

Keywords Text mining · Sentiment analysis · Ontology · Machine learning

1 Introduction

For a human being mostly it is very easy to sense the sentiment in the text using their trained mind. Humans have trained their mind by learning through experiences. An inexperienced person always demands an opinion from others while trying new things. An automated system that can correctly identify the polarity is the need of the hour. Although there is a huge advancement in field of natural language processing (NLP) and machine learning (ML), automated systems still have not achieved 100% accuracy in dealing with sarcasm or finding the polarity of the text. With the advance-

V. Vyas (✉) · V. Uma
Department of Computer Science, Pondicherry University,
Puducherry 605014, India
e-mail: vyasvishaluni@gmail.com

V. Uma
e-mail: umabskr@gmail.com

© Springer Nature Singapore Pte Ltd. 2018
P. K. Pattnaik et al. (eds.), *Progress in Computing, Analytics and Networking*,
Advances in Intelligent Systems and Computing 710,
https://doi.org/10.1007/978-981-10-7871-2_8

ment in the field of NLP and ML in the last decade, there is a growing need for sentiment analysis systems in order to help humans in getting accurate opinion which could subsequently help them in decision-making. Sentiment analysis (SA) is a field where we try to get the point of view, belief, and intensity toward entities such as organizations, manufactured items, creatures, occasion, and their elements by using ML [1], NLP and many other ontology-based mining algorithms. Sentiment analysis is a task that is becoming increasingly important for many companies because of the emergence of social media sites such as Facebook, Twitter, e-commerce Web sites, and the other trillions of them. Business organizations track tweets about their products to know about the people's demand and to modernize their impact over time, whereas politicians use them to track their campaign by looking around comments on the social media Web sites. With the comments and feedbacks on the Internet, it is necessary to have an automated system that can make sense out of them. Opinions are important both at personal and professional level. Either we ask for opinion or we get influenced by the advertisement that business organizations put on Internet after huge research. The existing approaches to deduce sentiments from the posts, reviews, tweets, and forums which are available in social media Web sites can be summarized in points stated below:

1. Text to analyze in the social media is unstructured in nature. While working in the noisy environment, the identification of the sentiment from the text is not an easy task. Forming a quintuple [2] reduces the noisy labels but in the presence of sarcasm and smaller sentences the formation of quintuple becomes difficult. The creation of emoticon vocabulary [3] is the other way to tackle the noise in the text. The vocabulary is used to train the ML classifiers such as support vector machine (SVM), Naive Bayes (NB), maximum entropy (MaxEnt). The trained SVM classifier has a high accuracy in analyzing the sentiment from the text.
2. To improve the sentiment classification accuracy, various approaches such as feature-based model and the tree kernel-based model, n-gram and lexicon features have been combined with machine learning methods [4].
3. Ontology can be defined as an explicit formal specification of concepts which is machine readable [5]. SA using ontology is done in two phases. (a) Creating a domain ontology which includes formal concepts analysis and ontology learning. (b) Analysis of the sentiment as per the concepts of ontology. The course of SA consists of classification process at different level, namely document-level sentiment analysis, sentence-level sentiment analysis, aspect-based sentiment analysis, and comparative-based sentiment analysis. In document-level sentiment analysis, whole document is considered as single information unit and classified as positive, negative, or neutral sentiment polarity. Sentence-level sentiment analysis considers each sentence as one information unit. In aspect-based sentiment analysis, classification of sentiment is with respect to particular aspect/entity and in comparative-based sentiment analysis, rather than having a direct opinion about a product, text have comparative opinions. The sole purpose of this survey is to cover the techniques for SA which comprises of machine learning techniques for automatic learning of patterns in data and ontology for better

visualization of data to determine sentiment. Over the years, much research work have been carried out in the field of machine learning. In the age of Semantic Web, there is a need to explore ontology and machine learning together to analyze and classify the sentiments. This survey follows the pattern of [1] for the analysis of articles but the perspective here is an empirical categorization of articles by considering different techniques for SA. This survey is beneficial for researchers in the field of SA in various ways. Firstly, categorization of articles is done based on the approaches used for SA. Secondly, in-brief explanation of essential steps involved prior to SA is provided. Thirdly, the year-wise categorization of recent articles is presented on the basis of concepts and techniques, dataset, and data resources. Finally, the categorization of articles is analyzed with the help of bar charts and future work is discussed which needs a separate attention of researchers to improve sentiment analysis.

2 Sentiment Analysis Using Various Approaches

Approaches used for SA are machine learning and lexicon based. When two or more approaches are combined then it becomes a hybrid approach. Various algorithms which are also known as the types of machine learning are supervised and unsupervised machine learning algorithms. Lexicon-based approach contains dictionary-based approach (DBA) and corpus-based approach. Ontology building is a series of process and Web 2.0 empowers us with ontology creation for SA. Mukherjee and Joshi [6], Weichselbraun et al. [7], and Penalver-Martinez et al. [8] show that using ontologies it is possible to achieve tasks of SA. Table 1 categorizes various articles based on the approaches used in SA. Third column in this table specifies the task performed in the article. The table shows that the same task can be achieved using different approaches.

3 Preliminary Steps Involved in Sentiment Analysis

SA is performed in stages and it is better to call it as multifaceted problem [19]. The ample availability of heterogeneous online resources gives rise to the first step required for SA, which is data acquisition. The analysis approaches change with the various forms of data or multimedia data. Application programming interface (API) provided by microblogging sites such as Twitter, Facebook makes it easy for collecting public data, whereas few other sources are available which provide domain-oriented (movie, car, etc.) datasets. Available APIs and datasets for public use are discussed in Table 2.

Preprocessing is the second step before actual analysis starts. The data acquired from various data resources in the first step is in raw form which requires formatting. Various techniques involved in preprocessing are highlighted in Table 3.

Table 1 Approaches for sentiment analysis

References	Approach	Task
Blair-Goldensohn et al. [9]	Supervised machine learning	Binary classification of text
Lu et al. [10]	Supervised machine learning	5-star rating
Jakob and Gurevych [11]	Supervised machine learning	Opinion mining
Titov and McDonald [12]	Unsupervised machine learning	Aspect detection
Lakkaraju et al. [13]	Unsupervised machine learning	Aspect detection
Wang et al. [14]	Unsupervised machine learning	Aspect rating prediction
Popescu and Etzioni [15]	Hybrid method	Aspect detection
Raju et al. [16]	Hybrid method	Aspect detection
Mukherjee and Joshi [6]	Ontology	Binary classification of text
Weichselbraun et al. [7]	Ontology	Binary classification of text
Penalver-Martinez et al. [8]	Ontology	Binary classification of text
Moghaddam and Ester [17]	Dictionary-based approach (DBA)	Binary classification of text
Zhu et al. [18]	Dictionary-based approach (DBA)	Aspect sentiment analysis

Table 2 Articles using different API/Datasets for SA

References	Name	API/Datasets	Purpose
Kumar et al. [20]	Twitter REST	API	To extract profile information
Khan et al. [21], Kontopoulos et al. [22]	Twitter4J	API	Extract streaming tweets
Ortigosa et al. [23], Li and Xu [24]	Facebook Graph	API	Extract posts
Cruz et al. [25]	TBOD	DATASET	Reviews
Kouloumpis et al. [26]	EMOT	DATASET	Tweets and emoticons

Table 3 Steps involved in preprocessing of text for SA

Steps	Description
TOKENIZATION	Breaks sentence into meaningful tokens
STOPWORD REMOVAL	Removing stopword
STEMMING	Brings word to its root form
POS TAGGING	Recognizes different part of speech in the text
FEATURE EXTRACTION	Tackles the extreme noise in data captured

4 Literature Survey and Categorization of Articles

The survey is done with the aim to know the various concepts and technologies being used for SA. For this purpose, seventeen articles are summarized in Table 4. Table 4 contains five columns, where the first and second columns have the details regarding the survey papers and the year of publications, respectively. Third column shows the various concepts and technologies used in different articles. Fourth column specifies the domain of the data used for SA. Fifth column specifies the well-known datasets used in different articles.

Table 4 Categorization of articles

References	Year	Concept and technology	Type of data	Data set/Data source
Penalver-Martinez et al. [8]	2014	Ontology, DBA	Movie review	SWN
Bravo-Marquez et al. [27]	2014	Logistic regression	Microblog	Ten dictionaries
Mukherjee and Joshi [6]	2014	Ontology, DBA	Product review	SWN, GI, OL
Mukherjee and Joshi [30]	2014	DBA	Movie review	WN
Cambria et al. [31]	2014	DBA	Global domain	CN, DBPedia, WN
Poria et al. [32]	2014	Ontology, DBA	Global domain	AffectiveSpace
Poria et al. [33]	2014	Ontology, DBA	Global domain	SN 3, WNA
Weichselbraun et al. [7]	2014	Ontology, DBA	Product review	WN, CN
Krishnamoorthy [34]	2015	SVM	Product review	Amazon review datasets
Nakov et al. [35]	2016	NN	Tweets	Twitter API
Saif et al. [36]	2016	Lexicon-based senticircle	Tweets	STS-Gold
Wang and Cardie [37]	2016	SVM, RBF Kernal	Conversation	Wikipedia talk
Palomino et al. [38]	2016	Qualitative method	Nature health	Twitter API, Alchemy API
Poria et al. [29]	2016	MKL, CNN	Video	MOUD, ICT-MMMO
Poria et al. [39]	2017	Chi-square	Health	Health media collaboration
Ali et al. [40]	2017	Fuzzy ontology	Tweets, reviews	REST-API
Giatsoglou et al. [28]	2017	LBA	Tweets	Twitter API

Fig. 1 Percentage and number of articles analyzing various text domains over the past 4 years

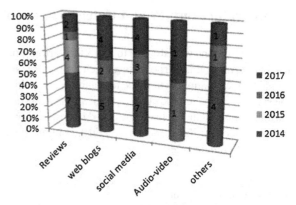

Fig. 2 Percentage and number of articles based on the approaches used over the past 4 years

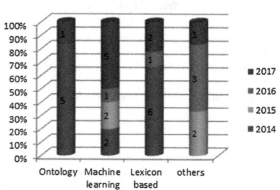

Figure 1 shows that using product reviews and social media nearly 43% articles published in 2014, whereas [8, 27, 28] represent usage of microblogs for SA. Penalver-Martinez et al. [8] analyzed tweets using REST-API which is a publicly available dataset. Analysis of audio–video is done by Poria et al. [29] in 2016 using MKL and CNN.

Figure 2 shows nearly 80% of articles published in 2014 considered ontology approach for SA. Machine learning algorithm remains the best approach for SA in past 4 years. 60% of articles in 2014 and 20% in 2017 considered lexicon-based approach as a best way for SA.

5 Conclusion

Over the years, researchers have focused on the binary classification of the text by collecting posts from social networking Web sites, reviews from e-commerce Web sites, etc. Problem arises when it comes to conditional sentence. It is hard to identify the sentiment expressed by conditional sentence such as "If I find his address, I will send her an invitation." Narayanan et al. [41] proposed an approach for the above-said problem. Using SVM classifier, they have achieved 75.6% and 66% accuracy for binary and ternary classification, respectively. High accuracy in the case of conditional sentences is to be achieved. Our future work will include comparing semantic and hybrid approaches to identify which will perform better when analyzing conditional sentences to identify the technique that will perform better.

References

1. Medhat, W., Hassan, A., Korashy, H.: Sentiment analysis algorithms and applications: A survey. Ain Shams Engineering Journal 5(4) (2014) 1093–1113
2. Liu, B.: Web data mining: exploring hyperlinks, contents, and usage data. Springer Science & Business Media (2007)
3. Read, J.: Using emoticons to reduce dependency in machine learning techniques for sentiment classification. In: Proceedings of the ACL student research workshop, Association for Computational Linguistics (2005) 43–48
4. Barbosa, L., Feng, J.: Robust sentiment detection on twitter from biased and noisy data. In: Proceedings of the 23rd International Conference on Computational Linguistics: Posters, Association for Computational Linguistics (2010) 36–44
5. Studer, R., Benjamins, V.R., Fensel, D.: Knowledge engineering: principles and methods. Data & knowledge engineering 25(1–2) (1998) 161–197
6. Mukherjee, S., Joshi, S.: Sentiment aggregation using conceptnet ontology. In: IJCNLP. (2013) 570–578
7. Weichselbraun, A., Gindl, S., Scharl, A.: Enriching semantic knowledge bases for opinion mining in big data applications. Knowledge-Based Systems 69 (2014) 78–85
8. Penalver-Martinez, I., Garcia-Sanchez, F., Valencia-Garcia, R., Rodriguez-Garcia, M.A., Moreno, V., Fraga, A., Sanchez-Cervantes, J.L.: Feature-based opinion mining through ontologies. Expert Systems with Applications 41(13) (2014) 5995–6008
9. Blair-Goldensohn, S., Hannan, K., McDonald, R., Neylon, T., Reis, G.A., Reynar, J.: Building a sentiment summarizer for local service reviews. In: WWW workshop on NLP in the information explosion era. Volume 14. (2008) 339–348
10. Lu, B., Ott, M., Cardie, C., Tsou, B.K.: Multi-aspect sentiment analysis with topic models. In: Data Mining Workshops (ICDMW), 2011 IEEE 11th International Conference on, IEEE (2011) 81–88
11. Jakob, N., Gurevych, I.: Extracting opinion targets in a single-and cross-domain setting with conditional random fields. In: Proceedings of the 2010 conference on empirical methods in natural language processing, Association for Computational Linguistics (2010) 1035–1045
12. Titov, I., McDonald, R.: Modeling online reviews with multi-grain topic models. In: Proceedings of the 17th international conference on World Wide Web, ACM (2008) 111–120
13. Lakkaraju, H., Bhattacharyya, C., Bhattacharya, I., Merugu, S.: Exploiting coherence for the simultaneous discovery of latent facets and associated sentiments. In: Proceedings of the 2011 SIAM international conference on data mining, SIAM (2011) 498–509
14. Wang, H., Lu, Y., Zhai, C.: Latent aspect rating analysis without aspect keyword supervision. In: Proceedings of the 17th ACM SIGKDD international conference on Knowledge discovery and data mining, ACM (2011) 618–626
15. Popescu, A.M., Etzioni, O.: Extracting product features and opinions from reviews. In: Natural language processing and text mining. Springer (2007) 9–28
16. Raju, S., Pingali, P., Varma, V.: An unsupervised approach to product attribute extraction. In: European Conference on Information Retrieval, Springer (2009) 796–800

17. Moghaddam, S., Ester, M.: Opinion digger: an unsupervised opinion miner from unstructured product reviews. In: Proceedings of the 19th ACM international conference on Information and knowledge management, ACM (2010) 1825–1828
18. Zhu, J., Wang, H., Tsou, B.K., Zhu, M.: Multi-aspect opinion polling from textual reviews. In: Proceedings of the 18th ACM conference on Information and knowledge management, ACM (2009) 1799–1802
19. Liu, B.: Sentiment analysis: A multifaceted problem. IEEE Intelligent Systems **25**(3) (8 2010) 76–80
20. Kumar, S., Morstatter, F., Liu, H.: Twitter data analytics. Springer Science & Business Media (2013)
21. Khan, F.H., Bashir, S., Qamar, U.: Tom: Twitter opinion mining framework using hybrid classification scheme. Decision Support Systems **57** (2014) 245–257
22. Kontopoulos, E., Berberidis, C., Dergiades, T., Bassiliades, N.: Ontology-based sentiment analysis of twitter posts. Expert systems with applications **40**(10) (2013) 4065–4074
23. Ortigosa, A., Martín, J.M., Carro, R.M.: Sentiment analysis in facebook and its application to e-learning. Computers in Human Behavior **31** (2014) 527–541
24. Li, W., Xu, H.: Text-based emotion classification using emotion cause extraction. Expert Systems with Applications **41**(4) (2014) 1742–1749
25. Cruz, F.L., Troyano, J.A., Enríquez, F., Ortega, F.J., Vallejo, C.G.: A knowledge-rich approach to feature-based opinion extraction from product reviews. In: Proceedings of the 2nd international workshop on Search and mining user-generated contents, ACM (2010) 13–20
26. Kouloumpis, E., Wilson, T., Moore, J.D.: Twitter sentiment analysis: The good the bad and the omg! Icwsm **11**(538–541) (2011) 164
27. Bravo-Marquez, F., Mendoza, M., Poblete, B.: Meta-level sentiment models for big social data analysis. Knowledge-Based Systems **69** (2014) 86–99
28. Giatsoglou, M., Vozalis, M.G., Diamantaras, K., Vakali, A., Sarigiannidis, G., Chatzisavvas, K.C.: Sentiment analysis leveraging emotions and word embeddings. Expert Systems with Applications **69** (2017) 214–224
29. Poria, S., Chaturvedi, I., Cambria, E., Hussain, A.: Convolutional mkl based multimodal emotion recognition and sentiment analysis. In: Data Mining (ICDM), 2016 IEEE 16th International Conference on, IEEE (2016) 439–448
30. Mukherjee, S., Joshi, S.: Author-specific sentiment aggregation for polarity prediction of reviews. In: LREC. (2014) 3092–3099
31. Cambria, E., Olsher, D., Rajagopal, D.: Senticnet 3: a common and common-sense knowledge base for cognition-driven sentiment analysis. In: Proceedings of the twenty-eighth AAAI conference on artificial intelligence, AAAI Press (2014) 1515–1521
32. Poria, S., Cambria, E., Winterstein, G., Huang, G.B.: Sentic patterns: Dependency-based rules for concept-level sentiment analysis. Knowledge-Based Systems **69** (2014) 45–63
33. Poria, S., Gelbukh, A., Cambria, E., Hussain, A., Huang, G.B.: Emosenticspace: A novel framework for affective common-sense reasoning. Knowledge-Based Systems **69** (2014) 108–123
34. Krishnamoorthy, S.: Linguistic features for review helpfulness prediction. Expert Systems with Applications **42**(7) (2015) 3751–3759
35. Nakov, P., Ritter, A., Rosenthal, S., Sebastiani, F., Stoyanov, V.: Semeval-2016 task 4: Sentiment analysis in twitter. Proceedings of SemEval (2016) 1–18
36. Saif, H., He, Y., Fernandez, M., Alani, H.: Contextual semantics for sentiment analysis of twitter. Information Processing & Management **52**(1) (2016) 5–19
37. Wang, L., Cardie, C.: A piece of my mind: A sentiment analysis approach for online dispute detection. arXiv:1606.05704 (2016)
38. Palomino, M., Taylor, T., Göker, A., Isaacs, J., Warber, S.: The online dissemination of nature-health concepts: Lessons from sentiment analysis of social media relating to nature-deficit disorder. International journal of environmental research and public health **13**(1) (2016) 142
39. Poria, S., Peng, H., Hussain, A., Howard, N., Cambria, E.: Ensemble application of convolutional neural networks and multiple kernel learning for multimodal sentiment analysis. Neurocomputing (2017)

40. Ali, F., Kwak, D., Khan, P., Islam, S.R., Kim, K.H., Kwak, K.: Fuzzy ontology-based sentiment analysis of transportation and city feature reviews for safe traveling. Transportation Research Part C: Emerging Technologies **77** (2017) 33–48
41. Narayanan, R., Liu, B., Choudhary, A.: Sentiment analysis of conditional sentences. In: Proceedings of the 2009 Conference on Empirical Methods in Natural Language Processing: Volume 1–Volume 1. EMNLP '09, Stroudsburg, PA, USA, Association for Computational Linguistics (2009) 180–189

Verification and Validation of Trust-Based Opportunistic Routing Protocol

Sandeep A. Thorat, P. J. Kulkarni and S. V. Yadav

Abstract Data routing is an essential operation in working of a MANET. Many researchers have proposed novel routing protocols for MANET. Working of the routing protocols differs with each other. Each routing protocol follows a set of rules and has different characteristics. Various network simulators are popularly used to test performance and working of the novel routing protocols. However, there is a need to formally verify working of any novel routing protocol and to statistically validate experimental results collected from simulation. Our last research contribution proposed a novel trust-based opportunistic routing protocol, viz. ORPSN. This paper presents formal verification of ORPSN protocol using analytical proofs. The paper gives analytical proofs about optimality of the algorithm and loop freedom. The paper uses t-test to validate experimental results and observations. It compares performance of ORPSN and CORMAN opportunistic routing protocols in various test conditions. After statistical validation of experimental results, it is observed that performance of ORPSN is significantly better than CORMAN.

Keywords MANET · Routing protocol · Opportunistic routing · Verification
Analytical proofs · Validation · Hypothesis testing

S. A. Thorat (✉) · S. V. Yadav
Department of Computer Science and Engineering, Rajarambapu Institute
of Technology, Islampur, India
e-mail: sathorat2003@gmail.com

S. V. Yadav
e-mail: shital2303@gmail.com

P. J. Kulkarni
Walchand College of Engineering, Sangli, India
e-mail: pjk_walchand@rediffmail.com

© Springer Nature Singapore Pte Ltd. 2018
P. K. Pattnaik et al. (eds.), *Progress in Computing, Analytics and Networking*,
Advances in Intelligent Systems and Computing 710,
https://doi.org/10.1007/978-981-10-7871-2_9

1 Introduction and Motivation

Mobile ad hoc network (MANET) is infrastructure less, peer-to-peer wireless network. Data routing is as essential task in any network. In MANET, each node acts as packet router. MANET routing protocols conventionally assume that all participating nodes are honest and cooperative. A packet sent by the source node successfully reaches to the destination only if all nodes on the path forward that packet. It is practically infeasible to consider that all participating nodes in an open MANET are honest and cooperative. Non-cooperation of a node with other nodes causes disruption to the network service. Such selfish behaviour by the participating nodes degrades the performance of network to great extent [1, 2].

In opportunistic routing (OR) protocol, a route towards the destination is selected dynamically by making use of broadcast nature of the wireless communication [3]. As discussed above, OR protocols also assume that nodes participating in the network operations are honest and cooperative. We observed that OR protocol performance degrades significantly if selfish nodes are participating in the network operations. To overcome this problem, we proposed a novel trusted OR protocol, viz. opportunistic routing in presence of selfish nodes (ORPSN) [4]. The ORPSN overcomes presence of selfish nodes in the network by using trustworthy candidates nodes for packet forwarding. The ORPSN paper [4] gives details about working of algorithm, mathematical modelling and experimental results.

A protocol is nothing but set of rules required for exchanging a message between nodes in a network. Each routing protocol follows a different set of rules. The characteristics of opportunistic routing protocols are different than traditional MANET routing protocols. There is a need to verify if the ORPSN protocol is working as per standard expectations. This includes steps to ensure that routing protocol is error free, loop-free, absolute and functionally correct [5, 6].

The performance a routing protocol depends on various parameters such as node density, node movement speed, percentage of selfish nodes in the network. In [4], working and performance of ORPSN are tested using NS2 [7] simulator tool. The paper used various test conditions to compare performance of CORMAN and ORPSN by taking a large number of observations. There is a need to statistically validate experimental results to check if performance of ORPSN is significantly better than CORMAN.

Thus for any novel routing protocol, there is a need to verify that protocol works as per the expectations. Also it is needed to validate the experimental results obtained using simulator. This paper addresses these two issues, viz. verifying working of ORPSN protocol and validating experimental results of the ORPSN. The research contributions of this paper are as follows:

1. Analytical proofs related with working of ORPSN are presented. The proof verifies optimality of the ORPSN algorithm and its loop freedom.
2. t-test is used to verify validity of the statistical results and observations which are obtained using simulation. This verified that the performance of ORPSN

protocol is better than CORMAN in presence of selfish nodes under different test conditions.

The paper is organized as follows: Section 2 presents literature survey on opportunistic routing and verification of routing protocols. Section 3 gives an overview of ORPSN protocol. Section 4 presents various analytical proofs related to working ORPSN protocol. Section 5 gives validation of experimental results to compare performance of the ORPSN and CORMAN. The last section presents conclusion of the proposed research work and gives directions for future research work.

2 Related Work

ExOR [8] is considered as the first opportunistic routing protocol. Chakchouk et al. [9] is a literature survey on opportunistic routing protocol. The paper discusses evolution of routing paradigm and applications of OR in different areas. The paper classifies OR protocols as probabilistic, link state aware, optimization-based, cross-layer and geographical routing protocols. Patel et al. [10] reviewed existing opportunistic routing protocols in wireless sensor networks. The paper described components of opportunistic routing, viz. coordination method and candidate selection. SOAR (Simple Opportunistic Adaptive Routing) [11], PRIOR (Prioritized Forwarding for Opportunistic Routing) [12], EOpR [13] are few more examples of opportunistic routing protocols.

Thorat et al. [14] discussed various issues in designing a trust-based routing protocol. Salehi et al. [15] and MCOR [16] are examples of trust-based opportunistic routing protocols. These protocols build trust model depending on a node's packet forwarding behaviour. The derived trust values are used to choose cooperative nodes as packet forwarders.

Formal verification has become an increasingly important technique towards establishing the correctness of any protocol [5]. Bhargavan et al. [17] proved properties of routing protocol using automated reasoning methods. The authors discuss possibility and need of verification of routing protocols. Bourke et al. [18] provided automated proof of AODV protocol. De Renesse et al. [19], demonstrated formal verification of ad hoc routing protocol using SPIN tool.

Vamsi et al. [20] used Sequential Hypothesis Testing (SHT) to detect malicious node which affect entire network with Sybil attack. The authors collected experimental results using NS2 simulator. They concluded that SHT is robust method against detection of Sybil attack. Ho et al. [21] used sequential hypothesis testing to detect replica attack. Here, Sequential Probability Ratio Test (SPRT) process is considered to take decision about false positive and negative rate to overcome against replica cluster detection problem.

3 Overview of ORPSN Opportunistic Routing Protocol

This research work does verification and validation of ORPSN [4] opportunistic routing protocol. The protocol is a representative example of trust-based opportunistic routing. Though discussion in the paper is in the context of ORPSN, with few variations the concepts can be applied to other opportunistic routing protocols. A brief overview of ORPSN working is given below.

ORPSN extends functionality of CORMAN [22] opportunistic routing protocol using trust to overcome selfish nodes in the network. Here, packets are forwarded in form of batches with the help of nodes that are close to the destination. Each packet consists of a forwarding list which contains identities of candidate nodes; these candidate nodes are selected for transferring a packet from source node to the destination. At the initial stage, source generates a forwarding list. Each time when packets are forwarded towards the destination, intermediate nodes may update the forwarding list after taking into consideration instantaneous conditions.

ORPSN uses a novel metric, viz. *path goodness* to prioritize the available candidate nodes to forward packet towards a particular destination. *Path goodness* depends on two components, viz. path trust and closeness of the node towards the destination. A node's trustworthiness is calculated based on past packet forwarding behaviour of that node. For this, behaviour of the node is passively monitored. Path trust depends on trustworthiness of nodes which are lying on the path. Here, it is equivalent to trustworthiness of most untrustworthy node on the path. ORPSN calculates the closeness between any node and the destination in the form of Estimated Transmission Count (ETX).

ORPSN chooses two best candidate, nodes, viz. *Next Expected Forwarder* (NXF) and *Second Best Forwarder* (SBF) for forwarding each packet towards the destination. The NXF takes first chance to forward a packet; if it fails then SBF does forwarding. Experimental results given in [4] observed that ORPSN increases network throughput in the presence of selfish nodes.

4 Verification of ORPSN Protocol

This section gives various analytical proofs related to working of ORPSN protocol. An analytical proof uses algebraic methods to design proofs of the theorems. Structure of analytical proof is simple. Here it is necessary to ensure that given proofs do not go beyond the assumptions of the research work [23].

Theorem 1 *Let NL_i contain neighbour nodes of i having ETX less than i for the destination d. Using ORPSN, node i chooses node j which is part of NL_i as NXF using* path goodness (PG) *metric. For any other node k which is part of NL_i following statement holds true: $PG_{i,d,k} \leq PG_{i,d,j}$ where $PG_{i,d,k}$ = path goodness for path from i to d via k.*

Proof Let's consider an exceptional case: NL_i contains only one node, viz. j. In this case node i does not have any choice other than choosing j as NXF. Then above theorem is true.

If NL_i contains more than one nodes, viz. {j, k, l, m, n, ...}, then the ORPSN chooses node j as NXF. If there exist node k which has better *path goodness* than node j, this contradicts with the ORPSN algorithm, which ensures the node with maximum *path goodness* is chosen as NXF. Hence above theorem is true.

Theorem 2 *If R_i is the trusted cooperative route from node i to d chosen by ORPSN having optimal path goodness, and m is any intermediate node on the route, then sub-route from m to d denoted by R_m also have optimal path goodness among all routes to the destination d.*

Proof This is proven by contradiction. Suppose, R'_m is route with optimal *path goodness* from node m to d, hence $PG_{R'_m} \geq PG(R_m)$. So, the *path goodness* of newly formed route from node i to d, which consists of the sub-route R'_m from m to d is optimum. However, this contradicts with the assumption that R_i is the route with optimal path. Therefore, above theorem is true.

Theorem 3 *The ORPSN algorithm gives an optimal solution.*

Proof This is proven by contradiction. Suppose ORPSN identifies R_i as optimal route from node i to reach destination d. Assuming that the optimal route is R'_i instead of R_i, so $PG_{R'_i} \geq PG_{R_i}$. Now as R_i is not having optimal *path goodness* route from node i to d, there exists at least one node m in R'_i meeting the condition: $PG_{R'_m} \geq PG_{R_m}$.
As per Theorem 2, above claim is not possible as it contradicts with the assumption that all sub-routes of R_i are optimum. Therefore, above theorem is true.

Theorem 4 *The ORPSN algorithm is loop-free.*

Proof This is again proven by contradiction. Let's assume that (i, j, k, l, i) is the loop present in the route as shown in Fig. 1. As ORPSN does not select any selfish node in the route, all nodes in the loop are trusted. Above loop is directed, and each node in the loop has the corresponding *path goodness* with respect to node d, viz. $PG_i^*, PG_j^*, PG_k^*, PG_l^*$.
Following inequality is obtained from Theorem 1: $PG_i^* < PG_j^* < PG_k^* < PG_l^*$. As node i calculates the *path goodness* of its route to d, viz. PG_i^*, every node in the

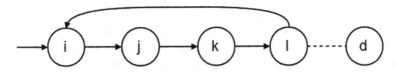

Fig. 1 An example of a loop existing in network

route has influence on the PG_i^*. Let PG_l' be the *path goodness* of the route from l to d due to existence of the loop. As $PG_i^* > PG_j^*$, if node j is deleted then PG_i^* can be updated with PG_i'. Hence it is observed that $PG_l' > PG_l^*$. This leads to a contradiction with the assumption that PG_l^* is the optimal *path goodness* between node l and node d. Therefore, ORPSN algorithm is loop-free.

5 Validating Experimental Results

ORPSN paper discussed experimental set-up and collected observations in details. Statistical validation of the experimental results using hypothesis testing is presented here. Hypothesis testing is a formal process which helps to evaluate a statistical hypotheses [24]. Here, IBM SPSS version 20.0 [25] is used for statistical analysis of the results. It helps to check whether difference between performance of CORMAN and ORPSN protocols is statically significant.

ORPSN addresses presence of selfish nodes and its impacts on opportunistic routing. As selfish nodes perform packet dropping attack, the packet delivery ratio is the most significant measurement parameter. Null hypothesis considered is—mean packet delivery ratios obtained by CORMAN and ORPSN are same. In other words, there is no statically significant difference between performance of ORPSN and CORMAN. Thus, ORPSN does not improve the performance in presence of selfish nodes. The alternative hypothesis is "mean packet delivery ratio for ORPSN is higher than CORMAN". In other words, ORPSN performance is significantly higher than CORMAN.

In the validation work, significance level (α) considered is 0.05. If significance value is less than or equal to 0.05, it indicates to have strong evidence against the null hypothesis. In that case alternative hypothesis is accepted. The 0.05 significance level indicates 5% chances of rejecting a null hypothesis when it is true.

The research work compares two mean values which are continuous in the nature. The population standard deviation is unknown. In this case results may be interesting in any direction, i.e. either CORMAN performance dominates ORPSN or vice versa. Hence two-tail t-test with paired samples is useful. The formula for two-tail t-test is given in Eq. 1.

$$t = \frac{\overline{x1} - \overline{x2}}{\sqrt{\frac{s_{12}}{n_1} + \frac{s_{22}}{n_2}}} \tag{1}$$

Here The n1 and n2 are number of values in each set. The $\overline{x1}$ and $\overline{x2}$ are means of values, with S1 and S2 standard deviations.

ORPSN used three test conditions for testing performance of CORMAN and ORPSN. These test conditions are: varying dimensions, selfish nodes and speed of the nodes. The experimental set-up used six different values for grid dimensions; and for each dimension, the experiment was repeated 20 times. Thus, total 120

Table 1 Protocol performance in different test conditions

Sr.	Test condition	Protocol	Mean	Std. deviation	Std. error
1	Varying dimension	CORMAN	71.68	15.48	1.41
		ORPSN	76.07	13.35	1.21
2	Varying selfish nodes	CORMAN	61.72	16.54	1.51
		ORPSN	66.40	15.09	1.37
3	Varying speed	CORMAN	53.03	14.80	1.35
		ORPSN	60.24	14.04	1.28

Table 2 Paired different between performance of protocols

Sr.	Test condition	Paired difference					t	df	P
		M	SD	SE	95% CI				
					L	U			
1	Varying dimension	−4.3914	7.2207	0.6591	−5.6966	−3.0862	6.662	119	0.000
2	Varying selfish nodes	−4.6789	8.2932	0.7570	−6.1779	−3.1798	−6.180	199	0.000
3	Varying speed	−7.2296	9.3670	0.8550	8.9228	−5.5365	−8.455	119	0.000

observations have been made available by varying grid dimensions. In similar way for varying selfish nodes and speed, there are 120 observations each. The values of mean (M) and standard deviation (SD), standard error (SE) for individual protocols, viz. CORMAN and ORPSN for various test conditions are given in Table 1.

Table 2 gives details about paired differences between CORMAN and ORPSN. It gives details about lower (L) and upper (U) values for 95% CI, t value, significance (p) and N = 120.

In above table, values for p are significantly less than 0.05. Thus, difference between performances of the CORMAN and ORPSN is statistically significant. Therefore, the null hypothesis is rejected and there is acceptance to alternative hypothesis. Thus, mean packet delivery ratio for ORPSN protocol is higher than CORMAN in all test conditions.

6 Conclusion and Scope for Future Work

Verifying working of a routing protocol and validating experimental results is a crucial task. The research work verified working of ORPSN routing protocol using analytical proofs. It is found that ORPSN is loop-free and chooses candidate nodes in optimal way. Performance of routing protocols varies according to different scenarios and network settings. Research work applied t-test to statistically validate the performance of ORPSN protocol. It is observed that packet delivery ratio of ORPSN is significantly better than CORMAN in different test conditions. The research work can be further extended to verify working of other newly proposed routing protocols. The protocols can be further verified using automated model checking tools like SPIN and HOL.

References

1. Djahel, Soufiene, Farid Nait-Abdesselam, and Zonghua Zhang: Mitigating packet dropping problem in mobile ad hoc networks: proposals and challenges. In: IEEE communications surveys & tutorials 13, no. 4, 658–672, 2011.
2. Govindan, Kannan, and Prasant Mohapatra: Trust computations and trust dynamics in mobile adhoc networks: a survey. In: IEEE Communications Surveys & Tutorials 14, no. 2, 279–298, 2012.
3. Jadhav, Payal, and RachnaSatao: A survey on opportunistic routing protocols for wireless sensor networks. In: Procedia Computer Science 79, 603–609, 2016.
4. Thorat, Sandeep A., and P. J. Kulkarni: Opportunistic routing in presence of selfish nodes for MANET. In: Wireless Personal Communications 82.2, 689–708, 2015.
5. Yasin, Daniyal, Kashif Saghar, and Shahzad Younis: Formal modeling and verification of Rumor Routing protocol. In: 13th IEEE International Bhurban Conference on Applied Sciences and Technology (IBCAST), 2016.
6. Šimoňák, Slavomír: Verification of communication protocols based on formal methods integration. In: Acta Polytechnica Hungarica 9.4, 117–128, 2012.
7. NS2, https://www.isi.edu/nsnam/ns/, 2017.
8. Biswas, Sanjit, and Robert Morris: ExOR: opportunistic multi-hop routing for wireless networks. In: ACM SIGCOMM Computer Communication Review 35.4, 133–144, 2005.
9. Chakchouk, Nessrine: A survey on opportunistic routing in wireless communication networks. In: IEEE Communications Surveys & Tutorials 17.4, 2214–2241, 2015.
10. Patel, Tejas, and Pariza Kamboj: Opportunistic routing in wireless sensor networks: A review. In: IEEE International on Advance Computing Conference (IACC), 2015.
11. Rozner, Eric: SOAR: Simple opportunistic adaptive routing protocol for wireless mesh networks. In: IEEE transactions on Mobile computing 8.12, 1622–1635, 2009.
12. Yamazaki, Taku: Forwarding mechanism using prioritized forwarders for opportunistic routing. In: 18th IEEE Asia-Pacific Network Operations and Management Symposium (APNOMS), 2016.
13. Shabani, S., N. Moghim, and A. Bohlooli: EOpR: An opportunistic routing algorithm for adhoc networks. In: 5th IEEE International Conference on Computer and Knowledge Engineering (ICCKE), 2015.
14. Thorat, Sandeep A., and P. J. Kulkarni: Design issues in trust based routing for MANET. In: 5th IEEE International Conference on Computing, Communication and Networking Technologies (ICCCNT), pp. 1–7, 2014.

15. M. Salehi, A. Boukerche, A. Darehshoorzadeh, and A. Mammeri: Towards a Novel Trust-based Opportunistic Routing Protocol for Wireless Networks. In: Wireless Networks, vol. 22, no. 3, pp. 927–943, 2016.
16. Bo, Wang: Trust-based minimum cost opportunistic routing for Ad hoc networks. In: Journal of Systems and Software 84.12, 2107–2122, 2011.
17. Bhargavan, Karthikeyan, Davor Obradovic, and Carl A. Gunter: Formal verification of standards for distance vector routing protocols. In: Journal of the ACM (JACM) 49.4, 538–576, 2002.
18. Bourke, Timothy, Rob van Glabbeek, and Peter Höfner: A mechanized proof of loop freedom of the (untimed) AODV routing protocol. In: International Symposium on Automated Technology for Verification and Analysis. Springer International Publishing, 2014.
19. De Renesse, F., and A. H. Aghvami: Formal verification of ad-hoc routing protocols using SPIN model checker. In: Proceedings of the 12th IEEE Mediterranean Electro-technical Conference. MELECON 2004.
20. Vamsi, P. Raghu, and Krishna Kant: Sybil attack detection using sequential hypothesis testing in wireless sensor networks. In: IEEE International Conference on Signal Propagation and Computer Technology (ICSPCT), 2014.
21. Ho, Jun-Won: Sequential hypothesis testing based approach for replica cluster detection in wireless sensor networks. In: Journal of Sensor and Actuator Networks 1.2, 153–165, 2012.
22. Wang, Zehua, Yuanzhu Chen, and Cheng Li: CORMAN: A novel cooperative opportunistic routing scheme in mobile ad hoc networks. In: IEEE Journal on Selected Areas in Communications 30.2, 289–296, 2012.
23. Analytical Proofs, https://en.wikipedia.org/wiki/Analytic_proof.
24. Hypothesis Testing, https://en.wikipedia.org/wiki/Null_hypothesis.
25. IBM SPSS, https://www.ibm.com/analytics/us/en/technology/spss/.

Adaptive MAC Protocol in Wireless Sensor Networks for Disaster Detection

Anshu Katiyar, Jitendra Kumar and Pabitra Mohan Khilar

Abstract The real-time applications of wireless sensor networks (WSNs) make it as a vast area of emerging research. An energy efficient and reliable medium access control (MAC) protocol plays an important role to monitor a natural disaster such as volcano eruptions. Area of interest is to handle the emergency situation when the vibrations from earth surpass a threshold value, reliable and immediate delivery of data is required. To fulfill these dynamic scenarios, Adaptive MAC protocol (A-MAC) is used to give QoS services in normal as well as emergency situations. A-MAC protocol uses the standard IEEE 802.15.4 protocol in normal traffic, while in emergency traffic it uses IEEE 802.15.4 protocol with different backoff mechanism. In the emergency traffic, this mechanism is able to give better results as compared to standard mechanism.

Keywords IEEE 802.15.4 · Adaptive MAC · Variable traffic · Disaster detection · Energy consumption

1 Introduction

WSNs are very useful in telecommunication fields as they are capable of storing and processing the data using less energy and hardware. The efficient use of WSNs is challenging. WSNs are designed to store the data correctly, to process the data efficiently, and to monitor the environment. These networks consist of some sensor nodes. These sensor nodes are very simple with respect to hardware and software and follow the alarm-driven model which makes it perfect for real-time applications.

A. Katiyar (✉) · J. Kumar · P. M. Khilar
National Institute of Technology, Rourkela 769008, India
e-mail: anshukiot09@gmail.com

J. Kumar
e-mail: jtndr969@gmail.com

P. M. Khilar
e-mail: pmkhilar@nitrkl.ac.in

© Springer Nature Singapore Pte Ltd. 2018
P. K. Pattnaik et al. (eds.), *Progress in Computing, Analytics and Networking*,
Advances in Intelligent Systems and Computing 710,
https://doi.org/10.1007/978-981-10-7871-2_10

Such type of sensor nodes are used in many applications such as healthcare monitoring [1], disaster detection, temperature monitoring, machine surveillance, and soil moisture checking [2]. For disaster detection such as earthquake monitoring and volcano eruption monitoring, sensor networks are very useful. These sensors can be used to detect the vibrations of the earth by locating it to the disaster-prone area.

In this paper, we proposed an Adaptive MAC protocol (A-MAC) which follows the baseline of IEEE 802.15.4 MAC protocol as it is a low power and efficient MAC protocol used for wireless personal area networks (WPANs). This A-MAC is capable of transmitting the data to the base station and handling two types of traffic patterns: (i) normal traffic and (ii) emergency traffic. When the vibrations from earth are exceed the threshold value, then it generates emergency traffic and this information should be delivered with certain Quality of Service (QoS) parameters immediately. Otherwise, the normal traffic is generated. The performance of the proposed protocol is represented in terms of generic parameters such as delay, power consumption, and packet delivery ratio. In normal traffic, the protocol broadcasts the beacon packets to synchronize with other sensor nodes, while in emergency traffic it broadcasts the alarm packets to inform others. At that time, the normal backoff mechanism is preempted and the modified backoff mechanism is opted to deliver the data.

2 Related Work

Fei et al. [3] described the role of MAC protocol in the real-time communication. In the work, different categories of MAC protocol are discussed and pros and cons of different categories also elaborated. Nadeem et al. [4] described the applications of wireless sensors networks with respect to healthcare monitoring. The work showed the use of body area sensor network (BASN) in activity analyzing, posture guessing, military surveillance, etc. Koubaa et al. [5, 6] proposed an approach to improve the performance of IEEE 802.15.4 MAC protocol by varying the backoff time and change the value of parameters to calculate the backoff period. Du et al. [7] explained the detailed working of IEEE 802.15.4. and proposed two hardware models to implement it, which is able to take different parameters of superframe order (SO) and beacon order (BO). Samal et al. [8] proposed a HC-MAC protocol in the healthcare networks. This protocol is able to handle the variable type of health data. Ko et al. [9] described the effect of different ranges for backoff period in IEEE 802.15.4. It showed that backoff delay can be reduced by lowering the standard range of backoff exponent (BE) that is three by default.

3 Proposed Work

In this paper, we proposed a novel disaster detection MAC protocol to guarantee a QoS with respect to emergency traffic without affecting the normal traffic. The base line of this protocol is IEEE 802.15.4 [10], slotted CSMA/CA-based approach. Two types of packets are used to provide synchronization among nodes, beacon packets, and alarm packets.

3.1 System Model and Assumption

In the proposed system model, all nodes are directly connected to the head of respective cluster and form a star topology, and head nodes are connected to the base station, so the base station acts as a sink node for all the nodes. The sensor nodes are placed in the disaster-prone area, and they are connected by the cluster heads. Most of the time these sensor nodes are having normal traffic but sometimes when the vibrations from the earth increase its intensity and crossed some threshold, sensor nodes are having emergency traffic. At that time, it should consume less energy because sensor nodes are having less power and it should also transmit the data as quickly as possible. Figure 1 presents the system model of A-MAC protocol.

3.2 Proposed A-MAC

At first, all the nodes broadcast their location to the head nodes. The head nodes broadcast the beacon packets to synchronize the nodes in their communication range. The proposed A-MAC protocol uses the same backoff mechanism of the standard IEEE 802.15.4 in normal traffic and different backoff mechanism for emergency traffic, which is described in following parts:

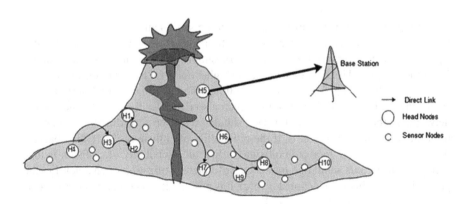

Fig. 1 Disaster detection sensor network

3.2.1   Backoff Mechanism in IEEE 802.15.4

IEEE 802.15.4 works on the mechanism of CSMA/CA for medium access. This mechanism adopts a binary exponential backoff (BEB) algorithm to avoid the collisions and control the channel access. Whenever nodes are contending the medium and a collision occur, nodes have to wait for a randomly chosen backoff period. After this period only they can contend again. However, this mechanism depends on parameters. These parameters are (i) initial value of contention window (CW_{init}), (ii) minimum backoff exponent (macMinBE), (iii) maximum number of backoffs (macMaxCSMABackoffs), (iv) maximum backoff exponent (aMaxBE). The default values of these parameters are shown as: macMinBE = 3, aMaxBE = 5, macMaxC-SMABackoffs = 4, aMaxframeRetries = 3.

Initially, the values are fixed as $CW_{init} = 2$, NB = 0 (number of backoffs), and BE = 3 (backoff exponent). While nodes are transferring the data and if a collision occurs, then each node has to wait for a random amount of time between $[0, (2^{BE} - 1)]$, after this time node can transmit the data. For a particular node, if the backoff period is over, then the algorithm performs the first clear channel assessment (CCA), if the channel is idle during that, then it performs second CCA, if the channel is still idle, then the node can transmit the data immediately; otherwise, in the middle of any assessment if the channel is busy, then at that time the value of BE and NB is incremented by one and node has to wait randomly during that time; meanwhile, if the value of BE reaches to limit (5) or the number of backoffs reaches to max (4), then the algorithm returns as failure and discard the packet; otherwise, node can transmit the data after waiting random backoff period accordingly. For the same frame after failure, nodes can try for three times only after that they have to contend for next frame.

3.2.2   Modified Backoff Mechanism in IEEE 802.15.4

The standard backoff mechanism depends on the static nature of the networks, and it does not take the real art of communication into consideration which includes dynamic aspect. The range for backoff period should consider the dynamic changes. If the backoff period is large, then it leads to higher delay for transmission and reflects inefficient utilization and energy consumption, whereas if the backoff period is too small, then it reflects high collisions, which also degrades the performance of the network. So the range for backoff period should be chosen according to the real scenario of communication; that is, if the probability of collision is high, then backoff period should be high to avoid collisions; when the probability of collision is low, then backoff periods should be low in order to better utilization of channel. Let the probability of collision is denoted by p(c), this probability of collision for kth updating period can be calculated as Eq. 1.

$$P(c) = \frac{NC^K}{NS^K} \tag{1}$$

Table 1 Simulator parameters

Simulator	NS2.35
Channel type	Channel/Wireless channel
Antenna	Antenna/Omni Antenna
Simulation area	100 m × 1000 m
Mobile nodes	30, 60, 90, 12, 01, 50, 180
Traffic sources	CBR (UDP)
Packet size	800 Bytes
Simulation time	300 s
Data rate	250 kbps

where NC^k and NS^k are the numbers of collisions and the number attempts to send data of kth updating period.

Now the backoff period will take the probability of collision into the consideration. Let the backoff period is denoted as BT, and in order to efficient delivery of data the backoff period should be chosen according to Eq. 2.

$$BT \in [0, P(c) * (2^{BE} - 1)] \qquad (2)$$

So now the backoff period depends on the probability of collision; if the probability of collision is high, then the large backoff period is chosen in order to avoid a collision, and if the probability of collision is low, then the small backoff period is chosen in order to better resource utilization. If the collision occurs during data transmission, then nodes have to wait a random amount of time according to the Eq. 2. If during CCA again collision occurs, then the probability of collision get changes which also reflect the different range for backoff period.

4 Performance Analysis

The simulation for the proposed A-MAC protocol is performed in NS-2.35.[1] The head nodes are fixed as 18 nodes, and all nodes are having equal transmission range. The capacity of the channel is fixed as 300 kbps. All the parameters used in the simulation are shown in Table 1.

In our simulation, first, we evaluate the effect of the simulation time in seconds of A-MAC protocol. We vary the range from 50 to 300 s.

Figure 2 represents the graph between the simulation time and PDR. When the time increases, the PDR of nodes also increases because more number of nodes able to take part to transmit the data. Emergency data shows better PDR as compare to nor-

---

[1] http://www.isi.edu/nsnam/ns/.

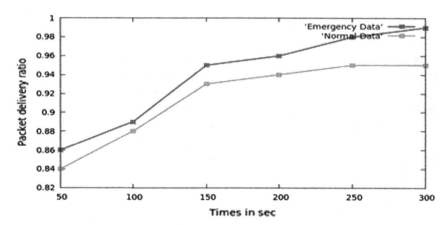

Fig. 2 PDR versus Time

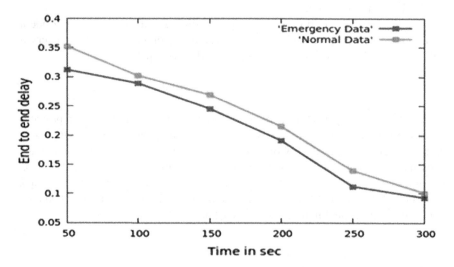

Fig. 3 End to end delay versus time

mal data as it uses modified backoff scheme. The packet loss decreases with increase in time. The A-MAC protocol is able to achieve almost 100.

Figure 3 represents the graph between average end to end delay and time in seconds. By simulation, it is clear that emergency data shows the less delay compare to normal data as it has high PDR also. Figure 4 represents the average energy consumed by the node with time. It is clear that initially, energy consumption is high; however, it decreases with time because of delivery of a high number of packets. Except for this emergency traffic is able to reduce the energy consumption by choosing a better range of backoff time.

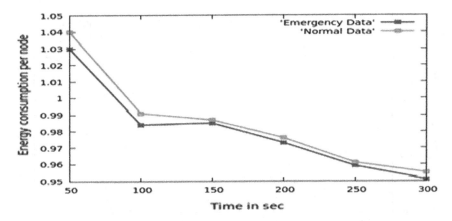

Fig. 4 Energy consumption per node versus time

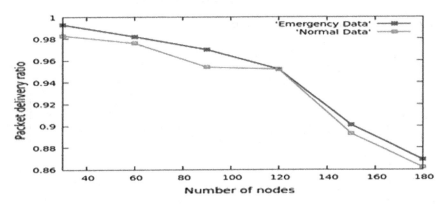

Fig. 5 PDR versus number of nodes

Secondly, we observe the behavior of the proposed algorithm with respect to number of nodes. We take the range from 30 to 180 sensor nodes.

Figure 5 represents the PDR with the increasing number of nodes. As we increase the number of nodes, the PDR decreases but still able to transfer more than 80% of the packets. Figure 6 represents the graph of end to end delay with respect to increasing number of nodes. As the number of nodes increases, the average end to end delay among nodes also increases. Emergency traffic shows less delay as it reduces the number of failures during transmission. Figure 7 shows the graph between energy consumption and number of nodes. Energy consumption per node increases as the network grows. Emergency traffic consumes less energy comparatively.

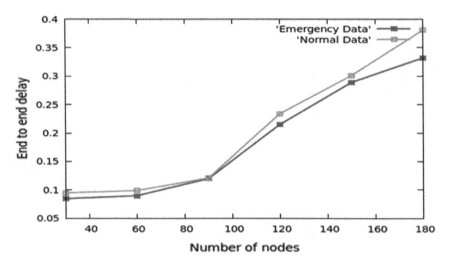

Fig. 6 End to end delay versus number of nodes

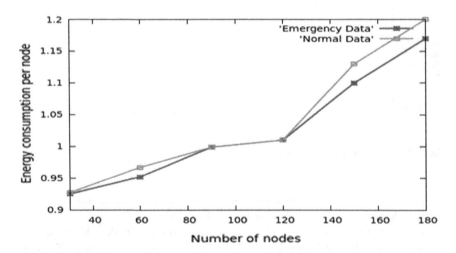

Fig. 7 Energy consumption per node versus number of nodes

5 Conclusion

This paper shows the real art of communication by representing variable data traffic with respect to disaster detection. We proposed a energy efficient protocol, which is able to choose a better range as backoff period when the emergency situation occurs and giving better performance. The system architecture involves the head nodes and the common nodes. Head nodes are transferring the information to the base station.

The simulation results show that the proposed protocol is able to give good PDR, more than 80% in all the cases and consuming less power, so it ensures a reliable and energy efficient delivery of data.

References

1. M. A. Hanson, H. C. Powell Jr, A. T. Barth, K. Ringgenberg, B. H. Calhoun, J. H. Aylor, and J. Lach, "Body area sensor networks: Challenges and opportunities," *Computer*, vol. 42, no. 1, 2009.
2. G. R. Mendez, M. A. M. Yunus, and S. C. Mukhopadhyay, "A wifi based smart wireless sensor network for an agricultural environment," in *2011 Fifth International Conference on Sensing Technology*, Nov 2011, pp. 405–410.
3. L. D. P. Fei, "Energy-efficient mac protocols for wireless sensor networks," *information and communications technologies, Beihang University, Beijing*, vol. 100083, 2009.
4. A. Nadeem, M. A. Hussain, O. Owais, A. Salam, S. Iqbal, and K. Ahsan, "Application specific study, analysis and classification of body area wireless sensor network applications," Computer Networks, vol. 83, pp. 363–380, 2015.
5. A. Koubâa, M. Alves, and E. Tovar, "IEEE 802.15.4: a federating communication protocol for time-sensitive wireless sensor networks," *Sensor Networks and Configurations: Fundamentals, Techniques, Platforms, and Experiments*, pp. 19–49, 2006.
6. A. Koubaa, M. Alves, B. Nefzi, and Y.-Q. Song, "Improving the IEEE 802.15. 4 slotted CSMA/CA MAC for time-critical events in wireless sensor networks," 2006.
7. W. Du, D. Navarro, and F. Mieyeville, "Performance evaluation of IEEE 802.15. 4 sensor networks in industrial applications," International Journal of Communication Systems, vol. 28, no. 10, pp. 1657–1674, 2015.
8. T. Samal, M. Dash, R. R. Swain, and M. R. Kabat, "A media access control protocol for healthcare sensor networks," in *Next Generation Computing Technologies (NGCT), 2015 1st International Conference on*. IEEE, 2015, pp. 331–337.
9. J.-G. Ko, Y.-H. Cho, and H. Kim, "Performance evaluation of IEEE 802.15.4 MAC with different backoff ranges in wireless sensor networks," in *Communication systems, 2006. ICCS 2006. 10th IEEE Singapore International Conference on*. IEEE, 2006, pp. 1–5.
10. A. V. Patil and A. Y. Kazi, "Performance analysis of IEEE 802.15.4 sensor networks," in *2013 Fourth International Conference on Computing, Communications and Networking Technologies (ICCCNT)*, July 2013, pp. 1–6.

Dynamic Security Risk Assessment in Cloud Computing Using IAG

Gopi Puppala and Syam Kumar Pasupuleti

Abstract Cloud computing is one of the most emerging technologies because of its benefits. However, cloud security is one of the major issues that attracting lot of research. In cloud computing environment, cloud users may have privilege to install their own applications, Particularly in Infrastructure as a Service (IaaS) clouds provide privileges to users to install applications on their virtual machines (VMs), so users may install vulnerable applications. In this case, identifying zombie's exploitation attack is difficult. Many attack graph-based solutions were proposed to detect compromised VMs, but they focus only on static attack scenario. In this paper, we propose a dynamic risk assessment system by incorporating Bayes theorem into attack graph model, namely improved attack graph (IAG) to assess the dynamic risks and decide appropriate countermeasure based on IAG analytical models. The effectiveness and efficiency of the propose system are demonstrated in security and performance analysis, respectively.

Keywords Cloud computing · DDoS attack · Vulnerability · Attack graph · Risk management · Bayesian theorem

G. Puppala (✉)
University of Hyderabad, Hyderabad, India
e-mail: puppala.nagasaran@gmail.com

S. K. Pasupuleti
Institute for Development and Research in Banking Technology (IDRBT), Hyderabad, India
e-mail: psyamkumar@idrbt.ac.in

© Springer Nature Singapore Pte Ltd. 2018
P. K. Pattnaik et al. (eds.), *Progress in Computing, Analytics and Networking*,
Advances in Intelligent Systems and Computing 710,
https://doi.org/10.1007/978-981-10-7871-2_11

1 Introduction

Cloud computing is one of the most prominent computing models in IT industry. Particularly, all characteristics of other computing models (distributed, grid, and ubiquitous computing) are comprised in cloud computing. Especially, on-demand elasticity and rapid elasticity are the most desirable features of cloud computing attracting organizations toward cloud computing. However, cloud security is one of the major concerns, and lot of research is taking place.

Currently, considerable amount of research is taking place to address above cloud security threats. Chung et al. [2] introduced a Network Intrusion Detection and Countermeasure Selection (NICE) in Virtual Network Systems to detect the compromised VM and resolve by countermeasure. In NICE implementation, they incorporate analytical attack graph model with intrusion detection system (IDS) processes. NICE has two main phases: in first phase, NICE decides whether or not to put a virtual machine in network inspection state based on severity of identified vulnerabilities and in second phase, deep packet inspection is applied. However, NICE focuses on static risk assessment strategy; i.e., it uses local conditional probability only to assess the security risk.

In this paper, we proposed a dynamic security risk assessment and risk mitigation strategy to address above problems. In our scheme, we use an improved attack graph (IAG) model to detect DDoS attacks and countermeasure selection to counter the attack. The contributions of our work in this paper are presented as follows:

- we built the improved attack graph, which is a collection of all possible attack paths where vulnerabilities are nodes and conditions are edges.
- By using Common Vulnerability Scoring System [3] (CVSS), we initialize base score for each node in the attack graph. Once the attacker exploits a node in any attack path, we dynamically calculate likelihood probability of exploiting the other nodes in that attack path toward target node by using Baye's theorem of conditional probability.
- If the exploitation probability of any node exceeds the threshold probability value then we choose an optimum countermeasure from a pool of countermeasures to counter the attack.
- Through security analysis and performance analysis, we prove security and performance of the system.

"The rest of the paper is organized as follows: Sect. 2 describes the related work, Sect. 3 explains the proposed method, Sect. 4 analyze the security of our scheme, Sect. 5 analyze the performance of our scheme and Sect. 6 gives Conclusion".

2 Related Work

In this related work, we presented literature of research areas related to zombie detection and prevention, intrusion detection system and alert correlation, attack graph construction, security metrics and analysis, and Bayesian attack graph. Considerable amount of research has been taking place in the area of detecting zombie systems. Duan et al. [4] followed an approach called SPOT to detect compromised machines which are serving as spam zombies. This approach basically scans the outgoing messages sequentially to identify compromised hosts. Bot-Hunter [5] assumes that a malware detection process can be divided into number of stages which helps in associating intrusion alarms due to incoming traffic with outgoing communication patterns. Using the above facts, they identified compromised hosts. Bot-Sniffer [6] detects zombies by exploiting compromised machine's uniform behavior characteristics (spatial, temporal). In this approach, they grouped flows based on server connections and they identified zombies by searching for alike behavior in the flow. For detection of suspicious events in network, firewall and IDS are used. But they have limitations in their implementation such as large volumes of raw alerts from IDS and false alarms. Sadoddin et al. [7] stated that alert correlation gives a comprehensive view of a attack. In a network, series of exploits can be represented using attack graph. An atomic attack is a series of exploits which makes a system state undesirable. Many automation tools are available for attack graph construction. Sheyner et al. [8] implemented a model by incorporating modified symbolic model checking NuSMV [9] and Binary Decision Diagrams (BDDs), though it generates all possible attack paths, scalability is an issue in this model. P. Amman et al. [10] in their work they considered the principle of monotonicity, according to monotonicity principle attacker need not to backtrack. Therefore, this model generates incisive and scalable attack graphs for encoding attack trees. MulVAL is another tool to generate attack graphs, proposed by Ou et al. [11]. MulVAL follows logic programming, and to model and analyze the network, it uses datalog language. Because of polynomial number of facts in the system, the termination of attack graph construction process is appropriate. There are many standardized security metrics available such as Common Vulnerability Scoring System (CVSS) [3] and Common Weakness Scoring System (CWSS) [12], where CVSS deals with ranking the known vulnerabilities and CWSS deals with software weaknesses. The above metrics form the basis to find ways to assign numerical scores to know vulnerabilities stored in National Vulnerability Database (NVD) [13]. Network security metrics have garnered a lot of attention. In [14], Markov model proposed time and effort required by potential adversaries as a security metric. Apart from them, other metrics are lengths of shortest path attacks, etc. In subsequent work [15], number of shortest paths is used as a metric; in [16], the easiest path among sequence of attacks used by attackers in an attack tree is considered as a security metric. Another work [17] considers arithmetic mean of all attack path lengths as a security metric.

3   Proposed Method

In order to address DoS and DDoS attacks in cloud, we propose a dynamic security risk assessment system using IAG. The propose system consists of attack graph construction, risk assessment, and countermeasure selection. These phases are explained in detail in the following sections.

3.1   Attack Graph Construction

In this section, we describe the attack graph construction for given sample network in Fig. 1. Attack graph provides the logical representation for the information such as number of vulnerable virtual machines present in the network, relationship between the vulnerabilities of different VMs, all possible ways by which an attacker can enter and reach the target. An attack graph consists of number of paths, each path illustrates a way in which the network can be put in an unsafe state by an attacker. We give description about the procedure for attack construction based on the property AG ($\neg unsafe$). It takes set of states Q_r and transaction relation between the states T, set of initial states Q_0, and a safety property p as input, and it constructs the attack graph. The set of states Q_r reachable from the initial states will be discovered in first step. In second step, it determines another set of reachable states Q_{unsafe} which reach unsafe sates. An iterative algorithm obtained from a fix-point characterization of the attack graph operator [18] is used to determine the set of states Q_{unsafe}. Let T be the transaction relation of the model, i.e.,$(q, q^1) \in T$ if and only if there exists a transition from q to q. We get a transition relation T^p that confine edges of attack graph by limiting the domain and range of T to Q_{unsafe}. Therefore, the attack graph $(Q_{unsafe}, T^p, Q_0^p, Q_s^p)$, where Q_{unsafe} and T^p represent set of nodes and set of edges of the graph, respectively. $Q_0^p = Q_0 \cap Q_{unsafe}$ is the set of initial states, and $Q_s^p = \{q | q \in Q_{unsafe} \wedge unsafe \in L(q)\}$ is the set of success states.

3.2   Dynamic Security Risk Assessment

In this section, we assess the dynamic risk based on the IAG. In IAG, all external nodes represent main sources of threats with their effect on other attributes of network. A few of these attributes acts as precondition for an exploit. These preconditions put network in a favorable state for subsequent exploits when an attacker executes them successfully.

Figure 1 shows our test network, from which we can take a sample attack scenario and constructed a simple IAG showed in Fig. 2 for our security risk assessment.

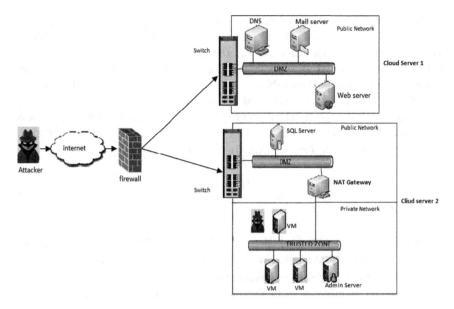

Fig. 1 Test network

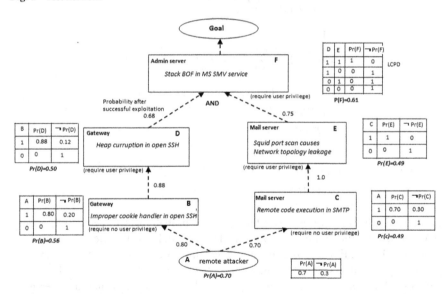

Fig. 2 Sample attack scenario

The probability of success of those attack node will become one, leading to re-evaluation of risk level estimations. Successor of the attack node with probability 1 will be updated by forward propagation. The initial assumptions on all prior probabilities during static risk assessment will be corrected with backward propagation. The updated unconditional probabilities are known as posterior probabilities. Given a set of attacks s_i' for which we have evidence of exploit, the probability of success for those attack nodes is now 1. Thus, we need to determine the probability of success for the attack nodes that are affected by s_i', i.e., the set of $s_j \in \{S - s_i'\}$. We compute the posterior probability, $Pr(s_j|s_i')$ using Bayes theorem given Eq. (1):

$$Pr(s_j|s_i') = \frac{[Pr(s_i'|s_j) \times Pr(s_j)]}{Pr(s_i')} \tag{1}$$

where $Pr(s_j)$ and $Pr(s_i')$ are the prior unconditional probabilities of the corresponding nodes. The conditional probability of joint occurrence of s_i' given the states of s_j is denoted by $Pr(s_i'|s_j)$. If we have evidence of goal state, i.e., F being compromised, we can compute its effect on Node D probability by using Eq. (2) as follows:

$$Pr(D|F) = \frac{[Pr(F|D) \times Pr(D)}{Pr(F)}$$

Where,

$$Pr(F|D) = \sum_{E \in T,F} [Pr(F|D, E = T) \times Pr(E)]$$

$$= (1.00 \times 0.49)_T + (1.00 \times 0.51)_F \tag{2}$$

$$Pr(F|D) = 1$$
$$Pr(D) = 0.50$$
$$Pr(F) = 0.61$$

Therefore,

$$Pr(D|F) = 0.82$$

In the similarly way, we compute the posterior probabilities of remaining nodes. Here, the unconditional probability for the D was initially 0.50. After the happening attack incident at F, D's posterior probability increased to 0.82. After computing posterior probabilities for all the nodes in network, based on this probability score network administrator figures out the most vulnerable nodes which attacker may target to exploit. The administrator selects the nodes which have posterior probability value greater than threshold to apply optimal countermeasure.

3.3   Counter Measure Selection

Algorithm: Counter Measure Selection
Input: Alert,G(E,V),C
Output: Optimal counter measure

```
 1  Let V_Alert = Source node of the Alert
 2  if Distance_to_Goal(V_Alert) >threshold then
 3  │   Update_BAG;
 4  │   return;
 5  end
 6  Let P = Descendant(V_Alert) ∪ V_Alert
 7  Set Pr(V_Alert) = 1
 8  Calculate _Risk _Prob(P)
 9  Let benefit[|P|, |C|] = φ
10  for each p ∈ P do
11  │   for each c ∈ C do
12  │   │   if c.condition(t) then
13  │   │   │   Pr(p)=Pr(p) * (1- c.effectiveness);
14  │   │   │   Calculate _Risk _Prob(Descendant(t));
15  │   │   │   benefit[t, c] = ΔPr(goal_node);
16  │   │   end
17  │   end
18  end
19  Let ROI[|P|, |C|] = φ
20  for each p ∈ P do
21  │   for each c ∈ C do
22  │   │   ROI[t,c]= benifit[t,c] / cost.c+intrusiveness
23  │   end
24  end
25  Update _BAG
26  return Select _Optimal _C(ROI)
```

In this section, we define the way to choose the optimal countermeasure for the attack scenario that we considered in previous section. Attack graph G, *alert*, and a set of countermeasures C are taken as input by the procedure listed in Table 1.

This procedure begins with determination of node v_{Alert} that relates to generated alert. Before choosing a countermeasure, we measure the distance from v_{Alert} to the *Goalnode*. We update the alert correlation graph *ACG* to keep track of alerts, but no need to perform countermeasure when measured distance is higher than the threshold value. Set of all nodes P, which reachable from source node v_{Alert} (including source node), is determined. We set the v_{Alert} probability as 1, because after attacker performing action only the alert has raised. Now, we compute the new probabilities for all the child nodes which belong to set P. Now, $\forall\, p \in P$ the countermeasures in C which can be applied are chosen and new set of probabilities are computed based on the gravity of chosen countermeasure. We compute benefit of applied countermeasure based on the change in *Goal* node probability. For each *benefit* of applied countermeasure, we compute the *ReturnofInvestment*(ROI). We choose the optimal countermeasure, when we apply that on a node gives minimum value of ROI.

4 Security Analysis

In this section, we analyze the security of our system against various attacks in cloud in order to determine the effectiveness of proposed risk assessment system. In this experiment,we have taken a test network showed in Fig. 1. A sample attack graph for the test network is showed in Fig. 2., initially, with a probability measure for successful exploitation of each node, node is shown in that attack graph without any countermeasures. In the following sections, we discussed about different attack scenarios and attacker capabilities with respect to his/her position in the virtual network. We listed set of some possible countermeasures in Table 1, whenever we encountered a evidence in IAG, i.e., $Pr(S_i = 1)$, our proposed framework will select a optimal countermeasure from a pool of countermeasures by using the Algorithm 2 to counter an attack.

4.1 Attack Model 1

In attack1, the attacker is an insider to the virtual network. As such they might be having user access privileges and install and run any vulnerable applications, might be able to do authentication bypass with an easy effort, and might be having a chance to know decent information about vulnerabilities in virtual nodes. As this kind of attacker knows the authentication procedure, there is a chance for him/her to add zombie nodes as legitimate nodes to the existing virtual network. The main motive here is to compromise a virtual system. In this scenario, using least privileged service accounts to run processes and access resources is an optimal countermeasure.

4.2 Attack Model 2

In attack2, the attacker does not have the same capability as the previous attack model. As such, he/she will not able to compromise a virtual node. But by making use of the known vulnerability information, he/she can send and run malicious code remotely on any virtual node, by that attacker can get root level access privileges or considerable information about open ports. Once attacker comes to know about open ports information it will leads to network topology leakage. In this scenario, *BlockPort* is an optimal countermeasure.

4.3 Attack Model 3

The attacker in this scenario is an outsider and he/she is nor more concern about virtual node compromising, rather he/she is interested in disrupt available services and as suck jam communication frequencies, overload virtual nodes with suspicious message packets and so on. In this scenario, most tempting attack will destroy the virtual nodes. For this kind of scenarios, *DeepPacketInspection* is an optimal countermeasure. By inspecting the packets deeply, compromised nodes and target/Goal node can be identified and mitigation can be done by *Traffic isolation*.

5 Performance Analysis

In performance analysis, we analyze the performance of our dynamic risk assessment scheme. We implemented our proposed scheme on top of OpenStack open source cloud platform. Openstack allows customers to load and manage various server instances of Windows/Linux platforms.

We conducted the experiments on a local cloud platform that built on OpenStack newton 2.13.0 and created a test environment using Linux machine having Intel i7 Quad-Core CPUSs with a clock speed of 3.0 GHz and each has 16GB of RAM and 64-bit Ubuntu 16.04. This machine is connected via a Gigabit switch to an OpenStack cloud platform having 2 VLANs connecting two cloud servers, each one having a set of VMs. The architecture of the OpenStack Neutron network is shown in Fig. 2. The connectivity between the nodes is presented in Table 1, which includes virtual machines across two cloud servers and configured each Virtual Machine as a target node to create a IAG.

In our proposed system, attack graph construction, dynamic security risk assessment, and countermeasure selection are the prime concerns. Performance of proposed model depends on the performance of individual process. For attack graph construction, we incorporated extended MulVAL tool, this MulVAL reasoning engine takes a set of Datalog tuples (**Host1, Host2, Protocol_P, and Port number**) as input. These datalog tuples give information about the pattern of communication between the nodes in cloud network. We experimented many times with different number of hosts in the two cloud servers connected through 2 VLANs connected using different topologies. Essentially, we checked scalability of a model by increasing number of nodes exponentially. In Fig. 3, we compared the CPU utilization for attack graph construction of our proposed model with NICE [2].

Figure 3a shows that CPU utilization of our scheme is lower than existing scheme [2]. After the attack graph is constructed for a cloud network, security risk assessment for that attack graph gives a security measure value at every node that represents the level of a network security at that particular node. In this paper, we used the probability of exploiting an vulnerability as security measure. Computational cost of risk depends on the number of VMs in the network, number of vulnera-

Table 1 List of
countermeasures

Countermeasure list			
No.	Countermeasure	Intrusiveness	Cost
1	Traffic redirection	3	3
2	Traffic isolation	4	2
3	Deep packet inspection	3	3
4	Creating filtering rules	1	2
5	MAC address change	2	1
6	IP address change	2	1
7	Block port	4	1
8	Software patch	5	4
9	Quarantine	5	2

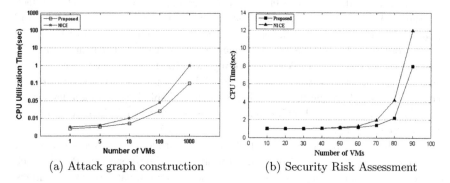

(a) Attack graph construction   (b) Security Risk Assessment

Fig. 3 **a** Attack graph construction. **b** Security risk assessment

bilities in each VM, and the relationship between VMs. Now, we measure the CPU
utilization for dynamic risk assessment. Figure 3b illustrates the comparison of computational cost for security risk assessment between our model and NICE [2], and
it shows that our scheme will take less CPU time than NICE [2]. Because we used
Bayesian network-based attack graph that assigns the probabilities to exploits while
later assigns probabilities to edges.

After security risk assessment process cloud network administrator able to find
out most vulnerable nodes in the network, so that when an attack starts he can counter
the attack by applying a countermeasures at most vulnerable nodes. By executing
procedure countermeasure, an optimal countermeasure will be selected and applied.

We listed the countermeasures along with their cost in Table 2, which are applicable to cloud network.

6 Conclusion

In this paper, we address the problem of assessing the risk and choosing a countermeasure in cloud networking environment. One of the important contributions of our solution is the usage of IAG modeling technique to perform attack prediction, detection, and countermeasure selection. We have presented formal definitions for attack graph and performance measure for this solution model. We also presented that usage of a IAG helps to understand the casual relationship between preconditions, vulnerability exploitation, and post conditions. We have shown how the IAG can be used to amend likelihoods of various outcomes possible as a result of the cause-consequences relationships in the event of attack incidents.

References

1. Coud Security Alliance, "Top Threats to Cloud Computing v1.0," https://cloudsecurityalliance.org/topthreats/csathreats.v1.0.pdf, Mar. 2010.
2. Chun-Jen Chung, Tianyi Xing and Dijiang Huang, "NICE: Network Intrusion Detection and Countermeasure Selection in Virtual Network Systems", IEEE TRANSACTIONS ON DEPENDABLE AND SECURE COMPUTING, VOL. 10, NO. 4, JULY/AUGUST 2013.
3. P. Mell, K. Scarfone, and S. Romanosky, Common Vulnerability Scoring System (CVSS), http://www.first.org/cvss/cvss-guide.html, May 2010.
4. Z. Duan, P. Chen, F. Sanchez, Y. Dong, M. Stephenson, and J. Barker, Detecting Spam Zombies by Monitoring Outgoing Messages, IEEE Trans. Dependable and Secure Computing, vol. 9, no. 2, pp. 198–210, 2012.
5. G. Gu, J. Zhang, and W. Lee, BotSniffer: Detecting Botnet Command and Control Channels in Network Traffic, Proc. 15th Ann. Network and Distributed Sytem Security Symp. (NDSS 08), Feb. 2008.
6. R. Sadoddin and A. Ghorbani, Alert Correlation Survey: Framework and Techniques, Proc. ACM Intl Conf. Privacy, Security and Trust: Bridge the Gap between PST Technologies and Business Services (PST 06), pp. 37:1–37:10, 2006.
7. O. Sheyner, J. Haines, S. Jha, R. Lippmann, and J.M. Wing, Automated Generation and Analysis of Attack Graphs, Proc. IEEE Symp. Security and Privacy, pp. 273–284, 2002.
8. NuSMV: A New Symbolic Model Checker, http://afrodite.itc.it:1024/nusmv. Aug. 2012.
9. P. Ammann, D. Wijesekera, and S. Kaushik, Scalable, graphbased network vulnerability analysis, Proc. 9th ACM Conf. Computer and Comm. Security (CCS 02), pp. 217–224, 2002.
10. X. Ou, S. Govindavajhala, and A.W. Appel, MulVAL: A Logic Based Network Security Analyzer, Proc. 14th USENIX Security Symp., pp. 113–128, 2005.
11. The MITRE Corporation. Common weakness scoring system. http://cwe.mitre.org/cwss/ 2010.
12. National vulnerability database. available at: http://www.nvd.org, May 9, 2008.
13. OpenStack Open Source Cloud Software (2014). [Online]. Available: http://openstack.org/.
14. M. Dacier. Towards quantitative evaluation of computer security. Ph.D. Thesis, Institut National Polytechnique de Toulouse, 1994

15. R. Ortalo, Y. Deswarte, and M. Kaaniche. Experimenting with quantitative evaluation tools for monitoring operational security. IEEE Trans. Software Eng., 25(5):633650, 1999.
16. D. Balzarotti, M. Monga, and S. Sicari. Assessing the risk of using vulnerable components. In Proceedings of the 1st ACM QoP, 2005.
17. W. Li and R. B. Vaughn. Cluster security research involving the modeling of network exploitations using exploitation graphs. In Proceedings of the Sixth IEEE International Symposium on Cluster Computing and the Grid, CCGRID 06, pages 26, Washington, DC, USA, 2006. IEEE Computer Society.
18. E. Clarke, O. Grumberg, and D. Peled. Model Checking MIT Press, 2000.
19. Nayot Poolsappasit, Rinku Dewri, and Indrajit Ray, Member, Dynamic Security Risk Management Using Bayesian Attack Graphs, IEEE TRANSACTIONS ON DEPENDABLE AND SECURE COMPUTING, VOL. 9, NO. 1, JANUARY/FEBRUARY 2012. pp. 61–74.

Time-Efficient Advent for Diagnosing Flaws in Hadoop on the Big Sensor Type Data

Mehta Jaldhi Jagdishchandra and Bhargavi R. Upadhyay

Abstract Hadoop is a MapReduce-based distributed processing framework used in the area of big data analytics in every organizations. Big sensor data is difficult to manage with the traditional data management tools. Thus, Hadoop challenges to manage it in high scalable amount in a time-efficient manner. In this paper, for fast detection of flaws in big sensor data sets, a different type of approach in diagnosing flaws with the time efficiency is used. Due to the wireless transfer of data across the nodes in a wireless sensor networks, there can be loss of data which will result in wrong interpretation of data at the nodes. The proposed approach of this paper is to form a group of sensors as a cluster. If any sensor detects violations, then the energy of that sensor has to be compared with the other sensors. The sensor having the highest energy will become the cluster head, and it will send the sensed data to the data center. The data center then diagnoses the flaw with respect to the sensed data in the big sensor data.

Keywords HDFS · Hadoop · MapReduce · Big sensor data

1 Introduction

In the current situation, sensor networks is in a boom with their different applications in many areas such as industrial, commercial, and environmental fields. Usually, sensor network comprises of various nodes which monitors a particular region and extract the data about its surroundings.

M. J. Jagdishchandra (✉) · B. R. Upadhyay
Department of Computer Science & Engineering, Amrita School of Engineering,
Amrita Vishwa Vidyapeetham, Amrita University, Bengaluru, India
e-mail: jaldhi.mehta13@gmail.com

B. R. Upadhyay
e-mail: u_bhargavi@blr.amrita.edu

© Springer Nature Singapore Pte Ltd. 2018
P. K. Pattnaik et al. (eds.), *Progress in Computing, Analytics and Networking*,
Advances in Intelligent Systems and Computing 710,
https://doi.org/10.1007/978-981-10-7871-2_12

Wireless sensor networks comprises the specially dispersed and the self-regulated sensors which can coordinate with each other and monitor the conditions of the environment constituting the sound, temperature, pressure, and motion. Each node of the sensor network is loaded with the radio transceivers or few of the other wireless devices with minute microcontroller, and the source of energy of these nodes is mostly from cells or batteries. The nodes in the network cooperate with each other and deploy themselves accordingly in a random manner.

There are three responsibilities of a node in the sensor network, that is, sensing, processing, and transferring the data. The most common applications of sensor networks are fire sensors, bomb sensors, earthquake sensors, camera sensor, etc. Therefore, sensors can be very much useful in several areas such as health care, defense services and also the environment services. These sensors generate considerable amount of data which can be used for a specific application or a related field, which affects the other unused services. Thus, massive amount of services gets waste. Now for accelerating the creation of services, we need to incorporate the sensors with the help of boundless services by distributing each others' valuable data.

An innovation in wireless communication has directed to the growth of the smart sensors. These sensors facilitate to sensing, processing, and transferring the data through wireless connection. The group of massive number of these sensors are called wireless sensor network (WSN). In sensor networks, the purpose of sensor nodes is to diagnose events or environmental changes by sensing, processing, and transferring data to the interested user.

In this proposed paper, we are trying to aim the sensor transmission for cluster-based WSNs (CWSNs) where the clusters are fashioned dynamically and in periodic manner. In CWSNs, each cluster has cluster head (CH) which gathers the data from the leaf nodes (non-CH sensor nodes) and then directs the combined data to the data center (base center). Signature must be generated for the each sensor using a secured hash function SHA256. When the sensor sends the information to the data center, then the signature gets verified. When any intruder sensor gets into the cluster and pretend to be an actual sensor and the data sends to data center, then the signature verification gets failed and thus the false data shall not be sent to the data center.

Primarily, cluster of sensors should be classified and henceforth gathered the data by WSNs. WSNs play a vital role in improving the supervision and communication of a person with his physical environment. Wireless sensor networks have improvised itself with Hadoop and created an established system. Wireless sensor networks have become troublesome issue with Hadoop while implementing in real-time application.

2   Literature Survey

Chi Yang et al. [1] proposed the different advent of diagnosing flaws with the complete potential of Cloud platform in sensor networks. The proposed advent is based on the scalable topology which is on sensor networks, and many diagnosing tasks can be directed in limited temporal or spatial data blocks instead of the big data set. This paper diagnoses the errors using Cloud.

Javier Solobera [2] describes in his article about the products developed by Libelium which aim to provide the capability of alert management and provide the early warning alarms. This product is implemented in North Spain region covering the 210 ha area.

Kechar Bouabdellah et al. [3] proposed an analytical learning using a real experimental approach of two forest fire detection methods (Canadian and Korean). With the study of both the approach, they conclude that the Canadian approach is appropriate.

In [4], they proposed integrating the tools of big data for the storage, gathering and analysis of data generated by WSN that monitors air contamination levels in city.

Subhash Chandra et al. [5] proposed the optimal approach to improve the performance of Hadoop framework. The different clustering approaches of Hadoop are used. K-medoids clustering algorithms have been developed giving the better and efficient result in Hadoop with the multinode environment.

In-Yong Jung et al. [6] presented management system which is based on Hadoop using MapReduce and distributed file system. This paper describes efficient ways for managing the big data sets and multiple nodes. Apart from this, the Hadoop-based distributed sensor node management system also provides the flexibility of re-configuring the configurations and data format of the sensor nodes.

Parth Gohil et al. [7] proposed about the Hadoop file system and improved the handling of small files in Hadoop. The combining of small file is done with the help of MapReduce model.

Maneesha V. Ramesh [8] discusses the real-time implementation of WSN for detecting landslides and development of algorithms for efficient data collection and data aggregation.

Sethuraman Rao et al. [9] discuss the disasters that happens due to fires and gas leaks in a building via WSN. An algorithm is also proposed for detecting fires and gas leaks using WSN with minimum number of ZigBee nodes.

S. Saravanan et al. [10] analyzed the Web log files of NASA which results the number of hits the Web site gets in each webpage, total number of hits the Web site gets in each hour using Hadoop and takes less response time to produce accurate results.

P. K. Rahul et al. [11] discuss the security issues in Hadoop framework and implement novel authentication framework for clients. The framework will use the different functions such as public and private key cryptography, hashing functions, and random number generator for each client, and the new key will authenticate all the clients and services.

Sabrina Boubiche et al. [12] presented the study on integrating big data tools for collecting, storing, and studying the data generated by WSNs.

In the above papers, different technologies were used with sensors networks to monitor the environmental changes. As the nodes in the sensor networks are continuously monitoring and sending the data, lot of data is generated. At times, processing such massive amount of data becomes time-consuming due to which

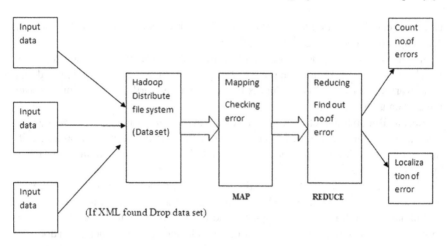

Fig. 1 Data flow diagram

there can be some delay in conveying the messages. To overcome the issue of such big sensor data, the Hadoop framework has been collaborated with the wireless sensor networks. This combination of Hadoop with wireless sensor networks will be able to process large amount of data, which will keep us timely updated.

3 Proposed Design

According to the proposed design, the flaw detection system is deployed on the network topology and most of the process of diagnosis can be performed on the restricted or spatial blocks of data instead of processing the whole data set. Hence, the diagnosis and the process of the location can be hastened up in the dramatic manner. And thus, detection and responsibilities of the location can be distributed to the Hadoop platform for using it in appropriate manner in large amount. Using Hadoop platform, it is demonstrated that this proposed design does debases the time for the diagnosing of flaw and the location in the big data sets which is regulated by the network of large-scale type with the acceptable flaw in diagnosing the precision arrived.

The paper focuses in detecting the flaws with large amount of data, scalability, and the location of the flaw where it has happened from the sensors of the network. The data flow diagram for the MapReduce of this proposed system is shown in the Fig. 1.

4 Implementation

Basically, while implementing on the real-time scenario, it will be more efficient with Hadoop. Currently, this is implemented on virtual machine using 8 GB RAM size. The implementation details are as follows:

4.1 Sensors

All three respective sensors do regulate those sets of data and progress to the server of the data. Cluster head only send the set of data to the respective server of data. Cluster head dynamically amends reckoned on the status of energy. It selects the cluster head basically for sending the respective data set to the HDFS.

4.2 Servers

Receive all the sets of data especially from the sensors. Upload the set of the data into the directory of HDFS. To find out how the XML found especially for the flaw of injection.

4.3 HDFS

Reserves set of data regulated by the respective sensor node. If map does calls mapping for the respective sets of the data. Mapper part herein discovers out where actually appeared in the respective set of data. If set of data consist of any flaws it results in accumulation of flaws in reducer part. We need to discover the location of the flaw in the set of data. Mapper herein works to conveniently ease out the flaw in the respective data sets.

For diagnosing the error in the sensed data from the sensor, we need to maintain a certain threshold for all the generated data. Hereby, we consider the following threshold value for the data sensed as shown in the Table 1.

Figure 2 shows information of all attributes in the big sensor data sets.

In this approach, we are finding out the errors in the sensed data as well as localizing it. And finally graph will be plotted based on the time taken by the Hadoop to find out the error from the data set.

Table 1 Attribute's information

No.	Attributes	Attribute information	Values
1	X	X-axis coordinates within the map of Montesinho park	1–9
2	Y	Y-axis coordinates within the map of Montesinho park	2–9
3	Month	Month of year	"Jan"–"Dec"
4	Day	Day of week	"Mon"–"Sun"
5	FFMC	Fine fuel moisture code from fire weather index	18.7–96.20
6	DMC	Duff moisture code from fire weather index	1.1–291.3
7	DC	Drought code from fire weather index	7.9–860.6
8	ISI	Initial spread index from fire weather index	0.0–56.10
9	Temp	Temperature in celsius degrees	2.2–33.30
10	RH	Relative humidity in percentage	15.0–100
11	Wind	Wind speed in km/h	0.40–9.40
12	Rain	Outside rain in mm/m^2	0.0–6.4
13	Area	The burned area of forest (ha)	0.00–1090.84

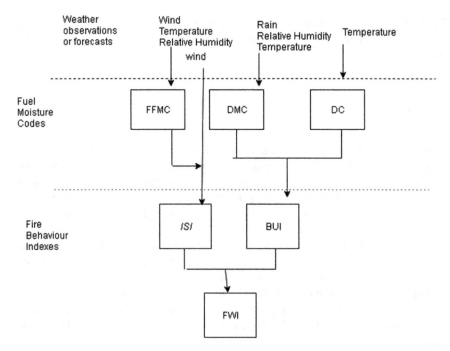

Fig. 2 Attribute information of big sensor data

Table 2 Duration for detecting errors

No.	No. of errors	Time (s)
1	1	102.8
2	5	278.7
3	10	400.7
4	20	412.5
5	25	504.4

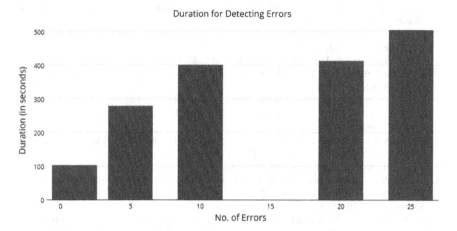

Fig. 3 Graph of duration for detecting errors

5   Results

Results shows time efficiency for the detection of errors in the Table 2.

Graph shows the time duration for detecting errors using Hadoop in the Fig. 3.

In the previous approaches, diagnosing the flaws in the sensor data was a bit time-consuming. In the proposed system, for detecting 1 error takes 102.8 s, 5 errors it takes 278.8 s, 10 errors it takes 400.7 s, and so on. From the results, we can observe that the proposed system is very much time efficient and therefore we can conclude that the combination of Hadoop with wireless sensor networks provides better results.

6   Conclusion and Future Works

We herein ascertain that for diagnosing flaws in big data sets, which does bring efficient results rather than the traditional methods or tools with the utilization of MapReduce. The management of database can be easily managed through Hadoop and also it is more time efficient. In this paper, the diagnosis of flaws in data and locating flaws in nodes are proposed. The improvement in finding errors at large scale can be future direction.

References

1. Chi Yang, Chang Liu, Xuyun Zhang, Surya Nepal, and Jinjun Chen: A Time Efficient Approach for Detecting Errors in Big Sensor Data on Cloud. In: IEEE Transactions on Parallel And Distributed Systems, Vol. 26, No. 2, February 2015.
2. Detecting Forest Fires using Wireless Sensor Networks, http://www.libelium.com/wireless_sensor_networks_to_detec_forest_fires/.
3. Kechar Bouabdellah, Houache Noureddine, and Sekhri Larbi: Using Wireless Sensor Networks for Reliable Forest Fires Detection. In: Procedia Computer Science, Vol. 19, 2013, Pages 794–801.
4. Lidice Garcia Rios, and Jos'e Alberto Incera Diguez: Big Data Infrastructure for analyzing data generated by Wireless Sensor Networks. In: IEEE International Congress on Big Data, 2014–06, Pages 816–823.
5. Subhash Chandra, and Deepak Motwani: An Approach to Enhance the Performance of Hadoop MapReduce Framework for Big Data. In: International Conference on Micro-Electronics and Telecommunication Engineering (ICMETE), 2016.
6. In-Yong Jung, Ki-Hyun Kim, Byong-John Han, and Chang-Sung Jeong: Hadoop-Based Distributed Sensor Node Management System. In: International Journal of Distributed Sensor Networks, Vol. 10, 2014.
7. Parth Gohil, Bakul Panchal, and J. S. Dhobi: A novel approach to improve the performance of Hadoop in handling of small files. In: IEEE International Conference on Electrical, Computer and Communication Technologies (ICECCT), 2015.
8. Maneesha V. Ramesh: Real-Time Wireless Sensor Network for Landslide Detection. In: Third International Conference on Sensor Technologies and Applications, 2009. SENSORCOMM '09.
9. Sethuraman Rao, G. K. Nithya, and K Rakesh: Development of a wireless sensor network for detecting fire and Gas leaks in a collapsing building. In: International Conference on Computing, Communication and Networking Technologies (ICCCNT), 2014.
10. Saravanan S, and B. Uma Maheswari: Analyzing Large Web Log Files in a Hadoop Distributed Cluster Environment. In: International Journal of Computer Technology and Applications (IJCTA), Vol. 5, Issue 5, (2014).
11. Rahul, P. K., and K.T. Gireesh: A Novel Authentication Framework for Hadoop. In: Artificial Intelligence and Evolutionary Algorithms in Engineering Systems: Proceedings of ICAEES 2014, Volume 1, Springer India, Number 324, New Delhi, Pages 333340 (2015).
12. Sabrina Boubiche, Djallel Eddine Boubiche, and Bilami Azzedine: Integrating Big data paradigm in WSNs. In: International Conference on Big Data and Advanced Wireless Technologies, Article No. 56, 2016.

Anomaly Detection System Using Beta Mixture Models and Outlier Detection

Nour Moustafa, Gideon Creech and Jill Slay

Abstract An intrusion detection system (IDS) plays a significant role in recognising suspicious activities in hosts or networks, even though this system still has the challenge of producing high false positive rates with the degradation of its performance. This paper suggests a new beta mixture technique (BMM-ADS) using the principle of anomaly detection. This establishes a profile from the normal data and considers any deviation from this profile as an anomaly. The experimental outcomes show that the BMM-ADS technique provides a higher detection rate and lower false rate than three recent techniques on the UNSW-NB15 data set.

Keywords Intrusion detection system (IDS) · Anomaly detection system (ADS)
Beta mixture model (BMM) · Outlier detection

1 Introduction

An intrusion detection system (IDS) has become an essential application to defend against cyber attackers. The methodologies of IDS can be categorised into misuse-based, anomaly-based or hybrid of the previous two [2, 16]. On the one hand, a misuse-based IDS monitors the activities of hosts or networks to match observed instances with a well-known blacklist in which includes the existing signatures of known attacks. Though this method provides higher detection rates (DR) and lower false positive rates (FPR), it cannot detect new attacks (i.e. zero-day attacks). Additionally, it demands a huge effort to regularly update its blacklist with the new rules of

N. Moustafa (✉) · G. Creech · J. Slay
The Australian Centre for Cyber Security, University of New South Wales,
Canberra, Australia
e-mail: nour.moustafa@unsw.edu.au

G. Creech
e-mail: G.Creech@adfa.edu.au

J. Slay
e-mail: j.slay@adfa.edu.au

© Springer Nature Singapore Pte Ltd. 2018
P. K. Pattnaik et al. (eds.), *Progress in Computing, Analytics and Networking*,
Advances in Intelligent Systems and Computing 710,
https://doi.org/10.1007/978-981-10-7871-2_13

suspicious activities [3]. An anomaly-based IDS, on the other hand, constructs a profile from legitimate data and detects any variation from the profile as an anomaly. This method can identify existing and zero-day attacks, so it will be better than misuse–based if its potential procedures are successfully designed. However, constructing a normal profile is very difficult due to the difficulty of involving all possible patterns of normal data [11].

Therefore, we propose constructing a normal profile using statistical models, in particular a beta mixture model (BMM) for several reasons [4, 8, 15]. Firstly, statistical models can simply determine potential properties of network patterns for both features and vectors [14]. Secondly, mixture models can precisely fit Gaussian and non-Gaussian data with specifying data edges. This means that any data outside of these edges will be handled as outliers/anomalies. Thirdly, a BMM can be designed by scaling data edges between a finite range ($[x, y], x, y \in R$) in order to control data boundaries within this range.

In this paper, we suggest an anomaly-based IDS based on the theory of beta mixture models in order to establish a profile from normal data. To recognise suspicions observations, we propose a decision-making method for detecting existing and new attacks using a baseline of the lower-upper interquartile range (IQR) [17]. This method measures the lower and upper boundaries of the normal profile and treats any observation outside of this range as an anomaly. The proposed BMM-ADS technique is evaluated on the UNSW-NB15 data set[1] [13], providing a higher DR and lower FPR than three compelling techniques.

The rest of this paper is organised as follows. Section 2 explains the background and related studies to the IDS technology. The new anomaly detection system based on the beta mixture model is explained in Sect. 3. The experimental results and discussions are provided in Sect. 4. Finally, we summarise the paper.

2 Background and Previous Work

An intrusion detection system (IDS) is a mechanism for monitoring host or network activities to recognise possible threats by estimating their vulnerabilities of Confidentiality, Integrity and Availability (CIA) principles [12, 15, 16, 20]. There are two kinds of IDSs depending on the data source: a host-based IDS inspects the activities of a computer system by accumulating information which take place in a client system, whereas a network-based IDS monitors network traffic to define network attacks that happen throughout that network [15].

An anomaly-based IDS (ADS) is a type of IDS for monitoring events that happen in a host or network to recognise possible threats. A classic ADS comprises three components of a data source, data pre-processing and decision-making method. The data source involves data gathered from host traces or network traffic, while the data

---

[1]"The UNSW-NB15 data set", https://www.unsw.adfa.edu.au/australian-centre-for-cyber-security/cybersecurity/ADFA-NB15-Datasets/, January 2017.

pre-processing includes the construction of attributes from the data that are then sent to the detection method, which is utilised for identifying malicious activities [3, 11]. This technique establishes a profile from legitimate patterns and considers the variations from this profile as attacks [15]. Nevertheless, identifying the boundaries of such a profile and the method of recognising outliers is still challenging [2, 4, 11, 14].

Several studies have been conducted to address this challenge. For example, Greggio [5] developed ADS based on the Gaussian Mixture Model. The mixture component was specified by estimating the parameters of the normal data and handling any data outside of this range as anomalies. Tan et al. [20] suggested a multivariate correlation technique for establishing a DoS identification mechanism using a triangular method of the lower correlation matrix used for estimating the correlation between attributes in order to help in identifying malicious instances.

Fan et al. [7] proposed a Bayesian inference method for designing a network collaboration framework for data via gathering feedback from distributed nodes and modelled by a beta distribution to classify the error rates for different ADS techniques. Singh et al. [19] suggested a distributed ADS based on the random forest algorithm for identifying botnets from a large-scale network. Fortunati et al. [6] proposed a statistical ADS using a generalised version of the inequality for random observation. The results of this technique slightly improved the accuracy detection using the KDD99 data set.

Most of the studies above enhanced the detection rate because they used a particular baseline/threshold in the classification stage that would be either a binary value, which is 1 for attack and 0 for normal, or static value that did not estimate from real network environments. Nevertheless, the results were often biased towards normal observations that provided high FPRs [9]. In our recent work [15], we developed a Geometric Area Analysis mechanism using trapezoidal area estimation for each instance calculated from the BMM parameters for network attributes and the distances between instances, but this paper proposes estimating the baseline from the processed network data with flexible inference overlays using a BMM-ADS in order to improve the DR and decrease the FPR.

3   Beta Mixture Model-ADS

The mixture technique is a robust probabilistic model for representing a subset multivariate data that demonstrates the whole data set. The beta mixture model (BMM) precisely fits the bounded property data with less complexity than the Gaussian mixture model (GMM) [10]. However, the GMM can model any random distribution with appropriate mixture components. There are some components do not correctly characterise boundaries when testing data are bounded or semi-bounded [4].

The features of network data cannot accurately fit a normal distribution because they do not fit its unbounded and symmetric edges (i.e.] $-\infty, \infty[$) [14]. As in the data sets of NSLKDD[2] and UNSW-NB15, their features can be represented in a semi-bounded range of $[0, N]$, such that N denotes an asymmetric number. A beta distribution can fit data in a more elastic form than a normal distribution and models arbitrary features that have a finite range of $([x, y], x, y \in R)$, such as $[0, 1]$. Consequently, we use BMM for building the normal profile of ADS [8, 10].

A beta distribution's probability density function (PDF) is calculated by

$$Beta(x; \upsilon, \omega) = \frac{1}{beta(\upsilon, \omega)} x^{\upsilon-\omega}(1 - x)^{\omega-1}, \upsilon, \omega > 0 \qquad (1)$$

such that x is the random variables/attributes, $beta(\upsilon, \omega)$ is the beta function, $beta(\upsilon, \omega) = \Gamma(\upsilon)\Gamma(\omega)/\Gamma(\upsilon + \omega)$, υ and ω refer to the shaped parameters that model the beta distribution, and $\Gamma(.)$ denotes the gamma function $\Gamma(c) = \int_0^\infty \exp(-t)t^{c-1} dt$.

In our new BMM-ADS technique, a BMM is used for estimating the network feature's PDFs. It is noted that network features are independent [20], while multivariate attributes are dependent in many situations. Nonetheless, for any attribute (x) containing L values, the dependence between values $x_1, \ldots, x_L$ is indicated using a mixture technique even if each component can design observations with independent attributes. We declare the PDF multivariate BMM for some observations as

$$f(x; \pi, v, \omega) = \sum_{i=1}^{I} \Pi_i Beta(X, v_i, \omega_i)$$

$$= \sum_{i=1}^{I} \Pi_i \prod_{l=1}^{L} Beta(x_l, v_{li}, \omega_{li}) \qquad (2)$$

where I indicates component number $(X = \{x_1, ..., x_L\}$, $\prod = \{\Pi_1, .., \Pi_I\}$, $v = \{v_1, ..., v_I\}$, $\omega = \{\omega_1, ..., \omega_I\})$, Π_i refers to the mixing component (where $\sum_{i=1}^{I} \Pi_i = 1, 0 < \pi < 1$), $\{v_i, \omega_i\}$ are the parameter instances of the ith mixture component, $Beta(X; v_i, \omega_i)$ is the component parameters, and $\{v_{li}, ..., \omega_{li}\}$ indicate the beta parameters for attribute x_l.

To explain the BMM, given two random variables $(x_1$ and $x_2)$, their parameters are computed using the EM technique, as detailed in [10]. Figure 1 shows an example for modelling two variables by BMM, where parameters of $x_1(\pi, v, \omega)$ be $(0.55, 30, 10)$ and parameters of x_2 be $(0.45, 10, 30)$. We estimate the BMM parameters for the data set features in order to construct a normal profile, which has a wide range of PDFs that could represent the entire observations of normal behaviours.

The learning process of BMM is a significant task for estimating the parameters and selecting the number of components (M). We use the maximum likelihood suggested in [10] to estimate the parameters of the finite BMM and choose the number of components.

---

[2]"NSLKDD data set", https://web.archive.org/web/20150205070216/, http://nsl.cs.unb.ca/NSL-KDD/, January 2017.

Fig. 1 BMM for two
random variables

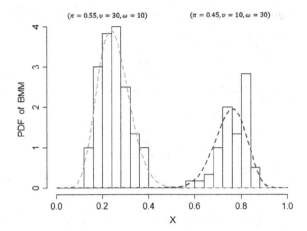

In this study, we suggest a new BMM-ADS technique for recognising anomaly instances. In the training phase of the technique, we establish the legitimate profile using BMM parameters, PDFs and a lower-upper IQR baseline for learning legitimate network data, whereas the abnormal instances which are outside of the baseline are considered as suspicious instances in the testing phase, as detailed in the following two sections.

3.1 Training phase

The BMM-ADS technique has to learn using purely legitimate observations in order to make sure that the technique can correctly detect malicious ones. Given a set of normal observations ($r_{1:n}^{normal}$) in which each vector consists of a set of features, where $r_{1:n}^{normal} = \{x_1, x_2, ..., x_D\}^{normal}$, the legitimate profile involves only statistical measures from $r_{1:n}^{normal}$. They involve the estimated parameters (π, v, ω) of the BMM to calculate the PDF of the beta distribution ($Beta(x; \pi, v, \omega)$) for each vector in the training set.

Algorithm 1 presents the suggested process for establishing a legitimate profile (pro) using the parameters of the BMM estimated for all the legitimate instances $r_{1:n}^{normal}$ using the equations proposed in [10], and then the PDFs of the features ($x_{1:D}$) are computed using Eq. 2. After that, IQR is calculated by subtracting the first quartile from the third quartile of the PDFs to specify a baseline for identifying suspicious observations in the testing phase. Quartiles can divide a range of data into contiguous intervals with equal probabilities [17].

Algorithm 1 Normal profile construction of normal instances

Input: normal observations ($r_{1:n}^{normal}$)
Output: normal profile (pro)

1: **for** each record i in ($r_{1:n}^{normal}$) **do**
2:     calculate the parameters ($\pi_i, v_{,i}, \omega_i$) of the BMM as in [14]
3:     calculate the PDFs using equation 2 using the parameters of Step 2
4: **end for**
5: calculate $lower = quartile(PDFs, 1)$
6: calculate $upper = quartile(PDFs, 3)$
7: calculate $IQR = upper - lower$
8: pro $\leftarrow \{(\pi_i, v_{,i}, \omega_i), (lower, upper, IQR)\}$
 * **return** pro

3.2   Testing Phase and Attack Detection

For testing each observed record, the Beta PDF ($PDF^{testing}$) of each instance ($r^{testing}$) is calculated using the same parameters of the normal profile (pro). Algorithm 2 describes the steps in the testing phase and decision-making method for recognising the Beta PDFs of the malicious records, with step 1 describing the PDF of each observed instance using the normal parameters ($\pi_i, v_{,i}, \omega_i$).

Algorithm 2 Testing phase and decision-making method

---

input : observed record ($r^{testing}$), pro
output : normal or attack

1: calculate the $PDF^{testing}$ using equation 2 using the parameters ($\pi_i, v_{,i}, \omega_i$)
2: **if** ($PDF^{testing} < (lower - w * (IQR))$) || ($PDF^{testing} > (upper + w * (IQR))$) **then**
3:     **return** attack
4: **else**
5:     **return** normal
6: **end if**

Steps 2 to 6 explain the steps of the decision-making method. The IQR is the length of the box in the box-and-whisker plot, specifying outliers as values that locate more than 1.5 the length of the box from either end of the box. In more detail, the IQR of the normal instances is calculated for identifying the anomalies of any observed record ($r^{testing}$) in the testing phase which is treated as any instance located below ($lower - w * (IQR)$) or above ($upper + w * (IQR)$), such that w refers to the interval values between 1.5 and 3 [17]. The decision of detection depends on considering any $PDF^{testing}$ falling outside of this range as a malicious record, otherwise normal.

4 Empirical Results and Discussion

4.1 Evaluation Criteria

Multiple experiments were conduced on the UNSW-NB15 data set in order to appraise the performance of the BMM-ADS technique using the metrics of accuracy, DR, FPR and ROC curves, defined as in the following points.

- The **accuracy** is the proportion of all legitimate and malicious observations correctly categorised, that is,

$$accuracy = \frac{(TP + TN)}{(TP + TN + FP + FN)} \tag{3}$$

- The **detection rate (DR)** is the proportion of correctly identified malicious observations, that is,

$$DR = \frac{TP}{(TP + FN)} \tag{4}$$

- The **false positive rate (FPR)** is the proportion of incorrectly identified malicious observations, that is,

$$FPR = \frac{FP}{(FP + TN)} \tag{5}$$

where TP (true positive) refers to the number of actual malicious observations categorised as attacks, TN (true negative) indicates the number of actual normal records categorised as normal, FP (false positive) means the number of actual normal records categorised as attacks, and FN (false negative) refers to the number of actual malicious observations categorised as normal.

4.2 Description of Pre-processing Stage

The UNSW-NB15 data set was used for evaluating the effectiveness of the proposed BMM-ADS technique, which has a collection of recent normal and attack observations. Its size is nearly 100 GBs extracted 2,540,044 records, which are kept in four CSV files. Each record includes 47 attributes and its label. It includes ten different classes, one legitimate and nine kinds of malicious events. A part of the data set is prepared for training and testing NIDS techniques in [14]. The proposed technique was assessed using eight features selected from the UNSW-NB15 using the principal component analysis technique listed in Table 1.

Table 1 Feature selected from UNSW-NB15 data set

Data set	Selected features
UNSW-NB15	ct_dst_sport_ltm, tcprtt, dwin, ct_src_dport_ltm, ct_dst_src_ltm, ct_dst_ltm, smean, service

In order to carry out the experiments, arbitrary samples are selected from the UNSW-NB15 data set with sizes vary between 50,000 and 200,000. In each one, legitimate instances were approximately 55–65% of the total size, with some used to create the legitimate profile and the testing set.

5   Empirical Results

The performance of the BMM-ADS mechanism was evaluated using the overall accuracy, DR and FPR on the feature adopted from the UNSW-NB15 data set, demonstrated in Table 2. Furthermore, the ROC curves which represent the relationship between the DRs and FPRs with different w values are presented in (Fig. 2). The DR and accuracy increased from 82.4% to 92.7% and 84.2% and 93.4%, respectively; however, the FPR decreased from 10.3% to 5.9 % while the w value increased from 1.5 to 3.

Table 3 shows that the proposed mechanism identified observation types of the UNSW-NB15 data set with normal DRs fluctuating between 83.4% and 94.0% when the w value increased from 1.5 to 3. Likewise, the DRs of the malicious kinds increased gradually from an average of 35.7% to an average of 89.6%.

Some attack types achieved higher DRs within the gradual increase of the w value, while others do not produce high DRs due to the small similarities between malicious and legitimate observations. Since the UNSW-NB15 data set is similar to real networks with broad variations of legitimate and malicious patterns, applying a feature reduction method could make a clear difference between these patterns, improving the performance of the proposed technique. We observe that the variances of the selected feature are close, leading an overlap the PDFs of the attacks in normal ones.

Table 2 Performance of features selected from UNSW-NB15 data set

w value	DR (%)	Accuracy (%)	FPR (%)
1.5	82.4	84.2	10.3
2	84.5	86.3	8.8
2.5	90.5	91.5	7.2
3	92.7	93.4	5.9

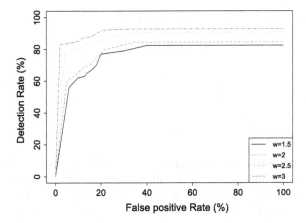

Fig. 2 ROC curves of UNSW-NB15 data set with w values

Table 3 Comparison of DRs (%) on UNSW-NB15 data set

	w values			
Record type	1.5 (%)	2 (%)	2.5 (%)	3 (%)
Normal	81.2	85.4	90.5	93.4
DoS	82.6	85.3	86.1	89.6
Backdoor	55.3	61.2	62.3	63.8
Exploits	60.2	67.1	73.6	79.4
Analysis	72.6	71.2	77.1	83.4
Generic	80.5	86.3	86.3	86.3
Fuzzers	42.4	50.1	50.8	52.8
Shellcode	42.2	44.3	47.2	48.7
Reconnaissance	50.8	54.2	54.2	55.6
Worms	35.7	40.3	42.2	47.8

We compare our proposed technique with three recent techniques, namely Multivariate Correlation Analysis (MCA) [20], Artificial Immune System (AIS) [18] and Filter-based Support Vector Machine (FSVM) [1] on the UNSW-NB15 data set. As listed in Table 4, the findings obviously show the superiority of our mechanism in terms of detection and false positive rates. This is because our technique is designed to model the normal data with a flexible shape, which includes a wide range of normal PDFs, and the decision method of IQR can therefore find the outliers from the profile as anomalies.

The MCA technique depends on only finding correlations between features with the Gaussian mixture model to recognise the DoS attacks, which sometimes cannot specify accurate edges between normal and attack PDFs. The other two techniques rely on learning normal and abnormal data in the training stage, which is the

Table 4 Comparison of performance of four techniques

Technique	DR (%)	FPR (%)
MCA [20]	88.3	11.6
AIS [18]	83.5	15.7
FSVM [1]	90.4	8.5
BMM-ADS	92.7	5.9

principle of rule-based. Such techniques demand a huge number of instances to be properly learned which makes it in online learning. Although these techniques reflected a higher performance evaluation on the outdated KDD99 data set or its improved version NSLKDD, our technique outperforms them in terms of DRs and FPRs. This is an indication that our technique can achieve better than these mechanisms on real network data, as it is hard to receive all security events and malware at the same time from different nodes.

6 Conclusion

This paper covers a proposed anomaly detection system based on the beta mixture model for establishing a profile from normal network data. In order to recognise malicious observations, we suggest the lower-upper interquartile threshold as a baseline of legitimate profile and any variations from this threshold are considered as an attack. The experimental results showed the higher performance evaluation of this technique and its superiority compared with three recent mechanisms. In future, we are planning to investigate feature reduction methods to find clear differences between selected features, further improving the performance of these techniques.

References

1. Ambusaidi, M.A., He, X., Nanda, P., Tan, Z.: Building an intrusion detection system using a filter-based feature selection algorithm. IEEE transactions on computers **65**(10), 2986–2998 (2016)
2. Bhuyan, M.H., Bhattacharyya, D.K., Kalita, J.K.: Network anomaly detection: methods, systems and tools. IEEE communications surveys & tutorials **16**(1), 303–336 (2014)
3. Creech, G., Hu, J.: A semantic approach to host-based intrusion detection systems using contiguousand discontiguous system call patterns. IEEE Transactions on Computers **63**(4), 807–819 (2014)
4. Escobar, M.D., West, M.: Bayesian density estimation and inference using mixtures. Journal of the american statistical association **90**(430), 577–588 (1995)
5. Fan, W., Bouguila, N., Ziou, D.: Unsupervised anomaly intrusion detection via localized bayesian feature selection. In: Data Mining (ICDM), 2011 IEEE 11th International Conference on, pp. 1032–1037. IEEE (2011)

6. Fortunati, S., Gini, F., Greco, M.S., Farina, A., Graziano, A., Giompapa, S.: An improvement of the state-of-the-art covariance-based methods for statistical anomaly detection algorithms. Signal, Image and Video Processing **10**(4), 687–694 (2016)
7. Fung, C.J., Zhu, Q., Boutaba, R., Ba, T., et al.: Bayesian decision aggregation in collaborative intrusion detection networks. In: Network Operations and Management Symposium (NOMS), 2010 IEEE, pp. 349–356. IEEE (2010)
8. Gupta, A.K., Nadarajah, S.: Handbook of beta distribution and its applications. CRC press (2004)
9. Gyanchandani, M., Rana, J., Yadav, R.: Taxonomy of anomaly based intrusion detection system: a review. International Journal of Scientific and Research Publications **2**(12), 1–13 (2012)
10. Ma, Z., Leijon, A.: Beta mixture models and the application to image classification. In: Image Processing (ICIP), 2009 16th IEEE International Conference on, pp. 2045–2048. IEEE (2009)
11. Moustafa, N., Slay, J.: A hybrid feature selection for network intrusion detection systems: Central points (2015)
12. Moustafa, N., Slay, J.: The significant features of the unsw-nb15 and the kdd99 data sets for network intrusion detection systems. In: Building Analysis Datasets and Gathering Experience Returns for Security (BADGERS), 2015 4th International Workshop on, pp. 25–31. IEEE (2015)
13. Moustafa, N., Slay, J.: Unsw-nb15: a comprehensive data set for network intrusion detection systems (unsw-nb15 network data set). In: Military Communications and Information Systems Conference (MilCIS), 2015, pp. 1–6. IEEE (2015)
14. Moustafa, N., Slay, J.: The evaluation of network anomaly detection systems: Statistical analysis of the unsw-nb15 data set and the comparison with the kdd99 data set. Information Security Journal: A Global Perspective **25**(1-3), 18–31 (2016)
15. Moustafa, N., Slay, J., Creech, G.: Novel geometric area analysis technique for anomaly detection using trapezoidal area estimation on large-scale networks. IEEE Transactions on Big Data **PP**(99), 1–1 (2017). 10.1109/TBDATA.2017.2715166
16. Pontarelli, S., Bianchi, G., Teofili, S.: Traffic-aware design of a high-speed fpga network intrusion detection system. IEEE Transactions on Computers **62**(11), 2322–2334 (2013)
17. Rousseeuw, P.J., Hubert, M.: Robust statistics for outlier detection. Wiley Interdisciplinary Reviews: Data Mining and Knowledge Discovery **1**(1), 73–79 (2011)
18. Saurabh, P., Verma, B.: An efficient proactive artificial immune system based anomaly detection and prevention system. Expert Systems with Applications **60**, 311–320 (2016)
19. Singh, K., Guntuku, S.C., Thakur, A., Hota, C.: Big data analytics framework for peer-to-peer botnet detection using random forests. Information Sciences **278**, 488–497 (2014)
20. Tan, Z., Jamdagni, A., He, X., Nanda, P., Liu, R.P.: A system for denial-of-service attack detection based on multivariate correlation analysis. IEEE transactions on parallel and distributed systems **25**(2), 447–456 (2014)

Optimization of Handoff Latency Using Efficient Spectrum Sensing for CR System

Rohini S. Kale and J. B. Helonde

Abstract Cognitive radio (CR) is a new technology in wireless communications. Presently, we are facing spectrum scarcity problem. CR gives solution to spectrum scarcity problem. The idea behind cognitive radio is the utilization of unused frequency bands of primary or licensed users (PU) by secondary or unlicensed users (SU). This unused frequency band is called white spaces or spectrum hole. This scenario needs the demand of cognitive radio. Spectrum sensing is the main task in CR. Proposed system has used energy detection method for spectrum sensing by using new threshold formulations. Novel algorithm for optimized handoff decision using fuzzy logic and artificial neural network and proactive strategy is used for channel allocation. The proposed system saves the power and optimized handoff delay.

Keywords Cognitive radio · Threshold · RSS · Bit rate · CPE
Fuzzy logic · ANN · Handoff · Idle to busy ratio · SSC

1 Introduction

Today we have spectrum scarcity problem, so available spectrum should be used intelligently. CR technology will enable the users to determine spectrum sensing, spectrum management, spectrum sharing, and spectrum mobility. Spectrum sensing, spectrum analysis, and spectrum decision are the main steps of the cognitive cycle [1, 2]. Identifying the utilized spectrum is called spectrum sensing. The success of CR depends on efficient spectrum sensing. The complexity of the energy detection method is low and sensing accuracy depends upon selection threshold level [3]. Interfaces suggested by IEEE 1900.6 standards. Store sensed information

R. S. Kale
MAEERs MIT Polytechnic, Pune, India
e-mail: rohiniskale@gmail.com

J. B. Helonde (✉)
ITM College of Engineering, Nagpur, India
e-mail: jbhelonde60@gmail.com

© Springer Nature Singapore Pte Ltd. 2018
P. K. Pattnaik et al. (eds.), *Progress in Computing, Analytics and Networking*,
Advances in Intelligent Systems and Computing 710,
https://doi.org/10.1007/978-981-10-7871-2_14

uses data archive interface. Cognitive engine interface is used to utilize cognitive capabilities. This interface also carries out the implementation of spectrum access policies. Get sensing information sensor interface is used. A spectrum sensing mechanism to detect the possible presence of incumbent users such as analog TV, Digital TV, and low power licensed users such as wireless microphones is supported by wireless regional area network (WRAN) standard IEEE 802.22 [3, 4]. Wireless regional area network (WRAN) working group is developing a point to multipoint fixed wireless access network standard intended to operate worldwide in the unused segments of the terrestrial TV broadcast bands. WRAN cell radius lies between $17.1 < R < 32.4$ km. WRAN BS power 36 dBm EIRP [5]. Proposed system has increased the accuracy of the signal detection. Fuzzy logic controller (FLC) used with parameters bit rate (BR) and received signal strength (RSS). BR has taken randomly, and RSS has calculated from distance formula. The patterns of FLC are trained by neural network (NN). If handoff decision is 'Y' (yes) then other FLC operated with the inputs minimum number of handoff (p1), and maximum idle to the busy ratio (p2). WRAN cell is divided in the microcell. This WRAN cell is divided into seven clusters, i.e., 49 microcells. In this paper, a novel system has been proposed that gives optimized handoff latency. The paper is organized as follows: Sect. 2 explains related work, Sect. 3 proposed system model, Sect. 4 simulation results, and Sect. 5 concludes the paper.

2   Related Work

J. Eric Salt et al. [3] analyze the energy detector that is commonly used to detect the presence of unknown information-bearing signals. The algorithm simply compares the energy (or power) in a sliding window to a threshold definition of white spaces [6, 7]. The unutilized frequency spectrum in the licensed band is called white spaces. New networking paradigm is called dynamic spectrum access (DSA) [8]. Spectrum sensing scheme is able to achieve higher throughput and lower delay [9]. Implementation issues of the MRSS techniques [1, 10, 11]. The effects of in phase (I) and quadrature (Q) gain and phase mismatch are explained using various modulation types. They conclude that the quadrature-phase voltage controlled oscillator (VCO) should be optimized to keep I/Q phase orthogonal. IEEE 802.22 is the first worldwide standard based on the cognitive radio technology [12]. The optimization of delay in proactive decision spectrum handoff by target channel sequence selection scheme which can realize the minimum probability of spectrum handoff failure and obtained a desirable expected number of handshake trials till success [5]. Qualitative comparison of various handoff strategies with regard to handoff, these are no handoff, pure reactive, pure proactive, and hybrid handoff, and he suggested adaptive multiple handoff strategies approach to achieve optimal performance in dynamic spectrum environment. He focused on decentralized architecture [2, 4, 5, 10, 11, 13, 14]. With the consideration of above-related work, the optimized handoff is must in any CR system. Spectrum sensed properly means detection probability is 100%. Our modified threshold formula gives detection of a signal from 20 to −20 dB. Novel system has considered fuzzy logic and ANN [5, 9–11, 13–15], for handoff decision in CR network [16]. Nobody has carried such work before as per my knowledge.

3 Proposed System Model

The proposed system model is shown in Fig. 1. The system model is based on following assumptions.

(1) A microcell is a geographical representation of an area divided into small cells. Group of such seven cells forms a cluster.
(2) Cognitive radio operates in TV UHF band (T_f) ranging from 470 to 890 MHz with 6 MHz bandwidth (i.e., 70 channels).
(3) All CPEs are stationary and equipped with the self-intelligence system.
(4) The data archive stores the result of sensing and updates it periodically. Distributed sensing is done by BS and CPE. The proposed system architecture is shown in Fig. 2.

(A) **System Input:** System input is restricted to geographical location, number of channels, microcell which is given in Eqs. (1), (2), and the requirement microcell is given in Eq. (3).

$$G = \{\{G_i\}|1 \leq i \leq R\}. \tag{1}$$

$$C = \{r, loc, ch|\{M_c\}|1 \leq i \leq 7\}. \tag{2}$$

Fig. 1 Proposed system model

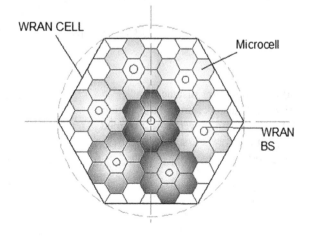

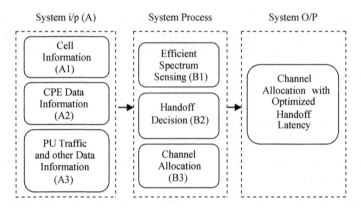

Fig. 2 Proposed system architecture

$$M_c = \{Id, r, loc, ncep, RSS, BR\}. \tag{3}$$

where

G = Geographical area, C = cell
R = rational number, M_c = microcell
RSS = received signal strength
BR = bit rate, r = radius
Loc = GPS location

Users: User is an asset of primary and secondary users is given in Eq. (4).

$$U = \{\{P_u\}, \{S_u\}\}. \tag{4}$$

CPEs have self-intelligence. CPEs are updated with their values like RSS, BR, and channel in use, present frequency in use, previous channel, and frequency. For calculation of received signal strength, Eq. (5) is used.

$$RSS = P0 - 10n \log_{10} \frac{d1}{d0}. \tag{5}$$

d0 = 10 reference distance
d1 = CPE distance from base station
P0 = minimum power = 10 assumed
n = path loss = 2 assumed
d1 ≥ d0

(B) System Process

(i) Efficient Spectrum Sensing

Efficient spectrum sensing, threshold for presence and absence of the primary user is clear from Eqs. (6) and (7).

$$Ys(t) = n(t) \ldots < \lambda_n \ldots H0 \ldots PUabsent. \tag{6}$$

$$Ys(t) = s(t) + n(t) \ldots > \lambda_n \ldots H1 \ldots PUpresent. \tag{7}$$

Comparing energy of the signal with a new threshold and decide PU present or not, we derived new threshold formula as Eq. (8).

$$\lambda_n = 10 \log[Q^{-1}(pfa)(\sqrt{2N} + N)] \left(\sqrt{\frac{\sigma}{100}}\right)^2 \xi \tag{8}$$

where ξ = multiplication factor.

False detection of PU gives unnecessary handoff. Approximately 96.06% of the average receiving energy or 110.75% of the average transmitting energy is consumed by the single spectrum handoff. We have modified this formula, as Eq. (9) without Q inverse function, independent of pfa, and independent of number of samples. This formulation also gives accurate PU detection from SNR = 20 to −20 dB. Modification factor (mf) has a specific value is given in Eq. (10).

$$\lambda_m = 30 + 10 \log_{10}(2\pi mf \sigma) \tag{9}$$

$$mf = 0.005(SNR) + 0.48. \tag{10}$$

(ii) Handoff Decision

For quick decision related to handoff, we have use Fuzzy logic and neural network. Figure 3 gives FLC for handoff decision.

Parameters for training are (1) SSC (2) BR (3) RSS. A fuzzy set is a very convenient method to represent a form of uncertainty. It is simple, low complexity implementation and quick spectrum mobility [17]. Fuzzy logic makes use of fuzzy logic controllers (FLC). FLC has been designed to qualitatively determine whether a spectrum handoff should be realized or not. Linguistic variables are considered in terms of three fuzzy sets, respectively, 'Low,' 'Medium,' and 'High.' The term set

Fig. 3 FLC for handoff decision

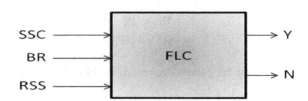

Table 1 Fuzzy rules for FLC2

Fuzzy rule	If		Then
	p1	p2	Channel allocation
1	L	H	B
2	H	H	C
3	H	M	C
4	M	H	C
5	M	M	C
6	L	M	C
7	M	L	N
8	H	L	N
9	L	L	N

the output linguistic variables consists of two fuzzy sets 'Y,' 'N.' Table 1 gives fuzzy rules for handoff decision. The original parameters are normalized in the scale of 0–1, by using normalization equation. 'Low' means linguistic value lies between '0'–'2.5,' and its pattern is '0000.' 'Medium' means its value lies between '2.5'–'7.5,' and its pattern is '0101.' 'High' means its value lies between '7.5'–'1.'

Membership Function:
Figures 4, 5, and 6 give triangular membership function for SSC, BR, and RSS, respectively.

$$\mu_f(x, a, b, c) =
\begin{cases}
0 & \text{if } x < a \\
(x-a)/(b-a) & \text{if } a \leq x \leq b \\
(c-x)/(c-b) & \text{if } b \leq x \leq c \\
1 & \text{if } x > c
\end{cases} \tag{10}$$

$$P_1 = \{x | x \in R, 1 \leq x \leq 100\} \tag{11}$$

$$P_2 = \{x | x \in R, 5 \leq x \leq 70\} \tag{12}$$

$$P_3 = \{x | x \in R, -95 \leq x \leq -10\} \tag{13}$$

P1, P2, and P3 are rational values of SSC, BR, and RSS, which is given in Eqs. (11), (12), and (13). Normalize P1, P2, P3, 0–1

P1 $SSC = (P1 - 10)/90$
P2 $BR = (P2 - 5)/65$
P3 $RSS = ((P3 - (-95))/(-10 - (-95))$

Training the patterns generated by FLC ANN is used.

Fig. 4 SSC membership
function

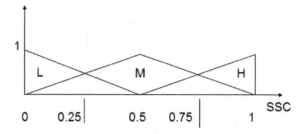

Fig. 5 BR membership
function

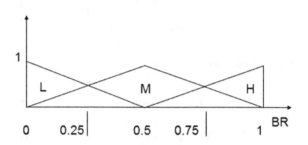

Fig. 6 RSS membership
function

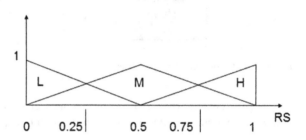

(iii) **Spectrum Handoff Process**

Efficient spectrum sense with 100% detection probability. Proposed system has used proactive handoff strategy, so handoff delay is very low. Figure 7 shows spectrum handoff process. As shown in Fig. 8, handoff decision is 'N' transmission of CPE or SU is continuous on the same channel. When handoff decision is 'Y' then FLC2 is used to search backup channel. For new channel detection, parameters used are minimum handoff (p1) and maximum idle to the busy ratio (p2). Three linguistic variables are considered, respectively, 'Low,' 'Medium,' and 'High.' The term set the output linguistic variables consists of three fuzzy sets 'B,' 'C,' and 'N.'

Table 1 gives backup and candidate channel with consideration of minimum handoff and maximum idle to busy ratio.

Number of channels = N, Current channel = M.

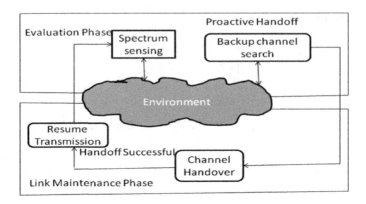

Fig. 7 Handoff process

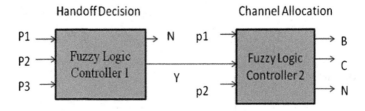

Fig. 8 FLC for optimized handoff latency

Assigned channel (Bk) is a set of channels given in Eq. (14); it should have minimum handoff and idle to busy ratio maximum as per Eq. (15).

$$B_k = B_k \in \{1, 2, 3, \ldots .N\}_{k=1}^{M} M \leq N \tag{14}$$

Fc = Fk then Hd = 'Y'
p1 = Handoff, p2 = ibratio
Optimized Handoff Channel = ϑ

$$\vartheta = \arg \min p1 \ and \ \arg \max p2 \ldots \vartheta \in N \tag{15}$$

4 Simulation Results

(A) **System Input**
(i) **Cell Information:** Channels allocated randomly consecutive ten for each cell.

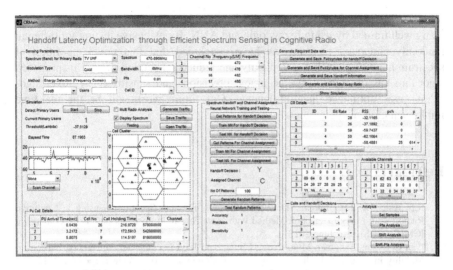

Fig. 9 System graphical user interface (GUI)

(ii) **CPE Information:** All CPEs have self-intelligence. CPE inflation will get as shown in Fig. 9.

(iii) **PU Traffic and Other Data Input:** the traffic of PU using Poisson distribution.

(B) **System Process**

(i) **Efficient Spectrum Sensing**

New formulation for the threshold is derived with rigorous analysis of SNR, pfa, and multiplication factor.

(ii) **Handoff Decision**

Fuzzy rules are generated using parameters SSC, BR, and RSS. The pattern generated through fuzzy rule is of 12 bit. For 100% training, 10000 iterations are required.

(iii) **Channel Allocation with Optimized Handoff Latency**

Handoff decision given by FLC1 is 'N' then data transmission of CPE is continued as before. If handoff decision is 'Y', then FLC2 will work. FLC2 will work on two parameters. These parameters are a minimum handoff and maximum idle to busy ratio. An overall system with all interfaces is shown in Fig. 9.

5 Conclusion

In frequency domain analysis, the accuracy of proposed new threshold formulation is of 96.56%. SNR and pfa analysis show proposed formulation that gives stable system. The proposed new algorithm gives handoff decision in the cognitive radio network. In this system, each microcell contains different CPEs with each CPE being well trained by using fuzzy logic and ANN. By extensive testing for different randomly generated patterns, we have concluded that this novel algorithm of spectrum handoff gives low complexity and reduced execution time. This proposed algorithm has obtained 100% accuracy, precision, and sensitivity. A novel algorithm gives optimized handoff latency. Our future work will be the real-time implementation of the system.

References

1. R.S. Kale, Dr. J.B. Helonde, Dr. V.M. Wadhai, "Efficient Spectrum Sensing in Cognitive Radio Using Energy Detection Method with New Threshold Formulation", IEEE conference ICMICR 2013, 4–6 June 2013
2. Ivan Christian, Sangman Moh, Ilyong Chung, and Jinyi Lee, Chosun University, "Spectrum Mobility in Cognitive Radio Networks" IEEE Communications Magazine • June 2012
3. J. Eric Salt, Member, IEEE, and Ha H. Nguyen, Senior Member, IEEE, "Performance Prediction for Energy Detection of Unknown Signals", IEEE TRANSACTIONS ON VEHICULAR TECHNOLOGY, VOL. 57, NO. 6, NOVEMBER 2008
4. Shilian Zheng, *Member, IEEE*, Xiaoniu Yang, Shichuan Chen, and Caiyi Lou, "Target Channel Sequence Selection Scheme for Proactive-Decision Spectrum Handoff", IEEE COMMUNICATIONS LETTERS, VOL. 15, NO. 12, DECEMBER 2011
5. Shunqing Zhang, Tianyu Wu, and Vincent K. N. Lau, "A Low-Overhead Energy Detection Based Cooperative Sensing Protocol for Cognitive Radio Systems" IEEE TRANSACTIONS ON WIRELESS COMMUNICATIONS, VOL. 8, NO. 11, NOVEMBER 2009 5575
6. Shukla, A.; "Cognitive Radio Technology: A Study for of com – Volume 1." QINETIQ/06/00420 Issue 1.1, February 12th, 2007
7. FCC Spectrum Policy Task Force, November 2002, *ET Docket No. 02 135,* Washington DC
8. XG Working Group. The XG vision. Request for comments. Version 2.0. Technical report, BBN Technologies, 2005
9. Ayman A EI Saleh, "Optimizing Spectrum Sensing Parameters for Local and Co-operative Cognitive Radios" ISBN 978-89-5519-139-4 Feb. 15–18, ICACT 2009
10. Eric Salt, *Member, IEEE,* and Ha H. Nguyen, *Senior Member, IEEE,* "Performance Prediction for Energy Detection of Unknown Signals" IEEE TRANSACTIONS ON VEHICULAR TECHNOLOGY, VOL. 57, NO. 6, NOVEMBER 2008
11. Yonghong Zeng, Ying-Chang Liang, and Rui Zhang, "Blindly Combined Energy Detection for Spectrum Sensing in Cognitive Radio", IEEE SIGNAL PROCESSING LETTERS, VOL. 15, 2008 649
12. C. Cordeiro, K. Challapali, D. Birru, S. Shankar, and IEEE 802.22: the first worldwide wireless standard based on cognitive radios, in Proc. IEEE DySPAN 2005, November 2005, pp. 328–337
13. Park, "Implementation Issues of Wide Band Multi Resolution Spectrum Sensing (MRSS) Technique for Cognitive Radio (CR) System", IEEE 2006
14. E. Del Re, R. Fantacci and G. Giambene, ——A Dynamic channel Allocation Technique Based on Hopfield Neural Networks‖, IEEE Transactions on Vehicular Technology, Vol. VT-45, no. 1, pp. 26–32, 1995
15. S. Rajasekaran, G.A. Vijayalakshmi Pai, "Neural Networks, Fuzzy Logic, and Genetic Algorithms"

16. R.S. Kale, Dr. J.B. Helonde, Dr. V.M. Wadhai, "New Algorithm for Handoff Optimization in Cognitive Radio Networks Using Fuzzy Logic and Artificial Neural Network" ERCICA 2013
17. L. Giupponi, Ana I. Perez-Neira, "Fuzzy-based Spectrum Handoff in Cognitive Radio Networks", 2010

Performance Comparison of Deep VM Workload Prediction Approaches for Cloud

Yashwant Singh Patel and Rajiv Misra

Abstract With the exponential growth of distributed devices, the era of cloud computing is continued to expand and the systems are required to be more and more energy-efficient with time. The virtualization in cloud manages a large-scale grid-of-servers to efficiently process the demands while optimizing power consumption and energy efficiency. However, to ensure the overall performance, it is critical to predict and extract the high-level features of the future virtual machines (VMs). To predict its load deeply, this paper investigates the methods of a revolutionary machine-learning technique, i.e., deep learning. It extracts the multiple correlation among VMs based on its past workload trace and predicts their future workload with high accuracy. The VM workload prediction helps the decision makers for capacity planning and to apply the suitable VM placement and migration technique with a more robust scaling decision. The effectiveness of deep learning approaches is extensively evaluated using real workload traces of PlanetLab and optimized with selection of model, granularity of training data, number of layers, activation functions, epochs, batch size, the type of optimizer, etc.

Keywords Cloud computing · Deep learning · Energy efficiency
Physical machine (PM) · Virtual machine (VM) · Workload prediction

1 Introduction

Billions of smart devices, i.e., sensors and smart phones that compose the cyber physical systems (CPS) and Internet of things (IoT), will continuously generate huge amount of data than any individual Web application. The digital universe

Y. S. Patel (✉) · R. Misra
Department of Computer Science and Engineering,
Indian Institute of Technology, Patna 801106, India
e-mail: yashwant.pcs17@iitp.ac.in

R. Misra
e-mail: rajivm@iitp.ac.in

© Springer Nature Singapore Pte Ltd. 2018
P. K. Pattnaik et al. (eds.), *Progress in Computing, Analytics and Networking*,
Advances in Intelligent Systems and Computing 710,
https://doi.org/10.1007/978-981-10-7871-2_15

resides escalating in a computing cloud, higher than terra firma of huge hardware data centers connected to billions of distributed devices, all monitored and controlled by intelligent softwares [1]. Cloud computing is undoubtedly a fine approach to address these staggering requirements. To address the data boom caused by the devices like IoT requires fully controlled cloud services. The cloud service providers have to guarantee the levels of interoperability, portability, and manageability that are almost far away to achieve with the current solutions. Service providers help the companies to select suitable communication hardware and software to support cloud protocols as well as secure remote upgrades. To offer fully managed private, public, and hybrid cloud solutions from a simple development to resource-intensive applications, the cloud infrastructure and platform technologies have to ensure elastic scalability and high-throughput event processing services. To achieve this, the companies have designed open-source distributed database systems for accumulating, processing, and managing large amount of data across commodity clusters and servers. In order to extract the knowledge from the collected data and to feed users of smart city applications, such system follows a typical three-layer architecture. Firstly, the collection layer is responsible to collect data from individual devices and send it to the gateways. In the transmission layer, data is moved from gateways to distributed cloud platforms. At last, at the processing layer data is convoluted in the platform of cloud where the knowledge is extracted and makes available to applications [2]. During such complex process, cloud has promised the vision of computing resources and advances the faster network with lower latency. As the services of cloud computing become well-liked, more and more data centers persisted to be deployed around the globe to remotely deliver the computational power over the Internet. Such data centers acquired a larger fraction of the planet's computing resources. During its management, the service providers will definitely suffered from critical business challenges such as security, privacy, interoperability, portability, reliability, availability, bandwidth cost, performance, cost management, complexity of building cloud, and its environmental impact. But, the major worries while providing the light-speed transfer of data are the increased carbon emissions due to servers. In this reference, energy-efficient management of data center resources is a critical and challenging task while considering operational costs as well as CO_2 emissions to the surroundings. In a data center, the long-term operation of servers will not only wear out the equipment, but will also carry the problems of high temperature and energy consumption [3]. A recent report on power consumption of server farms is of evidence that the electricity consumed by servers around the globe accounts to 3% of the global electricity production and about 2% of total greenhouse gas emissions.

Virtual machine (VM)-based distributed and scalable on-demand resource allocation techniques, load balancing approaches, and energy-performance trade-offs while reducing cost and power consumption at the large-scale data centers are the need of time. VM allocation methods try to deploy multiple heterogeneous VMs on each physical machine (PM). In case of high overload situation, i.e., higher than specified threshold of CPU utilization, more VMs are reallocated from one operating PM to another to avoid the violation of service-level

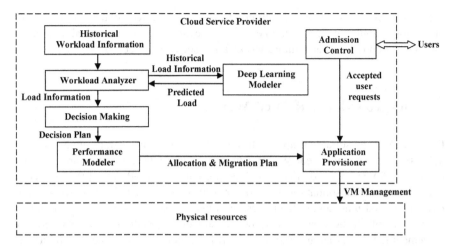

Fig. 1 Utilization-aware workload prediction framework in cloud

agreement (SLA) [4] while the under-utilization, i.e., lower than specified threshold of CPU utilization, will scale down the performance. During such live migration, the overall performance of running applications inside the VM can be impacted negatively [5]. Therefore, by predicting the future workload of VM will not only enhance the overall utilization of resources but also minimize the problem of energy consumption. The prediction of the workload will help the decision makers for capacity planning and applying suitable VM placement as well as migration technique as depicted in Fig. 1 [6].

In this work, we present multi-layer neural networks or popularly known deep learning models to predict the VM workload based on its past workload traces. Deep learning, however, is become a new era of machine learning. It has modernized the machine learning to another level of creating algorithms and to make the system much better analyzer. In recent years, deep learning has reignited the grand challenges of artificial intelligence and become a third boom of AI. It helped the researchers to identify ordinary characteristics of certain objects from the massive amounts of data. The proposed deep learning models will learn the inherent correlated features of VMs workload trace and more effectively predict the workload of future VMs. The predicted load information will be transferred to workload analyzer and then given to the decision-making modeler. It will generate a decision plan of VM management and provide it to performance modeler, and then, the allocation and migration plan choice will be transferred to application provisioner. The application provisioner will receive the accepted user request and apply the suitable VM placement strategy to map the VM to physical servers. In case of overloading, the best migration plans will be selected.

The rest part of this paper is structured as follows: Sect. 2 describes recent works. Section 3 presents performance modeling for utilization-aware workload prediction. Section 4 elaborates different deep learning techniques for workload prediction. Simulation design and performance evaluations are described in Sect. 5. Finally, the conclusion and future works are discussed in Sect. 6.

2 Background and Related Works

Dynamic VM consolidation approaches are widely known for improving resource utilization and maintain energy efficiency in data centers. In literature, various strategies of VM consolidation have been presented. Bobroff et al. [7] proposed a dynamic server consolidation method for a given workload. In their work, they have integrated bin-packing heuristics and time series-based forecasting to reduce the amount of physical capacity needed to support a specific rate of service-level agreement (SLA) violations. Secron et al. [8] used a threshold value assumption to prevent CPUs from reaching 100 percent utilization that may lead to performance degradation. Beloglazov and Buyya [5] applied a statistical analysis of the historical data and used two thresholds, i.e., upper and lower thresholds. They have divided the VM consolidation technique into detection of (i) host under-load situation, i.e., lower than specified threshold of CPU utilization; (ii) host overload situation, i.e., higher than specified threshold of CPU utilization; followed by (iii) VM selection, i.e., to pick best VMs for migration; (iv) VM placement; and (v) balancing of workload among physical machines, i.e., servers. Therefore, it is superior to predict the future workload rather than monitoring the current workload and applying the migration techniques. Prediction of workload will facilitate the decision maker to plan and deal with the capacity of resources. Such advance load prediction will not only improve the performance of overall system but also make it energy-efficient.

In the field of VM workload prediction, numerous approaches have been proposed. Dorian and Freisleben [9] proposed artificial neural networks (ANNs)-based distributed resource allocation approach to find best VM allocations while optimizing utility function. Bitirgen et al. [10] used ANN-based model to support online model training by predicting the performance. In their work, they have considered resource allocation at the multiprocessor chip level. Zhen et al. [11] presented an exponentially weighted moving average (EWMA) approach for short-term prediction of CPU load. Kousiouris et al. [12] proposed a GA-based approach based on the artificial neural networks (ANNs) for workload prediction. Calheiros et al. [13] proposed a proactive method for dynamic provisioning of resources. It is based on autoregressive integrated moving average (ARIMA) model that employs linear prediction structure and predicts future workload by using real-world traces. Fahimeh et al. [14] proposed k-nearest neighbor regression-based model to predict the future utilization of resources. Their utilization prediction-aware best fit decreasing (UP-BFD) method optimizes the VM placement by considering present and upcoming resource requirements. Feng et al. [15] proposed a deep belief network (DBN) that contains multiple-layered restricted Boltzmann machines (RBMs) and a regression layer to predict the workload of future VM. Authors have evaluated its performance with the existing literature work such as EWMA and ARIMA method. All of these existing approaches have used a linear prediction model and implemented a very low dimension structure. These approaches give low performance when long-time workload prediction is required and inherent VM features required to be extracted in complex cloud network. To resolve these issues, this work applies and investigates deep learning techniques to identify inherent correlation of VMs from the massive amounts of workload trace and predict the future workload of VMs.

3   Performance Modeling for Utilization-Aware Prediction

Let $X(t)$ be the set of all past CPU utilization trace as the time intervals of every 5 min and $Y(t)$ be the CPU utilization at the next time $(t + 1)$. To predict the CPU utilization at $(t + 1)$, the past information of CPU utilization at previous time intervals $(t - 1)$ and $(t - 2)$ will be used. This problem can be modeled as a regression problem, where the input time values are $(t - 2)$, $(t - 1)$, t is given, and the predicted output value is $(t + 1)$. The mean absolute error can be calculated by Eq. (1):

$$\text{Mean Absolute Error} = \frac{1}{n} \sum_{i=1}^{n} \frac{\left| x_i^a - x_i^p \right|}{x_i^a} \tag{1}$$

where n is the prediction intervals, x_i^a is the actual CPU utilization value, and x_i^p is the predicted CPU utilization value.

The performance modeler will use this predicted CPU utilization for allocation or migration of VM at the destination host with the following constraints of Eq. (2) [14]:

$$PU_{cpu}(VM) + CU_{cpu}(PM) \le TH_{cpu} X\, TU_{cpu}(PM) \tag{2}$$

where $PU_{cpu}(VM)$ is a predicted CPU utilization of VM, $CU_{cpu}(PM)$ is the current CPU utilization of PM, TH_{cpu} is the threshold value, and $TU_{cpu}(PM)$ is the total CPU utilization of PM. If the Eq. (2) is satisfied, the VM placement can be performed at destination PM and the status of PM will be updated as shown in Eq. (3):

$$TU_{cpu}(PM) = PU_{cpu}(VM) + CU_{cpu}(PM) \tag{3}$$

During the case of hot spot mitigation or VM migration, the new PMs are required to be searched (or) the idle PMs are to be switched in active state. The violation can be formulated by Eq. (4):

$$PU_{cpu}(VM) + CU_{cpu}(PM) \ge TH_{cpu} X\, TU_{cpu}(PM) \tag{4}$$

Overall CPU load of PM denoted by $L_{cpu\ (PM)}$ can be calculated by Eq. (5):

$$L_{cpu(PM)} = \frac{CU_{cpu(PM)}}{TU_{cpu(PM)}} \tag{5}$$

where $CU_{cpu}(PM)$ is the current CPU load of PM, and $TU_{cpu}(PM)$ is the total CPU load of PM. Threshold values of PM can be defined though Eq. (6):

$$TH_{Lcpu}(PM) \leq TU_{cpu}(PM) \leq TH_{Ucpu}(PM) \tag{6}$$

where $TH_{Lcpu}\ (PM)$ denotes lower threshold value of PM, and $TH_{Ucpu}\ (PM)$ denotes upper threshold value of PM.

Case of host under-load situation, i.e., lower than specified threshold of CPU utilization, is shown in Eq. (7):

$$TU_{cpu}(PM) \leq TH_{Lcpu}(PM) \tag{7}$$

This is also called the case of cold spot; if it is satisfied, then there is a need of VM migration so that the PM can be switched off or switched to sleep state and rest PM can be utilized. It will reduce the number of active PMs and improve the degree of energy efficiency.

Case of host overload situation, i.e., higher than specified threshold of CPU utilization, is shown in Eq. (8):

$$TU_{cpu}(PM) \geq TH_{Ucpu}(PM) \tag{8}$$

This is also called the case of hot spot; if it is satisfied, then there is a need of VM migration so that the unnecessary SLA violation can be avoided and other PMs will be searched to satisfy the increased demand of particular VM.

4   Deep Learning-Based Workload Prediction Techniques

The existing workload prediction approaches apply the statistical analysis of the workload trace, i.e., CPU, memory, disk, and bandwidth and predict the future workload by identifying variations in workload trace. To deeply analyze the workload variations, the depth of layers in a neural network becomes a critical factor and gave birth to "deep learning—a revolutionary machine-learning technique." The problem of workload prediction is assumed to be a time series-based regression problem and solved with powerful deep learning approaches. The input of these models is workload trace of VMs recorded in different time intervals, and output is predicted load of future VMs. These approaches apply the technique of unsupervised learning, where only a little knowledge of resources is provided. Accuracy of prediction can be improved with the number of hidden layers, epochs, batch size, activation functions, and type of optimizer. Different deep learning models that are used in this work are discussed as follows:

4.1   Recurrent Neural Network (RNN) Model

Recurrent neural networks (RNN) [16, 17] are known to be a complement set of classical neural networks, i.e., feed-forward network. It removes the constraint of passing the information in forward manner and improves the model by providing at least one feed-backward edge.

4.2   Long Short-Term Memory (LSTM) Network Model

LSTM model was proposed by Hochreiter et al. in 1997 [18], Wang and Raj [17]. It tries to contest the vanishing gradient problem with the help of gates and an explicitly defined memory cell. Each neuron has three gates, i.e., input, output, and forget, along with memory cell. The input gate decides that how much information of the previous layer is required to be stored in the cell. The output layer decides how much of cell state to be known by the next layer, and the forget gate is for erasing the few content of previous layer. LSTM has been widely applied in several real-world problems.

4.3   Boltzmann Machine Model

It is also known as a hidden unit version of Hopfield network. It is a fully connected network made by hidden and visible units. In this model, few neurons are marked as input while others are hidden. It initiates with random weights and learns through contrastive divergence. The process of training and running is similar to Hopfield. It is inspired from physics where the rise in temperature causes the state transfer. The energy function of Boltzmann machine can be represented by Eq. (9):

$$E(v, h) = -\sum_i v_i b_i - \sum_k h_k b_k - \frac{1}{2}\sum_{i,j} v_i v_j w_{i,j} - \frac{1}{2}\sum_{i,k} v_i h_k w_{i,k} - \frac{1}{2}\sum_{k,l} h_k h_l w_{k,l} \quad (9)$$

where v defines visible units, h defines hidden units, w defines weights, and b is for bias. The global temperature value controls the activation; if it is minimized, then the energy of the cells decreases. The right temperature to the network achieves an equilibrium state [17].

4.4   *Convolution Neural Network (CNN) Model*

CNN is also known as LeNet. It is based on traditional multiple layer perceptrons. It was proposed by LeCun et al. in 1998 [19]. It applies convolution and sub-sampling operation alternatively on input data by using different computational units in convolutional and sub-sampling layers. After this, the data represented in higher layers fed to a fully connected network and complete the task.

5   Simulation Design and Performance Evaluation

5.1   *Simulation Design*

To evaluate the efficiency of deep learning approaches, a real workload trace of PlanetLab [20, 21] is used. It is a widely popular open platform that contains the CPU utilization of over 1000 VMs. This data is collected in every five minutes and stored in different files. For one VM, there are total 288 observations per day [22].

5.2   *Performance Evaluation*

In this work, the input of model is the CPU utilization of VMs and output is future CPU utilization. The data set is divided into two parts, i.e., training set and test set. The training set includes the CPU utilization of VMs recorded in 7 days, and remaining is kept for test set. For single VM workload prediction, there are total 2880 time intervals out of which 70% is used for training and 30% is used for test. Then, the deep learning models are trained with different sizes and features as shown in Table 1 and tested with unknown data set. The performance of deep learning models, i.e., multi-layer NN, convolutional NN, recurrent NN, Boltzmann, and LSTM NN for single VM workload prediction during long time intervals of testing data, is represented in Fig. 2. It can be observed that the predicted utilization of CPU by LSTM network is too close to actual workload, while the convolutional network gives low performance in comparison with other techniques.

Table 1 Experimental configuration

Layers	Epochs	Batch size	Activation function	Loss function	Optimizer
3	50	10	Relu, SoftMax	MSE	SGD
5	100	50	Relu, SoftMax	MSE	Adam
10	150	100	Relu, SoftMax	MSE	Adamax

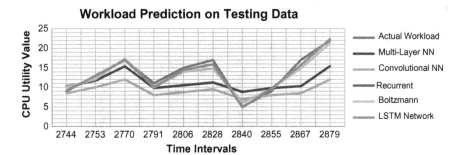

Fig. 2 Performance comparison of deep learning approaches for long-term workload prediction of single VM

Overall analysis of mean absolute error for single VM is represented in Fig. 3. The deep learning models are also depended on the amount of training data. As much as we increase the amount of training data, it will improve the accuracy of prediction. In case of multiple VMs, we have selected 10 continuously running VMs and plotted its average mean absolute error in Fig. 4. The LSTM network model gives minimum average mean absolute error and performs better than other deep learning models. It is advantageous in the case of multiple VM workload prediction during long time intervals. These deep learning models are beneficial during VM management and help the decision makers to pre-plan the VM placement and migration strategies. The overall performance of deep learning models can be arranged as:

$$(Low)Convolutional < Multi-layer < Recurrent < Boltzmann < LSTM(High)$$

Fig. 3 Performance comparison for single VM workload prediction

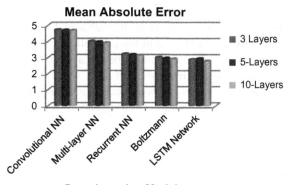

Fig. 4 Performance comparison for 10 VMs workload prediction

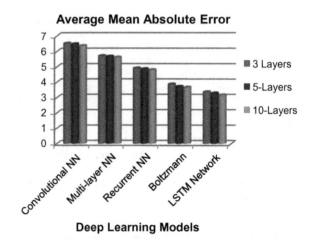

6 Conclusion and Future Works

In this work, we have presented different utilization-aware prediction models of deep learning approaches. It extracts the high-level features from the workload trace of past VMs and predicts their future workload with high accuracy. The prediction of the workload can help the decision makers to estimate the overall capacity and to apply the suitable VM placement as well as migration technique. The proposed framework will support the prediction of large-scale data intensive systems for distributed decision making such as hot spot mitigation, cold spot mitigation, threshold violation, and SLA violation. The accuracy of deep learning approaches is evaluated using real workload traces and shown with the help of experimental results. The results are promising and show that the LSTM-based networks improve the performance of workload prediction while convolutional NN gives low performance. Deep learning approaches are suitable for long-term prediction of workloads. The performance of the deep learning approaches can be improved further by increasing size of training data and depth of the model. This will help the model to find more correlation between workload patterns and determine the load with dynamic requirements. In future, we will try to investigate more robust and efficient approaches of workload estimation while coordinating with multi-tier applications and multi-tier VMs running on heterogeneous PMs in real cloud platform.

References

1. The digital universe in 2020, https://www.emc.com/leadership/digital-universe/2012iview/executive-summary-a-universe-of.htm (2012).

2. F. Tao, L. Zhang, V.C. Venkatesh, Y. Luo, and Y. Cheng, Cloud manufacturing: A computing and service-oriented manufacturing model, in Proc. Inst. Mech. Eng. B—J. Eng. Manuf., 225 (10), (2011) 1969–1976.

3. C.C. Lin, P. Liu, and J.J. Wu, Energy-efficient virtual provision algorithms for cloud systems, 4th IEEE International Conference on Utility and Cloud Computing (2011) 81–88.

4. M. Mishra, A. Das, P. Kulkarni, and A. Sahoo, Dynamic resource management using virtual machine migrations, IEEE Communications Magazine (2012) 34–40.

5. A. Beloglazov and R. Buyya, "Optimal online deterministic algorithms and adaptive heuristics for energy and performance efficient dynamic consolidation of virtual machines in cloud data centers," Concurrency and Computation: Practice and Experience, 24 (13), (2012) 1397– 1420.

6. R. N. Calheiros, E. Masoumi, R. Ranjan and R. Buyya, Workload Prediction Using ARIMA Model and Its Impact on Cloud Applications' QoS, in IEEE Transactions on Cloud Computing, 3(4), (2015) 449–458.

7. N. Bobroff, A. Kochut, and K. Beaty, Dynamic placement of virtual machines for managing sla violations, in Integrated Network Management, IM'07. 10th IFIP/IEEE International Symposium (2007) 119–128.

8. A. Murtazaev and S. Oh, Sercon: Server consolidation algorithm using live migration of virtual machines for green computing, TE Technical Review, 28(3), (2011) 212–231.

9. D. Minarolli and B. Freisleben, "Distributed Resource Allocation to Virtual Machines via Artificial Neural Networks," 22nd Euromicro International Conference on Parallel, Distributed, and Network-Based Processing, Torino (2014) 490–499.

10. R. Bitirgen, E. Ipek, and J.F. Martinez. Coordinated management of multiple interacting resources in chip multiprocessors: A machine learning approach. In Proc. 41st Annual IEEE/ACM International Symposium on Microarchitecture (2008) 318–329.

11. Z. Xiao, W. Song and Q. Chen. Dynamic resource allocation using virtual machines for cloud computing environment, IEEE Transactions on Parallel and Distributed Systems, 24(6), (2013) 1107–1117.

12. G. Kousiouris, A. Menychtas, D. Kyriazis, et al. Parametric design and performance analysis of a decoupled service-oriented prediction framework based on embedded numerical software, IEEE Transactions on Services Computing, 6(4), (2013) 511–524.

13. R. Calheiros, E. Masoumi, R. Ranjan and R. Buyya. Workload Prediction Using ARIMA Model and Its Impact on Cloud Applications' QoS, IEEE Transactions On Cloud Computing, 3 (4), (2015) 449–458.

14. F. Farahnakian, T. Pahikkala, P. Liljeberg, J. Plosila and H. Tenhunen, Utilization Prediction Aware VM Consolidation Approach for Green Cloud Computing, IEEE 8th International Conference on Cloud Computing, New York City, NY, (2015) 381–388.

15. F. Qiu, B. Zhang and J. Guo, "A deep learning approach for VM workload prediction in the cloud, 17th IEEE/ACIS International Conference on Software Engineering, Artificial Intelligence, Networking and Parallel/Distributed Computing (SNPD), Shanghai (2016) 319–324.

16. Ken-ichi Funahashi, Yuichi Nakamura, Approximation of dynamical systems by continuous time recurrent neural networks, Neural Networks, 6(6), (1993) 801–806.

17. H. Wang and B. Raj, A survey: Time travel in deep learning space: An introduction to deep learning models and how deep learning models evolved from the initial ideas, arXiv preprint arXiv:1510.04781 (2015).

18. Sepp Hochreiter and Jürgen Schmidhuber, Long short-term memory. Neural computation 9 (8), (1997) 1735–1780.

19. LeCun, Yann, et al., Gradient-based learning applied to document recognition, Proceedings of the IEEE, 86(11), (1998) 2278–2324.

20. K. Park and V. Pai, CoMon: a mostly-scalable monitoring system for PlanetLab, ACM SIGOPS Operating Systems Review, 40, (2006) 65–74.

21. R.N. Calheiros, R. Ranjan, A. Beloglazov, C. Rose and R. Buyya, CloudSim: a toolkit for modeling and simulation of cloud computing environments and evaluation of resource provisioning algorithms, Software: Practice and Experience, 41(1), (2011) 23–50.
22. Beloglazov A, Energy-efficient management of virtual machines in data centers for cloud computing, PhD thesis (2013).

A New Neural Network-Based IDS for Cloud Computing

Priyanka Joshi, Ritu Prasad, Pradeep Mewada and Praneet Saurabh

Abstract Services provided by cloud computing are the very fascinating as it offers of free access or paid access to the buyers. This paradigm facilitates a verity of facets to the users. Being such an interesting concept and having so many beneficial features, the cloud also suffers from several security risks. This results in creating a lot of challenges at the time of implementation. Since, cloud services are not confined to limited boundaries therefore chances of misadventure leading to compromise is immense. Intrusion detection system (IDS) within the cloud environment is an interesting idea and this paper presents "A neural network-based intrusion detection system for cloud computing (NN-IDS)". It discusses the various integrated methods that provide detection in cloud environment and also takes prevention measures for the malignant functions found within the cloud. Experimental results show that NN-IDS performs much better than existing work and shows significant improvement in accuracy and precision.

Keywords Intrusion · Intrusion detection · Cloud computing
Identity-based encryption

P. Joshi (✉) · R. Prasad · P. Mewada
Department of Information Technology and Engineering, Technocrats Institute
of Technology (Excellence), Bhopal 462021, India
e-mail: priyankajsh92@gmail.com

R. Prasad
e-mail: rit7ndm@gmail.com

P. Mewada
e-mail: pradeepmewada07@gmail.com

P. Saurabh
Department of Computer Science and Engineering, Technocrats Institute
of Technology, Bhopal 462021, India
e-mail: praneetsaurabh@gmail.com

© Springer Nature Singapore Pte Ltd. 2018
P. K. Pattnaik et al. (eds.), *Progress in Computing, Analytics and Networking*,
Advances in Intelligent Systems and Computing 710,
https://doi.org/10.1007/978-981-10-7871-2_16

1 Introduction

With the emergence of the Internet and increasing rate of IT trends, concept of cloud has become the very beneficial aspect for users [1]. Cloud computing offers a way of achieving services of computing for which there is no requirement of having the expert knowledge of the various technologies and as per the business point of view, the cloud computing may provide various latest types of services for the users and also for the organization easily, which can provide the large scale and various services to the users in order to speed up the innovation and also helps in the better process of decision-making [2]. Various users handle humongous amount of data and in this paradigm, users are basically dependent on the services on the Internet for any type of business or personal communication also for performing various activities related to sending or storing of data [3]. This paradigm has also introduced new aspect of software development along with their deployment with various resources [4]. Consequently, it lowers the development, implementation, and deployment cost [5].

Cloud demonstrates four types of deployment schemes that are found and represented as the private cloud, public cloud, community cloud and, finally, the hybrid cloud [6]. These schemes offer lot of flexibility and add efficiency to the users. But somehow this open and flexible architecture becomes vulnerable for attacks [7]. Intrusion detection system (IDS) is not a new concept, indeed it is an appealing concept that monitors the incoming packets analyses them and then filter out the potential attacks while letting go the legitimate packets [8]. Since cloud is a distributed concept, it is more prone of attacks; therefore, IDS becomes crucial concept for making computing in cloud environment secure [9]. Lately, it has also been seen that IDS in many cases fails to detect new and novel attacks, thus lowering the detection rate; therefore, a lot of attention is paid in development of IDS that must have the potential to successfully filter out the potential attacks more proficiently and correctly [10].

A multilayer perceptron (MLP) is a type of artificial neural network with minimum three layers of neurons, namely an input layer, one or more hidden layers, and an output layer. Entry layer is not taken into consideration as a "actual" layer. Neurons within the enter layer actually distribute the additives of an input pattern vector to neurons inside the hidden layer without any other processing [11]. This paper proposes a neural network-based intrusion detection system for cloud computing (NN-IDS) that incorporates the neural network concepts to design and develop an IDS that can successfully filter out the new attacks in order to instill trust in the system. Rest of the paper is organized in the following manner; Sect. 2 presents the related work while Sect. 3 introduces the proposed work. Section 4 explains the results and analysis while Sect. 5 concludes the paper.

2 Related Work

This section describes the various concepts of cloud computing, intrusion detection, and neural networks. Cloud computing is the next Web-based computing that provides straightforward and customizable services to the users for accessing or to figure with numerous cloud applications [12]. Cloud computing is the next Internet technology primarily based on Internet which offers easy and flexible software, hardware, or services. Cloud computing gives a lot of flexibility that saves lot of time and brings ease by using connecting the cloud application using Internet [13]. Security in cloud computing is the major concern that needs to be addressed. If security measures are not provided properly for data operations and transmissions, then data is at high risk [14]. Since cloud computing provides the flair for a bunch of users to access the stored information, there is a chance of getting high data risk [15]. Significant security measures need to be enforced after identifying prominent security challenge which can lead to solutions for such challenges. Securing cloud is very important as if these are not properly taken care will evntually lead in creating security vulnerabilities [16]. Therefore, this paradigm needs most powerful safety options by working out security understandings that should have the potential to deal with these challenges. Intrusion detection system (IDS) is a type of software or the hardware element which monitors process to identify potential attacks [17]. Due to this fact, IDS is one of the fastest growing technologies to impart security. IDS works on mainly three aspects: monitoring, analyzing, and then making decision about any packet. IDS can be divided in two categories such as signature-based IDS and anomaly-based IDS. Signature-based IDS detects known attacks through matching signature in pre-stored attack signature base. Signatures are the well-formatted patterns found in the attack. Thus, they are limited to detecting known attacks. Anomaly-based IDS stores the behavior of previous events and constructs a model to predict the behavior of the incoming events [18]. These systems are able to detect both known as well as an unknown attack, however produce high false alarm and high computational cost. The IDS service may raise the alarm if it encounters an attack automatically since the process of analysis is automatically [19].

Popovi and Hocenski mentioned concerning the security problems, necessities, and challenges that are faced by cloud service providers throughout cloud engineering [4]. Behl explores the safety problems regarding the cloud atmosphere. This paper mentioned concerning existing security approaches to secure the cloud infrastructure and applications and their drawbacks [5]. Sabahi [20] discussed about the security problems, responsibility, and accessibility for cloud computing. This paper also planned a possible resolution for few security problems [6]. In another work, Mohamed et al. [21] bestowed the information security model of cloud computing supported the study of cloud design. They conjointly enforced the knowledge to develop a security paradigm for cloud computing. Later on, Wentao [22] introduced some cloud computing systems and analyzes cloud computing security issues and its strategy in step with the cloud computing ideas [8].

Mathisen [23] mentioned concerning a number of the key security problems that cloud computing will witness in future and put forward some potential solutions for the same. Also, Sondhiya and Shreevastav [11] analyzed the maximum use of neural networks and its learning abilities that have been defined in order to categorize the intrusions. They also stated about the soft computing approach like MLP algorithm for identifying the unknown found attack over the network within the cloud. Mathew in his work described the problems that are found within the architecture of the cloud [12] by highlighting various types of threats that create issues within the cloud infrastructure extended in [16]. Recently bio-inspired advances [24] also gained attention in realizing different goals on this domain [25–27]. Next section presents the proposed "A neural network-based intrusion detection system" for cloud to overcome the threat perception.

3 Proposed Method

This section presents the proposed "A neural network-based intrusion detection system (NN-IDS)." The proposed NN-IDS is meant for securing the cloud environment. Major steps in NN-IDS are generation of desired dataset and classify the dataset. The flowchart of proposed NN-IDS is described in Fig. 1 followed by the algorithm given below.

Algorithm for NN-IDS

```
// read dataset X having three classes normal, known attack, and unknown attack.
// having n number of record. X having X.data for data and X.class having classes
1.    Start
2.    For i=1 to n
3.      {
4.        If X.class!=normal
5.        {
6.          data(i)=X.data(i)
7.        }
8.      }
9.    Data.train, Data.test = Divide(data)
10.   trainModel = Train.MultilayerPerceptronClassifier (data.train, classes.train)
11.   predictedClass = Test. MultilayerPerceptronClassifier (trainModel, data.test)
12.   conf = confutionMatrix(predictedClass, data.test)
13.   Accuracy=sum(conf(i, i))/sum(conf(i, j)) for every I, j=1,2;
14.   End
```

In the beginning data, cleaning is done and dataset is categorized into two and the first belongs to the normal category while another belongs to attack category. Now, dataset is divided into training set and test set; then, proper classifier is used for the identification of legitimate or attack pattern. Under training phase, the classifier gets trained and becomes ready for the testing of any new attack in testing. Testing phase uses confusion matrix for the analysis of the performance of the proposed NN-IDS.

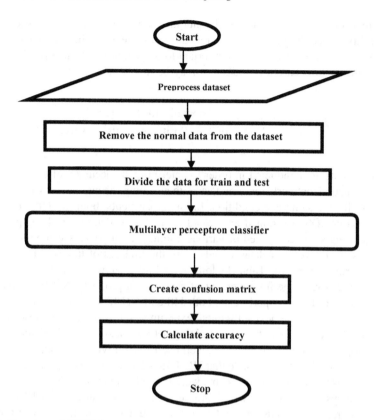

Fig. 1 Flowchart of NN-IDS

4 Result Analysis

This section discusses the different experiments conducted on the developed NN-IDS for cloud under different scenarios to validate its efficiency. Kyoto dataset has been used for both training set and test set for all the experiments, and then, comparison has been drawn with the current state of the art. Results are calculated on accuracy and precision.

(i) Accuracy: It is a parameter that is used to find the efficiency of the work. This will show the effectiveness of the classification of the true positive and true negative given in Eq. (1).

$$\text{Accuracy} = \frac{\text{True Positives} + \text{True Negative}}{\text{TP} + \text{TN} + \text{FP} + \text{FN}} \tag{1}$$

(ii) Precision: It is a description of random errors, a measure of statistical variability stated in Eq. (2). Precision attribute specifies the characteristics of features in great detail and is important to realize, however, that precision data no matter how carefully measured may be inaccurate.

$$\text{Precision} = \frac{\text{Number of True Positives}}{\text{Numbeof True Positives} + \text{False Positives}} \tag{2}$$

Experiments are conducted in order to determine the accuracy of the developed IDS with neural network for cloud, and then, comparisons are drawn with J48 algorithm for the same test condition. In the experiments, both the J48 and neural network-based IDS are trained and tested using Kyoto dataset. In the experimentation, training set is composed of various training set of packets while test dataset is composed of several of dataset. Below are the findings of the experiments.

In experimental result, Table 1 along with Fig. 2 shows the evaluation of the accuracy and percentage improvement of accuracy in proposed NN-IDS over J48, when compared. In the experiments, both J48 and NN-IDS were trained with 10% of the dataset, and in the next subsequent experiments, it was increased from 10% to 20%, 30%, ..., 60%. This change in training set size also reflects the efficiency of the developed NN-IDS as it performs well even trained with low training set size. Results in Table 1 and Fig. 2 state that NN-IDS achieves 0.9631% accuracy against 0.9565% of J48 when both the systems were trained with 10% of dataset. Accuracy of both the systems increases with increase in size of dataset and NN-IDS reports 0.9643 accuracy while J48 reports 0.92340% accuracy when trained with 60% of dataset. With these results, it is evident that the proposed NN-IDS achieves higher accuracy than the J48 algorithm and these are visible in percentage increase of accuracy.

Next experiment is conducted in order to determine the precision of the developed IDS with neural network for cloud, and then, comparisons are drawn with J48

Table 1 Accuracy of existing and NN-IDS	Training set (%)	J48 (%)	NN-IDS (%)	% Improvement
	10	0.9565	0.9631	0.066
	20	0.9526	0.9664	0.138
	30	0.9491	0.9596	0.105
	40	0.9419	0.9665	0.246
	50	0.9324	0.9654	0.333
	60	0.9234	0.9643	0.409

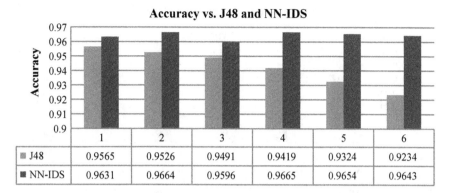

Fig. 2 Accuracy comparison between J48 and NN-IDS

Table 2 Precision of J48 and NN-IDS

Training set (%)	J48 (%)	NN-IDS (%)	% Improvement
10	0.9463	0.9796	0.033
20	0.9546	0.9678	0.132
30	0.9705	0.9943	0.208
40	0.9419	0.9665	0.336
50	0.9633	0.9718	0.455
60	0.9566	0.9613	0.477

algorithm for the same test condition. In the experiments, both the J48 and neural network-based IDS are trained and tested using Kyoto dataset. In the experimentation, training set is composed of various training set of packets while test dataset is composed of various dataset. Below are the findings of the experiments.

In experimental result, Table 2 along with Fig. 3 shows the evaluation of the precision and percentage improvement of precision in proposed NN-IDS over J48, when compared. In the experiments, both J48 and NN-IDS were trained with 10% of the dataset, and in the next subsequent experiments, it was increased from 10% to 20%, 30%, ..., 60%. This change in training set size also reflects the efficiency of the developed NN-IDS as it performs well even trained with low training set size. Results in Table 2 and Fig. 3 state that NN-IDS achieves 0.9796% precision against 0.9463% of J48 when both the systems were trained with 10% of dataset. Precision of both the systems increases with increase in size of dataset and NN-IDS reports 0.9613% precision while J48 reports 0.9566% precision when trained with 60% of dataset. With these results, it is evident that the proposed NN-IDS achieves higher precision than the J48 algorithm and these are visible in percentage increase of precision.

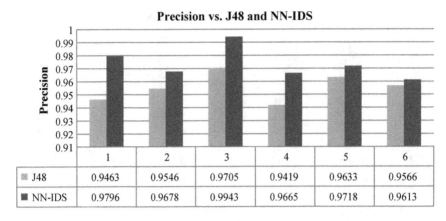

Fig. 3 Precision comparison between J48 and NN-IDS

5 Conclusion

This paper highlighted that there are several types of attacks are there within the layered protection of the cloud environment and which is also distract from having the trust in between cloud users and their providers which also consists of the some illegal type of access, loss of data, bad services utilizations, etc., within cloud, and some types of hackers or attacks are also present. In quest to overcome this situation, this paper proposed "A neural network-based intrusion detection system (NN-IDS) for cloud environment." The proposed NN-IDS integrated methods provide detection in cloud environment and also take prevention measures for the malignant functions found within the cloud. Experimental results show that NN-IDS performs much better than existing work and shows significant improvement in accuracy and precision.

References

1. Arshad, J., Townsend, P. and Xu, J.: A novel intrusion severity analysis approach for Clouds. Future Generation Computer Systems, 29 (2013) 416–428.
2. Casola, V., Cuomo, A., Rak, M. and Villano, U.: The Cloud Grid approach-Security analysis and performance evaluation. Future Generation Computer Systems, 29 (2013) 387–401.
3. Chen, D., and Zhao, H.: Data Security and Privacy Protection Issues in Cloud Computing. International Conference on Computer Science and Electronics Engineering (2012) 647–651.
4. Han, J., Susilo, W. and Mu, Y.: Identity-based data storage in cloud computing. Future Generation Computer Systems, 29 (2013) 673–681.
5. Yin, X.Z., Liu, H.: An Efficient and Secured Data Storage Scheme in Cloud Computing Using ECC-based PKI. IEEE 16th International Conference on Advanced Communication Technology (ICACT) (2014) 523–527.

6. Yang, C.: Protecting Data Privacy and Security for Cloud Computing Based on Secret Sharing. International Symposium on Biometrics and Security Technologies (ISBAST) (2013) 259–266.

7. Alzain, M.A., Soh, B. & Pardede, E.: A Survey on Data Security Issues in Cloud Computing: From Single to Multi-Clouds, Journal of Software, Vol. 8 No. 5 (2013).

8. Mohod, A.G., Alaspurkar, S.J.: Analysis of IDS for Cloud Computing. International Journal of Application or Innovation in Engineering & Management (IJAIEM), Vol. 2, Issue 3 (2013) 344–349.

9. Van, R.: Comparison of Network Intrusion Detection Systems in cloud computing environment. Computer Communication and Informatics (ICCCI), International Conference on 10–12 Jan. (2012).

10. Parag, K., Gawande, A. D.: Intrusion Detection System for Cloud Computing. International Journal of Scientific & Technology Research Volume 1, Issue 4, ISSN 2277–8616, (2012).

11. Sondhiya, R., Shreevastav, M.: To Improve Security in Cloud Computing with Intrusion detection system using Neural Network. International Journal of Soft Computing and Engineering (IJSCE), Volume-3, Issue-2 (2013).

12. Mathew, S.: Securing Cloud from Attacks based on Intrusion Detection System. International Journal of Advanced Research in Computer and Communication Engineering Vol. 1, Issue 10, (2012).

13. Gupta, S.: IDS Based Defense for Cloud Based Mobile Infrastructure as a Service. IEEE Eighth World Congress on Services (2012).

14. Vaishali, B.: Intrusion Detection System in Cloud Computing: An Overview. International Journal on Recent and Innovation Trends in Computing and Communication, Volume: 4 Issue: 1 (2016).

15. Kresimir, P., Zeljko H.: Cloud computing security issues and challenges. MIPRO Proceedings of the 33rd International Convention (2010) 344–349.

16. Bhel, A.: Emerging Security Challenges in Cloud Computing. Information and Communication Technologies, World Congress on, Mumbai (2011) 217–222.

17. Mishti, D.: Intrusion Detection System for DoS Attack in Cloud. International Journal of Applied Information Systems (IJAIS), Volume 10, No. 5 (2016).

18. Patil, D.: To Implement Intrusion Detection System for Cloud Computing Using Genetic Algorithm. International Journal of Computer Science and Information Technology Research, Vol. 3, Issue 1 (2015).

19. Nassif, A.B., Danny Ho b, Capretz, L.F.: Towards an early software estimation using log-linear regression and a multilayer perceptron model. Journal of Systems and Software, 86 (2013) 144–160.

20. Sabahi, F.: Cloud Computing Security Threats and Responses. IEEE 3rd International Conference on Communication software and Networks (ICCSN) (2011) 245–249.

21. Mohamed, E.M., Abdelkader, H.S., Etriby, S. EI.: Enhanced Data Security Model for Cloud Computing. 8th International Conference on Informatics and Systems (INFOS), Cairo, (2012) 12.

22. Liu, W.: Research on Cloud Computing Security Problem and Strategy. 2nd International Conference on Consumer Electronics. Communications and Networks (CECNet) (2012) 1216–1219.

23. Mathisen, E.: Security Challenges and Solutions in Cloud Computing. International Conference on Digital Ecosystems and Technologies (IEEE DEST) (2011) 208–212.

24. Saurabh, P., Verma, B.: An Efficient Proactive Artificial Immune System based Anomaly Detection and Prevention System. Expert Systems with Applications, Elsevier, 60 (2016) 311–320.

25. Saurabh, P., Verma, B.: Cooperative Negative Selection Algorithm. International Journal of Computer Applications (0975–8887), vol 95, Number 17 (2014) 27–32.

26. Saurabh, P., Verma, B, Sharma, S.: An Immunity Inspired Anomaly Detection System: A General Framework. Proceedings of Seventh International Conference on Bio-Inspired Computing: Theories and Applications (BIC-TA 2012), vol 202 of the series Advances in Intelligent Systems and Computing, Springer (2012) 417–428.
27. Saurabh, P., Verma, B, Sharma, S.: Biologically Inspired Computer Security System: The Way Ahead, Recent Trends in Computer Networks and Distributed Systems Security the Way Ahead. Recent Trends in Computer Networks and Distributed Systems Security, Communications in Computer and Information Science, Springer, vol 335 (2011) 474–484.

Designing of an Orchestration Mechanism for the Efficient Web-Services Composition

Reena Gupta, Raj Kamal and Ugrasen Suman

Abstract Service-oriented architecture (SOA) is an emerging paradigm to build complex applications and business processes. SOA is described by the interactions between the loosely coupled, coarse-grained, and autonomous services. The interactions take place in a distributed environment. The services need interoperability for the heterogeneous applications and complex business processes. Web-services composition (WSC) is thus an important aspect of applications and processes. Two major approaches for the WSCs are orchestration and choreography. The orchestration offers number of advantages over choreography during the WSC. The paper gives a literature review of different approaches and of the tools, which are available for Web-services orchestration (WSO). The paper describes a comparison of earlier WSO approaches taking into account different benchmarks and identifies the needs of the improvements. The paper suggests an orchestration-based improved approach during the WSC and needed steps for that.

Keywords Service-oriented architecture · Web-services · Web-services composition · Orchestration · Choreography · Dynamic

1 Introduction

Service-oriented architecture (SOA) is an architectural way used for designing complex distributed systems. It is a way to organize and utilize the distributed capabilities. SOA services are interoperable in distributed environment. With the

R. Gupta (✉) · R. Kamal · U. Suman
School of Computer Science & Information Technology, Devi Ahilya University,
Indore 452001, Madhya Pradesh, India
e-mail: gupta.reena865@gmail.com

R. Kamal
e-mail: dr_rajkamal@hotmail.com

U. Suman
e-mail: ugrasen123@yahoo.com

© Springer Nature Singapore Pte Ltd. 2018   171
P. K. Pattnaik et al. (eds.), *Progress in Computing, Analytics and Networking*,
Advances in Intelligent Systems and Computing 710,
https://doi.org/10.1007/978-981-10-7871-2_17

advent of WWW services, interoperability is required on the Web. Various standard languages, the format of interfaces and protocols supports interoperability among the Web-services. These are Xtensible Markup Language (XML), Hyper Text Transfer Protocol (HTTP), Web-Services Description Language (WSDL), Simple Object Access Protocol (SOAP), and Universal Description, Discovery and Integration (UDDI) [1].

The current researches in Web-services include many challenging areas starting from service publication to service mining. The most vital among them is WSC. A single atomic service has limited functionality. Therefore, WSC is required to design a complex business process. Quality of Service (QoS), which is a non-functional property of a Web-service, plays an important role in composition [2]. XML-based approaches provide a way to compose such Web-services either through orchestration or choreography.

1.1 Two Approaches: Orchestration and Choreography

Web-services orchestration (WSO) and Web-services choreography (WSCh) are two approaches for coordination and orderly execution of services.

WSO: One central controller (CC) enables orderly execution of services. The services do not directly interact with each other. They pass messages and communicate via this CC only [3]. CC invokes a service, which responds and communicates with the CC. Orchestration functionalities for the executable business processes use the XML-based Business Process Execution Language (BPEL). BPEL includes sequencing of process activity, message correlation, failure recovery, and relationship between process roles [4].

WSCh: There is no CC and services can directly interact with each other. Each service involved in a composition knows with whom it takes to interact [3]. Choreography works for multiparty collaboration with the help of XML-based Web-Services Choreography Interface (WSChI) [4, 5]. The interfaces provide dynamic collaboration, message correlation, sequencing rules, and exception handling during the transactions [5].

WSO has following advantages over WSCh when composing the Web-services to execute business process [3, 4]:

- The coordination among component Web-services centrally manages through a CC.
- Web-services are unaware that they are participating in creating a larger business process.
- Alternate solution is available in case of a Web-service fault.
- Design and execution of choreography models are more complex and challenging than orchestration.

- The process of orchestration is well defined and understood while choreography is an open-research challenge.

The organization of the paper is as follows. Section 2 describes a literature review for orchestration-based existing approaches and summarizes them based on various benchmarks. Section 3 gives a discussion and identifies issues for WSO. Section 4 gives a design and explains suggested approach and sequences required. Section 5 concludes the results.

2 Comparison of the Orchestration-Based Approaches

Various approaches [6–20] have been adopted for orchestration-based WSC. Liu et al. [6] analyzed service domain features on a Web-service optimal composition. It improves the optimization strategies based on artificial bee colony and uses improved artificial bee colony algorithm (S-ABC$_{SC}$). Chitra and Guptha [7] proposed a tree-based strategy for a QoS-aware service composition. The proposed work also analyzed the parameters such as server maximum capacity, server's current load. This provided the alternative services with improved response times.

Mohamed et al. [8] suggested a clonal selection algorithm-based solution for the semantic WSC. The solution used the QoS attributes and semantic similarity. They compared with a genetic algorithm-based solution. Yu et al. [9] proposed a QoS optimization technique for data-intensive Web-services. Proposed approach considered a parallel structure for the composition. It also introduced a Benefit Ratio of Composite Services (BROCS) model. That balanced the throughput and cost. It calculated the degree of parallelism based on the proposed BROCS model.

Mohamed et al. [10] designed an adaptive replication framework for orchestration enabled WSC. The framework improved the Web-service availability in case of failure or load balancing. Arul and Prakash [11] introduced a fault-handling strategy for orchestration-based WSC using WS-BPEL. A separate fault-handling module identifies the fault and handles that during composition of the business process.

Zhao et al. [12] proposed a hybrid-service selection algorithm for WSC. Their proposed approach was based on the combination of clonal selection algorithm and particle swarm optimization algorithm. Further, proposed algorithm compared with the genetic algorithm-based solution CoDiGA and particle swarm optimization-based solution iPSOA. Their comparative study showed that hybrid approach gives better performance. Liu et al. [13] proposed a branch and bound-based algorithm to resolve QoS-aware service composition problem. A universal QoS model was used for solution. A flexible constraint satisfaction framework was also developed.

Baird et al. [14] designed a flexible and self-adaptable workflow with the help of BPEL. Next-generation Workflow Toolkit (NeWT) supported runtime flexibility to BPEL. Lin et al. [15] proposed a relaxable QoS-based service selection algorithm

(RQSS) for a dynamic composition. The QoS attributes such as execution time, reliability, availability, reputation, and price-based service selection lead to a dynamic and flexible solution. WS-BPEL was used to demonstrate the RQSS with the implementation of a framework.

Wu et al. [16] gave a solution for the large-scale WSC. Firstly, the solution converts multi-dimensional QoS model into single objective multi-constraints problem. Then the Genetic Algorithm Embedded Local Searching (GAELS) solves the composition problem. Wu and Wang [17] proposed a Web-service global selection algorithm, which used a multi-objective genetic algorithm. The proposed algorithm also overcomes the limitations of local selection.

Bin et al. [18] proposed a model, which supports semantic data-links and QoS. The model provides efficient composition with End-to-End QoS. The approach uses greedy algorithm for optimal selection. Wang et al. [19] proposed an improved particle swarm optimization algorithm (iPSOA) for QoS-aware service selection and proposed a detailed strategy. Haung et al. [20] suggested single QoS-based service discovery and QoS-based optimization. The integrated programming and multiple criteria decision making approaches enable the discovery and optimization.

Various benchmarks taken in the literature are degree of dynamicity, QoS support, functional user preferences, compositional structure, fault handling, time complexity calculation, and testing over large dataset.

A comparison based on the benchmarks identifies the various approaches for WSOs. Table 1 gives the results of the comparison.

3   Discussion and the Issues for Web-Services Orchestration

WSC deploys various approaches, technologies, and tools. Although earlier studies provide good solutions for the WSCs, several gaps exist that need to be addressed. These gaps include the efficient dynamic composition, user's functional preferences, QoS support, compositional structure, efficient fault handling, reduced time complexity, and testing on the large datasets.

3.1   Efficient Dynamic Composition

Dynamic behavior during the composition leads to a faster composition, greater user interaction, and provides the results efficiently. Flexibility also achieves with the dynamic composition. Manual selection of services does not produce better results in the absence of automation. The literature review showed that many

Table 1 Comparison of orchestration approaches based on the different benchmarks

Approaches	Degree of dynamicity	QoS support	Functional user preference	Compositional structure	Fault handling	Time complexity calculation	Testing over large dataset
Liu et al. [6]	High	RT, REL, TP, Success rate	No	Sequence, conditional, parallel	No	No	Average
Chitra and Guptha [7]	High	RT, AVL, TP, REL, Successability, Latency	Yes	All	No	No	Yes
Mohamed et al. [8]	High	RT, EC	Yes	Sequential	No	No	Yes
Yu et al. [9]	Average	EC, RT, TP	No	Parallel	No	No	Yes
Mohamed et al. [10]	Average	Server availability, performance and load	No	Not mentioned	Yes	No	Yes
Arul and Prakash [11]	Average	No	Yes	Not mentioned	Yes	No	Yes
Zhao et al. [12]	Average	EC, RT, AVL, REL	No	All	No	No	Yes
Liu et al. [13]	High	EC, ED, REP, AVL, REL	No	All	No	Yes	Yes
Baird et al. [14]	High	RT, AVL, REL, EC	Yes	Linear	Yes	No	Average
Lin et al. [15]	Average	ET, REL, AVL, REP, EC	Yes	Sequence, conditional, parallel	Average	Yes	Average
Wu et al. [16]	Average	REP, EC, AVL	Yes	Sequence, conditional, parallel	No	No	Yes

(continued)

Table 1 (continued)

Approaches	Degree of dynamicity	QoS support	Functional user preference	Compositional structure	Fault handling	Time complexity calculation	Testing over large dataset
Wu and Wang [17]	High	EC, RT, REL, REP	No	Sequence, conditional, parallel	No	No	Yes
Bin et al. [18]	Average	RT, TP, AVL, REL, EC	Yes	Sequence, conditional, parallel	No	Yes	Yes
Wang et al. [19]	Average	EC, RT, AVL, REP	No	Sequential	No	No	Average
Haung et al. [20]	High	RT, AVL, REL, EC	Yes	All	No	Yes	Yes

RT Response time, *TP* Throughput, *AVL* Availability, *REL* Reliability, *EC* Execution cost, *REP* Reputation, *ET* Execution time, *ED* Execution duration

approaches are available to automate the composition process but some approaches [9–12, 15, 16, 18, 19] did not consider in degree of dynamicity.

3.2 User's Functional Preferences

The major problems, which associate with the automation, are selection and verification of a candidate service, which closely relate to the user requirements. Degree of dynamism increases with the selection of appropriate approach that is best suited to the user's requirement and produces more efficient results, which earlier available approaches [6, 9, 10, 12, 13, 17, 19] did not took into account.

3.3 QoS Support

The QoS deals with the non-functional properties of a particular service. The considerations of QoS parameters are important during the dynamic composition of Web-services. Most of the researchers considered the QoS parameters with their approaches to provide dynamic features. Current major researches [8, 9, 12, 14, 16–20] in the field of QoS are limited to the availability, response time, throughput, reputation, reliability, and execution cost of Web-services. The need exists to further take into account the advanced attributes.

3.4 Composing of Structure

Orchestration mechanism considers four basic structures when composing the Web-services: sequential, parallel, conditional, and loop. A hybrid structure, that is, a combination of these four basic structures is needed in the complex business processes. An efficient composition is thus required. Earlier approaches [6, 8, 9, 14–19] need to modify for consideration of hybrid compositions.

3.5 Efficient Fault Handling

Fault can arise in a Web-service at any stage of dynamic composition and can degrade the performance of the composition process. A reliable composition process should handle different kind of faults such as logic fault and network fault. Most of the currently available approaches [6–9, 12, 13, 16–20] need to incorporate a fault-handling module. Results more efficiently produced when providing reliability at the component as well as composition level.

3.6   Reducing Time Complexity

A measure of effectiveness of an approach is time complexity calculation. Most of the reviewed approaches [6–12, 14, 16, 17, 19] needed to consider time complexity calculation and those who calculated [13, 15, 18, 20] did not produce the efficiently. Searching for a large number of Web-services can increase time complexity badly. There should be some filtering mechanism to reduce search time complexity effectively.

3.7   Testing on the Large Datasets

Some composition processes work well for less number of Web-services. Results can fluctuate when test is applied on large number of datasets and services. Although most of the research work supported testing over large dataset yet, few of them needs to scale up the datasets for testing [6, 14, 15, 19]. Therefore, testing should be applied on the large dataset in order to produce the accurate results.

4   Proposed Orchestration Model

4.1   Functional Description of Modules

Figure 1 shows the proposed orchestration model that considers identified issues. The functional description of various modules defined in model is following:

Services UDDI Registry Module: Initially, all the atomic candidate services get registered in UDDI. Service interaction then takes place via this UDDI registry module only.

User Request Module: This module resolves an issue of *user's functional preferences* through designing of the user interfaces. A user places their runtime functional service request using the GUIs.

Functional Matchmaking Module: This module considers an issue of *reduced time complexity* by providing a Web-service filtration technique. Multiple service providers can have multiple functionally identical services. Searching for a user request for all the services will increase time complexity. The technique reduces searching process and leads to reduction in search time complexity. This module also achieves component level reliability through calculation of trust rate for each service provider. Functional preferences will be searched only for the trustworthy service provider's services.

Optimal Web-Service Selection Module: This module considers an issue of *QoS support* by enabling multiple QoS attributes. Multiple qualified services can fulfill user's functional requirements. This module calculates QoS attributes for

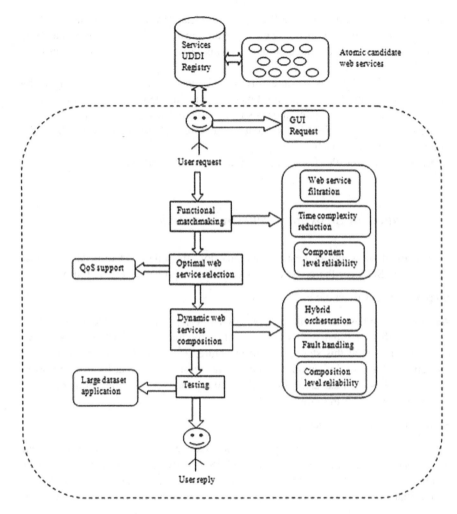

Fig. 1 Web-services orchestration model

each qualified service and dynamically selects one optimum service for user request. The major QoS considered are response time, throughput, availability, reliability, and execution cost for the Web-services and one additional parameter trust rate for service providers.

Dynamic Web-Services Composition Module: This module gives a solution of defined issues of *efficient dynamic composition* by using hybrid orchestration, *a compositional structure* by supporting all compositional structures, and *efficient fault handling* using composition-level reliability. The module adopts a dynamic orchestration mechanism for the WSCs and models a hybrid orchestration. A fault can arise in an atomic Web-service during composition process. A fault-handling module provides best alternate solution at this level to achieve composition-level reliability.

Testing Module: This module solves an issue of *testing on large dataset* by applying the approach in a specific business domain. Defined orchestration-based composition technique applies and tests using a large dataset business application of Electronic Supply Chain Management System (e-SCMS) in order to show the efficiency of the approach.

User Reply Module: User receives the requested composite service.

4.2 Sequential Steps for Orchestration Actions

Sequences of steps and orchestrator actions flow from the start to result in a final WSC in the SOA for the complex service business processes are as follows:

Step 1: Efficient dynamic composition

Action: An orchestrator will compose dynamically selected services of various tasks through an optimal Web-service selection module for e-SCMS at this step. An orchestrator used at this step is hybrid in nature. The hybrid orchestrator uses the concept of global optimization. Global optimization ensures that locally optimized atomic services selected using optimal module guarantees for the optimization of composite service at the global level.

Step 2: Composition structure

Action: The basic composition structures are sequential, parallel, conditional, and loop. A complex business process of e-SCMS can use any one these structures or combination of all depends on the nature of their tasks. Therefore, hybrid orchestration that is, combination of all basic composition structures is used at this step.

Step 3: Efficient fault handling

Action: The process of dynamic composition may fail if any atomic Web-service of any task of e-SCM fails to perform its functionality due to any kind of fault. The hybrid orchestrator will handle the fault efficiently by providing a fault-handling module at the composition level. The module will detect and recover faulty service by selecting alternate optimum service. The selected optimum service will be replaced by the faulty service and orchestrator will continue with the composition process. The user will receive an orchestrated composite service.

5 Conclusion

The major challenge in the present era of changing demand in WSC is to meet the customer satisfaction without any interruption. Dynamic and reliable WSC considers bridging the gap between these two fundamental requirements.

Present study highlights the advantages of orchestration. Although earlier researches provide the good solutions for the WSCs, several gaps exist that need to be addressed. These gaps include, for examples, the efficient dynamic composition, user's functional preferences, QoS support, and compositional structure, efficient fault handling, reduced time complexity, and testing on the large datasets.

A WSO model proposes sequences of steps and orchestrator actions for a WSC in the SOA for a complex service business processes. The model addresses the needed consideration during the WSCs.

References

1. Josuttis, N.M.: SOA in Practice: The Art of Distributed System Design. O'Reilly Media, Sebastopol, CA, USA (2007).
2. Rathore, M., Suman, U.: A Quality of Service Broker Based Process Model for Dynamic Web Service Composition. J. Comput. Sci. 7(8), 1267-1274 (2011).
3. Juric, M.B.: A Hands-on Introduction to BPEL http://www.oracle.com/technetwork/articles/matjaz-bpel1-090575.html.
4. Karande, A., Karande, M., Meshram, B.B.: Choreography and Orchestration using Business Process Execution Language for SOA with Web Services. Int. J. Comput. Sci. Issues 8(2), 224–232 (2011).
5. Albreshne, A., Fuhrer, P., Pasquier, J.: Web Services Orchestration and Composition. Working Paper (2009).
6. Liu, Z., Wang, H., Xu, X., Wang, Z.: Web services optimal composition based on improved artificial bee colony algorithm with the knowledge of service domain features. Int. J. Serv. Comput. 4(1), 27–38 (2016).
7. Chitra, A., Guptha, M.N.: QoS Aware Adaptive Service Composition. Res. J. Appl. Sci. Eng. Technol. 7(19), 4072–4078 (2014).
8. Mohamed, M., Amine, C.M., Amina, B.: Immune-inspired method for selecting the optimal solution in semantic web service composition. Int. J. Web Semant. Technol. 5(4), 21–31 (2014).
9. Yu, D., Li, C., Yin, Yu.: Optimizing web service composition for Data-intensive applications. Int. J. Database Theor. Appl. 7(2), 1–12 (2014).
10. Mohamed, M.F., ElYamany, H.F., Nassar, H.M.: A study of an adaptive replication framework for orchestrated composite web services. SpringerPlus 2, 511 (2013).
11. Arul, U., Prakash, D.S.: Towards Fault Handling In B2b Collaboration Using Orchestration Based Web Services Composition. Int. J. Emerg. Technol. Adv. Eng. 3(1), 388–394 (2013).
12. Zhao, X., Huang, P., Liu, T., Li, X.: A Hybrid Clonal Selection Algorithm for Quality of Service-Aware Web Service Selection Problem. Int. J. Innov. Comput. Inf. Control 8(12), 8527–8544 (2012).
13. Liu, M., Wang, M., Shen, W., Luo, N., Yan, J.: A quality of service (QoS)-aware execution plan selection approach for a service composition process. Future Gener. Comput. Syst. 28, 1080–1089 (2012).

14. Baird, R., Jorgenson, N., Gamble, R.: Self-adapting workflow reconfiguration. J. Syst. Softw. 84(3), 510–524 (2011).
15. Lin, C.F., Sheu, R.K., Chang, Y.S., Yuan, S.M.: A relaxable service selection algorithm for QoS-based web service composition. Inf. Softw. Technol. 53(12), 1370–1381(2011).
16. Wu, M., Xiong, X., Ying, J., Jin, C., Yu, C.: QoS-driven global optimization approach for large-scale web services composition. J. Comput. 6(7), 1452–1460 (2011).
17. Wu, Y., Wang, X.: Applying multi-objective genetic algorithms to QoS-aware web service global selection. Adv. Inf. Sci. Serv. Sci. 3(11), 473–482 (2011).
18. Bin, X., Sen, L., Yixin, Y.: Efficient Composition of Semantic Web Services with End-to-End QoS optimization. Tsinghua Sci. Technol. 15(6), 678–686 (2010).
19. Wang, W., Sun, Q., Zhao, X., Yang, F.: An improved particle swarm optimization algorithm for QoS-aware web service selection in service oriented communication. Int. J. Comput. Intell. Syst. 3(1), 18–30 (2010).
20. Haung, A.F.M., Lan, C.W., Yang, S.J.H.: An optimal QoS-based web service selection scheme. Inf. Sci. 179, 3309–3322 (2009).

Influence of Parameters in Multiple Sequence Alignment Methods for Protein Sequences

P. Manikandan and D. Ramyachitra

Abstract Protein sequence alignment is necessary to specify functions to unknown proteins. The alignment of protein sequences is used to determine the relatedness of organisms. Constructing a perfect multiple sequence alignment (MSA) for protein/ DNA sequences without having similarity is a difficult task in computational biology. Nucleotide and amino acid sequence are ordered with feasible alignment, and minimal quantity of gap values is treated by multiple sequence alignment that expresses to the evolutionary, structural, and functional relationships between the protein/DNA sequences. This research work compares the various multiple sequence alignments such as Artificial Bee Colony (ABC), Bacterial Foraging Optimization (BFO), and online MSA tools, namely T-Coffee, Clustal Omega, and Muscle to predict the best method for aligning the sequences. The parameters such as single and double shift for ABC algorithm and swim length for BFO algorithm have been analyzed using 19% gap penalty values. The experiments were examined on different protein sequences, and the final result proves that the BFO algorithm obtains better significant results as compared with the other methods.

Keywords Multiple sequence alignment · Artificial bee colony
Bacterial foraging optimization · T-Coffee · Clustal Omega · Muscle

1 Introduction

In computational biology, the multiple sequence alignment plays a fundamental problem to determine the relatedness between the organisms. And also the MSA is used to predict the similar proteins from different organisms to regulate the

P. Manikandan · D. Ramyachitra (✉)
Department of Computer Science, Bharathiar University,
Coimbatore 641046, Tamil Nadu, India
e-mail: jaichitra1@yahoo.co.in

P. Manikandan
e-mail: manimkn89@gmail.com

© Springer Nature Singapore Pte Ltd. 2018
P. K. Pattnaik et al. (eds.), *Progress in Computing, Analytics and Networking*,
Advances in Intelligent Systems and Computing 710,
https://doi.org/10.1007/978-981-10-7871-2_18

183

relationship [1]. For alignment of at least three protein/DNA sequences of equal length, multiple sequence alignment is utilized [2]. Applications of MSA include structure prediction, phylogenetic tree construction, sequence homology, functional site prediction, critical residue identification and so on. Several approaches have appeared to resolve the problem of multiple sequence alignment (MSA) including dynamic programing, progressive, iterative, stochastic, and the combinations between the approaches. In later years different techniques have been put into illuminate the inconvenience of multiple sequence alignment includes, ClustalW [3], Clustal-X [4], Match-Box [5], DIALIGN [6], T-Coffee [7], MUSCLE [2] and Clustal Omega [8], are based on the methodologies of progressive and iterative. To handle huge number of sequences, stochastic technique can be applied. The well-known approach of this technique is Gibbs sampling [9]. The optimization and evolutionary algorithms are also used to solve the MSA problems such as genetic algorithm [10], GAPM [11], MSA-GA [12], SAGA [13], ant colony optimization (ACO) [14], particle swarm optimization (PSO) [15, 16], artificial bee colony (ABC) [17], and genetic algorithm with ant colony optimization (GA-ACO) [18]. The remaining section of this research work is formulated as follows: The Sect. 2 explains the framework of MSA for the existing algorithms, Sect. 3 emphasizes the experimental outcomes for the benchmark databases, and finally, Sect. 4 spotlights the conclusion and gives the scope for further enhancement.

2   Methodology

In this research work, the existing algorithms such as ABC, BFO and online MSA tools, namely T-Coffee, Muscle, and Clustal Omega are compared to predict the best algorithm for multiple sequence alignment problems. Classically, the Sum of Pairs (SP) and Total Column Score (TCS) performance measures are used to find the optimal solution for the MSA problem. The multi-objective functions such as similarity, Non-Gap Percentage (NGP), and Gap Penalty (GP) are calculated for the existing algorithms such as ABC and BFO techniques. According to the objectives, the values of similarity and NGP have been maximized and the GP value is minimal for predicting the best optimal algorithm for MSA.

2.1   Optimization Techniques

This research work compares two optimization techniques such as ABC and BFO algorithms. And besides the performance measures have been compared with several online tools.

2.1.1 Artificial Bee Colony Algorithm

The swarm-based evolutionary algorithm named artificial bee colony algorithm is created by [19], and it is impelled by the clever actions of the honey bees. In ABC algorithm, the colony of bees is recognized as the population of entity, in which we get three cases of bees such as employed, onlooker, and watch [20]. The initial case of colony bees is employed to an exact food resource, and the second case of onlooker colony bees has stayed in the colony of bees and inspecting the hop of the employed colony bees with the aim of developing those food resources with huge quantity of nectar and lastly, the scout colony bees is in the direction of penetrating other food resources when a food resource turn out to be bushed.

2.1.2 Bacterial Foraging Optimization Algorithm

The BFO technique has several advantages concerning its local minima, route of the bacteria progress, attractant and repellent, randomness, swarming, etc. [21]. The parameters of BFO algorithm are optimized to characterize the location of bacteria. The parameters used in BFO algorithm are chemotaxis, swarming, reproduction, and elimination—dispersal. All the parameters in BFO algorithm are iterated when the greatest amount of elimination dispersal was achieved [22].

Aligning sequences $s_1, s_2, ...s_n$

Step 1: Elimination and Dispersal-k=k+1
Step 2: Bacteria Reproduction-m=m+1
Step 3: Chemotaxis phase-l=l+1
    i) For d=$s_1, s_2, ...s_n$ take chemotaxis step for all bacterium 'd'
    ii) Compute the fitness function
    iii) Tumble and move the bacterium using swim phase
Step 4: Continue the chemotaxis step up to the end of all the bacterium
Step 5: Reproduction Phase
Step 6: Increment the reproduction step
Step 7: Eliminate and Dispersal Phase

Algorithm 1: Pseudo code for the Bacterial Foraging Optimization (BFO) algorithm

The prediction of best position of gaps in MSA problems is a complicated problem in bioinformatics. Hence, the bacteria will hold the location of these gap values in every sequences of the dataset. The amount of dimensions for the bacteria will be identical to the amount of gap values required to be included to the protein/DNA sequences. The pseudocode of the bacterial foraging optimization algorithm is shown in Algorithm 1.

3   Experimental Results

In this research work, the algorithms are tested with the well-known benchmark datasets for analyzing the performance of the algorithms based on the effectiveness. In summation, the execution of the algorithms has been assessed by comparing the optimization techniques, namely artificial bee colony, bacterial foraging optimization, and existing online tools, namely T-Coffee, Muscle, and Clustal Omega.

3.1   Performance Measures

This research focuses on the performance measures such as the ratio of pairs correctly aligned namely sum of pairs (SP), the ratio of the columns correctly aligned namely total column score (TCS). The datasets that can be utilized for multiple sequence alignment are collected from different benchmark databases. Nine different datasets with specific enzyme are chosen. Based on the existing literature, 100 individuals are used as primary population range. The datasets used in this research work are reported in the Table 1.

Figures 1, 2, and 3 show the average result values for 19% of gap value and 300 numbers of generations. In this study, two types of trial outcomes are acquired, where the initial outcome is to compute the objective functions value such as similarity, GP and NGP for ABC and BFO. The subsequent one is to calculate the performance measure values such as SP and TCS. The algorithms have been carried out for 15 times as well as the average values are shown. For the optimization algorithms, different gap penalty values have been used to evaluate the functioning of the algorithms. The result shown in Figs. 1, 2, and 3 suggests that the BFO algorithm performs better than the ABC algorithm by using 19% gap penalty value.

Table 1 Datasets utilized in this experiment

Dataset	Classification	Total sequence	Shortest sequence length	Longest sequence length	Alignment length
1AU7	Binding protein	9	54	130	155
1NDH	Electron transport	11	71	270	321
1H3G	Hydrolase	28	79	597	710
1SER	Ligase	6	265	504	600
4ENL	Lyase	7	343	436	519
1DJN	Oxidoreductase	23	98	729	868
1BRU	Sereine	5	219	229	273
1OHV	Transferase	18	97	461	549
1B35	Virus	4	220	282	336

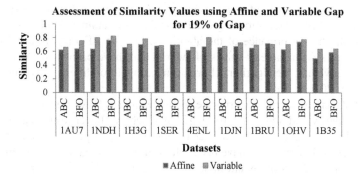

Fig. 1 Comparison of similarity values for the optimization algorithms with respect to affine and variable gap penalty

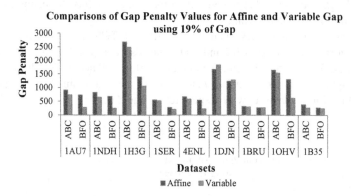

Fig. 2 Comparison of GP values for the optimization algorithms using affine and variable gap

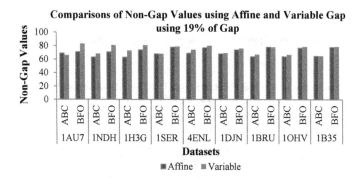

Fig. 3 Comparison of NGP values for the optimization algorithms with respect to affine and variable gap penalty

The experiment is carried out using different parameter values for the optimization algorithms. In ABC algorithm, single and double shift parameters have been used for analyzing the performance of the algorithm. For the BFO algorithm, forward and backward shift parameter values of swim length have been used. Also for all the parameter values, the algorithms have been executed for different iterations such as 5, 10, 15, 20, and 25%.

In initial iterations, the performance values cannot achieve better results such that the similarity and non-gap percentage value achieve lower results and the gap penalty achieves higher values. In later iterations, the gap penalty values lead to negative results. Better results have been achieved in 10% iteration with single shift parameter for ABC algorithm and forward shift parameter in BFO algorithm as the results shown in Figs. 1, 2, and 3. From the results, it is recognized that the bacterial foraging optimization (BFO) method accomplishes superior results than the ABC, for each multi-objective values. For all the MSA datasets, the BFO method gives more expert values for the similarity, GP, and NGP values. It is also established that the variable gap penalty value is better than the values attained by using an affine gap for similarity and NGP values.

The performance measures such as the SP and TCS are compared for the existing algorithms such as ABC and BFO and also compared with online tools. Figures 4 and 5 show the performance outcomes of the SP and TCS values at 19%. From the figures, it is accomplished that the BFO method attains superior performance values for all datasets with respect to SP and TCS.

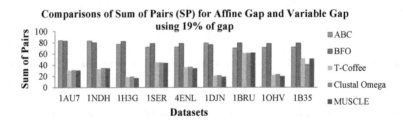

Fig. 4 Comparison of sum of pairs (SP) for the protein sequence datasets with 19% gap

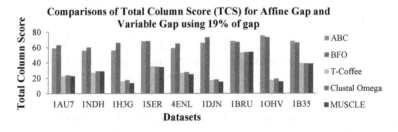

Fig. 5 Comparison of total column score (TCS) for the protein sequence datasets with 19% gap

Table 2 Statistical significance of the existing algorithms for the protein sequence dataset

	T-Coffee	Clustal Omega	MUSCLE	ABC	BFO
T-Coffee		0.139	0.097	0.008	0.008
Clustal Omega	0.028		0.173	0.008	0.008
MUSCLE	0.086	0.021		0.008	0.008
ABC	0.008	0.008	0.008		0.008
BFO	0.008	0.008	0.008	0.011	

Every performance measure value is oscillated during the first four runs of the research. In the afterward runs, consistency values were observed for the performance measures. The final stage yields the statistical significance of the BFO algorithm which is calculated using the Wilcoxon matched-pair signed-rank test for every pair of techniques by utilizing significant confidence level of 5% (P-value < 0.05). Each entry in the Table 2 consists of P-value allocated by Wilcoxon matched-pair signed-rank test for the divergence between the pair of methods. The upper right corner of the matrix is attained from SP score, and the lower left corner is obtained from TCS score.

4 Conclusion and Future Enhancement

In the modern universe, MSA problems are an open problem for the researchers involved in the field of computational biology. The goal of this study is to evaluate the optimization algorithms such as ABC and BFO and discovering the ways to additional progress its performance to accomplish finest solution. After careful study of the existing algorithms, this study suggests that the BFO algorithm can be enhanced to perform MSA and express the outcome toward a finest result. The multi-objective technique is applied to resolve the MSA crisis which minimizes the value of GP and maximizes the similarity, NGP, which goes to the Pareto—optimal result. The statistical implication is computed to evaluate the significance of the algorithms. From the experimental analysis, it is exposed that the BFO algorithm does better than the other algorithm in terms of all multi-objectives and performance measures. In future, the BFO algorithm can be blended or run with additional evolutionary algorithm to acquire the finest outcomes. Several objective functions might be initiated to find most tremendous outcomes of MSA.

Acknowledgements The authors are thankful to the DST, New Delhi, India (Grant Number: DST/INSPIRE Fellowship/2015/IF150093) for the financial grant under INSPIRE Fellowship scheme for this work.

References

1. Keehyoung Joo, et al. Multiple Sequence Alignment by Conformational Space Annealing. Biophys J. 2008 Nov 15;95(10):4813–9.
2. Robert C. Edgar. MUSCLE: multiple sequence alignment with high accuracy and high throughput. Nucleic Acids Res. 2004 Mar 19;32(5):1792–7.
3. J D Thompson, D G Higgins, and T J Gibson. CLUSTAL W: improving the sensitivity of progressive multiple sequence alignment through sequence weighting, position-specific gap penalties and weight matrix choice. Nucleic Acids Res. 1994 Nov 11;22(22): 4673–4680.
4. Julie D. Thompson, Toby J. Gibson, Frédéric Plewniak, François Jeanmougin, Desmond G. Higgins. The CLUSTAL_X windows interface: flexible strategies for multiple sequence alignment aided by quality analysis tools. Nucleic Acids Res. 1997 Dec 15;25(24):4876–82.
5. Depiereux E, Baudoux G, Briffeuil P, Reginster I, De Bolle X, Vinals C, Feytmans E. Match-Box_server: a multiple sequence alignment tool placing emphasis on reliability. Comput Appl Biosci. 1997 Jun;13(3):249–56.
6. B. Morgenstern, K. Frech, A. Dress, T. Werner. DIALIGN: finding local similarities by multiple sequence alignment. Bioinformatics, (Apr. 1998), 14 (3), pp. 290–294.
7. Cedric Notredame, Desmond G Higgins, Jaap Heringa. T-coffee: a novel method for fast and accurate multiple sequence alignment. J Mol Biol. 2000 Sep 8; 302(1):205–17.
8. Sievers F, Higgins DG. Clustal Omega, accurate alignment of very large numbers of sequences. Methods Mol Biol. 2014; 1079:105–16.
9. Lawrence, et al., Detecting subtle sequence signals: a Gibbs sampling strategy for multiple alignment. Science. 1993 Oct 8;262(5131):208–14.
10. Marco Botta, Guido Negro. Multiple Sequence Alignment with Genetic Algorithms. Computational Intelligence Methods for Bioinformatics and Biostatistics: 6th International Meeting, CIBB 2009, Genoa, Italy, October 15–17, Springer chapter, Volume 6160, pp 206–214.
11. F. Naznin, R. Sarker, D. Essam. Progressive alignment method using genetic algorithm for multiple sequence alignment. IEEE Trans. Evolutionary. Computation. 2012 Oct 16 (5): 615–631.
12. Ruchi Gupta, Dr. Pankaj Agarwal, Dr. A. K. Soni. MSA-GA: Multiple Sequence Alignment Tool Based On Genetic Approach. International Journal Of Soft Computing And Software Engineering, 2013 Aug 3(8): 1–11.
13. Cédric Notredame, Desmond G. Higgins. SAGA: sequence alignment by genetic algorithm. Nucleic Acids Res. 1996 Apr 15;24(8): 1515–1524.
14. Simeon Tsvetanov, Desislava Ivanova, Boris Zografov. Ant Colony Optimization Applied for Multiple Sequence Alignment. Biomath communications, 2015 Jun 2(1):599–1.
15. Fasheng Xu, Yuehui Chen. A Method for Multiple Sequence Alignment Based on Particle Swarm Optimization. Springer Chapter, Emerging Intelligent Computing Technology and Applications. With Aspects of Artificial Intelligence, 2009. Volume 5755: 965–973.
16. Long HX, Xu WB, Sun J. Binary Particle Swarm Optimization algorithm with mutation for multiple sequence alignment. Rivista di Biologia. 2009 Jan–Apr;102(1):75–94.
17. Xiujuan Lei, Jingjing Sun, Xiaojun Xu, Ling Guo. Artificial bee colony algorithm for solving multiple sequence alignment. IEEE Fifth International Conference on Bio-Inspired Computing: Theories and Applications (BIC-TA), 2010, https://doi.org/10.1109/bicta.2010.5645304.
18. Zne-Jung Lee, Shun-Feng Su, Chen-Chia Chuang, Kuan-Hung Liu. Genetic algorithm with ant colony optimization (GA-ACO) for multiple sequence alignment. Applied Soft Computing 8 (2008) 55–78.
19. D. Karaboga. An Idea Based on Honey Bee Swarm for Numerical Optimization. Technical report-tr06, Erciyes University, Engineering Faculty, Computer Engineering Department (2005).

20. Álvaro Rubio-Largo, Miguel A.Vega-Rodríguez, David L.González-Álvarez. Hybrid multi-objective artificial bee colony for multiple sequence alignment, Applied Soft Computing, 2016 Apr 41:157–168.
21. R. Ranjani Rani & D. Ramyachitra. Multiple sequence alignment using multi-objective based bacterial foraging optimization algorithm. Biosystems. 2016 Dec;150:177–189.
22. Passino,K.M., 2010. Bacterial foraging optimization. Int. J. Swarm Intell. Res. 2010. 1 (1), 1–16.

Analyzing Cloud Computing Security Issues and Challenges

Neeti Mehra, Shalu Aggarwal, Ankita Shokeen and Deepa Bura

Abstract Cloud computing is the model of computing based on Internet. This is used for completing the computer's need by providing necessary data and computer resources. Most of the companies use cloud computing for avoiding the purchasing cost of servers. Therefore, it becomes essential to study various issues associated with cloud computing. One of major issues that industries face is security issue. In this paper, we aim to study various key attributes of cloud computing, important characteristics of cloud model. Further, the paper discusses security issues, limitations of existing approach, and possible solutions associated with cloud computing approach.

Keywords Cloud computing · Security issues · Services over Internet

1 Introduction

Cloud computing is referred to as delivery of services over Web. It is a technology which provides extra resources to the industries. Most of the companies use cloud computing for avoiding the purchasing cost of servers. In 2009, cloud computing became more popular because it provided high capability of storage ability for data which in turn reduced the cost of computer resources and increased the performance of computers. It is a platform over which the communication is done between the

N. Mehra · S. Aggarwal · A. Shokeen · D. Bura (✉)
Faculty of Engineering and Technology, Department of Computer Science & Engineering,
Manav Rachna International University, Faridabad, India
e-mail: deepa.fet@mriu.edu.in

N. Mehra
e-mail: neetimehra23@gmail.com

S. Aggarwal
e-mail: aggarwalchahak1997@gmail.com

A. Shokeen
e-mail: ankitashokeen28596@gmail.com

© Springer Nature Singapore Pte Ltd. 2018
P. K. Pattnaik et al. (eds.), *Progress in Computing, Analytics and Networking*,
Advances in Intelligent Systems and Computing 710,
https://doi.org/10.1007/978-981-10-7871-2_19

clients and server application by using Internet. This process involves abstraction between the resources of computers and their low-level structure. The existence of this platform is not physical; however, it is logical. The platform is based on the concept of virtualization. Cloud computing is also known as big storage platform that is shared by many users. Most of the companies adopted this platform due to the benefits like high level of manageability, reduced cost of hardware, full utilization of resources, improved flexibility. It was examined that 76% of institutes used cloud computing for storing their records in cloud and 35% of institutes have 1TB of data which was uploaded to the cloud and 43% of high level of institutes solved the problem of cloud computing by using some existing technologies [1]. For emphasizing the concept of cloud computing, paper discusses various issues and challenges associated with cloud computing.

2 Related Work

For representing the Internet as a metaphor in network diagrams, the term of cloud was made [2]. The Internet-based computing services are provided by the cloud computing. By using the existing technologies of cloud computing such as grid computing and virtualization, the technical meaning of Internet is increased and distributed among the computing technology. During the interaction of systems, applications, and end users, the virtualization hides the complexity of cloud computing by providing characteristics of resources. With the help of grid computing, the users can access the computers and data without the knowledge of operating system, locations, and account administration. The cloud computing has its own distinct characteristics and also shares some of the characteristics with grid computing and virtualization [3]. Application service provision (ASP) provides the numerous definitions of cloud computing that are used for the business over the Internet in the IT models [4]. HP provided the definition of cloud computing as "Everything as a Service" [5], whereas Microsoft provided the importance of cloud computing of the end user and also give the value of cloud computing [6]. T-Systems define the cloud computing according to their bandwidths, software, and infrastructure or utility also under the condition of services. These components are used according to the needs of users, availability and the security of cloud computing between the end-to-end service level agreements (SLAs), and the dependent services of users [7]. The National Institute of Standards and Technology (NIST) said, the cloud computing is a model that shred the resources' according to the demand of users [8]. According to the IT executives, the security of cloud computing is collecting from 263 IT professional by discussing the questions related to the cloud computing and executives also worried about the security [9]. Nowadays, the use of cloud computing has become the first priority by the customer in the technical field [10].

3   Assets and Liabilities of Cloud

Though many business enterprises are shifting its data on the cloud to get the benefits of less cost and less maintenance, cloud computing comes with certain liabilities as threats also as shown below in Fig. 1:

1. Cost Savings: With cloud computing, no in-house application or server storage is required, substantial capital costs can be saved. According to M. Armbrust study, to finish computations faster, "cost associativity" of cloud computing can be used by the organizations that perform batch analytics that uses 1000 EC2 machines for 1 h instead of using 1 machine for 1000 h [11].
2. Manageability: Enhanced and simplified IT management with maintenance capabilities are provided by cloud computing through service level agreement. As the service providers maintain all resources, updates and maintenance of IT infrastructure are eliminated.
3. Disaster Recovery: All size of businesses, small or big, invests in vigorous disaster recovery. As expressed by Aberdeen group, to implement cloud-based backup and recovery solutions, small businesses are twice of larger companies, that rolls up a third party expertise as part of deal, avoid large investment and saves time. Gharat in 2015 gave some mechanisms that were used during disaster recovery techniques so that back up the data can be recovered by some mechanisms [12]. Some of the backup sites explained were: Hot backup site, Cool backup site, Warm backup site.
4. Reliability and Flexibility: As compared to in-house IT infrastructure, cloud computing provides much more reliable services. Sultan in 2011 described that to manage the company's projects and to make it reliable and flexible, a software named Scrum Wall was developed which used a Microsoft Animation Technology called Silverlight. This software attracted customer's interest which encouraged them to use Windows Azure in order to make it a hosted service [2].
5. A3 services: Cloud gives A3 (Anywhere, Anytime, Anyplace) services. Cloud offers services which can be availed anytime, which adds on to the benefits of cloud computing.

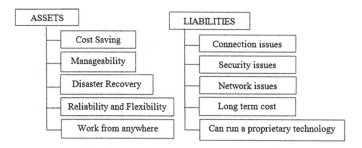

Fig. 1 Assets and liabilities of cloud computing

One of the major bottlenecks in cloud computing is bandwidth problem faced by organizations who switched from local networked applications to cloud-based applications in addition to the concern about attacks on the cloud infrastructure which may creep in after shifting the valuable data on cloud.

4 Challenges in Cloud Computing

As discussed cloud computing suffers from several issues such as connection, security and organizations enjoying its benefits also face certain challenges as well. Figure 2 shows some of the challenges that business enterprises encounter:

1. Migration of Virtual Machine (VMM): Virtualization provides several benefits by enabling Virtual Machine Migration. Currently, during the detection of workload hotspots and initiating a migration, there is a lack of agility in response to sudden workload changes. Voorslyus et al. have performed a model that is used to analyze the negative impact, when the application is running in virtual machine during the migration and designed benchmark architecture for reducing the effect of migration in virtual machine [13].
2. Authentication and Identity Management: By using different identity tokens and negotiation protocols, interoperability drawbacks arise in Identity Management (IDM). Gopalakrishnan et al. introduced a openID mechanisms to overcome the authentication problem in the cloud [14]. Nuñez et al. give the Federated Identity Management (FIM) that is used for reducing the negative impact of identity and authentication management problem in cloud [15].
3. Trust Management and Policy Integration: The challenges such as policy evaluation management, semantic heterogeneity, and secure interoperability should be addressed by cloud's policy integration tasks. Takabi et al. proposed the semantic-based policy management framework that is used for solving the policy integration problem in cloud computing [16]. Vaquero et al. tells us about the virtual TPM that are developed by IBM at the time of facing that challenge [17].
4. Secure-Service Management: Security is major concern in cloud computing, mainly service providers use Web Services Description language, but this

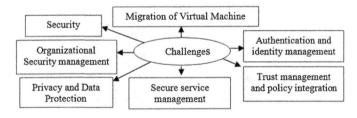

Fig. 2 Challenges in cloud computing

language also does not fulfill the security requirements of customers. Sabahi et al. tells us about the use of virtual machines that helps to overcome this problem by using ARP spoofing [18].

5. Privacy and Data Protection: All security solutions must be embedded by privacy-protection mechanisms. Sasse et al. explained the privacy penetration testing for the protection of data in cloud [19]. Squicciarini et al. introduced the auditing or monitoring techniques for resolving the protection problem. Wood et al. discussed that US Safe Harbor Privacy protocol is also used for the data protection in cloud [20].

6. Organizational Security Management: If this issue is not properly addressed, it becomes a major issue. Fears can also be raised by depending on external entities about disaster recovery plans and timely responses to security incidents. Kretzschmar et al. presented the organizational security policy and interoperability challenges based on cloud for managing the organizational security [21].

7. Security: Security solutions vary from cryptographic techniques, public key infrastructure (PKI) to use of multiple cloud providers, that leads to improvement of virtual machine support. Wang et al. discussed the client data privacy policy for the security of cloud [22].

5   Cloud Computing Threats and Their Effects

This section discusses various threats and their issues faced in cloud computing environment (Table 1).

In 2013, CLOUD SECURITY ALLIANCE (CSA) reported nine major threats of security based on the cloud computing, which are discussed below:

1. **Data Breaches**—Most of the organization that store their data in cloud, lost their sensitive information and data to their competitor organization. Chou et al. surveyed data breaches involved the malicious attack up to the 37% [23]. Srinivasan et al. by the malicious attack, data breaches are increased up to 26% in the cloud [24].

2. **Data Loss**—The data of any customer will be loosed by some natural hazards like earthquake and fire. Information can be shared between different equipment in cloud such that the problem of data can be solved and the cloud computing gives the dependable data storage center for the users [25].

3. **Account or Service Traffic Hijacking**—For avoiding this major security problem of data, the individuals and the authorities protected their data references and password and sharing them only between the users and services. Some other techniques are also used for protecting the data.

4. **Insecure Interfaces and APIs**—It is important to secure the software interfaces and APIs by using encryption key of data and authentication.

Table 1 Cloud computing threats and their effects

Threats	Effect	Limitations	Solutions
Data breaches	The data lost automatically, if the user lost their encryption key of that data	If and only if workload is parallelizable, then compute power is elastic. Data is replicated and stored at untrusted host	One can craft an encryption policy and enforce it. We can perform vulnerability assessments
Data loss	Due to the problem of security, user lost their personal data	One can never get back the data that is once lost. And data blows up in processing	Data can be prevented by end-to-end encryption
Account or service hijacking	It occurs when one of the users accesses another user's data password and their information of account	It may lead the client to redirect to illegitimate Website	It can be controlled by adopting security policies and strong authentication
Insecure interfaces and APIs	Used API and software interfaces to protect the data between users and the providers	It allows unauthorized access to services and improper use of API's would often result in clear-text authentication, Tx of content, improper authorizations and many more	It can be controlled and protected by ensuring strong authentication and encrypted transmission
Denial of service	System resources became slowdown by attackers, that is why response time became slow and the users only wait for their work	It overwhelms the victim resources and makes it difficult rather impossible for the legitimate users to use them	One can provide control and monitoring system on offered services
Malicious insider	It contained all the data and references when the security has not well managed	It can manipulate data and can destroy the whole infrastructure. Systems are at greater risk that depends on Cloud service provider for security	Can provide transparency to management and breach notification can be used
Abuse of cloud services	Sharing the servers makes easy release of key for attackers	These types of threats are challenging to address. Due to large traffic between sites, attackers take advantage of this	Registration and authentication should be stronger

(continued)

Table 1 (continued)

Threats	Effect	Limitations	Solutions
Insufficient due diligence	Many authorities adopted the cloud services, but they are unknown for the problem of security and the knowledge of cloud	If a company's development team lacks familiarity with cloud technologies, architectural and infrastructural issues can arise	CSA can remind organization that they must perform due diligence so that they understand the risk
Shared technology vulnerabilities	By sharing the platform of cloud and software, a single user does not impact for another tenant	An error in a single integral component, it can destroy the entire environment to potential breach and compromise	Strong authentication and can inspect vulnerability and configuration

5. **Denial of Service (DOS)**—The problem of Denial of service (DOS) is increased day by day due to the effective characteristics of cloud computing. The vulnerability of DOS exists across all the platform of SDN [26].

6. **Malicious Insiders**—People who have authorized access to an organization's network system or data can be a threat to an organization and are known as malicious insider. Rocha et al. suggested to use cryptographic techniques for protecting the data from unauthorized users in the cloud [27].

7. **Abuse of Cloud Services**—Cloud computing shares the resources between many users, that is why the organization does not purchase any resources and also reduced the maintaining cost of resources.

8. **Insufficient Due Diligence**—Without the knowledge of cloud computing, many organizations purchased the platform of cloud and suffered from many problems of security risks.

9. **Shared Technology Vulnerability**—Most of the components like CPU CACHES, GPUs are not capable for multi-tenant and these components do not offer the isolation for multiple deployments.

5.1 Possible Solutions

Many technologies, concept, application, and methods are used for protecting the cloud infrastructure and the servers of cloud. The four-layered framework is needed for securing the cloud. The first layer of framework is used for securing the layer of virtual machine in cloud. Second framework layer is used for the storage of data. This layer is used to build up the virtual storage system. The fourth and last layer is used for connecting the solution of both software and hardware in first layer of framework to control the problem of cloud.

For public security of cloud, some tricks are used at the time when security solution transferred from the services to the users.

Verify the Access Control—Apply the data in correct manner and then checked and control the data by service providers of cloud, at the time when the cloud user used that data. Consumer implements that data and the service of cloud protect the data from unauthorized users.

Control the Consumer Access Devices—The devices that are used by users must be secure. By the security, it is possible to secure the loss of devices and maintain the functioning and features of the devices by the cloud computing users.

Monitor the Data Access—Cloud providers monitored that whom, when, and what the data is used.

6 Conclusion

In this paper, we discussed about security threats include network security, application security, data security. The main agenda is to safely store and handle data that is not managed by the owner of the data. By reading this paper, we conclude that the security issues associated with cloud computing should be handled properly and cannot be taken for granted. The security of the data should be perfectly verified and encrypted. One of the major security issues with the cloud computing model is distribution of services. The cloud suppliers need to educate their customers that they are providing them with suitable security measures that will help to secure the data of their customer and also help in gaining confidence for their service. There is one way through which they can attain this, is through the use of third-party auditors or listeners. The new security abilities required to be advanced and more developed, whereas the older security abilities required be modifying or altering completely to be able to perform or work with the clouds architecture. Plugging in security technology which already exists will not work as this new delivery model brings new changes to the way in which one can utilize and access computer resources. There are many other security challenges which include security outlook of virtualization. We believe that because of several complications and difficulties of the cloud, it will be difficult to attain end-to-end security. However, the challenges we face is to ensure safer performance even if some parts of cloud fail. For most of the software, we not only need information assurance but also mission assurance. Therefore, raising trust applications from the untrusted constituents will be a major or main aspect with respect to the cloud security.

Acknowledgements Authors would like to express the gratitude Dr. Kiran Khatter, Research Mentor of CL Educate—Accendere Knowledge Management Services Pvt. Ltd. for her constant guidance and comments on an earlier version of the manuscript. Although any errors are our own and should not tarnish the reputations of these esteemed persons.

References

1. Singh, H. (2015). A Review Of Cloud Computing Security Issues. International Journal Of Education And Management Engineering (Ijeme), 5(5), 32.
2. Sultan, N. A. (2011). Reaching for the "cloud": How SMEs can manage. International journal of information management, 31(3), 272–278.
3. Weinhardt, C., Anandasivam, A., Blau, B., Borissov, N., Meinl, T., Michalk, W., & Stößer, J. (2009). Cloud computing–a classification, business models, and research directions. Business & Information Systems Engineering, 1(5), 391–399.
4. Susarla, A., Barua, A., & Whinston, A. B. (2003). Understanding the service component of application service provision: empirical analysis of satisfaction with ASP services. MIS quarterly, 27(1), 91–123.
5. Robison, S. (2008). The next wave: Everything as a service. Executive Viewpoint: www.hp. com.
6. Wang, B., & Xing, H. (2011, June). The application of cloud computing in education informatization. In Computer Science and Service System (CSSS), 2011 International Conference on (pp. 2673–2676). IEEE.
7. El-Gazzar, R. F. (2014, June). A literature review on cloud computing adoption issues in enterprises. In International Working Conference on Transfer and Diffusion of IT (pp. 214–242). Springer, Berlin, Heidelberg.
8. Mell, P., & Grance, T. (2011). The NIST definition of cloud computing.
9. Alvi, F. A., Choudary, B. S., Jaferry, N., & Pathan, E. (2012). Review on cloud computing security issues & challenges. iaesjournal.com, 2.
10. Zhang, S., Zhang, S., Chen, X., & Huo, X. (2010, January). Cloud computing research and development trend. In Future Networks, 2010. ICFN'10. Second International Conference on (pp. 93–97). Ieee.
11. Armbrust, M., Fox, A., Griffith, R., Joseph, A. D., Katz, R., Konwinski, A., ... & Zaharia, M. (2010). A view of cloud computing. Communications of the ACM, 53(4), 50–58.
12. Gharat, M. A. A., & Mhamunkar, M. D. E. Disaster Recovery in Cloud Computing.
13. Voorsluys, W, Broberg, J, Venugopal, S, Buyya, R. (2009) Cost of virtual machine live migration in clouds: A performance evaluation. Proceedings of the 1st International Conference on Cloud Computing (CloudCom 2009), Springer, Beijing, China, 33.
14. Gopalakrishnan, A. (2009). Cloud computing identity management. SETLabs briefings, 7(7), 45–54.
15. Nuñez, D., & Agudo, I. (2014). BlindIdM: A privacy-preserving approach for identity management as a service. International Journal of Information Security, 13(2), 199–215.
16. Takabi, H., & Joshi, J. B. (2012). Semantic-based policy management for cloud computing environments. International Journal of Cloud Computing, 1(2–3), 119–144.
17. Vaquero, L. M., Rodero-Merino, L., & Morán, D. (2011). Locking the sky: a survey on IaaS cloud security. Computing, 91(1), 93–118.
18. Sabahi, F. (2011, May). Cloud computing security threats and responses. In Communication Software and Networks (ICCSN), 2011 IEEE 3rd International Conference on (pp. 245–249). IEEE.
19. Probst, C. W., Sasse, M. A., Pieters, W., Dimkov, T., Luysterborg, E., & Arnaud, M. (2012). Privacy penetration testing: How to establish trust in your cloud provider. In European Data Protection: In Good Health? (pp. 251–265). Springer Netherlands.
20. Squicciarini, A., Sundareswaran, S., & Lin, D. (2010, July). Preventing information leakage from indexing in the cloud. In Cloud Computing (CLOUD), 2010 IEEE 3rd International Conference on (pp. 188–195). IEEE.
21. Kretzschmar, M., & Hanigk, S. (2010, October). Security management interoperability challenges for collaborative clouds. In Systems and Virtualization Management (SVM), 2010 4th International DMTF Academic Alliance Workshop on (pp. 43–49). IEEE.

22. Wang, Q., Wang, C., Li, J., Ren, K., & Lou, W. (2009, September). Enabling public verifiability and data dynamics for storage security in cloud computing. In European symposium on research in computer security (pp. 355–370). Springer Berlin Heidelberg.
23. Chou, T. S. (2013). Security threats on cloud computing vulnerabilities. International Journal of Computer Science & Information Technology, 5(3), 79.
24. Srinivasan, M. K., Sarukesi, K., Rodrigues, P., Manoj, M. S., & Revathy, P. (2012, August). State-of-the-art cloud computing security taxonomies: a classification of security challenges in the present cloud computing environment. In Proceedings of the international conference on advances in computing, communications and informatics (pp. 470–476). ACM.
25. Zhang, S., Zhang, S., Chen, X., & Huo, X. (2010, January). Cloud computing research and development trend. In Future Networks, 2010. ICFN'10. Second International Conference on (pp. 93–97). Ieee. Account and service hacking.
26. Yan, Q., Yu, F. R., Gong, Q., & Li, J. (2016). Software-defined networking (SDN) and distributed denial of service (DDoS) attacks in cloud computing environments: A survey, some research issues, and challenges. IEEE Communications Surveys & Tutorials, 18(1), 602–622.
27. Rocha, F., Gross, T., & van Moorsel, A. (2013, March). Defense-in-depth against malicious insiders in the cloud. In Cloud Engineering (IC2E), 2013 IEEE International Conference on (pp. 88–97). IEEE.

An Online Review-Based Hotel Selection Process Using Intuitionistic Fuzzy TOPSIS Method

Saikat Pahari, Dhrubajyoti Ghosh and Anita Pal

Abstract Nowadays, online review on tourism Web site to select hotels has a great impact on hotel industry. According to existing studies, it is highly likely that the decisions of tourists will be modified after browsing the online reviews given by other tourists on tourism Web site. How to utilize the online reviews on tourism Web site to select hotels and help tourists is a problem to be investigated. Online reviews of one hotel have been given by different previous tourists with respect to different criteria; hence, each tourist can be treated as a decision maker. The problem of selecting hotels based on these online reviews on tourism Web site is a multicriteria decision-making (MCDM) problem. TOPSIS is a widely used method for MCDM problem. We have used this method combined with intuitionistic fuzzy set to choose a suitable hotel. Finally, a numerical example with a case study of TripAdvisor.com is conducted for hotel selection to illustrate the function of intuitionistic fuzzy TOPSIS method.

Keywords Multicriteria decision making · Hotel selection · Intuitionistic fuzzy set · TOPSIS

S. Pahari (✉) · D. Ghosh
Department of Computer Science & Engineering, OmDayal Group of Institutions,
Howrah, India
e-mail: saikat.pahari@gmail.com

D. Ghosh
e-mail: krizz27@gmail.com

A. Pal
Department of Mathematics, National Institute of Technology, Durgapur, India
e-mail: anita.buie@gmail.com

© Springer Nature Singapore Pte Ltd. 2018
P. K. Pattnaik et al. (eds.), *Progress in Computing, Analytics and Networking*,
Advances in Intelligent Systems and Computing 710,
https://doi.org/10.1007/978-981-10-7871-2_20

1 Introduction

With the advancement of information technology, people are getting help from Internet almost all situations in their daily life [1]. Tourists are also following the same. When a tourist wants to go for a tour, they would make a plan beforehand [2, 3]. For this, they browse online reviews to select a particular hotel. However, online reviews given by other tourists have both positive and negative impacts on choosing hotels [4]. While choosing a hotel, a huge number of reviews may increase the difficulty in the process of choosing the appropriate hotels [5, 6]. Then how to select hotels on a tourism Web site based on online reviews would be a question worthy of study. This is because (a) several decision makers participate and give their opinions, (b) decision-making process is multidimensional, and (c) the requirement for effectively modeling imprecision is inherent in the decision-making process. On the other hand, hotels are also greatly affected by the reviews of the previous tourists. So, for successful dealing with the hotel selection problem, structured approaches are desirable.

Online reviews have become significantly important in the process of making decision, especially when consumers are unable to judge a product or service by themselves. Chatterjee [7] found that reviews of online affect the decisions of consumers who read them. Gretzel et al. [8] found that tourists would plan their trips four or more months in advance. Also, they enjoy this process of browsing the reviews on the Web site, which was an important part of planning their trips. Ngai et al. [9] proposed a hotel advisory system (HAS) using fuzzy logic to help tourists in selecting hotel. As several criteria are considered and several decision makers are giving remarks in the decision process, so it can be considered as multicriteria decision-making (MCDM) method. Various MCDM approaches are considered to choose optimal alternative [10–14]. Hung et al. [15] proposed a decision-making trial and evaluation laboratory (DEMATEL) to evaluate and develop expert services of marketing which is a hybrid MCDM model. Peng et al. [16] proposed an MCDM method based on fuzzy preference ranking organization method for enrichment evaluations (PROMETHEE) to rank alternative products based on online customer reviews of products. Zhang et al. [17] used social information for tourists on TripAdvisor.com for restaurant decision support model.

The main challenge to work with online review data is as follows:

1. Dataset is not normalized; for example, number of users who have given reviews are different for different hotels (alternatives).
2. Users are opting for different options (criteria) for different hotels.
3. Different decision group contain different number of users (decision makers) for different hotels.

In our paper, we have used a multicriteria group decision-making model based on intuitionistic fuzzy TOPSIS method based on online reviews for hotel selection problem. Each decision-making group includes many decision makers (users). The importance of the decision-making group and the impact of criteria on alternatives (hotels) provided by decision makers are complicated to accurately express by crisp data in the process of hotel selection. Intuitionistic fuzzy sets introduced by Atanassov [18] can precisely deal these issues, and hence, it is used for various decision-making problems under a hesitant situation. Aggregation of user opinions to form a group opinion is very important for proper assessment method. Hence, IFWA operator is used to combine all decision makers' opinion to form a group opinion for rating the importance of criteria and the alternatives. One widely used method to solve multicriteria decision problem is TOPSIS method which considers both ideal and negative-ideal solution. When TOPSIS is combined with intuitionistic fuzzy set, then the result is expected to be more accurate.

This paper is organized as follows. Section 2 presents proposed intuitionistic fuzzy TOPSIS model. In Sect. 3, a numerical example with a case study of Trip Advisor is established. Finally, Sect. 4 ends with the conclusion of this paper.

2 Intuitionistic Fuzzy TOPSIS Method for Hotel Selection Based on Online Review

Online reviews are given by past tourists who have already stayed in a particular hotel for some time. Based on the experience, they give their opinion. Users of any online system are of various categories such as family, friends, couples. They are decision-making groups. Users of a group give a rating in linguistic term for various criteria such as food quality, room service, location. We have assumed that all group will give reviews for a common set of criteria.

Let the set of alternatives (hotels) be denoted as $A = \{A_1, A_2, …, A_m\}$ and set of criteria denoted as $X = \{X_1, X_2, …, X_n\}$, and then, the proposed TOPSIS method combined with intuitionistic fuzzy set is described below:

Step 1: Cumulated intuitionistic fuzzy rating matrix for each linguistic term for any decision-making group for rating the alternatives is determined.

Say n_{ki} is number of user of ith linguistic term in any decision-making group k; giving decision in any of t number of linguistic options, then weight of decision-making group k is obtained by

$$w_{km} = \frac{n_{k,i}}{\sum_{i=1}^{t} n_{k,i}} \tag{1}$$

Let (μ_j, ϑ_j) be IFN for any linguistic value used for rating the alternatives. Then, the cumulated IFN f_w for each decision-making group is obtained by using intuitionistic fuzzy-weighted averaging operator [19].

$$f_w(\mu_j, \vartheta_j) = \left(1 - \prod_{k=1}^{t} \left(1 - \mu_{ij}^{(k)}\right)^{w_k}, \prod_{k=1}^{t} \left(v_{ij}^{(k)}\right)^{w_k}\right) \tag{2}$$

Step 2: Decision makers' weights are determined as follows.

Let there are l decision-making group. Linguistic terms expressed in intuitionistic fuzzy numbers are used to denote the importance of the decision group.

Say $D_k = [\pi_k, v_k, \mu_k]$ be an intuitionistic fuzzy number for a rating of kth decision group. Then, the weight of kth decision group can be obtained as:

$$\lambda_k = \frac{\left(\mu_k + \pi_k \left(\frac{\mu_k}{\mu_k + v_k}\right)\right)}{\sum_{k=1}^{l} \left(\mu_k + \pi_k \left(\frac{\mu_k}{\mu_k + v_k}\right)\right)} \quad \text{and} \quad \sum_{k=1}^{l} \lambda_k = 1 \tag{3}$$

Step 3: Obtain intuitionistic fuzzy-cumulated decision matrix based on the opinions of decision group.

Say $R^{(k)} = \left(r_{ij}^{(k)}\right)_{mxn}$ be an intuitionistic fuzzy decision matrix of each decision maker. Let $\lambda = \lambda_1, \lambda_2, \lambda_3 \ldots \lambda_l$ be the weight of each assessment maker and $\sum_{k=1}^{l} \lambda_k = 1$. As we are considering group decision process, so all the individual decision opinions need to be merged into a group opinion to construct cumulated intuitionistic fuzzy decision matrix. For that, we use IFWA operator, proposed by Xu [20]. $R^{(k)} = \left(r_{ij}^{(k)}\right)_{mxn}$, where

$$r_{ij} = IFWA\left(r_{ij}^{(1)}, r_{ij}^{(2)}, \ldots, r_{ij}^{(l)}\right)$$
$$= \left[1 - \prod_{k=1}^{l}\left(1 - \mu_{ij}^{(k)}\right)^{\lambda_k}, \prod_{k=1}^{l}\left(v_{ij}^{(k)}\right)^{\lambda_k}, \prod_{k=1}^{l}\left(1 - \mu_{ij}^{(k)}\right)^{\lambda_k} - \prod_{k=1}^{l}\left(v_{ij}^{(k)}\right)^{\lambda_k}\right], \tag{4}$$

where $r_{ij} = \mu_{Ai}(x_j), v_{Ai}(x_j), \pi_{Ai}(x_j)$

The cumulated intuitionistic fuzzy decision matrix R is denoted as:

$$\begin{bmatrix} (\mu_{A1}(x_1), v_{A1}(x_1), \pi_{A1}(x_1)) & (\mu_{A1}(x_2), v_{A1}(x_2), \pi_{A1}(x_2)) & \cdots & (\mu_{A1}(x_n), v_{A1}(x_n), \pi_{A1}(x_n)) \\ (\mu_{A2}(x_1), v_{A2}(x_1), \pi_{A2}(x_1)) & (\mu_{A2}(x_2), v_{A2}(x_2), \pi_{A2}(x_2)) & \cdots & (\mu_{A2}(x_n), v_{A2}(x_n), \pi_{A1}(x_n)) \\ & & \cdot & \\ & & \cdot & \\ (\mu_{Am}(x_1), v_{Am}(x_1), \pi_{Am}(x_1)) & (\mu_{Am}(x_2), v_{Am}(x_2), \pi_{Am}(x_2)) & \cdots & (\mu_{Am}(x_n), v_{Am}(x_n), \pi_{Am}(x_n)) \end{bmatrix}$$

Step 4: Criteria weights can be determined as follows.

Generally, different criteria have different importance. Let $W_j^{(k)} = \left[\mu_j^{(k)}, v_j^{(k)}, \pi_j^{(k)}\right]$ be IFN for the criteria x_j by kth decision group. Then, the criteria weights can be calculated using IFWA operator:

$$w_j = IFWA\left(w_j^{(1)}, w_j^{(2)}, \ldots, w_j^{(l)}\right)$$

$$= \left[1 - \prod_{k=1}^{l}\left(1 - \mu_j^{(k)}\right)^{\lambda_k}, \prod_{k=1}^{l}\left(v_j^{(k)}\right)^{\lambda_k}, \prod_{k=1}^{l}\left(1 - \mu_j^{(k)}\right)^{\lambda_k} - \prod_{k=1}^{l}\left(v_j^{(k)}\right)^{\lambda_k}\right], \quad (5)$$

where $w_j = \left(\mu_j, v_j, \pi_j\right)$

Step 5: Let R' be the cumulated weighted intuitionistic fuzzy decision matrix which is formed according to following definition [18].

$$R \otimes W = \{x, \mu_{Ai}(x) \cdot \mu_w(x), v_{A1}(x) + v_w(x) - v_{A1}(x) \cdot v_w(x)) \quad (6)$$

And

$$\pi_{Ai.w}(x) = 1 - v_{Ai}(x) - v_w(x) - \mu_{Ai}(x) \cdot \mu_w(x) + v_{Ai}(x) \cdot v_w(x) \quad (7)$$

Step 6: Now intuitionistic fuzzy positive-ideal solution A^* and intuitionistic fuzzy negative-ideal solution A^- is obtained.

Let j_1 and j_2 be profit and cost criteria, respectively.

$$A^* = \mu_{A^*w}\left(x_j\right), v_{A^*w}\left(x_j\right) \text{ and } A^- = \mu_{A^-w}\left(x_j\right), v_{A^-w}\left(x_j\right) \quad (8)$$

where

$$\mu_{A^*w}\left(x_j\right) = ((\max \mu_{Ai^*w}\left(x_j\right) \, j \in j_1), \, (\min \mu_{Ai^*w}\left(x_j\right) \, j \in j_2)) \quad (9)$$

$$v_{A^*w}\left(x_j\right) = ((\min v_{Ai^*w}\left(x_j\right) \, j \in j_1), \, (\max v_{Ai^*w}\left(x_j\right) \, j \in j_2)) \quad (10)$$

$$\mu_{A^-w}\left(x_j\right) = ((\max \mu_{Ai^-w}\left(x_j\right) \, j \in j_1), \, (\max \mu_{Ai^-w}\left(x_j\right) \, j \in j_2)) \quad (11)$$

$$v_{A^-w}\left(x_j\right) = ((\max v_{Ai^-w}\left(x_j\right) \, j \in j_1), \, (\max v_{Ai^-w}\left(x_j\right) \, j \in j_2)) \quad (12)$$

Step 7: Positive- and negative-idle solutions are calculated using normalized Euclidean distance [21].

$$S^* = \sqrt{\frac{1}{2n}\sum\left[\left(\mu_{A_iw}\left(x_j\right) - \mu_{A^*w}\left(x_j\right)\right)^2 + \left(v_{A_iw}\left(x_j\right) - v_{A^*w}\left(x_j\right)\right)^2 + \left(\pi_{A_iw}\left(x_j\right) - \pi_{A^*w}\left(x_j\right)\right)^2\right]} \quad (13)$$

$$S^- = \sqrt{\frac{1}{2n}\sum\left[\left(\mu_{A_iw}\left(x_j\right) - \mu_{A^-w}\left(x_j\right)\right)^2 + \left(v_{A_iw}\left(x_j\right) - v_{A^-w}\left(x_j\right)\right)^2 + \left(\pi_{A_iw}\left(x_j\right) - \pi_{A^*w}\left(x_j\right)\right)^2\right]} \quad (14)$$

Step 8: The overall performance index of an alternative A_i is calculated as

$$C_{i^*} = \frac{S_i^-}{S_{i^*} + S_i^-} \quad \text{where} \quad 0 \le C_{i^*} \le 1 \tag{15}$$

Step 9: All the alternatives now can be ranked according to downward order of C_i.

3 Numerical Example with Case Study

One of the world's leading tourism communities is TripAdvisor.com with more than 300 million guest reviews. The visitors of TripAdvisor.com include both unregistered and registered users. The users are of five categories—family, couple, solo, business, and friends. We call each one a decision-making group. Users give their reviews and rating for various criteria such as geographical position, food quality, room quality, services, cost. Reviews are of five categories such as excellent, good, average, poor, and terrible. Figure 1 shows a snapshot of TripAdvisor.com for particular hotel showing linguistic rating, criteria, and decision-making group.

We consider four criteria as follows:

X_1: Geographical Location X_2: Facilities X_3: Food quality X_4: Price

We have taken three hotels for numerical analysis and raking purpose.

Procedure for the selection of hotels based on online reviews contains the following steps:

Step 1: Determine the aggregated intuitionistic fuzzy rating matrix.
First find the weight of each linguistic term for a particular group using Eq. (1).
Table 1 shows weight matrix. Then, aggregated intuitionistic fuzzy rating matrix is obtained using Eq. (2) and Table 4, and the result is shown in Table 2 .
Step 2: Decision maker's weights are determined.
Rating of each decision-making group and criteria using linguistic terms are given in Table 3, and importance and obtained weight of each group is shown in Table 5. Equation (3) is used to find the weights.
Step 3: Cumulated intuitionistic fuzzy decision matrix R based on the decision group's opinions using Eq. (4) for three alternatives is as follows:

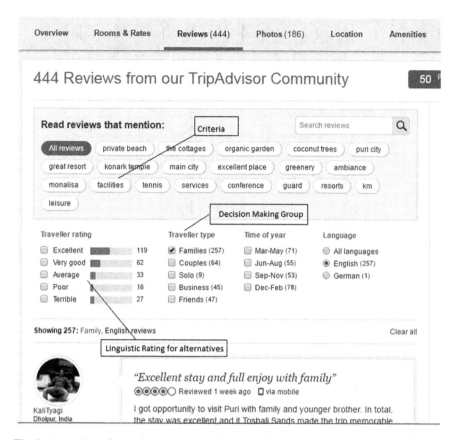

Fig. 1 A snapshot of reviews given by users on TripAdvisor.com

$$
R = \begin{array}{c} A_1 \\ A_2 \\ A_3 \end{array}
\begin{array}{cccc}
X_1 & X_2 & X_3 & X_4 \\
\end{array}
$$

$$
R = \begin{array}{c} A_1 \\ A_2 \\ A_3 \end{array}
\left[
\begin{array}{cccc}
(0.76, 0.22, 0.02) & (0.80, 0.16, 0.03) & (0.73, 0.22, 0.06) & (0.74, 0.21, 0.05) \\
(0.78, 0.18, 0.04) & (0.81, 0.16, 0.03) & (0.77, 0.18, 0.05) & (0.79, 0.17, 0.04) \\
(0.69, 0.23, 0.08) & (0.67, 0.25, 0.07) & (0.73, 0.23, 0.06) & (0.71, 0.25, 0.04)
\end{array}
\right]
$$

Step 4: Weights of the criteria using Eq. (5) are shown below (use Table 6):

$$
W_{(X_1, X_2, X_3, X_4)} = \begin{bmatrix}
(0.77, 0.20, 0.03) \\
(0.80, 0.18, 0.02) \\
(0.70, 0.23, 0.07) \\
(0.60, 0.31, 0.09)
\end{bmatrix}^T
$$

Table 1 Weight matrix for each linguistic term for a decision group

Criteria	Alternatives	Family					Couple					Solo					Business					Friends				
		Exc	VG	Av	P	T	Exc	VG	Av	P	T	Exc	VG	Av	P	T	Exc	VG	Av	P	T	Exc	VG	Av	P	T
X1	A1	82	45	11	3	1	8	20	0	1	0	0	0	0	0	0	1	0	0	0	0	3	6	1	0	0
		0.58	0.32	0.08	0.02	0.01	0.28	0.69	0.00	0.03	0.00	0.00	0.00	0.00	0.00	0.00	1.00	0.00	0.00	0.00	0.00	0.30	0.60	0.10	0.00	0.00
	A2	119	62	33	16	27	28	17	8	4	7	2	5	1	0	1	18	17	6	2	2	20	14	4	4	5
		0.46	0.24	0.13	0.06	0.11	0.44	0.27	0.13	0.06	0.11	0.22	0.56	0.11	0.00	0.11	0.40	0.38	0.13	0.04	0.04	0.43	0.30	0.09	0.09	0.11
	A3	21	49	25	20	15	6	9	9	2	3	1	0	1	0	0	0	0	0	0	0	5	5	0	0	0
		0.16	0.38	0.19	0.15	0.12	0.21	0.31	0.31	0.07	0.10	0.50	0.00	0.50	0.00	0.00	0.00	0.00	0.00	0.00	0.00	0.50	0.50	0.00	0.00	1.00
X2	A1	56	48	34	4	3	45	23	6	4	2	4	3	2	0	0	6	3	2	1	0	7	3	2	2	0
		0.39	0.33	0.23	0.03	0.02	0.56	0.29	0.08	0.05	0.03	0.44	0.33	0.22	0.00	0.00	0.50	0.25	0.17	0.08	0.00	0.50	0.21	0.14	0.14	0.00
	A2	43	32	10	6	3	12	23	7	2	2	2	3	0	0	0	3	2	0	0	0	5	7	2	1	0
		0.46	0.34	0.11	0.06	0.03	0.27	0.52	0.16	0.05	0.00	0.40	0.60	0.00	0.00	0.00	0.60	0.40	0.00	0.00	0.00	0.33	0.47	0.13	0.07	0.00
	A3	12	14	23	3	0	3	2	4	2	0	0	1	1	0	0	0	2	4	0	1	0	3	2	0	1
		0.23	0.27	0.44	0.06	0.00	0.27	0.18	0.36	0.18	0.00	0.00	0.50	0.50	0.00	0.00	0.00	0.29	0.57	0.00	0.14	0.00	0.33	0.67	0.00	0.14
X3	A1	35	42	46	21	2	12	16	8	2	2	3	4	7	0	0	2	4	7	0	0	6	3	12	0	0
		0.24	0.29	0.32	0.14	0.01	0.32	0.42	0.21	0.05	0.01	0.21	0.29	0.50	0.00	0.00	0.15	0.31	0.54	0.00	0.00	0.29	0.14	0.57	0.00	0.00
	A2	67	45	33	5	1	18	14	13	4	2	2	5	2	1	0	3	2	1	1	0	4	2	2	1	1
		0.44	0.30	0.22	0.03	0.01	0.35	0.27	0.25	0.08	0.04	0.20	0.50	0.20	0.10	0.00	0.43	0.29	0.14	0.14	0.00	0.40	0.20	0.20	0.10	0.10
	A3	23	34	30	7	2	8	12	20	0	1	0	3	1	0	1	2	1	1	0	0	2	3	2	1	1
		0.24	0.35	0.31	0.07	0.02	0.20	0.29	0.49	0.00	0.02	0.00	0.75	0.25	0.00	0.00	0.50	0.25	0.25	0.00	0.00	0.22	0.33	0.22	0.11	0.11
X4	A1	56	78	67	12	6	11	23	3	1	0	0	2	1	0	0	0	2	2	0	0	2	5	1	0	0
		0.26	0.36	0.31	0.05	0.03	0.29	0.61	0.08	0.03	0.00	0.00	0.67	0.33	0.00	0.00	0.00	0.67	0.33	0.00	0.00	0.25	0.63	0.13	0.00	0.00
	A2	125	68	45	12	3	17	12	6	2	3	0	2	1	1	0	2	1	0	0	0	12	8	4	2	0
		0.49	0.27	0.18	0.05	0.01	0.45	0.32	0.16	0.05	0.01	0.00	0.67	0.33	0.00	0.00	0.67	0.33	0.00	0.00	0.00	0.46	0.31	0.15	0.08	0.00
	A3	12	8	3	2	1	24	34	7	2	1	0	0	0	0	0	1	2	1	0	0	8	12	2	0	0
		0.46	0.31	0.12	0.08	0.04	0.36	0.51	0.10	0.03	0.04	0.00	0.00	0.00	0.00	0.00	0.25	0.50	0.25	0.00	0.00	0.36	0.55	0.09	0.00	0.00

Table 2 Aggregated intuitionistic fuzzy number for rating the alternatives

Criteria	Hotels	IFNs of decision-making groups				
		Family	Couple	Solo	Business	Friends
X1	Alt1	(0.84, 0.14)	(0.80, 0.16)	(0.00, 1.00)	(0.90, 0.10)	(0.80, 0.17)
	Alt2	(0.79, 0.17)	(0.78, 0.17)	(0.75, 0.20)	(0.79, 0.17)	(0.79, 0.17)
	Alt3	(0.68, 0.22)	(0.69, 0.23)	(0.78, 0.20)	(0.20, 0.40)	(0.84, 0.14)
X2	Alt1	(0.78, 0.18)	(0.83, 0.14)	(0.80, 0.17)	(0.81, 0.16)	(0.80, 0.16)
	Alt2	(0.81, 0.16)	(0.77, 0.19)	(0.83, 0.15)	(0.86, 0.13)	(0.79, 0.17)
	Alt3	(0.71, 0.23)	(0.70, 0.22)	(0.65, 0.28)	(0.56, 0.33)	(0.60, 0.32)
X3	Alt1	(0.71, 0.21)	(0.77, 0.19)	(0.71, 0.24)	(0.68, 0.26)	(0.72, 0.24)
	Alt2	(0.80, 0.17)	(0.75, 0.19)	(0.74, 0.20)	(0.79, 0.16)	(0.76, 0.19)
	Alt3	(0.73, 0.22)	(0.70, 0.25)	(0.70, 0.24)	(0.81, 0.17)	(0.70, 0.22)
X4	Alt1	(0.74, 0.21)	(0.79, 0.17)	(0.69, 0.25)	(0.69, 0.25)	(0.79, 0.18)
	Alt2	(0.81, 0.16)	(0.80, 0.16)	(0.69, 0.25)	(0.86, 0.13)	(0.80, 0.16)
	Alt3	(0.80, 0.16)	(0.80, 0.17)	(0.00, 1.00)	(0.76, 0.20)	(0.81, 0.17)

Table 3 Linguistic terms and corresponding IFNs for rating decision groups and criteria

Linguistic terms	IFNs
Very important	(0.85, 0.15)
Important	(0.75, 0.2)
Medium	(0.5, 0.35)
Unimportant	(0.3, 0.6)
Very unimportant	(0.15, 0.85)

Table 4 Linguistic for rating the alternatives

Linguistic terms	IFNs
Excellent	(0.9, 0.1)
Very good	(0.75, 0.2)
Average	(0.5, 0.4)
Poor	(0.4, 0.5)
Terrible	(0.2, 0.7)

Table 5 Importance of decision-making groups and weights

	Families	Couples	Solo	Business	Friends
Linguistic terms	Very important	Important	Very important	Medium	Very unimportant
Weights	0.313	0.291	0.22	0.121	0.055

Table 6 Weights of criteria

Criteria	Families	Couples	Solo	Business	Friends
X1	Very important	Important	Medium	Very important	Important
X2	Important	Very important	Important	Very important	Important
X3	Important	Important	Medium	Important	Medium
X4	Medium	Medium	Very important	Unimportant	Medium

Step 5: Cumulated weighted intuitionistic fuzzy decision matrix R' is formed according to Eqs. (6) and (7) and shown as follows:

$$
\begin{array}{ccccc}
& X_1 & X_2 & X_3 & X_4 \\
A_1 & (0.579, 0.374, 0.047) & (0.642, 0.311, 0.048) & (0.507, 0.400, 0.094) & (0.446, 0.453, 0.100) \\
A_2 & (0.597, 0.314, 0.062) & (0.646, 0.311, 0.043) & (0.537, 0.373, 0.090) & (0.476, 0.429, 0.095) \\
A_3 & (0.526, 0.383, 0.091) & (0.537, 0.385, 0.075) & (0.506, 0.406, 0.088) & (0.426, 0.483, 0.091)
\end{array}
$$

Step 6: Now intuitionistic fuzzy positive-ideal solution A^* and intuitionistic fuzzy negative-ideal solution A^- can be obtained by using geographical location, facilities, and food quality which are benefit criteria and price be cost criteria; then using Eqs. (8–12), we find

$$
A^* = \left\{ \begin{array}{l} (0.597, 0.314, 0.062), (0.646, 0.311, 0.043) \\ (0.537, 0.373, 0.090), (0.426, 0.483, 0.091) \end{array} \right\} \quad A^- = \left\{ \begin{array}{l} (0.526, 0.383, 0.091), (0.537, 0.385, 0.075) \\ (0.506, 0.406, 0.088), (0.476, 0.429, 0.095) \end{array} \right\}
$$

Step 7: The positive- and negative-idle solution is calculated using Eqs. (13, 14), and overall performance index of an alternative A_i is calculated using Eq. (15) as shown below:

Alternatives	S*	S⁻	C_{i*}
A_1	0.0777043	0.1512361	0.6605916
A_2	0.0321029	1.6143423	0.9805017
A_3	0.1770174	1.5647394	0.8983685

Step 8: As per the performance index, alternatives are ranked according to descending order of C_{i*} as $A_2 > A_3 > A_1$. So second hotel becomes the most appropriate for selection.

4 Conclusion and Future Work

In this paper, we have proposed an intuitionistic fuzzy TOPSIS approach to conduct the ranking of hotel on the basis of online reviews to assist tourists finding hotels on TripAdvisor.com. Although the reliability of TOPSIS method is proved, other decision-making approaches should be compared with the proposed method in future research. In addition, only linguistic rating has been taken into account, but there are some users who provide text reviews for some criteria. Now how to include text reviews into dataset of linguistic rating is a major challenge, which is necessary to study in future.

References

1. G.Q. Zhang, J. Shang, P. Yildirim, Optimal pricing for group buying with network effects, Omega 63 (2016) 69–82.
2. D. Buhalis, R. Law, Progress in information technology and tourism management: 20 years on and 10 years after the internet-The state of Tourism research, Tourism Management. 29 (4) (2008) 609–623.
3. S. Litvin, R. Goldsmith, B. Pan, Electronic word of mouth in hospitality and tourism management, Tourism Management. 29 (3) (2008) 458–468.
4. P.F. Limberger, F.A. Dos Anjos, J.V. de Souza Meira, et al., Satisfaction in hospitality on TripAdvisor.com: An analysis of the correlation between evaluation criteria and overall satisfaction, Tourism & Management Studies, 10 (1) (2014) 59–65.
5. B. Fang, et al., Analysis of the perceived value of online tourism reviews: influence of readability and reviewer characteristics, Tourism Management. 52(2016) 498–506.
6. C.W. Huang, F.N. Ho, Y.H. Chiu, Measurement of tourist hotels' productive efficiency, occupancy, and catering service effectiveness using a modified two-stage DEA model in Taiwan, Omega. 48 (2014) 49–59.
7. P. Chatterjee, Online review: do consumers use them? Advances in Consumer Research. 28 (2001) 129–133.
8. U. Gretzel, Online travel review study: Role and impact of online travel reviews, 2007.
9. E.W.T. Ngai, F.K.T. Wat, Design and development of a fuzzy expert system for hotel selection, Omega. 31 (4) (2003) 275–286.
10. Y. Peng, G. Kou, G.X. Wang, et al., FAMCDM: A fusion approach of MCDM methods to rank multiclass classification algorithms, Omega. 39 (6) (2011) 677–689.
11. Z.P. Tian, J. Wang, J.Q. Wang, et al., Simplified neutrosophic linguistic multi-criteria group decision-making approach to green product development, Group Decision and Negotiation. (2016) https://doi.org/10.1007/s10726-016-9479-5.
12. J.Q. Wang, J.J. Peng, H.Y. Zhang, et al., An uncertain linguistic multi-criteria group decision-making method based on a cloud model, Group Decision and Negotiation. 24 (1) (2015) 171–192.

13. E.K. Zavadskas, M.J. Skibniewski, J. Antucheviciene, Performance analysis of civil engineering journals based on the web of science® database, Archives of Civil and Mechanical Engineering. 14 (4) (2014) 519–527.
14. E.K. Zavadskas, Z. Turskis, Multi-criteria selection of a construction site for a deep-water port in the Eastern Baltic Sea, Applied Soft Computing. 26 (2015) 180–192.
15. Y.H. Hung, T.L. Huang, et al., Online reputation management for improving marketing by using a hybrid MCDM model, Knowledge-Based Systems. 35 (2012) 87–93.
16. Y. Peng, G. Kou, J. Li, A fuzzy promethee approach for mining customer reviews in Chinese, Arabian Journal for Science and Engineering. 39 (6) (2014) 5245–5252.
17. H.Y. Zhang, P. Ji, J.Q. Wang, et al., A novel decision support model for satisfactory restaurants utilizing social information: A case study of TripAdvisor.com, Tourism Management. 59 (2017) 281–297.
18. Atanassov, K.T, Intuitionistic fuzzy sets. Fuzzy Sets and Systems, 20, (1986) 87–96.
19. Yager, R.R.: On ordered weighted averaging aggregation operators in multi-criteria decisionmaking. IEEE Trans. Syst., Man Cybernetics 18(1), 183–190 (1988).
20. Xu, Z. S. Intuitionistic fuzzy aggregation operators. IEE Transaction of Fuzzy Systems, 15(6), (2007). 1179–1187.
21. Szmidt, E., & Kacprzyk, J., Distances between intuitionistic fuzzy sets. Fuzzy Sets and Systems, 114, (2000) 505–518.

A Layered Approach to Network Intrusion Detection Using Rule Learning Classifiers with Nature-Inspired Feature Selection

Ashalata Panigrahi and Manas Ranjan Patra

Abstract Intrusion detection systems are meant to provide secured network computing environment by protecting against attackers. The challenge in building an intrusion detection model is to deal with unbalanced intrusion datasets, i.e., when one class is represented by a small number of examples (minority class). Most of the time it is observed that the performance of the classification techniques somehow becomes biased toward the majority class due to unequal class distribution. In this work, a layered approach has been proposed to detect network intrusions with the help of certain rule learning classifiers. Each layer is designed to detect an attack type by employing certain nature-inspired search techniques such as ant search, genetic search, and PSO. The performance of the model has been evaluated in terms of accuracy, efficiency, detection rate, and false alarm rate.

Keywords Layered approach to intrusion detection · Rule-based classifier
Ant search · Genetic search · Particle swarm optimization

1 Introduction

Pervasiveness of Internet and growing dependence on Web-based applications has greatly influenced the present-day computing world. At the same time, the number of security breaches leading to misuse of network resources has also increased alarmingly. Malicious attackers constantly try to bypass the security provisions of a computer network and sometimes succeed in accessing important network resources. Therefore, protecting against such attackers has become a major concern for organizations. One of the ways to achieve this is to build effective intrusion

A. Panigrahi (✉)
Department of Computer Science & Engineering, VITAM, Berhampur, India
e-mail: ashalata.panigrahi@yahoo.com

M. R. Patra
Department of Computer Science, Berhampur University, Berhampur, India
e-mail: mrpatra12@gmail.com

© Springer Nature Singapore Pte Ltd. 2018
P. K. Pattnaik et al. (eds.), *Progress in Computing, Analytics and Networking*,
Advances in Intelligent Systems and Computing 710,
https://doi.org/10.1007/978-981-10-7871-2_21

detection systems (IDS) which can monitor the behavior of the network users and raise alerts whenever any suspicious behavior is observed. A typical intrusion detection system has certain capabilities such as analyzing activities around a network system, identify patterns of typical attacks, analyze suspicious activity patterns, and track usage policy violations. Certain types of attacks occur very frequently, and others may be less frequent or very rare. On the basis of this, attacks can be categorized into majority and minority classes. The attack type User-to-Root (U2R) belongs to minority or rare class of attacks. The minority attacks are more dangerous than the majority ones because of the difficulty in detecting such attacks at an early stage. In most cases, intrusion detection systems cannot detect U2R attacks within a permissible accuracy level. In this paper, a novel layered approach has been proposed by combining three nature-inspired search algorithms such as ant search, genetic search, and particle swarm optimization (PSO) search along with the rule learning algorithms, viz. decision table, ripple down rule learner (RIDOR), non-nested generalized exemplars (NNGE), JRip, decision table/naïve bayes (DTNB). The objective of this hybrid approach is to improve upon the detection accuracy for different attack categories, especially U2R attacks. The proposed layered model is presented in Sect. 2, and a brief outline of the rule-based classification techniques applied in our work is presented in Sect. 3. Finally, details of the experiments conducted with analysis of results are presented in Sect. 4. Section 5 sums up the work with concluding remarks.

2 Proposed Layered Model

The proposed model consists of four layers of processing (Fig. 1) such that each layer is capable of dealing with a specific type of attack. The aim of the proposed model is to apply the rule learning classifiers to build an intrusion detection model which is capable of achieving high accuracy, low false alarm rate, and reduced computation time to detect anomalous activities. The four layers of the model correspond to four different types of network attacks such as Denial-of-Service (DOS), Probe, Remote-to-Local (R2L), and User-to-Root (U2R).

3 Rule-Based Classification Algorithms

Here, we present five rule-based classifiers that are used in the proposed model.

3.1 Decision Table (DT)

The DT classifiers [1] fall into two types, viz. DT majority (DTM) and DT local (DTL). Further, DTM comprises a schema (features set) and a body

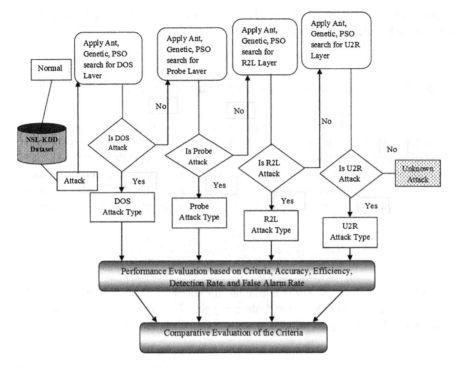

Fig. 1 A layered model for IDS

(labeled instances set). Given a set of unlabeled instances, a decision table classifier looks close matches in the decision table for those features in the schema. One can find many matching instances in the table. If no instances are found, the majority class of the DTM is identified; otherwise, the majority class of all matching instances is identified. In order to develop a DTM, one has to decide on the features to be considered for the induction algorithm.

3.2 Ripple Down Rule Learner (RIDOR)

RIDOR is a rule learning mechanism. It can generate exceptions by identifying default rules. Exceptions are produced by reducing errors incrementally through an iterative process. Here, a rule can be linked with other rules with exceptions. One can build a new rule that has effect on its parent rules in a given context. Such new rules can be inserted into the list [2]. Here, the rules are neither deleted nor modified but are only patched locally [3].

3.3 Non-nested Generalized Exemplars (NNGE)

Here, exemplars are combined to form generalization [4] and each time a new example is added to the database by joining it to its nearest neighbor within the same class. NNGE neither allows nesting nor overlapping of hyper-rectangles. It prevents overlapping by ensuring that no negative examples are included during generalization.

Here, new examples are classified by finding the nearest neighbors in the exemplar database by applying the Euclidean distance function, D(T, H) as in Eq. 1:

$$D(T, H) = W_H \sqrt{\sum_{i=1}^{n} \left[Wi \frac{d(Ti - Hi)}{Tmaxi - Tmini} \right]^2} \qquad (1)$$

where $T = (T_1, T_2,...,T_m)$ are the training instances, H is an exemplar, W_H is the exemplar weight, and W_i is the feature weight. T_i^{min} and T_i^{max} are the range of values for the training set which correspond to the ith attribute.

3.4 JRip

There are four phases in JRip algorithm [5, 6], viz. growth, pruning, optimization, and selection. A sequence of individual rules produces in the growth phase by adding predicates until a stopping criterion is satisfied by the rules. Then each rule is optimized by adding attributes to the original rule or by generating new rules using the first and second phases. In the final phase, the promising rules are picked up while the remaining rules are ignored.

3.5 Decision Table/Naïve Bayes (DTNB) Classifier

Here, at each point during the search operation, the classifier divides the features into two disjoint subsets corresponding to DT and NB [7]. The overall class probability is generated by combining the individual class probability of DT and NB as in Eq. 2.

$$Q(y|X) = \alpha \times QDT(y|XA) \times QNB(y|XB) / Q(y) \qquad (2)$$

where QDT(yXA) and QNB (yXB) are the estimates of class probabilities w.r.t. DT and NB, Q(y) is the prior probability of the class, and α is a normalization constant.

4 Experimentation and Result Analysis

4.1 Dataset

We have conducted our experiments using the NSL-KDD dataset which is widely used by researchers to conduct such experiments [8]. It consists of 41 attributes along with one class label. After removal of redundant data, there remain 125973 records in the dataset out of which 67343 represent normal and 58630 represent attack data. There are 24 different types of attacks represented in the dataset which fall into four main categories, viz. Denial-of-Service (DOS), Probe, Remote-to-Local (R2L), and User-to-Root (U2R). In this dataset, U2R belongs to the minority class and the rest belong to the majority class.

4.2 Feature Selection

The nature-inspired search methods, namely ant search, genetic search, and particle swarm optimization search are applied to select relevant features. Each of the four layers of our model (Fig. 1), namely DOS, Probe, R2L, and U2R selects specific features based on the type of attack as described in Table 1.

4.3 Performance Measurement

The performance of an intrusion detection system can be determined by its capability to predict attacks as accurately as possible. Essentially, IDS try to distinguish between an attack data and a normal data. Here, a confusion matrix has been built to measure the performance of different classifiers as expressed in Eqs. 3, 4, 5, and 6. A confusion matrix is a tabular representation of false positives (FP), false negatives (FN), true positives (TP), and true negatives (TN).

$$Accuracy = \frac{TP + TN}{P + N} \qquad (3)$$

$$Efficiency = \frac{TN}{N} \qquad (4)$$

Table 1 Selected features at each layer

Feature selection method	Attack category	Number of features selected	Selected features
Ant search	DOS	10	Pro_type, Service, Flag, Src_bytes, Land, Logg_in, Sev_coun, Sa_srv_rt, Di_srv_rt, Dst_h_co
	Probes	9	Flag, Src_bytes, Count, Rer_rt, Dst_h_co, Ds_ho_s, Ds_rate, Ds_p_rt, Ds_d_h_rt
	R2L	8	Src_bytes. Dst_bytes, Urgent, Num_f_cr, Rer_rt, Sr_di_ho, Dst_h_co, Ds_h_r
	U2R	7	Flag, Src_bytes, Dst_bytes, Num_f_cr, Dst_h_co, Ds_ho_s, Ds_rate
Genetic search	DOS	10	Pro_type, Service, Flag, Src_bytes, Land, Num_com, Sev_coun, Sa_srv_rt, Di_srv_rt, Dst_h_co
	Probes	20	Service, Src_bytes, Urgent, Logg_in, R_shell, Num_f_cr, Is_ho_lg, Count, Se_se_rt, Rer_rt, Sa_srv_rt, Sr_di_ho, Ds_ho_sr, Ds_ho_s, Ds_Rate, Ds_p_rt, Ds_d_h_rt, D_h_sr, Ds_hrr, D_hsrr
	R2L	18	Pro_type, Flag, Src_bytes, Dst_bytes, N_f_login, R_shell, Num_f_cr, Nu_ac_fl, Is_gu_lg, Ser_rate, Sr_rr_rt, Sr_di_ho, Ds_ho_sr, Ds_ho_s, D_h_sr, Ds_h_r, Ds_hrr, D_hsrr
	U2R	7	Pro_type, Src_bytes, Logg_in, Num_f_cr, R_shell, Ds_ho_s, Ds_p_rt
PSO search	DOS	10	Pro_type, Service, Flag, Src_bytes, Dst_bytes, Land, Sev_coun, Sa_srv_rt, Di_srv_rt, Dst_h_co
	Probes	8	Flag, Src_bytes, N_f_login, Sev_coun, Dst_h_co, Ds_rate, Ds_p_rt, Ds_d_h_rt
	R2L	10	Flag, Src_bytes. Dst_bytes, Urgent, N_f_login, Sr_rr_rt, Ds_ho_sr, D_h_sr, Ds_h_r
	U2R	5	Pro_type, Src_bytes, N_shell, Dst_h_co, Ds_ho_s

$$\text{Detection Rate} = \frac{TP}{TP + FN} \qquad (5)$$

$$\text{False Alarm Rate} = \frac{FP}{TN + FP} \qquad (6)$$

4.4 Result Analysis

Experiments were conducted by applying possible combinations of five classifiers, viz. decision table, ripple down rule learner, non-nested generalized exemplars, JRip, and decision table/naïve bayes with three search algorithms, viz. ant search, genetic search, particle swarm optimization search on the NSL-KDD dataset. Performance of each classifier was computed using the tenfold cross-validation technique. A comparison of performance of the five classifiers with different feature selection methods is presented in Tables 2, 3, and 4.

It can be observed from the tables that the degree of accuracy, efficiency, detection rate, and false alarm rate achieved in case of DOS attack is much better than the other attack types. Moreover, the result with respect to U2R, which is a rare attack type, is quite encouraging while using DTNB as the classifier and PSO as the feature reduction method.

Table 2 Performance of rule-based classifiers with ant search feature selection

Classifiers	Attack category	Accuracy (%)	Efficiency (%)	Detection rate (%)	False alarm rate (%)
Decision table	DOS	99.9978	99.9978	100	0.0022
	Probe	99.2622	99.2925	99.1942	0.7074
	R2L	98.6935	99.2908	25	0.7092
	U2R	71.1538	40.9091	93.3333	59.0909
RIDOR	DOS	99.9978	99.9978	100	0.0022
	Probe	99.7769	99.789	99.7499	0.211
	R2L	99.0955	99.7974	12.5	0.2026
	U2R	75	50	93.3333	50
NNGE	DOS	100	100	100	0
	Probe	99.674	99.8014	99.3887	0.1986
	R2L	99.4975	99.7974	62.5	0.2026
	U2R	86.5384	81.8182	90	18.1818
JRip	DOS	99.9956	100	99.7908	0
	Probe	99.7769	99.7518	99.8333	0.2482
	R2L	98.8945	99.5947	12.5	0.4053
	U2R	**75**	**50**	**93.3333**	**50**
DTNB	DOS	99.9978	99.9978	100	0.0022
	Probe	99.6482	99.7145	99.4999	0.2855
	R2L	99.196	99.696	37.5	0.3039
	U2R	76.923	59.0909	90	40.9091

Table 3 Performance of rule-based classifiers with genetic search feature selection

Classifiers	Attack category	Accuracy (%)	Efficiency	Detection rate (%)	False alarm rate (%)
Decision table	DOS	99.9978	99.9978	100	0.0022
	Probe	98.6874	98.5354	99.0275	1.4646
	R2L	98.593	99.2908	12.5	0.7092
	U2R	75	54.5454	96.6666	54.5454
RIDOR	DOS	99.9978	99.9978	100	0.0022
	Probe	99.6997	99.6897	99.7221	0.3103
	R2L	99.0955	99.696	28.5714	0.3039
	U2R	82.6923	72.7273	90	27.2727
NNGE	DOS	100	100	100	0
	Probe	99.5367	99.6897	99.1942	0.3103
	R2L	99.196	99.696	37.5	0.3039
	U2R	**92.3077**	**86.3636**	**96.6667**	**13.6364**
JRip	DOS	99.9956	100	99.7908	0
	Probe	99.7683	99.7269	99.8611	0.2731
	R2L	98.8945	99.5947	12.5	0.4053
	U2R	80.7692	63.6364	93.3333	36.3636
DTNB	DOS	99.9978	99.9978	100	0.0022
	Probe	99.245	99.578	98.4996	0.43
	R2L	98.6935	99.3921	16.6667	0.6079
	U2R	78.8461	54.5454	96.6666	45.4545

Table 4 Performance of rule-based classifiers with PSO search feature selection

Classifiers	Attack category	Accuracy (%)	Efficiency	Detection rate (%)	False alarm rate (%)
Decision table	DOS	99.9978	99.9978	100	0.0022
	Probe	98.6788	98.4856	99.1109	1.5142
	R2L	98.4925	99.0881	25	0.9118
	U2R	76.923	45.4545	100	54.5454
RIDOR	DOS	99.9978	99.9978	100	0.0022
	Probe	99.7769	99.7766	99.75	0.2234
	R2L	99.0955	99.696	25	0.3039
	U2R	80.7692	68.1818	90	31.8182
NNGE	DOS	100	100	100	0
	Probe	99.6482	99.6897	99.5554	0.3103
	R2L	98.8945	99.2908	50	0.7092
	U2R	84.6154	77.2727	90	22.7273

(continued)

Table 4 (continued)

Classifiers	Attack category	Accuracy (%)	Efficiency	Detection rate (%)	False alarm rate (%)
JRip	DOS	99.9956	100	99.7908	0
	Probe	99.734	99.7145	99.7777	0.2855
	R2L	99.2965	100	12.5	0
	U2R	80.7692	59.0909	96.6667	40.9091
DTNB	DOS	99.9978	99.9978	100	0.0022
	Probe	99.2622	99.2305	99.3331	0.7695
	R2L	99.2965	99.7974	37.5	0.2026
	U2R	**78.8461**	**50**	**100**	**50**

5 Conclusions

This paper deals with building of an efficient intrusion detection system that can analyze different network attack scenarios and raise alerts to deal with them appropriately. In order to deal with each of the attack types more rigorously, a layered model has been adopted. Combinations of five different rule-based classifiers with three feature reduction techniques have been experimented. Results indicate that the proposed model performs better for minor attacks like U2R when the combination of PSO (as the feature reduction technique) and decision table/naïve bayes (as the classifier) is used.

References

1. Kohavi, R., The Power of Decision Tables. In Proc. of the European Conference on Machine Learning (ECML), LNAI, Springer Verlag, Heraclion, Crete, Greece (1995). 174–189.
2. Sharma, P., Ripple-Down Rules for Knowledge Acquisition in Intelligent System. Journal of Technology and Engineering Sciences Vol. 1 (2009) 52–56.
3. Compton, P., Preston, P. and Kang, B., Local Patching Produces Compact Knowledge Bases. A Future in Knowledge Acquisition Springer Verlag, Berlin, 104–117, 1994.
4. Salzberg, S., A nearest hyperrectangle learning method. Machine Learning (1991). 277–309.
5. Cohen, W.W., Fast effective Rule Induction, In Proc. of the 12th International Conference on Machine Learning (1995). 115–123.
6. Yang, J., Tiyyagura, A., Chen, F., and Honavar, V., Feature Subset Selection for Rule Induction using RIPPER, In Proc. of the Genetic and Evolutionary Computation Conference, Oriando, Florida, USA (1999).
7. Hall, M., and Frank, E., Combining Naïve Bayes and Decision tables, In Proc. of the 21st Florida Artificial Intelligence Society Conference (FLAIRS), Florida, USA (2008), 318–319.
8. Tavallaee, M., Bagheri, E., Lu, W., and Ghorbani, A., A detailed analysis of the KDD CUP 99 data set, In Proc. of the IEEE Symposium on Computational Intelligence in Security and Defense Applications (CISDA-2009), Ottawa (2009), 1–6.

Fractal Dimension of GrayScale Images

Soumya Ranjan Nayak, Jibitesh Mishra and Pyari Mohan Jena

Abstract Fractal dimension (FD) is a necessary aspect for characterizing the surface roughness and self-similarity of complex objects. However, fractal dimension gradually established its importance in the area of image processing. A number of algorithms for estimating fractal dimension of digital images have been reported in many literatures. However, different techniques lead to different results. Among them, the differential box-counting (DBC) was most popular and well-liked technique in digital domain. In this paper, we have presented an efficient differential box-counting mechanism for accurate estimation of FD with less fitting error as compared to existing methods like original DBC, relative DBC (RDBC), and improved box-counting (IBC) and improved DBC (IDBC). The experimental work is carried out by one set of fourteen Brodatz images. From this experimental result, we found that the proposed method performs best among the existing methods in terms of less fitting error.

Keywords Fractal dimension · DBC · RDBC · IBC · IDBC
Grayscale image

S. R. Nayak (✉)
Department of Information Technology, College of Engineering and Technology,
Bhubaneswar, India
e-mail: nayak.soumya17@gmail.com

J. Mishra
Department of Computer Science and Application, College of Engineering and Technology,
Bhubaneswar, India
e-mail: mishrajibitesh@gmail.com

P. M. Jena
Department of Computer Science and Engineering, College of Engineering and Technology,
Bhubaneswar, India
e-mail: mohanjena.cse@gmail.com

© Springer Nature Singapore Pte Ltd. 2018
P. K. Pattnaik et al. (eds.), *Progress in Computing, Analytics and Networking*,
Advances in Intelligent Systems and Computing 710,
https://doi.org/10.1007/978-981-10-7871-2_22

1 Introduction

Fractal dimension (FD) is a term used in fractal geometry to evaluate surface roughness of complex objects found in nature like cloud, mountain, and coastlines. However, most of the objects residing in nature are irregular pattern and complex in nature and that cannot be characterized by Euclidean geometry reported in [1, 2]. In order to describe these complex objects, fractal dimension comes into existence and it was initially presented by Mandelbrot [3]. Nowadays fractal dimension becomes most popular in many kinds of applications such as pattern recognition, texture analysis, medical signal analysis, and image segmentation reported in [4]. Many researchers contributed their effort in the area of fractal geometry. Thus, different techniques have different results. Voss described and partitioned these techniques into three key concepts such as box-counting, variance, and spectral method reported in [5]. The box-counting is one of the most successful and widely used techniques for estimating FD in various fields of application due to its simplicity and easy implementation [6]. In this regard, many box-counting techniques and their improved versions come into existence and found in many literatures [7–12]. Sarkar and Chaudhuri [8] proposed most appropriate algorithm like differential box-counting (DBC) for digital images by taking maximum and minimum intensity point described in many literatures [13–17]. Jin et al. [10] presented relative DBC by adopting a convenient process for computing roughness. Biswas et al. [18] presented the modified version of DBC by taking a parallel algorithm for efficient estimation. Chen et al. [1] presented another approach similar to RDBC called shifting DBC by using the concept of shift operation. The improved box-counting (IBC) technique was described by Li et al. [11] based on three major issues such as selection of the height of box, box-number computation, and partitioning of the surface. Liu et al. [12] presented another improved version of DBC approach called improved DBC (IDBC) by adopting three concepts such as revising box-counting approach, shifting box in spatial coordinate, and choosing suitable size of the grid for better FD estimation.

2 Related Background Work

The FD is a major characteristic of fractal geometry to estimate surface roughness of whole image. The basic rules behind this estimation are based on the concept of self-similarity. From the property of self-similarity, we can say a fractal is normally an irregular shape. When a large fractal object is divided into smaller parts and each part is same as whole object. While in this regard, many techniques have been projected for better estimation of FD, still the precise roughness calculation of complex objects is a great challenge. The following subsections describe the existing well-liked methods which we have taken into consideration for our experimental analysis purpose. Fractal dimension of digital images is evaluated based on the (Eq. 1), which as follows:

$$D = \log(N)/\log(1/r) \tag{1}$$

2.1 Principle of DBC Algorithm

Sarkar et al. [8] projected the differential box-counting (DBC) method for evaluation of FD of digital images. In order to implement this algorithm, they represent grayscale image in $3D$ space, where $2D$ space like (x, y) represents an image plane, and third coordinates like z represents the gray level. Consider the image of size as $M \times M$ and partitioned into $L \times L$ grids. Each and every grid comprises a stake of boxes of size $L \times L \times H$, where H indicates the height of an every box and this height can be calculated in terms of $L \times G/M$, where G represents the total number of gray levels. Let the maximum and minimum gray values of (i, j) grid fall in L and K box, respectively, then the box count $n_r(i, j)$ can be calculated (Eq. 2) as follows:

$$n_r(i, j) = L - K + 1 \tag{2}$$

By taking involvement from all blocks, N_r is counting for different values of L based on (Eq. 3).

$$N_r = \sum_{i,j} n_r(i, j) \tag{3}$$

2.2 Principle of RDBC Algorithm

Based on original DBC, Jin et al. [10] presented an improved version of DBC called relative DBC (RDBC) by adopting same maximum and minimum intensity point on the grid and taking the scale limit such as upper and lower limits of scale ranges for accurate FD estimation of texture images. Finally, N_r is evaluated (Eq. 4) as follows:

$$N_r = \sum_{i,j} ceil[k^*((K - L)/L')] \tag{4}$$

where k represents the coefficient in z-direction and ceil (.) is used to set the nearest integer.

2.3 Principle of IBC Algorithm

Similar to DBC and RDBC, Li et al. [11] presented another improved DBC mechanism by adopting three major parameters like selection of height of the box, estimation of box number, and partition of intensity surface. They are selecting box height by using the formula (Eq. 5) as follows:

$$r' = \frac{L}{1 + 2a\sigma} \tag{5}$$

where a is a positive integer and set the appropriate value a as 3, σ represents standard deviation, and $2a\sigma$ represents image roughness. Finally $n_r(i,j)$ can be evaluated (Eq. 6) as follows:

$$n_r(i,j) = \begin{cases} ceil(\frac{K-L}{r'}) & \text{if } K \neq L \\ 1 & \text{otherwise} \end{cases} \tag{6}$$

N_r can be calculated by taking the contribution of all grids based on (Eq. 3).

2.4 Principle of IDBC Algorithm

Liu et al. [12] proposed another improved version of DBC called improved differential box-counting method (IDBC) for estimating FD of grayscale image. In their proposed method, three modifications have been done such as concepts such as revising box-counting approach, shifting box in spatial coordinate, and choosing suitable size of the grid and nr calculated by taking maximum contribution from (Eq. 2) and (Eq. 7).

$$n_r(i,j) = \begin{cases} ceil(\frac{I_{max} - I_{min} + 1}{s'}) & I_{max} \neq I_{min} \\ 1 & \text{otherwise} \end{cases} \tag{7}$$

N_r can be calculated by taking the contribution of all grids, and final FD can be evaluated by means of least square regression line of $\log(N_r)$ verses $\log(1/r)$.

3 Proposed Methodology

After analyzing original DBC and its improved version in terms of fitting error, we conclude that no proper box-counting methods are presented to estimate fractal dimension accurately. Therefore, this chapter presents an extended version of original DBC approach to provide wider range of fractal dimension by using slope of the linear fit $\log(N_r)$ verses $\log(1/r)$ as well as provides smallest error fit not only in the average value but also to every image.

Our proposed methodology took an image of size $M \times M$ which has scaled down into smaller size of $L \times L$, where L indicates the individual box size ranging between 2 and $M/2$. The image can be represented in 3D spatial space, where (x, y) representing 2D spatial space and 3rd coordinate Z representing gray level G. To evaluate this proposed method, we estimate the mean of each box size L × L. Then, this mean value of each block size compared with each corresponding pixel of block. If the pixel value is greater than the mean value, then count of max (MA) is accumulated otherwise, and it can be accumulated as min (MI). As the fractal dimension varies from 2 to 3 for grayscale images. In this case, we have multiplied 3 with maximum and 2 with minimum intensity point for better estimation. For calculation of $n_r(i,j)$, DBC uses the (Eq. 2), RDBC uses (Eq. 4), IBC uses (Eq. 6), and IDBC uses (Eq. 7). For more reasonable our proposed method $n_r(i,j)$ is calculated on (Eq. 8). However, if $L' = L \times G/M$ is less than one, then n_r should be larger than one. Therefore, n_r should be defined as one box when maximum intensity value is not equal to minimum intensity value. Then, $n_r(i,j)$ can be evaluated as follows:

$$n_r(i,j) = \begin{cases} \frac{3 \times MA \times \max(i,j) - 2 \times MI \times \min(i,j)}{L' \times L} & if \max(i,j) \neq \min(i,j) \\ 1 & otherwise \end{cases} \qquad (8)$$

N_r can be calculated by taking the contribution of all grids, and final FD can be computed by using slope of the linear fit $\log(N_r)$ verses $\log(1/r)$.

4 Result and Discussion

This section describes the performance of our proposed method in terms of fitting error. The experiments are carried out on a system with a MATLAB14(a) in windows 8, 64 bit operating system, Intel (R) i7—4770 CPU @ 3.40 GHz. In this experimental analysis, we have considered four well-liked methods such as DBC, RDBC, IBC, and IDBC and finally compared with proposed method through one experiment, which have a set of standard original fourteen real Brodatz images [19] represented in Fig. 1.

Fig. 1 Fourteen real Brodatz texture images

4.1 Tests on Real Brodatz Texture Images

In this section, we are using a set of 14 real texture images [19] of size 256×256 from Brodatz database for our experimental analysis which is represented in Fig. 1. For this study, we used four existing well-liked algorithms like DBC, RDBC, IBC, and IDBC along with our proposed method. However, fractal dimension can be calculated using linear fit straight line verses $\log(N_r)$ and $\log(1/r)$. Then, the error fit can be estimated from the root mean square distance of the data points from the line by using (Eq. 9). Their corresponding FD and error fit are listed on Table 1 and Table 2, and there corresponding graphical comparison figures are presented on Fig. 2 and Fig. 3, respectively. The FD generated from DBC technique falls within the range between 2.20 and 2.61; similarly the other measures like RDBC, IBC, IDBC, and proposed methods ranging from 2.28 to 2.68, 2.29 to 2.69, 2.31 to 2.67,

Table 1 Computational FD of the Brodatz images presented in Fig. 1

Image name	Fractal dimension				
	DBC	RDBC	IBC	IDBC	PROPOSED
a11	2.60	2.68	2.69	2.67	2.74
a23	2.59	2.62	2.62	2.64	2.76
a38	2.52	2.59	2.60	2.57	2.70
a56	2.53	2.61	2.62	2.63	2.72
a62	2.50	2.55	2.58	2.55	2.74
a69	2.52	2.54	2.55	2.56	2.64
a71	2.54	2.55	2.57	2.59	2.68
a89	2.43	2.50	2.52	2.51	2.55
a90	2.30	2.43	2.46	2.48	2.50
a91	2.20	2.28	2.29	2.31	2.32
a93	2.61	2.65	2.67	2.66	2.75
a98	2.42	2.50	2.51	2.47	2.72
a99	2.41	2.48	2.49	2.49	2.65
a100	2.57	2.66	2.67	2.62	2.75

Table 2 Computational error fit of the Brodatz images presented in Fig. 1

Image name	Error fit				
	DBC	RDBC	IBC	IDBC	PROPOSED
a11	0.053	0.055	0.056	0.045	0.041
a23	0.066	0.068	0.068	0.059	0.048
a38	0.045	0.048	0.050	0.036	0.028
a56	0.066	0.068	0.069	0.058	0.053
a62	0.066	0.068	0.070	0.056	0.052
a69	0.056	0.055	0.056	0.046	0.040
a71	0.063	0.062	0.063	0.055	0.045
a89	0.065	0.067	0.069	0.056	0.054
a90	0.057	0.068	0.070	0.063	0.062
a91	0.067	0.076	0.075	0.064	0.028
a93	0.049	0.047	0.050	0.038	0.032
a98	0.065	0.069	0.070	0.055	0.045
a99	0.067	0.069	0.070	0.059	0.054
a100	0.053	0.057	0.058	0.042	0.043

and 2.32 to 2.76, respectively, are listed in Table 1, and individual error fit of Brodatz images using five methods is listed in Table 2. The average error fit is estimated from each method like DBC, RDBC, IBC, IDBC, and PROPOSED are 0.060, 0.063, 0.064, 0.052 and 0.045, respectively, are listed in Table 3, and presented on Fig. 4. The lower error fit indicates higher accuracy. We have seen from this experimental analysis that only proposed method provides smallest error fit not only in the average value but also to every image. Hence, it is crystal clear that the proposed method accurately estimates fractal dimension with less fit error because

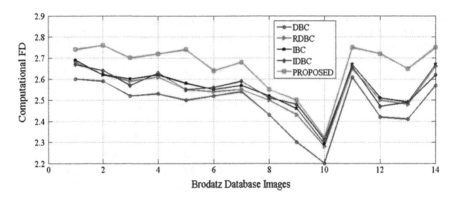

Fig. 2 Computational FD of the images in Fig. 1, by different approach

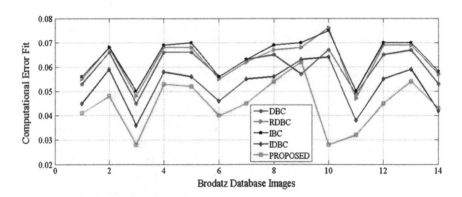

Fig. 3 Computational error fit of the images in Fig. 1, by different approach

Table 3 Computational average error fit

Average error fit				
DBC	RDBC	IBC	IDBC	PROPOSED
0.060	0.063	0.064	0.052	0.045

this method counted accurate number of boxes as compared to other existing method; hence, resulted error fit is quite less as compared to DBC, RDBC, IBC, and IDBC.

$$errorfit = \frac{1}{n}\sqrt{\sum_{i=1}^{n} \frac{(dx_i + c - y_i)}{1 + d^2}} \qquad (9)$$

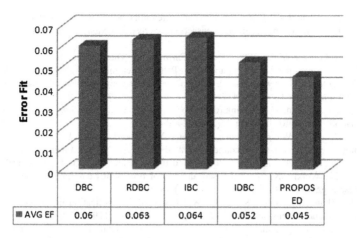

Fig. 4 Computational average error fit

5 Conclusion

In this study, we have proposed an extended version of DBC method; the improvement is based on the changing the means of the number of counting boxes in the box of block. In order to evaluate proposed method, we have carried out our experiment work with standard Brodatz database images and compared with original DBC and other improved DBC methods. The result illustrates that the proposed method has better performance in terms of less fit error as compared to other methods like DBC, RDBC, IBC, and IDBC. It is a robust and more precise method. Further systematic validation is needed on more kinds of images to analyze fractal dimension on specific objects.

References

1. Chen, W.S., Yuan, S.Y., Hsieh, C.M.,: Two algorithms to estimate fractal dimension of gray-level images. Optical Engineering. 42 (2003) 2452–2464
2. Asvestas, P., Matsopoulos, G.K., Nikita, K.S.,: A power differentiation method of fractal dimension estimation for 2-D signals. Journal of Visual Communication and Image Representation 9 (1998) 392–400
3. Mandelbrot, B.B.,: Fractal Geometry of Nature. San Francisco: Freeman (1982)
4. Lopes, R., Betrouni, N.,: Fractal and multifractal analysis: A review, Medical Image Analysis. 13 (2009) 634–649
5. Balghonaim, A.S., Keller, J.M.,: A maximum likelihood estimate for two-variable fractal surface. IEEE Transactions on Image Processing. 7 (1998) 1746–1753.
6. Peitgen, H.O., Jurgens, H., Saupe, D.,: Chaos and Fractals: New Frontiers of Science, first ed, Springer, Berlin (1992)
7. Gangepain, J.J, Carmes, C.R.,: Fractal approach to two dimensional and three dimensional surface roughness. Wear 109 (1986) 119–126

8. Sarker, N., Chaudhuri, B.B.,: An efficient differential box-counting approach to compute fractal dimension of image. IEEE Transactions on Systems Man and Cybernetics 24 (1994) 115–120
9. Buczkowski, S., Kyriacos, S., Nekka, F., Cartilier, L.,: The modified box-counting method: analysis of some characteristics parameters. Pattern Recognition. 3 (1998) 411–418
10. Jin, X.C., Ong, S.H., Jayasooriah, A practical method for estimating fractal dimension. Pattern Recognition Letter. 16 (1995) 457–464
11. Li, J., Du, Q., Sun, C.,: An improved box-counting method for image fractal dimension estimation. Pattern Recognition 42(2009) 2460–2469
12. Liu, Y., Chen, L., Wang, H., Jiang, L., Zhang, Yi., Zhao, J., Wang, D., Zhao, Y., Song, Y.,: An improved differential box-counting method to estimate fractal dimensions of gray-level images. Journal of visual communication and Image Representation 25 (2014) 1102–1111
13. Wenlu, X., Weixin, X.,: Fractal-based analysis of time series data and features extraction. Chinese Signal Processing Journal 13 (1997) 98–104
14. Yu, L., Zhang, D., Wang, K., Yang, W.,: Coarse iris classification using box-counting to estimate fractal dimensions. Pattern Recognition 38 (2005) 1791–1798
15. Nayak, S.R., Ranganath, A., Mishra. J.: Analysing fractal dimension of color Images. Computational Intelligence and Networks (CINE), International Conference on. IEEE. (2015) 156–159.
16. Nayak, S.R., Mishra, J.,: An improved method to estimate the fractal dimension of colour images. Perspectives in Science. 8 (2016) 412–416
17. Nayak, S.R., Mishra, J.,: An improved algorithm to estimate the fractal dimension of gray scale images. SCOPES2016. 3 (2016) 1109–1114
18. Biswas, M.K., Ghose, T., Guha, S., Biswas, P.K.,: Fractal dimension estimation for texture images: a parallel approach. Pattern Recognition Letters. 19 (1998) 309–313
19. Brodatz, P.,: Texture: A Photographic Album for Artists and Designers, New York

Dominant and LBP-Based Content Image Retrieval Using Combination of Color, Shape and Texture Features

Savita Chauhan, Ritu Prasad, Praneet Saurabh and Pradeep Mewada

Abstract Content-based image retrieval based on color, texture and shape are important concepts that facilitate quick user interaction. Due to these reasons, humongous amount of explores in this direction has been done, and subsequently, current focus has now shifted in improving the retrieval precision of images. This paper proposes a dominant color and content-based image retrieval system using a blend of color, shape, and texture features. K-dominant color is extracted from the pixels finding and can be gathered in the form of cluster or color clusters for forming a cluster bins. The alike colors are fetched on the basis of distance calculations between the color combinations. Then the combination of hue, saturation, and brightness is calculated where hue shows the exact color, and the color purity is shown by saturation, and the brightness of the percentage degree increases from black to white. Experimental results clearly indicate that the proposed method outperforms the existing state of the art like LBP, CM, and LBP and CM in combination.

Keywords Dominant color · Content retrieval · Color · Shape and texture

S. Chauhan (✉) · R. Prasad · P. Mewada
Department of Information Technology and Engineering,
Technocrats Institute of Technology (Excellence), Bhopal 462021, India
e-mail: savichauhan9143@gmail.com

R. Prasad
e-mail: rit7ndm@gmail.com

P. Mewada
e-mail: pradeepmewada07@gmail.com

P. Saurabh
Department of Computer Science and Engineering,
Technocrats Institute of Technology, Bhopal 462021, India
e-mail: praneetsaurabh@gmail.com

© Springer Nature Singapore Pte Ltd. 2018   235
P. K. Pattnaik et al. (eds.), *Progress in Computing, Analytics and Networking*,
Advances in Intelligent Systems and Computing 710,
https://doi.org/10.1007/978-981-10-7871-2_23

1 Introduction

Content-based image retrieval (CBIR) is not a new concept and deals with searching to retrieve images from the large database [1]. Content based basically implies that it searches the image based on its content rather than the metadata, such as keywords, tags, or descriptions associated with the image [2, 3]. Investigation on content-based image retrieval and similarity matching has expanded significantly in recent decade [3]. A significant measure of examination work has been done on image retrieval by various investigators, reaching out in both significance and extensiveness [4, 5]. The term content-based image retrieval (CBIR) seems to have begun with the work of Kato [6] which discussed modified recuperation of the photographs from a database, in perspective of the shading and shape display. Starting now and into the foreseeable future, the term has by and large been used to depict the technique of recuperating pined for pictures from an extensive social occasion of database, on the basis of picture components (color, texture and shape).

Image data provide the information separated from pictures using electronic or reproduced estimations [7]. An area vector is marked from every image in the database, and the strategy of all highlight vectors is enclosed as a database record [8, 9]. Most of the CBIR systems work similarly, component vectors are removed from each image in the database [10]. This paper introduces a dominant color and content-based image retrieval system using a blend of color, shape and texture features, Sect. 2 of this paper outlines the related work, Sect. 3 put forward the proposed work, while Sect. 4 covers experimental results, and Sect. 5 concludes the paper.

2 Related Work

CBIR illustrates the practices of salvaging the preferred images on the basis of syntactical image features from a significantly large set [11]. It uses several procedures, algorithms, and tools from different fields which include statistics, signal processing, pattern recognition, and computer vision [12, 13]. Das et al. [14] suggested a CBIR system that can be applied on different feature of images like shading and highlights it in an image. They proposed a shading-based recuperation structure that used fluffy abilities to fragment HSV shading space and also fuzzified the new image. Later on, Chaudhari et al. [15] recommended that the CBIR utilizes the visual properties of a picture, for example shading, shape, surface, and spatial format highlight the content of the image. They also proposed a calculation and hybridization with various productive calculations to enhance the exactness and execution of image retrieval. Thereafter, Bhagat et al. [16] proposed execution of electronic outline that is crucial for applications written in different languages and then can be linked to different data sources. It also displayed CBIR framework using assorted procedures for shading, surface, and shape examination. The basic target is to consider the unmistakable methodologies for picture mapping. Recently, bioinspired approaches [17] also gained attention in achieving different goals on this domain [18–20]. Mathur et al. [21] introduced CBIR as stated it as a compelling technique for recovering pictures from huge picture assets. Later on, Jenni et al. [22] highlighted multimedia contents and its associated complexity in nature that leads to exceptionally compelling recovery frameworks. They have also displayed review in the field of CBIR framework and exhibited and highlighted the photograph importance of preprocessing, highlight extraction and ordering, system learning, benchmarking datasets, similarity organizing, criticalness feedback, execution evaluation, and its portrayal. Next section presents the proposed work.

3   Proposed Method

This section introduces "Dominant color and content-based image retrieval system" using combination of color, shape and texture features. K-dominant color is extracted from the pixels finding approach. Then it is gathered and stored in cluster form or color clusters therefore forming a cluster bins. Now, alike colors are fetched on the basis of distance calculations between different color combinations. Thereafter, combination of hue, saturation, and brightness are calculated. In this approach, hue shows the exact color, color purity is shown by saturation, and brightness keeps on increasing from black to white. It extracts cluster of dominant colors, before isolating the shading traits of an image. All the pixels on database images are orchestrated into practically identical sorts of social occasions according to the likeness of their tones. Shading will be browsed with predefined tones that remain particularly near picture to pixel shading and is put away as another pixel. The distance between colors can be calculated and is given in Eq. (1) below

$$D_c = \min \left(\sqrt{(R_i - R_{iT})^2 + (Gi - G_{iT}) + (B_i - B_{iT})^2} \right) \tag{1}$$

where D_c represents the distance between colors, red, green, and blue and color intensity is represented by R_i, G_i, and B_i, respectively. The color table indexes are represented by R_{iT}, G_{iT}, and B_{iT}. The maximum percentage color component is selected as the dominant color and stored.

Local binary pattern (LBP) is used for efficient extraction of the local information. It helps in removing nearby elements of a question. The primary idea driving utilizing the LBP system is to ascertain the nearby structure of a picture by contrasting the pixels and the area given in Eq. (2).

$$LBP(C1, C2) = \sum_{n=0}^{n-1} 2^n G(PI_n - PI_c) \tag{2}$$

where C1 and C2 denote the central pixel. G can be expressed as follows:

$$G(X) = \begin{cases} 1 & if\ x \geq 0 \\ 0 & otherwise \end{cases} \tag{3}$$

where neighbor pixel intensity is denoted by PI_n and central pixel intensity is denoted by PI, then the positions of neighbors based on the center vector C1 and C2 are calculated and are given in Eqs. 4 and 5 as follows:

$$C1 = C1 + R\cos\frac{2\pi n}{S} \tag{4}$$

$$C2 = C2 - R\sin\frac{2\pi n}{S} \tag{5}$$

where R and S are the radius and sample point, respectively.

Now, color moment is calculated, and it is a strong estimation which can be utilized to separate pictures in light of the shading highlight. It is ascertained in light of the closeness of pictures. This can be essentially controlled by the ordinary circulation or by ascertaining their mean and difference. It demonstrates an example of minute which can help in distinguishing the picture in light of shading. Three minutes are utilized for the most part mean, standard deviation, and skewness. The shading can be characterized as the tint, immersion, and splendor. At that point, the minutes are computed for the different divert in the photograph. Firstly, it is calculated as the average color of the image by the following formula in Eq. (6):

$$C_i = \sum_{j=1}^{N} \frac{1}{N} P_{ij} \tag{6}$$

where the number of pixels is represented by N and P_{ij} shows the value of the j pixel of i color image. Now, standard deviation is calculated for the mean deviation calculation which is given in Eqs. 7 and 8 as follows:

$$\sigma_X = \sqrt{\sigma_X^2} \tag{7}$$

$$\sigma_X = \sqrt{\frac{1}{n}\left\{ \sum_{i=1}^{n} X_i^2 - \frac{1}{n}\left(\sum_{i=1}^{n} X_i \right)^2 \right\}} \tag{8}$$

Then, skewness is calculated to measure the asymmetric of the color distribution which is given in Eq. (9) as follows:

$$sk = \frac{\mu - \text{mode}}{\sigma} \tag{9}$$

Since, the proposed work is based on dominant color, LBP, color, shape and texture features, therefore it uses these features for efficient image retrieval. It can finish higher recuperation viability using transcendent shading. The components drawn from unexpected co-occasion histograms between the photograph tiles and relating supplement tiles, in RGB shading space, fill in as neighborhood descriptors of shading, shape, and surface. Now, coordination of the above mix, and then pack considering alike properties, is applied for overpowering tones and recuperate the practically identical images. Thereafter, histograms of edges are created and image information is discovered with respect to edge pictures figured using gradient vector flow fields. Invariant minutes are used to record the shape highlights, and then closeness measures is applied. The mix of the shading, shape, and surface components amidst picture and its supplement in conjunction with the shape components give a healthy rundown of capacities to picture recuperation. Reasonability estimation, precision, and audit can help in exhibiting the results. The proposed Algorithm 1 is given below as follows:

Algorithm 1

Input: Image database
Output: Image retrieval based on the similarity index
Step 1: Image data are selected.
Step 2: Pixels data preprocessing is started.
Step 3: Dominant color feature extraction.
Step 4: The mean of the separated index is then calculated and applied.

$$\text{Mean} = \frac{\sum Ci}{n} \tag{10}$$

$$\text{Standard Deviation} = \sqrt{1/N \sum_{i=1}^{N} (ci - \mu)^2} \tag{11}$$

$$\mu = \frac{y2 - y1}{x2 - x1} \tag{12}$$

Step 5: It is then send to the color moment process and LBP extraction process.
Step 6: Then feature vector extracted in the form of matrix.
Step 7: Based on the Euclidean distance, similarity measure has been calculated.

$$\sqrt{\sum_{i=1}^{N} (xi - yi)^2} \tag{13}$$

Step 8: Finally, similar images are extracted.

The working mechanism of the proposed work suggests that the image is selected first and then preprocessing is applied. Then dominant color-based extraction is performed. It is then processed for LBP mechanism. Then feature vector calculation is performed for similarity matching, and then finally based on the similar features, data are extracted.

4 Result Analysis

This section demonstrated and put forward the experiments carried to ascertain the performance of the proposed work, and then comparisons have been drawn with the current state of the art. All the experiments are conducted using Wang database consisting of 1000 images grouped in a total of 10 different categories with 100 different images in each. The proposed work strives to group these images one by one. Precision and accuracy are metric used for result evaluation and comparisons. The respective calculations are given below in Eqs. (13) and (14).

(i)
$$\text{Precision (P)} = \frac{TP}{TP + FP} \tag{13}$$

where

TP = True positive
FP = False positive
TN = True negative

(ii)
$$\text{Accuracy} = \sum \frac{P}{n} \tag{14}$$

Accuracy and precision tell about the performance of the proposed system, any system attempt to achieve high accuracy and high precision. Results obtained by the for accuracy in proposed methodology and various other state of the art is shown in Table 1, against different classification categories ranging from African man, Beaches, Buildings, Buses, Dinosaurs, Elephants, Flowers, Horses, Mountains, and Food. This table also shows that the proposed work outperforms other approaches and reports highest accuracy for all the ten categories. Also, Fig. 1 shows the graphical representation of the comparison shown in the table.

Figure 2 illustrates the precision of the proposed method along with other state of art. From the results, it is evident that the proposed method reports highest precision among all the methods.

Table 1 Comparison table of accuracy

S. no	Category	Proposed method DLBP–CBIR	Hybrid approach [15]	CM [15]	LBP [15]
1	African man (Classification 1)	0.9	Not calculated	Not calculated	Not calculated
2	Beaches (Classification 2)	0.8	0.5	0.31	0.35
3	Buildings (Classification 3)	0.85	0.7	0.28	0.3
4	Buses (Classification 4)	1	0.98	0.31	0.8
5	Dinosaurs (Classification 5)	1	1	0.93	0.97
6	Elephants (Classification 6)	0.6	0.6	0.44	0.19
7	Flowers (Classification 7)	1	0.89	0.61	0.79
8	Horses (Classification 8)	0.95	0.8	0.28	0.32
9	Mountains (Classification 9)	0.9	0.7	0.49	0.12
10	Food (Classification 10)	0.55	0.6	0.28	0.34
Overall accuracy		0.85	0.75	0.43	0.46

Fig. 1 Comparision of accuracy with different methods

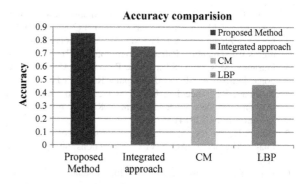

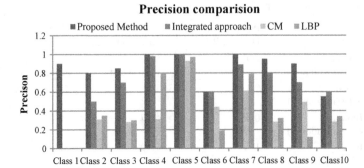

Fig. 2 Comparison of precision with different methodologies

5   Conclusion

This paper presented a dominant color and content-based image retrieval system using color, shape and texture features. In this method, K-dominant color is extracted from the pixels and formed a cluster. Same colors are fetched on the basis of distance calculations between the color combinations. Experimental results clearly indicate that the proposed method outperforms the existing state of the art like LBP, CM, and LBP and CM in combination and establishes the effectiveness of the proposed approach.

References

1. Datta, R., Joshi, D., Li, J., Wang, J.Z.: Image retrieval: Ideas, influences, and trends of the new age. ACM Computing Surveys (Csur) (2008) 40(2) 5.
2. Liu, Y., Zhang, D., Lu, G., Ma, W.Y.: A survey of content-based image retrieval with high-level semantics. Pattern recognition (2007) 40(1) 262–82.
3. Prasanna, M.K., Rai, S.C.: Image Processing Algorithms-A Comprehensive Study. International Journal of Advanced Computer Research Jun (2014) 1 4(2) 532.
4. Anandan, P., Sabeenian, R.S.: Curvelet based Image Compression using Support Vector Machine and Core Vector Machine-A Review. International Journal of Advanced Computer Research Jun 1 (2014) 4(2) 673.
5. Ghosh, P., Pandey, A., Pati, U.C.: Comparison of Different Feature Detection Techniques for Image Mosaicing. ACCENTS Transactions on Image Processing and Computer Vision (TIPCV). 1: 1–7.
6. Kato, T.: Database architecture for content-based image retrieval. In SPIE/IS&T 1992 symposium on electronic imaging: science and technology. International Society for Optics and Photonics. Apr 1 (1992) 112–123.
7. Flickner, M., Sawhney, H., Niblack, W., Ashley, J., Huang, Q., Dom, B., Gorkani, M., Hafner, J., Lee, D., Petkovic, D., Steele, D.: Query by image and video content: The QBIC system. Computer. Sep; 28(9) (1995) 23–32.
8. Gupta, A., Jain, R.: Visual information retrieval. Communications of the ACM. May 1 (1997) 40(5) 70–9.

9. Pentland, A., Picard, R.W., Sclaroff, S.: Photobook: Content-based manipulation of image databases. International journal of computer vision. Jun 1 (1996) 18(3):233–54.

10. Smith, J.R., Chang, S.F.: VisualSEEk: a fully automated content-based image query system. In Proceedings of the fourth ACM international conference on Multimedia. Feb 1 (1997) 87–98.

11. Wang, J.Z., Wiederhold, G., Firschein, O., Wei, S.X.: Content-based image indexing and searching using Daubechies' wavelets. International Journal on Digital Libraries. Mar 1(1998) 1(4) 311–28.

12. Carson, C., Belongie, S., Greenspan, H., Malik, J.: Blobworld: Image segmentation using expectation-maximization and its application to image querying. IEEE Transactions on Pattern Analysis and Machine Intelligence. Aug (2002) 24(8) 1026–38.

13. Wang, J.Z., Li, J., Wiederhold, G.: SIMPLIcity: Semantics-sensitive integrated matching for picture libraries. IEEE Transactions on pattern analysis and machine intelligence. Sep (2001) 23(9) 947–63.

14. Das, S., Garg, S., Sahoo, G.: Comparison of Content Based Image Retrieval Systems Using Wavelet and Curvelet Transform. The International Journal of Multimedia & Its Applications (2012).

15. Chaudhari, R., Patil, A.M.: Content based image retrieval using color and shape features. International Journal of Advanced Research in Electrical, Electronics and Instrumentation Engineering. Nov (2012) 1(5).

16. Bhagat, A.P., Atique, M.: Web based image retrieval system using color, texture and shape analysis: comparative analysis. International Journal of Advanced Computer Research (2013) 58–66.

17. Saurabh, P., Verma, B., Sharma, S.: Biologically Inspired Computer Security System: The Way Ahead, Recent Trends in Computer Networks and Distributed Systems Security, Springer (2011) 474–484.

18. Saurabh, P., Verma, B.: Cooperative Negative Selection Algorithm. International Journal of Computer Applications (0975–8887), vol 95—Number 17 (2014) 27–32.

19. Saurabh, P., Verma, B., Sharma, S.: An Immunity Inspired Anomaly Detection System: A General Framework A General Framework. Proceedings of 7th International Conference on Bio-Inspired Computing: Theories and Applications (BIC-TA 2012) Springer (2012) 417–428.

20. Saurabh, P., Verma, B.: An Efficient Proactive Artificial Immune System based Anomaly Detection and Prevention System. Expert Systems with Applications, Elsevier 60 (2016) 311–320.

21. Mathur, A., Mathur, R.: Content Based Image Retrieval by Multi Features using Image Blocks. International Journal of Advanced Computer Research. Dec 1 (2013) 3(4) 251.

22. Jenni, K., Mandala, S.: Pre-processing image database for efficient Content Based Image Retrieval. In Advances in Computing, Communications and Informatics (ICACCI, 2014) International Conference (2014) 968–972.

Proof of Retrieval and Ownership for Secure Fuzzy Deduplication of Multimedia Data

S. Preetha Bini and S. Abirami

Abstract With explosive growth of digital data and users wanting to outsource the data, there is great need for securely storing the data and utilization of storage space. Data deduplication eliminates redundant data from the storage and, thereby reducing the backup window, improves the efficiency of storage space and utilization of network bandwidth. Multimedia data such as images and videos are a good choice for deduplication, as it is one of the most frequent shared types of data found on data storage. A conventional secure deduplication employs exact data deduplication which is too rigid for multimedia data. Perceptually similar data maintain human visual perception and consume a lot of storage space. The proposed approach provides a framework for secure fuzzy deduplication for multimedia data and further strengthens the security by integrating proof of retrieval and proof of ownership protocols.

Keywords Multimedia data deduplication · Proof of retrieval
Proof of ownership

1 Introduction

Data deduplication is an effective data reduction practice for removing duplicate copies of redundant data, and it improves the utilization of storage and network bandwidth. With incremental outburst of digital data, the requirement for data storage service providers to manage their utilization of storage and bandwidth for data transfer in a cost-effective manner has become higher than ever [1].

S. Preetha Bini (✉) · S. Abirami
Department of Information Science and Technology,
College of Engineering, Anna University, Chennai, India
e-mail: preethabini94@gmail.com

S. Abirami
e-mail: abirami@auist.net

© Springer Nature Singapore Pte Ltd. 2018
P. K. Pattnaik et al. (eds.), *Progress in Computing, Analytics and Networking*,
Advances in Intelligent Systems and Computing 710,
https://doi.org/10.1007/978-981-10-7871-2_24

With the services provided by data storage service providers and users wanting to outsource their data, security of the data has become a major factor. The service providers for data storage though it is supposed to act according to the protocol; it cannot be trusted fully and are considered to be curious and semi-honest. For this issue, a deduplication scheme where the clients encrypt their data before storing it in the data storage and make it secure against malicious users and semi-honest data storage service provider.

Multimedia data such as images and videos are a good choice for deduplication, since they are one of the common types of data stored in data storages. Conventional deduplication schemes are too rigid for multimedia data since it performs exact deduplication. Modifications such as compression, resizing maintains human visual perceptions. The elimination of perceptually similar images saves storage space and increases the storage efficiency.

2 Background and Related Works

Xuan L. et al. [2] proposed a privacy-preserving fuzzy deduplication framework that addresses data storage and security. It accomplishes deduplication of images based on the estimation of their similarity over encrypted data. A secure perceptual similarity deduplication (SPSD) scheme is proposed which consists of pHash generation and encryption of hash and the image before uploading it to the CSP to provide security. Fuzzy deduplication is carried out on the storage by computing the hamming distances between the hash received by the CSP from the user and with hashes present in the server's database.

Navajit S. et al. [3] proposed a scheme that derives fingerprints from the perceptual data portions of the videos. This scheme is robust in opposition to the usual data protecting functions on the videos.

Rashid F. et al. [4] proposed an approach which employs a partial encryption and a distinctive image hashing over image compression using set partitioning in hierarchical trees (SPHIT) compression algorithm to achieve deduplication of images in data storage. The framework ensures security of data against a curious and dishonest cloud service provider or any malevolent user. It performs exact deduplication as even minor changes are detected.

Rashid F. et al. [5] proposed an original proof of retrieval and ownership protocols for images that are compressed using SPIHT. The POR procedure is invoked by the clients to make sure that their images are kept safely in the cloud, and the POW procedure is invoked by the cloud storage provider to validate the rightful proprietor of the images. The effectiveness of this method is because only a division of the data is used for encoding as the data is compressed.

Rashid F. et al. [6] proposed the proof of storage procedure for video deduplication in cloud storage. POR procedure is meant to allow the user to check the correctness of video stored in the cloud, and it ensures security by encoding the data and using error-correcting codes. The POW protocol is invoked by the CSP to validate the rightful proprietor of the video before giving access to the user.

Chen M. et al. [7] proposed a framework for high-precision duplicate image deduplication approach that involves eliminating the duplicate images by five stages where the features are extorted, high-dimensional indexing is done and the accurateness is increased. Then the centroid is decided on and the assessment of the deduplication scheme is computed. The framework fails to recognize a variety of image alteration.

Katiyar A. et al. [8] proposed a scheme for deduplication of videos where the redundancy eliminates not just by exact deduplication but also eliminates data that are similar at the application level. The framework consists of video signature generation, video segmentation, video sequence comparison, clustering, centroid selection, and video segment indexing and referencing.

3 Architecture of Proof of Storage for Secure Fuzzy Deduplication

The proposed approach provides a framework for proof of retrieval and ownership for secure fuzzy deduplication for multimedia data as shown in Fig. 1. Multimedia data such as images and videos are a good choice for deduplication as they are one of the most frequently shared types of data found on storage. Traditional deduplication scheme only eliminates exact copies of data. Perceptually similar images and videos consume a lot of storage space, as they maintain same human visual view. The framework provides a secure fuzzy deduplication framework for data storage services and further integrates proof of retrieval and proof of ownership to strengthen the security of the deduplication scheme. The framework involves pHash generation for image/video. The data are encrypted before sending it to the servers, to protect them against semi-honest data storage service providers and malevolent users. The hash value is sent to the server to check for duplicates by computing hamming distance. If a duplicate hash is not available, it will notify the user to upload the data. If not, it will update the pointer of the data ownership to the new client and will eliminate the duplicate copy of the data, thereby saving only one instance of the data. Proof of storage procedures further strengthens the security of the framework.

3.1 pHash Generation

Digital signature of the data (image/video) which are derived from various features of its content is considered as pHash of the data. In pHash generation, the hash value of the data (image/video) is calculated. Perceptually similar data have similar

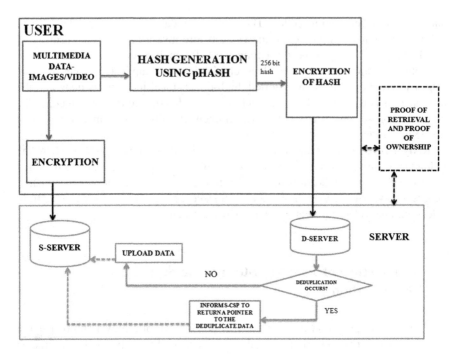

Fig. 1 Architecture for proof of retrieval and ownership for secure fuzzy deduplication of multimedia data

hash values. The image/video is given as the input and it produces a hash vector (H). The hash value is encrypted using a cryptographic hash function such as MD5 before it is uploaded to the server. The hash value for images is generated using perceptual hashing technique as follows:

1. N = predetermined bit extent of the pHash (N = m * m).
2. The image is normalized as I $\rightarrow$ I' with the dimension (m * m).
3. The average of the pixel gray values is computed.

4.
$$h(i,\ j) = \begin{cases} 0, & \text{Gray}\,(i,j) < \text{Avg} \\ 1, & \text{Gray}\,(i,j) \geq \text{Avg} \end{cases}$$

5. H = {h_1, h_2, ..., h_N} can be acquired by screening h(i, j).

The hash value for videos is generated using perceptual hashing technique [9] as follows:

1. Divide the video into a group of frames.
2. Boundary frame detection.
3. Evaluate the disparity between two frames using color intensities and their histogram.

4. For each frame, compute the distance measurement for boundary frame detection.
5. Determine the boundary frames using threshold.
6. Key frame selection.
7. Compute the hash value from the key frames that represent the video.

3.2 Encryption of Image/Video

The data are encrypted using symmetric encryption. Symmetric encryption includes:

- **Key stream generation**: A secret key (k) is employed to produce a key stream (K).
- **Data encryption**: It uses the key stream (K) to encrypt the data (PT) and produces the cipher data (CT).
- **Data decryption**: The key stream (K) can be obtained if we are aware of secret key using which the cipher data (CT) can be decrypted and produce the original data (PT).

3.3 Duplicate Check

The server exhibits two functions—the D-server to determine duplicates and the S-server to store the data. When the server receives the hash from the user, the D-server checks for duplicates by calculating hamming distance (d) between the received hash and the hashes already present in the database. T is the threshold value which is preset for similarity index. If hamming distance is less than the threshold, then a duplicate is present in the database and the D-server informs the S-server to update the pointer of the duplicate data. If hamming distance is greater than threshold, it requests the user to update image which is encrypted to ensure security.

3.4 Proof of Storage Protocols

The proof of retrieval is provoked by the user to check whether the data stored by user are secure against a semi-honest data storage service provider or malicious users. It ensures correctness of data and ensures the availability of data for retrieval by the user. The proof of ownership [10] is provoked by the server to authenticate the user who is requesting the data whether he is the rightful proprietor or not,

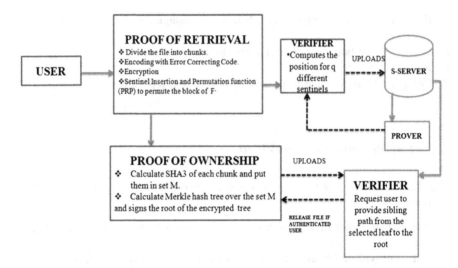

Fig. 2 Proof of storage protocols

before releasing the data. Figure 2 shows the Proof of Storage procedure which strengthens the security of the framework.

The proof of retrieval is invoked by the client to check the integrity and correctness of the data. It involves the following steps:

1. The file is divided into chunks.
2. Error-correcting codes are applied to each chunk.
3. MAC values of the encoded portions are computed and these are appended at the end of the chunks.
4. The verifier (user) invokes the query by signifying the index locations of the chunks to be verified and the index location of the MAC.
5. The prover (server) sends the equivalent chunks and the consequent MAC.
6. The verifier computes the MAC of the chunks sent by the server and compares it against the corresponding MAC returned by the server.
7. If there is an equivalent chunk, then the consequent blocks are kept whole; if not, the verifier employs an error correction code to recover the $d/2$ errors in the chunks.

The proof of ownership is provoked by the server to authenticate the right user, to give access of the data to the client.

1. The file is divided into portions.
2. The SHA3 hash of each portion is computed and kept in a set M.
3. The client computes a binary Merkle Hash tree (MHT) over the set M and marks the root of the encrypted tree. The tree and the set are sent to the server while uploading the data for the first time.

4. The server to authenticate the user selects a random leaf index j in M.
5. The client demanding the data will need to give a sibling path from the leaf index j demanded by the server to the root.
6. The path from the user is acquired by the server. The server will rebuild the tree from the path given by the client and will validate the root over the one marked when the initial upload is done.
7. In case of an equivalent path, the client demanding the data will be acknowledged as the rightful proprietor and the server will provide access for the data else it will not provide access for the data to the client.

4   Results and Analysis

By using MATLAB, the experiments were performed on the dataset (Standard images like lena, bridge, mandrill, and classic videos). The pHash for images and videos are generated, and the hash values are encrypted and calculation of hamming distance is calculated to determine whether the data are the same (perceptually similar images/video) or different data as shown in Fig. 3.

Figure 4 shows that the data are encrypted as using symmetric encryption before uploading to server to protect the privacy of the user against the semi-honest data storage service provider and malicious users.

Proof of retrieval and ownership is provoked to further strengthen the security of the framework. Proof of retrieval is done by file chunking and applying error-correcting codes such as Reed Solomon codes which is implemented using MATLAB Communication Systems toolbox. The correctness and availability of the data are tested. Figure 5 shows proof of ownership is provoked by computing Merkle Hash Trees for the data file. The POW procedure is resourceful in terms of computational cost as it will not require any computation of the data individually, as it utilizes the data from the POR scheme.

After hash comparison using hamming distance, the hash values are stored in the database using MySQL server. If a hash value of a new data is inserted, then the master table is updated by uploading the data along with hash. If a duplicate is already present, then it updates the linker table by only setting the reference of the image. Figures 6 and 7 show the master table where there are no duplicates based on hash value comparison and the linker table where data references are updated.

The performance of deduplication can be calculated by determining recall and precision using (1) and (2) and the deduplication ratios are evaluated for various parameters (Table 1).

$$Recall = \frac{Number\ of\ duplicate\ copies\ to\ be\ detected}{Number\ of\ total\ copies} \quad (1)$$

$$Precision = \frac{Number\ of\ duplicate\ copies\ correctly\ detected}{Number\ of\ duplicates\ detected} \quad (2)$$

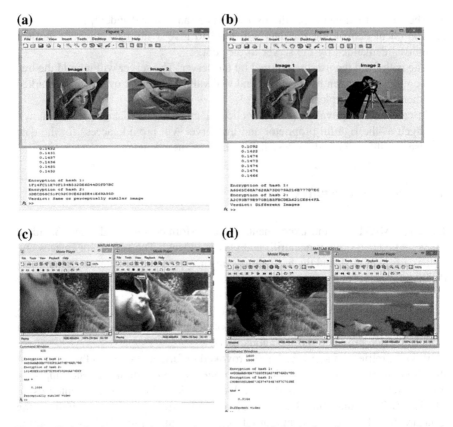

Fig. 3 pHash for images and videos is generated, and the hash values are encrypted and calculation of hamming distance is calculated to determine whether the data are the same (perceptually similar images/video) or different data

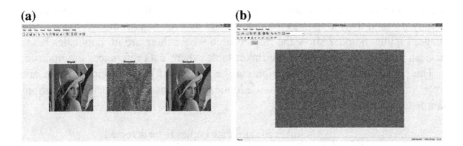

Fig. 4 Encryption of data using symmetric encryption

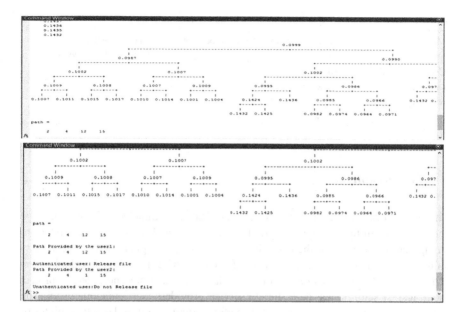

Fig. 5 Proof of ownership using Merkle hash tree

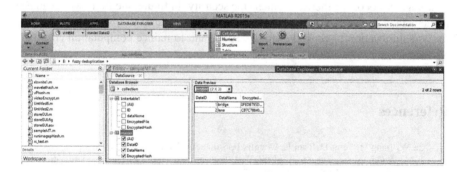

Fig. 6 Table with no duplicates based on hash comparison

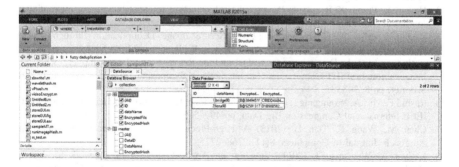

Fig. 7 Table for reference update

Table 1 Evaluation of deduplication for various parameters

Modification	Maximum ratio tested for modification parameters	Ratio to which deduplication occurs
Compression (%)	40–80	50
Contrast enhancement (%)	40–80	60
Resizing (%)	40–80	50
Rotation	180°	90°

5 Conclusion

The framework provides a secure fuzzy deduplication framework for data storage services and further integrates proof of retrieval and proof of ownership to strengthen the security of the deduplication scheme. Deduplication of perceptually similar data provides better storage efficiency since traditional deduplication scheme only deduplicates exact copies of data. The data are encrypted to protect them against semi-honest data storage service providers and malicious users. The hash value is sent to the server, and if there is a duplicate it updates the pointer of the duplicate data, else data are uploaded along with the hash. Integration of proof of storage protocols further strengthens the security. In future, the framework can be implemented in a real cloud environment and further study can be done on secure fuzzy deduplication to conserve storage space and to reduce computation cost and resources.

References

1. Xia W, Jiang H, Feng D, Tian L, Douglis F, Shilane P, Yu H, Min F, Yucheng Z, Yukun Z (2016) A Comprehensive Study of the Past, Present, and Future of Data Deduplication. In: Proceedings of the IEEE, 104(9):1681–1710.
2. Xuan L, Jin L, Faliang H. (2016) A Secure Cloud Storage System Supporting Privacy-Preserving Fuzzy Deduplication. Journal of Soft Computing, 20(4):1437–1448.
3. Navajit S, Prabin K B. (2014) Perceptual Hash Function for Scalable Video. International Journal of Information Security, 13(81):81–93.
4. Rashid F, Miri A, Woungang I. (2016) Secure Image Deduplication through Image Compression. Journal of Information Security and Applications, 27(28):54–64.
5. Rashid F, Miri A, Woungang I. (2014) Proof of Retrieval and Ownership Protocols for Images through SPIHT Compression. 6th International Symposium on Cyberspace Safety and Security, pp 835–838.
6. Rashid F, Miri A, Woungang I. (2015) Proof of Storage for Video Deduplication in the Cloud. IEEE International Congress on Big Data, pp 499–505.
7. Chen M, Wang S, Tian L. (2013) A High-Precision Duplicate Image Deduplication Approach. Journal of Computers, 8(11):2768–2775.
8. Katiyar A, Weissman J. (2011) Videdup: an Application-Aware Framework for Video De-duplication. 3rd USENIX Conference on Hot Topics in Storage and File Systems, p 7.

9. Roover C D, Vleeschouwer C D, Lefebvre F, Macq B (2005) Robust Video Hashing based on Radial Projections of Key Frames. IEEE Transaction on Signal Processing, 53(10):4020–4037.
10. Halevi S, Harnik D, Pinkas B, Shulman-Peleg A. (2011) Proofs of Ownership in Remote Storage Systems. 18th ACM Conference Computer Communications Security, pp 491–500.

Maintaining Consistency in Data-Intensive Cloud Computing Environment

Sruti Basu and Prasant Kumar Pattnaik

Abstract Cloud is a service that offers its users to access the shared pool of computing resources based on pay per use basis. Presently, cloud computing is adopted by most of the start-up companies and research areas. Data-intensive cloud computing is adopted in order to handle enormous amount of transactional data. This paper proposes a model in order to achieve the consistency under data-intensive cloud computing environment and compares the proposed model with an existing improved consistency model.

Keywords Data-intensive cloud computing environment · Consistency
CAP · Replica servers

1 Introduction

Cloud framework consists of the services namely Platform as a Service (PaaS), Infrastructure as a Service (IaaS), Software as a Service (SaaS) and Data base as a Service (DaaS). DaaS is a cloud computing service that enables its users to access the data base through Internet without any requirement of setting hardware or installing software [1]. So, DaaS helps the cloud users when they demand to store or retrieve any information using the data base [2]. Data-intensive computing is recommended for handling and managing a large amount of data. Data-intensive cloud computing is related to the analysis of both the programming techniques and platforms that are used to perform data-intensive assignments [3]. For any kind of data base system, transaction management is one of the most important considerations. For the static environment, cloud supports ACID-based transaction processing but for the moving environment ACID is not performed well [4]. So, for

S. Basu (✉) · P. K. Pattnaik
School of Computer Engineering, KIIT University, Bhubaneswar, India
e-mail: srutibasu1991@gmail.com

P. K. Pattnaik
e-mail: patnaikprasant@gmail.com

© Springer Nature Singapore Pte Ltd. 2018
P. K. Pattnaik et al. (eds.), *Progress in Computing, Analytics and Networking*,
Advances in Intelligent Systems and Computing 710,
https://doi.org/10.1007/978-981-10-7871-2_25

moving environment, cloud may support CAP theorem which ensures consistency, availability and partition tolerance [5].

2 Related Work

To achieve scalability and availability is a big issue for data-intensive cloud computing environment. Availability can be achieved by using data replication technique. But to provide the correctness of a transaction, maintaining consistency is also an essential issue for transaction processing system. Some related works are discussed below:

In 2010, Islam and Vrbsky [6] introduced a tree-based consistency approach for cloud data base. This approach helps to get better performance by reducing response time through minimizing the interdependency among the replica servers.

In 2011, Iskander et al. [7] proposed a modified version of two-phase commit protocol namely "Two-phase Validation Protocol" to give the assurance of a safe transaction. They also suggested this protocol for ensuring data consistency.

In 2012, Salinas et al. [8] suggested an architecture for distributed storage system combining cloud and traditional data base replication concept for providing transactional support and high availability. The architecture offers different levels of consistency in accordance with the demands of client applications to provide high availability along with elastic service in transactional system.

In 2012, Aye [9] proposed an analytical model. This model is used to maintain consistency on private cloud storage system by using M/M/1 queuing. They also introduced an approach to achieve better readability after update operation.

In 2014, Radi [10] proposed a technique to improve update propagation in cloud data storage. He introduces the technique to maintain the consistency of replica server. This technique is able to achieve both consistency and reliability along with better performance.

In 2014, Jeevarani and Chitra [11] introduced a model for improving consistency in cloud computing data bases. They suggested prioritized read–write mechanism using the Prioritized Operation Manager (POM) to obtain consistency as well as reliability. But this model is not able to reduce response time when the number of client request increases.

In 2015, Pati and Pattnaik [12] suggested a set of twelve criterions for cloud data base so that the cloud data base becomes standardized like traditional data bases.

In 2016, Bugga and Kumar [13] suggested a framework to ensure the security of distributed transactions in cloud computing environment. They enhanced two-phase commit protocol in their algorithm to provide secure transactions by ensuring ACID properties.

3 Proposed CCSA

For the distributed and cloud data base environment, data replication technique is heavily used to provide high availability [14]. As a result, most of the cloud services go for eventual consistency for data propagation throughout the system [7]. So, it becomes a challenge to maintain consistency along with availability especially when the servers of different locations are connected. This paper proposes an algorithm namely Cloud Consistency Satisfying Algorithm (CCSA) for ensuring consistency as well as availability in data-intensive cloud computing environment.

Figure 1 consists of one global transaction manager (GTM) and many local transaction managers (LTMs). All the nodes are represented as replica server, and edges are represented as network connection between them. Each node connected with all the other nodes that means each replica server has a connection with all other replica servers. Each replica server has one LTM which controls all operations particularly for that server. GTM controls the operations for all servers. So, GTM directly linked with all issuing LTM.

For read operation, data can be read from any replica server. But for update operation, the node for which the update request came becomes the primary node for that operation, and other nodes become the secondary nodes. So, here is no fixed primary node for every update operation. For which node the update request came becomes the primary node for that particular update operation. The primary node is updated first and after that the secondary nodes are updated.

Fig. 1 A scenario of proposed model

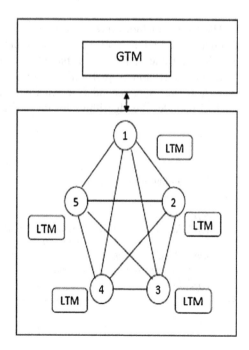

Table 1 Algorithm for request processing

Step1. Begin
Step2.   If (WaitQ!=Empty)
Step3.   Ri=Dequeue(WaitQ)
Step4.   Else
Step5.   Ri=Dequeue(RequestQ)
Step6.   End If
Step7.   If({Ri→type}==R)
Step8.   If({Ri→data}!=locked)
Step9.   Process Read operation
Step10.   Else
Step11.   Enqueue Ri the WaitQ
Step12.   go to Step5
Step13.   End If
Step14.   Else if({Ri→data}!=locked && {Ri→node}!=busy)
Step15.   Ri→data=locked
Step16.   Ri→node=busy
Step17.   Process update operation
Step18.   Else
Step19.   Enqueue Ri the WaitQ
Step20.   go to Step5
Step21.   End If
Step22.   End If
Step23. End

The CCSA includes three stages known as request processing, read operation, and update operation. All the stages are represented using algorithm and presented in Table 1, Table 2, Table 3, Table 4 and Table 5, respectively.

Update operation is performed by dividing into three sites called LTM and primary replica site, secondary replica site and GTM site. Table 3, Table 4 and Table 5 includes the algorithms for these sites, respectively.

Table 2 Algorithm for read operation

Step1. Begin
Step2. Ri sends {Ri→data} to the LTM of node N
*   //N is the node in which the request is come*
Step3. Raed{Ri→data}
Step4. Process Request Processing
Step5. End

Table 3 Algorithm for update operation in LTM and primary replica site

Step1. Begin
Step2. Ri sends {Ri→data} to the LTM of node N
                        //N is the node in which the request is come
Step3. update{Ri→data}
Step4. adj[N]=busy // adj[N] are the adjacent nodes of N
Step5. node N forward message update{Ri→data} to adj[N]
Step6. send ack(Ri) to GTM
Step7. Process Request Processing
Step8. End

Table 4 Algorithm for update operation in secondary replica site

Step1. Begin
Step2. Receive the message update{Ri→data} from node N
Step3. For each adj[N]
Step4.   update{Ri→data}
Step5.   send ack(Ri) to GTM
Step6. End For
Step7. End

3.1 Working Principle

The working principles of CCSA are as follows:

All requests are put into a queue referred as RequestQ and consider each request has three parameters say type, data and node.

Another queue called WaitQ is used to store the waiting requests. Initially, WaitQ is empty. At first, all the requests which came from the client side are stored in the RequestQ. Then, WaitQ is checked. As per our proposed algorithm, if the WaitQ is empty, then the request is deleted from the RequestQ otherwise the request is deleted from the WaitQ. After that we check the type of the request.

If the type of the request is Read, then check whether the data is locked or not. If the data is not locked, then Read operation is processed otherwise the request is put into the WaitQ. Then, next request is processed. For processing Read operation, Request Ri sends the Ri → data to the local transaction manager (LTM) of node N. Then, read the data from the node in which the request has come. After that the primary node makes all of its adjacent nodes busy and also forwards the "update data" message to its adjacent nodes.

Table 5 Algorithm for update operation in GTM site

```
Step1. Begin
Step2.   For each request Ri
Step3.       Initialize count=0
Step4.       For each node
Step5.           If(Receive ack(Ri)==1)
Step6.               node=free
Step7.               Increase count by 1
Step8.           End If
Step9.       End For
Step10.      If(count==n)
Step11.          send ack(Ri) to the client
Step12.          {Ri→data}=unlocked
Step13.      End If
Step14.  End For
Step15. End
```

If the type of the request is Update, then first check two conditions: whether the data for which the update request came is locked or not and also the node for which the request came is busy or not. If these two conditions are satisfied, then global transaction manager (GTM) makes the data (in which the request is come) locked and also makes the node (in which the request is come) busy. Then process the update operation. Otherwise put the request into WaitQ. For the update operation, the node in which the update request is come becomes the primary node for that operation and all other nodese become the secondary nodes. So, here is no fixed primary node. For which node the update request is come becomes the primary node only for that particular update operation. For processing update operation at primary site, Request Ri is sent to the LTM of node N (N is the primary node of that operation). Then, the primary node N updates the data in its own site. After that the primary node makes all of its adjacent nodes busy and also forwards the message update data to its adjacent nodes. Then, it sends acknowledgement to the GTM and process request processing algorithm to process the next request. In the secondary site, the adjacent nodes of primary node receive the update message from the primary node. Each node updates the data value for which the request is come and sends acknowledgement to the GTM. In GTM site, GTM receives the acknowledgement from each node and makes them free. When GTM gets the acknowledgement from all nodes for a particular request, then it sends the acknowledgement to the client and unlock the data.

Fig. 2 Number of
inconsistent read versus
probability of update
operation

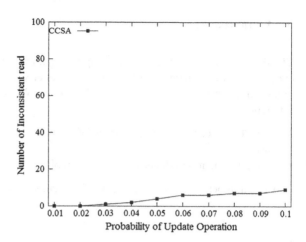

4 Result and Comparison

In this segment, we evaluate the performance of our model CCSA on the basis of
consistency. This analysis consists of two parameters: number of inconsistent read
and probability of update operation. Figure 2 shows that number of inconsistent
read is almost zero when the probability of update operation is very low. But with
the increasing of probability of update operation, the inconsistent read is increased
though the increment of inconsistent read is negligible.

We also compare our CCSA model with another model described by Jeevarani
and Chitra [11]. Their POM consistency model is also able to provide consistency
for cloud data base. The following table shows the comparison of CCSA model and
POM model (Table 6).

Table 6 CCSA model versus POM model

Attributes	CCSA	POM
Type of topology used for network connection	Mesh	Ring
Number of replica server increases	Response time increases	Response time increases
Number of update operation increases	Response time increases	Response time increases
Probability of update operation increases	Maintain consistency	Maintain consistency
When any network failure occur	The system will continue its processing	The system will be temporarily out of service

5   Conclusion

Cloud data base consistency is becoming very popular for medium-size and start-up companies. The maintenance of consistency property is becoming a challenge to the implementation of transactional cloud data bases. We conclude our work with the followings:

- The CCSA technique gives a model for maintaining consistency in cloud data base.
- The experiment conducts for only five replica servers.

More number of replica servers will be included as future scope of work.

References

1. Shehri, W.A.: Cloud Database as a Service. International Journal of Database Management System (IJDMS), vol. 5, No. 2, (April 2013)
2. Pasayet, S., Pati, S., Pattnaik, P.K.: Classification and Live Migration of Data-intensive Cloud Computing Environment. Communications in Computer and Information Science. Springer (2013)
3. Shamsi, J., Khojaye, M. A., Qasmi, M. A: Data-Intensive Cloud Computing: Requirements, Expectations, Challenges, and Solutions. Springer (2013)
4. Pattnaik, P.K., Kabat, M.R., Pal, S.: Fundamentals of Cloud Computing. 1st ed., Vikas Publishing House Pvt. Ltd., ISBN: 9789325976108. (2015) 85–98
5. Simon, S.: Brewer's CAP Theorem. CS341 Distributed Information Systems, University of Basel (HS2012)
6. Islam, M. A., Vrbsky, S. V. : Tree-Based consistency approach for cloud databases in Cloud Computing Technology and Science (CloudCom). International Conference on IEEE (2010) 25–44
7. Iskander, M. K., Wilkinson, D. W., Lee, A. J. : Enforcing Policy and Data Consistency of Cloud Transactions. Distributed Computing Workshops (ICDCSW) (2011)
8. Salinas, I.A., et al.: Classic Replication Techniques on the Cloud. IEEE Seventh International Conference on Availability, Reliability and Security (2012)
9. Aye, Y. N. : Data Consistency on Private Cloud Storage System. International Journal of Emerging Trends & Technology in Computer Science (IJETTCS) Volume 1, Issue 1 (May–June 2012)
10. Radi, M.: Improved Aggressive Update Propagation Technique in Cloud Data Storage. International Journal of Emerging Trends & Technology in Computer Science (IJETTCS) (2014) 102–105
11. Jeevarani, B., Chitra, K.: Improved Consistency Model in Cloud Computing Databases. IEEE International Conference on Computational Intelligence and Computing Research (2014)
12. Pati, S., Pattnaik, P. K.: Criterions for Databases in Cloud Computing Environment. Springer India (2015)
13. Bugga, N., Kumar, A.S.: A New Framework and Algorithms for secure cloud Transactions. International Journal of Computer Science and Mobile Computing (IJCSMC) Vol 5, Issue 6, (2016) 87–94
14. Souri, A., Pashazadeh, S., Navin, A.H.: Consistency of Data Replication Protocols In Database Systems: A Review. International Journal on Information Theory (IJIT), Vol. 3, No. 4, (October 2014)

Cryptographic Key Generation Scheme from Cancellable Biometrics

Arpita Sarkar, Binod Kr Singh and Ujjayanta Bhaumik

Abstract The cryptographic algorithms in current use are facing the problem of maintaining the secrecy of private keys which need to be stored securely to prevent forgery and loss of privacy. Stored private keys are saved by user chosen passwords are often acquired by brute-force attacks. Also, the user finds it difficult to remember large keys. So, it is a major issue in asymmetric cryptography to remember, protect, and manage private keys. The generation of cryptographic key from individual user's biometric feature is a solution to this problem. In this approach, it is too hard for the attacker to guess the cryptographic key without the prior knowledge of the user's biometrics. But the problem with biometrics is that compromise makes it unusable. To solve the above issue, cancellable biometrics has been proposed. In this present work, there is an attempt to generate cryptographic key from the user's cancellable fingerprint template.

Keywords Asymmetric cryptography · Cryptographic key generation
Cancelable template · Fingerprint biometrics

1 Introduction

In this digital age, the large amount of information at stake has made information security a burning issue. An unauthorized user with an illicit mind can cause havoc, and thus, cryptography is the necessity to prevent such wrongdoing. Cryptographic schemes can be asymmetric, for example RSA; symmetric algorithms include data

A. Sarkar (✉) · B. K. Singh · U. Bhaumik
Department of Computer Science and Engineering, NIT Jamshedpur,
Jamshedpur, India
e-mail: asarkar.cse@nitjsr.ac.in

B. K. Singh
e-mail: bksingh.cse@nitjsr.ac.in

U. Bhaumik
e-mail: 2014ugcs085@nitjsr.ac.in

© Springer Nature Singapore Pte Ltd. 2018
P. K. Pattnaik et al. (eds.), *Progress in Computing, Analytics and Networking*,
Advances in Intelligent Systems and Computing 710,
https://doi.org/10.1007/978-981-10-7871-2_26

265

encryption standard (DES), 3DES [1] and advanced encryption standard (AES), and others. It is very difficult to remember such a long keys used in these encryption standards. Smart cards and password-based authentication are viable options but are prone to social engineering and dictionary attacks. Thus, biometrics has been incorporated with cryptography to create better robust security techniques and there is no need to carry passwords or tokens. Cryptographic key is created using user features, for instance finger prints, iris, and face and saved so that biometric authentication is mandatory to reveal those stored keys. As the biometric traits are fixed in a person, if either the biometric trait or the cryptographic key is compromised anyway, then both become useless forever. Since the biometric trait used in key generation must be private, it should not tell anything about the biometric information of user. Cancellable template is such a popular option utilized in crypto-biometric system to solve the problems that are mentioned above. In different persons, fingerprints are statistically independent and that is what gives rise to the uniqueness which can be used for random cryptographic key generation from fingerprint templates. In case cancellable template is compromised, it can be cancelled easily. The present work uses the randomness present in fingerprint data of the user in place of his authentication. In this paper, a cancellable template is acquired from fingerprint of a user. Keys can be updated easily by updating the cancellable template. In this approach, a new cancellable template can be generated by updating shuffle key.

2 Related Works

The present effort contains transformation of biometric template and cryptographic key generation from transformed cancelable template. Some previous work related to the current work is described in this section. Cancelable biometrics was developed so that biometric template could be cancelled like a password and is unique to every application [2, 3]. The procedures are mainly (a) biometric salting and (b) non-invertible transformation. For example, biometric salting, user-specific random projection, is used [4]. Later, non-invertible transformation was brought into notice, where the fingerprint is distorted by a sequence of three non-invertible transformation functions which are Cartesian, polar, and surface folding transformation [5]. Tulyakov et al. proposed a method to generate hashed value of fingerprint minutiae points and doing fingerprint matching more excellently [6]. It is really very difficult to regenerate original template with resulting hash values because of one-way-ness of hash function. Ang et al. gave an idea of geometric transformation-based approach to create a key-dependent cancelable template [7]. Maiorana et al. in 2009 did works on similar fields that involved digital signatures [8]. Nanni et al. in 2010 proposed that the different matching trained using cancelable template that could be also used to improve the online signature verification performance [9]. Cryptographic key generation from biometric traits:-There are a few methods that are available for cryptographic key generation from different biometric traits. Monrose et al. devised a way where user voice using a passphrase is used to create cryptographic key [10]. Feng et al. made a method, BioPKI, where user's online signature is used to engender a private key [11]. Face biometrics can also be used to devise cryptographic key [12]. Similarly, iris feature is also used to generate cryptographic keys [13–15].

3 Proposed Method

This part discusses the proposed approach. An outline of proposed scheme is shown in Fig. 1.

This present work generates a pair of private and public key for Elgamal cryptosystem from the cancelable fingerprint template of the user. The different tasks involved in this approach are deliberated as follows.

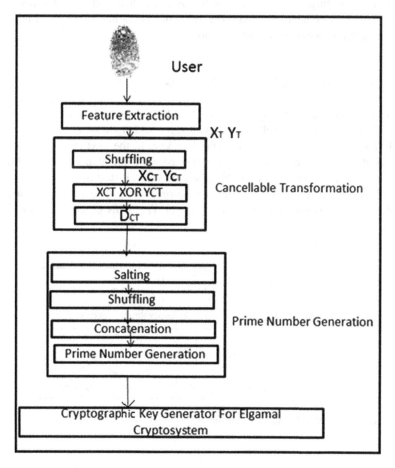

Fig. 1 Schematic diagram of proposed scheme

3.1   Feature Extraction from Fingerprint of the User

The methods for minutia extraction involve image enhancement, binarization, morphological operation followed by minutiae extraction often obtained by Principal Curve Analysis [16]. This algorithm yields (x, y, θ, q) as a minutiae point where (x, y) is the coordinate value, θ characterizes the alignment angle, and q signifies the quality of a minutiae point. For our purpose, Fx comprises x-coordinate values and in vector Fy-coordinate values of minutiae points are stored. $Fx = [xi]$ and $Fy = [yi]$, where $i = 1$ to n.

3.2   Cancellable Template Generation

In this step, the fingerprint template of the user is transformed into non-invertible forms, called cancellable template. The steps of generating transformed template from extracted minutia points are as follows.

3.2.1   Shuffling of X and Y Vector Elements

In this technique, a randomly generated key K of length N is taken. X_T is the biometric feature vector which is divided into L equal lengths blocks which are then synchronized with the N bits of the shuffling key. In the next step, two different parts containing biometric features are formed. The initial part has the blocks aligning to the position with the shuffling key bit value 1. Rest is taken into the next part. These two parts are now coupled to form biometric feature X_{CT} which is shuffled. Same process is applied to Y_T to get Y_{CT}. This process is depicted in Fig. 2.

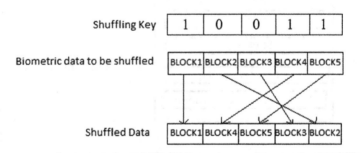

Fig. 2 Shuffling of X and Y vectors elements

The algorithm for transformed template generation is as follows.

```
//X_CT and X_T are vectors of size N. X_T is divided into 10
   blocks. b is a matrix of size 10. //
   Input: Vector X_T of size N
   Output: Shuffled X_T as X_CT
   Begin
   b=[1,1,1,1,1,1,1,1,1,1];
for q=1:10
  b(q)=random number that is either 1 or 0
end
X_CT =X_T;
jj=0; mm=aa; bs=N/10; ic=1;
for i=1:10
   if b(i)==1
     for q=1:bs
        jj=jj+1;
        X_CT(jj)=X_T(ic);
        ic=ic+1;
     end
end
if b(i)==0
   mm=mm-bs;
   for q=1:bs
     X_CT (mm+1)=X_T(ic);
     ic=ic+1;
     mm=mm+1;
   end
     mm=mm-bs;
   end
   end
   End
```

3.2.2 Shuffled Vectors Concatenation

Each and every element of vector X_{CT} and Y_{CT} are merged using bitwise XOR operation to get D_{CT} vector. $D_{CT}i = X_{CT}\char`^Y_{CT}$, $1 <=i <=N$.

3.3 Prime Number Generation from Cancellable Template for Elgamal Cryptosystem

If the total bits in D_{CT} are less than 1024, random bits are added; otherwise, first 1024 bits are selected to get vector U. U is then shuffled. The algorithm is as follows:

Input: Vector U
Output: Prime number p
p = Concatenation of all numbers in U
If p is even, add 1 to p
Keep on adding 2 to p until p is prime.

3.4 Key Generation and Encryption Decryption

For this purpose, we follow the standard protocol for Elgamal cryptosystem. Only the prime number used is obtained as above from fingerprint minutiae points.

4 Experimental Results

Database used: FVC 2002 DB1

Experimental Setup: This work is done with Intel® Core™ i7 Processor by 2.4 GHz clock speed in MATLAB12 using Windows 7OS.

Experimental Results: In this present research, work data of fingerprint is taken only for randomizing not for authentication of the user. Here, total 126 values for x-coordinates and so for y-coordinates are used to make shuffle key in MATLAB12. The corresponding values in X_T and Y_T are XORed in order to generate cancellable template consisting 252 values denoted as D_{CT}.

D_{CT} = [257 84 58 59 83 258 248 82 248 81 25 245 259 275 241 273 16 273 254 274 274 245 308 248 301 309 270 301 302 303 163 265 261 271 271 164 263 252 290 112 135 142 186 187 106 223 110 115 243 96 126 127 100 99 132 234 79 178 79 92 91 241 81 265 81 250 79 79 270 290 270 174 255 255 304 256 304 257 263 264 272 272 53 54 289 289 256 256 167 244 252 252 260 56 230 242 272 272 187 79 79 265 265 25 275 259 259 268 268 102 242]

After that cancellable template, D_{CT} first salted to extract the desired 1024 bits and stored in U vector. Then, the U vector is shuffled and all the numbers in U are concatenated to obtain a large prime number of 1024 bits.

Now, from these prime numbers cryptographic key is generated according to the key generation process of Elgamal cryptosystems.

5 Security Aspect

In this proposed approach, the user does not use their original template and the original template is not stored anywhere. Cancellable template is obtained by one-way transformation, and the reverse operation is not possible without the shuffle key that is fixed for the user and stored using some password. Hence, privacy of the biometric identity is preserved.

6 Conclusion

In traditional cryptographic approach, creating large keys and then respecting their secrecy are vital. The cryptographic keys being not correlated with user in a direct manner are difficult to recollect. This present work focuses on the above-mentioned issues and discussed a feasible method in which the cryptographic key is robustly related with the user's fingerprint traits. Here, the privacy of fingerprint template is maintained using the theory of cancellable fingerprint template.

References

1. W. Stallings, Cryptography and Network Security: Principles and Practice, 5th edition, Prentice Hall, 2010.
2. Soutar, C.; Roberge, A. and Vijaya Kumar, B.V.K., "Biometric Encryption using Image Processing", SPIE, pp. 178–188, 1998.
3. Bolle, R.M.; Connel, J.H. and Ratha, N.K., "Biometrics Perils and Patches", Elsevier - Pattern Recognition 35, pp. 2727–2738, 2002.
4. Teoh, Andrew B.J.; Goh, A. and Ngo, D.C.L., "Random MultispaceQuantisation as an Analytic Mechanism for BioHashing of Biometric and Random Identity Inputs", IEEE Transactions on Pattern Analysis and Machine Intelligence 28(12), pp. 1892–1901, 2006.
5. Ratha, N.K.; Chikkerur, S.; Connell, J.H. and Bolle, R.M., "Generating Cancelable Fingerprint Templates", IEEE Transactions on Pattern Analysis and Machine Intelligence, 29(4), pp. 561–572, 2007.
6. Tulyakov, S.; Farooq, F. and Govindaraju, V., "Symmetric Hash Functions for Fingerprint Minutiae", International Workshop on Pattern Recognition for Crime Prevention, Security and Surveillance (ICAPR 2005), 3687, pp. 30–38, 2005.
7. Ang, R.; Rei, S.N. and McAven, L., "Cancelable Key-Based Fingerprint Templates", Information Security and Privacy: 10th Australasian Conference (ACISP 2005), pp. 242–252, 2005.
8. Maiorana, E.; Campisi, P.; Fierrez, J. and Ortega-Garcia, J., "Cancelable Templates for Sequence Based Biometrics with Application to On-line Signature Recognition", IEEE Transactions on Systems, 40(3), pp. 525–538, 2010.
9. Nanni, L. and Lumini, A., "Cancelable Biometrics: Problems and Solutions for Improving Accuracy", NovaPublisher - Biometrics: Methods, Applications and Analysis, chap-7, pp. 153–166, 2010.

10. F Monrose, MK Reiter, Q Li, S Wetzel, "Cryptographic key generation from voice", Proceedings of IEEE Symposium on Security and Privacy, pp. 202–213, 2011.
11. H Feng, CC Wah, "Private Key generation from on-line hand written signatures", Information Management & Computer Security, 10(4), pp. 159–164, 2002.
12. B Chen, V Chandran, "Biometric Based Cryptographic Key Generation from Faces", Proceedings of 9th Biennial Conference of the Australian Pattern Recognition Society on Digital Image Computing Techniques and Applications, pp. 394–401, 2007.
13. A Jagadeesan, K Duraiswamy, "Secured Cryptographic Key Generationfrom Multimodal Biometrics: Feature Level Fusion of Fingerprint and Iris", Int. Journalon Computer Sc. & Information Security, 7(2), pp. 28–37, 2010.
14. A Jagadeesan, T Thillaikkarasi, K Duraiswamy, "Cryptographic KeyGeneration from Multiple Biometrics Modalities: Fusing Minutiae with Iris Feature", Int. J. Comput. Appl. 2(6), pp. 16–26, 2010.
15. C Rathgeb, A Uhl., "Context-based biometric key generation for Iris", IET Computer Vision, 5(6), pp. 389–397, 2011.
16. D. Milao Q. Tang, and W. Fu, "Fingerprint minutia extraction based on principal curves," Pattern Recognition Letters, Vol. 28, Issue 16, pp. 2184–2189, 2009.

Analytics Based on Video Object Tracking for Surveillance

Nagaraj Bhat, U. Eranna, B. M. Mahendra, Savita Sonali,
Adokshaja Kulkarni and Vikhyath Rai

Abstract An abandoned object in public places is one of the typical surveillance breaches. Detecting an abandoned object in surveillance video is very important to forecast terrorist activity. This work aims to develop a modular system with several individual stages where in at each stage different algorithm is employed. The overall task is to detect abandoned object in a video stream. This has been implemented in Math Work's MATLAB integrated development environment. The performance of the system is evaluated on test videos from standard publically available datasets and also custom dataset. The Abandoned Object Detection system is tested for two different datasets—publically available i-LiDS AVSS and custom dataset. The metric called system performance used to evaluate our system provided 85.71% result for AVSS dataset and 75% for custom dataset, with overall system performance reaching up to 78.125%.

Keywords AOD · I-LiDS · AVSS

N. Bhat (✉) · B. M. Mahendra · V. Rai
Department of ECE, RV College of Engineering, Bengaluru, India
e-mail: nbhat437@gmail.com

B. M. Mahendra
e-mail: mahendra.smvit@gmail.com

U. Eranna
Department of ECE, BITM Bellary, Bellary, India
e-mail: jayaveer_88@yahoo.com

S. Sonali
Department of ECE, RYMCOE, Bellary, India

A. Kulkarni
Department of ECE, TCE, Gadag, India
e-mail: adoksh_gadag@rediffmail.com

© Springer Nature Singapore Pte Ltd. 2018
P. K. Pattnaik et al. (eds.), *Progress in Computing, Analytics and Networking*,
Advances in Intelligent Systems and Computing 710,
https://doi.org/10.1007/978-981-10-7871-2_27

1   Introduction

The challenges faced by security operators today are ever increasing, so it is very much necessary to provide the best possible tools for their job. Security systems integrated with video management system will be the future of CCTV. An operator can manage large number of cameras easily. Conventional CCTV systems are used to retrieve frames of an event after it has occurred in general. Video analytics is a technique that makes use of analytical algorithms to automatically track and classify objects in surveillance providing an alarming or notifying function for real-time video information. Integrating the CCTV with video analytics technique with a VMS platform, security operators will be able to use these security devices as early warning detectors, enabling them to react to any possible threat or breach as and when it is happening.

This work attempt is to understand the tracking and identification of suspicious items in crowded places by performing video analytics on surveillance videos. A suspicious item in the context of this work is characterized as an object that is brought into the area of interest by a man and that is left behind while the individual leaves the area. Only if that item remains unmoved in that area for a fixed amount of time, it is considered as abandoned. Also, the system detects any removed item that was in the area of interest long enough and then evacuated. The extent of this project is to distinguish any such abandoned or removed item in the test video streams from both standard datasets as well as custom datasets and notify automatically without any intervention from humans. In the scope of the project, it is accepted that the information about the scene is accessible from just a single camera and from a settled perspective.

1.1   Applications of Video Analytics

1. Analysis of videotapes used in surveillance systems captured by CCTVs is one of the important one.
2. Perform a wide range of tasks ranging from analysis of video in real time for detection of events like breach of security or threat.
3. Analysis of a recorded video for forensic.
4. It also finds applications in object classification, virtual fence/perimeter breach, wrong direction indicator, facial recognition, motion tracking, abandoned item detection, removed item detection, vehicle counting, number plate recognition.

1.2   Literature Review

Due to its importance in anti-terrorism, a large number of researches have been undertaken in the domain of Abandoned Object Detection. Almost all the existing methods can be grouped into two: one that employs background modeling and subtraction and other that completely depends upon the tracking-based detection. Almost all of these methods use Gaussian Mixture Model [1] for BM&S. In GMM, each pixel's intensities are modeled to be weighted sum of two normal distributions, where one distribution represents background and the other foreground. The method in paper [2] models two backgrounds and uses the Bayesian tracking. Each frames dual backgrounds are then compared to estimate dual foregrounds. The approach in paper [3] uses Gaussian Mixture Model with three distributions for BM&S and uses these to classify the foreground into abandoned, moving, and removed items. A portion of the methodologies in view of alternate class of strategies, which are based on tracking, can be found in [4, 5]. The tracking and recognition of items carried out utilizing histograms in paper [4] where the missing hues in proportion histogram in between the different frames without and with the item are utilized to recognize the deserted item. The technique utilized as a part of paper [5] performs the task through a trans-dimensional Monte Carlo Markov chain display reasonable for tracking non-specific blobs and in this manner unequipped for recognizing people and different items while tracking. The yield of this following framework consequently should be subjected to further handling before the item can be distinguished and marked as abandoned.

2 Methodology

Methodology involves five fundamental stages as shown in Fig. 1.

Preprocessing: This stage is basically an extra module which makes use of contrast enhancement to enhance the nature of low-light recordings like those taken around evening time. The difference between max and min pixel intensity values is normalized and hence assisting to improve the quality of low-light conditions.

Background Modeling and Subtraction (BM&S): This stage makes a model of background and every next frame is differenced from it to distinguish the present foreground objects. The yield of this fundamental stage is normally pixels of set of objects that are in the current frame and not in the background. Two of the most used BM&S algorithms used are adaptive median technique and the running Gaussian average. A concise depiction of the two approaches is given underneath:

(a) Adaptive median: This BM&S strategy, portrayed in paper [6], operates on the presumption that the probability of background showing up at a pixel over a given time frame compared to forefront items, i.e., previous history luma values are probably going to contain most cases of background. This prompts the sensible assumption that the pixel remains in background for the greater part in history. Hence, the median is used for the model of background. In spite of the fact that this BM&S technique is generally simple to compute from a computational outlook, it has genuinely high memory necessities since the past m

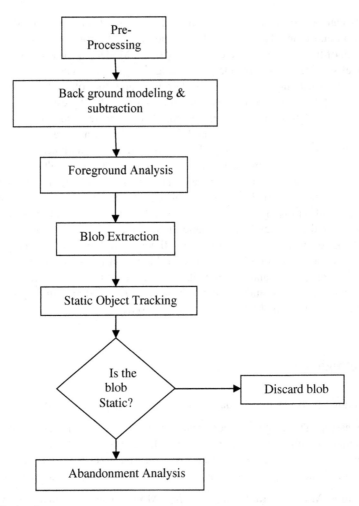

Fig. 1 Design flow

frames must be put away in a buffer and must be very substantial to get a decent gauge of the genuine background. So, an easier recursive adaptation of this calculation is all the more for all intents and purposes achievable. In this approach, the running assessment of the median is augmented by one if the present intensity is bigger than the current gauge and decremented by one in the event that it is littler. The gauge is left unaltered on the off chance that it breaks even with the present pixel estimation.

(b) Running Gaussian average: The essential thought here is like that in the last technique with the exception of that in this method, instead of median, the average of previous m frames is utilized in the background model. Making use of this method again needs a large buffer, thus the running average is taken.

Since the probability of recent background frames contribution is more than old frames, a weighted normal is utilized with higher weights appended to latest frames. The Gaussian average is acquired, whenever these weights fluctuate as per the Gaussian dissemination. The calculation executed in this approach is pointed in paper [7].

Foreground Analysis: The BM&S module is generally not able to adjust the rapid changes in the video stream. Also, there are chances that it maybe fuddle parts of a forefront item as background if they appear relatively similar, along these lines making a solitary item be part into different forefront blobs. Moreover, there may be certain unimportant forefront region that must be removed before further processing. The above components require an extra module to expel both false forefront items and right, however uninteresting forefront regions drawn over moving vehicles of corresponding width and height.

(a) Shadow detection: A formula-based approach is followed to detect shadows in the forefront mask. Shadows in general are actual foreground objects but also unessential for further analysis. So in order to make our system robust, a method based on normalized cross-correlation (NCC) is followed to identify shadow areas.
(b) Morphological operation: The shadow identification procedure is inclined to false detections and frequently give holes inside legitimate forefront items. Alongside, some deserted shadow pixels that might be identified as little blobs. These are evacuated by performing morphological processing like erosion and dilation. Dilation is a maximizing operation which causes brighter areas in the picture to grow, whereas erosion procedure is exact opposite causing the darker regions in the image to grow.

Extraction of Blob: The output of the forefront analysis is applied with a component labeling approach done by contour tracing to identify significant forefront items. A basic yet proficient method portrayed in paper [8] is utilized for this reason. The main method in this process is to make utilization of corner tracing to identify both internal and external contours and label them. The advantages of this method are that it utilizes a solitary pass over the frame; no relabeling is required as in other approaches and computationally inexpensive.

Tracking of Blobs: This module is generally the most important process in the Abandoned Object Detection procedure and is worried with identifying a relationship between existing blobs that have been tracked and present blobs of forefront. The initial step involves comparing every blob in the approaching frame to the current blobs to discover a match in view of position. For a current blob to coordinate another blob in the newest frame, their positions must contrast by not as more than a threshold. Any object is removed from the tracking system if it goes out of frame, or if its blob is not detected for too long or if the object is occluded for certain number of frames. The object is identified as static if it remains still for a certain number of frames set by the threshold. Then this object is sent to the next stage to classify whether the object is an abandoned item or a false positive like a very still human.

Abandonment Analysis: This is the last stage whose need is to avoid bogus identification of deserted items. The approach used is to check the internal variation of the blob for the time it has tracked followed to guarantee it is not still individual. The fundamental approach presented in paper [9] tells us that the presence of a genuine static item remains totally unaltered (given no occlusion) for many frames while a false static item identified because of still individual will demonstrate changes on its pixel values inside a bounded box (except if the individual is unnaturally still). These inside changes in blob are found out by running normal of differences in mean and if this esteem surpasses a specific limit, the item is named a still individual. The gradient pictures are used in place of actual images in order to compute mean differences to prevent, so that the procedure is insusceptible to any lighting changes. When an item is identified as deserted or abandoned, it makes a caution to rise instantly. So the final module distinguishes a blob identified as static in the previous module as one of the following: removed item, or abandoned item or a still individual. An alert is notified if an abandoned item stays in the scene for a specific measure of time.

3   Testing, Experimental Results and Comparisons

3.1   Details of Hardware and Software

Like most computer vision and image processing tasks, AOD is an extremely computationally intensive process and requires powerful hardware to run in real time. The present system has been tested on a fairly modern and moderately powerful computer with Intel core i5 processor having 4 GB Ram. The application has been coded entirely on MATLAB integrated development environment with the version MATLAB 2013a. The application is tested on both Windows 7 and Windows 8 operating systems.

3.2   Datasets

The testing is done for offline cases. The offline test video incorporates recordings from one openly accessible benchmark datasets: AVSS-i-LiDS [10]. It likewise incorporates a custom dataset comprising of 11 recordings shot utilizing a Sony DSC-W35 advanced camera. The video resolutions are 720 × 576 for open benchmark datasets and 640 × 480 for the exclusively arranged dataset. This framework has been tried on two unique databases, where one is freely accessible benchmark database and another one is a custom arranged dataset with recordings of different indoor and outside situations including both day and evening scenes. Below is a concise depiction of these datasets:

(a) AVSS i-LIDS: This dataset is accessible at [10] and comprises of CCTV film of two situations: Abandoned bag (AB) and illicitly Parked vehicle (PV). There are three distinct recordings of expanding trouble levels for both of these situations with the last likewise having an evening video. Testing was done on both situations since a stopped vehicle can likewise be considered as a deserted item

(b) Customized dataset: This dataset contains 11 recordings out of which 7 are open-air scenes while 4 are indoor ones; 8 of these were shot amid in sufficiently bright conditions while 3 were shot during the evening or in dim insides.

(c) *Results*

Testing was carried out on an Intel Core i5 processor with speed of 2.51 GHz and RAM size of 4 GB. Most of the time, half-resolution handling was adequate to recognize any abnormal events with minimum errors (false positives); full-resolution analysis was done only in few of the more unpredictable circumstances. Both the openly accessible dataset and the custom dataset have been tried for detecting abandoned items. The result summary for the publically available benchmark dataset AVSS-i-LiDS is provided in Table 1 [10].

The result summary for the custom dataset is provided in Table 2.

Spiting up the custom dataset categorically and then summarizing the results give us better understanding of the results. Table 3 shows results of custom dataset categorically.

After implementing the modules in MATLAB 2013a IDE and integrating them to form a single Abandoned Object Detection system, results can obtain and

Table 1 Result summary for the test videos from i-LIDS AVSS dataset

Set name	Number of events	Number of true detections	False detection (still person)	False detection (other objects)
AB-easy	1	1	0	0
AB-medium	1	1	0	0
AB-hard	1	1	0	0
AB-total	3	3	0	0
PV-easy	1	1	0	0
PV-medium	1	1	0	0
PV-hard	1	1	0	0
PV-night	1	0	0	0
PV-total	4	3	0	0
Overall	**7**	**6**	**0**	**0**

Table 2 Result summary for the test videos from custom dataset

Set number	Number of events	Number of true detections	False detection (still person)	False detection (other objects)
01	1	1	0	0
02	0	0	0	0
03	1	1	0	0
04	3	3	0	0
05	2	2	0	1
06	2	1	0	0
07	1	1	0	0
08	0	0	0	1
09	2	2	1	0
10	3	2	0	1
11	2	1	0	0
Overall	17	14	1	3

Table 3 Categorical distribution custom dataset results

Classification	Number of events	Number of true detections	False detection (still person)	False detection (other objects)
Outdoor	10	9	0	1
Indoor	7	5	1	2
well-lit or daytime	12	11	1	3
poorly lit or night	5	3	0	0

analyzed in terms of different datasets, location where the video stream is captured, lighting condition, number of true detections, and number of false positives. The overall system performance is measured in terms of a metric S. The system performance tells us how efficiently the AOD system works by considering the number of true detections and along with the false detections, scaled by an appropriate factor (Fig. 2).

An altered rendition of numerical metric given in paper [11] has been utilized in this project to gauge the general execution of this framework. The tool assesses the quantity of detections that identify actual abandoned item punished by the incorrect identifications and finally the metric is normalized.

The system performance used in this work is formulated as,

$$Sp = \frac{Ntrue - (0.25 * Nnp + 0.5 * Np)}{Ntot} \tag{3.1}$$

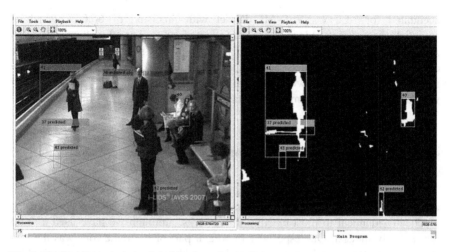

Fig. 2 Current frame and the foreground mask with detected abandoned object. Source: Video frames are taken from i-LiDs data sets

Table 4 Categorical distribution of system performance

Dataset	Category	System performance (S) in percentage
AVSSi-LIDS	Abandoned bag (AB)	100
AVSSi-LIDS	Parked vehicle (PV)	75
AVSSi-LIDS	Overall	85.71
Custom	Outdoor	87.5
Custom	Indoor	64.28
Custom	Well-lit/daytime	81.25
Custom	Poorly lit/dark	60
Custom	**Overall**	**75**
Combined	**Overall**	**78.125**

where N_{true} is the number of true detection of abandoned object, N_{tot} is the total number of events, N_{np} is the number of non-person objects (other objects) detected which are wrongly identified as abandoned item, and N_p is the number of still persons identified wrongly identified as abandoned item.

The system performance for both of the dataset, category based as well as overall is been given in Table 4.

In spite of the fact that AVSS i-LiDS dataset has been utilized for testing in numerous contemporary works in writing, not very many of these report adequately nitty gritty outcomes for direct correlation with our outcomes. Results for AVSS-AB dataset have been accounted for in [11]. Utilizing a comparative yet somewhat more casual metric, the general precision detailed there is 85.20%. The comparing figure for our framework is 84.71%; however, it should be noticed this has been acquired utilizing a stricter metric. The outcomes in [2] have been accounted for i-LiDS AVSS-AB dataset with precision of 66.67% which is essentially more regrettable than our after effect of 100%. The after effects of i-LiDS AVSS-PV dataset have likewise been accounted here but partly and cannot be contrasted with our outcomes. The framework in [3] has additionally been tried on i-LiDS AVSS-PV dataset with precision of 58.93%. Our framework performs better with this respect on the comparing dataset with 75% system performance.

4 Conclusion and Future Scope

The experiment was conducted on a substantial number of openly accessible and additionally handcrafted recordings and was found to give system performance practically identical to most existing frameworks, although we have used a setup that is fairly modest. One especially important part of its framework was the low rate of errors (false positives) gotten. Likewise, these outcomes were acquired by utilizing for all cases similar techniques and parameter values over every one of the test videos. Essentially better outcomes can be gotten if comprehensive testing and alterations are completed for every situation.

At last, and maybe above all, the techniques that have been exhibited and tried as a part of this project are those that are only part of initial actualization of this framework. These were particularly been moderately basic strategies, both to actualize and to execute, because of confinements of time and computational assets. But because of the modular approach followed in the project, it is very simple to add more advanced techniques to any of its module. This framework can, subsequently, be considered as the base for a really vigorous structure that exclusive requires a touch of calibration and modification to perform well in any practical situation.

The performance of our AOD system for the customized dataset is reasonably good. The real failures occur only in datasets 6, 8, 10, 11. The major reasons for the object not detecting are because the test item was black in color and is placed in shadowy region and was not properly visible to human eyes also. The reason failure for other test cases was because of shooting it in very dark conditions and the test item mixed with the background even on applying preprocessing by contrast enhancement.

Since our system follows modular approach, there is scope for further improvement by adding few more modules that can eliminate such false positives and further improve the system performance.

References

1. C. Stauffer and W. E. L. Grimson, —— "Adaptive background mixture models for real-time tracking, in Proc. IEEE Conference on Computer Vision and Pattern Recognition", Vol. 2, pp. 246–252, Feb. 1999.
2. Fatih Porikli, Yuri Ivanov and Tetsuji Haga ——"Robust Abandoned Object Detection Using Dual Foregrounds",‖ EURASIP Journal on Advances in Signal Processing, 2008.

3. Y. Tian, M. Lu and A. Hampapur, ——"Robust and efficient foreground analysis for real-time video surveillance",‖ in Proc. IEEE Conference on Computer Vision and Pattern Recognition, vol. 1, pp. 1182–1187, June 2005.

4. Xuli Li, Chao Zhang, Duo Zhang "Abandoned Objects Detection Using Double Illumination Invariant Foreground Masks" in Proc. 20th International Conference on Pattern Recognition, pp. 436–439, Aug. 2010.

5. Smith, K., Quelhas, P. and Gatica-Perez, D, ——"Detecting Abandoned Luggage Items in a Public Space",‖ in Proc. Ninth IEEE International Workshop on Performance Evaluation of Tracking and Surveillance, pp. 75–82, June 2006.

6. Abhineet Kumar Singh and Anupam Agarwal, "An Interactive Framework for Abandoned and Removed Object Detection in Video", *IEEE Indian Conference* (INDICON), https://doi.org/10.1109/tip.2011.2136352, 978-1-4799-2275-8/13, 2013.

7. K Jianting, Wen,Haifeng Gong, Xia Zhang and Wenze Hu Generative model for abandoned object detection.‖ IEEE International Conference on Image Processing, pp. 853–856, Nov. 2009.

8. F. Chang, C. Chen and C. Lu, "A linear-time component labeling algorithm using contour tracing technique" Computer Vision and Image Understanding, Vol. 93, Issue 2, pp. 206–220, Feb. 2004.

9. N. Bird, S. Atev, N. Caramelli, R. Martin, O. Masoud and N. Papanikolopoulos, -"Real Time, Online Detection of Abandoned Objects in Public Areas" in Proc. IEEE International Conference on Robotics and Automation, pp. 3775–3780, May 2006.

10. 2007 IEEE International Conference on Advanced Video and Signal basedSurveillance. http://www.eecs.qmul.ac.uk/~andrea/avss2007_d.html, June 2013.

11. S. Winkler, C. J. van den Branden Lambrecht, and M. Kunt, "Vision and Video: Models and Applications". In Christian J. van den Branden Lambrecht. Vision models and applications to image and video processing. Springer. pp. 209. ISBN 978-0-7923-7422-0, 2001.

Histogram of Oriented Gradients-Based Digit Classification Using Naive Bayesian Classifier

Shashwati Mishra and Mrutyunjaya Panda

Abstract Classification helps in grouping the objects according to their characteristics or features, which is essential for predicting the behavior of objects, simplifying the process of searching in a large database, detecting specific objects, etc. Advancement in information technology has increased the need for classification of text documents, image, video, audio dataset for easy and accurate retrieval of required information. Selecting features where the most relevant information lies is one of the important steps before classification. In this paper, gradient information is used for feature extraction with the help of histogram of oriented gradients technique. The simplicity of naive Bayesian classifier makes it suitable for large databases. The accuracy and ROC curve prove the effectiveness of the proposed method.

Keywords Histogram of oriented gradients · Bayes' theorem
Naive Bayesian classifier · Supervised learning · Digit classification

1 Introduction

The process of categorization where objects are identified and differentiated from each other is known as classification. In machine-learning, classification algorithms consider two groups of data, training dataset and test dataset. The class label information of training dataset is used to train the classifier and predict the class label information of test dataset. The classifiers can be probabilistic or non-probabilistic. Unlike non-probabilistic classifiers, probabilistic classifiers calculate the probability that an object or event belongs to a particular class. The class

S. Mishra (✉) · M. Panda
Department of Computer Science and Applications, Utkal University, Vani Vihar,
Bhubaneswar, Odisha, India
e-mail: shashwati.mishra@gmail.com

M. Panda
e-mail: mrutyunjayapanda@yahoo.in

© Springer Nature Singapore Pte Ltd. 2018
P. K. Pattnaik et al. (eds.), *Progress in Computing, Analytics and Networking*,
Advances in Intelligent Systems and Computing 710,
https://doi.org/10.1007/978-981-10-7871-2_28

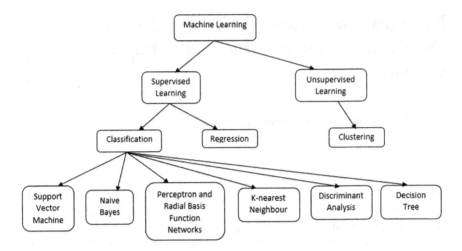

Fig. 1 Classification of machine-learning techniques

for which the probability is maximum is considered as the best class for that object or event under consideration. The ability to avoid error propagation and its suitability in large machine-learning problems make probabilistic classifiers popular as compared to the non-probabilistic classifiers.

Machine-learning techniques can be categorized as supervised learning and unsupervised learning as shown in Fig. 1. In the case of supervised learning, a predictive model is developed considering the input and output data. In unsupervised learning, the input data is used for getting an internal representation. Classification and regression come under supervised learning, and clustering belongs to unsupervised learning. Support vector machine, naive Bayes, nearest neighbor, discriminant analysis, and decision tree come under classification techniques. Both classification and regression techniques help in predicting the class label information [1].

In any classification technique, may it be an image or text or data in all cases, feature plays a very important role. The extraction of these features is the basic building block of classification techniques, and the result of classification is greatly affected by these feature vectors. Out of several classification methods, naive Bayes is one of the popular classification methods which is based on the assumption that for any class, these feature vectors are independent. This classifier uses the concept of Bayes' theorem for classifying the feature vectors. Some of the important applications of these classifiers include document classification, text categorization and automatic medical diagnosis. In these domains, this frequency-based classifier can compete with advanced classification methods like support vector machine.

2 Related Work

M. Nilsback and A. Zisserman [2] performed classification of flower images considering four different features such as local shape or texture, color, shape of boundary, and overall spatial distribution of petals. Support Vector Machine (SVM) classifier is applied on the extracted features for classification. Histogram of Oriented Gradients (HOG) features extracted help in getting the global spatial information. S. Jagannathan et al. [3] applied HOG and AdaBoost cascade classifier for detecting the object. To classify the detected objects, Convolutional Neural Network (CNN) is used. S. Tuermer et al. [4] developed a technique of vehicle detection using disparity maps and HOG features. A technique of pedestrian recognition was proposed by P. Geismann and G. Schneider [5] using HOG and Harr features. HOG features are also used for video forgery detection [6] and emotion recognition [7].

H. Zhang et al. [8] applied naive Bayes classifier to construct a prediction model for developmental toxicity. M. Zhang et al. [9] predicted the labels of test set applying multi-label naive Bayes classification technique on extracted features. Principal component analysis (PCA) is applied to remove redundant and irrelevant features followed by selection of subset of features using genetic algorithm.

T. Yamaguchi et al. [10] proposed a technique of classification of digits on signboards for recognizing telephone numbers. After extracting digit regions from the signboard images, the digits are further processed for slant and skew correction. Hough transformation is used for skew correction. Digits are circumscribed with tilted rectangles for correcting slant. P. Sermanet et al. [11] used convolutional neural networks for classifying digits in house numbers. Support Vector Machine (SVM) and Histogram of Oriented Gradients (HOG) features are used for handwritten digit recognition [12].

The process of assigning a document to one or more categories or classes is known as document classification or document categorization which can be done manually or with the help of computer programs. The manual classification is used in library science, whereas computer and information science basically deal with algorithmic classification. The document may consist of texts, images, digits, symbols, music etc. There are several techniques for document classification like expectation maximization, support vector machine, artificial neural network, K-nearest neighbor, decision trees, naive Bayesian classifier, etc. The applications of these classifiers include language identification, digit classification, sentiment analysis, readability assessment, spam filtering, routing of email, etc. In this paper, the naive Bayesian classifier is used for classification of digits.

3   Proposed Methodology

The proposed methodology is applied on publicly available digit image dataset for experimental analysis. Figure 2 diagrammatically represents the steps present in our proposed methodology.

The whole set of images is divided into training and test sets from which features are extracted separately using histogram of oriented gradients (HOG) feature extraction technique. After feature extraction, naive Bayesian classifier is used to construct a training model from the set of training images. The model obtained is used to predict the class labels of test dataset. The final step involves comparison of predicted class labels and actual class labels to find the accuracy of classification. The effectiveness of the proposed approach is proved from the calculated accuracy.

3.1   Histogram of Oriented Gradients

Histogram of oriented gradients (HOG) is a popular descriptor and widely used in detection of objects, human being, etc. Unlike SIFT algorithm which gives local descriptors, HOG feature extraction technique outputs interest point which is a global descriptor. This feature extraction technique calculates horizontal and vertical gradients, orientation and magnitude of gradients. The assumption is that the distribution of intensity gradients and direction of edges affect the appearance and shape of an object in the image. In this technique, the image is divided into small subsections called cells. The histogram of gradient directions is computed for each subsection separately. The histogram calculated from each subsection is concatenated together to obtain the final HOG descriptors. This descriptor is not affected by geometric and photometric transformations. So it is suitable for object detection in an image [13].

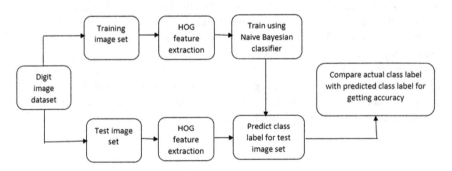

Fig. 2 Proposed methodology

Steps:-

a. **Gradient Computation**

In the first step, gradient values are calculated. Applying 1D centered point discrete derivative mask in the horizontal and vertical directions is the most common method. For this, one horizontal and one vertical filter kernel is applied on the grayscale image. These kernels are represented as

$$D_x = [-101] \text{ and } D_y = \begin{bmatrix} -1 \\ 0 \\ 1 \end{bmatrix} \tag{1}$$

Performing convolution operation,

$$I_x = I * D_x \text{ and } I_y = I * D_y \tag{2}$$

The gradient magnitude is

$$|G| = \sqrt{I_x^2 + I_y^2} \tag{3}$$

and gradient orientation is

$$\theta = \arctan \frac{I_y}{I_x} \tag{4}$$

b. **Orientation binning**

Depending on the calculated gradient values, each pixel in the cell is attached with a specific weight for the construction of an orientation-based histogram channel. These histogram channels are spread from 0 to 180° or 0 to 360°. This degree of orientation varies according to the sign of the gradient.

c. **Descriptor blocks**

To overcome the problem of change in contrast and illumination, the strength of gradients is normalized locally. This can be achieved by combining the cells together to create spatially connected large blocks. The components of all the normalized cell histograms obtained from all the blocks are combined together to generate the HOG descriptor. These blocks may overlap. Two popular block geometries are R-HOG blocks and C-HOG blocks.

d. **Block normalization**

Different approaches like L2-norm, L1-norm, and L1-sqrt are used to obtain the normalization factor and normalize the blocks using these factors [13].

3.2 Bayes' Theorem

Named after Reverend Thomas Bayes and later extended by Pierre-Simon Laplace, Bayes' theorem plays a vital role in the theory of probability. Bayes' rule calculates the posterior probability considering the prior probability and likelihood [14].

For two events X and Y, mathematically this theorem can be represented as

$$P(X|Y) = \frac{P(Y|X)P(X)}{P(Y)} \tag{5}$$

where

P(X)   is the probability of observing event X
P(Y)   is the probability of observing event Y
P(X|Y) is the probability of observing event X if the event Y is true
P(Y|X) is the probability of observing event Y if the event X is true

The ability of the Bayesian classifier to cope with a large number of features makes it popular for classification of digits, images, and text documents.

3.3 Naive Bayesian Classifier

The Bayes' theorem-based classifier, popularly known as naive Bayesian classifier, is widely used for classification of large datasets. The model based on this classifier is simple, easy to build, and gives better result as compared to other complex classification methods. The naive Bayesian classifier considers the attribute labels as categorical or nominal variables and is suitable for both binary and multi-class classification problems. This classification model also works well for large and frequently changing dataset. Naive Bayesian classifier is suitable when the input data has high dimensionality. This classifier uses the maximum likelihood method for estimating the parameter values. Another advantage is that for parameter estimation, it requires a small amount of training data. Let C represent the class label information and V is the predictor variable. The value of the variable V affects the value of the class C. Using Bayes' theorem, the posterior probability can be computed as

Posterior Probability = (Likelihood × Class Prior Probability)/Predictor Prior Probability

For a fixed prior probability of predictor X [14],

$$P(C|V) \propto P(V|C)P(C) \tag{6}$$

For more than one attribute values $V_1, V_2, ..., V_n$ of predictor variable V,

$$P(C|V) \propto P(V_1|C) \times P(V_2|C) \times \ldots P(V_n|C) \times P(C) \tag{7}$$

Prediction and classification using naive Bayesian classifier can be performed with the help of frequency tables. If the variables are numerical, then these are converted into categorical variables for the construction of frequency tables. One approach of calculating this frequency is to use the concept of binning. Another method is taking into consideration the distribution of the numerical variables. The distribution may be a normal (Gaussian) distribution or binomial distribution or multinomial distribution or kernel distribution, Bernoulli distribution, etc. For discrete features, Bernoulli and multinomial features are popularly used and Gaussian distribution is popular for continuous values. This paper concentrates on normal probability density function for finding the probability of a digit image belonging to a particular class.

Gaussian distribution also known as normal distribution or bell curve is a very important continuous probability distribution. This distribution works well when information from multiple sources acts independently and additively. Mean represents the center of Gaussian distribution where the value of relative frequency is the highest. The distribution is symmetric about the mean. For a variable x, if μ is mean and σ^2 is variance, then $x \sim N(\mu, \sigma^2)$. As the value moves away from the mean, relative frequency gradually decreases. Standard deviation indicates how the values are spread around the mean. Let μ represent mean and σ indicate standard deviation. The equation for probability density function in the case of Gaussian or normal distribution is

$$f(x) = \frac{1}{\sqrt{2\Pi}\sigma} e^{\frac{-(x-\mu)^2}{2\sigma^2}} \tag{8}$$

where $-\infty < x < \infty$.

For standard normal distribution, the mean value μ is 0 and standard deviation σ is 1.

4 Experimental Observations and Discussions

For applying our proposed methodology, publicly available digit images are taken and divided into training set and test set. Total number of images considered are 76, out of which 38 are training images and 38 are test images. Figure 3 shows a digit 7 and corresponding histogram plot obtained from the features extracted using Histogram of Oriented Gradients (HOG). In the next step, naive Bayesian classification algorithm is applied on these extracted features of training images to build a classification model. Since the normal distribution is considered for calculating the probability, the corresponding mean and standard deviation play a vital role in predicting the class labels. Calculated mean and standard deviation obtained from

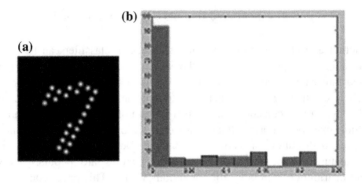

Fig. 3 Digit 7 (**a**) and corresponding histogram plot of extracted HOG features (**b**)

Table 1 Confusion matrix

		Predicted class labels			
Actual class labels		1	3	5	7
	1	6	0	1	1
	3	0	8	0	1
	5	0	0	10	1
	7	0	0	0	10

training images are applied on the extracted test image features to predict the class labels. The accuracy obtained using the above steps is 89.4737%. The confusion matrix representation is given in Table 1. Digits considered are 1 or 3 or 5 or 7, so there are four possible classes, class 1, class 3, class 5 and class 7. The confusion matrix obtained proves that 6 digits from class 1, 8 from class 3, 10 from class 5, and 10 from class 7 are correctly classified. Similarly, 2 from class 1, 1 from class 3, and 1 from class 5 are incorrectly classified.

$$\text{Accuracy in percentage} = (\text{Sum of correct classification})/(\text{Total number of classification}) \times 100$$
$$= (34/38) \times 100 = 0.89473684 \times 100 = 89.4737\%$$

Table 2 Precision, sensitivity, specificity, and false positive rate analysis

Class labels	Precision $(TP/(TP+FP))$	True positive rate or sensitivity or recall $(TP/(TP+FN))$	True negative rate or specificity $(TN/(TN+FP))$	False positive rate $(FP/(FP+TN))$
1	6/6 = 1	6/8 = 0.75	30/30 = 1	0/30 = 0
3	8/8 = 1	8/9 = 0.88	30/30 = 1	0/30 = 0
5	10/11 = 0.90	10/11 = 0.90	26/27 = 0.96	1/27 = 0.04
7	10/13 = 0.77	10/10 = 1	16/19 = 0.84	3/19 = 0.16

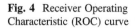

Fig. 4 Receiver Operating Characteristic (ROC) curve

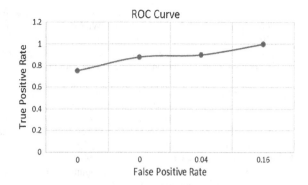

Precision, recall or sensitivity, specificity, and false positive rate for all classes are shown in Table 2. From these calculated values, Receiver Operating Characteristic (ROC) curve is plotted which is given in Fig. 4.

5 Conclusion

This paper focuses on HOG features and naive Bayesian classifier for digit classification. The invariance of extracted HOG features to geometric and photometric transformation helps in collecting better spatial information. Simplicity of naive Bayesian classifier helps in classifying large dataset. The classification results are analyzed by calculating precision, recall, specificity, and false positive rate. The ROC curve and accuracy obtained show the fruitfulness and efficiency of the proposed approach. The proposed work can be extended for classification of documents containing alphabets, numbers, and symbols from different languages.

References

1. Kotsiantis, S.: Supervised machine learning: A review of classification techniques. Informatica (2007) 249–268.
2. Nilsback, M., Zisserman, A.: Automated flower classification over a large number of classes. Sixth Indian Conference on Computer Vision, Graphics and Image Processing, IEEE (2008).
3. Jagannathan, S., Desappan, K., Swami, P., Mathew, M., Nagori, S., Chitnis, K., Marathe, Y., Poddar, D., Narayanan, S., Jain, A.: Efficient object detection and classification on low power embedded systems. International Conference on Consumer Electronics, IEEE (2017).
4. Tuermer, S., Kurz, F., Reinartz, P., Stilla, U.: Airborne vehicle detection in dense urban areas using HOG features and disparity maps. IEEE Journal of Selected Topics in Applied Earth Observations and Remote Sensing (2013).
5. Geismann, P., Schneider, G.: A two-staged approach to vision-based pedestrian recognition using Haar and HOG features. IEEE Intelligent Vehicles Symposium (2008) 554–559.

6. Subramanyam, A., Emmanuel, S.: Video forgery detection using HOG features and compression properties. International Workshop on Multimedia Signal Processing, IEEE (2012).

7. Dahmane, M., Meunier, J.: Emotion recognition using dynamic grid-based HOG features. Internatioanl Conference on Automatic Face and Gesture Recognition and Workshops, IEEE (2011) 884–888.

8. Zhang, H., Ren, J., Kang, Y., Bo, P., Liang, J., Ding, L, Kong, W., Zhang, J.: Development of novel in Silico model for developmental toxicity assessment by using naïve bayes classifier method. Reproductive Toxicology. https://doi.org/10.1016/j.reprotox. 2017. 04. 005 (2017).

9. Zhang, M., Peña, J., Robles, V.: Feature selection for multi-label naive bayes classification. Information Sciences, ELSEVIER (2009) 3218–3229.

10. Yamajuchi, T., Nakano, Y., Maruyama, M., Miyao, H., Hananoi, T.: Digit classification on signboards for telephone number recognition. International Conference on Document Analysis and Recognition, IEEE (2003).

11. Sermanet, P., Chintala, S., LeCun, Y.: Convolutional neural networks applied to house numbers digit classification. International Conference on Pattern Recognition, IEEE (2012).

12. Ebrahimzadeh, R., Jampour, M.: Efficient handwritten digit recognition based on histogram of oriented gradients and SVM. International Journal of Computer Applications, Vol. 104, No. 9 (2014) 10–13.

13. Tsai, G.: Histogram of Oriented Gradients. http://web.eecs.umich.edu/~silvio/teaching/EECS598_2010/slides/09_28_Grace.pdf (2010).

14. Han, J., Kambar, M.: Data mining concepts and techniques, Elsevier (2006).

Identifying Dissimilar OLAP Query Session for Building Goal Hierarchy

N. Parimala and Ranjeet Kumar Ranjan

Abstract Traditionally, a goal-oriented approach follows the goal decomposition technique to build a goal hierarchy in order to identify the schema for a data warehouse. In our earlier work, using reverse engineering approach, a goal hierarchy was built for an existing data warehouse schema using a single query session. The tasks of this hierarchy address some part of the warehouse. In this paper, we address the issue of identifying the next session to build a goal hierarchy. The sessions which provide the tasks and information goals distinct from existing goal hierarchy are desirable. To identify such a session, we define distance between sessions. The session whose distance from the current session is maximum is picked up.

Keywords Data analysis · Data warehousing · Goal decomposition
Goal hierarchy · OLAP · OLAP query · OLAP sessions · Session
distance · MDX

1 Introduction

A data warehouse is a collection of historical data gathered from heterogeneous sources to provide analytical information for the decision-making to improve the business process of the organisation [1]. Several requirement analysis techniques have been proposed for the design of the data warehouse schema. Some of them are goal-oriented approaches [2–5]. The goal-oriented approach identifies the goals of stakeholders of the organisation. The approach follows the goal decomposition technique to build the goal hierarchies in order to find the subject measures and

N. Parimala · R. K. Ranjan (✉)
School of Computer and Systems Sciences, Jawaharlal Nehru University,
New Delhi 110067, India
e-mail: ranjeetghitm@gmail.com

N. Parimala
e-mail: dr.parimala.n@gmail.com

© Springer Nature Singapore Pte Ltd. 2018
P. K. Pattnaik et al. (eds.), *Progress in Computing, Analytics and Networking*,
Advances in Intelligent Systems and Computing 710,
https://doi.org/10.1007/978-981-10-7871-2_29

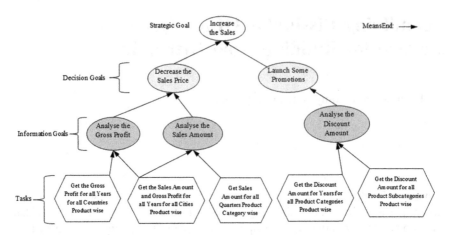

Fig. 1 Goal hierarchy example

contexts of analysis for the multidimensional schema [6]. An example of a goal hierarchy is given in Fig. 1, which shows the strategic goal, the decision goals, the information goals and the tasks. The strategic goal describes the strategic change for the organisation that requires the analysis of data. The decisions that are required to achieve a strategic goal are represented by the decision goals. The information required for a decision is given by the information goals, and finally, the tasks retrieve information for an information goal. The tasks have clear descriptions of subject measures and dimensions which need to be retrieved from the warehouse.

In many cases, data warehouse schema is arrived at based on the analysis of the data sources. The goal hierarchy which represents the requirements of a warehouse is missing. In this case, an approach for building the goal hierarchy using OLAP query recommendation technique has been proposed in [7]. The process of building a goal hierarchy is a reverse engineering process which identifies the part of the data warehouse used to achieve a strategic goal. The OLAP query recommendation system uses the queries of a single session. The queries of an analysis session are not just to get random information, but to get certain information which fulfils the requirements of the user's goal of analysis [8]. It is possible that multiple sessions may have to be used to arrive at a comprehensive goal hierarchy.

In this paper, we address the issue of selecting a session different from the current one for building the next goal hierarchy. Of the different sessions, a session has to be chosen in such a way that the session provides the maximum number of distinct tasks and information goals different from the existing goal hierarchy. Towards this, we define distance between sessions. The session with the maximum distance from the current one is likely to yield more tasks and information goals than the existing goal hierarchy. This session is chosen and a goal hierarchy is built using the approach proposed in [7].

In our system, every query has an attribute set consisting of measure and dimensional attribute sets associated with it. The measure set consists of all the measure attributes, and the dimensional attribute set consists of the entire dimensional attributes associated with the query. While building the goal hierarchy, the measure set as well as dimensional attribute set contributes to identifying the task and only the measure attribute set contributes to identifying the information goal. The aim is to find a session such that the queries of the session have measure sets and dimensional sets different than the current session as much as possible. The distance between two sessions *Session1* and *Session2* is defined using the measure and the dimensional attribute sets of *Session2* which are different from those in *Session1*. The session with maximum distance is considered as the most dissimilar sessions. This session is picked up to build a new goal hierarchy.

The remaining parts of this paper are organised as follows. Section 2 describes the goal-oriented requirement engineering techniques and the different approaches for the OLAP query session similarity. In Sect. 3, we have defined the terms used in this paper. In Sect. 4, we have briefly explained that how a goal hierarchy is built using a query session. The algorithm for computing the distance between sessions has been explained in Sect. 5. Section 6 explains the illustrative example for computing the distance between query sessions followed by conclusion in Sect. 7.

2 Related Work

There are several requirement analysis techniques that have been proposed for the design of the data warehouse schema where goal hierarchy has been used to represent the goal decomposition structure [2, 6, 9–11]. In [2], a goal-oriented requirement analysis approach has been proposed to build a model-driven architecture for the strategic goals and decomposed in hierarchies in order to identify the information required for the decision-makers. In [11], an extended rationale diagram has been created for an analysis goal to identify the OLAP queries in order to achieve the goal. Most of the recommendation systems take the OLAP queries or sessions as input and recommend next query or a group of queries [12–16]. In [15], a distance measure has been used to find the closest sessions from the current session and recommend the queries belonging to the closest sessions. In order to recommend OLAP sessions, [17] has identified some similarity measure techniques that can be suitable to calculate similarity between two OLAP sessions. Aligon et al. [8] have proposed a collaborative filtering approach for recommending OLAP sessions.

In this paper, we propose to find the dissimilar session in order to build a new goal hierarchy. We have proposed a new distance measure approach instead of using the existing approaches as our aim is to find sessions which identify tasks different from the ones already identified. In our case, distance between two sessions is calculated in terms of difference in measure and dimensional attribute sets of the queries of the sessions.

3   Basic Definitions

In this section, we have defined the OLAP query session and also introduced the OLAP query and attribute set which is given in [7].

Definition 1. OLAP Query Session: The OLAP queries used in this paper are the MDX (MultiDimensional eXpressions) queries [18]. These queries are executed for the schema *SalesSummary* shown in Fig. 2. The schema was generated using *SQL Server Data Tool* [19] and *AdventureWorks* data warehouse [20]. An OLAP query session is a sequence of OLAP queries which are executed one after another in order to complete an analysis task. Formally, we can define a session S consists of n queries as $S = \{q_1, q_2, ..., q_n\}$.

Definition 2. Attribute set: The attribute set associated with a query consists of measures and the dimensions or dimensional attributes. The set of attributes are grouped into two groups: measure set and the dimensional attribute set. The attribute set of a query q is defined as $a\_set(q) = \{ms(q), ds(q)\}$ where, $ms(q) = \{m_1, m_2, ..., m_i\}$ is the set of measure attributes and $ds(q) = \{d_1, d_2.., d_j\}$ is the set of dimensional attributes associated with the query q.

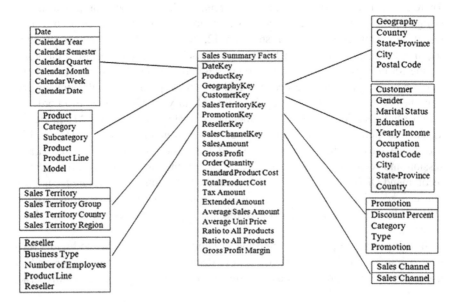

Fig. 2 Star schema of *SalesSummary*

For example, for the query

"SELECT
{([Measures].[Order Quantity]), ([Measures].[Sales Amount])} ON Columns,
{([Date].[Calendar Year].members, [Product].[Product Category].members,
[Geography].[Country].&[India])} ON Rows FROM [Adventure Works]",
the attribute set is {{Order Quantity, Sales Amount}, {Calendar Year, Product
Category, Country}}.

4 Building the Goal Hierarchy Using Queries of a Session

The goal hierarchy for an OLAP query session is built using a bottom-up approach. From the selected session, all the queries are picked up one by one. The queries are translated into tasks and related information goals. The decision goals and strategic goal are identified. The rules for creating the tasks, information goals, and decision goals and linking them using the *MeanEnds* edges are proposed in [7]. Only one strategic goal is created for the complete goal hierarchy built using the queries of the session.

5 Session Distance

A single session is used to build a goal hierarchy. A query log has multiple sessions. Each session contributes to building a goal hierarchy. If sessions are picked up at random, then there may not be tasks different from the tasks already identified in an earlier session. Since our main focus is to cover maximum parts of the data warehouse schema in the goal hierarchies, the next session for building a hierarchy has to be carefully chosen. To do so, we define distance between sessions.

The distance between the current session and a new session is measured in terms of how many different tasks and information goals of the new session are distinct from the current session.

As stated earlier, a task is created using the measure attributes as well as dimensional attributes though the information goal is created using the measure attributes only. If a query leads to create only a task, then the distance is incremented by one, and if a query contributes in creating a task as well as an information goal, then the distance is incremented by two.

Algorithm 1: To calculate the distance between sessions S' and S.

Input: $S = \{q_1, q_2, ..., q_n\}$, $S' = \{q_1', q_2', ..., q_m'\}$. Output: distance between sessions S' and S.

```
Session_Distance(S, S')                        {
1{                                                distance = distance+2
                                                  add qi' to new_S
  new_S = S, q_set= {}                         }
  distance = 0                                }4
  for i = 1 to m                             if (count' > 0)
  2{                                          {
    for j = 1 to len(new_S)                       distance = distance+2
    {                                             add qi' to new_S
      if (ms(qi') = ms(qj))                    }
      add qj to q_set                        }3
    }                                        else
    if (q_set = Φ)                           5{
    3{                                            count" =0
      count =0                                    for p =1 to len(q_set)
      count' = 0                                  {
      MS = {ms(q1) U ms(q2) U … U ms(q1en(new_s))}    if ds(qi')= ds(qp)
      for k = 1 to len(new_S)                         {
      {                                                 count" = 0
        if (ms(qi') ∩ ms(qk) = Φ)                       break
          count = count+1                             }
        else if ((ms(qi') - ms(qk) = Φ ||             else count"= count"+1
                  (ms(qi') - ms(qk)) ⊆ MS))           }
        {                                         if (count" > 0)
          distance = distance+1                   {
          add qi' to new_S                            distance= distance+1
          count' = 0                                  add qi' to new_S
          break                                   }
        }                                     }5
        else count' = count' + 1            }2
      }                                      return distance
      if (count= len(new_S))              }1
      4{
        if(attributes of qi' belongs to
               same strategic goal of G)
```

With each query q, $a\_set(q) = \{ms(q), ds(q)\}$ as given in *Definition 2* is associated. To check whether a query from one session is similar or distinct from the queries of another session, the measure and dimensional attribute sets of the queries are compared.

The following steps are followed in order to compute the session distance between a new session S' and the current session S:

(1) The first query q_1' of session S' is picked up. The measure set of the query, $ms(q_1')$, is compared with the measure sets all the queries of S.

(2) All the queries of S having the same measure set as $ms(q_1')$ are identified.

(3) The dimension set of the query q_1' of S', $ds(q_1')$, is compared with the dimension sets of the queries of S identified in the previous step. If it is equivalent to any query of S, then the distance remains unchanged. In case, there is no identical dimension set, then the distance is incremented by *one*.

(4) It is possible that there is no query of S having identical measure set to $ms(q_1')$. In this case, it is possible that there are one or more queries of S which, even though do not have identical measure set, may have some common measures with $ms(q_1')$.

(a) If some query of S has some common measure attributes with $ms(q_1')$, then the distance is incremented by *two*.

(b) If $ms(q_1')$ has a completely new measure set, then the user has to decide whether the attribute set of query q_1' can be part of the current goal hierarchy or not. In case, the user chooses to add the attribute set, the distance is incremented by *two*, otherwise the distance remains unchanged and the query q_1' is discarded from further considerations.

(5) Finally, the query q_1' is added to the session S if there is a change in the distance value. This step is required to check the redundant queries of S'.

(6) The above steps are followed for the remaining queries of the session S' one by one, and the final value of the distance is considered as the distance between the sessions.

6 Illustrative Example

In this section, we illustrate how the distance between two sessions is calculated using an example. We also explain which session should be picked up. Let us assume that the current session is $S = \{q_1, q_2, ..., q_{10}\}$ which has 10 queries and the session for which the distance we are calculating is $S' = \{q_1', q_2', ... , q_{10}'\}$ has also 10 queries. The measure and dimensional attribute sets of the queries of session S are shown in Table 1. The measure and dimensional attribute sets of the queries

Table 1 Attribute sets associated with the queries of session S

Query	Measure attribute set	Dimensional attribute set
q_1	{Sales Amount, Gross Profit, Order Quantity}	{Country, Calendar Year}
q_2	{Sales Amount, Gross Profit, Order Quantity}	{Country, Calendar Year, Calendar Quarter}
q_3	{Sales Amount, Gross Profit, Order Quantity}	{Calendar Year, Calendar Quarter, Calendar Week}
q_4	{Sales Amount, Gross Profit, Order Quantity}	{Calendar Month}
q_5	{Sales Amount, Gross Profit, Order Quantity}	{Calendar Month, Country}
q_6	{Sales Amount, Gross Profit, Order Quantity}	{Country, Calendar Month, Product}
q_7	{Sales Amount, Tax Amount}	{Country, Calendar Year}
q_8	{Gross Profit, Sales Amount}	{Sales Territory Country, Product Category}
q_9	{Gross Profit, Sales Amount, Total Product Cost}	{Calendar Year, Sales Territory Country, Product Category}
q_{10}	{Gross Profit, Sales Amount, Total Product Cost}	{Calendar Quarter, Sales Territory Country, Product Category}

of S' are shown in Table 2 with additional column indicating the distance incremented by the query to the session distance.

The query q_1' does not add anything to the distance because $ms(q_1')$ and $ds(q_1')$ are equivalent to $ms(q_1)$ and $ds(q_1)$, respectively. Similarly, the query q_8' *also* does not add anything to the distance. In the case of q_3', since the measure attributes of $ms(q_3')$ have not appeared in any of the measure sets of session S or in the measure sets $ms(q_1')$, $ms(q_2')$, the user will decide whether the query is to be considered to calculate the distance or not. We assume that the user said yes. So, the distance is incremented by two. For the query q_{10}', the distance is incremented by two because one of the measure attributes of $ms(q_{10}')$ appears for the first time. For each query q_2', $q_4'-q_7'$ and q_9', the distance is added by one. This is because the measure sets of each of these queries are either equivalent or have appeared in the measure sets of some of the queries of session S or previous queries in the same session S'. These queries have only distinct dimensional attribute sets. After adding the distance value of all the queries of session S', we get the distance of session S' from the session S as 10.

We have calculated the distance between the current session, $S1$, and twenty more sessions, $S2–S21$. The result is shown in Table 3. The session with maximum distance, i.e. *Session 18,* is picked up to build the goal hierarchy.

Table 2 Attribute sets associated with the queries of session S'

Query	Measure attribute set	Dimensional attribute set	Distance
q_1'	{Gross Profit, Sales Amount, Order Quantity}	{Country, Calendar Year}	0
q_2'	{Gross Profit, Sales Amount, Order Quantity}	{Country, Calendar Year, Product}	1
q_3'	{Total Product Cost, Freight Cost}	{Calendar Year, Country}	2
q_4'	{Total Product Cost, Freight Cost}	{Calendar Year, Country, Product}	1
q_5'	{Gross Profit, Sales Amount, Total Product Cost}	{Calendar Quarter, Sales Territory Region, Sales Territory Country, Product Category}	1
q_6'	{Sales Amount, Order Quantity}	{State-Province, Calendar Year, Product}	1
q_7'	{Sales Amount, Order Quantity}	{City, Calendar Quarter, Product Subcategory}	1
q_8'	{Sales Amount, Order Quantity, Gross Profit}	{Country, Calendar Month, Product}	0
q_9'	{Gross Profit, Sales Amount, Order Quantity}	{Calendar Year, Country, Product Category, Product}	1
q_{10}'	{Total Product Cost, Standard Product Cost}	{Product Category, Product Subcategory}	2

Table 3 Distances of sessions S2, S3, ..., S21 from the current session S1

Sessions	2	3	4	5	6	7	8	9	10	11	12	13	14	15	16	17	18	19	20	21
Distance	9	12	10	6	9	11	10	9	11	11	10	15	13	9	12	14	17	15	5	16

7 Conclusion

In this paper, we have proposed an algorithm to find a session that has maximum dissimilarity with the current session. Dissimilarity is measured using distance. The distance between sessions is defined using measure and dimensional attributes of the OLAP queries of the two sessions. The session with the maximum distance from the current one is chosen as it is likely to yield more tasks and information goals than other sessions.

All queries of a new session which belong to the strategic goal of the current session are retained. These queries are subsequently used to build a new goal hierarchy. We propose to integrate these two goal hierarchies in our future work. The integrated goal hierarchy will have wider perspectives in terms of tasks, information goals, and decision goals to achieve the strategic goal.

Acknowledgements This research was supported by Department of Science and Technology, Govt. of India, under the project "DST-PURSE Program, Phase- II".

References

1. Inmon, W.H.: Building the data warehouse. 4th edn. Wiley Publishing Inc, USA (1992).
2. Mazón, J.N., Pardillo, J., Trujillo, J.: A model-driven goal-oriented requirement engineering approach for data warehouses. In: ER Workshops 2007, LNCS, vol. 4802, pp. 255–264. Springer, Heidelberg (2007).
3. Salinesi, C., Gam, I.: A requirement-driven approach for designing data warehouses. In: Requirements Engineering: Foundations for Software Quality (REFSQ''06), p. 1. Luxembourg (2006).
4. Giorgini, P., Rizzi, S., Garzetti, M.: Goal-oriented requirement analysis for data warehouse design. In: Proceedings of the 8th ACM international workshop on Data warehousing and OLAP (DOLAP'05), pp. 47–56. Germany (2005).
5. Giorgini, P., Rizzi, S., Garzetti, M. (2008): GRAnD: A goal-oriented approach to requirement analysis in data warehouses. Decision Support Systems, vol. 45, no. 1, 4–21 (2005).
6. Golfarelli, M., Maio, D., Rizzi, S.: The dimensional fact model: a conceptual model for data warehouses. International Journal of Cooperative Information Systems, 7(02n03), 215–247 (1998).
7. Ranjan R.K., Parimala N.: A bottom-up approach for creating goal hierarchy using olap query recommendation technique, Int. J. Business Information Systems (Accepted 2017).
8. Aligon, J., Gallinucci, E., Golfarelli, M., Marcel, P., Rizzi, S.: A collaborative filtering approach for recommending olap sessions. Decision Support Systems, 69, 20–30 (2015).
9. Jensen, M., Holmgren, T., Pedersen, T.: Discovering multidimensional structure in relational data. In: Proceedings of International Conference on Data Warehousing and Knowledge Discovery, pp. 138–148. Zaragoza, Spain (2004).

10. Prakash, N., Gosain, A.: Requirements driven data warehouse development. CAiSE Short Paper Proceedings, Vol. 252. Springer (2003).
11. Parimala, N., Ranjan, R.K.: Mapping extended rationale diagrams to olap queries. ACM SIGSOFT Software Engineering Notes, vol. 38, no. 3, 1–6 (2013).
12. Adomavicius, G., Tuzhilin, A.: Toward the next generation of recommender systems: a survey of the state-of-the-art and possible extensions. IEEE Transactions on Knowledge and Data Engineering, vol. 17, no. 6, 734–749 (2005).
13. Aligon, J., Golfarelli, M., Marcel, P., Rizzi, S., Turricchia, E.: Mining preferences from olap query logs for proactive personalization. In: Proceedings ADBIS, pp. 84–97. Vienna, Austria, (2011).
14. Jerbi, H., Ravat, F., Teste, O., Zurfluh, G.: Preference-based recommendations for olpa analysis. In: Proceedings of the 11th International Conference on Data Warehousing and Knowledge Discovery (DaWaK'09), pp. 467–478. Springer-Verlag, Berlin, Heidelberg (2009).
15. Giacometti, A., Marcel, P., Negre, E.: A framework for recommending olap queries. In: Proceedings of the ACM 11th international workshop on Data warehousing and OLAP, pp. 73–80. ACM (2008).
16. Aissa, S., Gouider, M.S.: A new similairty measure for spatial personalization. International Journal of Database Management System, vol. 4, no. 4, 1–12 (2012).
17. Aligon, J., Golfarelli, M., Marcel, P., Rizzi, S., Turricchia, E.: Similarity measures for olap sessions. Knowledge and Information Systems, 39(2), 463–489 (2014).
18. Smith, B., Clay, C.: Microsoft sql server 2008 mdx step by step. Pearson Education, Washington, USA (2009).
19. Microsoft SQL Server 2012. https://www.microsoft.com/en-in/download/details.aspx?id=29062, last accessed 2016/08/01.
20. AdventureWorksDW: Microsoft sql server. https://msftdbprodsamples.codeplex.com, last accessed 2016/08/01.

Retinal Vessel Extraction and Fovea Detection Using Morphological Processing

Avik Banerjee, Soumyadeep Bhattacharjee and Sk. Latib

Abstract Extraction of blood vessels from retinal fundus images is a primary phase in the diagnosis of several eye disorders including diabetic retinopathy, a leading cause of vision impairment among working-age adults globally. Since manual detection of blood vessels by ophthalmologists gets progressively difficult with increasing scale, automated vessel detection algorithms provide an efficient and cost-effective alternative to manual methods. This paper aims to provide an efficient and highly accurate algorithm for the extraction of retinal blood vessels. The proposed algorithm uses morphological processing, background elimination, neighborhood comparison for preliminary detection of the vessels. Detection and removal of fovea, and bottom-hat filtering are performed subsequently to improve the accuracy, which is then calculated as a percentage with respect to ground truth images.

Keywords Diabetic retinopathy · Vessel extraction · Fovea detection
Fundus image · Bottom-hat filter · Neighborhood comparison

1 Introduction

According to the World Health Organization (WHO), diabetic retinopathy (DR) is one of the major causes of blindness and occurs due to long-term damage to the blood vessels in the retina. It is a microvascular disorder resulting due to prolonged, unrestrained suffering from diabetes mellitus and attributes to 2.6% of global

A. Banerjee (✉) · S. Bhattacharjee · Sk. Latib
Department of Computer Science and Engineering,
St. Thomas' College of Engineering and Technology, Kolkata, India
e-mail: bavik022@gmail.com

S. Bhattacharjee
e-mail: soumyadeep.bh1994@gmail.com

Sk. Latib
e-mail: sklatib@gmail.com

© Springer Nature Singapore Pte Ltd. 2018
P. K. Pattnaik et al. (eds.), *Progress in Computing, Analytics and Networking*,
Advances in Intelligent Systems and Computing 710,
https://doi.org/10.1007/978-981-10-7871-2_30

305

blindness [7]. Early detection/screening and suitable treatment have been shown to avert blindness in patients with retinal complications of diabetes. Retinal fundus images are extensively used by ophthalmologists for detecting and observing the progression of certain eye disorders such as DR, neoplasm of the choroid, glaucoma, multiple sclerosis, age-macular degeneration (AMD) [9]. Fundus photographs are captured using 'Charge-coupled Devices' (CCD), which are cameras that display the retina, or the light-sensitive layer of tissue in the interior surface of the eye [1, 9]. The key structures that can be visualized on a fundus image are the central and peripheral retina, optic disk and macula [1, 2]. These images provide information about the normal and abnormal features in the retina. The normal features include the optic disk, fovea, and vascular network [9]. There are different kinds of abnormal features caused by DR, such as microaneurysms, hard exudates, cotton-wool spots, hemorrhages, and neovascularization of blood vessels [3, 4]. Detection and segmentation of retinal vessels from fundus images is an important stage in classification of DR [5]. However, manual detection is extremely challenging as the blood vessels pictured in these images have a complex arrangement and poor local contrast, and the manual measurement of the features of blood vessels, such as length, width, branching pattern, and tortuosity, becomes cumbersome. As a result, it extends the period of diagnosis and decreases the efficiency of ophthalmologists as the scale increases [4]. Hence, automated methods for extracting and measuring the retinal vessels in fundus images are required to save the workload of the ophthalmologists and to aid in quicker and more efficient diagnosis.

The paper is organized as follows: Sect. 2 enlists previous attempts at deriving algorithms for segmentation of retinal features and detection of diabetic retinopathy. The proposed algorithm is an attempt to automate the process of retinal blood vessel detection as described in Sect. 3. Section 4 provides the result of application of the algorithm on the DRIVE database in terms of the accuracy of detection, sensitivity, and specificity. A comparison is provided between the average accuracies attained using existing algorithms and that of the proposed algorithm. It is seen that the proposed algorithm provides the highest accuracy of detection with a mean of 96.13%.

2   Literature Survey

Over the past decade, many image analysis methods have been suggested to interpret retinal fundus images based on image processing and machine learning techniques. Chaudhuri et al. [3] proposed an algorithm that approximated intensity profiles by means of a Gaussian curve. Gray-level profiles were derived along the perpendicular direction to the length of the vessel. Staal et al. proposed an algorithm for automated vessel segmentation in two-dimensional retinal color images, based on extraction of image ridges, which coincide approximately with vessel centerlines [11]. Chang et al. proposed a technique for the segmentation of retinal blood vessels

[2] that overcame the problem of Ricci and Perfetti [8] method which erroneously classified non-vessel pixels near the actual blood vessels, as vessel pixels. Fraz et al. proposed a hybrid method using derivative of Gaussian for vessel centerline detection and then combining them with vessel shape and orientation maps [4]. Zhang et al. proposed a method based on Derivative of Gaussian (DoG) filters and matched filters for vessel detection [4]. Soares et al. used Gabor filter at various scales to detect features of interest, followed by a Bayesian classifier for accurate classification of features [10]. Salazar-Gonzalez et al. proposed a method based on graph cut technique and Markov random field image reconstruction method for segmentation of the optic disk and blood vessels [9]. Miri et al. proposed a method based on curvelet transform to enhance vessel edges, followed by morphological operations to segment the vessels [6]. Marin et al. proposed a method based on neural network schemes for classification of pixels and a seven-dimensional vector for pixel representation [5].

3 Algorithm

3.1 Preprocessing

3.1.1 The green channel (I_g) from the RGB image is extracted, as all the essential features are prominent in this channel.

3.2 Vessel Enhancement

3.2.1 Bottom-hat filtering is applied on I_g to preserve the sharp bottoms and enhance contrast. The bottom-hat transform is obtained as the difference between the morphological closing of I_g, using a disk structuring element S, and I_g, as in Eq. (1)

$$I_1 = (I_g \cdot S) - I_g \qquad (1)$$

3.2.2 Contrast-limited adaptive histogram equalization is performed on image I_1 and then filtered with a 3 × 3 median filter to remove spurious non-vessel pixels, generating image I_2.

3.2.3 I_2 is then binarized using Otsu's threshold, to generate image I_3.

3.3 Separation of Image Background

3.3.1 The background I_B of image I_g is separated using a disk averaging filter of radius 30 units, corresponding to the size of the optic disk, the largest feature in the retinal fundus image.

3.3.2 The contrast of the image I_g is enhanced by scanning the entire image with a 9×9 window. For each 9×9 region, the average of the pixel intensities in the mask is calculated. The pixels whose intensities are less than the average intensity are suppressed.

3.3.3 The enhanced image I_4 is subtracted from the background I_B to obtain image I_5.

3.3.4 Pixel intensities in I_5 are amplified to obtain image I_6.

3.4 Vessel Reconstruction

3.4.1 The images I_3 and I_6 are compared, and the presence of common edge points in both the images is considered to be a vessel in the final image I_7.

3.4.2 The bridge morphological operation is applied on the image to eliminate discontinuities in the detected vessels, generating image I_8.

3.5 Removal of Fovea

3.5.1 I_g is closed with a structuring element S to obtain I_{close} using Eq. (2).

$$I_{close} = (I_g \oplus S) \ominus S \tag{2}$$

3.5.2 I_9 is generated through

$$I_9 = I_g \times I_r, \tag{3}$$

where I_r is the red channel of the RGB image.

3.5.3 $I_{ad} = adjust(I_9)$, where I_{ad} is the adjusted image I_9 obtained after mapping the intensities in gray scale image I_9 to new values in I_{ad} such that 1% of data is saturated at low and high intensities of I_9.

3.5.4 The image I_{ad} is filtered with a disk structuring element with size 10 units to obtain image I_{back}.

3.5.5 Image I_{10} is obtained by adding the closed image and the background image I_{back} using Eq. (4).

$$I_{10} = I_{close} + I_{back} \tag{4}$$

3.5.6 Image I_{11} is obtained by

$$I_{11} = (I_{10} \div I_M) + I_{mask}^c \tag{5}$$

where I_{mask} is the retinal mask. This is followed by suppressing the pixels greater than 1 down to 1.

3.5.7 Image I_{12} is generated by Eq. (6):

$$I_{12} = (I_{11}^c - adjust(I_g)) \times I_{11} \tag{6}$$

3.5.8 A 40×40 mask M_{fovea}, derived from a standard retinal scan, is used as a template, and the coordinates of the center pixel of the region in image I_{12} with the closest match to the template are taken as the centroid of the fovea (x_{fovea}, y_{fovea}).

3.5.9 The image I_{12} is scanned to determine the coordinates of each fovea pixel (x, y), where each such point satisfies the equation:

$$\left((x_{fovea} - x)^2 + (y_{fovea} - y)^2 \right) \le D_{fovea}^2 \tag{7}$$

All such pixels are raised to the maximum intensity, and all other pixels are suppressed in the binary image I_{fov}.

3.5.10 The final vessel extracted image I_{vess} is obtained by,

$$I_{vess} = I_8 - I_{fov} \tag{8}$$

Figure 1 illustrates the outputs of each stage of the algorithm for one of the images from the database.

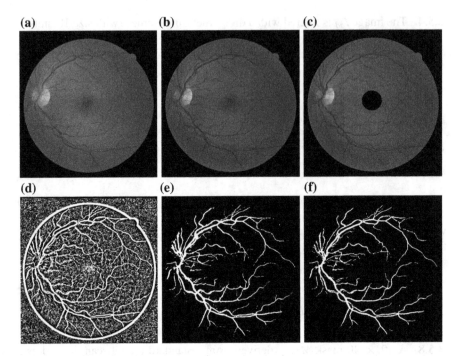

Fig. 1 **a** Input RGB image, **b** green channel extracted image, **c** fovea detected image, **d** output of background subtraction and subsequent binarization, **e** output of bottom-hat filtering and subsequent binarization, and **f** final vessel detected image

4 Results

The algorithm was applied on the DRIVE database and the accuracy of detection was calculated for each image, using the ground truth images provided in the database, with the help of the following concepts [4]:

- *True Positives* refer to vessel pixels that are correctly identified. TP refers to the number of pixels which have high intensity value both in the algorithm output and the ground truth.
- *True Negatives* refer to pixels that have not been identified both in the ground truth and the algorithm output; that is, they are correctly identified to be of no importance. TN refers to the number of pixels which have low intensity both in the algorithm output and the ground truth image.
- *False Positives* refer to pixels which have been incorrectly identified. FP refers to the number of pixels which have high intensity in the algorithm output but low intensity in the ground truth image.
- *False Negatives* refer to pixels which have been missed out incorrectly. FN refers to pixels that have low intensity in the algorithm output but high intensity in the ground truth image.

- *Sensitivity*, also called the true positive rate (TPR), refers to the proportion of positives correctly identified. It is calculated as

$$TPR = \frac{TP}{TP + FN} \tag{9}$$

- *Specificity*, also called the true negative rate, refers to the proportion of negatives correctly identified. It is calculated as

$$TNR = \frac{TN}{TN + FP} \tag{10}$$

- *Accuracy* refers to the accuracy of vessel detection and is calculated as

$$ACCURACY = \frac{TN + TP}{TN + TP + FN + FP} \tag{11}$$

Table 1 List of accuracy of detection for individual images in the DRIVE database

Image	Sensitivity	Specificity	Accuracy
1	85.0474	97.4018	96.4811
2	89.6314	97.2853	96.6372
3	82.8067	97.013	95.961
4	90.5944	96.7619	96.372
5	87.7838	97.6173	96.9557
6	88.6166	96.3499	95.8343
7	67.4681	98.014	95.5998
8	70.0436	98.12	96.1504
9	84.5238	96.8746	96.1232
10	83.3954	97.7128	96.8502
11	78.8614	97.4582	96.0504
12	77.9111	97.7181	96.2123
13	88.4261	95.7812	95.2658
14	69.7081	98.3221	95.8862
15	66.8843	97.6951	95.2355
16	86.5485	97.4616	96.6857
17	75.8418	97.9193	96.3296
18	86.4698	96.9589	96.1859
19	90.8799	96.5181	96.1026
20	87.4021	96.3836	95.7786

Table 2 Comparison of average accuracy of existing methods

Method	Average accuracy (%)
Chaudhuri et al. [3]	92.84
Staal et al. [11]	94.42
Soares et al. [10]	94.66
Ricci and Perfetti [8]	95.95
Zhang et al. [12]	93.82
Miri et al. [6]	94.58
Marin et al. [5]	94.52
Fraz et al. [4]	94.30
Gonzalez et al. [9]	94.12
Proposed method	96.13

Application of the algorithm on the DRIVE database images yielded accuracy of detection in the range of 95–97% with a mean of 96.13%. Table 1 lists out the individual accuracy of detection for each of the images. Table 2 tabulates the average accuracies of existing methods along with that of the proposed method.

5   Conclusion

The proposed algorithm extracts the retinal vessels in a fundus scan with a stable accuracy. The resulting vessel extracted image can be used as a tool for classification of various eye disorders like diabetic retinopathy (DR). This algorithm provides an integrated approach to a vital step in the diagnostic procedure of DR. The high accuracy of the proposed algorithm can thus improve the accuracy of detection of DR when used in conjunction with other relevant algorithms for detection of exudates, hemorrhages, and other retinal abnormalities.

References

1. Abramoff, Michael, Garvin, Mona, Sonka, Milan: Retinal Imaging and Image Analysis, IEEE Transactions on Medical Imaging, Jan. 2010
2. Chang, Samuel H, Gong Leiguang, Li, Maoqing, Hu, Xiaoying, Yan, Jingwen: Small retinal vessel extraction using modified Canny edge detection, International Conference on Audio, Language and Image Processing, 2008.
3. Chaudhuri, S, Chatterjee, S, Katz, N, Nelson, M, Goldbaum, M: Detection of blood vessels in retinal images using two-dimensional matched filters, IEEE Transactions on Medical Imaging, Volume: 8, Issue: 3, Sept. 1989
4. Fraz, M.M., Barman, S, Remagnino, P, Hoppe, A, Basit, A., Uyyanonvara, B, Rudnicka, A. R., and Owen, C.G.: An Approach To Localize The Retinal Blood Vessels Using Bit Planes And Centerline Detection, Comp. Methods and Progs in Biomed., vol. 108, no. 2, 2012

5. Marin, D., Aquino, A., Gegndez-Arias, M.E., and Bravo, J.M: A New Supervised Method For Blood Vessel Segmentation In Retinal Images By Using Gray-Level And Moment Invariants-Based Features, IEEE Trans. Med. Imaging, vol. 30, no. 1, pp. 146–158, 2011.
6. Miri, M.S. and Mahloojfar, A.: Retinal Image Analysis Using Curvelet Transform and Multistructure Elements Morphology by Reconstruction, IEEE Trans. on Biomed. Eng, vol. 58, pp. 1183–1192, May 2011.
7. Prevention of Blindness from Diabetes Mellitus, Report of a WHO consultation in Geneva, Switzerland, Nov. 2005.
8. Ricci, Elisa, Perfetti, Renzo: Retinal Blood Vessel Segmentation Using Line Operators and Vector Classification, IEEE Trans. on Medical Imaging, Volume: 26, Issue: 10, Oct. 2007
9. Salazar-Gonzalez, A., Kaba, D, Li, Y, and Liu, X: Segmentation Of Blood Vessels And Optic Disc In Retinal Images, IEEE Journal of Biomedical and Health Informatics, 2014.
10. Soares, J. V. B., Leandro, J. J. G., Cesar, R. M., H. Jelinek, F, and Cree, M.J.: Retinal Vessel Segmentation Using The 2-D Gabor Wavelet And Supervised Classification, IEEE Trans. Med. Imaging, vol. 25, no. 9, pp. 1214–1222, 2006.
11. Staal, Joel, Abramoff, Michael, Niemeijer, Meindert, Vuergever, Max, Ginneken, Bram van: Ridge-Based Vessel Segmentation in Color Images of the Retina, IEEE Transactions on Medical Imaging, Vol. 3 Issue 4, Apr. 2004.
12. Zhang, B, Zhang, L, Karray, F: Retinal Vessel Extraction by Matched Filter with First Order Derivative of Gaussian, Comp. in Bio. And Med., vol 40, no 4, 2010.

Developing High-Performance AVM Based VLSI Computing Systems: A Study

Siba Kumar Panda and Dhruba Charan Panda

Abstract With the initiation of ancient Vedic mathematics (AVM) concepts, very large-scale integration technique becomes more powerful in developing various VLSI computing systems. In the last decade, people have tried to integrate the Vedic mathematics techniques with the VLSI theory. Hence, analyzing methods, designing and manipulating the performance from circuit- and system-level perspectives become a vital task and challenging too. Performance study of various diverse techniques that are used for developing high-performance VLSI computing systems is the central focus of this paper. This paper provides a comprehensive survey of different designing techniques, complementing the limits of existing reviews in the literature. The survey covers introduction to Vedic methods, motivation toward the work, various designing techniques with their limitations, etc. This paper can be seen as a foremost step to present a state-of-the-art impression of revision work carried in developing high-performance VLSI computing systems.

Keywords VLSI computing · VLSI signal processing · AVM
FPGA · HDL

1 Introduction

VLSI computing system includes countless arithmetic operations. Purposely, the application-specific operation has ample usage in various signal and image processing works. In signal processing application, addition, multiplication, division,

S. K. Panda (✉)
Department of ECE, Centurion University of Technology & Management,
Jatni 752050, Odisha, India
e-mail: panda.sibakumar08vssut@gmail.com

D. C. Panda
P. G. Department of Electronic Science, Berhampur University, Berhampur
760007, Odisha, India
e-mail: dcpanda@gmail.com

© Springer Nature Singapore Pte Ltd. 2018
P. K. Pattnaik et al. (eds.), *Progress in Computing, Analytics and Networking*,
Advances in Intelligent Systems and Computing 710,
https://doi.org/10.1007/978-981-10-7871-2_31

squaring, square root and cubing are the majority as well as repeated arithmetic operations. An adept arithmetic treatment helps in developing processor architectures that use high-performance computing systems. At present, computing is a hot research domain in computer science, VLSI as well as basic sciences and numerous engineering areas. Out of these, VLSI computing is one of them.

Establishing the veracity of the VLSI computing techniques and investigating the essential information have become an important and sizzling research in developing high-performance VLSI computing systems. The idolization in the field of VLSI signal processing and the fast advancement in manuscripts published in the past years have put significant right on creating an entire article. The topical articles represent a wide-range checklist of references on design of computing systems for low-power VLSI signal processing applications. Though there are some other available reviews, many of existing designing techniques are not cited and stay nameless. In this manuscript, we do not weigh focus on the niceties of exact methods or illustrate results and their domino effects. This work also does not hold articles from admired press or papers. It only provides general information about various designing and developing techniques. We tried straight away jump into the central theme of the manuscript. We expect that this work shall provide a platform to the researchers in high-performance VLSI computing system domain in finding new research problems and solutions. This is a strive to make this paper complete by listing most live references. The authors presented a blueprint by means of thorough arrangement and presented suitable references into this. To the superlative grasp of the authors, this survey plays the most complete circulated source of citations on developing high-performance computing systems through AVM.

The paper organization can be shown as follows: Sect. 2 describes the motivation toward the work. The high-end methods for developing VLSI computing systems are shown in Sect. 3. The performance study and discussion part are presented in Sect. 4. At the end, conclusions are found in Sect. 5.

2 Motivation

Development of high-performance VLSI computing systems for variety of VLSI signal processing applications becomes a very crucial task and interesting too. So many of the researchers had proposed various well-known techniques and methods for this design and development.

3 High-end Methods for Developing VLSI Computing Systems

The testimonial is classified into numerous categories and planned for every category, arranged from latest publication to old publication year wise.

Various computer arithmetic techniques developed and well presented by Parhami [1] that help in developing high-performance multiplier architectures, divider architectures, function evaluation circuits, etc. This leads to efficient implementation as well as development of VLSI computing systems for high-throughput arithmetic, low-power arithmetic and fault-tolerant arithmetic circuits. AVM consists of 16 mathematical sutras [2]. The volume written by (Maharaja [2]; Tirthaji, Vedic mathematics [2]) explains conceptually with examples. It is the heart of 16 sutras which were presented by Sri Bharti Krishna Tirthaji [2]. Ancient Vedic mathematics (AVM) explores unique approach of calculation on the basis of 16 sutras [1, 2]. This motivated to go forward in the design and development of various VLSI computing systems.

Discussing various state-of-the-art methods for developing VLSI computing systems, Sharma et al. [3] proposed design of 2-bit multiplier used for multiplication of two quadratic equations. They used 'Urdhva Tiryakbhyam' sutra of AVM. They also presented CMOS logic design of the 2-bit multiplier in this work.

In [4], Barik et al. projected a widespread cube architecture which is based on Vedic mathematics. They used Yavadunam sutra of AVM. The algorithm converts the cube of a large magnitude number into small magnitude number and addition operation. Here, the algorithm is applied to both decimal numbers as well as binary radix-2 number system. Here, the cubic architecture is designed using cadence tool. From the results, they concluded that the architecture is helpful for less area and high-speed VLSI application. FPGA implementation of pipelined square root circuit proposed by Panda et al. [5] which describes the design and simulation of square root circuit for various mathematical operations as well as the use of non-restoring algorithms in it. They presented the pipelined design by using controlled subtract-multiplex (CSM) block. The main principle of the presented method [5] is analogous with usual non-restoring algorithm, but it only uses subtract operation and append 01, while add operation and append 11 is not used. The projected design has been conducted to put into practice of FPGA successfully. Bansal et al. [6] proposed 16-bit Vedic multiplier by using Urdhva Tiryakbhyam sutra. They used compressor adders in multiplier architecture. In this work, the authors concluded that proposed multiplier shows good speed results over traditional multipliers. Srimani et al. [7] anticipated the design of high-piece Vedic multipliers and design of DSP operations using AVM. The authors presented the design of a 4×4 multiplier circuit based on 'Urdhva Tiryakbhyam' Vedic sutra.

Anjana et al. [8] proposed the design of a high-speed floating-point multiplier. They used the concept of AVM to design this. The authors presented the design of multiplier architecture by using ripple-carry adder and carry-lookahead adder.

Barik et al. [9] presented the design of squaring architecture. They also used a popular sutra of AVM called as 'Yavadunam' sutra. The anticipated scheme helps in the calculation of the deficit of the number from the nearest base in order to find the square of any operand. A novel high-speed Vedic divider architecture proposed by Panda et al. [10] also uses AVM. They used Paravartya sutra here. Here, a 32-bit divider circuit is presented and also simulated using Xilinx tool.

Khan et al. [11] stated the design of a novel multiplier by using AVM. This design is done by using a popular sutra called as 'Ekanyunena Purvena' of Vedic mathematics. Sethi et al. [12] anticipated multiplier less high-speed squaring circuit using the concept of ancient Vedic mathematics (AVM), where they used YTVY sutra. In common use, the squaring circuit uses fast multipliers. They also compared their results in terms of time delay, and area is compared with both modified Booth's algorithms.

In [13], Saha et al. stated a division method using AVM in transistor-level realization. They used the 'Dhvajanka' formula for the design. Here, the design was implemented by half of the divisor bit instead of the actual divisor, subtraction. Again Saha et al. [14] stated the design of matrix multiplier based on the transistor. They used matrix element transformation and multiplication in this article. They got the improved result in terms of speed by rearranging the matrix element into a two-dimensional array of processing elements.

In [15], Rahman et al. presented a new blueprint for finding square root of N-bit unsigned numbers. They used the modified non-restoring square root algorithm for this design. In this design, a sequential pipeline asynchronous architecture is designed with HDL code.

Pradhan et al. [16] proposed a high-speed multiplier architecture using ancient Vedic mathematics (AVM). They used the Nikhilam algorithm for their design. They stated that the designed multiplier helps in finding the complement of the large operand from its nearest base so as to do the multiplication. They also used carry save adder (CSA) in the design. Poornima et al. [17] stated in this article that by using AVM and various algorithms in it, many multiplier architectures can be designed.

Saravanan et al. explained the concept of reversible logic in [18] by which they designed an efficient multiplier. They used Nikhilam sutra of AVM and also used reversible logic. Due to the advantages in dissipating zero power reversible logic help in design of low-power multipliers.

Senthilpari et al. proposed the design of square root circuit [19] by using a 1-bit full adder circuit as well as Shannon's theorem concept. Here, the authors presented a clear blueprint of non-restoring and restoring square root circuits. The designed circuit uses the 65 nm CMOS technology. In [20], Sajid et al. planned a design of N-bit fixed point square root circuit. Here, the authors also used non-restoring algorithm for the design.

Saha et al. presented [21] a ASIC design of a circuit for calculating factorial of a given number. Note that, using iterative multiplication the factorial of a number can be calculated. Here, the author used the parallel implementation concept mixing with ancient Vedic mathematics (AVM). In Sutikno et al. [22], the authors come up with an idea to realize modified non-restoring algorithm in gate level. The architecture is designed with the help of a basic CSM as building blocks. Again in Sultana et al. [23], the authors present a novel reversible implementation of a square root circuit by means of array structure. In classical irreversible arena, we find different realizations of square root circuit. The author presented that the reversible circuit introduces a basic module called reversible controlled adder/subtractor (RCAS) block.

Kasliwal et al. [24] proposed an efficient squaring operation by using AVM concepts. Sutikno et al. [25] presented a digit-by-digit calculation method for calculating the complicated square root. The authors presented the concept of DTC and FPGA in their design. They stated that the proposed method is based on a 2-bit shifter and a subtractor-multiplexor operation which help in faster calculation.

Deshpande et al. [26] adduced the design of squaring units and its comparison with the multipliers. Here, the author introduced a dedicated squaring unit to carry out square operation. Due to the development of AVM [27], it helps in designing and developing many of the high-performance VLSI computing systems. Hence, many of the researchers are interested to apply this concept by coding it any hardware description languages [28].

Ramalatha et al. [29] stated a cubing operation for finite field arithmetic. Again the author stated that by increasing the radix of the number, the process becomes dense for designed circuit. But with the introduction of AVM, they introduced an efficient cubic circuit with different multiplier structures. Here, the author used Anurupyena sutra of Vedic mathematics and also they compared with various state-of-the-art techniques. The author here concluded that the Anurupyena sutra improves the design performance.

In [30], Meheta et al. stated the conventional versus Vedic multiplication on hardware platform. For Vedic multiplication, they used Urdhva Tiryakbhyam sutra of Vedic mathematics and also used HDL [31] for its implementation.

Samavi et al. [32] proposed a square root circuit using modular array structure. Similarly, wang et al. [33] also proposed decimal floating-point square root circuit using Newton–Raphson algorithm. In paper [34], the authors Thapliyal et al. suggested a parallel architectures using AVM for calculation of square and cube. Here, the author used duplex property of binary numbers, and the cubic circuit uses Anurupyena sutra. The authors Chidgupkar et al. [35] explained the implementation of Vedic algorithm in digital signal processing application. Thapliyal et al. [36] proposed a new multiplier and square architecture using AVM concepts. The design was done at both gate level and RT level. Here, the author used Verilog language [37] for the design.

Ercegovac et al. [38] explained some elementary function using small multipliers. Here, the authors presented the design of reciprocal circuit, square roots as well as inverse square root circuit. In [39], the authors Liddicoat et al. presented that distinctive multipliers are used to work out square and cube of number. Here, the authors presented a parallel square cube design. The design of circuits helps the researcher to go forward in a straight direction so as to design different claim-specific circuits for diverse VLSI signal processing applications as stated by Parhi [40]. In [41], the authors Li et al. explained the design of square root for floating-point numbers. In [42], again Li et al. proposed parallel implementation of non-restoring algorithm to design square root. They used carry save adder in their design. Guenther et al. [43] proposed various arithmetic functions in digital computer machine environment. Li et al. [44] and O'Leary et al. [45] stated a new square root circuit using non-restoring algorithm and also they implemented it in VLSI level.

The advancement in the digital system design, various computer architectures [46] and the concept of AVM [47] help the researcher to develop high-performance VLSI computing systems.

4 Performance Study and Discussion

To the preeminent of our comprehension, this manuscript contains whole review of all published papers as mentioned in the reference section. We believe that it can help the researchers in the field of VLSI signal processing as well as developing various VLSI computing systems. In addition to that, it will also help them to find new research challenges. The performance of all the circuits as stated in the literature is summarized in Table 1. The concert in terms of delay, power, gate count and area of all mentioned papers is clearly presented in Table 1.

Table 1 Performance study of various AVM-based units and systems presented in the literature

References	Delay	Power	Gate Counts	Areas
[2]	6–9 ns	–	–	–
[4]	33.18 ns	84,987,014.349 nW	5431	250,087.114 μm^2
[6]	32 ns	–	–	–
[7]	0.060 ns	9.2×10^{-5} W	–	–
[8]	Using CLA—30.934 ns Using CLA—3 35.286 ns Using carry save—70.064 ns Array multiplier—73.485 ns	1.042 W 1.042 W 1.042 W 1.042 W	1% 2% 1% 1%	–
[9]	21.760 ns	–	284	–
[10]	18.675 ns	–	224	–
[12]	75.236 ns	–	3766	0.253 W
[13]	299.92 ns	32.53 mW	–	17.39 mm^2
[14]	2 μs	3.12 mW	–	–
[16]	21.625 ns(Spartan 3:xc3s50:-4) 12.641 ns(Virtex2P:xc2vp2:-7)	–	–	–
[17]	28.27 ns	–	176	–
[18]	18.8 ns	–	28	–
[19]	0.027 ns	4.376 μW	–	714 μm^2
[21]	42.13 ns	58.82 mW	–	6 mm^2
[24]	33.391 ns	–	294	–
[29]	56.237 ns	108.80 mW	–	–
[33]	0.95 ns	–	–	–
[34]	38 ns (Vedic square) 54 ns (Vedic cube)	–	–	–
[35]	0.480 ms (For 2 digit) 1.042 ms (For 3 digit)	–	–	–
[38]	48 τs (Reciprocal, square root and inverse square root)	–	–	–

The presented papers in the literature [1–47] consisting of the design of various multiplier, divider, squaring circuit, cubic circuit, square root circuit, etc., are designed in either Verilog HDL or VHDL languages. The performance parameters like delay, power and areas are collected from the respective article and presented in Table 1 clearly. Commonly, we can utter that the state of the art of developing VLSI-based computing units assists the researchers to improve in designing emergent, high-performance computing systems.

5 Conclusion

The concert of the various published work as cited throughout the paper as well as stated in the reference section is presented neatly. This initiation of research work helps the researcher to understand the key aspects of developing ancient Vedic mathematics-based VLSI computing systems. We wish it will help in design and development of low-power, high-speed computing systems.

6 Further Research

This study in developing high-performance AVM-based VLSI computing system helps the researchers to go forward in key design and implementation of many higher order VLSI computing systems. The potential future work of this survey needs to design novel high-performance computing systems for efficient VLSI signal processing applications.

Acknowledgements All the studies are carried out at Centurion University of Technology and Management, Odisha, India. The authors also express their sincere gratitude to Centurion University of Technology & Management, Jatni, Bhubaneswar, Odisha for providing a high-end research platform.

References

1. Parhami, B.: Computer arithmetic: algorithms and hardware designs, 2nd edn., Oxford University Press (2010)
2. Maharaja, J.S.S.B.K.T.: Vedic mathematics: Motilal Banarsidass Publishers Pvt. Ltd, Delhi (2007)
3. Sharma, P., Singh, R.P., Singh, R., Pande, P.: Design of Quadratic Equations Multiplier (for up to 2-Bit Number) Using Vedic Technique. In: Proceeding of International Conference on Intelligent Communication, Control and Devices. Advances in Intelligent Systems and Computing, vol 479. Springer, Singapore (2017)
4. Barik, R.K., Pradhan, M.: Efficient ASIC and FPGA implementation of cube architecture. IET Computers & Digital Techniques vol. 11(1), pp. 43–49 (2017)

5. Panda, S.K., Jena, A.: FPGA-VHDL implementation of pipelined square root circuit for VLSI signal processing applications. International journal of computer application, vol. 142, pp. 20–24 (2016)
6. Bansal, Y., Charu, M.: A novel high-speed approach for 16 × 16 Vedic multiplication with compressor adders, Computer. Electr. Eng., 49, pp. 39–49. Comput. Electr. Eng. (2016)
7. Srimani, S., Kundu, D.K., Panda, S., Maji, B.: Implementation of High Performance Vedic Multiplier and Design of DSP Operations Using Vedic Sutra. In Computational Advancement in Communication Circuits and Systems. Lecture Notes in Electrical Engineering, vol 335. Springer, New Delhi (2015)
8. Anjana, S., Pradeep, C., Samuel, P.: Synthesize of high speed floating-point multipliers based on Vedic mathematics. Procedia Computer Science, vol. 46, pp. 1294–1302, December 2015
9. Barik, R.K., Pradhan, M.: Area-time efficient square architecture (Advances Series D, AMSE Press), vol. 20, no. 1, pp. 21–35 (2015)
10. Panda, S.K., Sahu, A.: A Novel Vedic Divider Architecture with Reduced Delay for VLSI Applications. International journal of computer application, vol. 120, pp. 31–36 (2015)
11. Khan, A., Das, R.: Novel Approach of Multiplier Design Using Ancient Vedic Mathematics. In Information Systems Design and Intelligent Applications. Advances in Intelligent Systems and Computing, vol 340, pp 265–272, Springer, New Delhi (2015)
12. Sethi, K., Panda, R.: Multiplier less high-speed squaring circuit for binary numbers. International journal of electronics, vol. 102, pp. 433–443. Taylor Francis (2014)
13. Saha, P., Kumar, D., Bhattacharyya, P., et al: Vedic division methodology for high-speed very large scale integration application, J. Eng., 1, (1), pp. 1–9. (2014)
14. Saha, P., et al.: Improved matrix multiplier design for high speed signal processing applications. IET Circuits Devices and Syst. 8(1), pp. 27–37 (2014)
15. Rahman, A., Al-Kafi, A.: New efficient hardware design methodology for modified non-restoring square root algorithm. In: International conference on informatics electronics and Vision, pp. 1–6. Dhaka (2014)
16. Pradhan, M., Panda, R.: High speed multiplier using Nikhilam sutra algorithm of Vedic mathematics, Int. J. Electron., 101, (3), pp. 300–307 (2014)
17. Poornima, M., et al.: Implementation of multiplier using Vedic algorithm. IJITEE 2(6), pp. 219–223 (2013)
18. Saravanan, P., Chandrasekar, P., Chandran, L., Sriram, N., Kalpana, P. Design and Implementation of Efficient Vedic Multiplier Using Reversible Logic. In: Progress in VLSI Design and Test. Lecture Notes in Computer Science, vol 7373. Springer, Berlin, Heidelberg (2012)
19. Senthilpari, B.C., Kavitha, S.: Proposed low power, high speed, adder-based, 65 nm square root circuit. Journal of Microelectronics, vol. 42, pp. 445–451. Elsevier Science (2011)
20. Sajid, I., Ahmed, M.: Pipelined implementation of fixed point square root in FPGA using modified non-restoring algorithm. In: 2nd International conference on computer and automation engineering, pp. 226–230. IEEE press, Islamabad (2011)
21. Saha, P., et al.: ASIC design of a high speed low power circuit for factorial calculation using ancient vedic mathematics, Microelectronics. J. 42, pp. 1343–1352 (2011)
22. Sutikno, T.: An efficient implementation of non-restoring square root algorithm in gate level. International journal of computer theory and engineering, vol. 3, pp. 46–51(2011)
23. Sultana, S., Radecka, K.: Reversible implementation of square-root circuit. In: 18th IEEE international conference on electronic circuits and systems, pp. 141–144. IEEE Press, Canada (2011)
24. Kasliwal, P.S., Patil, B., Gautam, D.: Performance evaluation of squaring operation by Vedic mathematics, IETE J. Res., 57, (1), pp. 39–41 (2011)
25. Sutikno, T., Zakwan, A.: A simple strategy to solve complicated square root problem in DTC for FPGA implementation. In: IEEE symposium on industrial electronics and application, pp. 691–695. IEEE press, Penang (2010)
26. Deshpande, A., Draper, J.: Squaring units and a comparison with multipliers. Proc. of 53th Int. Symp. on Circuits and Systems, pp. 1266–1269(2010)

27. Chakrabarty, S.M., Kolluru, R.: Enjoy vedic mathematics. The Art of Living (Diamond Books), 31 Oct 2010
28. Ashenden, P.J.: The designer's guide to VHDL. Morgan Kaufmann (2010)
29. Ramalatha, M., Thanushkodi, K., Deena Dayalan, K., et al: A novel time and energy efficient cubing circuit using Vedic mathematics for finite field arithmetic. Proc. of 09th Int. Conf. on Advances in Recent Technologies in Communication and Computing, pp. 873–875(2009)
30. Meheta, P., Gawali, D.: Conventional versus vedic mathematical method for hardware implementation of a multiplier. In: Proceedings of IEEE International Conferences on Advances in Computing, Control and Telecommunication, pp. 640–642, Trivandrum, Kerala (2009)
31. Pedroni, V. A.: Circuit design with VHDL. Cambridge, MA: The MIT Press (2008)
32. Samavi, S., Sadrabadi, A., Fanian, A.: Modular array structure of non-restoring square root circuit. Journal of system architecture, vol. 54, pp. 957–966. Elsevier Science (2008)
33. Wang, L., Schulte, M.: Decimal floating point square root using Newton-Raphson iteration. In: 16th International conference on application specific systems architecture processors, pp. 309–315. IEEE press, USA (2005)
34. Thapliyal, H., Kotiyal, S., Srinivas, M.: Design and analysis of a novel parallel square and cube architecture based on ancient Indian Vedic mathematics. Proc. of 48th Int. Symp. on Circuits and Systems, pp. 1462–1465(2005)
35. Chidgupkar, P. D., Karad, M.T.: The implementation of Vedic algorithms in digital signal processing. Glob. J. Eng. Educ., 8(2), pp. 153–158 (2004)
36. Thapliyal, H., Arbania, H.R.: A time-area-power efficient multiplier and square architecture based on ancient indian vedic mathematics. In: Proceedings of the 2004 International Conference on VLSI (VLSI '04), Las Vegas, Nevada, pp. 434–439, June (2004)
37. Palnitkar, S.: Verilog HDL: A guide to digital design and synthesis. Prentice Hall Professional (2003)
38. Ercegovac, M.D., Lang, T., Muller, J.M., et al: Reciprocation, square root, inverse square root, and some elementary functions using small multipliers. IEEE Trans. Comput., 49(7), pp. 628–637 (2000)
39. Liddicoat, A.A., Flynn, M.: Parallel square and cube computations. Proc. of 34th Int. Conf. on Signals, Systems and Computers, vol. 2, pp. 1325–1329 (2000)
40. Parhi, K.K.: VLSI Digital Signal Processing Systems: Design and Implementation. Wiley, London (1999)
41. Li, Y., Chu, W.: Implementation of single precision floating point square root on FPGAs. In: 5th IEEE symposium on FPGA for custom computing machines, pp. 226–232. California, USA (1997)
42. Li, Y., Chu, W.: Parallel array implementations of non-restoring square root algorithm. In: International conference on computer design, pp. 690–695. IEEE press, USA (1997)
43. Guenther, H.: Arithmetic operations of the machine fundamentals of digital machine computing, Springer publication (1996)
44. Li, Y., Chu, W.: A new non-restoring square root algorithm and its VLSI implementation. In: IEEE International Conference on computer design, pp. 539–544. Texas, USA (1996)
45. O'Leary, J., Leeser, M.: Non-restoring integer square root-A case study in design by principled optimization. Technical report, Cornell University (1994)
46. Morris Mano, M.: Computer System Architecture, 3rd edn, pp. 346–348. Prentice-Hall, New Jersey (1993)
47. Jeganathan Sriskandarajah: Secrets of ancient maths: vedic mathematics. Journal of Indic Studies Foundation, California

A Fuzzy Optimization Technique for Energy Efficient Node Localization in Wireless Sensor Network Using Dynamic Trilateration Method

Saroj Kumar Rout, Amiya Kumar Rath,
Pradyumna Kumar Mohapatra, Pradeep K. Jena
and Aparimita Swain

Abstract In wireless sensor network (WSN), localization has a vital role to improve the performance of sensor networks. The proposed fuzzy optimization technique determines the sensor node location in an efficient manner. The weights can be evaluated on the basis of received signal strength indicator (RSSI)-based Mamdani fuzzy inference system. To find the location of the un-localized node, centroid-based technique is proposed. The proposed efficient fuzzy method is represented for a sensor network, and the simulation result gives direction and enhanced the performance of the wireless sensor network. The above said method is an optimistic one for getting the location of the sensors with zero or less error in contrast to simple weighted centroid technique.

Keywords Global positioning system (GPS) · Localization · WSN
RSSI · Fuzzy logic

S. K. Rout (✉)
Department of Computer Science & Engineering, Gandhi Institute for Technology,
Bhubaneswar, Odisha, India
e-mail: rout_sarojkumar@yahoo.co.in

A. K. Rath
Department of Computer Science & Engineering, Veer Surendra Sai University
of Technology (VSSUT), Burla, Sambalpur, Odisha, India
e-mail: amiyaamiya@rediffmail.com

P. K. Mohapatra
Department of Electronics & Telecommunication, Orissa Engineering College,
Bhubaneswar, Odisha, India
e-mail: er_pradyumna@yahoo.co.in

P. K. Jena
Department of Mechanical Engineering, GITA, Bhubaneswar, Odisha, India
e-mail: praadeep1900@gmail.com

A. Swain
School of Computer Engineering, KIIT University, Bhubaneswar, Odisha, India
e-mail: aparimita19swain@gmail.com

© Springer Nature Singapore Pte Ltd. 2018
P. K. Pattnaik et al. (eds.), *Progress in Computing, Analytics and Networking*,
Advances in Intelligent Systems and Computing 710,
https://doi.org/10.1007/978-981-10-7871-2_32

1 Introduction

WSNs play important roles for specific occasion or use. Localization process creates a dynamic framework for sense the meaningful data of a particular environment. Exact and correct node location value shows the importance of localization process. For vehicle tracking system node coordinate values is defined efficiently in [1] and location computation of sensor node is also defined in [2] during localization process. In second way, it can be achieved with help of GPS devices, and very often, the use of a GPS device as a specific one is impossible, because energy consumption is huge and significantly reduced sovereign [3]. In some cases like inner areas, e.g. an inside building, indoors, GPS technology does not work effectively [4]. Wireless sensor network is represented different localization algorithms to solve localization problem.

Localization algorithms are of two types, range-based localization method and range-free localization method. Node localization uses various fuzzy optimization techniques to find accurate and efficient node location value [5–9] and Monte Carlo represents an optimization technique in [10], neural sensor node localized network as defined in [11]. The node localization is represented in efficient algorithms in different ways [12, 13]. The edge weights of anchor nodes help in node localization process. This proposed work is based on Mamdani fuzzy systems and RSSI value. The objective of the paper is to present a localization method. This is based on a Mamdani fuzzy logic system to provide an optimal node localization framework.

The remaining part of the paper is organized as: Sect. 2 discusses the related work of node localization process, Sect. 3 represents the proposed trilateration, centroid and fuzzy logic. Section 4 shows simulation and results work of the system, and Sect. 5 provides the concluding remarks.

2 Related Work

RSSI-based dynamic location system is represented by using three anchor nodes [14]. To compute unknown node location for three anchor node position and received signal strength indicator is necessary. This approach shows minimum error and power consumption in the localization process. The new subspace method shows that the deterministic approach gives dynamic peer node distance estimation value [15]. It is represented and defined with help of the RSSI or time of arrival (TOA) techniques. The new efficient point-in-triangulation test (APIT) algorithm is represented in WSN [16]. The APIT algorithm performs better than the original APIT algorithm. A framework for solving complex noise problems is defined in [17]. Due to high-dimension noisy series, one observations result shows low-dimensional value. Node localization faces many challenges in different situation [18]. RSSI use for estimate the distance between unknown node and anchor node during localization process. The association between RSSI signal strength (S_t) and the square of the distance is represented in [19, 20].

$$S_t \, \alpha \, \frac{1}{d^2} \tag{1}$$

In node localization process, the reference node without the help of the hardware design system can be implemented in efficient ways. This means it can be adapted to the priory of the location of the orientation node. The distance and the signal power of the receiver are represented as:

$$P_{rec}(d_{rec}) = P(d_{ref}) - 10\,n \, \log\left(\frac{d_{rec}}{d_{ref}}\right) \tag{2}$$

where $P_{rec}(d_{rec})$ represents the receiver's receiving signal power, and the transmitter and receiver distance is represented by d_{rec} and $d_{rec}(P_{rec})$ is the power when d_{rec} is reference distance d_{ref}. Hence, the estimated distance d_{rec} can be obtained. Figure 1 shows that three nodes with their respective transmission range of R1, R2 and R3 were intersecting a sensor node.

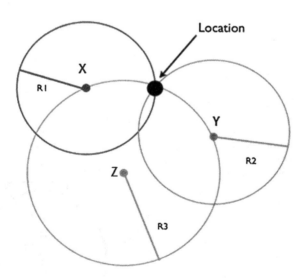

Fig. 1 Sensor's lies in the sensor field having distance R1, R2, and R3

3   Proposed Dynamic Trilateration, Centroid and Fuzzy Logic

3.1   Dynamic Trilateration

Unknown sensor node coordinate is calculated using the location of three anchors and distance of the anchor to sensor node. The unknown sensor node placed in the circumference of a circle, the sensor node is centred by the anchor node's coordinate points with a given radius length to the distance between an anchor node and sensor node.

The unknown node surrounded by three efficient anchor nodes. This association map is represented in Fig. 2, when three anchor nodes never intersect in a common point. Hence, it creates an overlapping region where an unknown node may be present in Fig. 3.

Fig. 2 RSSI-based trilateration of unknown sensor node

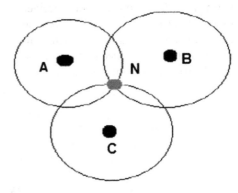

Fig. 3 RSSI-based trilateration of unknown sensor node. Unknown sensor node K is not intersected by anchor nodes (Trilateration problem)

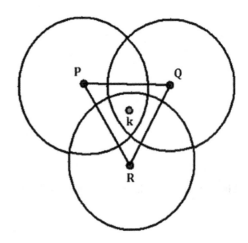

3.2 Fundamental Centroid

Find the innermost intersection points and then compute the coordinate point of unknown sensor node using general centroid method. In which unknown node is treated as the centroid of a polygon. Equation 4 represents unknown sensor node's estimated coordinate value after successful computation.

$$(X_{est}, Y_{est}) = \left(\frac{X_1 + \ldots X_n}{n}, \frac{Y_1 + \ldots Y_n}{n} \right) \tag{3}$$

$$(X_{est}, Y_{est}) = \left(\frac{X_1 w_1 + \ldots X_n w_n}{\sum_{i=1}^{n} w_i}, \frac{y_1 w_1 + \ldots y_n w_n}{\sum_{i=1}^{n} w_i} \right) \tag{4}$$

3.3 Fuzzy Logic

Fuzzy logic plays a vital role in WSN, and edge weights for anchor nodes can be designed in fuzzy system. FLS analyses and represents a fuzzifier along with fuzzy rules, also introduced inference engine, and defuzzifier data analytics. In this study we have applied Mamdani fuzzy inference system for optimization of unknown node location value. Triangular membership function has been used, and linguistic variables are quantified by fuzzy logic in terms of imprecise information for taking decision.

3.4 Fuzzy Logic-Based Localization Technique

The edge weights of sensor nodes can be estimated by fuzzy logic for weighted centroid localization technique. In this section, the proposed Mamdani fuzzy logic localization methods are discussed. The edge weights are obtained by the Mamdani fuzzy inference method and are optimized for calculating the weight of anchor nodes.

3.4.1 Edge Weight Calculation Using Mamdani Fuzzy Inference System

Node location estimation process is performed by help of Mamdani fuzzy system and RSSI input parameter as weight into different nine symmetrical triangular membership values: VVL, VL, L, ML, M, MH, H, VH and VVH.

Step 1. RSSI predicts the distance of the sensor node from the anchor node.
Step 2. The nine number of linguistic variables as defined below are used in Mamdani FIS:

(i) VVL, VL, L, ML, M, MH, H, VH and VVH.
(ii) Far, Intermediate, Near.

Step 3. The rule-based framework is formed using nine linguistic variables defined in Step 2 and computed the distance as output.

Step 4. Fuzzification is the next step after the fuzzy rules are framed, and then bins are allocated based on the fuzzy system.

Step 5. Jacobi's defuzzifier technique is used for constructing the bins. J_k value of anchor node is simply represented as:

$$J_k = (a, b, c) = \left(\left(\frac{\sum L_n}{|L|} \right)_x, (p_c)_x, \left(\frac{\sum G_n}{|G|} \right)_x \right) \tag{5}$$

where different parameters are represented as follows.

P defines centroid value of all node points of the column C.
L defines centroid value of every node points of the column C where the value shows its range, R < P.
G defines centroid value of every node points in column C where its range, R > P.

—

—

—

Step 6. The fuzzified location of nodes are calculated using the J_k value (x, y) using Jacobi equation

$$X = \{(P + (L - P)r, G - (G - L)r\} \tag{6}$$

where 'r' shows it values in lower bound 0 to its upper bound 10.

Step 7. By testing the number of iteration, the performance and final value of $X = \{x, y\}$ are acquired in anticipation of it converges. Data analytics of sensor node location are found out by the converged value.

3.4.2 Dynamic Trilateration Algorithm

The Dynamic trilateration algorithm has two phases:
Step 1: Trilateration based on three anchor nodes.
Step 2: Error analysis and calculation in trilateration are calculated using the Mamdani fuzzy system of weighted scheme with help of an efficient centroid technique using points of intersection which is redirected in Step 1.

Fig. 4 Innermost three
junction points

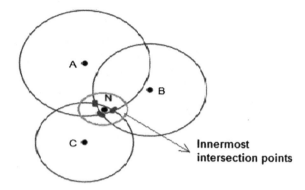

Innermost
intersection points

Step 2 describes as:

i. RSSI is used to measured distance between unknown node and mobile anchor
   node.
ii. In transmission radius, the unknown sensor node and anchor nodes are
   associated with each other and the centre as the anchor nodes.
iii. Six different intersection points are created by anchor A and B, anchor node A
   and C and anchor node B and C.
iv. Interior three junction points are given in Fig. 4.

4   Simulation and Results

Sensor node coordinate value is calculated using centroid method. In WSN, anchor
node's weight values are used in localization process using fuzzy system. RSSI
values are considered in Mamdani fuzzy input, and then it maps the outputs. RSSI
considers for membership function's input in Mamdani technique as shown in
Fig. 5. Nine separate triangular membership function is presented. The weighted
edges are set by the anchor node in range [0, E_{max}] where E_{max} stands for utmost
significance as 1(one). Unknown nodes nearer to and far from the anchor nodes are
associated with signal value. This is shown in Table 1.

   If-then rule expresses an idea to create the conditional statements that comprise
fuzzy logic. Using fuzzy rules, the weights are calculated based on the Table 1.
Figure 6 defines how RSSI related to fuzzy weight in localization process

   Table 2 describes the notion of fuzzy rules with two inputs and one output
applied to the residual energy management of node localization process in sensor
networks.

   Figure 7 shows that node energy utilization during the localization process
depends on RSSI distance and node residual energy managements. Figure 8
describes efficient energy utilization with respect to RSSI distance and node
residual energy.

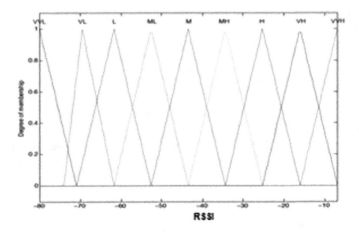

Fig. 5 Membership function for input value

Table 1 Data structure for RSSI with weight representation of fuzzy rules

Fuzzy rules	If RSSI value is	Then weight represents
R1	VVL	VVL
R2	VL	VL
R3	L	L
R4	ML	ML
R5	M	M
R6	MH	MH
R7	H	H
R8	VH	VH
R9	VVH	VVH

Figure 9 describes a dynamic fuzzy inference system; it prepares methodically the association from an input stream to an output stream using fuzzy logic. The association helps the decisions process, or patterns can be generated.

4.1   Coordinate Determination Algorithm

The Eq. (5) of centroid formula represents result analysis with help of reference nodes using the RSSI values. Figure 10 describes estimation of node location using centroid formula method, and Fig. 11 shows localization error rate with a constant area.

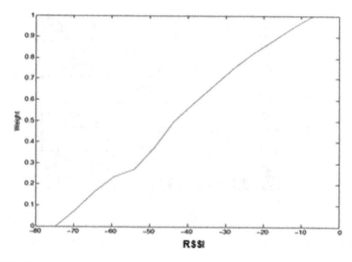

Fig. 6 RSSI signal versus fuzzy weight (surface)

Table 2 Data structure for fuzzy rules (residual energy management)

Fuzzy rules	RSSI distance	Residual energy	Node localization energy consumption
R1	Close	Low	Very small
R2	Close	Medium	Small
R3	Close	Medium	Small
R4	Medium	Low	Small
R5	Medium	Medium	Medium
R6	Medium	Medium	Large
R7	Far	Low	Large
R8	Far	Medium	Large
R9	Far	High	Very large

Fig. 7 Sensor node energy utilization in localization process

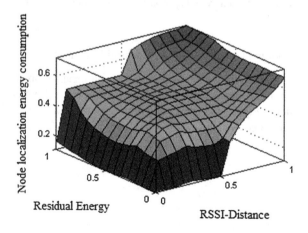

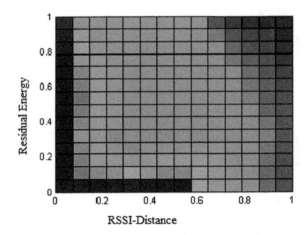

Fig. 8 RSSI distance vs Residual energy management in node localization process

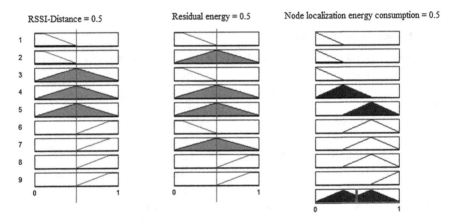

Fig. 9 Decision regarding controlling and utilizing energy consumption in the localization process

Coordinate determination in centroid method:

Figure 12 shows minimization of node localization error using the Mamdani fuzzy optimization technique. It defines random deployment of sensor nodes in sensor field. Figure 13 shows location accuracy with respect to the Mamdani fuzzy inference system.

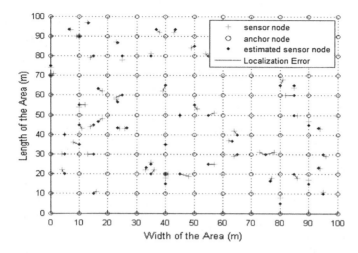

Fig. 10 Node location calculation

Fig. 11 Sensor node versus
localization error value (m)

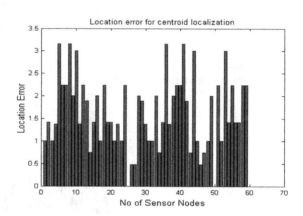

Location calculation in Mamdani Fuzzy Method:

The sensor node's exact position is identified by red circle points, and estimated
unknown sensor node is marked by empty circles points. The localization error is
marked as edges between exact and estimated node point (Table 3).

Figure 14 represents Mamdani fuzzy-based method and is more accurate in node
location calculation process. Proposed method gives better performance than centroid method.

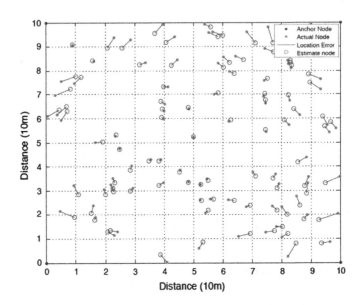

Fig. 12 Optimization of Mamdani fuzzy node localization process

Fig. 13 Sensor node
coordinate estimation error (m)

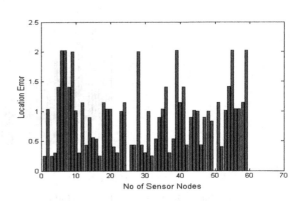

Table 3 Comparison between centroid method and proposed Mamdani technique

Methods	Maximum error value (m)	Minimum error value (m)	Average error value (m)
Centroid method	4.14321	0	1.4024
Proposed Mamdani method	3.15721	0	0.9745

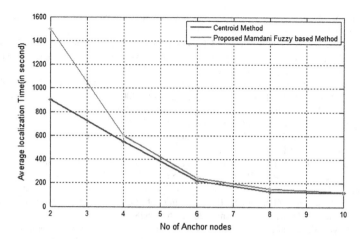

Fig. 14 Node location error versus anchor nodes represent in proposed Mamdani fuzzy system in wireless sensor networks

5 Conclusions

In a wireless sensor network, node localization is a great challenge and a tedious task. The proposed fuzzy optimization technique determines the sensor node location in an efficient manner using trilateration and weighted centroid method. Proposed RSSI with Mamdani fuzzy inference system plays a vital role in localization system. This system gives efficient and accurate role to minimizing localization error. This method provides energy efficient and node localization system.

References

1. Tubaishat, M., Peng, Z., Qi, Q., Yi, S.: Wireless sensor networks in intelligent transportation systems. Wireless Communication and Mobile Computing. (2009), Vol. 9, 287–302.
2. Aspnes, J., Eren, T., Goldenberg, D.K., Morse, A.S., Whiteley, W., Yang, Y.Y, Anderson, B. D., Belhumeur, P.N.: A theory of network localization. IEEE Transactions on Mobile Computing. (2006), vol. 5, No. 12, 1663–1678.
3. Zheng, K., Wang, H., Li, H., Xiang, W., Lei, L., Qiao, J., & Shen, X. S. (2017). Energy-Efficient Localization and Tracking of Mobile Devices in Wireless Sensor Networks. *IEEE Transactions on Vehicular Technology, 66*(3), 2714–2726.
4. Ren, W.: A rapid acquisition algorithm of WSN-aided GPS location. Proc. Int. Symp. Intell. Inf. Technol. Secur. Informatics, IITSI. (2009), 42–46.
5. Larios, D.F., Barbancho, J., Molina, F. J., Leon, C.: Locating sensors with fuzzy logic algorithms. IEEE Workshop On Merging Fields of Computational Intelligence and Sensor Technology—CompSens. (2011), 57–64.
6. Mustafa, A. M., Reza, A., Sener, U.: Range Free Localization of Wireless Sensor Networks Based on Sugeno Fuzzy Inference., SENSORCOMM August, (2012), 36–41.

7. Chuanhui, H., Zhan, X., Xiu, L. R.: Analysis and Improvement for MDS Localization Algorithm. IEEE. (2012). 12–15.
8. Velimirovic, A. S., Djordjevic, G. LJ., Velimirovic, M. M., Jovanovic, M. D.: *A Fuzzy Set-Based Approach to Range-Free Localization in Wireless Sensor Networks*. Facta Univ. Ser.: Elec. Energ., August (2010), vol. 23, no. 2, 227–244.
9. Sukhyun, Y., Jaehun, L., Wooyong, C., Euntai, K.: Centroid Localization Method in Wireless Sensor Networks using TSK Fuzzy Modeling, IEEE. 2009, 639–642.
10. Vasim B. M., Ramprasad, A.V.: Discrete Antithetic Markov Monte Carlo based Power Mapping Localization Algorithm for WSN, IEEE. (2012), 56–62.
11. Runjie, L., Kai, S., Jinyuan, S.: BP localization algorithm based on virtual nodes in wireless sensor network, IEEE. (2010), 1–4.
12. Tian, S., Zhang, X., Liu, P., Sun, P., Wang, X.: A RSSI-based DV-hop Algorithm for Wireless Sensor Networks. IEEE. (2007), 2555–2558.
13. Ding, Y., Tian, H., Han, G.: A Distributed Node Localization Algorithm for Wireless Sensor Network Based on MDS and SDP. Proceeding of International Conference on Computer Science and Electronics Engineering. (2012). 624–628.
14. Chaurasiya, V.K., Jain, N., Nandi, G.C.: A novel distance estimation approach for 3D localization in wireless sensor network using multi dimensional scaling. Information Fusion, vol. 15, no. 1, 5–18, (2014).
15. Slavisa, T., Marko, B., Rui, D., Goran, D., Milan T.: *Distributed {RSS}-Based Localization in Wireless Sensor Networks with Node Selection Mechanism*. Doctoral Conference on Computing, Electrical and Industrial Systems DoCEIS, vol. 450, 204–214, (2015).
16. Frankie, K. W. Chan., So, H.C., Ma, W.K.: A novel subspace approach for Co-operative Localization in Wireless Sensor Networks using Range measurements. IEEE Transactions on Signal Processing, IEEE Computer society. (2009), vol. 57, no. 1, 260–269.
17. Zeng, JI., Wang, H. Jin.: Improvement on APIT localization algorithm for Wireless Sensor networks. IEEE international conference on network security, wireless communication and trusted computing. (2011). 190–195.
18. Hamdoun, S., Rachedi, A., Benslimane, A.: *RSSI-based Localization Algorithms using Spatial Diversity in Wireless Sensor Networks*. International Journal of Ad Hoc and Ubiquitous Computing. Inderscience, vol. 19, no. 3, 157–167, (2015).
19. Jain, A., Ramana Reddy, B.V.: A Novel Method of Modeling Wireless Sensor Network Using Fuzzy Graph and Energy Efficient Fuzzy Based k-Hop Clustering Algorithm. Wireless Personal Communications, vol. 82, no. 1, pp. 157–181, (2015).
20. Xiaoyan, Li., Martin, R. P., Elnahrawy, E.: The Limits of Localization Using Signal Strength: A Comparative Study, *SECON*. (2004), 406–414.

Personalized Movie Recommendation System Using Twitter Data

Debashis Das, Himadri Tanaya Chidananda and Laxman Sahoo

Abstract Nowadays, we are living in an age recommendation, but the proper recommendation needs more accurate and relevant datas as their inputs. Rating databases like MovieLence or Netflix have long been popular and being widely used in recommendation system areas for research in past decades. But nowadays, they become irrelevant due to lack of new and relevant datas. Nowadays, social media like Facebook and Twitter become the most popular for researchers due to availability of large amount of new and relevant datas. In this paper, we have built a recommendation engine by analyzing rating datasets collected from Twitter to recommend movies to specific user using R.

Keywords Recommendation system · Type of recommendation system
Item-based collaborating filtering

1 Introduction

Data become the key factor for everything. But nowadays, the size of data is increasing exponentially. In June 2015, India had a Web client of around 354 million and is likely to reach 500 million in 2016, in spite of being the second biggest client hub on the planet. The infiltration of e-commerce of Web-based business is low appeared differently in relation to business areas like the USA (266 million, 84%) or France (54 million, 81%), yet is creating at an unprecedented rate, including around 6 million new members consistently every month [1]. This amount of datasets cannot be managed efficiently by the common database

D. Das (✉) · H. T. Chidananda · L. Sahoo
School of Computer Engineering, KIIT University, Bhubaneswar, India
e-mail: debashis.das.official@hotmail.com

H. T. Chidananda
e-mail: himadritanaya92@gmail.com

L. Sahoo
e-mail: lsahoofcs@kiit.ac.in

© Springer Nature Singapore Pte Ltd. 2018
P. K. Pattnaik et al. (eds.), *Progress in Computing, Analytics and Networking*,
Advances in Intelligent Systems and Computing 710,
https://doi.org/10.1007/978-981-10-7871-2_33

management system. The datasets in the form of semi-structured data and unstructured data like image, audio, video, JSON documents, Wet log, and search patterns, cannot be stored and handled by traditional databases, so the concept of Big Data came into the picture.

According to IBM, "every day, Internet user generates 2.5 quintillion bytes of information"—so much that 90% of the information on the planet today has been generated in the most recent 2 years alone [2]. This information originates from everywhere, for example, social media posts, images, videos, transition records of both e-commerce and no e-commerce, satellite data. These data are called Big Data. Tech America Foundation describes big data as "Big data is a term that defines huge volumes of high-velocity, complex, and varied data that require advanced techniques and technologies to enable the storage, capture, distribution, management, and analysis of the information" (Tech America Foundation's Federal Big Data Commission, 2012) [3].

Initially, Big Data is described by 3 V's (Variety, Volume, and Velocity). Volume is described as the quantity of information produced by individuals or organizations. The sources may be internal or external. Velocity is defined as the rate at which data are generated. Variety is represented as various sorts of information extracted from various sources like Facebook and Twitter in addition to various feedback Websites. In addition to the 3 V's, other V's have also been mentioned (Veracity, Variable, Value). IBM mentioned Veracity as the 4th V, which defines the uncertainty of information; Variability: SAS introduced Variability and Complexity as two more dimensions of big data; Value: Oracle presented Value as a defining attribute of big data.

Nowadays, we are living in an era of social media, and almost everyone is using it and sharing each small thing they do or going to and also to express their views. In this era of technology, we do not have to go to door to door to find out the reviews about the products or their preferred products. We can sit back and track down their activities on social media and can get almost everything what we need for, e.g., which product they like, which one they do not, past merchant history.

Twitter is an online news and social-networking site where users post and interact with messages "tweets" limited to 140 characters. Recently, Twitter has become a useful source for research due to the large amount of user-generated available data. In 2016, it has 319 million monthly active users and 250 million tweets per day.

Nowadays, we are living in an Age of Recommendation. In our day-to-day life, indeed, even to settle on requirements like which motion picture to watch, which novel to Paris, where to eat, we rely on our associates, news on the daily papers, what's more, common reviews, and so forward to help us find what is great for us. This support from our surroundings gives us an easy way to find out the best alternative without having much effort to filtering through the different choices available in the market. In this era of technology, the recommendation system is an application that filtered personalized information and gives the way to understand a user's taste and to suggest appropriate things to them by considering the patterns among their likes and ratings of various things. In recent years, RS becomes most popular research area. Many e-commerce sites like amazon and health kart use the personalized RS to maximize the profit and to attract more customers.

In this paper, we proposed a personalized movie recommended system which suggests movies to the specific user by analyzing the relevant tweets of the user, friends of the user, and friend of friends within two-degree of separation.

2 Recommendation System

Have you ever amused how the "People you may know" feature on Facebook or LinkedIn? This feature suggests a list of people whom you might know, who are similar to you based on your friends, friends of friends in your friend circle, current location or may be past location, skill sets, groups, linked pages, and so on. These recommendations are specific to you and differ from user to user.

Recommendation system is an approach to the issue to provide suitable things to the customer despite of searching lots of items. Although people's tastes vary from one to another, they also follow some pattern. RS is software tools and techniques that provide suggestion based on the individual's taste to discover new required content for them like useful products on e-commerce sites like Amazon. in, videos on YouTube, posts on the wall of the social media like Facebook, news recommendation on online news Websites automatically. RS perceives suggestions consequently to the customers by analyzing previous browsing history, the feedback assigned to the products, and different user's behavior.

There are two broad categories of recommended algorithm, i.e., user-based and item-based. RS is based on five filtering techniques as follows [5].

- Content-based filtering: This filtering approach is built on the item description and user preferences. Suggestions are related to the content related to the item and their property.
- Collaborative filtering: This type of filtering approach uses the users' past behavior (past purchasing or browsing history, etc.) or rating given to the item. This model recommended item the user may interest in. The recommendation based on the user relationship with item only.
- Demographic filtering: This type of RS only considers the data of the user like age, gender, employment status about the user only home possession and even location also. The recommends are made by considering demographic similarities to the user.
- Knowledge-based filtering: This type of system deployed in a specific domain where the perched history is small. In these types of system, the algorithm considers the knowledge about the item and its feature, user preference (asked explicitly), recommendation criteria before giving the recommendation.

- Hybrid filtering: This type of approach is built by joining different filtering approach to build a more robust framework by combing several filtering techniques; we can reduce the demerits of one method through the merits of one more system and accordingly construct a more robust system.

3 Related Work

Sajal Halder et al. [4] have proposed a data mining tool that gathers all important information which is required in a movie recommendation system by using the Movie Lens database. They have created a movie swarm for movie producers which are very helpful and can solve new item issues and also discovers which genres of a movie should be recommended among followers that solves new user's recommendation problem.

Wei Yang et al. [6] proposed IMRHN (interest-based movie recommendation in heterogeneous network) with user's information and users' influence on each other to implement personalized movie recommendation successfully. It also investigates the user's impact of interest in movies with others. Furthermore, the approach reduced time utilization efficiently to the scale of dataset to expand. Future work can be focused on how to design a parallel algorithm based on IMRHN.

RyuRi Kim et al. [7] in this paper proposed the movie recommendation system for in case trustworthy movie ratings. The vast majority of the movie recommendation systems does not consider the unfair routing problem but the emotion evaluation. At that point, our approach plays out the correct assessment against unfair rating. They collect opinion about the movie from Twitter and then find out users' feelings to analyze them. In this paper, they are able to provide a high recommendation based on trustworthy movie assessment.

Eva Oliveira et al. [8] developed an application for the movie and user emotion exploration as a way to access movies by analysis of user emotional profile. They also proposed novel interactive mechanism for movie emotion exploration.

Sneha Khatwani et al. [9] in this paper cover different systems which can be utilized for making personalized and non-personalized recommendations. This paper also investigates the different packages of R, i.e., Shiny, which is used to make Web applications, and R Markdown which is utilized to make dynamic documents. Additionally, they also discussed how to make a recommender model. They used different techniques of user-based and item-based collaborative filtering models.

4 Method

In this section, we described the models we used in building recommendation system.

4.1 Item-Based Collaborative Filtering

It is a model-based algorithm for recommendation system. This model suggests item based collaborative filtering approach on the users' past behavior like rating given or browsing history and recommended movies that are of highest similarity based on its features, such as genres, actors, directors, year of production.

We calculated similarities between the items from rating matrix, and based upon these similarities, user's preference for an item not rated by him/her is calculated. For similarities measured, here we used the Jaccard distance to measure the similarities between the user profile and the movies. It is because the Jaccard similarities are suitable for binary data. Then, the highly similar items are suggested to the users.

4.2 Jaccard Similarity Measure

Let we have two objects, P and Q each with n binary values. Each value of P and Q can either be 0 or 1. The total no. of each combination of attributes for both P and Q is specified as follows:

X_{11}: the total number of attributes where P and Q both have a value of 1.
X_{01}: the total number of attributes where the attribute of P is 0 and the attribute of Q is 1.
X_{10}: the total number of attributes where the attribute of P is 1 and the attribute of Q is 0.
X_{00}: the total number of attributes where P and Q both have a value of 0.

Each attribute must fall into one of these four categories, meaning that

$$X_{11} + X_{01} + X_{10} + X_{00} = n$$

The Jaccard similarity coefficient, J, is given as (1)

$$J = \frac{X_{11}}{X_{11} + X_{01} + X_{10}} \tag{1}$$

The Jaccard distance, d_j is given as (2)

$$d_j = \frac{X_{01} + X_{10}}{X_{11} + X_{01} + X_{10}} = 1 - J \tag{2}$$

5 Proposed Algorithm

We proposed a movie recombination engine using R. We have used the A Movie Rating Dataset Collected from Twitter [10]. The dataset will be updated regularly, and they have structured the dataset in different folders/latest snapshots. The/latest folder will always contain the complete dataset as available at the time of the commit, while the snapshots contain fixed portions of the dataset to allow experimentation and reproducibility of research. The proposed approach is as follows:

INPUT: Twitter Movie Rating datasets—Movies.csv, Ratings.csv, and Users.csv.
OUTPUT: Top recommended movies for specific users.

STEP-1: Make two objects (movies, ratings) and read the two data file Movies.csv and Ratings.csv using read.csv function.
STEP-2: Remove the unwanted columns like time stamps.
STEP-3: Calculate dot product of movie and genres, i.e., Movie$geners, and store in genres object.

```
genres <
-as.data.frame(movies$genres,stringsAsFactors = FALSE)
```

STEP-4: Obtain movie feature matrix, i.e., movie$genres matrix, but each genre is separated into columns by splitting the pipe ("|") to separate genres available in movie dataset using tstrsplit() function available in data.table package.

```
gen-
res2<as.data.frame(tstrsplit(genres[,1],'[|]',type.conver
t=TRUE), stringsAsFactors=FALSE)
```

STEP-5: Create a genre matrix with column containing every unique genre and row containing movie and indicates genre is present or not for each movie.

```
genre_list <- c("Action", "Adventure"......."Western")
genre_matrix[1,] <- genre_list #set first row to genre
list

#iterate through matrix
for (i in 1:nrow(genres2)) {
  for (c in 1:ncol(genres2)) {
    genmat_col = which(genre_matrix[1,] == genres2[i,c])
    genre_matrix[i+1,genmat_col] <- 1
  }
}
```

STEP-6: Convert rating matrix into binary format, i.e.

```
  if (binary_ratings[i,3] > 5)
    binary_ratings[i,3] <- 1
  else{
    binary_ratings[i,3] <- -1
```

STEP-7: Remove movies that never been rated, i.e., remove the rows that are not rated in movie dataset and also from the genre matrix.

```
movies<-movies[-which((movieIds%in%ratingmovieIds) ==
FALSE),]
rownames(movies2) <- NULL
genre_matrix <- genre_matrix[-which((movieIds %in%
ratingmovieIds) == FALSE),]
rownames(genre_matrix) <- NULL
```

STEP-8: Create a user profile matrix, i.e., output matrix by calculating dot product between Movie genre matrix and binary rating matrix. Convert all negative value to 0.

```
for (c in 1:ncol(binary_ratings))
  for (i in 1:ncol(genre_matrix3))
 output[i,c] <- sum((genre_matrix3[,i]) * (bina-
ry_ratings2[,c]))
```

STEP-9: Now, the user profiles created show the aggregated inclination of each user toward movie genres, each column represents a unique user ID, and positive values show a preference toward a certain genre and then simplified the values into binary matrix, i.e., positive values mapped to 1 represent likeness and negative values to 0.

if (output[i] < 0)

```
   output[i] <- 0
else {
   output[i] <- 1
```

STEP-10: Then, assume that users like similar items and retrieve movies that are closest in similarity to a user's profile, which represents a user's preference for an item's feature.

STEP-11: Use Jaccard similarity coefficient to measure the similarities between user profile and the movie genre matrix. The dist () function from the proxy library to calculate Jaccard distance.

STEP-12: Recommend the movie for specific user with highest similarities.

6 Results

We have applied the proposed algorithm on the Movie Rating Dataset Collected from Twitter [10] and got the list of movies for specific users with highest similarities (Table 1).

Table 1 Few example of movies recommended to Twitter users

Twitter id	Movie id	Movie title	Genres
31260677	115964	Crash (1996)	Drama
	120177	Spawn (1997)	Action|Fantasy|Thriller
	134847	Pitch Black (2000)	Action|Sci-Fi|Thriller
	356910	Mr. & Mrs. Smith (2005)	Action|Comedy|Romance
	890888	Vollidiot (2007)	Comedy
	1135092	The Limits of Control (2009)	Crime|Drama|Mystery|Thriller
	1500512	Private Romeo (2011)	Drama
18405182	43949	Quo Vadis (1951)	Drama|Romance
	64729	Nightmare in Wax (1969)	Horror|Mystery|Sci-Fi
	307479	Solaris (2002)	Drama|Mystery|Romance|Sci-fi
	988043	One-Eyed Monster (2008)	Comedy|Horror|Sci-Fi
	1513713	Baska Dilde Ask (2009)	Drama
	56262	The Music Man (1962)	Musical|Comedy|Family|Romance
	87597	The Last Starfighter (1984)	Action|Adventure|Family|Sci-Fi
	112461	The Basketball Diaries (1995)	Biography|Crime|Drama|Sport
	445990	Invincible (2006)	Biography|Drama|Sport
	1020543	Infestation (2009)	Action|Comedy|Horror|Sci-Fi

7 Conclusion

In this paper, we have presented our approach on building personalized movie recommendation engine. We tried to recommend a list of movies to specific Twitter users using content-based collaborative filtering approach by analyzing rating datasets collected from Twitter. This algorithm also can be applied to other products with small modification.

In the future, various other attributes like textual data analysis for sentiment evaluation and techniques can be developed and evaluated for efficient implementation of recommendation systems. Also by combining recommendation systems with machine learning (ML) and natural language processing (NLP), we can develop powerful and efficient recommendation systems which will consider various aspects. Using machine learning, we can train the system to provide better recommendations based on its past experiences.

Acknowledgements We are thankful to the faculty members of School of Computer Engineering Department of KIIT University, Bhubaneswar, for their cooperation and suggestions.

References

1. Website link https://en.wikipedia.org/wiki/E-commerce_in_India.
2. Website link https://www-01.ibm.com/software/data/bigdata/what-is-big-data.html.
3. J. Clerk Maxwell, A Treatise on Electricity and Magnetism, 3rd ed., vol. 2. Oxford: Clarendon, 1892, pp. 68–73.
4. Halder, Sajal, et al. "Movie swarm: Information mining technique for movie recommendation system." Electrical & Computer Engineering (ICECE), 2012 7th International Conference on. IEEE, 2012.
5. Debashis Das, Laxman Sahoo and Sujoy Datta. A Survey on Recommendation System. *International Journal of Computer Applications* 160(7): 6–10, February 2017.
6. Yang, Wei, et al. "User's Interests-Based Movie Recommendation in Heterogeneous Network." Identification, Information, and Knowledge in the Internet of Things (IIKI), 2015 International Conference on. IEEE, 2015.
7. Kim, RyuRi, et al. "Trustworthy Movie Recommender System with Correct Assessment and Emotion Evaluation." Proceedings of the International MultiConference of Engineers and Computer Scientists. Vol. 2. 2015.
8. Oliveira, Eva, Nuno Ribeiro, and Teresa Chambel. "Accessing movies' emotional information." Information Systems and Technologies (CISTI), 2015 10th Iberian Conference on. IEEE, 2015.
9. Sneha Khatwani, Dr. M.B. Chandak. "Building Personalized and Non Personalized Recommendation Systems." International Conference on Automatic Control and Dynamic Optimization Techniques (ICACDOT), 2016 International Institute of Information Technology (I2IT), Pune.
10. Dooms, Simon, Toon De Pessemier, and Luc Martens. "Movietweetings: a movie rating dataset collected from twitter." Workshop on Crowdsourcing and human computation for recommender systems, CrowdRec at RecSys. Vol. 2013. 2013.

Implementation of Chaotic-Based Hybrid Method to Provide Double Layer Protection

Shreela Dash, Madhabananda Das and Mamatarani Das

Abstract In the modern era, Internet is the most widely used transmission medium. While transmitting any secret information through any public channel, then that may be hacked in between. So to send data to the receiver without any kind of damage, here we have proposed a hybrid method by using both the cryptography and steganography technique. The secret message is first encrypted by using chaotic neural network. For encrypting data, we used CNN because of its random nature which is very challenging for hackers to know about the secret information. The secret key decides the position to hide the encrypted data. Only authorized users share the secret key. The receiver finds the original message by using secret key and then decryption is performed. Our experiment shows that PSNR of our method is very high as the technique modifies lesser number of bits. This method provides good security and less distortion to original image.

Keywords Chaotic neural network (CNN) · Matrix encoding
Least significant bit (LSB)

S. Dash (✉) · M. Das
Department of Computer Science and Engineering, C. V. Raman College of Engineering,
Bhubaneswar 752054, Odisha, India
e-mail: shreelamamadash@gmail.com

M. Das
e-mail: mamataparida2005@gmail.com

M. Das
School of Computer Engineering, KIIT University, Patia, Bhubaneswar 751024, Odisha,
India
e-mail: mndas_prof@kiit.ac.in

© Springer Nature Singapore Pte Ltd. 2018
P. K. Pattnaik et al. (eds.), *Progress in Computing, Analytics and Networking*,
Advances in Intelligent Systems and Computing 710,
https://doi.org/10.1007/978-981-10-7871-2_34

1 Introduction

Steganography is the most widely used technique for hiding data, i.e., image, audio, or video in the cover medium. The cover medium can also be any digital image, digital audio, or digital video. The technique is used for confidential communication, secret data storing, and protection of data modification by the hackers. Cryptography is the method for encrypting the data which the unauthorized user cannot access. It provides confidentiality, authenticity, and integrity of data. Both cryptography and steganography techniques attract the researchers for protecting data in the Internet era. Categorically steganography methods can be either spatial-domain- or frequency-domain-based. In this paper, spatial domain method is used where we are directly dealing with the intensity of pixels. This method is more simple and efficient than frequency domain. In the proposed method, the scrambled message is hidden inside the cover medium. Since this method combines both the concepts of cryptography and steganography, it provides high security to data.

The rest of the paper is organized as follows: Related Works in Sect. 2, Proposed Work in Sect. 3, Encryption using CNN is explained in Sect. 4, Embedding and Extraction algorithm is in Sect. 5, the analysis of simulation result in Sect. 6, and Conclusion in Sect. 7.

2 Related Works

Steganography strategies are based upon either spatial or frequency domain techniques. In spatial domain technique, we are straightforwardly dealing with the pixels of the cover picture. Spatial domain approach utilizes LSB-based steganography.

In [1], Cheng-Hsing Yang has proposed LSB substitution scheme. This approach saves time complexity for embedding. From the experiment, it is observed that the execution time is better than the previous schemes.

In [2], author has proposed that the LSB of color image is used for hiding data. This is done by directly substituting the least significant bits of three color planes red, green, and blue. It gives more capacity for storing secret data.

Jarno Mielikainen has described a steganography method in [3] for hiding message bits into a cover medium. In the LSBM methodology, the random choice is given to add or subtract one bit from the pixel of the cover image. The inserting is done utilizing a couple of pixels, where the first pixel conveys one piece of data, and a component of the two pixel values conveys another piece of data. This technique permits inserting an indistinguishable payload from LSB by coordinating however with fewer changes to the cover picture. The evaluation of this technique demonstrates better conventional LSB coordinating as far as distortion and resistance against existing steganalysis are concerned.

In [4], the author has proposed LSBMR algorithm which selects suitable region in the cover image for embedding data. By hiding secret data in the specific region of the pixels, the detection becomes difficult. The maximum embedding capacity can be improved by modifying the parameters of neighbor pixels.

In [5], steganography using edge adaptive image is given. In [6], chaos-based edge adaptive steganography is given. It uses *Canny's* edge detection algorithm for detecting edge pixels and data is embedded in the edge pixels. *Canny's* edge detection can detect almost all edges including weak and strong edges [7]. The secret message is twisted using chaotic cat map. Then the encrypted message is hidden in the edge pixels but not directly. More secrecy is incorporated by doing XOR operation. But the restriction is that only 2 secret bits are hidden in the edge pixel of red, green, and blue. So capacity to hide secret data is compromised.

In [8], the authors have proposed a Huffman encoding-based image steganography. In this scheme, the secret image is first encoded by Huffman encoding scheme. Then the number of bits is compressed up to 2 bits in different tires. Now these two bits are embedded in last or first pixel in two LSB positions of a cover image. This technique is more robust compared to others.

3 Proposed Work

In the proposed model, the benefits of both the steganography and cryptography techniques are combined. Images and multimedia data which are transmitted over the insecure channel must also be encrypted due to security reason. But image encryption through traditional cryptosystem is not efficient due to the following two reasons.

1. Images are comparatively larger in size than text.
2. Time to process image is more than text data.

However, a chaotic sequence shows random behavior through its sensitive dependence on initial condition. It is non-converging and also non-periodic. Changing the initial value alone will generate a large number of deterministic and reproducible signals in a random manner. These random sequences can be converted into integer-valued sequences and can be used for image encryption efficiently. The encrypted data is hidden inside the cover medium. The proposed framework for embedding and extraction is given in Fig. 1.

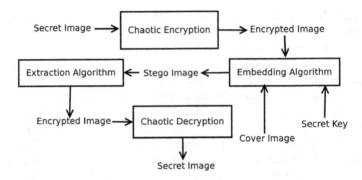

Fig. 1 Proposed framework for embedding and extraction

This method provides a double layer security by using both cryptography and steganography using secret key. So although the attacker knows the technique, it cannot extract the secret message.

4 Chaotic Encryption

To solve many real-world problems, a powerful technique called neural networks is used. Neural networks have the ability to learn from experience. Researchers found a considerable measure of enthusiasm because of the way of confusion which is utilized as a part of different building disciplines, where cryptography must be a standout among the most potential applications. The properties of chaos like ergodicity, semi-arbitrariness, affectability reliance on introductory conditions, and system parameters have allowed confused progression as a promising option for the traditional cryptographic calculations. Chaos-based cryptography depends on perplexing elements of nonlinear frameworks or maps which are deterministic in nature however straightforward. It can give a quick and secure means for information protection assurance, which is essential for digital media information transmission over the broadband Web correspondence.

Suppose any image of size m × n is to be encoded using CNN, then the algorithm is given below:

Algorithm 1: Chaotic Encryption algorithm using neural network
Input: Secret Image IMG
Output: Encrypted secret image EIMG

Step 1: Convert the gray scale image IMG of size m x n into binary and keep it in the one dimensional array of size L.
Step 2: Initialize two parameters μ and X (1) to generate chaotic sequence.
Step 3: Determine X (1), X (2) ....X (L) by using the formula $X(i) = \mu * X(i-1) * (1 - X(i-1))$;
Step 4: Create the binary representation of X(i) for i=0,1, ...L.
Step 5: Train the chaotic neural network by determining weight matrix.

    For n=0 to L-1 do
      Let $g(n) = (d_0 * 2^0 + d_1 * 2^1 + d_2 * 2^2 .... + d_7 * 2^7)$
        For P=0 to 7 do
          For q=0 to 7 do
              Set $W_{pq} = 0$ if p is not equal to q
              Set $W_{pq} = 1$ if p is equal to q and $b(8*n + p) = 0$
              Set $W_{pq} = -1$ if p is equal to q and $b(8*n + p) = 1$
      if $b(8*n + p) = 0$
      $\Phi_p = -\frac{1}{2}$
        else
            $\Phi_p = \frac{1}{2}$
      end
      $d_i = f(\sum W_{pq} * d_i + \Phi_p)$ (where i=0,1...7) if (x >= 0)
          $f(x) = 1$
    else
        $f(x) = 0$
    end
      $g'(n) = \sum d_i' * 2'$
  end

5 Secret Key-Based Steganography Approach

In this paper, the encrypted data is converted to 1D array and each bit is hidden inside the LSB of either the green or blue pixel using the secret key and red matrix.

The transformation of key into 1D circular array is given below. How the secret key is represented in 1D array is given in Fig. 2.

(1) Embedding Algorithm

The cover medium used here to hide the encrypted data is image. The decision to hide the data depends on red matrix and key. The key and the red matrix are

Fig. 2 Illustration of secret key in 1D array

combined to decide if 2 bits of hidden data are kept with green or blue matrix. This process continues till the secret information finishes. The authenticated receiver after receiving the stego image can extract the secret message.

Input: Cover Image, Secret Key, Encrypted message
Output: Stego Image
Procedure:
Step1: The Encrypted message (S) is converted into 1-D array of bit stream of Length L.
Step2: Convert the cover image (C) to binary with size r and c.
Step2: Convert the secret Key into 1-D circular array of bit stream K.
Step3: The cover image is segmented into three matrices i.e. R, G and B of size r and c.
Step4: Set k=1, Counter=0
Step5: While(Counter<L)
```
        {
        for (m=1; m<=r; m++)
          for (n=8; n<=c-8; n=n+8)
          if (R_{m,n} XOR k=1)
          {
          G_{m,n}= S(Counter);
          G_{m, n-1}= S(Counter+1);
          Counter+=2
          }
          else
          {
          B_{m,n}= S(Counter);
          B_{m, n-1}= S(Counter+1);
          Counter+=2
          }
        }
```
Step6: End

(2) Extraction Algorithm

To generate the secret image, the stego image S is separated into three matrices R, G, B. Using the reverse process of embedding, encrypted secret image M is generated.

Input: Stego Image, Secret Key
Output: Hidden Message
Procedure:
Step1: Stego Image is converted into three matrices R, G, B of size r and c.
Step2: Convert the secret Key into 1-D circular array of bit stream (Length L)
Step3: Set k=1, Counter=0
    while(Counter<L)
    {
      for (m=1; m<=r; m++)
       for (n=8; n<=c-8; n=n+8)
      {
      if ($R_{m,n}$ XOR k=1)
      {
      S(Counter)= $G_{m,n}$;
      S(Counter+1) = $G_{m,\ n-1}$;
      Counter+=2
      }
      else
      {
      S(Counter)= $B_{m,n}$;
      S(Counter+1) = $B_{m,\ n-1}$;
      Counter+=2
      }
    }
Step4: Repeat Step3 until all the bits of the hidden message gets extracted.
Step5: Finally reshape the 1-D Array into 2-D Array to get the actual information
    to get the Encrypted message.
Step 6: The Encrypted message is passed through Chaotic decryption to get the
    original secret message.
End

---

6 Result and Analysis

The simulation of the steganography techniques and chaotic neural network is done in MATLAB Version 7.13.0.564 (R2011b). After chaotic encryption of the following secret images Leena (150 × 150), Monarch (100 × 67), and Scene (86 × 60), given in Fig. 3a, we got the encrypted image. The cover image we have

(b)

(a)

Fig. 3 **a** List of secret images. **b** Cover image (green sunset)

taken is green sunset of different sizes (512 × 340), (806 × 536), and (1024 × 681), given in Fig. 3b.

The embedding algorithm has been tested by calculating the PSNR of cover and stego images and time taken to embed, security of the secret message and capacity of cover image to hold the amount of secret information, where MSE and PSNR are calculated as per Eqs. 1 and 2.

MSE is defined as the square of error between cover image (I) and stego image (K).

$$MSE = \frac{1}{N \times M} \sum_{i=0}^{N-1} \sum_{j=0}^{M-1} [X(i,j) - Y(i,j)]^2 \tag{1}$$

whereas PSNR is defined as the ratio of peak square value of pixels by MSE. It is used to detect the distortion present in the stego image comparing with original.

The PSNR is mathematically defined as below where L is the range of values a pixel can take, i.e., $2^8 - 1 = 255$.

$$PSNR = 10 \log_{10} \frac{L^2}{MSE} \tag{2}$$

Table 1 PSNR calculation for different secret images over a cover image of different sizes

Size of cover image green sunset	Size of secret Image	PSNR
512 × 340	Leena (150 × 150)	67.2
	Monarch (100 × 67)	61.2
	Scene (80 × 60)	55.6
806 × 536	Leena (150 × 150)	71.7
	Monarch (100 × 67)	65.7
	Scene (80 × 60)	59.6
1024 × 681	Leena (150 × 150)	73.3
	Monarch (100 × 67)	67.2
	Scene (80 × 60)	55.9

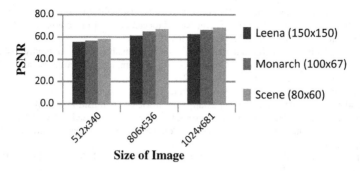

Fig. 4 Histogram representation of PSNR calculation in dB

The change in the stego image remains undetected with the human eye if PSNR is high. Table 1 shows the PSNR values for different sizes of secret image and cover image and the corresponding histogram is shown in Fig. 4, where the row represents the size of image and column represents PSNR in dB.

7   Conclusion

The proposed hybrid framework provides more security, but with lesser distortion to the secret message. It is extremely troublesome for the unapproved clients to distinguish any adjustments in the stego picture as PSNR is high. Even if anyone knows the presence of any secret communication and tries to retrieve the hidden data, then it is difficult because secret message is encrypted using chaotic encryption. Here, two random values of 'x' and 'µ' are chosen. From the experiment, it is seen that, by taking $x = 0.75$ and $µ = 3.9$, it provides better security. This technique is limited to secret image of less size. We can achieve more security with high capacity by using some compression technique.

References

1. Cheng-Hsing Yang And Shiuh-JengWang, "Transforming LSB Substitution for Image based Steganography in Matching Algorithms", Journal Of Information Science And Engineering, 26, 1199–1212 (2010).
2. Abbas Cheddad, Condell, Kevin Curran, Paul McKevitt, F. Hartung, "Information hiding-a survey" Proceedings of the IEEE: Special Issue on Identification and Protection of Multimedia Content, Volume: 87 Issue: 7, pp. I062–I078, July. 1999.
3. Jarno Mielikainen, "LSB matching revisited," IEEE signal processing letters, vol. 13, no. 5, May 2006.

4. S. M. MasudKarim, Md. Saifur Rahman, Md. Ismail Hossain "A New Approach for LSB Based Image Steganography using Secret Key" Proceedings of 14th International Conference on Computer and Information Technology (ICCIT) 2011.
5. G. KarthigaiSeivi, Leon Mariadhasan, K. L. Shunmuganathan "Steganography Using Edge Adaptive Image" International Conference on Computing, Electronics and Electrical Technologies [ICCEET] 2012, pp 1023–1027.
6. Qinhua Huang and Weimin Ouyang, "Protect Fragile Regions in Steganography LSB Embedding", 3rd International Symposium on Knowledge Acquisition and Modelling, 2010.
7. Ratnakirti Roy, Anirban Sarkar, Suvamoy Changder "Chaos based Edge Adaptive Image Steganography" international Conference on Computational Intelligence (CIMTA), 2013, vol 10, pp. 138–146.
8. Rig Das, Themrichon Tuitthung, "A Novel Steganography Method For Image Based on Huffman Encoding", IEEE, 2012.

Sentiment Analysis Using N-gram Technique

Himadri Tanaya Chidananda, Debashis Das and Santwana Sagnika

Abstract Dramatic growth of social media has created remarkable interest among Internet users nowadays. Information from these Web sites in the form of reviews, feedbacks, ratings, etc., can be utilized for various purposes like to find out users' taste or interest to develop a proper marketing strategy, maybe for a survey about the product by using sentiment analysis. Twitter is generally used for posting long comments in short status. Twitter offers organizations a fast and powerful approach to investigate customers' viewpoints toward the critical to success in the open market. Previously we calculate sentiment of each word for the sentiment, which may or may not be accurate because may be the same word used in past for negative review, but presently it is used for positive sense. We propose a method by applying both log function and N-gram techniques to find out the sentiment of the Twitter data in R to build a robust engine to achieve more accuracy.

Keywords Sentiment analysis · Preprocessing · N-grams

1 Introduction

Data is the backbone of the twenty-first century, and analytics are the combustion engine. Data is everywhere, in every industry in the form of videos, images, numbers, and text. There is no restriction of the information as it shows everywhere throughout the universe. As data continues to grow, so does the need to sort it out. Every second, there are around 8,23 tweets on Twitter, and every minute, nearly 520 comments are displayed, 294,000 statuses are updated, and 138,000 snapshots

H. T. Chidananda (✉) · D. Das · S. Sagnika
School of Computer Engineering, KIIT University, Bhubaneswar, India
e-mail: himadritanaya92@gmail.com

D. Das
e-mail: debashis.das.official@hotmail.com

S. Sagnika
e-mail: santwana.sagnikafcs@kiit.ac.in

© Springer Nature Singapore Pte Ltd. 2018
P. K. Pattnaik et al. (eds.), *Progress in Computing, Analytics and Networking*,
Advances in Intelligent Systems and Computing 710,
https://doi.org/10.1007/978-981-10-7871-2_35

are uploaded on Facebook, and every time, Walmart, a global discount department store chain, handles more than 1 million client transactions. Collecting such large amount of data would just be a waste of time, storage space, and effort if it cannot be put to any logical use. Organizations, independent entities, government, political parties, and police, among others, are finally investing time and money in unlocking the power of data. They analyze the data to understand and interpret market trends, study customer behavior, and take financial and logistical decisions. The need to sort, analyze, organize, and offer this critical data in a systematic manner which leads to the rise of the much-discussed term, big data.

According to the huge number of people are using social network sites to express their feelings, opinion and uncover about their everyday lives. However, people compose anything such as social activities or any comment on items. In addition, social media gives a chance for the business that giving a platform to interface with their customers, for example, social media to advertise or talk specifically to customers for associating with customer's point of view of products and services.

Twitter is a person-to-person communication and blogging Web site, which enables its users to read and post short tweets. Nowadays twitter becomes most popular data source for research because it has approximately 600 M of customers and over 250 M tweets per day generated. It became an essential platform where users express their sentiments and conclusion about any situation, product, etc. Generally, the tweets are limited to 140 characters in length, which may contain the noises like regional and SMS-type language data, sarcastic reviews, review that may not express any meaning, etc., so we have to eliminate this type of noises before performing sentiment analysis. SA has made it possible to analyze the state of mind of a person. It can push us to decide the positive, negative, or neutral perspective of a person based on his mentality on a given subject.

1.1 Sentiment Analysis

Sentiment analysis is a test that becomes very important for the companies because of emerging social media such as Facebook, Twitter, for example, a company wants to track tweets about their brands or products. Politicians can use this to track their campaigns, etc. Sentiment analysis or opinion mining is the process of knowing the people's attitude, opinions, their feelings, and emotions about any product or movie or any item. It is an information retrieval process as well as natural language processing task which is very challenging to carry out, but it is done due to its various applications in many areas. Opinion may differ from person to person in the same product. It may be positive or may be negative about the same product, because the product may have good feature or may have bad feature. On this basis, sentiment analysis can be of many types. It generally describes people's feelings and emotion toward an entity [1].

Different levels of sentiment analysis

Different levels of sentiment analysis are of three types [2]:

Document level: The whole file contains group's opinion. The file verifies whether it conveys the positive or negative sentiment.

Sentence level: It verifies whether a sentence conveys positive, negative, or neutral meaning.

Entity and aspect level: It verifies the emotions which are present at each level.

The rest of the paper is organized in the following manner. Section 1 is the introduction of Twitter sentiment and also the brief of big data. Section 2 states the associated work. Section 3 states a brief overview of our proposed design and information collection using R. Section 4 highlights our analysis results. The last area is based around conclusion and future work.

2 Related Work

A ton of work has been done in the field of sentiment analysis using social networks. There are different approaches to gathering user opinions on various subjects.

Anto et al. [3] proposed a technique to acquire user's feedbacks in the scenario where the most users fail to give feedbacks, by automatic extraction of data about the specific product from Twitter. They compare various text classifier techniques like Naive Bayes and found SVM to be 82% accurate, so they used SVM as text classifier. They used a third API Twitter4J for data extraction. Merits are more accurate; the rating can be done with the lack of direct information; demerits are application in another field which needs further investigation.

Ni et al. [4] proposed a new model to increase the efficiency of Naive Bayes. In his model, most efficient methods for computing the weight, classification, and feature extraction are applied. By using the term frequency, weight is calculated. Bayesian algorithm is used in this new model. In this, unique feature and representative features are used to adjust the weights of the classifiers. The information which represents a class is known as representative feature. The information which helps in differentiating between the classes is known as a unique feature. On the basis of weights, the probability for each classification is calculated and this feature improves the Bayesian algorithm.

Domingos et al. [5] concluded that Naive Bayes provides efficient results in case of certain problems where features are highly dependent, whereas Naive Bayes has a basic assumption that features must be independent of each other, but Naive Bayes gives better results.

Park et al. [6] generated a large amount of Twitter data by collecting the tweets automatically. Tweets are collected with the help of Application Programming Interface (API). He analyzed them by using emoticons. POS-tags and N-gram features are used by the Naive Bayes classifier. But in this method, there is a high probability of error, because the sentiments of tweets in the training dataset are considered as only on the basis of polarization of emoticons. Reason for less efficiency of the training set is that it considers only those tweets which have emoticons.

Aliza Sarlan et al. [7], in this paper, proposed a model to extract a huge amount of tweets from Twitter, to perform the sentiment analysis on that to classify the tweets into positive, negative and to represent the classification in the form of a pie chart and HTML page to deploy them in a Web application.

Zhao Jianqiang et al. [8], in this paper, have proposed a model to preprocessing the data before performing sentiment analysis on them by removing acronym, stop words, negation, etc., to increase the performance of classifiers for each dataset.

Monu Kumar et al. [9], in this paper, proposed a model to analyze and store the big data using Hadoop technology in a cloud environment to perform sentiment analysis.

Zhao Jianqiang et al. [10], in this paper, discussed the properties of a text preprocessing method on sentiment classification performance in two types of classification tasks and summed up the classification performances of six preprocessing methods using two feature models and four classifiers on five Twitter datasets. The experiments show that the accuracy using two component models and four classifiers on five Twitter datasets. The examinations demonstrated that the precision and F1-measure of Twitter sentiment classification classifier are improved when using the preprocessing methods.

Kuat Yessenov et al. [11] proposed an exact investigation of the effectiveness of machine learning methods in categorizing instant memos by semantic significance. They proposed different approaches in extracting text features such as bag-of-words model, handling negation, controlling to adverbs and adjectives hurdling word occurrences by a threshold, WordNet substitute's knowledge. The performance is

Fig. 1 Social media sentiment emojis

estimated to an accuracy of four machine learning techniques such as Decision Trees, k-means clustering, Maximum Entropy, and Naive Bayes. Merits are 1. It evaluates the fitness of different feature selection and learning algorithms on the classification of comments according to their subjectivity and their polarity (Fig. 1).

3 Proposed Model

3.1 What Is N-gram Techniques?

Traditionally, we take each word of a sentence to calculate the sentiment of the sentence, but there may be scenario that the word is previously used for positive sense, but now it is used for negative; let's consider, e.g., "what an awesome product, totally waste of money," if we consider "awesome" it is a positive word but if we consider the whole statement, it is expressing the negative sentiment. Due to these types of short comings, the N-gram technique came into the picture. An N-gram is a sequence of a "words" taken, in order, from a body of text. Basically, we consider one or more than one word at a time for evaluating the score of the sentence. It may be unary, binary, tertiary, and so on [12].

Example: "It's a surprisingly funny movie."
   Funny movie: 2 grams
   Surprisingly funny movie: 3 grams

Pre Processing:

1. Input a sentence: "a surprisingly funny movie."

2. Split it up: [a, surprisingly, funny, movie]

3. Cleanup: (remove stop words, punctuation, etc.):

   (Surprisingly, funny, movie)

4. Stem: [surprisingli, funni, movi]

Take the above key words and compare in training datasets.
       [Surprisingli, Funni, movi]
Funni occurs 0.1   movi occurs 0.7 of
Of all reviews   all reviews

[Funni, movi, I, recommend, it] // from training datasets

Score = 1/0.1 + 1/0.7
     = 10 + 1.43
     = 11.43

Suppose the reviews contain the word, i.e., very very rare. In this case, the word "Enigma," i.e., the name of the movie, then the fraction of time the word occurs in the training set is very small, maybe 1 in 1000 of reviews. When you divide it in score calculation, the contribution will become 1000 making all the other word scores irrelevant.

[Enigma, surprisingli, funni, movi]

Only occurs in   only occurs in   only occurs in
0.001 of reviews   0.1 of reviews   0.7 of reviews

[Enigma, funni, movi, I, recommend, it]

Score = 1/0.001 + 1/0.1 + 1/0.7
     = 1000 + 10 + 1.43
     = 1011.43

3.2 Log Function: "Squasher" (for Value > 1)

So we need to squash these greater larger numbers and make them small. The logarithm function is appropriate as long as we deal with the values >1.

Log (1) = 0
Log (5) = 0.7
Log (10) = 1
Log (100) = 2
Log (1000) = 3
Log (3000) = 3.7
$\vdots$
Log (100000000000000) = 14
Etc.

If we pass each result through log before counting the final score, we can see that the huge number of our rare word is squashing all the way down to 3 and the other word will contribute more comparable amount. If we want to more squash the number, we can use log base greater than 1.

[Enigma, surprisingli, funni, movi]

Only occurs in   only occurs in   only occurs in
0.001 of reviews   0.1 of reviews   0.7 of reviews

[Enigma, funni, movi, I, recommend, it]

Score = log (1/0.001) + log (1/0.1) + log (1/0.7)
     = log (1000) + log (10) + log (1.43)
     = 3 + 1 + 0.15
     = 4.15

3.3 Dataset

We used the movie review datasets consists of 5000 reviews available in text2vec package. We used this dataset because normal text takes a lot more memory as compared to vectorized text, because they are stored as sparse matrices. We divided the whole datasets into two parts: train dataset and test dataset.

3.4 Proposed Algorithm for Sentiment Analysis

Input: Enter the tweets for Twitter analysis
Output: Graphical representation of sentiment of all the tweets
Step1: Extracting the desired data from Twitter
Step2: Convert the tweet into text format
Step3: Data Preprocessing

- Remove the punctuation mark
- Convert the lower case
- Remove stop words like, and, or
- Remove the numbers
- Remove the white space

Step4: Break the tweets into individual words
Step5: Calculate the overall score of the tweet using N-gram techniques and log functions
Step6: Repeat steps 4–5 until all the tweets processed
Step7: Calculate the overall sentiment from the score array
Step8: Plot the sentiment graph for all the tweets

4 Result

We performed the sentiment analysis by considering 2 grams on testing datasets and got 92.68% accuracy (Fig. 2).

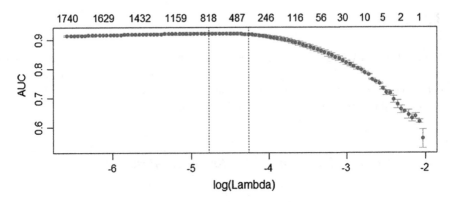

Fig. 2 Accuracy distribution on testing data

5 Conclusion

Sentiment analysis is a machine learning issue that has been a research concern for recent years. Although several notable works have come in this field, a completely automated and profoundly well-organized system has not been presented till now. This is because of the unstructured nature of natural language. Latest research shows the use of sentimental analysis in the development of the more precise recommender system. These types of approaches are usually used in the e-commerce business.

By considering each word of the review to find out the sentiment, it may or may not be accurate because may be the same word used in past for negative review but presently it is used for positive sense. So we have applied the bi-gram on movie review dataset and got 92% accuracy on test datasets.

Acknowledgements We are thankful to the faculty members of School of Computer Engineering Department of KIIT University, Bhubaneswar, for their cooperation and suggestions.

References

1. Web link-https://en.wikipedia.org/wiki/Sentiment_analysis.
2. Himadri Tanaya Chidananda, Santwana Sagnika and Laxman Sahoo. Survey on Sentiment Analysis: A Comparative Study. International Journal of Computer Applications 159(6): 4–7, February 2017.
3. Anto, Menara P., Kerala Thrissur, Mejo Antony, KM Muhsina, Nivea Johny, Vinay James, and Aswathy Wilson. "Product Rating Using Sentiment Analysis" International Conference on Electrical, Electronics, and Optimization Techniques (ICEEOT), 2016.
4. Niu, Zhen, Zelong Yin, and Xiangyu Kong. "Sentiment classification for microblog by machine learning." Computational and Information Sciences (ICCIS), 2012 Fourth International Conference on. Ieee, 2012.

5. Domingos, Pedro, and Michael Pazzani. "On the optimality of the simple Bayesian classifier under zero-one loss." Machine learning 29.2 (1997): 103–130.
6. Pak, Alexander, and Patrick Paroubek. "Twitter as a Corpus for Sentiment Analysis and Opinion Mining." LREc. Vol. 10. No. 2010. 2010.
7. Sarlan, Aliza, Chayanit Nadam, and Shuib Basri. "Twitter sentiment analysis." Information Technology and Multimedia (ICIMU), 2014 International Conference on. IEEE, 2014.
8. Jianqiang, Zhao. "Pre-processing Boosting Twitter Sentiment Analysis?" Smart City/ SocialCom/SustainCom (SmartCity), 2015 IEEE International Conference on. IEEE, 2015.
9. Kumar, Monu, and Anju Bala. "Analyzing Twitter sentiments through big data." Computing for Sustainable Global Development (INDIACom), 2016 3rd International Conference on. IEEE, 2016.
10. Zhao, Jianqiang, and Xiaolin Gui. "Comparison Research on Text Pre-processing Methods on Twitter Sentiment Analysis." IEEE Access (2017).
11. Kuat Yessenov, Sasa Misailovic, "Sentiment Analysis of Movie Review Comments", 6.863 Spring 2009 final project, pp. 1–17.
12. Web link-https://en.wikipedia.org/wiki/N-gram.

A Novel Edge-Supported Cost-Efficient Resource Management Approach for Smart Grid System

Jyotirmaya Mishra, Jitendra Sheetlani, K. Hemant K. Reddy and Diptendu Sinha Roy

Abstract The smart grids, a new-generation power supply system, have the capacity to lowering the cost, can increase service provision tremendously, and make surroundings greener as compared to conventional power supply systems. To interact with the physical world and widen its capabilities, integrated smart grid cyber-physical system (SG-CPS) can be used for computation, communication, and control. To support smart grid (SG), cloud components are employed for storing and processing users' power demand and control flow information generated at different control components like smart meter (SM), home energy management (HEM), phasor measurement units (PMUs), and soon. But storing smart grid data to cloud and processing incurs unacceptable delays. This paper addresses quality-of-service (QoS) requirements of SGs by integrating fog computing along with cloud computing infrastructure for realizing an Edge Computing integrated Smart Grid (EC-iSG). To that end, this paper presents novel heuristics for resource management of such integrated infrastructure that accounts for parameters such as uplink and downlink communication costs, cost for VM deployment, and cost for communicating among base stations. The results presented demonstrate the efficacy of the proposed methodology.

J. Mishra
Department of Computer Science and Engineering, Gandhi Institute of Engineering and Technology, Gunupur, India
e-mail: jyotirmayamishra75@gmail.com

J. Sheetlani
Department of Computer Science and Engineering, Sri Satya Sai University of Technology and Medical Sciences, Sehore, Madhya Pradesh, India
e-mail: Dr.jsheetlani@gmail.com

K. H. K. Reddy (✉)
Department of Computer Science and Engineering, National Institute of Science and Technology, Berhampur, India
e-mail: khemant.reddy@gmail.com

D. S. Roy
Department of Computer Science and Engineering, National Institute of Technology, Shillong, Meghalaya, India
e-mail: diptendu.sr@nitm.ac.in

© Springer Nature Singapore Pte Ltd. 2018
P. K. Pattnaik et al. (eds.), *Progress in Computing, Analytics and Networking*,
Advances in Intelligent Systems and Computing 710,
https://doi.org/10.1007/978-981-10-7871-2_36

Keywords Smart grid · Fog computing · Cloud computing
Cost optimization · HEM · PMU

1 Introduction

To interact with the physical world and widen its capabilities, cyber-physical system (CPS) can be used for computation, communication, and control [1]. The use of bidirectional connection between SG's physical components and computational elements significantly increases the efficiency, reliability, and cost-effectiveness of CPS [2]. As smart grid is a very complex system, it is very difficult to manage the operations in CPS optimally, and hence, it is a challenge to achieve high performance in real-time system with limited computational resources. Smart grids are complex engineering systems that seamlessly integrate computational network and cyber-resources with numerous physical processes, all encapsulated as a single unit [3]. EC-iSG holds a lot of promise toward power saving while fulfilling users' long-term QoS demands over time.

On the other hand, there has been a boom in population in the past years which has automatically led to an exponential growth in the number of houses and distribution points in the area. It has been estimated that this trend will be maintained in the years to come which will lead to increase data size as compared to a few years back. So, the old infrastructure of the cloud has to be modified to meet the new needs and also abide to the service quality assured to the users. The proposed approach is a coupling of edge computing and SM to make EC-iSG. It integrates the fog infrastructure with the SM to give a cost- and energy-effective model and give high standards of QoS than the previous SG model. The objective is to replace the conventional model of integrating SG with the cloud infrastructure. The communication between the devices of EMU is done using the cloud infrastructure. But this architecture is slowly being obsolete, the reason being that directly using the cloud to handle huge amount of generated data will create the huge amount of traffic in the servers. Accessing this information at different EMU levels from cloud directly will slow down the process, and delay incurred may reduce the QoS of entire system. It would be great if the load on cloud is distributed by a lower layer that uploads and downloads from the cloud only when necessary and handles most of the requests by itself. The remainder of this paper is organized as follows. Section 2 presents smart grid strategy and discusses its inherent limitations with an intuitive and illustrative example. Section 3 systematically presents the EC-iSG model and its underlying design principles. This section also presents the algorithm with a short discussion on the implementation details. Section 4 presents the efficacy of the proposed algorithm. Section 5 explains the experiments conducted on the aforementioned framework. Finally, the conclusions are presented in Sect. 6.

2 Literature Review

One of the major components of smart grid is base station and the policies associated with it. A number of studies have focused on base station-related technologies with myriad varieties in terms of model assumptions. For example, [4] develop a theoretical scheme for BS energy savings in conjunction with user association. Lee. S. et al. [5] addressed complications that arise one of temporal equality. Smart grid's two major components, namely PMUs as effective sensors for SGs, have been studied in [6], and a reliability study has been well studied in [7–9]. Similarly, home/residential management has been addressed in [10, 11].

2.1 Cloud-Enabled SG Model

Many research works have been dedicated to elaborate the benefits and opportunities of cloud-based smart grid system [3]. To manage the information of smart grid in cloud computing, [12, 13] proposes cloud-based smart grid information management models. An abstract of CSSGIM model is presented in Figs. 1 and 2, which shows how smart grid-generated data are uploaded to cloud for monitoring and billing purpose. In a cloud-enabled SG model, the major concern was the amount of delay incurred at different levels which fails to support the real-time services to give rapid response to consumers.

In this regard, we propose an enhanced fog-aided model that can effectively support QoS-enabled SG operations, as depicted in Fig. 2. There are also some works undertaken regarding the response time by giving direct communication among devices and consumers [14]. Simmhan et al. [15] have done an analysis for the benefits of integrating cloud platform with SG for demand response. Nagothu et al. [16] have discussed the contributions of different cloud technologies like

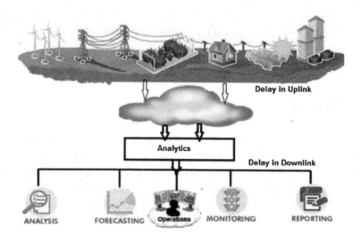

Fig. 1 Existing cloud-enabled smart grid

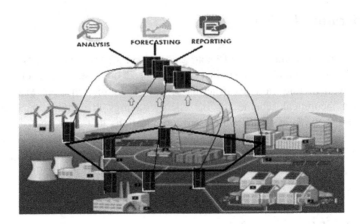

Fig. 2 Edge-computing enabled smart grid model

cloud storage and security to improve the disaster awareness level. Some of the research is also dedicated to develop the required cloud computing software methodology which can bring together energy service procedures and modern Web interoperable technologies [17]. Even though uses of cloud computing platform have been proven to be a boon to satisfy the computational requirements of smart grid system, it came across some challenges too like location of data, mixing of data, and term of agreement. All of these challenges were clearly defined and addressed by W. Deng et al. [18].

2.2 Fog Computing

Fog computing is proposed in [19], where cloud scenarios are offered much closer to SG devices and [20] present various technologies that are fundamental to realize fog computing. However, these works do not present concrete and working models, and this paper does that for SG's perspective under the proposed EC-iSG framework.

3 EC-ISG Model

This section consists of an introduction of our EC-iSG network model. It consists of the network model and the different types of constraints that exist in the model. Then, the cost function is formulated on the basis of different parameters like uplink cost, inter-BS communication, deployment, processing cost which can then be solved using those constraints earlier formulated. The notations that are used in this paper are given in Table 1.

Table 1 Notations

Constraints	
D, B & Q	Set of devices, set of base station (BS), and application set
Sub	The subcarrier set
$UCost_j^a$	The uplink cost at BS j of Application 'a'
$CCost_{j,k}$	The communication cost between BS j and k
AD^a	The delay constraint of a application 'A'
α_i^a	The arrival rate for application 'a' from device 'i'
L_i^a	The data length for application 'a' from device 'i'
$x_{i,j}$	The binary variable indicating if the device 'i' is in the coverage of BS 'j'
R	The data rate of one subcarrier
$Scap_j$	The storage capacity of BS 'j'
$Ccap_j$	The computation capacity of BS 'j'
Variables	
$ass_{j,i}$	A binary variable implying the association among BSs for devices i and j
$ass_{j,i}^{sc}$	Binary variable implying subcarrier BS$_j$'s allocation to device i or not
$p_{j,k}^a$	A binary variable indicating if data from BS j for app 'a' are processed in BS$_k$ or not
vm_k^a	Binary variable indicating if VM for app 'a' is placed in BS 'k' or not
$\lambda_{j,k}^a$	The request rate for app 'a' from BS$_j$ to BS$_k$
μ_k^a	The processing rate for processing a application 'a' in BSk
DT^a	Maximum delay tolerance for an application 'a'

3.1 EC-ISG Network Model

In this model, we are considering a connected wireless network as an undirected graph G = (N, E). Here, N represents the set of nodes consisting of union of set of generating devices and base stations B, i.e., N = D^{U}B, and E represents the edge links between the base stations. If the devices and base station are in the communication range of each other, then there is an edge Ei,j between them where i ∈ D and j ∈ B. Xi,j is a binary variable indicating the reachability of device 'i' and BSj in the transmission range. For a base station j ∈ B, let us consider the uplink cost at base station i and denote the communication cost between base stations i and j. It is assumed that the transmission delay is related to the network topology in the model and link capacities between the base stations are sufficient to take the load. The transmission delay on the edge Ei,j has been provided. The device is able to send the generated data to base stations using the uplinks. The base stations are composed of a subcarrier set Sub for uplink communication. Further, the number of subcarriers and bandwidth in all the base stations is same. Each base station b ∈ B in (1) EC-iSG has a server to host the VMs for different tasks as well as an antenna for wireless communication over a large area. Since the base station has a server, it has computation power as well as storage capacity. A renting cost Rj is charged for hosting a VM at the BS i. A device i $\in$ U carries a smartphone or a smart device when traveling around randomly in any area which will be in range of one or more base stations. Let the set of all application in the whole system be denoted by Q. The device sends its energy consumption request for a particular application to the associated base station. Let us represent the average arrival rate of data stream for application a in the home of device i. The length of the data stream uploaded by the device j for application 'a' is L_i^a. A VM is launched at the corresponding BS each time the data are uploaded. There exists a delay between the request by the device and its processing. The maximum delay tolerable by the device for application 'a' is denoted by DT^a.

3.2 Problem Statement

The main objective is to guarantee the QoS to the devices and to minimize the overall deployment cost of EC-iSG in the given edge infrastructure. We prefer the association of devices to the base station with the minimum uplink cost. But we cannot associate all the devices' connection with a single base station. In smart grid system, sensing devices are deployed in geographical area, these devices are in the range of one or two base stations and bandwidth, and cost of these base stations may change from ISP to ISP and vary from time-to-time due to availability. Depending upon availability of bandwidth, sensing devices need to select an appropriate base station for processing. The objective is to minimize the cost while finding a set of base stations to host the VM for each application. The main components of cost optimization are finding the best device association with BS, distributing the tasks and deployment of VM in the BS.

3.3 Problem Formulation

Hereafter, a heuristic for minimizing cost is presented that considers task skew and VMs deployed with the consideration of task distribution and VM deployment with the consideration of task distribution and VM deployment.

3.4 Device Association Constraints

If the base station j is connected to the device 'i', then the binary variable $a_{i,j}$ is set to 1, otherwise zero, i.e.

$$ass_{i,j} = \begin{cases} 1, & \text{if user } 'i' \text{ is associated with } BS_j \\ 0, & \text{Otherwise} \end{cases} \tag{1}$$

We define a binary variable $R_{i,j \forall i \in D \text{ and } j \in B}$ to denote whether the device 'D_i' is reachable from the base station j. This means that if device 'i' is associated with BS_j, then $R_{i,j} = 1$

$$\sum_{s \in Sub} ass^s_{i,j} \leq W_{i,j}, \forall \, i \in D, \, j \in B \tag{2}$$

Another constraint is that a device must be connected to only one base station.

$$\sum ass_{i,j} = 1, \quad \exists \, i \in D, \, j \in B \tag{3}$$

When the device is associated with the base station, a subcarrier is allocated to it so that device can communicate with the base station in a dedicated path irrespective of the other devices connected to that base station. We define a binary variable $A^s_{i,j}$ to represent whether the subcarrier s at base station j is allocated with the device$_i$ or not. Mathematically,

$$ass^s_{i,j} = \begin{cases} 1, & \text{if device } 'i' \text{ is associated with } BS \, j \text{ with subcarrier } s \\ 0, & \text{otherwise} \end{cases} \tag{4}$$

A subcarrier can be allocated to only one device, and there are no constraints on the number of subcarriers that are allocated to the device from a base station.

$$\sum ass^s_{i,j} \leq 1, \quad \forall \, i \in D, \quad s \in Sub \quad \text{and} \quad j \in B \tag{5}$$

3.5 Task Distribution Constraints

When the data are uploaded by the device to its corresponding base station, it can be processed either on the same BS or on any other BS. We define a binary variable $p^a_{i,j}$ to determine if the data for application a uploaded to its corresponding base station is then processed in BS k or not. Mathematically,

$$p^a_{i,j} = \begin{cases} 1, & \text{if data for } 'a' \text{ from } BS \, j \text{ is processed in } k \\ 0, & \text{otherwise} \end{cases} \tag{6}$$

Because of the fact that data are uploaded and processed in different base stations, we establish the following relationship between the psij and aij as follows.

$$p_{j,k}^s \leq \sum ass_{i,j} \leq 1, \quad j,k \in B, \quad i \in D \tag{7}$$

This equation signifies the fact that a base station can send the application data to other base station for processing if and only if it is associated with a device application.

3.6 VM Placement Constraints

Let binary variable P_k^a denote app a's VM hosting reality by B_k^s, and thus,

$$p_{j,k}^a \leq P_k^a, \quad \forall a \in A, \quad j,k \in B \tag{8}$$

where 'A' is the set of all application
Similarly, considering BS's data stream over apps' deployment, we can have

$$\mu_k^a / N \leq P_k^a \leq N^* \mu_k^a \tag{9}$$

Accordingly, BS's resource constraints can be denoted as

$$\sum P_k^a H^a \leq H_k, \quad \forall k \in B \quad and \quad a \in Q \tag{10}$$

and

$$\sum \mu_k^a \gamma^a \leq U_k, \forall k \in B \quad and \quad a \in Q \tag{11}$$

where μ_k^a is rate for app and γ^a, a scaling factor indicating correlation among rate and resource allocation.

3.7 QoS Considerations

In the proposed EC-iSG model, data request for subsequent processing undergoes 3 phases, namely

1. uploading data from SG device to its associated BS.
2. data transfer to appropriate base station for processing, and
3. processing delay at concerned BS.

Thus, uplink delays can be computed using (12) and (13).

$$r_{i,j} = \sum a_{i,j}^a R \quad \forall i \in D, \quad j \in B, \quad s \in Sub \tag{12}$$

$$T_{i,j}^a = L_i^a / r_{i,j} \tag{13}$$

4 Cost-Aware Scheduling Algorithm

Considering the above two QoS constraints (12) and (13), we presented our cost- and delay-aware heuristic algorithm for minimizing the delay and cost as delay is directly preoperational to cost.

Heuristic Algorithm:

Input :B[ ] – Set of Base stations

    D[ ]-Set of Generating Devices/users with required applications

Output :Tcost-Total allocation cost

---

1. *for all Base Station* $i \in B$ *do*
2.   *InitilizeFun*(B_i) *with random values within range*[x, y]
3. *end for*
4 *for all Device / Users* $j \in D$ *do*
5.   *InitilizeFun*(D_j) *with random values within range*[x, y]
6. *end for*
7. *for all Device / Users* 'j' $\in D$ *do*
8. $ass_{i,j} = Find$ *all* B_i, *an access range of* D_j
9.   *Sort* $ass_{i,j}$ *in decsending order*
10.   *if* $\exists ass_{i,j} | \sum ass_{i,j} \geq 1, \forall i \in D$ *and* $j \in B$ *then*
11. $min : ass_{i,j}.T cost \sum_{k=1, k \in a}^{n} \left[\left(Ucost_{i,j} * L_i^k \right) + \left(P_{i,j}^k * L_i^k \right) + \left(d cost_i^k \right) \right]$
12   *s.t.* (1) −(5) : *for assocationg a device* D_i *at a basestation* B_j
             (9), (10) : *deployment and computation*
             (12) *and* (13) : *delay incurred at network and BS*
             and (14)
13   *if current* $ass_{i,j}^t$ *not satisfying* (1) − (5) *or* (9) − (10) *or* (12) − (13) *then*
14.   *update* B_i *as* D_j
15.   *goto step* 8; / / − − − *for best search*
16.   *endif*
17.   *else*
18   *enqueue for next slot scheduling*
19.   .
20,   *endif*
21. *endfor*
22. *end*

5   Experimental Setup and Result Discussion Initialize

This section presents the performance results of our proposed algorithm, and same is compared with greedy approach. The proposed model finds all the base stations that are within the transmission range of a device and try to associate a device required application and VM with required computation to a base station with the minimum uplink cost and processing cost including VM deployment cost and interbase station communication cost. Figures 3 and 4 depict the performance difference between the proposed algorithm and greedy approach. Figure 3 depicts the total cost with respect to the number of devices with fixed number of applications, whereas Fig. 4 presents the performance effect on request arrival rate. It can be observed that in case of small arrival rate the performance of greedy approach is close to proposed heuristic approach, whereas performance of heuristic approach increases with respect to arrival rate. Our objective is to find the performance improvement of edge over cloud in smart grid application.

We simulated the network with a size of 500 × 500 area, 50 base stations with different communication ranges that range from 10 to 15 and 30 devices with different applications in order to create a simulation network close to realistic. We consider five different applications for different purposes. Each device with two applications with arrival rate of [0.1–0.5], and application data length is set within [10, 50]. Each base station has thee subcarriers with communication cost, VM deployment cost, and link delay costs that are randomly generated within [2–5], [1, 10], and [1, 3], respectively. It can be observed that heuristic achieves higher performance than the greedy approach.

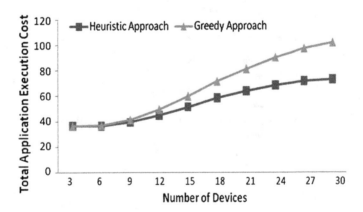

Fig. 3 Performance on total cost

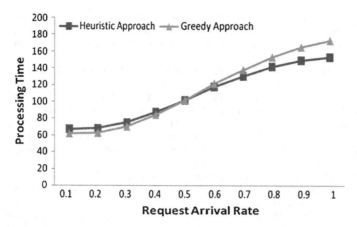

Fig. 4 Performance effect on request arrival rate

6 Conclusion

This paper presents a novel cost-minimizing approach for SGs that employ a fog-supported cloud infrastructure. The proposed EC-iSG model accounts for the interplay of three pertinent parameters, namely base station correlations, deployed VMs, and fork-programming distribution for cost optimization and QoS constraints. Experiments conducted demonstrate much superiority with respect to existing greedy approaches. The communication load on the cloud infrastructure and the heavy computation and storage demands make it difficult for the cloud providers to maintain the QoS to its devices leading to SLA violation. Thus, fog layer handles the load of the cloud in a lower edge level. Most of the computing thus can be done on the network edge, and only a fraction of the data and computation is transferred to the cloud for handling it.

References

1. Rajkumar, Ragunathan Raj, et al. "Cyber-physical systems: the next computing revolution." *Proceedings of the 47th Design Automation Conference*. ACM, 2010.
2. Jiang, B. (2015). Optimization and Management of Cyber-Physical Systems-Smart Grid and Plug-in Hybrid Electric Vehicles (Doctoral dissertation, Northeastern University Boston).
3. K. Hemant Reddy, D S Roy, D K Mohanta, "Cloud Based Cost Optimization Model for Effective Smart Grid Information Management". Part 8 (Big Data Analysis and Cyber Physical Systems) of edited volume Cyber-Physical Systems: A Computational Perspective, CRC Press, Taylor & Francis Group, LLC, Florida, USA; Eds. Patnaik L M, Srinivasa K G, Deka G C, Ganesh S.
4. Son, K., Kim, H., Yi, Y., & Krishnamachari, B. (2011). Base station operation and user association mechanisms for energy-delay tradeoffs in green cellular networks. IEEE journal on selected areas in communications, 29(8), 1525–1536.

5. N. Sung, N.-T. Pham, H. Yoon, S. Lee, and W. Hwang, "Base station association schemes to reduce unnecessary handovers using location awareness in femtocell networks," Wireless Networks, vol. 19, no. 5, pp. 741–753, 2013. [Online]. Available: https://doi.org/10.1007/s11276-012-0498-0.

6. Mohanta, D. K., Murthy, C., & Sinha Roy, D. (2016). A brief review of phasor measurement units as sensors for smart grid. Electric Power Components and Systems, 44(4), 411–425.

7. Behera, S., Pattnaik, B. S., Reza, M., & Roy, D. S. (2016). Predicting Consumer Loads for Improved Power Scheduling in Smart Homes. In Computational Intelligence in Data Mining —Volume 2 (pp. 463–473). Springer, New Delhi.

8. Murthy, Cherukuri, K. Ajay Varma, Diptendu Sinha Roy, and Dusmanta Kumar Mohanta. "Reliability evaluation of phasor measurement unit using type-2 fuzzy set theory"; Systems Journal, IEEE 8, no. 4 (2014): 1302–1309.

9. Murthy, Cherukuri, Anadi Mishra, Debashis Ghosh, Diptendu Sinha Roy, and Dusmanta Kumar Mohanta.; "Reliability analysis of phasor measurement unit using hidden Markov Model"; Systems Journal, IEEE 8, no. 4 (2014): 1293–1301.

10. Polaki, S. K., Reza, M., & Roy, D. S. (2015, June). A genetic algorithm for optimal power scheduling for residential energy management. In Environment and Electrical Engineering (EEEIC), 2015 IEEE 15th International Conference on (pp. 2061–2065). IEEE.

11. Murthy, C., Roy, D. S., & Mohanta, D. K. (2015). Reliability evaluation of phasor measurement unit: A system of systems approach. Electric Power Components and Systems, 43(4), 437–448.

12. Bera, Samaresh, SudipMisra, and Joel JPC Rodrigues. "Cloud computing applications for smart grid: A survey." IEEE Transactions on Parallel and Distributed Systems 26.5 (2015): 1477–1494.

13. Fang, Xi, et al. "Managing smart grid information in the cloud: opportunities, model, and applications." IEEE network 26.4 (2012).

14. Kim, Hongseok, et al. "Cloud-based demand response for smart grid: Architecture and distributed algorithms." Smart Grid Communications (SmartGridComm), 2011 IEEE International Conference on. IEEE, 2011.

15. Simmhan, Yogesh, et al. "An informatics approach to demand response optimization in smart grids." Natural Gas 31 (2011): 60.

16. Nagothu, Kranthimanoj, et al. "Persistent Net-AMI for microgrid infrastructure using cognitive radio on cloud data centers." IEEE Systems Journal 6.1 (2012): 4–15.

17. Nikolopoulos, Vassilis, et al. "Web-based decision-support system methodology for smart provision of adaptive digital energy services over cloud technologies." IET software 5.5 (2011): 454–465.

18. Deng, Wei, et al. "Harnessing renewable energy in cloud datacenters: opportunities and challenges." IEEE Network 28.1 (2014): 48–55.

19. Bonomi, Flavio, et al. "Fog computing and its role in the internet of things." Proceedings of the first edition of the MCC workshop on Mobile cloud computing. ACM, 2012.

20. J. Zhu, D. S. Chan, M. S. Prabhu, P. Natarajan, H. Hu, and F. Bonomi, "Improving web sites performance using edge servers in fog computing architecture," in Service Oriented System Engineering (SOSE), 2013 IEEE 7th International Symposium on. IEEE, 2013, pp. 320–323.

Task Scheduling Mechanism Using Multi-criteria Decision-making Technique, MACBETH in Cloud Computing

Suvendu Chandan Nayak, Sasmita Parida, Chitaranjan Tripathy and Prasant Kumar Pattnaik

Abstract Cloud computing is the new era of Internet technology which provides various utilities and computing resources from the pool of resources on the basis of "pay per Use". It is challenging one to allocate required on-demand resources for all the users' request. Meanwhile, the service provider aims toward a better resource utilization. These user requests are called task, if task execution is bounded by time limit which is called deadline-based task. The deadline-based tasks have different parameters. To schedule these tasks, researchers proposed many works based upon these parameters. However, in this work, we considered the scheduling of deadline-based task that is a Multi-criteria Decision-making problem due to different task's parameters associated with it. The work is proposed to implement Measuring Attractiveness through a Category-Based Evaluation Technique (MACBETH) to ranking the deadline-based task by which many tasks can meet their deadline. The results of the proposed work are quite good as compared to the existing mechanisms.

Keywords Cloud computing · Task scheduling · Resource utilization
Deadline-based task · MCDM · MACBETH

S. C. Nayak (✉) · S. Parida
Department of Computer Science and Engineering, C V Raman College of Engineering,
Bhubaneswar, India
e-mail: suvendu2006@gmail.com

S. Parida
e-mail: sasmitamohanty5@gmail.com

S. C. Nayak · C. Tripathy
Veera Surendra Sai University of Technology, Burla, India
e-mail: crt.vssut@yahoo.com

P. K. Pattnaik
School of Computer Engineering, KIIT University, Bhubaneswar, India
e-mail: patnaikprasantfcs@kiit.ac.in

© Springer Nature Singapore Pte Ltd. 2018
P. K. Pattnaik et al. (eds.), *Progress in Computing, Analytics and Networking*,
Advances in Intelligent Systems and Computing 710,
https://doi.org/10.1007/978-981-10-7871-2_37

1 Introduction

Task scheduling is an important aspect in cloud computing, and it directly impacts on resource utilization. It is challenging one due to the nature of task, cloud platform, and cloud utility. Moreover, the scheduling of tasks within a deadline while considering different task parameter is quite interesting and challenging one. The OpenNebula is one of the open-source cloud platforms [1]. Haizea is the scheduler used to schedule deadline-sensitive tasks in OpenNebula [2]. Deadline-sensitive tasks are best-effort leases or tasks. These two types of tasks are different with respect to allocating resources by time. The best effort allocates on-demand resources as soon as possible, whereas the deadline-sensitive task allocates resources within the deadline [3]. Several algorithms have been proposed for scheduling deadline-sensitive tasks, and backfilling algorithm is one of them. Backfilling algorithm is optimized first come, first served (FCFS) algorithm [4]. In backfilling, the tasks are sorted according to their start time. Some of the tasks need to be backfilled to get ideal resources for the new task. The selection of tasks is purely on FCFS basis. The scheduling performance of backfilling algorithm degrades with respect to a number of task schedules due to conflicts among the similar tasks [5]. The task selection must be carried out through a decision maker. In this work, we formulate the conflict among the similar tasks as a MCDM problem, due to the presence of different parameters of deadline-sensitive task.

Most of the research scheduling algorithm performance is evaluated using a priority and ranking among the tasks. These two processes must follow some mathematical concepts to rank the tasks during scheduling. The ranking is complex, mainly during scheduling of deadline-based tasks. So, we have taken an initiative to implement decision maker Measuring Attractiveness through a Category-Based Evaluation Technique (MACBETH) [6] to evaluate the ranking among the similar tasks along with other tasks. The aim of the implementation of MACBETH is to achieve a better resource utilization which can only achieve by scheduling number of tasks. The decision support system is an information system, which is used to evaluate and assist in making decision with a certain goal. Researchers have proposed many decision-making methods like weight product (WP), simple, addictive weighting (SAW), analytics hierarchy process (AHP), and technique for order of preference by similarity (TOPSIS) for the different application in different fields. MACBETH is one of them, and it is a simple method to respond to decision makers, introduced to qualitative and quantitative [6]. The ranking is computed by weight and range value of the parameters. Based upon these, a decision or ranking is computed to take a decision. Similarly, the conflicts among the tasks during scheduling can also be eliminated by ranking using MACBETH. Whenever there are similar tasks, the alternative came out, so the selection of a task should be carried out by the decision maker.

In this work, we introduce MACBETH to resolve the conflicts among the similar tasks in backfilling algorithm. The task close to the ideal resource utilization is selected by MACBETH among the similar tasks. The work is organized as follows:

In Sect. 2, the previous works related to the proposed work are discussed. The proposed algorithm with illustrations is presented in Sect. 3. Sections 4 and 5 deal with the performance, result analysis, and conclusions along with future work.

2   Related Work

In this section, we studied different deadline-based task scheduling algorithms proposed by researchers in a cloud computing environment. Sotomayor et al. [7] proposed an algorithm for predicting various run-time overheads involved in virtual machines for the AR lease. Recently, immediate and best-effort resource allocation policies are mostly used by cloud service providers to process user requests in IaaS [8, 9]. Nathani et al. [7] proposed a mechanism along with swapping and backfilling algorithm to schedule deadline-sensitive leases in OpenNebula platform, but the authors do not discuss about the similar types of leases. Moreover, based upon task deadline, many research works have been proposed. These works are based on priority or rank among the tasks. Recently, Byun et al. [10] proposed scheduling algorithm for cost optimization for deadline-based tasks. The authors considered a homogeneous type of resources instead of others. Li and Cai [11] introduced three priority rules for scheduling deadline-based tasks. These rules proposed allocating leases to the appropriate available time slots in a physical machine by which better resource utilization is achieved. Manimaran and Murthy [12] proposed scheduling non-preemptive tasks in a multiprocessor system. The work used parallelism in tasks to schedule within the deadline.

However, on-demand VM allocations have been assigned in different ways. But allocating VMs to the deadline-based task should be occurred using decision maker. Because, deadline-sensitive tasks have multiple criteria to allocate the VMs. MCDM mechanisms have been attracted by many researchers to evaluate and select the best compromise alternatives [13]. Among popular MCDM, MACBETH has attracted much to solve complex problems. It has an advantage in providing a ranking procedure for positive attributes and negative attributes when it is used for decision support and the best alternative is found out [14]. In the literature review, we studied very less attention is given by the research to implement MCDM in cloud computing. Gani et al. [15] proposed MCDM analysis to select cloud service. The authors focused to analyze different types of cloud services rather than task scheduling. Nayak et al. [5] implemented analytic hierarchy process (AHP) in the backfilling algorithm to resolve the conflicts. The authors suggested implementing and studying the other MCDM mechanisms in backfilling algorithm. Recently, a case study of MCDM in project resource scheduling is studied by Markou et al. [16]. The authors focused and discussed different MCDM methods through a case study, but not in a cloud computing environment. The MACBETH is successfully implemented and used in different manufacturing and production industries, whereas, there are very limited implementation in cloud computing. In this work, we implemented MACBETH with backfilling algorithm to find the rank among the tasks when similar tasks are in the scheduling queue.

3 Proposed Mechanism

3.1 Macbeth

The aim of the proposed work is to implement MCDM and MACBETH to schedule deadline-based tasks in cloud computing to enhance the performance of the existing backfilling algorithm. However, we have discussed MACBETH and its implementation in backfilling algorithm. The MACBETH technique is based on a linear additive model. It allows to evaluate the options against multiple criteria. It computes the difference of attractiveness between two tasks at a time to generate numerical scores for the alternatives in each criterion and to weight the criteria. The criteria are computed by the seven categories such as no, very weak, weak, moderate, strong, very strong, and extreme. It finds scores for the alternatives from the consistent set of judgments, uses mathematical programming to test consistency, and also finds suggestions to resolve inconsistencies if they arise [16–18]. The basic steps of MACBETH are as follows:

Step-1: Find the comparison of the most attractive and the least attractive option and must followed by the second most attractive option with the least attractive, and so on

Step-2: Compare the most attractive option with each of the other options, for increasing attractiveness, from right to left.

Step 3: Consider the first row of the matrix, and take as the fixed reference the most attractive option.

Step-4: Compare the most attractive option with the second most attractive option and the second most attractive with the third.

Step-5: Finally, the remaining judgments were assessed. The more preferential information provided greater the scale level of accuracy.

For consistent score, MACBETH suggests a numerical-scale V on M that must satisfy the following measurement rules:

Rule 1:

$$\forall\, m, n \in m : v(m) = v(n) \text{ if } m \text{ and } n \text{ are equally attractive}$$

$$\forall\, m, n \in m: v(m) > v(n) \text{ if } m \text{ is more attractive than } n$$

Rule 2:

$$\forall k, k' \in \{1, \dots x\}, \forall m, n, P, R \in m \text{ with } (m, n) \in C_k \text{ and } (P, R) \in C_k \colon k \geq$$
$$k' + 1 = > v(m) - v(n) > v(P) - v(R) \tag{1}$$

If m and n are not differentiated

$$v(m) - v(n) = 0$$

$$\text{If } (m, n) \in C_k \text{ and } (P, R) \in C_{k'} (k > k' \colon [v(m) - v(n)] > [v(P) - v(R)] \tag{2}$$

$$\text{That is } [v(m) - v(n)] - [v(P) - v(R)] > 0 \tag{3}$$

Or

$$[v(m) - v(n)] - [v(P) - v(R)] \geq \delta \, (\delta > 0) \tag{4}$$

where δ is the minimal difference between two alternatives.

3.2 Proposed Model

The proposed work followed the illustration; consider the deadline-based tasks as shown in Table 1. The tasks are associated with the parameters: the number of VMs (node), arrival time (AT), start time (ST), duration of execution (E), and deadline (DT). The tasks can be scheduled according to VMs, AT, ST, E, or DT [19]. Mainly, algorithms are proposed considering anyone parameter. The scheduling performance is also varied for these parameters. In backfilling algorithm, tasks are sorted according to the start time (ST) and tasks are scheduled in parallel if resources are available. A task must be selected to backfill and execute along with other task [20]. The task T1 executed at 12.30 and two VMs is allocated as per requirement for duration of 20 min. We can observe in Fig. 1 that at the same starting time there are four numbers of VMs out of which two are allocated to task T1. So the rest two VMs should be allocated to the next task as per the requirement. But the next task T2 requires four VMs. So T3 is selected to be scheduled along with T1 for duration of 30 min. It means T3 is backfilled. But the conflict arises between tasks T3 and T4 because both are similar task. This problem is studied by Nayak [5]. The author studied if T3 will be executed instead of T4, the task T5 does not meet its deadline as shown in figure. Whenever T4 is scheduled before T3, the task T5 meets its deadline and all tasks are executed with their required resources as shown in Fig. 2. It is observed the performance of backfilling algorithm can be improved by implementing decision maker, which can resolve conflicts among similar tasks Nayak [5, 21]. However, we have proposed resolving the above problem through MACBETH. It finds the relativeness among the similar tasks.

Table 1 Lease information [5]

Lease no.	Nodes	Submit time (AM)	Start time (PM)	Duration in minutes	Deadline (PM)
1	2	11.10	12.00	20	12.30
2	3	11.20	12.00	40	01.00
3	2	11.30	12.00	30	01.50
4	2	11.32	12.00	40	01.50
5	4	11.40	01.00	20	01.50

Figs. 1 and 2 Scheduling difference in the backfilling algorithm for similar tasks

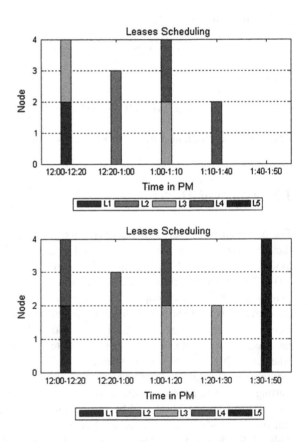

The proposed algorithm mainly implements MACBETH to handle the conflicts among the similar task in backfilling algorithm. In backfilling algorithm, it schedules the first task from the scheduling queue with its required VMs. The start time of scheduling is finding out at min $(T_i(ST))$. The number of VMs created throughout the execution or scheduling is computed as max $(T_i(n))$, where n is the number of VMs required by task T_i. After allocating the required resources to task T_i, the available resources are found out. As per scheduling principles of backfilling algorithm, a task T_x will be selected from the scheduling queue which can be fitted in time slot t_j. The challenge is if T_x and T_y both are same. So we proposed and resolve this problem using MACBETH. The MACBETH is invoked and finds the relativeness and weights over these tasks. Based upon these values, the task T_x or T_y is selected to be executed at time slot ti along with task T_i. In the proposed algorithm, the MACBETH is only involved whenever there are similar tasks in the queue. The meaning of similar task is expressed as follows: The tasks T_x and T_y are similar if and only if they satisfy the following conditions:

(a) if $T_x(ST) == T_y(ST)$, where $y = x + 1$ (5)

(b) And $T_x(n) == T_y(n)$,   where n is the number of VMs required   (6)

Proposed Algorithm

Step 1: Initialize Q with T number of tasks with respect to their start time (ST)

Step 2: Set scheduling time $t_i = \min(T_i(ST))$

Step 3: Create number of VMs at t_i as $N = \max(T_i(n))$

Step 4: Repeat the steps 5 to 10 until the queue is empty.

Step 5: Schedule first task (T_i) from the queue and allocate required VMs

Step 6: Find the available resource at time t_i: N available $= N - T_i(n)$

Step 7: select the next two tasks from the queue T_x and T_y where $T_x(n) <= N$ avaliable

Step 8: if T_x and T_y are similar

Invoke MACBETH

Resolve conflicts

Find weight over each other and select the task having higher weight

If end

Step 9: Select task T_x to schedule with task T_i at time t_i

Step 10: Update Q and execution time of task T_x

Step 11: Stop

Here, we are not considering execution time (E) and deadline of tasks, because these two parameters can be varied from task to task. However, these two parameters are used as criteria to evaluate the weight among the tasks. The weight among the tasks is computed using the credit, and the credits are computed based upon the task parameters. The credit set for execution E is computed as follows:

$T_x(E_c) = T_x(E)/10$, where $T_x(E_c)$ is always an integer number.

Similarly, the credit for deadline of a task T_x is computed in Eq. 7 as follows:

$$T_x(DT_c) = \frac{(T_x(DT) - T_x(ST))}{T_x(E)} \tag{7}$$

4 Performance and Result Analysis

In this work, we have implemented MACBETH for decision making and MATLAB R15a (32bit) for scheduling. We have considered a number of random datasets with different parameters of the tasks. The decision tree is formulated for similar tasks, and then, a credit is computed for the criteria. As we discussed, the criteria are execution time and deadline. Figures 3 and 4 show the credit matrix of deadline and duration of Table 1. Matrix values shown are consistently judged. The robustness found among the similar tasks is shown in Fig. 5. The robustness shows the judgment values of the tasks over another. As we discussed, there are two similar tasks in Table 1. Finally, we computed the difference profiles of these

Fig. 3 Credit matrix of deadline

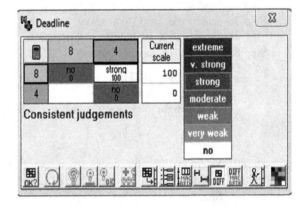

Fig. 4 Credit matrix of duration

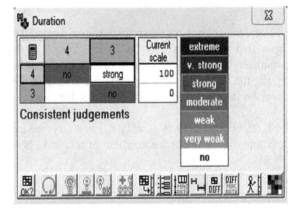

Fig. 5 Robustness analysis
of similar tasks

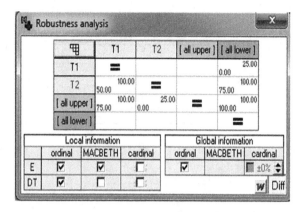

Fig. 6 Differences of T1
over T2

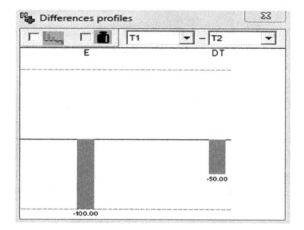

similar tasks that are shown in Figs. 6 and 7. The difference profile specifies the
difference among the similar tasks with respect to the criteria. In Fig. 6, the task T1
has negative robustness with respect to execution time (E) and deadlines; in execution, it is −100, and in deadline, it is −50 over T2. Moreover, T2 over T1 is
shown in Fig. 7. So the task T2 should execute before task T3. The task execution
of the table is shown in Fig. 2, in which all the tasks meet their deadline.

In this work, we consider five number task sets with different task's parameters
and observe the performance. The performance is shown in Table 2 and the graph
in Fig. 8. In this experiment, we considered different task's parameters and also
change the number of VMs on the physical machine. Moreover, we consider a
number of similar tasks in each random task set. In each task set, we observed a
number of tasks are scheduled. As we discussed the similar tasks, conflicts are
resolved by MACBETH 2.4.0 version in window platform. However, the performance of the backfilling algorithm is improved by implementing a decision maker

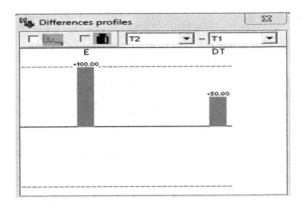

Fig. 7 Differences of T2 over T1

Table 2 Different task set parameters with scheduling performance

Serial no	No. of VMs	No. of tasks	No of similar tasks	Backfilling		Proposed mechanism	
				No. of tasks meeting deadline	No. of tasks missing deadline	No. of tasks meeting deadline	No. of tasks missing deadline
1	4	8	4	5	3	7	1
2	6	15	6	10	5	13	2
3	8	20	11	11	9	16	4
4	10	28	13	17	11	21	7
5	12	34	15	20	14	25	9

that is MACBETH. Though more tasks are scheduled, it implies that the proposed mechanism provides better resource utilization as compared to the existing algorithm.

Fig. 8 Comparison of task scheduling

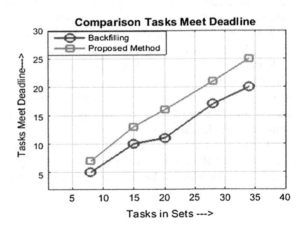

5 Conclusion

MCDM has been attracting many researchers to solve real-world decision problem in many fields. In this work, we proposed and implemented MACBETH as decision maker in backfilling algorithm. The deadline-sensitive task scheduling is treated as a MCDM problem. However, the proposed work performs better than the existing backfilling algorithm. We used MACBETH and MATLAB R2015a to implement the proposed work. The conflicts among the similar tasks are solved by MACBETH tool, and the tasks are scheduled. The comparison results of five different random datasets are shown in Fig. 8 which shows a better result in the proposed algorithm. Moreover, other MCDM methods may be implemented, and a comparative study may be observed in backfilling algorithm to improve its performance in future.

References

1. B. Sotomayor, R. S. Montero, I. M. Llorente, and I. Foster, "Virtual infrastructure management in private and hybrid clouds," IEEE Internet Comput., vol. 13, pp. 14–22, 2009.
2. O. Project, "OpenNebula 4.4 Design and Installation Guide," 2014.
3. A. Nathani, S. Chaudhary, and G. Somani, "Policy based resource allocation in IaaS cloud," Futur. Gener. Comput. Syst., vol. 28, no. 1, pp. 94–103, 2012.
4. D. G. Feitelson, "Experimental Analysis of the Root Causes of Performance Evaluation Results : A Backfilling Case Study," pp. 1–12.
5. S. C. Nayak and C. Tripathy, "Deadline sensitive lease scheduling in cloud computing environment using AHP," J. King Saud Univ. - Comput. Inf. Sci., 2016.
6. C. A. BANA E COSTA, J.-M. DE CORTE, and J.-C. VANSNICK, "Macbeth," Int. J. Inf. Technol. Decis. Mak., vol. 11, no. 2, pp. 359–387, 2012.
7. B. Sotomayor, R. S. Montero, I. M. Llorente, and I. Foster, "Resource Leasing and the Art of Suspending Virtual Machines," 2009 11th IEEE Int. Conf. High Perform. Comput. Commun., vol. 0, pp. 59–68, 2009.
8. I. Foster, "Virtual infrastrueture Manageent in Private and Hybrid Clouds," IEEE Internet Comput., 2009.
9. D. G. Feitelson, "Utilization and Predictability in Scheduling the IBM SP2 with Back lling 1 Introduction," Science (80-.).
10. E.-K. Byun, Y.-S. Kee, J.-S. Kim, and S. Maeng, "Cost optimized provisioning of elastic resources for application workflows," Futur. Gener. Comput. Syst., vol. 27, no. 8, pp. 1011–1026, 2011.
11. X. Li and Z. Cai, "Elastic Resource Provisioning for Cloud Workflow Applications," IEEE Trans. Autom. Sci. Eng., no. January, pp. 1–16, 2015.
12. F. Dong and S. G. Akl, "Scheduling Algorithms for Grid Computing: State of the Art and Open Problems," pp. 1–55, 2006.
13. A. S. Survey, "VIKOR and its Applications :," vol. 5, no. June, pp. 56–83, 2014.
14. Q. Z. D. L. Y. Yang, "VIKOR Method with Enhanced Accuracy for Multiple Criteria Decision Making in Healthcare Management," 2013.
15. A. Gani, N. B. Anuar, M. Shiraz, M. N. Haque, and I. T. Haque, "Cloud Service Selection Using Multicriteria Decision Analysis," vol. 2014, 2014.
16. C. Markou, G. K. Koulinas, and A. P. Vavatsikos, "Project Resources Scheduling and Leveling Using Multi-Attribute Decision Models: Models Implementation and Case Study," Expert Syst. Appl., vol. 77, pp. 160–169, 2017.

17. I. Solis Moreno, P. Garraghan, P. Townend, and J. Xu, "Analysis, Modeling and Simulation of Workload Patterns in a Large-Scale Utility Cloud," IEEE Trans. Cloud Comput., vol. PP, no. c, pp. 1–1, 2014.
18. H. Arabnejad, J. G. Barbosa, and R. Prodan, "Low-time complexity budget-deadline constrained workflow scheduling on heterogeneous resources," Futur. Gener. Comput. Syst., vol. 55, pp. 29–40, 2016.
19. S. Parida, S. C. Nayak, and C. Tripathy, "Truthful Resource Allocation Detection Mechanism for Cloud Computing," in WCI, 2015, pp. 487–491.
20. S. C. Nayak, S. Parida, C. Tripathy, P. K. Pattnaik, "Resource allocation policies in cloud computing environment," Advancing Cloud Database Systems and Capacity Planning With Dynamic Applications, 2017.
21. S. Parida, S. C. Nayak, P. Priyadarshi, P. K. Pattnaik, G. Ray, "Petri net: Design and analysis of parallel task scheduling algorithm," Lecture Notes in Electrical Engineering, vol-443, 2018.

Multi-objective Data Aggregation for Clustered Wireless Sensor Networks

Sukhchandan Randhawa and Sushma Jain

Abstract Maximizing the energy efficiency is one of the major challenges in Wireless Sensor Networks. Research works have shown that by cluster formation of nodes, energy can be more efficiently used. In this research work, a Multi-objective Data Aggregation Clustering (MDAC) technique is proposed based on multi-objective optimization approach. Non-dominated Sorting Genetic Algorithm-II is utilized for cluster formation which can consider the several objective functions defined simultaneously. The main objectives are to minimize the communication cost among cluster heads, base station and cluster members and also to maximize the number of nodes within a cluster. The selection of CH nearer to BS is also avoided in order to prevent the hot spot problem. NSGA-II presents different solutions in a solution set which result in different topologies. Every solution in a solution set represents the best solution based on objective functions. BS considers every solution instance in solution set and selects the most suitable solution based on the desired criteria. The experimental evaluation results show that the proposed MDAC technique performs better than existing multi-objective clustering techniques in terms of throughput, total energy consumption, network lifetime, number of active nodes, data received at BS and variation in network lifetime and energy with varying selection choices of NSGA-II algorithm.

Keywords Wireless sensor networks · Load balancing · Data aggregation Clustering · NSGA-2 · Multi-objective optimization

S. Randhawa (✉) · S. Jain
Computer Science and Engineering Department, Thapar University,
Punjab 147004, India
e-mail: Sukhchandan@thapar.edu

S. Jain
e-mail: sjain@thapar.edu

© Springer Nature Singapore Pte Ltd. 2018
P. K. Pattnaik et al. (eds.), *Progress in Computing, Analytics and Networking*,
Advances in Intelligent Systems and Computing 710,
https://doi.org/10.1007/978-981-10-7871-2_38

1 Introduction

A wireless sensor network (WSN) provides many advantages in terms of cooperative intelligence and cost [1]. The performance of a WSN is highly dependent on the life span of the network in order to provide required QoS level in continuous manner. The limited energy supply of nodes is the most important factor that effects the lifetime of the network, as the nodes die or become non-operational due to lack of energy which gets exhausted due to communication operations.

There is a need of a scalable routing algorithm, as huge amount of nodes are deployed in WSNs. Clustering is considered as the most commonly used energy-efficient routing mechanism in WSNs [2]. In clustering-based routing, nodes are classified in the form of clusters, and within each cluster, a cluster head (CH) is elected according to certain criteria based on homogenous or heterogeneous networks. In case of WSNs, there can be number of scenarios which can be modeled as multi-objective optimization formulations, in which multiple required objectives can be conflicting, and there is a requirement to choose one of the trade-off solutions [3].

In this research work, multi-objective optimization algorithm, i.e., Non-dominated Sorting Genetic Algorithm-II (NSGA-II) is utilized. A novel Multi-objective Data Aggregation Clustering (MDAC) technique is proposed, in which seven objective functions are defined: total energy needed by nodes for sending the data aggregated by CH to BS, total energy required for cluster member nodes which are transmitting their data directly to BS, inverse of overall energy level of CHs, the overall energy needed for cluster members to transmit their data to the CHs, overall energy of cluster member nodes, inverse of the count of cluster members, and the energy level required for sending the data by CH to the cluster nodes. Each solution based on NSGA-II algorithm in a solution set results in a different topology of network. According to the determined criteria, one of these topologies is chosen, based on different attributes such as overall residual network energy at the end of simulation iterations, number of iterations for which CHs can live, count of the data transmissions between CH and member nodes, and number of the data transmissions between BS and CHs. Additionally, in the proposed technique, BS determines the CHs and cluster members.

The rest of the paper is organized as follows: In Sect. 2, the existing work related to multi-objective optimization in WSNs is presented. Section 3 presents a brief description of NSGA-II algorithm. Section 4 presents the proposed MDAC technique and presentation of optimum solutions in solution set of the problem. In Sect. 5, the methodology is discussed to obtain the solutions from a set which includes optimum solutions and the simulation scenario is also presented along with clustering. The experimental setup is presented in Sect. 6 which is used for performance evaluation and results. Section 7 presents the conclusion and future scope.

2 Related Work

The main objective of multi-objective optimization algorithms is to optimize the conflicting goals in WSNs simultaneously. Most of these algorithms try to optimize the consumption of energy while considering other conflicting goals together. Jin et al. [4] presented a technique for cluster formation based on the minimum communication distance using genetic algorithm (GA). The fitness function utilized in this method is based on the total distance between the BS and CHs, total distance between the CHs and non-CHs nodes, and the difference between the number of all nodes and the number of CHs to optimize the number of CHs and communication distance. Weights are assigned to the input parameters, which transform the multi-dimensional optimization problem to single dimension.

Hussain et al. [5] presented a technique for cluster formation based on GA, in which fitness function is calculated in terms of the total distance between the BS and nodes, total distance between CHs and non-CH nodes and distance between CHs and BS, standard deviation of the distances from CHs, the energy dissipation for the transmission of gathered data from CH to BS, and the number of trans-missions. A weighting coefficient is assigned to each parameter in fitness function, which can adaptively be updated in each iteration. However, the multi-objective optimization problem is transformed as single objective.

Peiravi et al. [6] proposed an algorithm which is based on Pareto-optimal method and results in generation of number of optimum solution points rather than a single optimum solution. The main objective is to optimize the network lifetime and the number of the hops between nodes and BS. There is a need of centralized control in this approach. Ozdemir et al. [7] presented a Multi-objective Evolutionary Algorithm based on Decomposition (MOEA/D) to optimize the energy conservation and to maintain required coverage in clustering-based WSNs.

In data aggregation, the main objective is to find the optimal spanning tree in WSNs. The objectives of aggregation tree are defined in terms of four metrics. Lu et al. [8] presented a new algorithm, i.e., Jumping Particle Swarm Optimization (JPSO), which addresses this issue by presenting an adaptive double layer encoding scheme and results in Pareto-optimal solution. Jameii et al. [9] presented Multi-objective Optimization Coverage and Topology Control (MOOCTC), in which several conflicting objectives are optimized such as number of active sensor nodes, coverage, and network connectivity. The domain-specific knowledge is considered while obtaining the required solution along with learning automata which can adapt the mutation and crossover rates dynamically without external control.

Prasad et al. [10] proposed Multi-objective Particle Swarm Optimization Dif-ferential Evolution (MOPSO-DE) approach for efficient clustering of nodes in WSNs. CHs are selected based on fitness functions in terms of transmission energy and distance between source and destination. Residual energy and signal strength of neighboring nodes are also considered while routing the data and selection of CH. Ali et al. [11] presented a Multi-objective Particle Swarm Optimization (MOPSO) algorithm. The main objective is to provide an energy-efficient solution by optimizing the number of clusters in a WSN. It is based on calculated node degree and residual energy of nodes. It generates a solution set at a time. Attea et al. [12] utilized NSGA-II algorithm to take decision regarding location of mobile sensor nodes in order to provide longer network lifetime and high coverage. The main objective of this algorithm is to maximize both number of detected targets and network lifetime.

Xue et al. [13] utilized a Multi-objective Differential Evolution (MODE) algorithm in which latency and energy are considered to generate optimal routes between source and destination. Konstantinidis et al. [14] presented an optimized solution for the deployment and for determining the energy levels of transmission of sensors based on Multi-objective Evolutionary Algorithm based on Decomposition (MOEA/D).

3   NSGA-II Algorithm: A Brief Overview

Deb et al. [15] proposed NSGA-II algorithm for multi-objective optimization. NSGA-II is based on non-dominated sorting and genetic algorithm (GA). NSGA-II algorithm initializes a population with random deoxyribonucleic acid (DNA). All the objective functions are evaluated for each individual of the population, and values of results are captured in cost vector for each individual. An individual is said to be dominated, if the values of its cost vector are smaller than the element values of cost vectors of other individuals. The population is divided into several fronts in NSGA-II algorithm. In first front, those individuals are included which are non-dominated. In the next front, individuals which are influenced by first front individuals are included. Similarly, the successive fronts are generated. Rank value is maintained to store the information regarding the front to which an individual belongs. To analyze the similarity index between the solutions given by the individuals of the same front, crowding distance parameter is also calculated which is directly proportional to the diversity in the population.

4   The Proposed Multi-objective Data Aggregation Technique

The proposed method is based on centralized control architecture in which position of all nodes is known and stationary. Nodes adjust their transmitter range for long-range communication accordingly. Nodes can directly communicate with CH or a BS. CHs collect the gathered data in their clusters via data aggregation and send the aggregated data to the BS. Further, all nodes have equal chances to become CH in the homogenous network model assumed.

4.1 Multi-objective Data Aggregation Clustering Problem

Decision parameter 1: To determine the state of a node

Initially, the sequences are generated randomly based on population size used in NSGA-II and consist of 1 and 0. Table 1 represents the arbitrary sequences generated for 10 nodes apart from BS in a network. A solution for each individual is presented in each row in the population. For instance, for 'Individual' 1, 6, 5, 4, 3 are elected as CHs with value represented by 1 from right to left.

Decision parameter 2: Cluster Formation

Nodes are assigned to those CHs, with which they are having minimum distance than any other CH. The solutions for all individuals in a set are evaluated in the population based on NSGA-II algorithm one at a time.

Objective Functions: NSGA-II algorithm is used to solve multi-objective problems. Out of these 7 functions, six functions are based on energy parameter and the other one is based on CHs' count. The various objective functions in proposed MDAC are defined as in Table 2:

Table 1 Individual population

Node number	1	2	3	4	5	6	7	8	9	10
DNA of individual 1	0	0	1	1	1	1	0	0	0	0

Table 2 Objective functions in proposed MDAC

Objectives	Objective function
Objective 1: To minimize the total energy consumption of cluster member nodes for transmitting their data to their own CHs as given by (1)	$F_1 = \sum Energy_{Non - CH\,To\,CH}$ (1)
Objective 2: To minimize the total energy of non-CH nodes as defined by (2)	$F_2 = \sum Energy_{Non - CH}$ (2)
Objective 3: To maximize the total energy of CHs as given by (3)	$F_3 = \frac{1}{\sum Energy_{CH}}$ (3)
Objective 4: To maximize the number of non-CH nodes as given by (4)	$F_4 = \frac{1}{N}$ (4) Here, N denotes the number of cluster member nodes.
Objective 5: To minimize energy of CH, which dissipates the maximum energy to make a transmission to its member nodes as given by (5)	$F_5 = \max(Energy_{CH\,to\,Sink})$ (5)
Objective 6: To minimize the total energy consumption of CHs in order to send their aggregated data to BS as defined in (6)	$F_6 = \sum Energy_{CH - Sink}$ (6)
Objective 7: Minimizing the total energy consumption of cluster member nodes to communicate with BS directly as given in (7)	$F_7 = \sum Energy_{Non - CH\,to\,Sink}$ (7)

4.2 Using NSGA-II Algorithm for Clustering

The values of $F_1, F_2, F_3, \ldots\ldots\ldots F_7$ are calculated for each individual which is initialized by random DNA initially. Therefore, for each individual, costs of seven objective functions are calculated. Further, in order to choose between individuals and NSGA-II, four additional parameters are considered such as domination set, rank, crowding distance, and number of dominated individuals. Domination set is represented in the form of a vector which includes all those individuals which are influenced by a particular individual. Cost vector of an i individual and a j individual is given by (8).

$$Cost_i = [F_{1i} \quad F_{2i} \quad F_{3i} \quad F_{4i} \quad F_{5i} \quad F_{6i} \quad F_{7i}]; \ i = 1, 2 \ldots\ldots n_{pop}; \ i \neq j \quad (8)$$

$$Cost_j = [F_{1j} \quad F_{2j} \quad F_{3j} \quad F_{4j} \quad F_{5j} \quad F_{6j} \quad F_{7j}]; \ j = 1, 2 \ldots\ldots n_{pop}; \ j \neq i \quad (9)$$

In (8–9), F_{ki} represents the value obtained by ith individual from the kth cost function and also denotes the count of individuals utilized in NSGA-II. Conditionally, if the individual i dominates individual j, the relationship between $Cost_i$ and $Cost_j$ is given by (10):

$$F_{ki} \leq F_{kj}; \ k \, [1 \ldots 7] \quad (10)$$

If (10) is satisfied, then j must exist in the domination set for the individual i, which is given by (11):

$$ds_i = [j \, k \, l \, m] \, ; \ j \neq k \neq l \neq m \quad (11)$$

Based on (11), individual i dominates the individuals j, q, l, and m. The number of individuals which are dominated should be at least 1 for jth individual. Initially, the count of dominated value is initialized with 0 and is incremented for every domination by 1. The value of the number of dominated values is represented by (nd_j) for which jth individual will be updated by (12):

$$if \ F_{ki} \leq F_{kj} \ is \ true \ for \ k \ nd_j = nd_j + 1 \quad (12)$$

Assume that jth individual is dominated only by ith individual (nd_j). If individual i is not under the influence of any other individual, nd_i will be 0. Hence, rank of individual i is 1. Individual i and values of those individuals which are not dominated by other will be stored in vector V_1. In the next step, to obtain vector V_2, nd is decremented by 1 for all the individuals present in the domination set vector of i, since it is calculated as $nd_j = nd_j - 1 = 0$. Accordingly, 1 is decreased from nd_i of the individuals in domination set vectors of all other individuals in V_1 vector. Afterward, the process is repeated for the whole V_1 vector, in which those individuals are included which are not part of V_1 and having $nd = 0$ in V_2. The whole process is repeated to obtain vectors such as $V_3, V_4, \ldots \ldots \ldots V_p$. This process for getting V vectors is named as non-dominated sorting.

After this step, the calculation of crowding distance (c_d) is performed, for which individuals in a V_q, are sorted from smaller to larger or larger to smaller according to their cost values. A separate cost value and distance are calculated with respect to each objective function. The crowding distance of the individuals at the top or end is assigned as ∞ according to some cost. These values that are chosen by the individuals in vector V_1 from kth cost function are sorted in descending order, as given by (13):

$$[F_{k1}\ F_{k3}\ F_{k2}\ F_{k7}\ F_{k10}] \tag{13}$$

The individual number a will get the minimum value, and individual number b will get the maximum value from kth objective function according to sorting. The distance of the individuals included in V_1 vector to the kth objective function is given by (14):

$$d(3,k) = \frac{|F_{k2} - F_{k1}|}{|F_{k1} - F_{k0}|}\ ; d(2,k) = \frac{|F_{k7} - F_{k3}|}{|F_{k1} - F_{k10}|}\ ; d(7,k) = \frac{|F_{k10} - F_{k2}|}{|F_{k1} - F_{k10}|}\ ;$$
$$d(1,k) = \infty\ ; d(10,k) = \infty \tag{14}$$

In (14), $d(m,k)$ represents the distance value of individual m according to the kth objective function which is calculated for each individual in the same V vectors. The crowding distance value (cd_m) of mth individual is given by (15) as:

$$cd_m = \sum_{k=1}^{7} d(m,k) \tag{15}$$

According to the crowding distance and rank of individuals, sorting can be performed. After sorting, an individual is selected from the top position with high probability.

5 Selection of a Clustering-Based Network Topology

For every solution existing in set of solutions generated by NSGA-II algorithm, simulation is performed one after the other under the same scenario. NSGA-II simulations and solutions derived on the basis of NSGA-II are performed at BS which has sufficient energy resources to perform operations. In the last phase of every round, topology is decided by BS, which is further disseminated to every node by BS. Hence, every node will switch to listening mode. In addition, nodes which are elected as CH will disseminate Time Division Multiple Access (TDMA) schedule to all cluster members in every round. Data aggregation is performed by CHs within a cluster and transmitted to the BS.

Solution set includes the individuals obtained after NSGA-II algorithm's last iteration. Initially, the BS reduces the energy dissipated by the nodes in receiving the information related to network topology sent by BS itself. It is assumed that network topology will be determined by BS again in every K rounds. Some nodes already selected as CHs can have direct communication with BS based on the determined topology in NSGA-II algorithm, since some CHs do not have any other node apart from themselves. On the basis of TDMA, every node is assigned a transmission time. CHs send the information regarding TDMA schedule and energy level to its cluster members in each round. If a node fails to get TDMA schedule, it means that its CH's energy has exhausted and transmission by the node is interrupted until a topology is determined and communicated by the BS. Every node transmits its data to the respective CHs unless network topology is not determined and information regarding energy is not received. In the ending phase of each iteration, the values of variables given by (16) are calculated for each solution.

$$
\begin{aligned}
S_{1i} &= \frac{L_i}{Max(L_1, L_2...L_s)} \; ; \; S_{2i} = \frac{N_i}{Max(N_1, N_2...N_s)} \; ; \\
S_{3i} &= \frac{E_{toti}}{Max(E_{tot1}, E_{tot2}........E_{tots})} \\
S_{4i} &= \frac{CHS_{min_i}}{Max(CHS_{min_1}, CHS_{min_2}, CHS_{min_s})} \; ; \\
S_{5i} &= \frac{NCH_i}{Max(NCH_1, NCH_2......NCH_s)}
\end{aligned}
\tag{16}
$$

Based on above equations, five parameters are calculated named $S_{1i}, S_{2i}, S_{3i}, S_{4i}$ and S_{5i} for ith solution with solution S_{number} fetched by NSGA-II algorithm. Here, L_i depict number of rounds till the death of every cluster head, N_i depicts the count of active nodes, E_{toti} represents the total residual energy, CHS_{min_i} denotes number of times the CH which has the least number of communications with BS makes a communication, and NCH_i shows the count of packets received by CHs. The selected or all of the above discussed variables are gathered to select a solution type.

6 Experimental Setup and Results

The evaluation of performance of proposed MDAC technique is performed through NS2.34 simulator. The proposed MDAC technique is compared with existing MOOCTC [9], MOPSO [11], MOPSO-DE [10], and JPSO [8] in the terms of different parameters: number of data packets received, energy consumption, convergence rate, number of active nodes, network lifetime, and throughput. For the

Table 3 Simulation parameters

Simulation parameters	WSN1	WSN2
Area covered	100 × 100 m	100 × 100 m
Deployment mode	Randomly deployed	Randomly deployed
Location of sink	Center of area	100 m to closest node
Number of nodes	100	100
Packet length (k)	2000 bits	2000 bits
Initial node energy	0.5 J	0.5 J
E_{elec}	50 nJ/bit	50 nJ/bit
Data aggregation energy	5 nJ/bit	5 nJ/bit
ε_{mp}	100 pJ/bit/m^2	100 pJ/bit/m^2

calculation of energy loss in each node for communicating with the other nodes, an energy model of physical layer is assumed [16].

Table 3 enlists the experimental setup settings along with its values. The various NSGA-II parameters along their values are shown in Table 4 for proposed MDAC approach. The simulation results depend upon the updation time period of BS and parameters presented in (19). Furthermore, CH nodes can send advertisement message and have transmission range to reach all the nodes within a cluster in a single-hop manner.

Test Case 1: Energy Consumption with varying Node Density: The value of total energy consumption for the proposed MDAC technique and existing JPSO, MOPSO-DE, MOPSO, and MOOCTC techniques is calculated with varying number of nodes (20–100). As the node density is increasing, the energy consumption value also increases. Figure 1 depicts the lesser energy consumption in MDAC as compared to other techniques with varying number of nodes. The energy consumption value is minimum at 6.43 J in MDAC at 20 nodes. Average energy consumption in MDAC is 7.14%, 8.127%, 11.45%, 13.16%, and 15.69% lesser as compared to MOPSO, MOPSO-DE, MOOCTC, and JPSO, respectively. The reason for this huge variation in performance is as follows: In JPSO, intra-cluster routing optimal spanning tree is generated. Therefore, every time when there is occurrence of cluster reformation, it results in generation of optimal tree. With the increasing node density, the energy consumption also increases for the formation of network structure. In MOOCTC, the whole process of cluster generation is based on encoding scheme which further results in energy dissipation whenever a network change occurs. Although the energy consumption of MOOCTC and the MOPSO-DE is more or less same, still it is considered that the performance of proposed technique is better than existing techniques.

Test Case 2: Network Lifetime versus Node Density: The network lifetime value has been calculated for proposed MDAC and existing JPSO, MOPSO, MOPSO-DE, and MOOCTC with varying node density based on (Eq. 10). The value of network lifetime is decreasing, as the node density increases (20–100), for existing techniques. The reason behind this performance is incurred overhead in

Table 4 NSGA-II
parameters

Parameters	WSN1	WSN2
Mutation rate	0.1	0.1
Crossover rate	0.9	0.9
Population size	50	100
Number of iterations	150	150

Fig. 1 Energy consumption
versus number of nodes

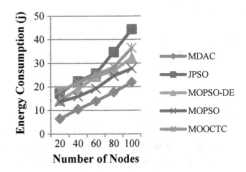

terms of communication during formation of topology. The value of network lifetime in MDAC is more as compared to MOOCTC, MOPSO-DE, MOPSO, and JPSO for varying number of nodes as depicted in Fig. 2. The network lifetime value is maximum at 129 s for 20 nodes. Average network lifetime in MDAC is 13.13%, 14.11%, 16.21%, and 19.07% more as compared to JPSO, MOPSO, MOPSO-DE, and MOOCTC, respectively.

Test Case 3: Number of active nodes versus Number of iterations: The number of active nodes values has been evaluated for MDAC, MOOCTC, MOPSO-DE, MOPSO, and JPSO with the increase in number of iterations (1–100). A node is considered as *active node* if its present residual energy is more than zero and there must be at least one CH within its range. As the number of iterations is increasing, the number of active nodes decreases due to energy dissipation. The value of number of active nodes is maximum for 86 at 19 iterations. Number of active node

Fig. 2 Network lifetime
versus number of nodes

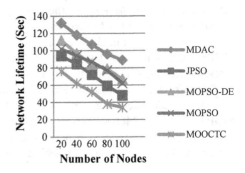

Fig. 3 Number of active nodes versus number of iterations

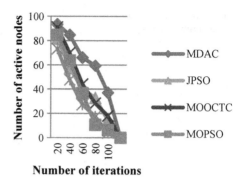

in MDAC is 16.28%, 15.18%, 11.79%, and 9.13% more as compared to MOOCTC, MOPSO, JPSO, and MOPSO-DE, respectively, as shown in Fig. 3.

Test Case 4: Residual Energy versus Data Packets Received: The value of data packets received is calculated with respect to *residual energy* for proposed MDAC technique and existing MOOCTC, MOPSO-DE, MOPSO, and JPSO techniques. As shown in Fig. 4, data packets' receiving rate is decreasing, with the decrease in residual energy. Initially, maximum number of packets is transferring at 7.9 J energy residual, but MDAC, JPSO, and MOPSO are receiving approximate similar amount of data packets.

At 7.45 J residual energy, MDAC receives 1.93%, 17.21%, 18.13%, and 18.26% more data packets than MOPSO, MOOCTC, MOPSO-DE, and JPSO, respectively. The maximum number of data packets received in MDAC is 7.91 at 7.9 J residual energy, and the minimum number of data packets received in MDAC is at 3.8 J. The average number of data packets received in MDAC is 2.69%, 12.76%, 13.91%, and 20.95% more than MOPSO, MOOCTC, JPSO, and MOPSO-DE, respectively.

Test Case 5: Network Lifetime variation wrt varying selection priorities of solutions from NSGA-II: Solution set which is calculated based on NSGA-II algorithm has desired characteristics and has maximum value of parameters in Eq. (17). By taking $K = 300$, $M = 5$, the influence of $S_{1i}, S_{2i}, S_{3i} \ldots S_{5i}$ is considered for calculating the required solution, and the performance for the selection of the nodes maximizing the values in (18), (19) by BS is analyzed.

$$T_i = S_{1i} + S_{2i} + S_{3i} + S_{4i} + S_{5i} \tag{17}$$

$$T_i = S_{1i} + S_{2i} + S_{3i} \tag{18}$$

$$T_i = S_{1i} + S_{2i} + S_{3i} + S_{4i} \tag{19}$$

In solutions based on the (17), the biggest solution is selected, which means those solutions are selected in which survival of more number of nodes is possible

Fig. 4 Received data packets
versus residual energy

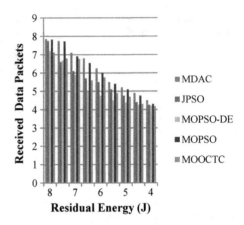

and the total residual energy of the active nodes is maximum as shown in Fig. 6.
Based on (19), those solutions are selected in which more active nodes survives,
nodes have maximum residual energy, and the communication distance between
CH and BS is maximum. Solutions obtained from (17) have solutions in which
survival of more nodes is possible, total residual energy of the active nodes is
maximized, and the communication between CH to BS and CHs to other nodes is
maximum. It is shown in Fig. 5 that the priority in a solution is given to maximize
the network lifetime and the solution having maximum value of (18) is selected.
Therefore, network lifetime will be longer as it can be expected.

*Test Case 6: Total packets received Variations at BS with varying selection
priorities of solutions from NSGA-II:* As shown in Fig. 6, selection of solutions to
maximize the parameter in (19) transmits a large amount of data to BS.

Fig. 5 Network lifetime
variation via varying selection
priorities of solutions

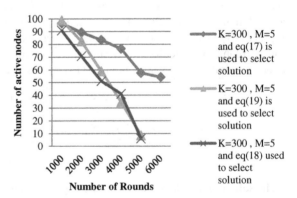

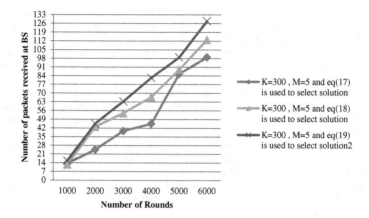

Fig. 6 Total received packets variation at BS via varying selection priorities of solutions

7 Conclusion and Future Scope

In this research work, a Multi-objective Data Aggregation Clustering (MDAC) technique is proposed, in which NSGA-II algorithm is utilized for providing optimal solutions in case multi-objectives which may be conflicting in nature. Seven objective functions are defined, out of which six are based on energy parameter and the last one is based on count of CHs. By utilizing NSGA-II algorithm which is primarily used for solving multi-objective problems, a solution set is generated in which each solution results in different topology. The performance evaluation shows that the proposed MDAC technique is better than existing techniques in terms of active number of nodes, network lifetime, total received packets, and energy consumption. In future, the proposed technique can be improved by considering mobility and multiple sinks in order to balance the load.

References

1. Akyildiz I. F., Su W., Sankarasubramaniam Y. & Cayirci E.: A survey on sensor networks. IEEE Communications magazine. 40(8), 102–114, (2002).
2. Akyildiz I. F. & Vuran M. C.: Wireless sensor networks. Networks. Vol. 4, (2010), John Wiley & Sons.
3. Iqbal M., Naeem M., Anpalagan A., Ahmed A. and Azam M.: Wireless Sensor Network Optimization: Multi-objective Paradigm. Sensors. 15, 17572–17620, (2015).
4. Jin S., Zhou M. & Wu A. S.: Sensor network optimization using a genetic algorithm. In Proceedings of the 7th World Multi-conference on Systematics, Cybernetics and Informatics. pp. 109–116, (2003).
5. Hussain S., Matin A. W., & Islam O.: Genetic algorithm for hierarchical wireless sensor networks. Journal of Networks. 2(5), 87–97, (2013).

6. Peiravi A., Mashhadi H. R. & Javadi S.H.: An optimal energy-efficient clustering method in wireless sensor networks using multi-objective genetic algorithm. International Journal of Communication Systems. 26(1), 114–126, (2013).

7. Ozdemir S., Bara'a A. A. & Khalil O. A.: Multi-objective evolutionary algorithm based on decomposition for energy efficient coverage in wireless sensor networks. Wireless personal communications. 71(1), 195–213, (2013).

8. Lu Y., Chen J., Comsa I., Kuonen P., Hirsbrunnera B.: Construction of data aggregation tree for multi-objectives in wireless sensor networks through jump particle swarm optimization. In: 18th International Conference on Knowledge-Based and Intelligent Information & Engineering Systems - KES2014. Vol. 35, 73–82, (2014).

9. Jameii S. M., Faez K., & Dehghan: M. Multi-objective optimization for topology and coverage control in wireless sensor networks. International Journal of Distributed Sensor Networks. Vol. 2015, 1–11, (2015).

10. Prasad D. R., Naganjaneyulu P. V., Prasad K. S.: Energy Efficient Clustering in Multi-hop Wireless Sensor Networks Using Differential Evolutionary MOPSO. Brazilian Archives of Biology and Technology. 59(2), 1–15, (2016).

11. Ali H., Shahzad W. & Khan F. A.: Energy-efficient clustering in mobile ad-hoc networks using multi-objective particle swarm optimization. Applied Soft Computing. 12(7), 1913–1928, (2012).

12. Bara'a A. A., Khalil E. A. & Cosar A.: Multi-objective evolutionary routing protocol for efficient coverage in mobile sensor networks. Soft Computing. 19(10), 2983–2995, (2015).

13. Xue F., Sanderson A. & Graves R.: Multi-objective routing in wireless sensor networks with a differential evolution algorithm. In: Proceedings of 2006 IEEE International Conference on Networking, Sensing and Control. pp. 880–885, (2006).

14. Konstantinidis A., Yang K., Zhang Q. & Zeinalipour-Yazti D.: A multi-objective evolutionary algorithm for the deployment and power assignment problem in wireless sensor networks. Computer networks. 54(6), 960–976, (2010).

15. Deb K., Pratap A., Agarwal S. & Meyarivan T. A. M. T.: A fast and elitist multi-objective genetic algorithm: NSGA-II. IEEE Transactions on Evolutionary Computation. 6(2), 182–197, (2002).

16. Randhawa S. and Jain S.: An intelligent PSO based load balancing in Wireless Sensor Networks. Turkish journal of Electrical Engineering and Computer Sciences. Online [accepted].

Multi-objective Assessment of Wind/BES Siting and Sizing in Electric Distribution Network

Kumari Kasturi and M. R. Nayak

Abstract The paper presents a multi-objective genetic algorithm (MOGA), which is used to allocate the wind/battery energy storage (BES) considering the annual operating cost and annual cost of power loss incorporated with distribution system. The developed platform is implemented on 69-bus radial distribution system (RDS) considering intermittent renewable power as wind which is supported by battery energy storage to overcome the power deficit. An efficient battery management strategy is adopted to prevent overcharging/discharging of the battery. The achieved results signify the high potential of optimizing algorithm for the studied system objectives and enhancing the techno-economics of the distribution system using MOGA.

Keywords Distribution system · Battery energy storage · Genetic algorithm
Wind

1 Introduction

The ever-increasing demand of energy and environmental concerns has increased the importance of hybrid power generation using renewable energy sources integrated to distribution systems. Unpredictability of natural resources gives raises to the problem of power reliabity, which can be mitigated by using battery energy storage (BES) system. The use of wind turbine and BES provides flexible injection of power to the utility grid [1] by storing the energy when price is low and giving at comparatively higher price to the grid.

K. Kasturi (✉) · M. R. Nayak
Department of Electrical Engineering, Siksha 'o' Anusandhan University,
Bhubaneswar 751030, Odisha, India
e-mail: kumari.kasturi1986@gmail.com

M. R. Nayak
e-mail: manasnk72@gmail.com

© Springer Nature Singapore Pte Ltd. 2018
P. K. Pattnaik et al. (eds.), *Progress in Computing, Analytics and Networking*,
Advances in Intelligent Systems and Computing 710,
https://doi.org/10.1007/978-981-10-7871-2_39

The research work on placement of distributed generation (DG) optimally has drawn the attention of researchers for the last 20 years [2]. Different methods are adopted to solve this problem. A methodology based on power production curve and average daily load is presented using genetic algorithm (GA) to find out optimal placing and sizing of DG units [3, 4]. A fuzzy decision-based multi-objective with a self-adaptive GA is used to get appropriate type for sustainable energy with considering power loss, voltage offset and operating cost [5]. The benefit of using BESS under time of use pricing (TOU) is evaluated referring to the optimal sizing of battery [6]. Determination of sizing of battery storage system using meta-heuristic algorithm for minimizing investment cost and losses of photovoltaic (PV)-wind hybrid system connected to the grid is given in [7, 8].

In the present article, a multi-objective genetic algorithm (MOGA) is promoted to optimize the allocation of both wind turbine and BES in distribution system to reduce the annual operating cost of wind, battery energy storage (BES) and annual cost of power loss in the grid. The technical advantages and computational cost scenarios for the proposed study using MOGA are discussed. Integration of wind turbine and BES in 69-bus radial distribution system considering intermittent nature of renewable resources incorporated with uncertain power demand and time of use pricing (TOU) is presented.

The residue of this paper is assembled as follows: in Sect. 2, modelling of system is described, whereas Sect. 3 presents the problem formulation. In Sect. 4, energy management strategy is briefed, and MOGA is described in Sect. 5. Result and discussion are illustrated in Sect. 6. At last, Sect. 7 concludes the paper.

2 Modelling of the System

Wind and BES units are connected to RDS at load bus. An inverter is used to convert the power as AC–DC or DC–AC as per the requirements of BES. As per the IEEE 1547 standard, active power and reactive power can be generated through wind and BES. Gelled Electrolyte Sealed Batteries which are a kind of valve-regulated lead acid battery (VRLA) are considered due to need of frequent charging and discharging. Backward and forward sweep-based algorithms have been used for distribution system load flow analysis [9].

2.1 Modelling of the Wind Turbine

The speed of the wind turbine varies with respect to height, so the measured wind speed must be calculated in terms of hub height as

$$v_w = v_{0,ref} \left(\frac{h_w}{h_{0,ref}} \right)^{\sigma} \tag{1}$$

where v_w is the wind speed at the hub height h_w and $v_{0,ref}$ is the wind speed at $h_{0,ref}$ height with σ is the coefficient of friction [10] which is generally taken as 1/7.

Power generated by the wind turbine can be calculated as

$$P_w = \begin{cases} 0 & v < v_{cut,in}, v > v_{cut,out} \\ v^3 \left(\frac{P_{rated}}{v_{rated}^3 - v_{cut,in}^3} \right) - P_{rated} \left(\frac{v_{cut,in}^3}{v_{raeted}^3 - v_{cut,in}^3} \right) & v_{cut,in} \le v < v_{rated} \\ P_{reated} & v_{rated} \le v \le v_{cut,out} \end{cases} \tag{2}$$

where P_{rated}, v_{rated} are the rated power and rated speed of wind turbine, respectively, v is the wind speed which is collected from the Indian Meteorological Department (IMD) of the location of Bhubaneswar for the year 2015 [11], $v_{cut,in}, v_{cut,out}$ are the cut-in and cut-out speed, respectively. For this study, a 6 kW of wind turbine is chosen, which has hub height of 15 m, cut-in velocity of 2 m/s, cut-out velocity of 20 m/s, rated velocity of 14 m/s associated with capital cost of ₹1,097,096 and operation with maintenance cost of ₹20,384.

2.2 Modelling of Battery Energy Storage (BES) System

The status of the BES system at hour t is related to its status at hour $t - 1$, the output power of PV panel and the load demand at time t. At time t, the available capacity of BES can be calculated as follows:

During peak hour,

$$C_{bat}(t) = \begin{cases} C_{bat}(t-1)(1-\sigma), & SOC(t) \le SOC^{min} \\ C_{bat}(t-1)(1-\sigma) - [\frac{P_{load}(t)}{\eta_{inv}} - P_w(t)] \eta_{bat}, & SOC(t) > SOC^{min} \end{cases} \tag{3}$$

During off-peak hour,

$$C_{bat}(t) = \begin{cases} C_{bat}(t-1)(1-\sigma), & SOC(t) \ge SOC^{max} \\ C_{bat}(t-1)(1-\sigma) + (P_w(t)) \eta_{bat}, & SOC(t) < SOC^{max} \end{cases} \tag{4}$$

where $C_{bat}(t)$ and $C_{bat}(t-1)$ are the capacity of BES at hour t and $t-1$, respectively, P_{load} = load demand at hour t, η_{bat} = battery round trip efficiency. The state of charge (SOC) of the battery is updated every hour with the charging and discharging of power to and from the battery.

Charging

$$SOC(t) = SOC(t-1) \times (1-\sigma) + \eta_{ch\ arg\ ing} \frac{P_{dc,bat}(t)}{C_{bat}(t) \times V} \tag{5}$$

Discharging

$$SOC(t) = SOC(t-1) \times (1-\sigma) - \eta_{disch\ arg\ ing} \frac{P_{dc,bat}(t)}{C_{bat}(t) \times V} \tag{6}$$

where $SOC(t)$ and $SOC(t-1)$ are SOC of the battery at hour t and $t-1$, respectively, $P_{dc,bat}(t)$ is the charging/discharging rate of the battery. $P_{dc,bat}(t)$ is defined by using the equation

$$P_{dc,bat}(t) = E_{bat}(t) - E_{bat}(t-1) \tag{7}$$

where $E_{bat}(t)$ and $E_{bat}(t-1)$ are the stored energy in the battery (kWh) at hour t and $t-1$, respectively.

AC output at the AC bus bar is calculated as follows:

$$P_{bat,ac}(t) = P_{dc,bat}(t) \times \eta_{inv} \times \eta_{inv\_sb} \tag{8}$$

where η_{inv} = inverter efficiency = 97%, η_{inv_sb} = 99% (AC cable loss accounting to the voltage drop between the inverter and the primary switchboard, not more than 1%). A 296 Ah with 12V BES is chosen which has self-discharging factor (σ) of 2.5% per month, minimum state of charge (SOC^{min}) = 30%, maximum state of charge (SOC^{max}) = 90%, minimum charging/discharging time(t_{min}) of 10 h, BES round trip efficiency (η_{bat}) = 81%, BES charging/discharging efficiency $(\eta_{ch\ arg\ ing})$ = 90%, capital cost of ₹67,270, operation and maintenance cost of ₹672 [12, 13].

2.3 Modelling of the Load

The 24-h load demand is assumed to follow the IEEE reliability test system load profile [14] and a lagging power factor. The predicted load at bus i at any desired time t can be calculated as follows:

$$P_{Li}(t) = w_h(t) \times P_i \tag{9}$$

where $w_h(t)$ = hourly weight factor, P_i = peak load at bus i.

3 Problem Formulation

3.1 Objective Functions

3.1.1 Annual Operating Cost (AOC)

$$f_{obj,1} = AOC = ACC_{wind} + ACC_{BES} + AOMC_{wind} + AOMC_{BES} \qquad (10)$$

where ACC_{wind}, ACC_{BES} are the annualized capital cost of wind turbine and BES, respectively, $AOMC_{wind}, AOMC_{BES}$ are the annualized operation and maintenance cost of wind turbine and BES, respectively.

3.1.2 Annual Cost of Power Loss in Distribution System $(ACPL)$

$$f_{obj,2} = ACPL = \left\{ \left[\sum_{i=1}^{N} P_{Loss,i} \times k_p \right] + \left[\left(\sum_{t=1}^{n_t} P_{Loss,i}(t) \times k_e(t) \times Lsf \right) \times T \right] \right\}$$

$$(11)$$

$$P_{Loss,i}(t) = R_i I_i^2(t) \qquad (12)$$

where $i =$ branch number, $n_t =$ time slots (24 h), $R_i =$ resistance of the ith branch, $I_i(t) =$ current at ith branch at time t, $P_{Loss,i}(t) =$ power loss of ith branch at time t, $k_p =$ annual demand cost per unit of power loss (₹/kW) = 2400 ₹/kW, $k_e =$ time of use pricing (TOU) which is taken as 7.00 ₹/kWh and 5.00 ₹/kWh for peak hours and off-peak hours, respectively, $T =$ time period in hours and $Lsf =$ loss factor considered as 0.2.

3.2 System Operational Constraints

The solution of the optimization problem considers the following constraints:

(a) Active and reactive power flow balance equations as follows:

$$P_{sub}(t) + P_w(t) + P_{ac,bat}(t) = P_L(t) + P_{Loss}(t) \qquad (13)$$

$$Q_{sub}(t) + Q_w(t) + Q_{ac,bat}(t) = Q_L(t) + Q_{Loss}(t) \qquad (14)$$

(b) System quality constraints of distribution system:

System quality constraint is defined as voltage limit of distribution system due to connection of the wind turbine and BES which can be written as follows:

$$U_j^{\min} \leq U_j(t) \leq U_j^{\max} \tag{15}$$

(c) Security constraints of distribution system:

Security constraints are of feeder line loading limit which can be written as follows:

$$I_i(t) \leq I_i^{\max} \tag{16}$$

(d) Power supply constraints of wind turbine:

The wind power generation units have a maximum and minimum generating capacity beyond which it is not feasible to generate due to technical reasons.

Generating limits are specified as upper and lower limits as follows:

$$P_w^{\min} \leq P_w(t) \leq P_w^{\max} \tag{17}$$

(e) Energy supply constraints of BES can be written as follows:

The lower and upper limit of the energy in the BES unit should be satisfied as follows:

$$P_{dc,bat}^{\min} \leq P_{dc,bat}(t) \leq P_{dc,bat}^{\max} \tag{18}$$

(f) SOC of BES should be maintained within a specified range:

$$SOC^{\min} \leq SOC(t) \leq SOC^{\max} \tag{19}$$

where $P_{sub}(t)$ and $Q_{sub}(t)$ are the active and reactive power injection of substation at time t, respectively, $Q_{pv\_ac}(t)$ is the reactive power output of the PV units at time t, respectively. $Q_{Loss}(t)$ is the total reactive power loss at time t, $U_j(t)$ is the voltage of bus j, $U_j^{\min}$ and $U_j^{\max}$ are the minimum and maximum voltage of bus j, $I_i^{\max}$ is the maximum current at ith branch, $P_w^{\min}$ and $P_w^{\max}$ are the minimum and maximum output power of wind turbine, respectively, $P_{dc,bat}^{\min}$ and $P_{dc,bat}^{\max}$ are the minimum and maximum DC output power of the battery, respectively.

4   Energy Management Strategy of Wind and BES

The proposed system generates the power based on the unpredictable load demand to operate the split power between wind, BES and grid. SOC of the BES should be within a specified range between $SOC^{\max}$ and $SOC^{\min}$. The power is drawn from utility grid to charge BES during off-peak hour, if SOC of BES is less than SOC^{max}. During peak hour, if soc of BES is greater than SOC^{min}, the battery discharges to the grid as well as the wind supplies power to the grid. If SOC of BES is less than or equal to SOC^{max}, the battery remains idle. The power delivering/consuming to the grid (P_{grid}) can be written as follows:

$$P_{grid}\ (t) = P_{L,i}\ (t) - P_w\ (t) - P_{bat,\ ac}^{disch}\ (t) \tag{20}$$

$$P_{grid}\ (t) = P_{L,i}\ (t) - P_w\ (t) \tag{21}$$

5 Genetic Algorithm

For global optimization, the operations of GA are explained in Fig. 1.

5.1 Genetic Algorithm Process

Initial population:

Initially, a population of size N_g is randomly generated in the feasible space. The population is encoded in "double vector" and then discrete in case of mixed integer programming. The number of individuals (population size) remains unchanged throughout the process, and the optimal solution accuracy depends on the size of population and number of generation.

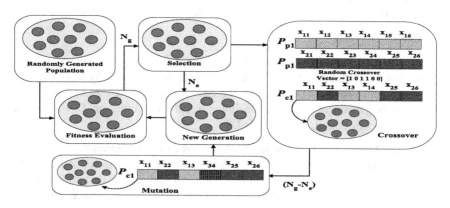

Fig. 1 Flow chart of GA and operation

Fitness evaluation:

The objective function is evaluated by utilizing each population group. Then a value on each individual solution is assigned that gives a measure of the solution quality. A rank is assigned to each individual solution for scaling of the objective function. In this process, the best individual is selected; i.e. the minimal function value receives the maximal fitness value with greater chance for survival and vice versa.

Selection:

The individuals from the population are selected pair wise for genetic operations after completing the fitness evaluation and create offspring/child population. In this selection process, the individual's selection probability is proportional to the individual's fitness. Thus, it ensures that the high-quality solutions will be selected and become parents of many child populations. The best selections are designed to maintain diverse population, whereas other selection process that does not take part is directly copied to the next generation called elitism which preserves the best solution for the next generation. The number of individuals with best fitness values in the current generation is guaranteed to survive to the next generation by the elite count (N_e).

Crossover or Recombination:

New individuals are produced by combining the information of two individuals, i.e. parents. The parents are selected by the selection process so that the child population are expected to inherit good genes. The scattered crossover is utilized for crossover operation in which a binary vector is created. The genes are selected from the first and second parents when the vector is a 1 and 0, respectively, in order to diversify genes in the expected child population. This crossover scheme is applied iteratively until the desired number of child population is generated. The crossover scheme will produce ($N_g - N_e$) child population.

Mutation:

It introduces random changes in the genes of the individual. The Gaussian scheme is employed for mutation operation. The new individual created by mutation does not vary a lot from the original one as the mutation fraction is kept low. Mutation reintroduces genetic diversity in the individuals. Thus, mutation GA helps the search for global optimization [15, 16].

Fuzzy Set Theory for Extracting the Best Compromised Solution

The fuzzy set theory is a reliable selection technique which is applied over the Pareto optimal set of non-dominated individuals to find out the best compromised solution. Due to the decision maker's inexact conclusion, the ith objective function H_i is represented by a membership function λ_i defined as follows:

$$\lambda_i = \begin{cases} 1 & H_i \leq H_i^{\min} \\ \dfrac{H_i^{\min} - H_i}{H_i^{\max} - H_i^{\min}} & H_i^{\min} \langle\, H_i \,\langle\, H_i^{\max} \\ 0 & H_i \geq H_i^{\max} \end{cases} \tag{22}$$

where $H_i^{\min}$ and $H_i^{\max}$ are the minimum and maximum value of ith objective function among all non-dominated solutions, respectively. For each non-dominated solution w, the normalized membership function λ^w is calculated as follows:

$$\lambda^w = \frac{\sum_{i=1}^{N_{obj}} \lambda_i^w}{\sum_{k=1}^{M} \sum_{i=1}^{N_{obj}} \lambda_i^w} \tag{23}$$

where M is the number of non-dominated solutions. The best compromised solution is that having the maximum value of λ^w.

6 Results and Discussion

The proposed MOGA optimization technique was tested in RDS for different cases. The parameters of MOGA used in simulation are crossover probability = 0.85, and the mutation probability are set to 0.3 and 0.5. The number of generation 100 with population size 50 was used as the termination criterion. The analysis of the proposed algorithm for allocation of wind and BES units in RDS was carried out at 0.86 leading power factor. The system is 69-bus large-scale RDS. Power flow calculation is performed using base value 100 MVA and 12.66 kV. The load bus is considered as location for wind and BES units. The bus voltage is limited to 0.95–1.05 pu. The peak hours of the day are considered as from 7 a.m. to 1 p.m. and 4 p.m. to 10 p.m., the rest of the hours as off-peak hours. The variables (location and size of wind and BES units) with best solutions are given in Table 1 with the distribution of Pareto solutions are shown in Fig. 2 using MOGA.

Table 1 Optimization results

Name of the parameter	Before integration of wind and BES	After integration of wind and BES
Optimal location of wind turbine	–	61
Optimal location of BES	–	19
Optimal no. of wind turbine	–	2
Optimal no. of BES	–	256
Annual operating cost (AOC) in ₹	–	5762512
Annual cost of power loss (ACPL) in ₹	170005022	74654394

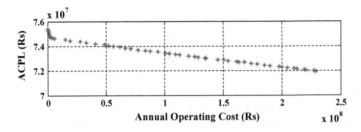

Fig. 2 Pareto front

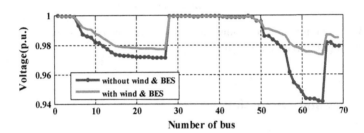

Fig. 3 Voltage profile of 69-bus system

Improved voltage profile after installation of wind and BES units for all buses are shown in Fig. 3.

As in Fig. 4, BES remains idle from the start of the day to 7 a.m. as it has maximum charge. After 7 a.m. as the peak hour starts, it discharges to supply the load until 1 p.m. Then during off-peak hour until 4 p.m., it charges. After 4 p.m., BES starts discharging until 7 p.m. during evening peak hour and reaches the minimum state of charge of 30%. Then it remains ideal and again starts charging at 11 p.m. as off-peak hour starts.

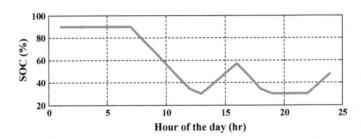

Fig. 4 Variation of SOC of BES

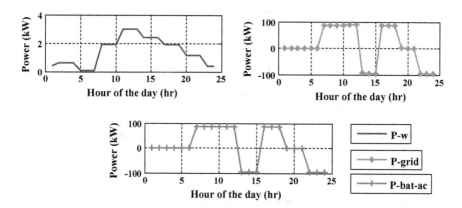

Fig. 5 Active power variation of wind, grid and BES

In Fig. 5, it is observed that, during the periods when loads are increasing, BES supplies the power to the grid and it charges during light load periods. During the peak hour demand, all the sources contribute significantly to the grid to maintain the voltage profile.

7 Conclusion

To find out the optimal allocation of wind, BES is the main benefaction of this paper. The proposed MOGA technique is used to find out compromised solution considering annual operating cost of wind, BES and annual cost of power loss in 69-bus RDS distribution system. The insertion of the wind and BES unit to the distribution system has a great advantage as it reduces voltage fluctuation, stores energy and discharges it when the distribution system needs. Overall, these advantages have been proven and demonstrated in the simulation results which show that the integration of wind and BES units into distribution system is a profitable system and offers techno-economical benefits.

References

1. Omran W. A., kazerani M and Salama M.M., "Investigation of methods for reduction of power fluctuations generated from large grid-connected photovoltaic system," IEEE Trans. Energy convers., vol. 26, (2011), pp. 318–27.
2. Georgilakis P.S., Hatziargyriou N.D., Optimal distributed generation placement in power distribution networks:, Models, methods and future research, IEEE Trans. Power Syst, vol. 28 (2013) pp. 3420–8.

3. Prenc R., Skrlec D., Komen V., "Distributed generation allocation based on average daily load and power production curves," Int. J. Electr. Power Energy Syst, vol. 53 (2013) pp. 612–22.
4. Sfikas E.E., katsigiannis Y.A., Georgilakis P.S., "Simultaneous capacity optimization of distributed generation and storage in medium voltage microgrid,", Electr. Power and Energy Syst., vol. 67 (2015) pp. 101–113.
5. Shanyi Xei, Ruicong Zhai et al., 'Self-adaptive genetic algorithm and Fuzzy decision based multi-objective optimization in microgrid with DGs.' The ope Electrical and Electronic Engg. J., (10) (2016) pp. 46–57.
6. Aksanli B. and Rosling T., "Optimal battery configuration in a residential home with time of use pricing," Proceedings of the IEEE Int. Conference on Smart grid Communication (2013).
7. Fathima,Hina & Palanisamy K., "Optimal sizing, selection & economic analysis of battery energy storage for grid-connected wind-PV hybrid system." Modelling and simulation in Engineering (2015) pp. 16.
8. Kornelakis, Aris & Yannis Marinakis, "Contribution for optimal siszing of grid- connected PV-systems using PSO," 35 (6) (2010) 1333–1341.
9. Nayak M.R.,. Nayak C.K, "Distributed generation optimal placement and sizing to enhance power distribution network performance using MTLBO" International Review of Electrical Engineering 6(8) (2013) pp. 1857–1869.
10. Diaf S., Notton G. Belhamel M., et.al., A design and technoeconomical optimization for hybrid PV/wind system under various meterological conditions, Elsevier-Appl. Energy (85) (2008) pp. 968–87.
11. 'Indian meteorolopgical department', Bhubaneswar, India, www.imd.gov.in.
12. D. T. Ton, C. J and G.H. a. J. D. Boyes, "Solar energy grid integration systems – energy storage (SEGIS-GS)," Sandia National Laboratories, Albuquerque, New Maxico 87185 and Livermore, california 94550 (2008).
13. T. Lambert, "Battery Roundtrip Efficiency," HOMER software, help index, (2004).
14. IEEE Standard For Interconnecting Distributed Resources With Electric Power Systems, IEEE Std. 1547 (2003).
15. Hong Y.Y. and. Lian R.C.. "Optimal sizing of hybrid wind/PV/diesel generation in a stand-alone power system using markov-based genetic algorithm," IEEE Trans. On Power Delivery, vol. 27 (2) (2012) pp. 640–647.
16. Senjyu T., Hayashi D., Urasaki N. and Funabashi T.,."Optimum configuration for renewable generating system in residence using genetic algorithm," IEEE Trans. On Energy Conversion, Vol. 21 (2) (2006) pp. 459–466.

Drowsiness Detection for Safe Driving Using PCA EEG Signals

S. S. Poorna, V. V. Arsha, P. T. A. Aparna, Parvathy Gopal
and G. J. Nair

Abstract Forewarning the onset of drowsiness in drivers and pilots by analyzing the state of brain can reduce the number of road and aviation accidents to a large extent. For this, EEG signals are acquired using a 14-channel wireless neuro-headset, while subjects are in virtual driving environment. Principal component analysis (PCA) of EEG data is used to extract the dominant ocular pulses. Two sets of feature vectors obtained from the analysis are: one set characterizing eye blinks only and another set where eye blinks are excluded. The temporal characteristics of ocular pulses are obtained from the first set. The latter is obtained from the spectral bands delta, theta, alpha, beta, and gamma. Classification using K-nearest neighbor (KNN) and artificial neural network (ANN) gives an accuracy of 80% and 85%, sensitivity of 33.35% and 58.21%, respectively, for these features. The targets used for classification are alert or awake, drowsy, and sleep state.

Keywords EEG · Drowsiness · Eye blinks · PCA · Energy
Blink rate · KNN · ANN · Accuracy · Sensitivity · Specificity
Precision

S. S. Poorna (✉) · V. V. Arsha · P. T. A. Aparna · P. Gopal · G. J. Nair
Department of Electronics and Communication Engineering, Amrita School of Engineering,
Amrita Vishwa Vidyapeetham, Amritapuri, India
e-mail: poorna.surendran@gmail.com

V. V. Arsha
e-mail: arshavenugopal96@gmail.com

P. T. A.Aparna
e-mail: aparna.adithyan.7@gmail.com

P. Gopal
e-mail: parvathygopal23@gmail.com

G. J. Nair
e-mail: gjnair08@gmail.com

© Springer Nature Singapore Pte Ltd. 2018
P. K. Pattnaik et al. (eds.), *Progress in Computing, Analytics and Networking*,
Advances in Intelligent Systems and Computing 710,
https://doi.org/10.1007/978-981-10-7871-2_40

1   Introduction

Drowsiness of drivers and pilots is a major cause of a large number of fatal road traffic and aviation accidents. Drowsiness decreases the individual's attention and alertness toward the tasks he or she is carrying out. Extended working hours, use of medication, sleeplessness, or continuous driving are some of the major reasons for drowsiness. Amir et al. report that US National Sleep Foundation (NSF) conducted a survey in 2009 which showed that 54% of adult drivers have driven a vehicle while feeling drowsy and 28% of them actually fell asleep [1]. A review of different sensing techniques to detect drowsiness is described in the published works of Sahayadhas et al. [2] and Jianfeng et al. [3]. These sensing techniques for drowsiness detection fall under three categories: First one used sensors mounted on the vehicle parts such as steering wheels or with the help of video cameras [4–6]. Second one senses the drowsiness with the help of behavior of the driver, usually by computer vision and imaging techniques [7, 3, 8] to detect the facial movements of the driver such as drooped head, yawning, and eye closures. The third set of techniques use the physiological parameters of the driver, which include eye activity by electrooculogram (EOG), muscle activity by electromyogram (EMG), heart rate variability by electrocardiogram (ECG), and brain states by electroencephalogram (EEG). Physiological changes related to the state of brain functions may help in determining drowsiness in an objective manner. Other characteristics are subject-specific and hence will be less reliable. They are also affected by illumination of the surrounding as well as the drivers postures.

EEG data analysis is one of the accepted methods for drowsiness detection. EOG-based techniques can also serve the same purpose, but the sensors of EOG, placed in and around the eyes, may cause disturbances to the driver if used for long time. These sensors have much lower SNR and can give false alarms. The electrical activity of the neurons inside brain, EEG, can provide the information regarding both muscular movements of the eye as well as the sleep stages. Hence, EEG-based drowsiness detection was considered in this work.

Several methods have been proposed to identify drowsiness from EEG. One such experiment used the analysis of alpha power spectrum changes of EEG signals by Dajeong Kim et al. [9], when subjects are feeling drowsy (with eyes open). Such eye activity cannot be detected by image processing methods. In their work, experiments were conducted on three subjects (age group of 24–25). Power spectrum of alpha, beta, theta, and delta signals was analyzed using fast Fourier transform. It was found from the experiments that alpha showed significant changes in power spectrum during drowsiness period even when eyes are open. In a similar study by Shaoda Yu et al. [10], EEG variations during sleep onset transitions were observed. In their work, the feature, EEG spectral bands divided into 1 Hz bin intervals and used these as input to support vector machine (SVM) classifier. From a set of optimized features, an accuracy and precision of 98.01% and 97.91%, respectively, was achieved. Research carried out by Roman Rosipal et al. [11] used an EEG-based probabilistic model to detect drowsiness using the spectral contents of four-second-long EEG segments. They modeled a real-time system using hierarchical Gaussian mixture model. Labeling was done using Karolinska drowsiness scoring method. Yabo Yin et al. [12] used k-means clustering and linear discriminant analysis (LDA) to find the correlation of alpha and beta waves with the states of drowsiness and consciousness.

In most of the literatures available, the features for drowsiness detection were based either on blink-related information or on spectral characteristics. In this paper, we try to integrate both these features and evaluate those using supervised learning techniques. PCA-based preprocessing will be used to combine the suitable channels from the headset. The performance of the system will be analyzed in terms of accuracy, sensitivity, specificity, and precision. The paper is organized as follows: In Sects. 2 and 3, the methodology of feature extraction and preprocessing is discussed in detail. Section 4 briefly explains the classification methods, and Sect. 5 gives the results obtained. The paper is concluded in Sect. 6 with further information on possible future works.

2 Methodology

In this section, we will be dealing with acquisition of EEG and preprocessing methods. We will begin with a brief discussion on human brain and conclude this section in feature extraction techniques.

2.1 Data Acquisition

EEG data was acquired by using the Emotiv EPOC device. The device has a resolution of 12 bits. It is an EEG signal acquisition and processing wireless headset that monitors 14 channels of EEG data. EPOC has a sampling frequency of 128 Hz and sends the EEG data to the computer via Bluetooth. EEG data of 18 subjects (nine males and nine females) of age group 20–22 was collected. Noise while recording was avoided by switching off other electronic devices nearby. The subjects were asked to undertake a virtual driving game for 2 h. The data was recorded while the subjects were virtually driving the vehicle. Subjects were slipping into stage of drowsiness when the data was taken. For virtual reality, VR box was used to give a 3D virtual image for purpose of providing a real driving scenario. To facilitate the contact of electrode with scalp, a saline solution was used. The 14 electrodes (AF3, F7, F3, FC5, T7, P7, O1, O2, P8, T8, FC6, F4, F8, and AF4) were placed according to the international 10–20 systems forming 7 sets of symmetric channels. The recordings were highly noisy as shown in Fig. 1.

Even though the recordings were taken from all the channels, the features pertaining to ocular pulses were dominant only in the electrodes placed in the frontal and occipital regions. Hence, only 9 channels—AF3, F7, F3, F6, O2, FC6, F4, F8,

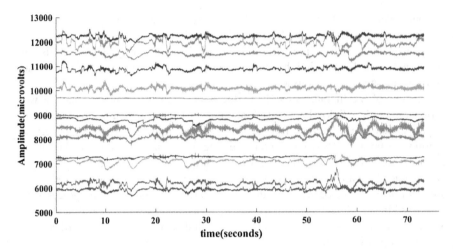

Fig. 1 EEG output plot of 14 channels

and AF4—were considered for this work. A video channel was also used to note down the presence and behavior of eye blinks. Video was taken from the instant when the EEG data was recorded. The onset of blinks was identified from the video and verified with EEG pulses obtained. The EEG pulses not matching the video record were not considered for analysis. The identified EEG portions for analysis varied between 6 and 10 min. In noisy data, to identify actual pulses it was necessary to have parallel video recording.

3 Feature Extraction

3.1 Principal Component Analysis and Preprocessing

3.1.1 Preprocessing for Blink-Dependent Features

All of the 9 selected channels give information regarding the state of the subject, and hence, the most relevant data should be selected from the available channels. For combining the appropriate channels, principal component analysis (PCA) was used. The EEG signal of channels AF4 and AF5 is given in Fig. 2a and b, respectively. The PCA output for the channels is shown in Fig. 2c. Since the eye blink-related features were considered, the PCA output with maximum energy (the output with maximum eigenvalue), i.e., the first channel, was considered. Along with the required output, the coefficients (or weights) and latent (or eigenvalues) were also obtained from PCA. This signal was further normalized as shown in Fig. 2d. Normalization was done by subtracting the mean from it and dividing the result with the maximum of that signal.

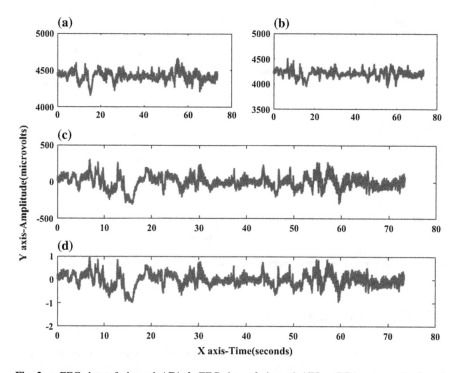

Fig. 2 **a** EEG data of channel AF4. **b** EEG data of channel AF5. **c** PCA output of selected channels. **d** Normalized PCA output

It is seen that a normal human blinks in between 2 and 10 s. Hence for eye blink-dependent features extraction, the EEG waveform was further segmented and analyzed with 10 s duration. An overlap of 2 s was also provided to prevent loss of data while segmenting. EEG recordings had baseline noise as shown in Fig. 3a. In order to remove the baseline variations, polynomial fitting was done on the normalized signal and was subtracted. The resultant gave smooth signals with peaks corresponding to the eye blinks. This is shown in Fig. 3b.

3.1.2 Preprocessing for Spectral Features

The output of PCA was for eye blink-independent features which are discussed below. All EEG channels have effects of blinks. In order to remove the signal corresponding to blink, processing was done using the outputs of PCA. The first output channel of PCA, having the maximum blink variability, was made zero. Inverse operation of PCA was done inorder to get back the EEG data from the 9 channels that are free from the effect of blinks. This was used for further power analysis in different blocks.

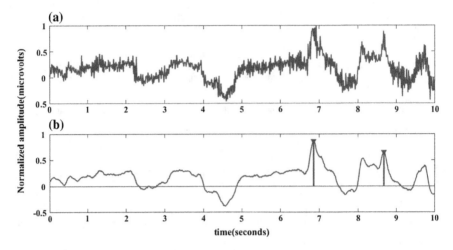

Fig. 3 **a** Segmented EEG before preprocessing. **b** Baseline removed and smoothed signal with detected eye blinks

3.2 Feature Extraction

As mentioned earlier, brain waves gamma, beta, alpha, theta, and delta play a significant role in determining the stages of alert, drowsy, and sleep. Two types of feature vectors were used for detecting drowsiness: One type was dependent on the eye blink information which included the blink rate, sum of blink heights inside the particular window and sum of blink duration widths in that window. Second feature vector was obtained by removing effects of eye blink. It includes the average and standard deviations of energy in the above-mentioned five frequency bands. Therefore, there were 2 types of features: First one was a temporal analysis in time domain while second one was in frequency domain.

3.2.1 Blink Features

Blink rate was calculated according to the number of times the subject blinks in a 10 s window. Blink width and blink height were also calculated from this window. It is a known fact that characteristics of blinks while a person is awake and when one is drowsy vary in a significant manner, which motivated us to take these features. Thus, three blink-dependent features, rate, height, and width/duration, were obtained for each subject.

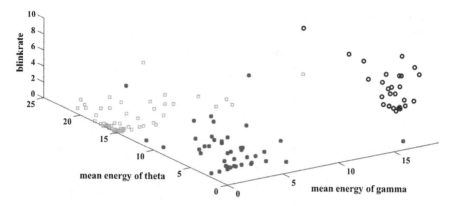

Fig. 4 Three-dimensional plot of the feature space comprising the features: mean energy of gamma and theta versus the blink rate

3.2.2 Spectral Features

The signal without blink data was further filtered using a set of FIR filters of order 60, tuned to different frequencies according to the frequency band of EEG's. A total of 10 feature vectors regarding the brain waves: mean energy and standard deviation of energy corresponding to each of 5 frequencies. The 3 blink features and 10 spectral feature vectors were combined to get a total of 13 feature vectors and used for classification purpose. Possible three-dimensional plots of the above feature combinations were taken to visualize the feature space. A sample three-dimensional plot of the feature space comprising the features mean energy of gamma and theta versus the blink rate is shown in Fig. 4.

4 Classification

Two supervised classification methods: K-nearest neighbor (KNN) and artificial neural network (ANN) [13, 14] were used to analyze the feature vectors. The classification was done for three cases: (i) using vectors having eye blink (ii) without eye blink, and (iii) combination of two feature vectors which include both. Eighty percentage of the data was used to train the classifiers while twenty percentage was used to test. The number of nearest neighbors are denoted by the variable k. K was iteratively chosen in the paper to aid maximum accuracy in classification; for our work, it was chosen as 11.

Table 1 Results for case (i) and case (ii)

Measures in (%)	Case (i)		Case (ii)	
	KNN	ANN	KNN	ANN
Accuracy	50	75	73.33	75
Sensitivity	37.97	41.2	54.67	44.43
Specificity	67.78	75.27	77.65	70.59
Precision	29.43	47.55	53.87	86.84

Table 2 Results for case (iii)

Measures in (%)	KNN	ANN
Accuracy	80	85
Sensitivity	33.35	58.21
Specificity	81.9533	83.24
Precision	84.36	65.73

5 Results

Our results show that the three stages were classified using the PCA EEG signals. Classification was done using KNN and ANN algorithms where ANN gave better performance in individual cases. The results were analyzed for three cases: (1) using blink-related features (2) using spectral features, and (3) with combination of both. The classifiers were evaluated for the performance measures accuracy, sensitivity, specificity, and precision.

From the analysis given in Table 1, it can be seen that for both cases, i.e., blink features and spectral features, ANN gave better classification performance measures accuracy, sensitivity, specificity, and precision. Using KNN, spectral parameters gave better performance measures, i.e., 73.33% accuracy, 54.67% sensitivity, 77.65% specificity, and 29.43% precision compared to the blink-based feature. Using ANN, the accuracy measure for both the cases (i) and (ii) were same, i.e., 75%. Table 2 shows the performance measures when combination of blink and spectral features was used. The combination of features was found to give highest accuracy, of the three cases. In case (iii) also ANN classified the stages: awake, onset of drowsiness and sleep with much better performance measures compared to the one with individual cases.

6 Conclusion

Amrita Vishwa Vidyapeetham has developed a system for forewarning drowsiness of pilots and drivers to prevent impending accidents. The analysis of this system has shown it is possible to detect drowsiness in pilots and drivers using PCA EEG signals with reasonable accuracy. Our observations conclude that accuracy obtained for drowsiness detection when the two set of features were used together was 80%

using KNN classifier and 85% using ANN classifier. In all the cases, ANN gives the best results in the performance measures considered. It is expected that eye tracking and heart rate variability may give a higher level of accuracy.

Acknowledgements We wish to thank Almighty God for the successful completion of this work. We also thank Amrita Vishwa Vidyapeetham, Amritapuri Campus, Kerala, for providing us support to carry out this project and permission to publish this work.

References

1. Amir Jalilifard and EdnaldoBrigante: An efficient K-NN approach for automatic drowsiness detection using single channel EEG recording, IEEE, 2016.
2. Sahayadhas A, Sundaraj K, Murugappan M: Detecting Driver Drowsiness Based on Sensors: A Review. Sensors (Basel, Switzerland). 2012; 12(12):16937–16953. https://doi.org/10.3390/s121216937.
3. Jianfeng Hu: Comparison of Different Features and Classifiers for Driver Fatigue Detection Based on a Single EEG Channel, Computational and Mathematical Methods in Medicine, Hindawi, Volume 2017 (2017) https://doi.org/10.1155/2017/5109530.
4. Samuel Lawoyin, Ding-Yu Fei, Ou Bai: Accelerometer-based steering-wheel movement monitoring for drowsy-driving detection Proceedings of the Institution of Mechanical Engineers, Part D: Journal of Automobile Engineering, Vol 229, Issue 2, pp. 163–173 October-31-2014 https://doi.org/10.1177/0954407014536148.
5. M. V. Ramesh, Nair, A. K., and Kunnathu, A. Thekkeyil: Intelligent Steering Wheel Sensor Network for Real-Time Monitoring and Detection of Driver Drowsiness, International Journal of Computer Science and Security (IJCSS), vol. 1, p. 1, 2011.
6. Ramesh, Maneesha V, Aswathy K. Nair, and Abishek Thekkeyil Kunnathu: Real-time automated multiplexed sensor system for driver drowsiness detection. Wireless Communications, Networking and Mobile Computing (WiCOM), 2011 7th International Conference on. IEEE, 2011.
7. Wei Zhang, Bo Cheng, Yingzi Lin: Driver Drowsiness Recognition Based on Computer Vision Technology, IEEE explore, pp 354–362 Volume 17, Number 3, ISSN:1007-0214-18/18, June 2012.
8. H. M. and R., S. Sundaram: Development of a nonintrusive driver drowsiness monitoring system, Advances in Intelligent Systems and Computing (AISC), vol. 1, pp. 737–743, 2014.
9. Dajeong Kim, Hyungseob Han, Sangjin Choand, Uipil Chong: Detection of drowsiness with eyes open using EEG based power spectrum analysis, IEEE, 2013.
10. Shaoda Yu, Peng Li, Honghuang Lin, Ehsan Rohani, Gwan Choi, Botang Shao and Quian Waing: Support Vector Machine based detection of drowsiness using minimum EEG features, IEEE, 2013.
11. Roman Rosipal, Björn Peters, Göran Kecklund, Torbjörn Åkerstedt, Georg Gruber, Michael Woertz, Peter Anderer, and Georg Dorffner1: EEG-Based Drivers' Drowsiness Monitoring Using a Hierarchical Gaussian Mixture Model. In: Schmorrow D.D., Reeves L.M. (eds) Foundations of Augmented Cognition. FAC 2007. Lecture Notes in Computer Science, vol 4565. Springer, Berlin, Heidelberg, 2007.
12. Yin Y., Zhu Y., Xiong S., Zhang J: Drowsiness Detection from EEG Spectrum Analysis Informatics in Control, Automation and Robotics (2012): 753–759. Lecture Notes in Electrical Engineering, vol 133. Springer, Berlin, Heidelberg, 2011.
13. S S Poorna, P M V D Sai Baba, Lakshmi Ramya Gujjalapudi, Prasanna Poreddy, Aashritha L. S, Renjith S, G J Nair: Classification of EEG based Control Using ANN and KNN- A Comparison, 2016 IEEE International Conference on Computational Intelligence and

Computing Research December 15–17, 2016, Chennai, 2016, pp. 1-6. https://doi.org/10.1109/ICCIC.2016.7919524.
14. Jain, Anil K., Jianchang Mao, and K. Moidin Mohiuddin: Artificial neural networks: A tutorial. Computer 29.3 (1996): 31–44.

Remote Healthcare Development Using Vehicular Ad Hoc and Wireless Sensor Networks

Suparna DasGupta, Soumyabrata Saha and Koyel Chatterjee

Abstract Wireless sensor networks along with vehicular ad hoc networks comprise of distributed sensor nodes which have sensing, communication, and meting out capabilities and work as emerging technology for diverse applications including healthcare industries. The objective of the proposed framework is to ensure the unremitting monitoring of vigorous parameters of patients without affecting the customary activities and provides the factual information to the end user. The proposed system includes smart vehicles outfitted with VANETs and body sensors embedded in the patients' body equipped by WBSNs. Smart vehicles carry health information collected from the patients and forward to the adjoining healthcare service provider. To better support the proposed framework, along with VANETs, WSNs can be adopted to design the framework for developing remote health consisting of the fundamental architecture of the system to provide unswerving communication with multicast data delivery in real time.

Keywords Wireless sensor networks · Vehicular ad hoc networks
Health care · Smart vehicle · System architecture

1 Introduction

The recent technological breakthrough has enabled cost-effective low-power wireless sensors and is interconnected with each other to find a growing number of healthcare applications of WSNs. WSNs consist of sinks and sensors. Sinks have

S. DasGupta (✉) · S. Saha · K. Chatterjee
Department of Information Technology, JIS College of Engineering, Kalyani,
West Bengal, India
e-mail: suparna.dasgupta@jiscollege.ac.in

S. Saha
e-mail: soumyabrata.saha@jiscollege.ac.in

K. Chatterjee
e-mail: koyel.chatterjee@gmail.com

© Springer Nature Singapore Pte Ltd. 2018
P. K. Pattnaik et al. (eds.), *Progress in Computing, Analytics and Networking*,
Advances in Intelligent Systems and Computing 710,
https://doi.org/10.1007/978-981-10-7871-2_41

been used to accumulate data, transmitted by sensors. Sensor nodes perceive the enviable corporeal phenomenon and perform the obligatory data aggregations necessary to avoid outmoded data transmissions.

A sensor node is embraced by four basic components such as: sensor, processing, radio, and power unit. The detection unit has been used to measure corporal condition; it has been used as a processing unit for collecting and meting out signals; the radio unit transfers signals from sensor node to the user through the gateway. All these units are supported by the power unit to provide the energy required to perform the tasks.

The wireless communication between moving vehicles is increasingly the focus of research in health, academic communities, and automotive industries. The vehicular ad hoc networks are an emerging technology that includes vehicles and road units (RSUs) as network nodes and allow Vehicle-to-Vehicle (IVC) communication and as well as with the Roadside-to-Vehicle communications (RVC). In VANETs, vehicles are used to form an automatic self-organization network without the use of immune infrastructure. Vehicles can communicate with nearby vehicles known as communication from Vehicle-to-Vehicle (V2V) and also with the side of the road infrastructure also known as Vehicle-to-Infrastructure (V2I). Establishing a competent and adaptable route between network nodes is one of the prerequisites in vehicle communication. It can offer diverse services that can benefit users, and the deployment of communication in VANETs is heavily reliant on their security and privacy features.

The requirements mentioned for the proposed architecture of the healthcare framework that is developed for remote distance have been achieved as: reliability, energy efficiency, routing, mobility of nodes, timeliness. Healthcare applications have required energy efficiency system to ensure unremitting operation within the life cycle of sensor nodes. In addition to energy efficiency, reliability is one of the overriding techniques for the accomplishment of the proposed framework together with network coding that has emerged as a viable technology for WSNs. Few applications of WSNs in healthcare are mentioned here, such as heart diseases; asthma; cancer detection; diabetes; blood pressure monitoring of pregnant women.

The proposed framework would make it easier for remote patients to reach physicians or the health center in the nearest urban or suburban area through the proposed solution. The system effectively includes an intelligent vehicle outfitted with VANETs and wireless body sensors connected to the patient's body equipped with WBSNs. These vehicles are used to collect personal sensitive health information from the patient and carry forward to the nearest healthcare provider.

The rest of the article is organized as follows. In Sect. 2, we have conducted surveys inclusive of existing approaches. In Sect. 3, it has presented the new architecture proposed system. The analysis is presented in Sect. 4. We conclude our article with the concluding remarks in Sect. 5.

2 Related Work

In this section we have discussed some of the remote healthcare monitoring frameworks using VANETs and WSNs.

In [1] authors presented the prototype for healthcare monitoring system using WSNs that consist of different types of sensors which are integrated onto the MicaZ and Telos motes. [1] ADMR used for multicast routing to discover nearby devices and its simple query interface allows caregivers to receive enduring data. MEDiSN [2] has been used to monitor the health of patients' physiological monitors and to transmit data collected through the network gateway. It has been used to optimize 1:1 and 1:M communication without explicitly using multicast communication. In [3], the authors proposed the reliable cluster-based communication scheme to collect real-time data related to patient care.

In [4] adjacent nodes created virtual clusters and used synchronization to establish general sleep schedules. S-MAC [4] has minimized power consumption and avoids the overload of time synchronization by suspending time warnings. In [5], the authors proposed the framework that provides lower latency and better scalability [4]. DS-MAC [5] is a dynamic work cycle technique that has been implemented in S-MAC [4] is enabled. MD-SMAC [6] is an amalgam of the mobile version of SMAC [4] and DS-MAC [5]. The main objective of [6] is to provide mechanisms to meet the constraints posed by applications sensitive to delays, together with the efficient management of mobility conditions. In [7], the routing metric is proposed combining jump and speed with the deliberation of the use of vehicle driving information and the reduction of the delay. An on-board information gathering module was designed and implemented using OBD technology to gather information on speed without modifying any other.

In [8] authors proposed framework which is based on the hot spot detection methodologies and executes a single hop or multi-hop fashion as communication requirements. In [9], authors have presented stable augmented throughput-based multi-hop protocol for link efficiency in wireless body area networks, where multi-hop communication is used to improve lifetime of the node and minimize the energy consumption. In [10], the authors have proposed the mechanism of communication in a single bound to send data from node to sink and this method is valuable to conquer delay but remote nodes have required more energy for communication purposes. Authors have proposed wireless autonomous spanning tree protocol [11] where messages are broadcasted to inform parent nodes for child nodes and data are used to bring about low delay and high network trustworthiness.

Tree algorithm based on priority for WBASNs [12] has used dedicated channels for emergency data communication, and normal data are presented for effective transmission after emergency data delivery. In [13], authors have proposed routing-based allocation of energy balancing speed where data are shrewdly transmitted through the adaptive routing path based on residual energy, and this framework guarantees a uniform distribution of the load at the nodes and increases the life of the network. The authors have proposed a multi-hop protocol [14] in

WBASNs, which is robust against frequent network changes and the use of an adaptive transmission mechanism for nodes and improves energy efficiency. A model based on the reputation event has been proposed in [15] to sieve the warning messages and based on the location of the vehicles to the interior of the model classifies the traffic into diverse roles.

Through an extensive review it has identified that different authors presented diverse techniques to monitor the health of the system and the transfer of the location of the detected data sensors for the end users was recognized, and it has been considered as one of the main problems of design in remote healthcare monitoring framework. In order to recover the deficiencies of aforementioned schemes, the challenge is to develop a new proposed framework that can meet up the conflicting requirements. The following section proposes a framework for remote healthcare development using vehicular ad hoc and sensor networks. The main objective of the proposed framework is to serve the people in accordance with the requirements.

3   Proposed Framework for Remote Healthcare Development

The previous section leads to the observation that the data collection has been executed continuously and that the collected data would be sent to the end user for proper execution purposes.

- Wireless body sensor integrated into the body of each selected patient and continuously collects physiological signals from the patient's body.
- Wireless multi-hop relay nodes are used to forward health data of patient from WBSN to VA-Cle.
- VA-Cle: The smart vehicle is equipped with VANET for receiving, carrying, and forwarding the required information to another VA-Cle or V-Server.
- V-Server: The receiving information through VA-Cle would be stored in the V-Server and analyzed for next level of execution. According to the decision, it would communicate to doctors or medical practitioners (Fig. 1).

Algorithm 1: Algorithm for Data Collection and Forwarding	
Step 1:	Embed wireless body sensors to different patients' body.
Step 2:	Body sensors collected data continuously and store in the corresponding buffer.
Step 3:	Collected information would be forwarded to relay node.
Step 4:	Wireless multi-hop relay node are act as cluster head and forward the patient's health data to the nearest smart vehicle (VA-Cle).
END	

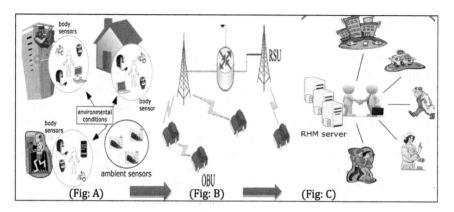

Fig. 1 Framework of Remote Healthcare Monitoring Using VANETs and WSNs

Algorithm 2: Algorithm for Patient Registration	
Step 1:	Smart vehicles (VA-Cle) received the patient's health data.
Step 2:	It checks for the patient registration, if the patient details are found in its database then it add the current collected information with the existing information, otherwise make a new entry of patient's information.
Step 3:	VA-Cle informs its other neighbors of the new patient's information.
Step 4:	Wireless multi-hop relay node are act as cluster head node and broadcast the patient's registration details to its neighbor vehicles.
END	

Algorithm 3: Algorithm for Data Processing	
Step 1:	Smart vehicles forward the collected information to the V-Server.
Step 2:	Same patient medical data may be received from different smart vehicles at different time interval and store in the V-Server.
Step 3:	V-Server checks the collected data and compare with the pre-defined threshold. If the collected data is differ from threshold values, and instant action would be taken care off.
Step 4:	Nearby available doctors or medical practitioners would receive the messages from the V-Server and they would take care the patient's health condition.
END	

By using the above three algorithms, any patients' health information would be reached to the medical experts, doctors, through VANETs and WSNs.

4 Analysis

In this proposed mechanism, layered approach has taken an important role for execution of the system. The main drawback with the centralized system is single point to failure. In a contrast, the layered approach provides support even when any node fails and as well as fault tolerance of the network is increased. It allows for the distribution of the load on more than one layer. This helps in solving the performance bottleneck problem. The simulation model consists of a network model that has a number of wireless nodes, representing the entire network to be simulated. We have executed simulations by using the simulation tool MATLAB to monitor performance and evaluate the performance of the proposed framework.

Normalized routing load (NRL) is the relationship between packet transmissions administrative and routing data packets delivered. A data packet is counted as delivered when received by the destination node. Each jump is counted separately at the time of transmission count. Let D be the total number of data packet received by the destination node and R be the number of routing packet needed to transmission of D packets, i.e., NRL = D/R. In Fig. 2, we have presented a relation between packet generation rates versus NRL.

End-to-end delay is the average difference between the time the first data packet is caused by an application and the time this packet is received on this destination.

In Fig. 3, we have presented the relationship between packet generation rate versus end-to-end delay.

Throughput is defined as the total number of messages sent or received per second. The packet drop ratio is defined as the fraction of data packets lost by an application in time data delivery. The reasons for the fall were mainly packet collisions with several expirations retry count too. In Fig. 4, we have presented the relationship between throughput and number of nodes.

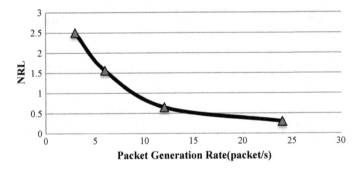

Fig. 2 NRL versus packet generation rate

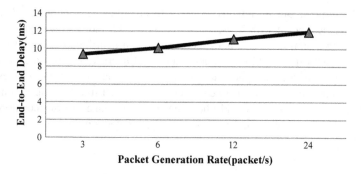

Fig. 3 Packet generation rate versus end-to-end delay

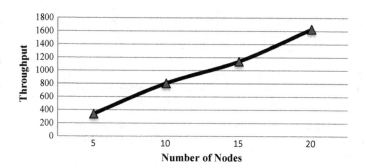

Fig. 4 Number of node versus throughput

5 Conclusion

In this paper, we have focused our discussion on the benefits of using VANET and wireless sensor networks for medical applications. The future of health care is increasingly aging world and would force the health surveillance everywhere with minimal physical interaction of physicians with their patients. Design networks for better medical wireless sensors seem to be a good solution for part of the problem.

As upshot, VANETs and WSNs are flattering gradually more important to observe patients both in the clinical setting and home again. The application of VANETs together with the health monitoring of the sensor network systems has been divided into three categories: monitoring of patients in clinical practice, supervision of chronic patients in the home and the elderly and the elderly, and the collection of clinical data long-term.

In this paper, the framework for remote health surveillance is offered using VANET and sensor networks. The impending benefits of deploying wireless sensor networks and VANETs in healthcare applications are easy to access patient data updated at any time and from anywhere. A test bed would be taken into consideration to test the performance of the required parameters as blood pressure, ECG, heart rate, temperature instantaneous retort to emergency situations, and rider of high-quality healthcare with low-cost individual health monitoring system.

The future vision of WSNs is to secure abundant distributed devices to control and interact with the world body phenomena and to make use of detection capabilities and performance space and temporarily dense detection devices. The potential apparition of WSNs is to entrench plentiful distributed devices to monitor and interact with corporeal world phenomena and to make use of detection capabilities, performance space and temporarily dense detection devices.

References

1. V. Shnayder, B.R. Chen, K. Lorincz, T.F. Fulfor Jones, M. Welsh, *"Sensor Networks for Medical Care: Technical Report TR-0805; Division of Engineering and Applied Sciences"*, Harvard University: Cambridge, MA, USA, 2005; pp. 1–14.
2. J. Ko, J.H. Lim, Y. Chen, R. Musvaloui, A. Terzis, G. Masson, T. Gao, W. Destler, L. Selavo, R. Dutton, *"MEDiSN: Medical Emergency Detection in Sensor Networks"*, published in the ACM Transactions Embedded Computing System, in 2010, vol. 10, pp: 1–29.
3. F. Hu, M. Jiang, L. Celentano, Y. Xiao, *"Robust Medical ad hoc Sensor Networks with Wavelet Based ECG Data Mining"*, published in Elsevier Journal of Ad Hoc Networking, in 2008, 6, pp: 986–1012.
4. W. Ye, J. Heidemann, D. EStrin, *"Medium Access Control with Coordinated Adaptive Sleeping for Wireless Sensor Networks"*, published in IEEE ACM Transaction on Networking in 2004, vol. 12, pp: 493–506.
5. P. Lin, C. Qiao, X. Wang, *"Medium Access Control with a Dynamic Duty Cycle for Sensor Networks"*, published in the proceedings of the IEEE Wireless Communication Networks Conference in 2004, pp: 1534–1539.
6. H. Pham, S. Jha, *"An Adaptive Mobility Aware MAC Protocol for Sensor Networks"*, published in the proceedings of the IEEE International Conference on Mobile Ad-hoc and Sensor Systems, in Fort Lauderdale, October 2004, pp. 558–560.
7. Y. Chen, Z. Xiang, W. Jian, W. Jiang, *"An Improved AOMDV Routing Protocol for V2V Communication"*, published in the proceedings of the IEEE Intelligent Vehicles Symposium, in 2009, pp. 1115–1120.
8. N. Javaid, Z. Abbas, M.S. Fareed, Z.A. Khan, N. Alrajeh, *"M-ATTEMPT: A New Energy–Efficient Routing Protocol for Wireless Body Area Sensor Networks"* published in the Procedia Computer Science, in 2014, pp: 224–231.
9. Q. Nadeem, N. Javaid, S.N. Mohammad, M.Y. Khan, S. Sarfraz, M. Gull, *"SIMPLE- Stable Increased Throughput Multi-hop Protocol for Link Efficiency in Wireless Body Area Networks"*, published in the 8th International Conference on Broadband and Wireless Computing, Communication and Application in 2013, pp. 221–226.
10. M. Quwaider, S. Biswas, *"DTN Routing in Body Sensor Networks with Dynamic Postural Partitioning"*, published in the Elsevier Journal of Ad Hoc Networks, in 2010, vol. 8, no. 8, pp. 824–841.
11. B. Braem, B. Latre, I. Moerman, C. Blondia, and P. Demeester, *"The Wireless Autonomous Spanning Tree Protocol for Multi-hop Wireless Body Area Networks,"* in published in the proceedings of the 3rd Annual IEEE International Conference on Mobile and Ubiquitous Systems in July 2006.
12. R. Annur, N. Wattanamongkhol, S. Nakpeerayuth, L. Wuttisittikulkij, J.I. Takada, *"Applying the Tree Algorithm with Prioritization for Body Area Networks"*, published in the proceedings of the International Journal of Distributed Sensor Networks, in 2011, pp. 519–524.

13. N. Ababneh, N. Timmons, J. Morrison, D. Tracey, *"Energy Balanced Rate Assignment and Routing Protocol for Body Area Networks"*, in published in the proceedings of 26th IEEE International Conference on the Advanced Information Networking and Applications Workshops in 2012, pp. 466–471.
14. M. Nabi, T. Basten, M. Geilen, M. Blagojevic, T. Hendriks, *"A Robust Protocol Stack for Multi-hop Wireless Body Area Networks with Transmit Power Adaptation"*, published in the proceedings of the 5th ACM International Conference on Body Area Networks, in 2010, pp. 77–83.
15. Q. Ding, X. Li, M. Jiang, X. Zhou, *"Reputation Based Trust Model in Vehicular Ad hoc Networks"*, published in the International Conference on Wireless Communications and Signal Processing, in 2010, pp 1–6.

Comparative Analysis of Subcontracting Scheduling Methods

Konstantin Aksyonov, Anna Antonova and Eugene Sysoletin

Abstract This paper considers the following methods of the work scheduling: network planning techniques (critical path method, program evaluation and review technique, and graphical evaluation and review technique), method of agents cooperation in the needs-and-means networks proposed by Skobelev P.O., method of simulation and genetic algorithms integration proposed by Kureichik V.V., and method of multiagent genetic optimization developed by the authors based on the Kureichik method. As a result of the comparative analysis, the advantages of the method of multiagent genetic optimization in terms of solving the problem of subcontracting scheduling have been revealed. The multiagent genetic optimization method takes into account the nonrenewable resources, allows implementing different resource allocation strategies using simulation and multiagent modeling, and allows optimizing subcontract resources via analysis of alternative work schedules using genetic algorithms and simulation.

Keywords Subcontracting scheduling · Network planning techniques
Genetic algorithms · Simulation · Multiagent modeling

1 Introduction

The subcontracting scheduling problem is part of the scheduling problem and is associated with the analysis of the bottlenecks of own resources distribution and optimization of the subcontracting resources. The subcontracting scheduling

K. Aksyonov · A. Antonova · E. Sysoletin (✉)
Department of Information Technology and Automation, Ural Federal University,
Mira str. 19, 620002 Yekaterinburg, Russian Federation
e-mail: unclesal@mail.ru

K. Aksyonov
e-mail: wiper99@mail.ru

A. Antonova
e-mail: antonovaannas@gmail.com

© Springer Nature Singapore Pte Ltd. 2018
P. K. Pattnaik et al. (eds.), *Progress in Computing, Analytics and Networking*,
Advances in Intelligent Systems and Computing 710,
https://doi.org/10.1007/978-981-10-7871-2_42

problem is relevant especially for enterprises, where number of employees is small. Subcontracting scheduling is aimed at the maximum loading of own resources and execution of all projects on time due to additional resources. The following objective functions can be used to solve the subcontracting scheduling:

(1) Minimization of the total subcontract cost value:

$$OF_1 = \sum_{i=1}^{P} \sum_{j=1}^{Ki} (SS(i,j) \cdot V_{SC}(i,j)) \rightarrow \min, \tag{1}$$

where

$SS(i, j)$ cost of the work j project i;
$V_{SC}(i, j)$ volume of subcontracting workforces on the work j project i;
K_i works amount in the project i;
P projects amount.

(2) Minimization of the total company departments downtime:

$$OF_2 = \frac{\sum_{t=0}^{T} \sum_{w=1}^{V} VF(t,w)}{T \cdot V} \rightarrow \min, \tag{2}$$

where

$VF(t, w)$ amount of free workforces of department w at the moment t;
V departments amount;
T the range scheduling duration. Constraints of the problem are time constraints of the early and late works start.

Let us consider a number of methods [1, 6, 8–10] for solving the problem of work planning and carry out comparative analysis in relation to the problem of subcontracting scheduling.

2   Network Planning Techniques

Network planning techniques are based on the idea of presenting project work as a network. In this network, the aimed arcs are associated with the works, the nodes— with the events of the work's start and finish. A network schedule construction is carried out according to the rules and necessarily reflected the relationship between the preceding and following works because the performance of the network planning techniques is based on the analysis of these relationships.

Let us consider the following network planning techniques: critical path method (CPM), program evaluation and review technique (PERT), and graphical evaluation and review technique (GERT).

2.1   CPM Method

The CPM method is intended to assess the standby time of works performance in the case of deterministic works durations. The found standby time of works performance is used to balance resource, which is carried out through a variety of heuristic algorithms to establish the priority of works [8, 9]. After resource balancing is finished, the only way to reduce the critical path is to attract subcontracting resources. To assess the feasibility of attracting subcontracting resources, a value of the average cost of reducing the duration of project per unit time is calculated for each work. Then the most profitable work from the viewpoint of acceleration of project implementation is selected to attract subcontracting resources.

2.2   PERT and GERT Methods

The PERT method is intended to assess the timing of the project completion taking into account the assignment of the works duration by using β distribution [9]. The GERT method is a development of the PERT method. The GERT method is intended to the analysis of stochastic network graph [10]. Each arc of the stochastic network (i.e., work) is characterized by the duration and the probability of realization in the project. The network implementation is a network section, in which some arcs are stored (realized), while others arcs are discarded. Each node of the stochastic network is identified with two events: event of the work end (input event) and event of the work start (output event). Two types of the output are defined in the GERT language for describing the output event: deterministic output (all arcs, originating from the node, are implemented) and probabilistic output (only one arc of all the arcs, originating from the node, is implemented).

The GERT method extends the use of the CPM method to solve the subcontracting scheduling taking into account stochastic work durations and the probabilistic occurrence of work in the project. The GERT method builds a branch of realized works, calculates works durations using distribution functions, and calculates a critical path. For works of the critical path, it is possible to calculate the feasibility of using subcontracts to accelerate the project processes.

3 Scheduling Method on the Basis of the Needs-and-Means Network

Scheduling method on the basis of the needs-and-means network is proposed by Skobelev P.O. and is intended to schedule by constructing a multiagent system of the operative resource allocation in real time [12]. The method takes into account the possibility of adjusting the composition and characteristics of the planned works and resources. The needs-and-means network (NM network) is a multiagent system where each agent is characterized by needs (N) and means (M). The NM network agent negotiates to achieve its needs with the help of other agent's means (Fig. 1).

In the method, the NM network is used to represent the set of orders, projects, works, and resources of the enterprise. Each item listed in the NM network is associated with an agent, e.g., resource #1 agent, work #1 agent, project #1 agent. During the agents' negotiations, the distribution of resources by works is carried; fragment of the negotiations protocol at the level of individual agents is shown in Fig. 1. As can be seen from the figure, the work #4 agent chooses the resource #1 agent from the three available resource agents (the first in the list), so the other alternative resources remain unanalyzed.

Scheduling method on the basis of the NM network includes an initial phase of the conflict-free scheduling and proactive phase of the rescheduling [11, 12]. The phase of the conflict-free scheduling involves the resources allocation between works. Each work generates the time interval (slot) of the employment of the resource, that is recorded in the planned slots of this resource. The phase of the proactive scheduling requires resolution for each resource the conflicts of the

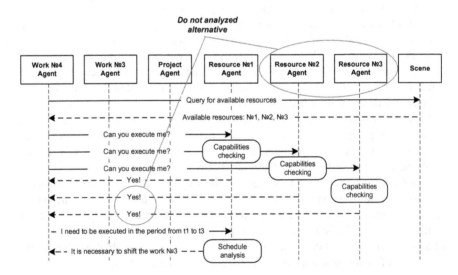

Fig. 1 A fragment of the negotiations protocol of the method on the basis of the NM network

planned slots set by different works. In the case of the new work emergence or new resource (i.e., subcontract resource) emergence, the system creates a new agent-work or agent-resource that is included in the negotiations, expressing its needs and means. Thus, the flexibility of the scheduling method regarding the subcontract assessment is achieved.

4 Scheduling Method on the Basis of the Simulation and Genetic Algorithm Integration

Scheduling method on the basis of the simulation and genetic algorithms integration is proposed by Kureichik V.V. and is intended to modeling discrete processes that occur in the organizational and technical systems and optimization of control process parameters by means of genetic algorithms [6]. Genetic algorithms (GA) are widely known as algorithms for solving the complex systems management problem in a short time [5]. Figure 2 shows a diagram of the Kureichik V.V. method.

According to the Kureichik V.V. method, the scheduling problem is solved by the GA, and the simulation model is used to calculate the multiobjective function of the suitability of individuals of the next generation. Expert system is used to analyze and correct parameters of the GA (the probability of genetic operators).

The proposed method has been implemented in the software RDO-studio [6], and with this help the scheduling problem of the shop works has been solved. The purpose of optimization was the selection of the optimal values of the controlled variables of the simulation model, which were the priorities of executive works. Fitness function was the function of penalties for failures orders.

The Kureichik V.V. method can be applied to solve the problem of subcontracting as follows. The simulation model evaluates the various options for subcontracting from the point of view of satisfying the objective functions (1) and (2). The optimization module based on the estimates obtained by the simulation model generates new variants of subcontracting when scheduling the project's works.

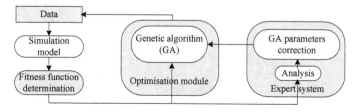

Fig. 2 A diagram of the Kureichik V.V. method

5   Method of Multiagent Genetic Optimization

The method of multiagent genetic optimization (MGO method) has been developed by the paper authors [1]. At the heart of the MGO method is a Kureichik V.V. method modified using the following methods and algorithms: (1) multiagent simulation [13] for description of the model of distribution of internal and external resources on works; (2) numerical methods of uncertainty removing with regard to the account for the probability of occurrence of additional projects; (3) simulated annealing algorithm [4] and search of novelty algorithm [7] in order to modification of the genetic algorithm to improve the quality of solutions found by the algorithm. The MGO method is implemented in the optimization module of the metallurgical enterprise information system (Fig. 3).

The metallurgical enterprise information system is a Web-oriented system for monitoring, modeling, analysis, and improvement processes of the steel products manufacturing [2, 3]. On Fig. 3, the decision of the problem of scheduling the number of employees in the two departments is shown. The optimal values of the input model parameters are found.

The modified genetic algorithm is designed to find the optimal values of controlled parameters of the simulation model. The simulation model is designed to evaluate the fitness function of each solution found by the genetic algorithm. Subcontract scheduling using the MGO method is performed by evaluating the

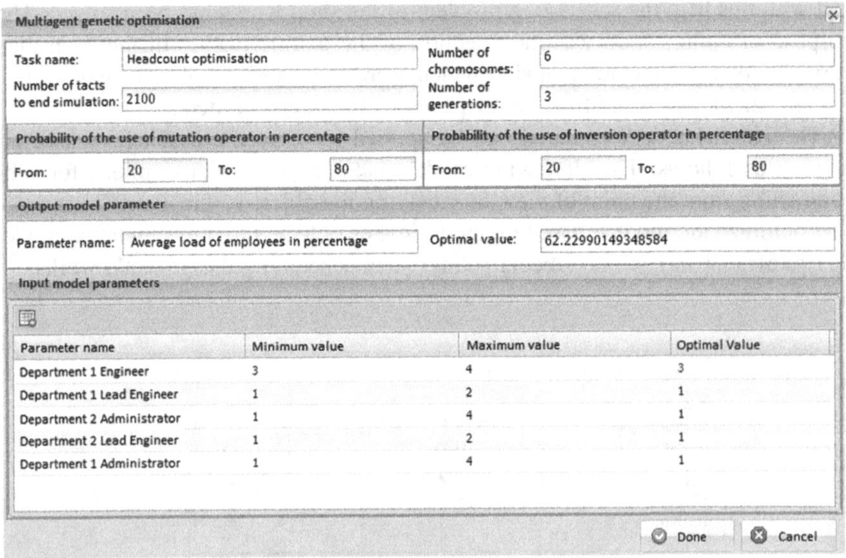

Fig. 3 User interface of the optimization module with the MGO method

objective functions (1) and (2) in the simulation model and further searching for the solution using a modified genetic algorithm. Fitness function of solutions is then used in selection to apply genetic operators to solutions.

6 Comparative Analysis of Subcontracting Scheduling Methods

Let us consider the following subcontracting scheduling methods: network planning techniques (NPT), scheduling method on the basis of the needs-and-means network (NMN), scheduling method on the basis of the simulation and genetic algorithms integration (SGA), and MGO method (MGO). Results of these methods comparative analysis are presented in Table 1. The criteria in the table are arranged in order of decreasing of the criterion importance for the subcontracting scheduling solution.

As follows from the table, all of the methods, except the MGO method, do not have the full functionality of the subcontracting scheduling.

Analysis of network planning methods reveals the following disadvantages:

1. The bulkiness and poor readability of the stochastic network diagrams are constructed by the GERT language. During conversion any stochastic network to this type of network, the number of arcs and nodes in the network increases, which complicates the perception and analysis of the network.
2. The CPM method allows assigning third-party resources to perform activities of the critical path and evaluate the effectiveness of the appointment. However, the CPM method does not have subcontracting optimization techniques.

Table 1 Comparative analysis of subcontracting scheduling methods

Criterion	NPT	NMN	SGA	MGO
Problems				
Scheduling	●	●	●	●
Renewable resources consideration	●	●	●	●
Subcontracting consideration	●	●	○	●
Rescheduling	○	●	○	●
Analysis of alternative plans	○	○	●	●
Subcontracting optimization	○	○	○	●
Nonrenewable resources consideration	○	○	○	●
Methods for solving the scheduling problem				
Heuristic algorithms	●	○	●	●
Expert modeling	○	●	●	●
Simulation	○	○	●	●
Multiagent modeling	○	●	○	●
Evolutionary modeling	○	○	●	●

3. Lack of means of formalizing the decision-making scenarios in the allocation of resources on the works (construction of models of decision-makers).

Scheduling method on the basis of the needs-and-means network uses the negotiations of intelligent agents, but these agents do not support the analysis of alternative solutions, cutting off the "extra" alternatives in the course of negotiations. The disadvantages of the NMN method also include the following:

1. The NMN method supports the description of the subcontracting agent but does not provide mechanism to determine the optimal number of such agents.
2. Failure to account for nonrenewable resources.

Analysis of the scheduling method on the basis of the simulation and genetic algorithms integration reveals the following disadvantages:

1. Method focuses on a wide class of the organizational and technical systems management tasks, which leads to the need to develop custom ontology of the subcontracting scheduling problem and develop of its own genetic algorithm.
2. The lack of mechanisms of subcontract optimization taking into account nonrenewable resources; lack of means of formalizing decision-making scenarios in the allocation of resources on the works.
3. The inability to reschedule the works with the appearance of additional work. At the same time, the method provides the ability to specify the probabilistic duration and cost of the work.

Thus, the MGO method is the most preferable when scheduling the work with subcontracting.

7   Conclusion and Future Work

In this paper, a comparative analysis in considering subcontracting scheduling problem has been conducted. The objective function of subcontracting scheduling is to maximize the load of own resources and minimize the cost of subcontracting resources.

Network planning techniques use subcontract to reduce the critical path of the works. To assess the feasibility of attracting subcontracting resources, a value of the average cost of reducing the duration of project per unit time is calculated for each work. Scheduling method on the basis of the NM network does not distinguish between own and subcontracted resources because both are agents who negotiate with the goal of efficient works scheduling with less cost. The Kureichik V.V. method evaluates the various options for subcontracting with the use of the simulation model and generates variants with the help of genetic algorithm. The MGO method modifies the Kureichik V.V. method by multiagent simulation, numerical methods of uncertainty removing, simulated annealing algorithm, and search of novelty algorithm.

As a result of the comparative analysis, the advantages of the method of multiagent genetic optimization in terms of solving the problem of subcontracting scheduling have been revealed. The multiagent genetic optimization method takes into account the nonrenewable resources, allows implementing different resource allocation strategies using simulation and multiagent modeling, and allows optimizing subcontract resources via analysis of alternative work schedules using genetic algorithms and simulation, reschedules the works using numerical methods of uncertainty removing and simulation.

The aim of future research is to extend and apply the developed MGO method for the technological and logistics scheduling. The technological and logistics scheduling is complicated by considering the production plan for the units of output and the availability of additional technological support operations, which are strictly related to the number of the completed basic technological operations on the industrial unit.

Acknowledgements This work is supported by Act 211 Government of the Russian Federation, contract No 02.A03.21.0006.

References

1. Aksyonov, K. and Antonova, A.: Multiagent genetic optimisation to solve the project scheduling problem under uncertainty. International Journal on Advances in Software, 7(1&2) (2014) 1–19
2. Aksyonov, K., Bykov, E., Aksyonova, O., and Antonova, A.: Development of real-time simulation models: integration with enterprise information systems. In: Proceedings of the Ninth International Multi-Conference on Computing in the Global Information Technology (2014) 45–50
3. Borodin, A., Kiselev, Y., Mirvoda, S., and Porshnev, S.: On design of domain-specific query language for the metallurgical industry. In: Proceedings of 11th International Conference BDAS: Beyond Databases, Architectures and Structures: Communications in Computer and Information Science (2015) 505–515
4. Goffe, V., Ferrier, G., and Rogers, J.: Global optimization of statistical functions with simulated annealing. Journal of Econometrics 60 (1994) 65–99
5. Goldberg, D.: Genetic algorithms. Addison Wesley, (1989)
6. Kureichik, V.M., Malioukov, S., Kureichik, V.V., and Malioukov, A.: Genetic Algorithms for Applied CAD Problems. Springer (2009)
7. Lehman, J. and Stanley, K.: Exploiting open-endedness to solve problems through the search for novelty. In: Proceedings of the Eleventh International Conference Artificial Life (ALIFE XI) (2008) 329–336
8. Moder, J. and Elmaghraby, S. (Eds.): Handbook of operations research: foundations and fundamentals, Vol. 1. New York: Van Nostrand-Reinhold, 2nd. ed., (1978)
9. Moder, J. and Elmaghraby, S. (Eds.): Handbook of operations research: models and applications, Vol. 2. New York: Van Nostrand-Reinhold, 2nd. ed., (1978)
10. Pritsker, A. and Happ, W.: GERT: graphical evaluation and review technique: Part I, Fundamentals. Journal of Industrial Engineering, 17(6), (1966) 267–274
11. Rzevski, G., Himoff, J., and Skobelev, P.: MAGENTA technology: a family of multi-agent intelligent schedulers. In: Proceedings of International conference on multi-agent systems: Workshop on Software Agents in Information Systems and Industrial Applications 2 (SAISIA), Germany: Fraunhofer IITB (2006)

12. Vittikh, V. and Skobelev, P.: Multiagent interaction models for constructing the needs-and-means networks in open systems. Automation and Remote Control, 64, (2003) 162–169
13. Wooldridge, M.: Intelligent Agent: Theory and Practice. Knowledge Engineering Review, Vol. 10 (2), (1995)

K-means Clustering: An Efficient Algorithm for Protein Complex Detection

S. Kalaivani, D. Ramyachitra and P. Manikandan

Abstract The protein complexes have significant biological functions of proteins and nucleic acids dense from the molecular interaction network in cells. Several computational methods are developed to detect protein complexes from the protein–protein interaction (PPI) networks. The existing algorithms do not predict better complex, and it also provides low performance values. In this research, K-means algorithm has been proposed for protein complex detection and compared with the existing algorithms such as MCODE and SPICi. The protein interaction and gene expression benchmark datasets such as Collins, DIP, Krogan, Krogan Extended, PPI-D1, PPI-D2, GSE12220, GSE12221, GSE12442, and GSE17716 have been used for comparing the performance of the existing and proposed algorithms. From this experimental analysis, it is inferred that the proposed K-means clustering algorithm outperforms the other existing methods.

Keywords PPI · Protein complex detection · MCODE · SPCi
K-means clustering · Yeast protein dataset · Gene expression dataset

1 Introduction

Biological functions generate huge data in the form of protein–protein interactions (PPI) which consists of molecular complex. Generally, protein complex is identified as molecular function that consists of numerous proteins that are connected with each other at the equal time. In protein complex detection, the PPI network is

S. Kalaivani (✉) · D. Ramyachitra · P. Manikandan
Department of Computer Science, Bharathiar University, Coimbatore 641046
Tamil Nadu, India
e-mail: kalaiero.bu91@gmail.com

D. Ramyachitra
e-mail: jaichitra1@yahoo.co.in

P. Manikandan
e-mail: manimkn89@gmail.com

© Springer Nature Singapore Pte Ltd. 2018
P. K. Pattnaik et al. (eds.), *Progress in Computing, Analytics and Networking*,
Advances in Intelligent Systems and Computing 710,
https://doi.org/10.1007/978-981-10-7871-2_43

constructed based on the interaction datasets and the complex detection is achieved by clustering techniques. Most of the complex predictions are done on the organism of Saccharomyces cerevisiae. Based on the literature, this research work also focused on the yeast organism. The PPI interaction benchmark datasets such as Collins, DIP, Krogan, Krogan Extended, PPI-D1, and PPI-D2 and gene expression datasets such as GSE12220, GSE12221, GSE12442, and GSE17716 are compared with the reference datasets such as Complex D1 and Complex D2 which are collected from the MIPS databases.

Several clustering algorithms have been projected to identify the protein complexes, and these algorithms include the merging and increasing the clusters. In this research, two existing algorithms such as MCODE and SPICi clustering algorithms are used. A new graph theoretic clustering algorithm named Molecular Complex Detection (MCODE) identifies the densely connected regions in huge protein–protein interaction networks that may signify molecular complexes [1, 2]. The MCODE algorithm considers complexes as dense regions developed from highly weighted vertices [3]. SPICi is known as Speed Performance In Clustering, and it creates clusters, which require high-weighted degree, and adding nodes that maintain the density of the clusters. SPICi uses a different seed selection criterion and integrates interaction confidences [4–6]. The algorithms have been compared with different performance measures for evaluating the quality of predicted complex. The remaining section of the paper is structured as follows: Section 2 describes the methodology for the protein complex detection, Sect. 3 describes the experimental result, and finally, Sect. 4 gives the conclusion and suggests the future work.

2 Methodology

In this research work, the existing algorithms such as MCODE, SPICi and the proposed algorithm, K-means clustering algorithm, are used to identify the protein complexes. From the results, it is concluded that the K-means algorithm provides better results than the existing algorithms.

2.1 Molecular Complex Detection (MCODE)

The MCODE algorithm is mainly used for finding molecular functions based on PPI networks. MCODE detects closely connected regions in PPI networks as protein complexes. This method employs in three steps: (i) vertex weighting (ii) complex prediction (iii) post-processing. In the first stage, the MCODE finds the k-core, and in second stage, it selects the seed vertex in highest weight in connected graphs and forms the threshold cluster. MCODE will repeat above steps until no more clusters can be detected. In the final stage, post-processing is performed to generate the overlapping clusters [1].

2.2 Speed Performance in Clustering (SPICi)

The insight underlying SPICi is related to DPClus [7]. SPICi algorithm is used to construct a cluster at a time. Every cluster extended from real seed pair of proteins. The initial data structure is a priority queue, DegreeQ, to select the seed proteins. Once a cluster is formed and output, its proteins are detached from DegreeQ, and the weighted degrees of all proteins adjoining to these are decreased to reproduce the connectivity to other unclustered proteins. Otherwise clusters are detached from the complex [8–10]. It is based on the sustain of (m, M). CandidateQ desires to support insertions, as neighbors of nodes added to M are added to it, and augment key operations for extracting the max ingredient, because M grows the chains of all vertices with deference to M raised [11–13].

2.3 K-means Clustering Algorithm

The K-means clustering algorithm is straightforward for vectors into set of groups. Preliminary cluster seeds are selected (at random). K-means algorithm consists of the separation of all information of an exact dataset into k different clusters which aggregate each one of the data [14–16]. The squared Euclidean distance from each entity to each cluster is computed, and every entity is assigned to the neighboring cluster. For every cluster, the new centroid is computed and each seed rate is now replaced by the individual cluster centroid. The cluster centroid is recalculated based on the new relationship task [17]. Algorithm 1 shows the pseudocode for the K-means clustering algorithm.

where

K Tree,
n Node,
K Middle candidate,
X Cell,
D Candidate set,
d* Nearest neighbor

```
filter(k Node n, CandidateSet  D)
{ X <- n.cell;
if(n is a leaf)
{d*<- the closest point in D to n.point;
d *.wgtMid,- d *.wgtMid+n.point;
d *.count,- d *.count+1;}
Else
{d *<-the closest point in D to X's midpoint;
for each (m €D \ {n*})
if (m.isFarther(d*,C))  M <- M \ { m };
if (|M |= 1)
{d *.wgtMid<- d *.wgtMid+ n. wgtMid;
d *.count <- d *.count+ n.count;}
Else {Filter (n.left, D);
Filter (n.right, D);}}}
```

Algorithm 1: Pseudo code for the K-Means Clustering Algorithm

The square geometric method from every object to every cluster is evaluated, and every object is assigned to the contiguous cluster. For every node of the k-tree, a set of candidate is preserved in the middle. The K-means algorithm separates the middle points that may serve as the adjacent neighbour for a number of positions lying within the coupled cell. The candidate middle for the origin consists of all K middle. The amount of connected data points n: calculated bias Midpoint; n: wgtMid, which distinct to be the vector summation of all the connected points. The real middle point is presently n:wgtMid = n:count. It is simple to change the k-tree structure to calculate this further information in the similar space and time limits, and then to propagate candidates as follows: For every node n, X indicates its group and K indicates its candidate set. Initially, calculate the candidate d*€ D. D is close to the middle of X. Subsequently, for each of the remaining candidates m € D \ {d*}, if no piece of X is more rapidly to m than it is to d*, it can assume that m is not the adjacent middle to any data position associated with n and, for this reason, can reduce, or filter, m from the list of candidates. If n is connected with a particular candidate (which be required to d*), then d* is the adjacent neighbor of all its data points. It can allocate them to d* by counting the linked node with the weighted middle node and add to d*. If not, if n is an internal node, then recurse on its offspring. If it is a leaf node, calculate the distance since its connected data point to all the candidates in D and allocate the data point to its adjacent middle.

3 Results and Discussion

In this research work, the well-known benchmark datasets namely Collins, DIP, Krogan, Krogan Extended, PPI-D1, PPI-D2, GSE12220, GSE12221, GSE12442, and GSE17716 are used to assess the performance of the proposed algorithm with the existing algorithms such as MCODE and SPICi. To evaluate the performance of the proposed algorithm with the existing algorithms, six performance measures, namely precision, recall, f-measure, sensitivity, positive predictive value (PPV) and accuracy are used in this work. From the experimental results, it is inferred that the proposed K-means algorithm provides better results than the existing algorithms.

For all the datasets and its complex detection, the proposed K-means clustering algorithm provides better accuracy than the existing algorithms. And also for the overall accuracy, the proposed K-means algorithm gives better results than the existing algorithms. The performance measures for the protein interaction datasets such as Collins, DIP, Krogan, Krogan Extended (2006), PPI D1, PPI D2 and gene expression datasets such as GSE12220, GSE12221, GSE12442, and GSE17716 are calculated. From the experimental results, it is inferred that the proposed algorithm achieves better performance values than the existing algorithms, and it is shown in Figs. 1, 2, 3, 4, 5, 6, 7, 8, 9, and 10.

With respect to Complex-D1 and Complex-D2 for the accuracy, the proposed algorithm performs better compared to all the existing algorithms as given in Table 1 and Fig. 11, respectively. Based on the experimental and statistical analysis, it is inferred that the proposed algorithm achieves better results than the existing algorithms for the protein complex datasets.

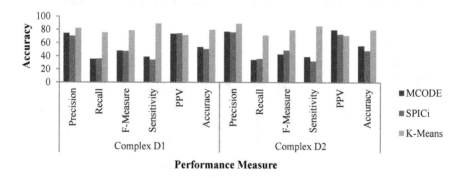

Fig. 1 Performance analysis for the existing and proposed algorithm for the collins dataset

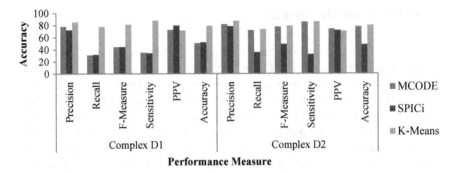

Fig. 2 Performance analysis for the existing and proposed algorithm for DIP dataset

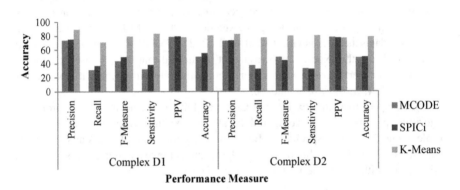

Fig. 3 Performance analysis for the existing and proposed algorithm for krogan dataset

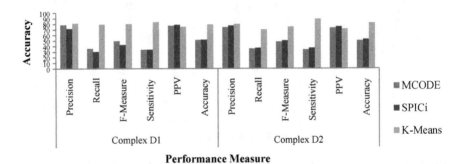

Fig. 4 Performance analysis for the existing and proposed algorithm for krogan-extended dataset

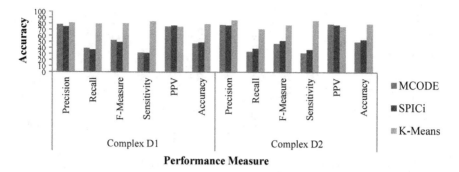

Fig. 5 Performance analysis for the existing and proposed algorithm for PPI-D1 dataset

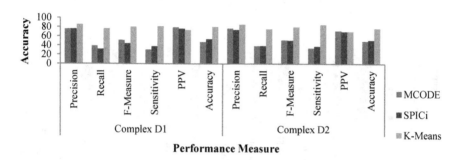

Fig. 6 Performance analysis for the existing and proposed algorithm for PPI-D2 dataset

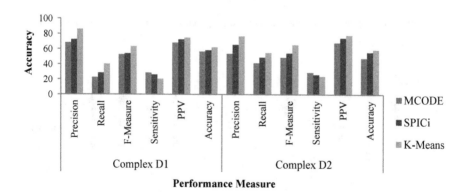

Fig. 7 Performance analysis for the existing and proposed algorithm for GSE12220 dataset

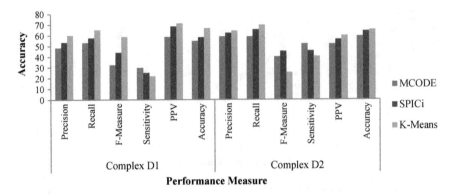

Fig. 8 Performance analysis for the existing and proposed algorithm for GSE12221 dataset

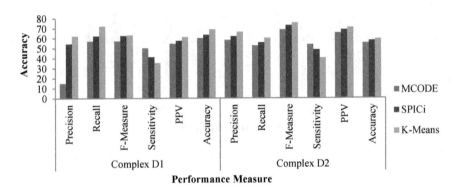

Fig. 9 Performance analysis for the existing and proposed algorithm for GSE12442 dataset

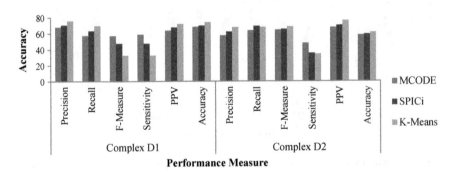

Fig. 10 Performance analysis for the existing and proposed algorithm for GSE17716 dataset

Table 1 Statistical comparison of proposed algorithm performance with existing algorithms with reference to Complex D1 and Complex D2

Datasets	% difference with respect to complex-D1		% difference with respect to complex-D2	
	MCODE	SPICi	MCODE	SPICi
Collins	30.22	39.4	30.22	39.4
DIP	2.68	40.06	2.68	40.06
Krogan	37.96	36.83	37.96	36.83
Krogan extended	39.3	35.79	39.3	35.79
PPI-D1	37.15	32.79	37.15	32.79
PPI-D2	35.91	33.27	35.91	33.27
GSE12220	9.06	6.33	19.17	5.73
GSE12221	17.86	12.73	8.96	1.79
GSE12442	12.74	8.05	6.84	2.73
GSE17716	7.93	6.26	5.67	4.02

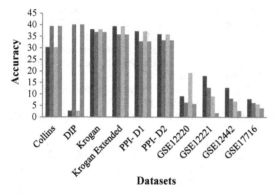

■ % difference with respect to Complex - D1 MCODE

■ % difference with respect to Complex - D1 SPICi

■ % difference with respect to Complex - D2 MCODE

■ % difference with respect to Complex - D2 SPICi

Fig. 11 Statistical comparison of accuracy for the proposed algorithm with the existing algorithms with reference to Complex D1 and Complex D2

4 Conclusion and Future Work

Clustering techniques are used to predict the protein complexes from the PPI networks. High-throughput experimental techniques have produced a large amount of protein interaction, which makes it possible to predict protein complex from protein–protein interaction (PPI) networks. However, the small amount of known physical interaction may limit protein complex detection. The protein interaction datasets such as DIP, Collins, Krogan, Krogan Extended, PPI-D1, PPI-D2 and gene expression datasets such as GSE12220, GSE12221, GSE12442, and GSE17716 are used for existing and proposed algorithms, namely MCODE, SPICi and K-means.

Compared with MCODE and SPICi, the proposed algorithm predicts protein complexes with higher quality and achieves higher precision values and lower sensitivity values. From the experimental results, it is proved that the proposed algorithm achieves higher performance in terms of accuracy, precision, recall, and f-measure values. In the future, the proposed algorithm will be applied on other types of protein complex datasets such as phenotype, pathways and evolutionary datasets.

Acknowledgements The authors thank the Department of Science and Technology (DST), New Delhi (DST/INSPIRE Fellowship/2015/IF150093), for the financial support under INSPIRE Fellowship for this research work.

References

1. Bader GD and Hogue CW. An Automated Method For Finding Molecular Complexes In Large Protein Interaction Networks. BMC Bioinformatics. 2003 Jan 13;4:2.
2. Tong AH, et al. A combined experimental and computational strategy to define protein interaction networks for peptide recognition modules. Science. 2002 Jan 11;295(5553):321–4.
3. Eileen Marie Hanna, et al. Detecting Protein Complexes In Protein Interaction Networks Modelled As Gene Expression Biclusters. PLoS One. 2015 Dec 7;10(12):e0144163.
4. Le Ou-Yang et al. Protein Complex Detection Based On Partially Shared Multi-View Clustering. BMC Bioinformatics. 2016 Sep 13;17(1):371.
5. Xueyong Li et al. Identification of protein complexes from multi-relationship protein interaction networks. Hum Genomics. 2016; 10(Suppl 2): 17.
6. Ou-Yang L, et al. A Two Layer Integration Framework For Protein Complex Detection. BMC Bioinformatics. 2016 Feb 24;17:100.
7. Altaf-Ul-Amin, M. et al. Development and implementation of an algorithm for detection of protein complexes in large interaction networks. BMC Bioinformatics. 2006;7:207.
8. S. Brohee and J. van Helden. Evaluation of clustering algorithms for protein-protein interaction networks. BMC Bioinformatics. 2006 Nov 6;7:488.
9. A.D. King, N. Przulj, and I. Jurisica. Protein complex prediction via cost-based clustering. Bioinformatics. 2004 Nov 22;20(17):3013–20.
10. Debomoy K Lahiri and Yuan-Wen Ge. Electrophoretic mobility shift assay for the detection of specific DNA–protein complex in nuclear extracts from the cultured cells and frozen autopsy human brain tissue. Brain Res Brain Res Protoc. 2000 Jul;5(3):257–65.
11. Jiang P and Singh M. SPICi: a fast clustering algorithm for large biological networks. Bioinformatics. 2010 Apr 15;26(8):1105–11.
12. Enright, A.J. et al. An efficient algorithm for large-scale detection of protein families. Nucleic Acids Res. 2002 Apr 1;30(7):1575–84.
13. Ashburner, M. et al. Gene Ontology: tool for the unification of biology. The Gene Ontology Consortium. Nat Genet. 2000 May;25(1):25–9.
14. Tapas Kanungo and David M. Mount. An Efficient k-Means Clustering Algorithm: Analysis and Implementation. IEEE Transactions on Pattern Analysis and Machine Intelligence. Vol. 24, No. 7, July 2002.
15. K. Alsabti, S. Ranka, and V. Singh, An Efficient k-means Clustering Algorithm, Proc. First Workshop High Performance Data Mining, Mar. 1998.

16. L. Kaufman and P.J. Rousseeuw. Finding Groups in Data: An Introduction to Cluster Analysis. New York: John Wiley & Sons, 1990.

17. O.L. Mangasarian.Mathematical Programming in Data Mining. Data Mining and Knowledge Discovery. vol. 1, pp. 183–201, 1997.

Automatic Generation of Fill-in-the-Blank Questions From History Books for School-Level Evaluation

Sumeet Pannu, Aishwarya Krishna, Shiwani Kumari, Rakesh Patra and Sujan Kumar Saha

Abstract Fill-in-the-blank questions (FIBs) play an important role in educational assessment. FIBs are effective to assess the understanding of well-defined concepts, and these are often used in school level. But manual preparation of FIBs is time-consuming and requires sufficient expertise on the content. This paper presents the proposed system for automatic generation of FIB questions that accepts school textbook as input. First, we identify the informative sentences that can act as the basis of FIBs. A parse structure-based module works on the sentences to identify the concept or knowledge embedded in the sentence. The knowledge is extracted in form of subject–predicate–object triplet or expanded triplet. Then, a hybrid algorithm chooses the most appropriate word/phrase that can be marked as a gap. Proposed system is tested using class VII-level history textbook as input. The quality of the system generated questions is then evaluated manually using three defined metrics. Experimental result shows that the proposed technique is quite promising.

Keywords Question generation · Fill-in-the-blanks · Educational NLP

S. Pannu · A. Krishna · S. Kumari · R. Patra · S. K. Saha (✉)
Department of CSE, BIT Mesra, Ranchi, India
e-mail: sujan.kr.saha@gmail.com

S. Pannu
e-mail: sumeetpannu79@gmail.com

A. Krishna
e-mail: aishwarya.krishna07@gmail.com

S. Kumari
e-mail: shiwani.4215@gmail.com

R. Patra
e-mail: rakesh9687@gmail.com

© Springer Nature Singapore Pte Ltd. 2018
P. K. Pattnaik et al. (eds.), *Progress in Computing, Analytics and Networking*,
Advances in Intelligent Systems and Computing 710,
https://doi.org/10.1007/978-981-10-7871-2_44

1 Introduction

Fill-in-the-blank questions (FIBs) play an important role in educational assessment. FIBs are effective to assess the understanding of well-defined concepts, and these are often used in school level. But manual preparation of FIBs is time-consuming and requires sufficient expertise on the content. The person needs to scan through each line of the chapter and see if that sentence is capable of becoming an FIB question or not. An acceptable FIB question can be formed from a particular sentence only if it contains some fact or information, so that if formed a question out of it has some value towards the gain in knowledge for students. Then, he needs to identify the words or phrases that will be marked as the blank.

For the automatic question generation task also, we follow similar steps. The system we develop for automatic generation of FIBs consists of four basic modules: (i) preprocessing of the text, (ii) identification of concept or knowledge embedded in the sentence, (iii) selection of sentences capable of generating FIBs and (iv) identification of key or the gap-word. Preprocessing module performs text conversion, text cleaning, pronoun resolution, etc. We feel that sentence selection is the most important step as the efficiency and accuracy of this step will decide what set of decent questions that finally we are going to have at the end of the complete process. Not all sentences of a chapter are capable of becoming a question. An algorithm is required to filter out only factual and informative sentences. A few approaches are proposed in the literature for sentence selection in various domains, like first sentence and other features based, context pattern based, summarization based, parse tree similarity based; these are discussed in Sect. 2. But applicability of a specific approach depends on its suitability on the target domain and application. Since we are working on a specific domain, history, there are certain characteristics of the subject that helped us to develop the algorithm for sentence selection. In this domain, the names play the most important role in question formation. When we study the available questions, given as review question at the end of each chapter of the book, we find that most of the questions deal with the names (e.g. king, ruler, kingdom, capital, region) or dates. Therefore, we use the availability of named entity words or date in a sentence as one of the selection criteria. Next, a parse structure-based module works on the sentences to identify the concept or knowledge embedded in the sentence. The knowledge is extracted in form of subject–predicate–object triplet or expanded triplet. Availability of an important predicate along with a set of required arguments becomes another clue for sentence selection as well as key selection. Then, a hybrid module, that uses named entity information, parts of speech information and the arguments of the predicates, is used to choose the most appropriate word or phrase that is marked as a gap.

To evaluate the performance of the system, we run it on NCERT class VII history textbook—Our Pasts II. The pdf version of the book is given as input to the system. The preprocessing module converts the pdf file into readable text format and cleans the text. Then, the system generates FIB questions from the clean sentences. The quality of the system generated questions is then evaluated manually. For the evaluation, we use three metrics, namely *is valid, sentence quality* and *key quality*. In our experiments, we observe that 84.73% of the questions are evaluated as valid questions. This value indicates that the system is effectual in FIB question generation. The details of the system are described in the subsequent sections of the paper.

2 Related Work

Development of an automatic FIB or MCQ generation system has become a popular research problem in the last few years. Here, we discuss a few systems available in the literature for fill-in-the-blanks generation. The process of MCQ generation is similar to the FIB generation, except MCQ generation requires an extra step for distractor generation. Therefore, here we also discuss the articles on MCQ generation, with special attention to the sentence selection and key selection phases.

Mitkov and Ha and Mitkov et al. developed semi-automatic systems for MCQ generation from a textbook on linguistics [1, 2]. They used several natural language processing (NLP) techniques like shallow parsing, term extraction, sentence transformation and computation of semantic distance for the task. They also employed natural language corpora and ontologies such as WordNet. Their system consists of three major modules: term extraction, stem generation and distractor generation. Term extraction from the text is basically done by using frequency count. Stem generation is for identifying eligible clauses where a set of linguistic rules are used. Brown developed a system for automatic generation of vocabulary assessment questions. In this task, they used WordNet for finding definition, synonym, antonym, hypernym and hyponym in order to develop the questions [3]. Aldabe et al. and Aldabe and Maritxalar developed systems to generate close questions in Basque language [4, 5]. They have divided the task into six phases: selection of text, marking blanks, generation of distractors, selection of distractors, evaluation with learners and item analysis. The generated questions are used for learners' assessment in the science domain. They did text selection based on level of the learners and the length of the texts. And marking of blanks was mostly done manually. Papasalouros et al. (2008) proposed an ontology-based approach for development of an automatic MCQ system [6]. They have used the structure of ontology that is the concepts, instances and the relationship or properties that relates the concepts or instances. First, they formed sentences from the ontology structure, and then, they found distractors from the ontology. Agarwal and Mannem presented a system for generating gap-fill questions from a biology text book [7]. They also divided their work into three phases: sentence selection, key selection and distractors generation. They used task-specific features for the individual phases. Bhatia et al. presented a system for generating MCQ questions from Wikipedia text. The system used a list of patterns or rules for sentence selection and key selection [8]. Majumder and Saha used a parse tree similarity-based approach for sentence selection for MCQ [9]. Narendra et al. used the MEAD summarizer for sentence selection and topic word extraction-based criteria for key selection in their MCQ system [10].

3 Methodology

The system is composed of multiple modules. Each module has its own strategy to follow. We discuss below the strategies we adopt to develop the individual modules of the system.

3.1 Preprocessing of Input Text

This step consists of some prerequisites of subsequent major steps to be taken towards the generation of automatic FIB questions. The first of them is to prepare the input text. To make the system robust, we make it capable of handling simple text document as well as pdf file. As our domain of interest is school education and most of the text books are available in pdf format only, we put an extra step for converting pdf files into text. This task is done with the help of the PDFMiner[1] tool. The next step is text cleaning. For the question generation, we need only the text portion of the book or chapter. But the text converted from the pdf book often contains images, sample questions and some other content that are not required for the task. Additionally, the sentence boundaries become erroneous in several sentences. Segregation of topic headings, subheadings and paragraphs is also necessary for question preparation from a desired portion of the book. To handle these issues, we run a semi-automatic phase to extract complete, bounded and meaningful sentences, tagged with *chapter_id* and *heading_id*, from the source text. This step leads to a well-formed clean text suitable for automatic question generation.

Pronoun resolution is the next important preprocessing phase. For the preparation of question from a sentence, the sentence should have complete set of information. Pronouns are required to be replaced by the corresponding nouns to make it complete. For the pronoun resolution task, we employ the ARKref[2] coreference resolution tool.

---

[1] https://euske.github.io/pdfminer/.
[2] https://github.com/brendano/arkref.

3.2 Sentence Selection

All the sentences in the text are not capable of generating FIB questions. A question can be prepared only from the sentences that contain a questionable fact. Sentence selection step aims to identify such sentences that can act as the basis of question formation. As named entities are the pivotal element of a sentence, occurrence of a name in a sentence increases the quantity of questionable fact in the sentence. But only occurrence of named entity in a sentence does not guarantee that the sentence is questionable. Therefore, we extract some additional information from the parse tree of the sentence to refine the selection. We discuss below the strategy for sentence selection.

NER Information. We deeply study the existing questions of this domain and observe that majority of the questions contain a named entity, like names of kings or other important people, name of a state, province, capital, and other locations, date or year of war or some historic event. So, the primary feature of our sentence selection is the availability of one or more NE in the sentence. Specifically, in this domain, we choose those sentences that contain person and location names or date. We plan to use Stanford NER tagger[3] for identifying the named entities in the sentence. But during the experiments, we observed that the Stanford NER system is trained with general or newswire domain corpus; therefore, it fails in recognizing a portion of the history domain names. Then, we semi-automatically create a few gazetteers lists that are incorporated with the output of Stanford NER. We also perform boundary refinement of the names. Boundary detection is important in MCQs. Sometimes the NER system is unable to do this NER boundary detection properly. This task we also perform with the help of the gazetteer lists and a few context patterns [11].

Predicate–Argument-Based Sentence Selection. To refine the sentence selection, next, we employ parse tree information in it. After a deep study of the domain, we observe that occurrence of certain verbs increases the content of questionable information in the sentence. Example of such verbs is 'defeated', 'conquered', 'born', 'defeat', 'succeeded', 'recruited', 'assassinate', etc. So, we compile a list (Histoty_Verb_List) of such important verbs. This list is created automatically through parse tree analysis of existing FIB questions. We collect a list of existing questions from the review questions of the textbook and other related materials. Then, we apply the Stanford Parser[4] on these sentences. The parse tree is analysed to find the deepest verb (VBD) in the main verb phrase (VP) of the sentence. These extracted verbs are incorporated in *History_Verb_List*.

After the set of verbs have been finalized, we search for the arguments (or parameters) of the verbs (or predicate) that describe different categories of information needed to make a full informative sentence. For example, the predicate 'defeated' can be associated with multiple arguments, like *defeated (Date, Ruler1,*

---

[3]https://nlp.stanford.edu/software/CRF-NER.shtml.

[4]https://nlp.stanford.edu/software/lex-parser.shtml.

Ruler2, Location). These parameters describe *Ruler1* defeated *Ruler2*, and the *Date* and *Location* imply when and where this fight took place. Some of these arguments are marked *as essential arguments* and some as *additional arguments.* List of essential and additional arguments is decided through the parse structure analysis of the existing questions. If a sentence contains an important predicate with a list of required arguments, then the sentence becomes a candidate for selection. To extract the predicates and the arguments, we primarily follow the method discussed in Rusu et al. [12].

Final Sentence Selection Procedure. Now we summarize our sentence selection procedure in Algorithm 1.

Algorithm 1: Procedure for selecting a sentence as a questionable sentence.
Input: One sentence.   *Output:* Selected or Not.

(1) Check the availability of any verb from the *Histoty_Verb_List.* If not available, then discard the sentence.
(2) Apply Stanford NER and Gazetteer list based NER on the sentence.
(3) Check the availability of Person, Location names and Dates in the sentence. If not available, then discard the sentence.
(4) Apply the Stanford Parser on the sentence.
(5) Analyze the parse tree to extract the triplets.
(6) Check the availability of the predicate with required arguments in the sentences. If not available, then discard the sentence.
(7) Else, the sentence is selected.

3.3 Key or Blank Word Identification

Next task is identification of the key. Here, in the task 'key' refers to the word or sequence of words or phrase that will be replaced by a blank. Key identification is done with the help of the output of the NER and the predicate–argument information extracted from the sentences.

We extract the set of triplets (subject–predicate–object) from the selected sentences with the help of the methodology discussed by Rusu et al. [12]. But to handle the application-specific and domain-specific requirements, we have modified the original Rusu triplet methodology. The actual algorithm prefers to pick the head noun or first noun in the NP subtree as the subject. But in this domain, most of the subjects are named entities and contain multiple words. So, we modify the methodology accordingly to pick the complete named entity as the subject. Sometimes a sentence contains multiple objects in this domain. The original triplet extraction methodology is able to identify these but unable to distinguish between them. We use the parts of speech tags (like IN) in the preposition phrases (PP) of the sentence to distinguish between the arguments. Let us consider an example sentence to make it clearer: the sentence "Sitaram Pande was recruited in 1912 as a sepoy in the Bengal Native Army". The predicate is "recruited", the subject is "Sitaram Pandey", but the sentence contains multiple objects like "1912", "sepoy", "Bengal Native Army". We distinguish these objects with the help of the IN-words like "recruited_as", "recruited_in", "recruited_in_date".

Now we use this triplet information and NER information to select the key. If both the subject and object are named entity, then we choose the subject as the key. If we find any object labelled as "in_Date", "at_Location", "of_Location", "over_Location", "from_Location", "to_Location", "from_Person", "since_date", "for_CD", or "as_post", then it is also selected as the key.

The system selects three different keys from the example sentence given above. These are *Sitaram Pandey, 1912, sepoy*. Similarly, from the sentence "Babur occupied much of northern India after his victory at Panipat in 1526", four keys are selected: *Babur, northern India, Panipat* and *1526*.

As per the key selection criteria, we use a sentence that may have multiple keys. That implies that multiple FIB questions are generated from one informative sentence. Therefore, this key selection approach increases the overall efficiency of the proposed FIB generation system.

4   Result and Discussion

To evaluate the proposed system, we apply it on NCERT class VII history text book—Our Pasts II. Three chapters of the book are given as input to the system for question generation from these. The system generates a total of 76 fill-in-the-blank questions. These questions are then manually assessed to measure the accuracy of the system. For the assessment, we use the feedback of five human evaluators.

The primary metric of evaluation is the quality of the question—whether the question is *valid* and can be used in any actual examination in a school. Additionally, we use two other metrics for evaluation of the core modules of the system. These are: *sentence quality* and *key quality*. Sentence quality quantifies how good the sentence selection approach is—that is whether the sentence is really a good sentence for FIB generation. Key quality indicates whether the key is properly selected or not. All these three metrics are considered as binary: the evaluator puts a score '1' if he is satisfied with it and '0' otherwise. Table 1 presents the score we obtain after the manual evaluation of the 76 system generated questions. These 76 questions were formed from 42 sentences. So, we measure *sentence quality* of these 42 sentences, and *key quality* and *is valid* are evaluated for all the 76 questions. From the table, we observe that the key selection module of the system is highly

Table 1 Evaluation of the system generated questions (total 76 questions)

Evaluator#	Sentence quality (42)	Key quality (76)	Is valid (76)
Evaluator 1	35	67	63
Evaluator 2	32	69	61
Evaluator 3	37	73	70
Evaluator 4	34	70	66
Evaluator 5	32	67	62
Average score	34/42 = 80.95%	69.2/76 = 91.05%	64.4/76 = 84.73%

efficient, as 91.05% of the keys are selected correctly. Accuracy of the sentence selection module is 80.95%. Also, 84.73% of the generated questions are labelled as valid questions. These values indicate that the system is quite efficient in automatically generating FIB questions.

5 Conclusion

This paper presented a technique for automatic generation of FIB questions from history textbook. Manual evaluation results demonstrate the efficiency of the proposed technique. Although the system contains some domain dependent features and resources, generalization can be made through use of proper alternative techniques or tools. Additionally, when we compute the recall of the system, that is the percentage of the total available sentences used in question generation, the value is not very high. If the questions were prepared manually in greedy manner, total number of questions would become quite higher than the system generated questions. Future improvement of the system can be made in this direction also.

Acknowledgements This work is supported by the project grant (project file no.: YSS/2015/001948) provided by the Science and Engineering Research Board (SERB), Govt. of India.

References

1. Mitkov, R., Ha, L.A., 2003. Computer-aided generation of multiple-choice tests. Proceedings of the HLT/NAACL Workshop on Building educational applications using Natural Language Processing, pp. 17–22.
2. Mitkov, R., Ha, L. A., and Karamanis, N., 2006. A computer-aided environment for generating multiple-choice test items. Natural Language Engineering, Vol. 12(2), pp. 177–194.
3. Brown, J. C., Frishkoff, G. A., and Eskenazi, M., 2005. Automatic question generation for vocabulary assessment. In Proceedings of HLT and EMNLP, pp. 819–826.
4. Aldabe, I., Lopez de Lacalle, M., Maritxalar, M., Martinez, E., Uria, L., 2006. ArikIturri: An Automatic Question Generator Based on Corpora and NLP Techniques. In ITS. LNCS 4053, pp. 584–594.

5. Aldabe, I., Maritxalar, M., 2010. Automatic Distractor Generation for Domain Specific Texts. Proceedings of IceTAL, LNAI 6233. pp. 27–38.
6. Papasalouros, A., Kanaris, K., Kotis, K,. 2008. Automatic Generation of multiple-choice questions from domain ontologies. IADIS e-Learning (2008).
7. Agarwal, M., and Mannem, P., 2011. Automatic gap-fill question generation from text books. In Proceedings of the 6th Workshop on Innovative Use of NLP for Building Educational Applications, pp. 56–64.
8. Bhatia, A. S., Kirti, M., and Saha, S. K., 2013. Automatic Generation of Multiple Choice Questions Using Wikipedia. In Proceedings of Pattern Recognition and Machine Intelligence, Springer Berlin Heidelberg, pp. 733–738.
9. Majumdar M, Saha S. K., 2014. Automatic Selection of Informative Sentences: The Sentences that can generate Multiple Choice Questions. Knowledge Management & E-Learning. Vol. 6, No. 4, pp. 377–391.
10. Narendra, A., Agarwal, M. and Shah, R., 2013. Automatic Cloze-Questions Generation. In Proceedings of Recent Advances in Natural Language Processing, Bulgaria, pp. 511–515.
11. Saha SK, Sarkar S, Mitra P. 2008. A Hybrid Feature Set based Maximum Entropy Hindi Named Entity Recognition. In proceedings of IJCNLP 2008, pp. 343–349.
12. Rusu, D., Dali, L., Fortuna, B., Grobelnik, M. and Mladenić, D. 2007. Triplet Extraction from Sentences. In Proceedings of the 10th International Multiconference "Information Society - IS 2007" Ljubljana, Slovenia, October 8–12, 2007, pp. 218–222.

Fault Control Using Triple Modular Redundancy (TMR)

Sharon Hudson, R. S. Shyama Sundar and Srinivas Koppu

Abstract Operating Systems have been widely expanding in terms of capabilities and resources. One of the many unavoidable concerns is the occurrence of a fault in the system. A fault is a violation of the existing system. A fault leads to a single or multiple failure in the system. In order to avoid this type of failure, we need to remove or control the fault. The commonly used techniques for controlling and isolating faults in the system are replication and check pointing. This paper aims to provide control over the detected fault by using the antique technique of triple modular redundancy (TMR) which is a type of N-modular redundancy techniques. Although it has the highest form of reliability, it has not been used to create a fault tolerant system. In our paper, we propose a system using the technique of triple modular redundancy to effectively mask and mitigate the detected faults to provide uninterrupted usage of the entire operating system.

Keywords Fault control · Triple modular redundancy · Fault
Fault isolation · Fault correction · Fault tolerance

1 Introduction

Operating Systems have been widely expanding in terms of capabilities and resources. One of the many unavoidable concerns is the occurrence of fault in the system. A fault is a violation of the assumptions made by or existing in a system [1]. An error is a condition which exhibits a fault. A failure is a visible variation

S. Hudson · R. S. Shyama Sundar (✉) · S. Koppu
School of Information and Technology (SITE), VIT University, Vellore 632014,
Tamil Nadu, India
e-mail: rsshyamasundar@gmail.com

S. Hudson
e-mail: sharon_helen@hotmail.com

S. Koppu
e-mail: srinukoppu@vit.ac.in

© Springer Nature Singapore Pte Ltd. 2018   471
P. K. Pattnaik et al. (eds.), *Progress in Computing, Analytics and Networking*,
Advances in Intelligent Systems and Computing 710,
https://doi.org/10.1007/978-981-10-7871-2_45

from specifications that exists externally. A fault doesn't always produce an error, neither does an error always produce a failure. If a memory location holds data and it is corrupted, whatever caused its corruption is called a fault and the data becomes erroneous. A program that crashes using this data is a failure.

1.1 Fault Control

Fault control is the detection, isolation, and correction of faults [2]. Fault detection determines whether the system contains a fault, the size of the fault and also determines if it can be corrected. Fault isolation is pinpointing the component or components where the fault is located. Fault correction is as the name suggests the correction of faults. Fault correction is the reconstruction of error-free data. The objective of fault control is to find the faults or errors in a system and correct them. To find the fault and rectify it accordingly, some redundancy (extra data) may be added to the message, which receivers can use to check the correctness of the delivered message, and to retrieve data which may be corrupted.

In this paper, we address and come up with a solution for an intermittent fault. This type of fault causes failure to the entire system. To locate this fault and find a solution is not easy. Our model makes use of replication and triple modular redundancy technique to overcome an intermittent fault.

1.2 Triple Modular Redundancy (TMR)

Modular redundancy is a basic concept that dates back to antiquity. It is a technique that uses an identical secondary system to back up the primary system [3]. The secondary system is additional like a spare and does not monitor the main system. Triple modular redundancy (TMR) is a process that uses a form of N-modular redundancy to control faults [3]. If a single indication of a critical operation resulted in an error, the entire mission would result in a disaster. A TMR-based system would ensure that three readings would be processed, thus avoiding a system shutdown due to a lone, false reading. Therefore, TMR technology provided both safety and availability to critical missions. In the present scenario, the concept of TMR still exists and is used widely in mission-critical environments [4].

We propose a simple system which makes use of the concept of TMR, which examines error signals provided by voters and discovers the system that causes the error. The two available systems can rectify and mask the fault in the occurrence of failure of one of the three systems.

2 Literature Survey

From the study of the papers [5–15], we concluded that if the OS design is static, it becomes expensive from the perspective of memory consumption and run times. Clock cycles and delay penalty can further be reduced. With smaller overheads, efficiency is improved. In many of the current high-performance computing applications, the mean-time-to-failure (MTF) of the system becomes significantly larger than the execution time. With that in mind, we propose a simple fault controlled system using the technique of triple modular redundancy.

Another major issue in existence is that the space requirements for replication increases enormously. This issue is resolved in our system by using remote storage of the data, for example, like the cloud environment.

S. no.	Author name and title	Technology	Drawback	Future work
1.	Gils, V. A triple modular redundancy technique providing multiple bit error protection without using extra redundancy [5]	Triple modular redundancy It detects and repairs the faulty bits in the faulty processor Fault detection is done over the air means at the same time By using TMR model, the faulty processor is detected as well as the administrator will be able to know that fault lies in which bit of which processor The timing simulation shows that time requires for fault detection and repair is in 8 ns, and it is very low	The space needed for replication is quite high If there are errors in two out of three devices, the result will also be erroneous	The space issue should be overcome
2.	Bharath Balasubramanian and Vijay K. Garg, fellow Fault tolerance in distributed systems using fused data structures [6]	Fused backups for linked lists Correcting crash faults Amazon dynamo Java collection framework	The recovery time is very expensive when compared to replication as replication has the time of O (mst), whereas the fusion technique	The ways to overcome the recovery time issue have to be taken care of The fused backup must be more effective

(continued)

(continued)

S. no.	Author name and title	Technology	Drawback	Future work
			requires O (mst2n) which is very high In fusion, the client needs to acquire the state of all the remaining data structures	
3.	Zizhong Chen and Jack Dongarra Algorithm-based fault tolerance for fail-stop failures [7]	ScaLAPACK matrix–matrix multiplication The mean-time-to-failure (MTTF) of these systems is becoming significantly shorter than the execution time of many current high-performance computing applications Avoids restarting computations from beginning after failures	Checksum relationship cannot be maintained in the middle of the computation	Need to find faster and more reliable methods
4.	Jasbir Kaur and Kinger Analysis of different techniques used for fault tolerance [8]	Fault tolerance manager architecture Message passing interface architecture Self-healing preemptive migration MapReduce	The current techniques are neither efficient nor reliable Existing techniques are very expensive	Need of a more efficient and reliable technique that is also cheaper than the existing techniques Need to explore more on MPI architecture in order to present a reliable and less costly technique for fault tolerance
5.	Kola, G., Kosar, T., & Livny, M. Faults in large distributed systems and what we can do about them [9]	Silent fail-stop stutter model Data provenance mechanism Automated fault location	This is only a theoretical concept. It was not successful on implementation	A more rigorous theoretical analysis of the silent fail-stutter model can be developed

(continued)

S. no.	Author name and title	Technology	Drawback	Future work
		Can transparently adapt applications to avoid faulty machines Has a data provenance mechanism that tracks the origin of the results, enabling scientists to selectively purge results from faulty components		The mechanisms can be deployed in real systems over a long period and evaluated Check if there are limits on failure fraction that will cause the mechanisms to not work
6.	Aniruddha Marathe Rachel Harris David K. Lowenthal Exploiting redundancy and application scalability for cost-effective, time-constrained execution of HPC applications on amazon EC2 [10]	Amazon EC2 Amazon Web Services (AWS) Elastic Block Store (EBS)	The program though is adaptive, but in the end, is only for amazon server and is not broad minded to develop for an open environment The system is still an undergoing and is prone to be of errors	Predicting of performance has to be added and should be let out in a broader MPI
7.	Hoffmann, M., Borchert, C., Dietrich, C., Schirmeier, H., Kapitza, R., Spinczyk, O., & Lohmann, D Effectiveness of fault detection mechanisms in static and dynamic operating system designs [11]	Fault injection CRC for error detection eCos kernel	Static design of OS is expensive at the price of memory consumption and run times Unreliable hardware	A static OS can be hardened at much lower price
8.	Chen, W., Gong, R., Dai, K., Liu, F., & Wang, Z. Two new space-time triple modular	Space-Time TMR (ST-TMR) Enhanced ST-TMR (EST-TMR) with double edge triggered registers	Not suitable to implement in critical environments	Research is required for protecting combinational circuits to improve the

(continued)

(continued)

S. no.	Author name and title	Technology	Drawback	Future work
	redundancy techniques for improving fault tolerance of computer systems [12]	Time redundancy is added to TMR		fault tolerance of the entire system

3 Proposed Architecture

The proposed architecture consists of three modules, namely the input module, the TMR module, and the output module in Fig. 1. A complete structure of the TMR module is specified in Fig. 2. The structure of its components is described in Figs. 3 and 4. A detailed description of the modules is furnished further on.

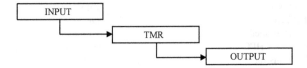

Fig. 1 Basic architecture

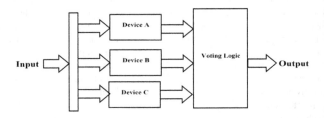

Fig. 2 Block diagram of proposed architecture

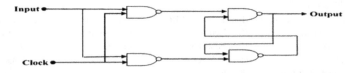

Fig. 3 D flip-flop

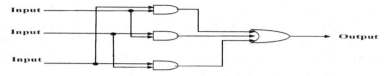

Fig. 4 Voting logic

3.1 Input Module

As the name suggests, this module provides input to the device. Under this module, all the user has to do is set the time intervals for the clock and input to be different. The inputs are generated randomly at the set time intervals. Once these details are set by the user, to proceed further the user has to run the simulation.

3.2 TMR Module

This module consists of the device utilizing the technique of triple modular redundancy. This device has three identical sub-devices (Device DFF1, Device DFF2, and Device DFF3) and one voting logic. It receives the input from the input module and sends the output to the output module. In this module, the input is replicated into three and fed into the devices DFF1, DFF2, and DFF3, simultaneously. The synchronized inputs from the devices are fed into the voting logic, where the majority of input becomes the output. Thus, even if there is an error in a single device, it is corrected with the help of the voter and the corrected output is got.

3.2.1 Device

The device is a D flip-flop. The input is sent through the NAND gate along with the clock time Q. The clock basically synchronizes the inputs. It is not used to change the outputs. Both the inputs are passed through the NAND gates to get the corrected input, and output is got. If the inputs are not synchronized, the inputs are referred through the NAND gates and the output is got. Two outputs that are fed are further fed into three NAND gates (six inputs are fed into three NAND gates), and the synchronized output is finally got.

3.2.2 Voting Logic

A device called the voting logic is used to check the correctness of the inputs. It takes the majority of the input values to be the output value. The synchronized inputs from the three devices are fed into the voter, and it gives the output value as the majority of inputs. If one of the three devices has an error due to fault in the system and gives a different output, this variability will be found and corrected by the voting logic. Thus, assuming that only a single error occurs, the voted output is always correct. When triple modular redundancy is applied to a system, all outputs of the system are voted; therefore, no error exists at the output.

3.3 Output Module

The output is generated in a waveform. Once the output is generated, it will be noted that the output is the same as the input. An inference report will be generated with the above results. This report proves that errors, if any, have been corrected. Hence, it also proves that our model is able to identify and correct faults, making our model fault controlled.

4 Results

The following results produced through the timing and functional simulation of the Altera Cyclone and Altera Quartus software kit show that system successfully tackles the faults (if any) and give the original or properly computed output through the STMR. Basically, the D pin is the input given to the processors, and CLK is the clock used to synchronize the computation processes across the entire system. The DFF1, DFF2, and DFF3 are outputs from each processor, and these are fed to the voting logic to produce the final output STMR.

In Fig. 5, it can be seen that the system detects the fault at DFF2 = 0 and produces the proper output STMR = 1, which is the majority value of the inputs to the voter.

Similarly, in Fig. 6, in the above waveform, the output produced is STMR = 0 irrespective of the CLK value as there is no input in D.

A sample table, Table 1, for the various inputs to the processors is given below. V_ERR is the assumption for a faulty voter in the system.

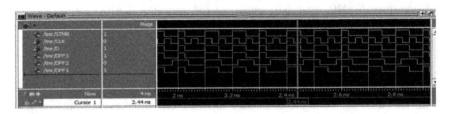

Fig. 5 Simulation 1

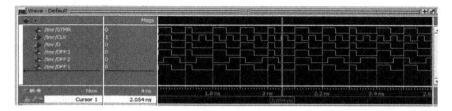

Fig. 6 Simulation 2

Table 1 Sample table of inputs and outputs of proposed architecture

CLK	D	DFF1	DFF2	DFF3	V_ERR	STMR
0	0	0	0	0	0	0
1	0	0	0	1	0	0
0	0	0	1	0	0	0
1	1	0	1	1	0	1
0	0	1	0	0	0	0
1	1	1	0	1	0	1
0	1	1	0	1	0	1
1	1	1	1	1	0	1

From Table 1, we can conclude that the input D will be the same as the output STMR, irrespective of change in DFF1, DFF2, DFF3. Thus, our model is proven to control faults.

5 Conclusion

The proposed system successfully detects a fault in the processor using the TMR architecture and also recovers from the fault. The system automatically prevents the system from failing as it has detected which processor is faulty. In order to recover from the fault, the system uses the output given out by the voting logic. The limitation of the system is the inability to detect multiple bit errors, and it can be overcome by using N-modular redundancy techniques. Further, the system occupies more space than other fault tolerant techniques due to the concept of redundancy, and this can be tackled by considering storage options in the cloud environment. In future, the development of this architecture into a real-time working system is the key challenge.

References

1. Avizienis, A., & Laprie, J. C. (1986). Dependable computing: From concepts to design diversity. Proceedings of the IEEE, 74(5), 629–638.
2. Patton, R. J. (2015). Fault-tolerant control. Encyclopedia of systems and control, 422–428.
3. NiGlobal (2015) Redundant Systems Basic Concepts – National Instruments. White paper.
4. Kim, E. P., & Shanbhag, N. R. (2012). Soft N-modular redundancy. IEEE Transactions on Computers, 61(3), 323–336.
5. Gils, V. (2013). A triple modular redundancy technique providing multiple-bit error protection without using extra redundancy. IEEE Transactions on Computers, 100(12), 623–631.
6. Balasubramanian, B., & Garg, V. K. (2013). Fault tolerance in distributed systems using fused data structures. IEEE transactions on parallel and distributed systems, 24(4), 701–715.
7. Chen, Z., & Dongarra, J. (2008). Algorithm-based fault tolerance for fail-stop failures. IEEE Transactions on Parallel and Distributed Systems, 19(12), 1628–1641.
8. Kaur, J., & Kinger, S. (2014). Analysis of different techniques used for fault tolerance. IJCSIT) International Journal of Computer Science and Information Technologies, 5(3), 4086–4090.
9. Kola, G., Kosar, T., & Livny, M. (2015, August). Faults in large distributed systems and what we can do about them. In European Conference on Parallel Processing (pp. 442–453). Springer Berlin Heidelberg.
10. Aniruddha Marathe Rachel Harris David K. Lowenthal (2015). "Exploiting Redundancy and Application Scalability for Cost-Effective, Time-Constrained Execution of HPC Applications on Amazon EC2". In IEEE Transactions on Parallel and Distributed Systems, 2015.
11. Hoffmann, M., Borchert, C., Dietrich, C., Schirmeier, H., Kapitza, R., Spinczyk, O., & Lohmann, D. (2014, June). Effectiveness of fault detection mechanisms in static and dynamic operating system designs. In Object/Component/Service-Oriented Real-Time Distributed Computing (ISORC), 2014 IEEE 17th International Symposium on (pp. 230–237). IEEE.
12. Chen, W., Gong, R., Dai, K., Liu, F., & Wang, Z. (2006, September). Two new space-time triple modular redundancy techniques for improving fault tolerance of computer systems. In Computer and Information Technology, 2006. CIT'06. The Sixth IEEE International Conference on (pp. 175–175). IEEE.
13. Chen, Y. H., Lu, C. W., Shyu, S. S., Lee, C. L., & Ou, T. C. (2014). A multi-stage fault-tolerant multiplier with triple module redundancy (TMR) technique. Journal of Circuits, Systems, and Computers, 23(05), 1450074.
14. George, C., & Vadhiyar, S. (2015). Fault tolerance on large scale systems using adaptive process replication. IEEE Transactions on Computers, 64(8), 2213–2225.
15. Distler, T., Cachin, C., & Kapitza, R. (2016). Resource-efficient Byzantine fault tolerance. IEEE Transactions on Computers, 65(9), 2807–2819.

Internet of Things-Enabled Smart Campus Energy Management and Control with Soft Computing Approach

Ramasamy Mariappan

Abstract Nowadays, sensor devices found widespread applications in multiple fields such as smart grids, smart buildings, Internet of things, and cyber-physical systems. One such significant application is energy management in buildings, which monitors the energy consumption and accordingly control. It may be equipped with wired sensor devices or wireless sensor devices to form a distributed sensor network over an optical backbone network. This paper proposes interconnected buildings for networked energy management system using Internet of things (IOT). In this system, wireless fiber optic sensors will be used to provide multiple types of energy management information for campus buildings through the existing information and communication network. This research work investigates on practical steps to realize the integration of IOT-enabled microgrid with campus area network (CAN)—Wi-Fi network for the campus energy management using soft computing-based energy management system (EMS).

Keywords Smart energy management · Internet of things · Soft computing

1 Introduction

In the recent years, the utilization of electrical energy and hence the demands are growing enormously. Challenges are growing about the environmental and social impacts on the consumption of fossil fuels, which include air pollution including emission of green house gases, etc. Therefore, it is necessary to save energy in generation, distribution, and utilization. While energy management system [1] for smart and microgrids is aimed at large-scale implementation, this can also be implemented for small-scale off-grid power systems such as domestic power system. Hence, it is the need of the hour to develop a good energy management system for smart buildings using real-time energy monitoring and control with Internet of

R. Mariappan (✉)
Sri Venkateswara College of Engineering, Tirupati 517507, Andhra Pradesh, India
e-mail: mrmrama2004@rediffmail.com

© Springer Nature Singapore Pte Ltd. 2018
P. K. Pattnaik et al. (eds.), *Progress in Computing, Analytics and Networking*,
Advances in Intelligent Systems and Computing 710,
https://doi.org/10.1007/978-981-10-7871-2_46

things (IOT) connectivity. An efficient energy management system monitors the load scheduling and distributed energy sources in the system and also manages the efficient utilization of the loads. This can be accomplished by minimizing overall operating cost for distributed generation while maximizing the energy utilization by the user.

2 Related Work

The recent evolution of information and communication technology [1] allows an existing communication network that can carry energy utilization information, etc., so that it can be accessed anywhere. This smartgrid development migrates the current system of generation, distribution, and utilization of energy. Hence, the future electric power grid needs ICT, whereas ICT needs electricity. This research paper is proposed to realize the integration of wireless sensor network for the campus energy management and control by deploying the Internet of things (IOT).

Applying distributed wireless sensor network for energy management has many quality of service (QoS) issues related to delays for getting the energy consumption data, loss of energy-related data, false alarm or control, etc. Increasing the number of sensing devices gives more knowledge about energy information, but increases the burden of underlying communication network, leading to congestion, packet loss, delay, etc., which degrades the QoS performance of energy management system, which lacks user comfort. Hence, the QoS problem for an efficient energy management in a campus building is a challenging task to do. Addressing this issue, we have differentiated the most prioritized energy-related data for alarm or control from that of non-prioritized data such as accounting and billing information by means of differentiated QoS. Internet of things reduces the effort of humans by introducing machine-to-machine interaction, which is used in [2] for implementing smartgrid through IoT using cloud data storage. Ashok Jhunjhunwala, IITM, Solar-DC Microgrid for Indian homes, 2016. The author, Ashok Jhunjhunwala, presents the method for using DC microgrid for home appliances and for electric vehicles. The authors [3] focus on the implementation of DC microgrid to check its viability and sustainability on rural electrification in India. The paper [4] proposed that coordinated control strategy for AC islanded microgrids, with available power in renewable energy sources (RES) and storage capacity of energy storage systems (ESS). The paper [5] presents a home automation system (HAS) using Intel Galileo by integration of cloud networking and wireless communication, for smart control of appliances within their home and storing the data in the cloud. The authors in [6] made a comprehensive survey on challenges over power management in hybrid AC/DC microgrid systems.

3 Proposed Work

An intelligent sensor network is one, which is running on reliable and secure information and communication technology network [7], and information access is the key to such communication system. This research work proposes a smart energy management system in campus buildings, which incorporates monitoring, analysis, control of energy conservation and communication capabilities to improve quality of service (QoS), reliability, and security. The major objectives of this research paper are as follows:

   i. Integration of wireless optical sensor network with Wi-Fi-campus area network through Internet of things (IOT).
  ii. Smart monitoring and controlling of campus energy utilization system to increase the energy efficiency through intelligent sensor network converged through Wi-Fi-campus area network with differentiated QoS and reliability.

3.1 Implementation Methodology

The intelligent sensor network will be designed to plug in various low power wireless optical sensor devices such as OptoEMU sensor, smart meter, luminescence sensor, temperature sensor, and object movement sensor, which exchange data through Zigbee-based wireless communication protocol. Various smart energy devices like load control device, luminescence control, and temperature control are communicated through power line communication through a PLC gateway. A centralized energy management server is deployed to collect all data such as energy consumption and generation from the smart sensing devices such as smart meter installed in the campus premises through a Zigbee gateway and accordingly to control the energy utilization load through PLC.

A Web portal for energy management will be implemented, which can monitor, manage, and control the energy utilization, energy loss, etc., through smart devices connected through IOT in the campus buildings. Also, utility events, alerts and messages through GSM/cellular gateway will be made available to the users through the Web portal. This EMS Web server is implemented using Microsoft Web server. The layers of IOT-enabled EMS are shown in Fig. 1.

3.2 Smart EMS Design Methodology

The parameters which are dependent on the optimal QoS performance of the energy management system are delay, packet loss, false alarms, etc. The threshold values of the control parameters will be determined to get the optimum performance.

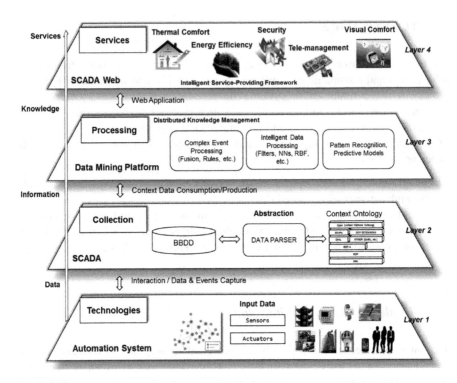

Fig. 1 Different layers of IOT for home EMS

The design methodology for QoS improvement is as follows:

  i. Identify the correlated QoS parameters
 ii. Tune the energy control performances
iii. Determine threshold values of control parameters
 iv. Evaluate the performance of EMS within these thresholds
  v. If it is not optimal QoS, retune until you get the optimal configuration.

The smart campus energy management test bed will be deployed using wireless optical sensor devices such as OptoEMU sensor and smart meter on each laboratory with each electrical device considered as a node and a set of nodes connected through a Zigbee gateway for data gathering as well as PLC gateway for energy control. Similar setup will be done on each laboratory, and all the gateways will be communicated through a central energy management server for monitoring the energy data as well as for controlling the energy utilization and generation. An EMS Web portal application will be created to display all information about the energy generation as well as utilization. A prototype model for the smart campus energy management system is shown in Fig. 2.

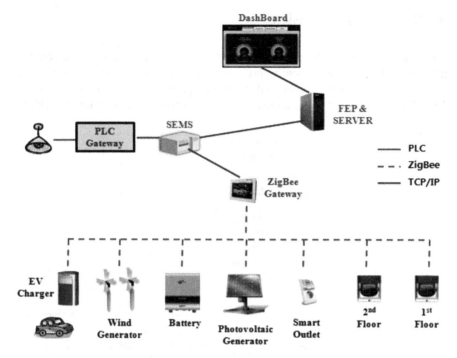

Fig. 2 Prototype of DC microgrid test bed for smart EMS

3.3 Outcomes

The outcomes and deliverables from this research work are manifold and designed for intelligent management of energy with the help of existing information communication technology. Both of the collaborating bodies and the respective institutions are responsible for the delivery of the outcomes. The targeted outcomes of this research are as follows:

i. A standardized network with integrated flow of information and electrical signal will be framed.
ii. An IOT-enabled microgrid with integrated network will be deployed.
iii. Publication of investigated methodologies, framework, results, and performance analysis in referred international journals and conferences.
iv. Energy conservation in campus building will be optimized and also increases the efficiency of utilization of energy while reducing loss of energy.
v. Enhancing the quality of service for the flow of information pertaining to energy conservation.

4   Results and Discussion

This section discusses about the results obtained through simulation of energy
management and optimization algorithm applied with DC microgrid for smart
buildings. The EMS is implemented using the optimization toolbox of MATLAB
15R. The smart EMS optimization algorithm is shown in Fig. 3. In this algorithm,

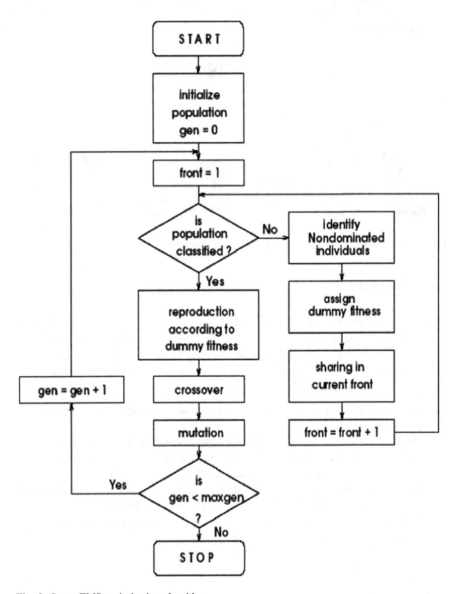

Fig. 3 Smart EMS optimization algorithm

after population classifying, crossover and mutation are done till the predefined maximum threshold of gen is reached.

4.1 Simulation Results

In MATLAB 15R, the EMS-optimized load power with varying load hours is measured and plotted in graph as shown in Fig. 4. In comparison with EMS without optimization, the new proposed EMS optimization approach reduces the peak hour load power and saves the energy consumption. Figure 5 shows the variation of energy consumption cost versus iteration number. The cost is steeply decreasing

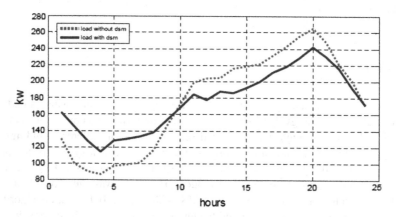

Fig. 4 Simulated results of load with microgrid EMS with optimization

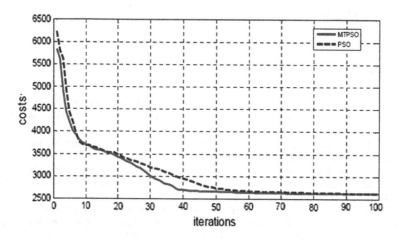

Fig. 5 Convergence of energy optimization algorithm for smart EMS

with increasing iteration number. After 50 iterations, our approach reaches the constant cost. This shows that our EMS optimization approach outperforms than existing EMS method.

4.2 Discussion

The MATLAB simulated results show that the load consumption is reduced with EMS with optimization algorithm as shown in Fig. 4. In other words, it reduces the energy loss. As the number of simulation iteration increases, it converges after reaching N = 50. After 50 iterations, the energy cost reaches minimal. This shows that the EMS optimization outcome is achieved after 50% time of simulation period as shown in Fig. 5.

5 Conclusion

The energy management system is an ever-growing research field, where smartgrid is the vital role for energy distribution as well as monitoring and control of electrical energy utilization through interconnected sensor devices in different buildings. In this paper, a microgrid in a smart campus energy management system is equipped with Internet of things with networked EMS for the energy efficient system with soft computing approach for EMS to reduce the energy wastage. The MATLAB simulated results show that the smart EMS with energy optimization algorithm reduces the maximum load power and the energy utilization cost is minimized with maximizing the energy utilization. Hence, this proposed system provides better quality of service with offering maximum energy utilization with minimum cost for the microgrid in campus EMS.

References

1. Bhim Singh, Krishna Kant and Chinmay Jain, "Small Hydro-Wind-Photo-Voltaic Based Standalone Microgrid System," Pending Indian Patent No. 2031/DEL/2015 Filed on: 03 July 2015.
2. Ashok Jhunjhunwala, IITM, Solar-DC and Electric Vehicles, An Opportunity for India, 2016.
3. Ashok Jhunjhunwala, IITM, Solar-DC Micro-grid for Indian homes, 2016.
4. Debojyoti Sen, Varun Singhal, Vijay Kumar, Solar Dc Microgrid for Rural Electrification-A Case Study, International Advanced Research Journal in Science, Engineering & Technology (IARJSET), Vol. 2, Special Issue 1, May 2015.
5. IA. Arachana, A Grid Connected Solar PV Array with Power Quality Analysis Using MPPT Technique, International Journal of Advanced Research in Biology Engineering Science and Technology (IJARBEST) Vol. 2, Special Issue 10, March 2016.

6. Vinay sagar K N, Kusuma S M, Home Automation Using Internet of Things, International Research Journal of Engineering and Technology (IRJET) e-ISSN: 2395-0056 Volume: 02 Issue: 03 June-2015 ISSN: 2395-0072 © 2015, Page 1965.

7. C. Natesan et al., Chitra Natesan, SenthilKumar Ajithan, Swathi Chozhavendhan, Anitha Devendhiran, Power Management Strategies in Microgrid: A Survey, International Journal of Renewable Energy Research, Vol. 5, No. 2, 2015.

Deep Learning Approaches for Detecting Objects from Images: A Review

Ajeet Ram Pathak, Manjusha Pandey and Siddharth Rautaray

Abstract Detecting objects from images is a challenging problem in the domain of computer vision and plays a very crucial role for wide range of real-time applications. The ever-increasing growth of deep learning due to availability of large training data and powerful GPUs helped computer vision community to build commercial products and services which were not possible a decade ago. Deep learning architectures especially convolutional neural networks have achieved state-of-the-art performance on worldwide competitions for visual recognition like ILSVRC, PASCAL VOC. Deep learning techniques alleviate the need of human expertise from designing the handcrafted features and automatically learn the features. This resulted into use of deep architectures in many domains like computer vision (image classification, visual recognition) and natural language processing (language modeling, speech recognition). Object detection is one such promising area immensely needed to be used in automated applications like self-driving cars, robotics, drone image analysis. This paper analytically reviews state-of-the-art deep learning techniques based on convolutional neural networks for object detection.

Keywords Computer vision · Convolutional neural network · Deep learning
Object detection · Visual recognition

A. R. Pathak (✉) · M. Pandey · S. Rautaray
School of Computer Engineering, Kalinga Institute of Industrial Technology (KIIT)
University, Bhubaneswar, India
e-mail: ajeet.pathak44@gmail.com

M. Pandey
e-mail: manjushapandey82@gmail.com

S. Rautaray
e-mail: sr.rgpv@gmail.com

© Springer Nature Singapore Pte Ltd. 2018
P. K. Pattnaik et al. (eds.), *Progress in Computing, Analytics and Networking*,
Advances in Intelligent Systems and Computing 710,
https://doi.org/10.1007/978-981-10-7871-2_47

1 Introduction

The past four years witnessed great improvement in performance of computer vision tasks making use of deep learning techniques. According to Gartner's prediction of technology trends for 2017 governing the future smart digital network, trends like artificial intelligence and advanced machine learning are on the top position and so the deep learning [1]. Factors like availability of large datasets and fast graphics processors have made deep learning techniques to be applicable in different domains like big data analytics, image and video processing, natural language modeling, speech processing, and computer vision. The market of computer vision technology will strike $33.3 billion by 2019 with significant growth in consumer, robotics, and machine vision [2]. It can be understood that deep learning would definitely play an active role for making the computer vision-based systems more accurate and efficient.

After obtaining significant results on image classification using deep learning [3], deep learning techniques especially convolutional neural networks (CNN) have been found to be significantly outstanding for object detection. This paper aims to give analytical review of deep learning techniques for object detection from images.

The contents of the paper are portrayed as follows. Section 2 discusses visual recognition system and formulation of object detection. State-of-the-art deep learning techniques for object detection are discussed in Sect. 3. Section 4 concludes the paper.

2 Object Detection

In many computer vision-based products, scene understanding is the preliminary step to take possible actions. Visual recognition systems generally follow the sequence of steps in order to understand the scene [4] as shown in Fig. 1. Object detection is one of the steps in visual recognition systems.

- The first step *verification* deals with checking whether the object of interest is present in the image or not.

Fig. 1 Steps in visual recognition systems

- *Object detection* and *localization* determines location and scale of all the instances of objects present in the image by outputting bounding box around the detected objects along with associated class label and confidence score. Classification deals with identifying the categories of different objects present in the given image. Object detection is classified into two kinds as single object detection and multiple object detection. Single object detection aims to detect instance/instances of object belonging to single class, while the later focuses on detecting instances of objects belonging to multiple classes.
- The next step deals with *naming* all labels of different objects in the image.
- The last step is *scene description* in which association between different objects is found out using the contextual information of image and the actions depicted in the image are illustrated.

Mathematically, object detection can be formulized in the following manner as adopted by worldwide competitions like PASCAL VOC, ImageNet ILSVRC. Given an image, show the annotated set (c_i, b_i, s_i) where c_i denotes class labels, b_i represents bounding boxes, and s_i denotes confidence scores. In case of classification, the algorithm produces class labels c_i, $i = 1, 2, 3, ..., n$ in decreasing order of confidence score and bounding boxes are depicted as b_i, $i = 1, 2, 3, ..., n$. Generally, n is set to 5 so that classifier predicts 5 probable class labels for the detected object and corresponding bounding boxes. The ground truth table for class labels is given as GC_k, $k = 1, 2, 3, ..., n$, n being class label and ground truth bounding boxes given by GB_{km}, $m = 1, 2, 3, ..., M_k$. M_k denotes number of instances of kth object in the respective image. For comparison of predicted class label and bounding box with corresponding ground truth label and bounding box, function is defined. The value of function $d(c_i, GC_k)$ is set to 0 if predicted class label matches with ground truth label.

$$d(c_i, GC_k) = \begin{cases} 0, & c_i = GC_k \\ 1, & \text{Otherwise} \end{cases} \tag{1}$$

Similarly, if there is 50% overlap of predicted bounding box b_i with ground truth bounding box GB_k, value of function is set to 0.

$$f(b_i, GB_{km}) = \begin{cases} 0, & 50\% \text{ overlap of } b_i \text{ with } GB_k \\ 1, & \text{Otherwise} \end{cases} \tag{2}$$

The error e is calculated as the average of corresponding error across all test images.

$$e = \frac{1}{n} \sum_k min_i min_m max\{d(c_i, GC_k), f(b_i, GB_{km})\} \tag{3}$$

3 State-of-the-Art Deep Learning Techniques for Object Detection

Deep learning techniques for object detection from images are mainly focused on two aspects, viz., (1) accurate object detection (improving detection accuracy) and (2) faster object detection (speedup of training, testing, and computation). Each deep learning approach is associated with performance trade-off associated with accuracy and faster processing. Tables 1 and 2 compare deep learning techniques for object detection based on accuracy improvement and faster object detection, respectively. The comparison is done on the basis of approach, base model of deep learning, pooling layer, training strategy, method of regularization to handle overfitting, and the corpus used.

3.1 Deep Learning Techniques Emphasizing Accurate Object Detection

Region proposal-based approaches exhaustively search for all the possible places in the image where object can be located and produces large number of bounding boxes for probable places of objects. The regions of interest with bounding box are called as region proposals. Once the region proposal is obtained, it is decided whether it belongs to target class or background using some technique. Region proposal network (RPN) is used for pruning out areas or regions where probability of occurrence of object is very less and thereof speeds up the overall object detection system.

Girshick et al. used region with CNN feature (R-CNN) [5] model for object detection. In this paper, category-independent region proposals are treated with deep CNN to get fixed length feature vector from each region. These feature vectors are provided as input to class-wise linear SVM to classify the object. For improving localization, bounding-box regression is applied.

R-CNN requires more space and time since it works in multistage pipeline and object detection is slow. R-CNN has been used as base model for many object detection papers employing deep learning. Similar approach based on object proposals—namely regionlets—is given in [6] for generic object detection. Its Support Pixel Integral Image (SPPI) exhibits different kinds of features like dense histogram of gradients (HOG), local binary patterns (LBP), covariance features, and sparse deep CNN. This approach detects objects independent of context information. Before advent of deep learning, deformable part-based model (DPM) was considered as fundamental and effective approach for object detection [20]. This approach exhaustively detects objects at all scales and locations in the image using multi-scale deformable part model. The detection pipeline for generic object detection is put forth in DeepID-Net [8]. Authors introduced constrained deformation pooling layer (def-pooling) which has ability to handle deformation

Table 1 Comparative study of state-of-the-art approaches for object detection emphasizing accuracy

Approach	Ref.	Base model of deep learning	Pooling	Training	Regularization	Corpus
Region proposal model approach	R-CNN [5]	ImageNet [3]	Max pooling and second-order pooling	Supervised pre-training, bounding-box regressor training	Hard negative mining	PASCAL VOC 2012, ILSVRC 2013
	Regionlets [6]	DeCAF [7]	Max pooling	RealBoost algorithm for cascaded classifier training	–	PASCAL VOC 2007 & 2010, ILSVC 2013
Part-based model approach	DeepID-Net [8]	ZFNet [9], R-CNN [5]	Def-pooling	Multistage deep training	–	PASCAL VOC, ILSVC 2014
	TPPL [10]	ZFNet [9], R-CNN [5]	Spatial pyramid (SPP-Net)	Supervised training	L2 loss and L1 regularization	Caltech-UCSD Birds-2000–2011
Saliency inspired approach	DeepMultiBox [11]	ImageNet [3]	Max pooling	Adaptive gradient algorithm based on stochastic optimization	Hard negative mining	PASCAL VOC 2007, ILSVRC 2012
Hybrid approach	OverFeat [12]	ImageNet [3]	Max pooling	DropOut	Hard negative mining	ILSVRC 2013
	segDeepM [13]	R-CNN [5]	Second-order pooling	–	Hard negative mining	PASCAL VOC 2010

Table 2 Comparative study of state-of-the-art approaches for faster object detection

Approach	Ref.	Base model of deep learning	Pooling	Training	Regularization	Corpus
Saliency inspired approach	MSV [14]	ImageNet [3]	Max pooling	Multi-scale training, data augmentation	Hard negative mining	PASCAL VOC and highway vehicles dataset
Region proposal model approach	FRCN [15]	R-CNN [5]	RoI Pooling	Multi-scale training, data augmentation	Bounding-box regressor training	PASCAL VOC 2012
	Faster R-CNN [16]	VGGNet and ZFNet [9]	RoI Pooling	Alternating training	–	PASCAL VOC 2007, 2012, and MS COCO datasets
	PVANET [17]	Faster R-CNN [16]	Max pooling	Training based on Batch normalization and residual structure	Learning rate control using plateau detection	PASCAL VOC 2007 & 2012
Similar to Region proposal model	YOLO [18]	GoogLeNet [19]	Max pooling	Pre-training on ImageNet using DarkNet framework	DropOut, data augmentation	PASCAL VOC 2007, PASCAL VOC 2012

properties of object parts. The mean average accuracy obtained by this method outperforms R-CNN. Most of the approaches rely on independent designing and training of part-based detector and object classifier. Huang et al. have combined the part detector and object classifier for fine-grained object recognition in task-driven progressive part localization (TPPL) framework [10]. They have used Part-SPP (Spatial Pyramid Pooling) as a baseline detector and particle swarm optimization approach to discriminatively search the image region.

In saliency inspired approach, salient object parts are detected from the image by suppressing the background scenes. Based on the obtained salient regions, features are extracted and objects are classified. Generally, detector and classifier are designed separately and trained independently of each other. In order to detect multiple instances of the same object in the image, DeepMultiBox model put forth in [11] follows saliency inspired approach and handles all the instances of object in class-agnostic manner, making it scalable. This model is trained on ImageNet, and it uses Adagrad for controlling learning rate of network. This approach predicts set of class-agnostic bounding boxes and supports cross-class generalization across multiple datasets. OverFeat is the integrated framework performing classification, localization, and detection [12]. It works on hybrid approach based on multi-scaling and sliding window approach. This is end-to-end trainable feature extractor requiring large amount of training data. Another category of hybrid approach, namely segDeepM, used combined methodology of segmentation and context modeling for improving accuracy of object detection [13]. Markov random field model is used for scoring appearance and context for each detection; in addition to this, iterative sequential localization scheme is used for scoring and positioning of the bounding box. The combination of multi-scale structure and context modeling is employed in multi-scale volume (MSV) model for object detection and localization [14]. Multi-scale volumes of deep feature pyramids are used to jointly detect and localize objects with large-scale variation and also small objects.

3.2 Deep Learning Techniques Emphasizing Faster Object Detection

A region of interest (RoI) pooling used as neural network layer for object detection task was first put forth by Girshick in Fast R-CNN (FRCN) [15].

This approach improved R-CNN by multitask training and multi-scale training; thus, speeding up training and testing of network is still maintaining high accuracy of detection. This approach suffers from computations associated with generating region proposal. This problem is alleviated in extended work of Girshick in Faster R-CNN [16] using region proposal network (RPN). RPN being fully convolutional network simultaneously outputs bounding boxes along with score of detection.

In order to detect multiple category objects from image at real time, PVANET [17] redesigned the feature extractor part in shallow CNN. Shallow CNN is marked by less number of connected channels among network but large number of layers in NN. The approach is based on region proposals following the pipeline architecture for object detection in which feature extraction is followed by region proposals and then region of interest classification.

For real-time processing, You Only Look Once (YOLO) framework [18] modeled object detection as a regression problem to bounding boxes and corresponding class probabilities. YOLO scans image only once during training and testing to infer contextual and appearance-based information as opposed to the iterative scanning method of regional proposal-based approaches and sliding window approaches.

4 Conclusion

The analytical review of deep learning techniques for object detection from images has been carried out in this paper. Object detection has already been used for traditional face recognition applications and industry-related automation processes. Nowadays, due to proliferation of deep learning, it has been possible to apply object detection for advanced applications like detecting faulty tracks on the railway route [21], abandoned object detection at public places, surveillance areas like line of control, detecting drowsiness of drivers carrying cargo on highways. Convolutional neural networks have proved to be the game changers for object detection yielding excellent performances on complex datasets and proving to be essential for automated systems like self-driving cars, robotics.

It can also be observed that before the advent of deep learning, the focus of object detection methods was more on improving the accuracy of detection. But now, the use of deep learning techniques expedited the process of object detection to get the results at real time. The graphics processor, multitask learning, multi-scale learning, parallel implementation of algorithms, transfer learning are major pillars for real-time detection of objects from images and videos.

References

1. Technology Trends, http://www.gartner.com/newsroom/id/3482617
2. Computer Vision Technology Market to Reach $33.3 Billion by 2019, https://www.tractica.com/newsroom/press-releases/computer-vision-technology-market-to-reach-33-3-billion-by-2019/
3. Alex Krizhevsky, et al.: ImageNet classification with deep convolutional neural networks. In: Advances in Neural Information Processing Systems. (2012)
4. P. Perona: Object Categorization: Computer and Human Perspectives, Cambridge University Press. pp. 55–68. (2009)
5. R. Girshick, J. Donahue, T. Darrell, et al.: Rich feature hierarchies for accurate object detection and semantic segmentation. In: Proceedings of CVPR. (2014)

6. X. Wang, M. Yang, S. Zhu and Y. Lin.: Regionlets for Generic Object Detection. In: IEEE Transactions on Pattern Analysis and Machine Intelligence, vol. 37, no. 10, pp. 2071–2084. (2015)
7. J. Donahue, et al: DeCAF: A deep convolutional activation feature for generic visual recognition. In: arXiv preprint arXiv:1310.1531. (2013)
8. W. Ouyang, et al.: DeepID-Net: Multi-stage and deformable deep convolutional neural networks for object detection. In: Proceedings of the CVPR. (2015)
9. M. D. Zeiler, R. Fergus.: Visualizing and understanding convolutional neural networks. In: ECCV. (2014)
10. C. Huang, Z. He, G. Cao, and W. Cao.: Task-Driven Progressive Part Localization for Fine-Grained Object Recognition. In: IEEE Transactions on Multimedia, vol. 18, no. 12, pp. 2372–2383. (2016)
11. E. Dumitru, C. Szegedy, A. Toshev, and D. Anguelov.: Scalable object detection using deep neural networks. In: IEEE Conference on Computer Vision and Pattern Recognition, pp. 2147–2154. (2014)
12. Pierre Sermanet, et al: OverFeat: Integrated Recognition, Localization and Detection using Convolutional Networks. In: ICLR. (2014)
13. Zhu, Yukun, et al: segDeepM: Exploiting segmentation & context in deep neural networks for object detection. In: IEEE Conference on Computer Vision and Pattern Recognition, pp. 4703–4711. (2015)
14. Ohn-Bar, E., and Trivedi, M.: Multi-scale volumes for deep object detection and localization. Pattern Recognition, 61, pp. 557–572. (2017)
15. R. Girshick.: Fast R-CNN, In: Proceedings of the ICCV. (2015)
16. S. Ren, K. He, R. Girshick and J. Sun.: Faster R-CNN: Towards Real-Time Object Detection with Region Proposal Networks. In: IEEE Transactions on Pattern Analysis and Machine Intelligence, vol. 39, no. 6, pp. 1137–1149. (2017)
17. Kim, Kye-Hyeon, Sanghoon Hong, Byungseok Roh, Yeongjae Cheon, and Minje Park.: PVANET: Deep but Lightweight Neural Networks for Real-time Object Detection. In: arXiv preprint arXiv:1608.08021. (2016)
18. Redmon, Joseph et al: You only look once: Unified, real-time object detection. In: IEEE Conference on Computer Vision and Pattern Recognition, pp. 779–788. (2016)
19. Szegedy, C. et al.: Going deeper with convolutions. In: IEEE Conference on Computer Vision and Pattern Recognition, pp. 1–9. (2015)
20. P. F. Felzenszwalb, R. B. Girshick, D. McAllester and D. Ramanan.: Object Detection with Discriminatively Trained Part-Based Models. In: IEEE Transactions on Pattern Analysis and Machine Intelligence, vol. 32, no. 9, pp. 1627–1645. (2010)
21. Gibert, X., Patel, V. M., & Chellappa, R.: Deep Multitask Learning for Railway Track Inspection. In: IEEE Transactions on Intelligent Transportation Systems, vol. 18, no. 1, pp. 153–164. (2017)

Dynamic Load Balancing with Advanced Reservation of Resources for Computational Grid

Sophiya Sheikh, Aitha Nagaraju and Mohammad Shahid

Abstract The primary requirement of heterogeneous computing is minimization of task waiting time in order to well regulate services to the users with efficient resource utilization. In this paper, we propose a dynamic load balancing with advanced reservation (DLBAR) of resources that commits advanced reservation of resources to tasks to minimize load imbalance on nodes with optimum makespan. The objective of this work is to allocate and calculate load earlier in advance on each resource before task execution started to efficiently distribute load among available resources, and other parameters like makespan are computed for performance evaluation. In order to show the effectiveness of proposed model, an unbiased comparative performance analysis is carried out with other well-known load balancing heuristic approach available in the literature. The simulation study reveals the motivation of algorithm with the superior performance of the proposed algorithm on account of all considered parameters under study.

Keywords Computational grid · Dynamic load balancing · Waiting time
Advanced reservation

S. Sheikh (✉) · A. Nagaraju
Department of Computer Science, Central University of Rajasthan,
Kishangarh, Ajmer, India
e-mail: sophiya.sheikh@gmail.com

A. Nagaraju
e-mail: nagaraju@curaj.ac.in

M. Shahid
Department of Commerce, Aligarh Muslim University,
Aligarh, Uttar Pradesh, India
e-mail: mdshahid.cs@gmail.com

© Springer Nature Singapore Pte Ltd. 2018   501
P. K. Pattnaik et al. (eds.), *Progress in Computing, Analytics and Networking*,
Advances in Intelligent Systems and Computing 710,
https://doi.org/10.1007/978-981-10-7871-2_48

1 Introduction

Since the grid is the collection of large and geographically dispersed resources, the basic authority of grid system is to manage all resources effectively. The grid is responsible for accepting user requests and for allocating it to most suitable and available resources [1]. In view of the proper usages of underutilized resources, resource allocation technique must be efficient enough to process a large number of computational jobs. To enhance utilization of resources in decentralized architecture, task scheduling needs to be done efficiently [2]. Job scheduling and load balancing are the key issues in computational grid. Task allocation to the right resources at the right time has always been a challenging problem in grid [3]. The purpose of the grid is to work in a geographically dispersed environment which is dynamic and heterogeneous in nature. Millions of users are waiting to execute their tasks. The main objectives of grid architecture are as follows: Resources need to be fully utilized to process a large number of computationally intensive jobs, waiting time should be minimized for the users to execute their tasks on time, and load should be balanced among processors to equally utilize all heterogeneous resources for all users.

In this paper, we propose a dynamic load balancing with advanced reservation (DLBAR) of resources to minimize task waiting time and to balance load distribution on nodes with minimum makespan. Each user has a group of tasks to execute. Allocation of resources will be done in advance for each independent task of a user. The objective of this work is to calculate load of each resource earlier before allocating it to a task. Then resource with the minimum load will be allocated to the task. Users may have multiple tasks to execute. Although it is not necessary that each user has an equal number of tasks to execute, yet maximum task limits can be set.

Many techniques have been reported in the literature, but none of them has the feature of advanced load allocation of multiple resources that will work for multiple users and their tasks. It is different from other strategies as it allocates load to resources in advance in order to balance the level of load among resources resulting to optimize Makespan. The rest of the paper is organized as follows: Sect. 2 presents some related work reported in the literature. Section 3 discusses the system description, optimization parameters, and DLBAR with an illustration. Experimental setup with simulation study and results is presented in Sect. 4. Finally, this paper ends with the conclusion in Sect. 5.

2 Related Work

This section refines various traditional and dynamic approaches related to load balancing, efficient task execution time, and resource allocation. Scheduling in a heterogeneous and dynamic environment has been proven to be NP complete.

Henceforth, many techniques for effective solutions for scheduling have been proposed. There are several nature-inspired optimization techniques used in the area of optimization and load balancing. Ant-based heuristic approach to scheduling and workload distribution (AHSWDG) for efficient load balancing among the available resources has been proposed [4]. In this chain, two new distributed swarm intelligence-inspired load balancing algorithms have been proposed in order to minimize makespan and average response time with minimum communication overhead to overcome problems that occur in dynamic load balancing [5]. Some load balancing algorithm has been designed using a hierarchical approach to improve user's response time in order to utilize the resources efficiently. In this regard, enhanced load balancing mechanism based upon deadline control in a direction is implemented to promote an idle system so that no resource will be overloaded and none will be under loaded [6]. A load balancing scheme is proposed for regional grids in the form of clusters around broker sites considered network transfer delay and organized in fully decentralized fashion [7]. A hierarchical load balancing technique based upon the variable threshold value has been designed to maintain the resource utilization and response time with the help of sender initiative policy [8]. Although advanced reservation of resources introduced earlier in terms of efficient processing time and cost yet it failed to optimized load among resources [9]. Many techniques have been reported in literature for the purpose, but none of them has featured with advanced load allocation for multiple resources with optimized grid parameters. A load balanced min-min algorithm for task scheduling firstly schedules the tasks, then remaining task which has not been executed yet will be rescheduled to balance load among processors [10]. Load balancing can also be achieved with the availability of the machine. Traditional opportunistic load balancing (OLB) provides poor makespan time and both min-min and max-min are not good in consideration of availability and load on machine [3]. On the other hand, without grouping algorithm (WGA) is a random approach for task selection and completion. Due to its randomized nature, it will fail to produce balanced load and optimized running time. To overcome its limitations, grouping algorithm is introduced that executes tasks in a group to save communication cost and processing requirement [11]. Existing OLB, grouping algorithm, and WGA are having a lack of machine availability and resource optimization. Apart from that a rigorous amount of considered task waiting time shows their failure; therefore, we cannot consider them as efficient load balancing and optimization techniques.

DLBAR is proposed with the advantage of both load balancing and optimum makespan. DLBAR is an efficient, advanced load reservation technique that assigns load on resources before task execution getting started so that task will never wait for resources and task waiting time will be zero. Due to its advanced load allocation nature, load balancing can be done efficiently and resultant rational amount of level of load balancing can be found with optimum makespan value.

3 The Proposed Model

This section describes proposed DLBAR approach with its system description and optimized parameters details with an illustrative example.

3.1 System Description

Figure 1 illustrates the queue architecture of DLBAR. Here, users have a set of tasks that are waiting to get executed. All tasks were in spooler at that time. The length of tasks will be calculated in MI whereas resource capability will be calculated in MIPS. Each task arrives at a specific time called arrival time and is completed by its completion time. Initial capability of the resource is known, given in MIPS. Another measurement needs to be taken to execute a task is the size of task in MI. The resource which is capable enough to execute that much MI (task) will be allocated to that particular task dynamically. The allocation decision for task depends upon both resource capability and task's size. Once a resource is getting allocated, then the task will be moved from the spooler to allocation queue. Thereafter running time taken from the resource needs to be fetched. Total time, which has been taken to execute that task, will be calculated as resource running time.

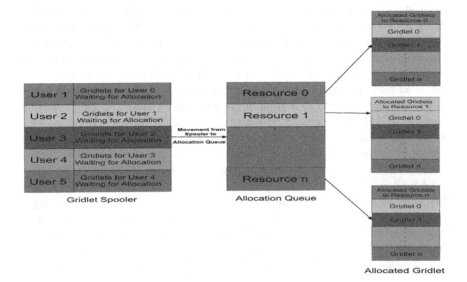

Fig. 1 Allocation strategy for reservation of resources

3.2 Optimization Parameters

In the considered system, users $u_i = u_1, u_2, \ldots, u_n$ have number of tasks $t_i = t_1, t_2, \ldots, t_n$ that will be executed on $k_j = k_1, k_2, \ldots, k_n$ computational resources. $ETC[t_i][k_j]$ is the expected computation time of each task t_i on resource. A number of optimizing parameters are calculated to check the effect of load variations among processors. Running time of task t_i on resource k_j is represented by $RT[t_i][k_j]$, and it is the difference between task arrival time and completion time that can be computed as given in Eq. 1:

$$RT[t_i][k_j] = AT[t_i][k_j] - CT[t_i][k_j] \tag{1}$$

Completion time $CT[k_j]$ can be computed by adding the running times of all tasks assigned on the node k_j given in Eq. 2:

$$CT[k_j] = \sum_{\forall t_i \to k_j} RT[t_i][k_j] \tag{2}$$

Load upon individual resource U_k can be calculated as given in Eq. 3:

$$U_k = \frac{CT[kj]}{\max(CT[kj])} \tag{3}$$

Average utilization U_j of the system can be estimated by using equation as given in Eq. 4:

$$U_j = \frac{\sum CT(k_j)}{k * \max(CT(k_j))} \tag{4}$$

Level of load balancing (LLB) is a parameter for measuring load imbalance on the resources used for execution of tasks and can be computed as given in Eq. 5.

$$LLB = 1 - \frac{\sqrt{\frac{1}{k}\left(\sum_{j=1}^{k}(U_j - U_k)^2\right)}}{U_j} \tag{5}$$

Makespan time is finishing time of the last executed task that can be expressed in terms of the completion time of resources as given in Eq. 6:

$$MT = \max\{CT[k_j] | k_j \in Resources\} \tag{6}$$

3.3 Dynamic Load Balancing with Advanced Reservation (DLBAR)

The complete flow of advanced reservation can be discerned from Fig. 2. For the first user, availability of first resource will be checked dynamically. If resource is available, then calculate the running time to execute tasks. Every time running time will be added in load shared (LS) queue in order to make a decision as to which resources would be allocated to the next task to optimize all resources in an efficient way. Initially, all resources are free so that all can be reserved for tasks, but after the first iteration, total running time needs to be compared for each resource. Next reservation will be based upon the minimum load of a resource because the load has to be balanced among resources. The resource with minimum running time will be reserved for the next task dynamically. Then, the total running time will be calculated for the resource. Once all tasks have been allocated to the resource, then execution will be started one by one for all tasks. After execution of a task, it will be removed from allocation queue and resource load will be reduced for that resource from load shared queue. Similar procedure would run till all users get executed by the resources which have been committed in advance to them. The total running time of all resources is used to calculate the level of load balancing (LLB) and makespan time.

```
Input: user List with its id, and gridlets
        gridlet List for each user with its id, size, count and user id
        resource_List with its id, name, PE and MIPS
Each Task will works in three modules
        Available[k]    //Check for availability of resource k
        Queue[k][t]    //Corresponding task instructions t for k resource
        LS[k]    //Load on resource in terms of running time for advanced committed task
        When a new task tₖ arrives
                1. Find index of k resource at which LS is minimum
                2. Queue[k][t]=tₖ                               //Add task to resource queue
                3. LS[k]=LS[k]+Length of task tₖ          //Compute total load on each
                resource
        When a task goes for execution to Resource k
                1. Available[k]=false  //If resource is not available
                2. LS[k]=LS[k]-length of Queue[k][1] //Reduce first task length from
                Load Share Queue
                3. Queue[k][t]=Queue[k][t+1]; //Queue length is increased by one
        When a Resource k finishes its execution
                1. Calculate Run Time of k
                2. Available[k]=True
Similar process will run for all user's gridlets.
Then calculate total running time of each resource as Total_RT
        for k:=0 to N do
                Calculate load among individual processor with eq-1
                Calculate Average Utilization, LLB and makespan with eq-4,5,6 respectively
        endfor
```

Fig. 2 Dynamic load balancing using advanced reservation of resources

3.4   An Illustration of DLBAR

Running time for five resources has been calculated as:
$RT_1 = 305.74$, $RT_2 = 358.24$, $RT_3 = 350.31$, $RT_4 = 364.25$, $RT_5 = 365.83$.
Load upon individual resources can be calculated as:

$Uk_1 = 0.8357$, $Uk_2 = 0.9792$, $Uk_3 = 0.9575$, $Uk_4 = 0.9956$, $Uk_5 = 1.0$ By Eq. 4.

Average Utilization: $U_j = 1744.39/(365.83) * 5 = 0.9536 = 95\%$ By Eq. 5.

Level of load balancing: $LLB = 1 - (0.004965/0.9536) = 0.99$ By Eq. 6.

4   Simulation Study and Results

The experiments are conducted using GridSim 5.2 on i7 processors having seven cores and 8 GB RAM. Experimental study with results is given as follows.

4.1   Experimental Setup

In the proposed work experiment, single machine contains multiple resources that are heterogeneous in nature. Multiple machines can be included as per our requirement. Resources and users can be from different time zones. The total number of gridlets (tasks) is being varied from 250 to 1000 while length of gridlets can be varied from 0 to 50,000 MI. The simulator accepts users with their gridlets. Each gridlet has predefined processing requirements or million instructions (MI) that have to be executed by processors. After creation of a first user entity, it will be inserted in the user list. All generated gridlets of that user will be stored in gridlet list. The system randomly generates gridlets as per given average MI. The scheduler will check the availability of resources dynamically. Each gridlets will be stored with its corresponding resource ID, processing cost, and running time. In the proposed work, we have considered five resources R1 to R5. Total processing elements are varying from 4 to 16. Resources have different MIPS ratings and bandwidth speed.

4.2   Results and Discussion

Simulations are processed to analyze and compare static approaches like OLB and dynamic approach like grouping algorithm and WGA. Same environment is considered for the comparison of LLB and makespan in order to perform the evaluation of the proposed work. The proposed work DLBAR is compared with other

Fig. 3 Level of load
balancing

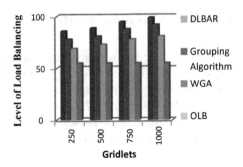

Fig. 4 Makespan

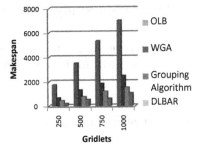

approaches which are implemented using gridsim environments with similar conditions. Proposed DLBAR is refined aptly through the difference between existing and proposed approach which would be further divided by existing approaches thereafter multiplied by 100. LLB and makespan for multiple traditional heuristics and DLBAR have been calculated in Figs. 3 and 4. Ideal load and load upon independent resource have been calculated initially. Here, load estimation has been made earlier to check overloaded and under loaded resources; therefore, the load can be distributed equally. With balanced load DLBAR also minimized makespan time. In DLBAR, resources are allocated to task in advance with minimum load in order to provide better resource optimization resulting in better makespan value. Makespan is compared with a number of existing approaches grouping algorithm, WGA, and OLB, and DLBAR is found to be the best among all approaches presented in Fig. 4. OLB executes jobs as per the availability of resourcing while WGA executes jobs in a random manner. Grouping algorithm, however, produces optimum results in comparison with WGA and OLB because sending and receiving jobs in a group will reduce processing requirement and communication cost. DLBAR provides optimum makespan over grouping algorithm because of its advanced allocation strategy and negligible waiting time as well as communication cost.

The result shows that DLBAR provides 20–32% optimum load balancing as compared to grouping algorithm, while grouping algorithm, which is better than WGA, provides 9–12% balanced load among resources. The WGA has high processing requirement still better than OLB with 7–10% of load optimization. OLB is based upon the availability of resources which are found to be worst among all approaches. DLBAR provides 30–53% optimum makespan as compared to grouping algorithm while grouping algorithm, which is better than WGA, provides 33–42% efficient makespan. WGA is better than OLB with 62–65% optimal makespan.

5 Conclusion

One of the key objectives of grid environment is efficient utilization of resources. The heterogeneous system is only useful if we properly exploit its all resources. In this research, we have investigated the effectiveness of advanced reservation of resources in grid environment. In this paper, a dynamic load balancing with advanced reservation (DLBAR) of resources that commits advanced reservation of resources to users to minimize load imbalance on nodes has been proposed. The proposed strategy is quite suitable for applications where minimum task waiting time is an essential requirement. The task will be never in task waiting queue as resources are allocated in advance before execution started. The advanced commitment of resources properly utilizes resources with equal load distribution with an optimum makespan but not suitable to minimize TAT and flow time. The performance evaluation of proposed strategy has been carried out by comparing the proposed work with state-of-the-art algorithms. The experimental results show that DLBAR outperforms among all considered algorithm on almost all parameters under study.

References

1. Xhafa, F., Abraham, A.: Computational models and heuristic methods for Grid scheduling problems, Vol. 4. Future generation computer systems. 1(2010) 608–621.
2. Shah, R., Veeravalli, B., Misra, M.: On the design of adaptive and decentralized load balancing algorithms with load estimation for computational grid environments, Vol. 18. IEEE Transactions on parallel and distributed systems, (2007) 1675–1686.
3. Braun, T. D., Siegel, H. J., Beck, N., Bölöni, L. L., Maheswaran, M., Reuther, A. I., Freund, R. F.: A comparison of eleven static heuristics for mapping a class of independent tasks onto heterogeneous distributed computing systems, Vol. 61. Journal of Parallel and Distributed computing. (2001) 810–837.
4. Saxena, R., Kumar, A., Kumar, A., & Saxena, S.: AHSWDG: An Ant Based Heuristic Approach to Scheduling and Workload Distribution in Computational Grids. In Computational Intelligence & Communication Technology (CICT), 2015 IEEE International Conference. 2(2015) 569–574.
5. Ludwig, S. A., & Moallem, A.: Swarm intelligence approaches for grid load balancing, Vol. 3. Journal of Grid Computing. 3(2011) 279–301.

6. Hao, Y., Liu, G., & Wen, N. An enhanced load balancing mechanism based on deadline control on GridSim, Vol. 28. *Future Generation Computer Systems*, 4(2012) 657–665.

7. Rajavel, R.: De-centralized load balancing for the computational grid environment. Communication and Computational Intelligence (INCOCCI), 2010 International Conference, 10(2010) 419–424.

8. Rathore, N., & Chana, I. A sender initiate based hierarchical load balancing technique for grid using variable threshold value. In *Signal Processing, Computing and Control (ISPCC), IEEE International Conference.* (2013, September) 1–6.

9. Sulistio, A., Buyya, R.: A grid simulation infrastructure supporting advance reservation. 16th International Conference on Parallel and Distributed Computing and Systems (PDCS 2004). 11(2004) 9–11.

10. Kokilavani, T., Amalarethinam, D. G.: Load balanced min-min algorithm for static meta-task scheduling in grid computing, Vol. 20. International Journal of Computer Applications, 2(2011) 43–49.

11. Muthuvelu, N., Liu, J., Soe, N. L., Venugopal, S., Sulistio, A., Buyya, R.: A dynamic job grouping-based scheduling for deploying applications with fine-grained tasks on global grids. Proceedings of the 2005 Australasian workshop on Grid computing and e-research, Vol. 44. Australian Computer Society, Inc. (2005, January) 41–48.

Automatic Generation of Named Entity Distractors of Multiple Choice Questions Using Web Information

Rakesh Patra and Sujan Kumar Saha

Abstract This paper presents a novel technique for automatic generation of distractors for multiple choice questions. Distractors are the wrong choices given along with the correct answer (key) to befuddle the examinee. Various techniques have been proposed in the literature for automatic distractor generation. But none of these approaches are suitable when the key is a named entity. And named entity key or distractors are dominating in many domains including sports and entertainment. Here, we propose a technique for generation of named entity distractors. For generating good named entity distractors, we first detect the class of the key and collect a set of attribute values, classified into generic and specific categories. Based on these attributes, we retrieve a set of candidate distractors from a few trusted Web sites like Wikipedia. Then, we find the similarity between the key and a candidate distractor. The close ones are chosen as the final set of distractors. A set of human evaluators assess the distractors by using a set of parameters. In our evaluation, we observe that the system-generated distractors are good in terms of relevance and close to the key.

Keywords Distractors · MCQ · Question generation · Named entity

1 Introduction

Multiple choice question (MCQ) is quite popular in assessment in various fields. In MCQ, the respondents are asked to select the best possible answer out of a set of choices. Development of automatic MCQ generator has become a popular research problem in recent years [1–5, 8, 10, 12]. A MCQ is composed of three basic parts:

R. Patra · S. K. Saha (✉)
Department of CSE, Birla Institute of Technology Mesra, Mesra, Ranchi, India
e-mail: sujan.kr.saha@gmail.com

R. Patra
e-mail: rakesh9687@gmail.com

© Springer Nature Singapore Pte Ltd. 2018
P. K. Pattnaik et al. (eds.), *Progress in Computing, Analytics and Networking*,
Advances in Intelligent Systems and Computing 710,
https://doi.org/10.1007/978-981-10-7871-2_49

stem, key, and distractors. The stem is the question sentence, key or the target word is the correct answer, and distractors are the set of wrong choices.

Distractor can be defined as a concept semantically close to the key. In the literature, we find that in general domain or vocabulary test-related MCQs similar words (similar with key: like synonym) are extracted using the WordNet or domain ontologies [1, 2, 6, 11]. But such distractor generation techniques do not work when the key is a named entity (NE). In many domains (e.g., sports, entertainment, travel, biomedical), NE keys are dominant. For a NE key, the distractors should also be the NEs that are 'close' to the key. Here, closeness is not only belonging to same NE class, but several other domain-specific parameters are required to be considered. McKenna and Bull stated that good distractors should not be too close to the correct answer [9]. However, in case of NE distractors, if these are not too close to the key, then the MCQ becomes unattractive.

Let us consider a question from the sports domain: 'Who was the highest run scorer of the India side in the final match of ICC World Cup 2011?' The answer is 'Gautam Gambhir.' If the distractors are given as Adam Gilchrist, Hasim Amla, and Ricky Ponting, then the quality of the MCQ is degraded because, among these options, 'Gautam Gambhir' is the only name who is from India and becomes the obvious choice. Again, if the distractors are Sunil Gavaskar, Harbhajan Singh, and Zaheer Khan, then also the MCQ fails to meet the quality because they are Indian but either not played in 2011 World Cup or are bowlers who are unlikely to become the highest run scorer. In the question, if the distractors are generated as Sachin Tendulkar, Yuvraj Singh, and MS Dhoni, then the MCQ becomes attractive.

In this paper, we present a novel technique for generation of NE distractors. The system takes the stem and the key as input. For generating the distractors, it first extracts some information regarding the key from the Web. To do this, first it determines the entity category of the key. Then, it finds a set of generic attributes that represent the key category from certain trusted Web sites. A set of specific attributes, if any such is there, is extracted from the stem. Then, a set of candidate distractors are retrieved from the Web with the help of the attributes. Class-specific repository is created, semiautomatically using the Web, that contains the generic attribute values of the possible entities belonging to a category. Next, a similarity metric is proposed that finds the distance between the key and a candidate set member using the values stored in the repository. The entities that have maximum similarity are chosen as the final set of distractors. The proposed technique is applied in cricket domain. The generated distractors are evaluated manually. The evaluation results demonstrate that the proposed technique is highly accurate.

2 Named Entity Distractor Generation

2.1 Distractor Generation

For generating NE distractors here we use Web information, specifically semi-structured or tabular information, extracted from a couple of trusted Web sites like Wikipedia. Like in other approaches, we have not used any domain ontology or WordNet in the task. In this article, we have focused on distractor generation, not the complete MCQ system. The system assumes that the stem and key are available to the system as input.

For distractor generation, basically we retrieve similar names from the Web. Similar name indicates the names that are having attribute values close to the key. Here, we propose two different types of attribute sets for representing the names: generic attribute and specific attribute; these are discussed in Sect. 2.2 in detail.

2.2 Identify the Class of the Key

For automatic generation of distractors using the Web first we need to identify the named entity category of the key. To identify the category of the key, we use a hybrid approach combining gazetteer list matching and a named entity recognition (NER) system. Creation of a gazetteer list that contains all names of a particular category is very difficult as new names are constantly included. Therefore, we plan to use the hybrid approach by considering a few gazetteer lists and an in-house NER system. The gazetteer lists are rapidly prepared; therefore, these may not be complete but contain most the names that are likely to occur in MCQs. If the key is not from numeric category like date, number and not available in the gazetteer list, then we use the NER system. The NER system works on sentences, not on a word. Again, the NER system works better in statements than questions. Therefore, we replace the question word (e.g., who, which team) by the key to form assertive sentence and the sentence is analyzed by the NER system in order to identify the NEs.

Gazetteer List-Based Identification. We use the Web to prepare a few gazetteer lists. First, we identify the major categories of key in this domain. These are: person name (cricketer, batsman, bowler, captain, wicketkeeper, team owner, board president, etc.), organization name (franchise name, team name, country name, cricket boards like ICC), location name (cricket ground, city, etc.), event name (tournament, cup, championship, trophy, etc.). We make a list of relevant and trusted Web sites and extract lists of names. For instance, for the name of cricketers we use the sources like Wikipedia, ESPNcricinfo, Yahoo Cricket players lists. From these various sources, we compile a cricketer gazetteer list containing a total of 3978 names. In Table 1, we have summarized the gazetteer lists prepared for the task.

NER System-Based Identification. The NER system is developed using the conditional random fields (CRF) classifier [7]. The training data is collected from cricket-related Wikipedia pages and consists of approximately 200,000 words. The data is manually annotated using the aforementioned cricket-specific NE classes. A feature set containing word window, word orthographic information, affix information, parts of speech, and parse information is used to train the classifier. Active learning-based semi-supervised learning is used to improve the classifier. The system achieves a f-score of 88.34 with 92.2% precision.

Table 1 Gazetteer lists in cricket domain

Name category	Source	Size
Cricketer name	Wikipedia, Yahoo Cricket, ESPNcricinfo, Cricbuzz	3978
Umpire and referee	ICC Cricket, Wikipedia	590
Other officials and owners	Wikipedia, Country Boards like ecb.co.uk	536
Cricket teams	ESPNcricinfo, Yahoo Cricket, Cricbuzz	325
Governing body	ICC Cricket, Wikipedia	147
Cricket event	ESPNcricinfo and Cricbuzz archive	2324
City and ground	Wikipedia, ESPNcricinfo	742

2.3 Attribute Set

For each of the name categories, a set of attributes are defined. This attribute set will help to generate the search query as well as it will play a major role in selecting the best option. For the task, we have considered two types of attributes: generic and specific. Generic attributes are the set of general information that helps to distinguish a particular member from other members of the category. And we define specific attributes as the set of predefined features extracted from the question, i.e., the stem. For example, the generic attribute for the category batsman includes date of birth, team name, span, last match, batting style, total run, strike rate, batting average, number of century, highest score, etc. Specific attribute can be whether played a particular match or tournament (if the stem is focusing on it), statistics in a particular match or tournament, man of the match, captain of team, etc. Specific attribute set is dependent on the stem; therefore, it can be empty.

Generic attributes are motivated by the fields used for summarizing the entity (e.g., career or the personal details in case of cricketer) in Wikipedia-, ESPNcricinfo-, and Cricbuzz-like Web sites. The Wikipedia pages often contain an information template (at the top-right portion of the page) that summarizes a set of basic properties defining the class. Additionally, majority pages in Wikipedia or other related Web sites hold a table that summarizing the statistics. The fields of the tables are taken as generic attribute set. Similarly, the ESPNcricinfo and Cricbuzz entity-specific pages contain semi-structured and tabular data from which generic attributes are extracted. Such attributes are manually extracted for a few popular members of a particular class. Then, the duplicates and synonyms are removed to prepare the final generic attribute set for the class.

Specific attributes are a set of information occurring in the stems that will help to restrict the search space. For making a list of specific attributes, we study a number of MCQs available in various relevant Web sites. We aim to make a list of such properties that can distinguish a few members from the possible set of distractors. For example, when the key is focused on a particular tournament then the distractors must have a close relationship with that tournament. Similarly, name of a series, name of a trophy, name of a ground, a particular match, a particular team, etc., act as specific attributes. In sports domain, many questions deal with records or statistics. Examples of such information are maximum number of century, fastest century, maximum distance of over boundary, number of hat tricks, most five wickets in an innings, most catches as non-wicketkeeper, largest ground, most expensive team, etc. We consider these records as specific attribute too. We compile such list of records from various sources and search whether these present in the stem.

2.4 Entity-Attribute Repository Creation

Next, we create class-specific repositories that contain the list of entities with their generic attribute values. The repositories are created semiautomatically. The base information of the repository is extracted automatically from the Wikipedia. Wikipedia 'list_of_Indian_ODI_cricketer'-like pages contain list of entities with a list of attribute values in tabular format. But, our generic attribute sets normally contain more attributes. Additional attribute values are collected by accessing respective pages of the individual entities. We employ a focused crawler to automatically go through the pages given a list and a set of patterns, which extracts specific information from the pages.

The repository is kept as simple file during storage in a matrix-like format, where each row represents an entity and the columns are the attributes. First column refers to the name of the entity. All the attribute values may not be available for some of the entities; unavailable fields are filled with 'NULL' indicator.

2.5 Retrieving Candidate Distractors

Next, we need to retrieve a set candidate distractors. If any specific attribute is not found in the stem, then the task becomes simpler. We find a set of similar entities from the repository. Similar entity refers to the entities that have the same value in certain attributes compared to the key. A set of attributes are tagged as 'important' for each class. For example, in the cricketer class we pick important attributes as: same country, batting average (difference < 10), bowling average (difference < 5), span (overlapping of 1 year). Similarly, for the ground class, country attribute is taken as important; for the team class, we take the country and common tournament attributes as important. The entities having match in important attributes are considered as candidate attributes.

If the stem contains any specific attribute, then a search query is formed using it. To identify the specific attributes in the stem, we run the NER system. If the NER system detects any named entity (of types: team, tournament, ground, city), then the entity is considered as specific attribute. Then depending on the key, we form a query to find the distractors that are related to the attribute. For example, consider the stem: 'who was the wicketkeeper of Bangladesh during ICC World Cup 2015?' and the key: 'Mushfiqur Rahim.' The NER system identifies two special attributes from the stem team: 'Bangladesh' and tournament: 'ICC World Cup 2015.' Then, the query is formed as 'list cricketer Bangladesh ICC World Cup 2015.' These queries are searched in three Web sites namely, Wikipedia, ESPNcricinfo, and Cricbuzz. From the resultant pages, we automatically extract top ten candidate distractors that are commonly appeared.

Another category of specific attribute is records. There are several types of records available in the cricket domain. We made a list of possible records from the 'Records' section of espncricinfo.com. For each type of record, we manually identify the keywords or phrases that are likely to occur in the stem as record indicator. The stem is searched for the record indicator terms from the list (of size: 52 terms). If any term is present, then the corresponding ESPNcricinfo record page is accessed by the system and top 10 record rank holder entities are extracted as candidate distractors.

2.6   Final Distractors: Similarity Between Candidate Set and the Key

Now, the similarity between the candidate distractor set entities and key is computed in order to select the final set of distractors. To obtain the similarity, we use the corresponding vectors (row) from the entity-attribute repository. Dimension of the vectors is represented by the attributes; few of which possess numerical values (e.g., number of innings), and others take non-numeric values (e.g., country). The distance between the non-numeric attributes is considered as binary: 0 if there is a match and 1 otherwise; then normalized by total number of non-numeric attributes. To compute the distance between the numeric attributes, we employ the distance computation metric given in Eq. 1.

$$D(P, Q) = \frac{1}{L} \sum_{i=1...L} \frac{(P_i - Q_i)}{\max(P_i, Q_i)} \tag{1}$$

where 'P' and 'Q' represent two vectors corresponding to the target entities. 'L' is the total number of numeric attributes, and 'i' is the index that iteratively considers all individual attributes P_i. Finally, the distance of the numeric and non-numeric attributes is combined.

The distance computation metric returns the distance as close to zero when the attributes of two target entities (one is the key, and other one is a candidate distractor) are close. We select three entities that return lower distance value as the final set of distractors.

3   Result and Discussion

We do not find any openly available dataset for the task. Therefore, we use a set of self-generated key-MCQ pair for the evaluation of the system. The test set contains 100 cricket-related MCQs and corresponding keys collected from the Web. The system generates three distractors for each question. For the evaluation, two metrics have been used: (i) relevance and (ii) closeness. *Relevance* refers to the affinity of the distractors with the stem. *Closeness* is the metric to indicate whether the distractors are close to the key. These metrics are considered as binary: For a particular distractor, if it satisfies the quality, then the score is 1 and 0 otherwise.

The system-generated distractors are then evaluated manually by three human evaluators, who are having decent knowledge in the domain. The evaluators check the distractors and put their relevance and closeness scores against each distractor. Then, we take average of these scores which is considered as the accuracy of the system. Table 2 presents the assessment scores of the system. The system achieves an average accuracy of 87.7% on relevance. Individual and average relevance scores imply that most of the system-generated distractors are relevant to the stem. The closeness score reflects whether the machine-generated distractors are as good as the human-generated distractors. The developed system finds the distractors based on some statistics retrieved from the Web. Only statistical information might not be sufficient in case of named entity distractors. In this domain, we found sometimes the best possible (human-generated) distractors do not have much statistical closeness with the key. Still the system achieves an average score of 79.3% on closeness. These values indicate that the system picks the distractors with reasonable efficiency.

Table 2 Evaluation of the system-generated distractors (total 100 keys)

Evaluator#	Relevance			Closeness		
	D1	D2	D3	D1	D2	D3
Evaluator 1	90	84	82	82	78	78
Evaluator 2	93	90	86	81	81	80
Evaluator 3	91	91	83	84	76	74
Average (individual distractors)	91.3	88.3	83.6	82.3	78.3	77.3
Average (all distractors)	87.7			79.3		

D1, D2, and D3 indicate the first, second, and third distractors, respectively

4 Conclusion

The paper presents a novel technique for generating distractors for the named entity keys. The experimental results demonstrate the efficiency of the technique.

There is no standard dataset or evaluation metrics defined for the task; we would like to work on creating a larger dataset and investigate other metrics for evaluation. In future, we would also like to investigate the portability of the approach by applying in another domain like history and entertainment.

Acknowledgements This work is supported by the project grant (project file no.: YSS/2015/ 001948) provided by the Science and Engineering Research Board (SERB), Govt. of India.

References

1. Agarwal Manish and Mannem Prashanth. 2011. Automatic Gap-fill Question Generation from Text Books. Proceedings of the Sixth Workshop on Innovative Use of NLP for Building Educational Applications, pp. 56–64.
2. Aldabe Itziar and Maritxalar Montse. 2010. Automatic Distractor Generation for Domain Specific Texts. IceTAL 2010, LNAI 6233, pp. 27–38.
3. Bhatia Arjun Singh, Kirti Manas and Saha Sujan Kumar. 2013. Automatic Generation of Multiple Choice Questions using Wikipedia. Proc. of Pattern Recognition and Machine Intelligence (PReMI -13), LNCS Vol. 8251, pp. 733–738.
4. Brown JC., Frishkoff GA and Eskenazi M. 2005. Automatic question generation for vocabulary assessment. Proceedings of Human Language Technology Conference and Conference on Empirical Methods in Natural Language Processing (HLT/EMNLP), pp. 819–826.
5. Coniam David. 1997. A Preliminary Inquiry into Using Corpus Word Frequency Data in the Automatic Generation of English Language Cloze Tests. CAL-ICO Journal, 14 (2):15–33.
6. Correia, R., Baptista, J., Mamede, N., Trancoso, I., and Eskenazi M. 2010. Automatic Generation of Cloze Question Distractors. In Second Language Studies: Acquisition, Learning, Education and Technology.
7. Lafferty John D., McCallum Andrew and Pereira Fernando C. N. 2001. Conditional Random Fields: Probabilistic Models for Segmenting and Labeling Sequence Data. Proc. of Eighteenth International Conference on Machine Learning, pp. 282–289.
8. Majumdar Mukta, Saha Sujan Kumar. 2015. A System for Generating Multiple Choice Questions: With a Novel Approach for Sentence Selection. Proceedings of the 2nd ACL Workshop on Natural Language Processing Techniques for Educational Applications (NLP-TEA), pages 64–72.
9. McKenna Colleen and Bull Joanna. 1999. Designing effective objective test questions: an introductory workshop. Technical Report: CAA Centre, Lough-borough University.
10. Mitkov R. and Ha L.A. 2003. Computer-aided generation of multiple-choice tests. Proceedings of the HLT/NAACL 2003 Workshop on Building educational applications using Natural Language Processing. pp. 17–22.
11. Mitkov, R., Ha, L.A., Varga, A. and Rello, L. 2009. Semantic similarity of distractors in multiple-choice tests: extrinsic evaluation. Proceedings of EACL 2009 Workshop on GEMS: GEometical Models of Natural Language Semantics, pp. 49–56.
12. Papasalouros A., Kanaris K and Kotis K. 2008. Automatic Generation of multiple-choice questions from domain ontologies. IADIS e-Learning.

Spatial Domain Blind Watermarking for Digital Images

Maharshi Parekh, Shiv Bidani and V. Santhi

Abstract In modern technological world, digital manipulation of images and video data has become very common. It is required to bring out some mechanism to protect copyright and authentication of digital data. In this work, a new blind digital watermarking algorithm is proposed for protecting copyright of digital images. In this work, embedding process is carried out in spatial domain by modifying luminance components of cover images. The cover image is divided into many blocks of size 8 × 8, and its correlation values are used as key in selecting blocks for inserting watermark. The image to be watermarked is called host image, and it could be in color or grayscale format. The secret data to be inserted is called watermark, and it is considered to be in monochrome format of size 32 × 32 bytes. This paper shows a novel approach in inserting a watermark in spatial domain. The obtained results show the efficiency of the proposed approach, and it could be classified as fragile watermarking.

Keywords Spatial · Correlation · Watermark · Copyright protection
Embedding · Extraction · Fragile · Luminance

M. Parekh (✉) · S. Bidani · V. Santhi
School of Computer Science and Engineering, Vellore Institute of Technology, Vellore, India
e-mail: maharshig.parekh2014@gmail.com

S. Bidani
e-mail: shivbidani@gmail.com

V. Santhi
e-mail: vsanthinathan@gmail.com

© Springer Nature Singapore Pte Ltd. 2018
P. K. Pattnaik et al. (eds.), *Progress in Computing, Analytics and Networking*,
Advances in Intelligent Systems and Computing 710,
https://doi.org/10.1007/978-981-10-7871-2_50

1   Introduction

In the last few years, there has been a vast amount of data generated in the form of images, video, and audio. This data has been prone to be copied by unauthorized users and distributed. It is important to have a process to identify owners of images and such data. The process of watermarking has been an active field of research. In the past, algorithms have been proposed to embed random sequences of real numbers in a particular set of DCT coefficients [1]. Such methods have utilized the frequency domain for embedding watermarks. The watermarking in spatial domain has included some methods wherein the image is watermarked by randomly modifying the intensity values of image pixels [2]. In this method, the original image is not required as the pixel intensity values are compared with the global mean intensity.

The idea of having uniform criteria for watermarking quality measures had been missing for a long time, and it was imperative that key performance indicators be explicitly defined. In paper [3], authors have proposed a method to identify benchmarking standards. It is therefore important to understand the various quality measures in order to incorporate such standards in today's research. The process of verifying whether an image received from a service provider is indeed the original image, and it has been a case for studies in the past. The design of a completely secure process of watermarking has been proposed by a few researchers. They do so by employing existing cryptographic concepts and perception quality concepts [4]. The other methodologies of block-oriented and modular arithmetic-based watermarking for logos have been proposed in [5].

The organization of this paper is as follows. In Sect. 2, a brief literature review is presented. Section 3 discusses about basics of correlation coefficient. The proposed methodology is presented in Sect. 4. The performance evaluation of the proposed system is presented in Sect. 5. Section 6 concludes the proposed work.

2   Literature Review

In certain schemes, the watermark image is taken to be a binary image with a fixed size (32 × 32 bits). A pseudo-random sequence is generated using a secret key and bitwise XOR operation. The watermarked image is not susceptible to cropping, filtering, compression, and such attacks. It accounts for such attacks by embedding the watermark image at four different positions in the host image [6]. The process of watermarking in some methods does not make any changes to the host image which results in the image being watermarked without any visible changes. An algorithm that saves the position of corresponding watermark and host image pixel values as the key for embedding and extraction is used. The algorithm used is called "Save Algorithm" [7]. In [8], information preserving transformations and alterations susceptibility is minimized by creating an algorithm for semi-fragile watermarking. Operations are carried out in the DCT domain as in the other papers. Another approach utilizes the blue component of the host image because the human eyes are least susceptible to the blue color range [9].

The method that is used in [10] compares the objective and the subjective quality of the watermarking algorithm. The algorithm requires two main processes which are bit embedding and recovering. Introduction of new techniques like multi-resolution property has been proposed in [11]. The procedure used in video watermarking is similar to that of image watermarking. The watermark is embedded into the DCT blocks in [12]. Frames that have the same group of pictures (GOP) are given the same watermark. The coefficients are first selected based on the DCT. It is then embedded as a 4 × 4 block.

The digitization of 3D models has led to the increased importance of protecting and copyrighting 3D models. The method used in [13] embeds a watermark in the host 3D model by using the algorithm of redundant embedding. In order to retrieve the watermark, there are two processes; they are: watermark extraction in which the original mesh data is accessed and the key is used. Secondly, it is the correlation test. The attack used for this technique is the DCT test. A technique that involves both frequency domain and spatial domain watermark embedding is proposed in [14]. Data importance and user preference are taken into consideration in order to determine the frequency domain embedding or spatial domain embedding.

3 Basics of the Correlation Coefficient

Correlation is a mathematical model that helps understand the possible linear relation between two continuous variables. Correlation as a statistical method was proposed in 1885 by Sir Francis Galton. The correlation coefficient (Pearson's) was published in 1895 by Karl Pearson. Pearson's coefficient "r" is a computational index used to measure bivariate association. The restriction for correlation is that only bivariate settings must be considered. The mathematical representation was given by Pearson in 1895 [15], and it is given in Eq. (1)

$$r = \frac{\sum (X_i - \bar{X})(Y_i - \bar{Y})}{\sqrt{\sum (X_i - \bar{X})^2 \sum (Y_i - \bar{Y})^2}} \qquad (1)$$

The product-moment correlation coefficient is a dimensionless index. In the numerator, the values are calculated by subtracting the mean from every value and performing a sum of the cross products. The denominator performs the necessary adjustments to ensure the unit remains dimensionless. The Pearson coefficient value lies between -1 and $+1$. When the value of the correlation coefficient is 0, there is no relationship between the two variables being analyzed. If the value is -1, there exists perfect inverse relation, i.e., when the value of first variable increases, the value of the second decreases. If correlation coefficient is $+1$, then there exists perfect linear relation, i.e., the value of the second variable increases, when the value of the first variable increases. On comparison, it is known that Spearman's correlation coefficient fares much better against outliers, than the Pearson correlation coefficient [16]. Few of the various applications of calculating correlation coefficient values include model vector analysis [17], measuring the reliability of quantitative scales, setting its equivalence with kappa [18], and in medical research.

4 Proposed Methodology

In this section, a novel blind watermarking method is proposed to embed a binary image as watermark in a digital image. The proposed method is implemented using MATLAB to analyze performance of the proposed work. The embedding process is carried out in luminance components of a host image by converting it from RGB domain to YC_bC_r domain. In YC_bC_r domain, Y represents brightness values of pixel, whereas C_bC_r represents chrominance blue and red components of signal. In order to test the proposed work, host images of sizes 512×512 and a binary watermark of size $32 * 32$ are considered. The watermark image and the Y component of the host image are divided into sub-images of size $8 * 8$ pixels. The host image is converted into two sub-images which are then required to compute correlation values between two corresponding blocks of sub-images. The obtained correlation values are sorted in descending order to insert watermark. The embedding algorithm requires spatial domain operations based on the binary value of the sub-images. The sub-images are used to insert watermark and then restructured according to corresponding index numbers to form the complete Y components. The Y component of the image is then converted back into the RGB image. In order to extract the binary watermark image, the correlation matrix is obtained and an extraction algorithm is applied. The proposed approach could be classified as semi-blind watermarking algorithm as it is assumed that the correlation matrix is available, and both the sizes of the watermark image as well as host image are known. The embedding algorithm is given below.

$I' = Embedding\ Algorithm\ (I, J)$

---

1. Divide luminance component (Y) of host image I into blocks of size 8x8 and number of blocks (R) of host image in Y component:

$$R = Blocks(Y) = (M' * N')/(8 * 8) \qquad (2)$$

2. Divide watermark image J into blocks of size 8x8 and number of blocks is

$$S = \frac{K' * L'}{8 * 8} \qquad (3)$$

3. Divide host image into two sub images as:

$$I1 = I2 = (M'/2) * N \qquad (4)$$

4. Number of blocks in each sub image is calculated as follows.

$$R1 = R2 = Z = (M'/2 * N')/(8 * 8) \qquad (5)$$

5. Calculate the correlation factor of each corresponding pair of blocks using Eq. (1), let $r1, r2 \ldots rz$ correlation coefficients of different blocks

6. Sort correlation coefficients in descending order, where $r_1, r_2 \ldots r_z$ are correlation coefficients $\forall r_i \in corr\_values$, and $r_i < r_{i-1}$

7. Number of corresponding block pairs required (P) to embed watermark in host image, by descending order:

$$P = S/2 \qquad (6)$$

8. In order to embed the watermark into image blocks, modify each pixel in the host image as follows

   //If watermark pixel is zero then the procedure to be followed is given below//

   // If mod(pix_h /2) != 0, then pixel value pix_h = pix_h + 1 else pixel value pix_h is left as it is. Also pix_w represents watermark pixel and pix_h represents host image pixel//

   if (pix_w=0), // pix_w represents black.

   {
   if (modulus(pix_h) = 0) pix_h = even then pix_h = pix_h + 0;
   else if (modulus(pix_h) = 1) pix_h = odd; then pix_h = pix_h + 1;
   }

   //If Watermark Pixel is white then the procedure to be followed is given below//

   // If mod(pv/2) != 0, then pixel value pix_h = pix_h else pixel value pix_h is left unchanged//

   if (pix_w=1) // pix_w represents white.
   {
   if (modulus(pix_h) = 0) pix_h = even; then pix_h = pix_h + 1;elseif (modulus(pix_h) = 1) pix_h = odd; pix_h = pix_h + 0;}

9. Convert luminance components back to color components to construct watermarked Image.

Similarly, the watermark extraction algorithm is given below.

$I' =$ *Extraction Algorithm (I,J)*

---

1. Calculate the Y (luminance), Cb (, and Cr as follows for host image:

$$Y = 0.299 * R + 0.587 * G + 0.114 * B$$
$$Cb = 0.596 * R - 0.275 * G - 0.321 * B$$
$$Cr = 0.212 * R - 0.523 * G - 0.311 * B \qquad (7)$$

2. Divide the luminance component (Y) of host image I into blocks of size 8*8. Number of blocks (R) of host image in Y component given by:

$$R = (M' * N')/(8 * 8) \qquad (8)$$

3. Divide host image into two sub-images as:

$$I1 = I2 = (M'/2) * N, \text{ and Number of blocks:}$$
$$R1 = R2 = (M'/2 * N')/(8 * 8), \qquad (9)$$

4. Calculate the correlation factor of each corresponding pair of blocks using Eq.(1) Store the values with index number.

5. Sort correlation coefficients in descending order, where $r_1, r_2....r_z$ represents correlation coefficients $\forall r_i \in corr\_values, r_i \neq NaN$ and $r_i < r_{i-1}$

6. Number of embedded watermark blocks is S and required pairs $(P) = S/2$ (10)

7. In order to extract watermark for P pairs of blocks of host image the following Procedure is adopted:

//If host pixel pix_h is even, extracted watermark pixel pix_w is black (0) else if host pixel value pix_h is odd, then watermark pixel pix_w is white (1)//

$if\ (\ modulus(pix\_h) = 0)\ then\ pix\_h = even\ and\ pix\_w = 0,$

$\qquad else\ if\ (\ modulus(pix\_h) = 1)then\ pix\_h = odd\ and\ pix\_w = 1,$

8. Watermark image is constructed using P pairs of blocks.

5 Performance Evaluation

The performance evaluation of the proposed work is discussed in this section. The original watermark image is shown in Fig. 1. Similarly, original test images used for inserting watermark are shown in Fig. 2. The watermarked images are shown in

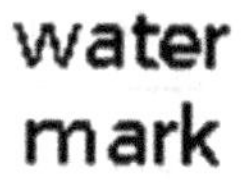

water
mark

Fig. 1 Original watermark

Fig. 2 Sample RGB test images

Table 1 with the calculated values of mean square error (MSE) and peak signal-to-noise Ratio (PSNR). In Table 2, the computed values of MSE and PSNR after implementing various attacks are shown. The attacks considered in this proposal are noise addition and compression attacks.

6 Conclusion

In this proposed work, a novel spatial domain watermarking approach using correlation coefficient matrix is discussed. The proposed approach could be classified as blind watermarking, and it is invisible. As spatial domain watermarking techniques are not robust to any attacks, it could also be called fragile watermarking. The performance of the proposed watermark is tested with simple attacks such as noise addition and compression. The proposed spatial domain watermarking could be used for data authentication.

Table 1 Watermarked images and calculated peak signal-to-noise ratio

Image Name	Watermarked Image	MSE	PSNR
Airplane		0.0740	59.4746
Baboon		0.0728	59.542
House		0.0727	59.5523
Lena		0.0700	59.7138
Peppers		0.0733	59.5167

Table 2 Results after implementing noise addition and JPEG compression attack on RGB images

Image name	Salt and pepper noise addition		Gaussian noise addition		JPEG compression	
	MSE	PSNR in dB	MSE	PSNR dB	MSB	PSNR dB
Airplane	0.0054	70.8642	0.0513	61.0662	0.0481	61.3437
Baboon	0.0051	71.0662	0.0542	60.8249	0.0503	61.1497
House	0.0046	71.5009	0.0535	60.8840	0.0508	61.1078
Lena	0.0054	70.8642	0.0508	61.1078	0.0498	61.1921
Peppers	0.0034	72.8271	0.0474	61.4104	0.0483	61.3217

References

1. Barni, M., Bartolini, F., Cappellini, V., & Piva, A. (1998). A DCT-domain system for robust image watermarking. *Signal processing, 66*(3), 357–372.
2. Nikolaidis, N., & Pitas, I. (1998). Robust image watermarking in the spatial domain. *Signal processing, 66*(3), 385–403.
3. Kutter, M., & Petitcolas, F. A. (1999, April). Fair benchmark for image watermarking systems. In *Electronic Imaging'99* (pp. 226–239). International Society for Optics and Photonics.
4. Karybali, I. G., & Berberidis, K. (2006). Efficient spatial image watermarking via new perceptual masking and blind detection schemes. *IEEE Transactions on Information Forensics and security, 1*(2), 256–274.
5. Lin, P. L. (2000). Robust transparent image watermarking system with spatial mechanisms. *Journal of systems and software, 50*(2), 107–116.
6. Jun, L., & LiZhi, L. (2008, December). An improved watermarking detect algorithm for color image in spatial domain. In *Future BioMedical Information Engineering, 2008. FBIE'08. International Seminar on* (pp. 95–99). IEEE.
7. Murch, G. M. (1984). Physiological principles for the effective use of color. *IEEE Computer Graphics and Applications, 4*(11), 48–55.
8. Lin, E. T., Podilchuk, C. I., & Delp III, E. J. (2000, May). Detection of image alterations using semifragile watermarks. In *Electronic Imaging* (pp. 152–163). International Society for Optics and Photonics.
9. Megalingam, R. K., Nair, M. M., Srikumar, R., Balasubramanian, V. K., & Sarma, V. S. V. (2010, February). Performance comparison of novel, robust spatial domain digital image watermarking with the conventional frequency domain watermarking techniques. In *Signal Acquisition and Processing, 2010. ICSAP'10. International Conference on* (pp. 349–353). IEEE.
10. Sun, J., Yang, N., Liu, J., Yang, X., Li, X., & Zhang, L. (2010, July). Video watermarking scheme based on spatial relationship of DCT coefficients. In *Intelligent Control and Automation (WCICA), 2010 8th World Congress on* (pp. 56–59). IEEE.
11. Meerwald, P., & Uhl, A. (2001, August). Survey of wavelet-domain watermarking algorithms. In *Photonics West 2001-Electronic Imaging* (pp. 505–516). International Society for Optics and Photonics.
12. Hajisami, A., Rahmati, A., & Babaie-Zadeh, M. (2011, March). Watermarking based on independent component analysis in spatial domain. In *Computer Modelling and Simulation (UKSim), 2011 UkSim 13th International Conference on* (pp. 299–303). IEEE.
13. Singh, A. K., Sharma, N., Dave, M., & Mohan, A. (2012, December). A novel technique for digital image watermarking in spatial domain. In *Parallel Distributed and Grid Computing (PDGC), 2012 2nd IEEE International Conference on* (pp. 497–501). IEEE.
14. Shih, F. Y., & Wu, S. Y. (2003). Combinational image watermarking in the spatial and frequency domains. *Pattern Recognition, 36*(4), 969–975.
15. Lee Rodgers, J., & Nicewander, W. A. (1988). Thirteen ways to look at the correlation coefficient. *The American Statistician, 42*(1), 59–66.
16. Mukaka, M. M. (2012). A guide to appropriate use of correlation coefficient in medical research. *Malawi Medical Journal, 24*(3), 69–71.
17. Allemang, R. J., & Brown, D. L. (1982, November). A correlation coefficient for modal vector analysis. In *Proceedings of the 1st international modal analysis conference* (Vol. 1, pp. 110–116). SEM, Orlando.
18. Fleiss, J. L., & Cohen, J. (1973). The equivalence of weighted kappa and the intraclass correlation coefficient as measures of reliability. *Educational and psychological measurement, 33*(3), 613–6 http://file.scirp.org/Html/22029.html.

An Approach to Improve Load Balancing in Distributed Storage Systems for NoSQL Databases: Mongodb

Sudhakar and Shivendra Kumar Pandey

Abstract The ongoing process of heterogeneous data generation needs a better NoSQL database system to accommodate it. NoSQL database stores data in the distributed manner in their globally deployed shards. The data stored in these databases should have high availability, and the system should not compromise with the scalability and partition tolerance. The distributed storage systems have the main challenge to address the skewness in the data. The process of distribution of data items over the nodes in the system causes skewness of data. To address this problem, we propose a different approach to balance load in the distributed environment is the partitioning of data into small chunks that can be relocated independently.

Keywords NoSQL · Data load balancing · MongoDB · Chunk migration
Big data

1 Introduction

Recent developments in size of data have heightened the need for storing world digital data exceeds the limit of a zettabyte (i.e., 10^{21} bytes); it is a challenge as well as necessity to develop a powerful and efficient system that has the capacity to accommodate data. For example, a system using a very dense storage medium like deoxyribonucleic acid (DNA). DNA can encode two bits per nucleotide (NT) or 455 exabytes per gram of single-stranded DNA [1]. Taken into account the fact that

Sudhakar (✉)
Indian Computer Emergency Response Team, Ministry of Electronics
& Information Technology, New Delhi, India
e-mail: sudhak82_scs@jnu.ac.in

Sudhakar · S. K. Pandey
School of Computer & Systems Sciences, Jawaharlal Nehru University,
New Delhi, India
e-mail: shivaiert@gmail.com

© Springer Nature Singapore Pte Ltd. 2018
P. K. Pattnaik et al. (eds.), *Progress in Computing, Analytics and Networking*,
Advances in Intelligent Systems and Computing 710,
https://doi.org/10.1007/978-981-10-7871-2_51

ton of genetic material is prerequisite by DNA as to store zettabyte of information. The argument can simply be made that data storage needs to be distributed for quantitative reasons alone.

For this, the distributed storage systems need to be available and scalable when needed. This amount of storage will only be possible if it is distributed geographically and should exhibit the property of being accessible by millions of users besides its raw storage capacity.

Web giants like Google, Amazon, Facebook, and LinkedIn are the industries that use distributed storage systems. To fulfill their requirements, they have deployed thousands of data centers globally so that they can make data available all the time with scalability at any level. Furthermore, in the case of failure that occurs in scaling process is either the failure of the software or the hardware components. Therefore, these failures need to be handled during the planning and implementation phases.

In addition to this, the traditional distributed large-scale storage systems are inefficient to store the enormous heterogeneous data (structured, semi-structured, or unstructured) [2, 3] as they do not satisfy the 7 Vs (volume, variety, velocity, veracity, validity, volatility, and value) [4]. The way it is accessed and stored in traditional databases may pose many limitations. These new horizons of the data bring *big data* [5] into reality. Therefore, we require more powerful and efficient solutions to process big data.

Big data requires a new kind of database system to handle heterogeneous data sets. One of the most popular and well-known databases for big data is NoSQL (Not Only SQL) that has the capability to process big data for mining valued information. As a result, many industries have developed various NoSQL databases depending on their requirements such as Facebook's Cassandra [3], Amazon's Dynamo [6], Yahoo! Pnuts [7], Google's BigTable [8] or Riak, and MongoDB [9]. These systems scale very well over the trade-offs of consistency, availability, and partition tolerance as mentioned in the CAP theorem [10]. Each one of them is using the shards to store their data. Since deploying shards globally is the main challenge for big data to handle as it suffers from load balancing problem.

The load balancing techniques used in NoSQL systems do not consider chunk migration as performance indicator rather they prefer high availability and partition tolerance as their key indicator. In this work, we aim to bridge this gap by proposing an improvement over existing load balancing techniques by taking into account shard utilization and the migration of chunks to increase the efficiency of NoSQL databases, considering the particular NoSQL, e.g., MongoDB. Here, in this work, we have proposed a new approach to improve load balancing for MongoDB and compared our results with automatic load balancing algorithm of MongoDB, which clearly shows the better performance of our approach without affecting memory utilization of the shards. The main contribution of this article is:

- A naive and holistic approach is proposed for load balancing for MongoDB based NoSQL systems.

- Our proposed method is computationally cost-effective as the number of chunk migrations among shards are less compared to the traditional load balancing algorithms for MongoDB.
- Consistent performance is achieved by the proposed method irrespective of number and size of the shards.

The rest of the article is organized as follows: Sect. 2 comprises literature survey of NoSQL. Section 3 explains the maintenance and structure of the data being stored in the shards in MongoDB. In Sect. 4, we present our proposed approach for load balancing in MongoDB. Section 4.3 presents experiments and evaluation. Finally, Sect. 5 concludes the paper with some of the future research directions.

2 Related Work

Facebook's Cassandra [3, 11] is a distributed database designed to store structured data in a key-value pair and indexed by a *key*. Cassandra is highly scalable from both perspectives; one is that of storage and the second is that of request throughput while preventing from single point failure. Additionally, Cassandra's store's data in the form of *tables* that is very similar to the distributed multi-dimensional maps is also indexed by a *key*. It belongs to the column family like BigTable [8]. In a single row key, it provides atomic per-replica operation. In Cassandra, *consistent hashing* [12] is used for the notion of data partitioning to fulfill the purpose of mapping keys to nodes in a similar manner like Chord distributed hash table (DHT). Partitioned data is stored in a Cassandra cluster that would contain the moving nodes on the ring. To facilitate the load balancing, it uses DHT on its *keys*.

Amazon's Dynamo [6] is distributed key-value store database. It mainly focuses on scalability and availability rather than consistency. To address the problem of non-uniformity of node distribution in the ring, it uses the concept of virtual nodes (vnodes). Also, it follows a different strategy for partition-to-vnode assignment which results into the better distribution of load across vnodes and therefore over the physical nodes.

Scatter [13] unlike Amazon's Dynamo, it is a distributed *consistent* key-value store database, which is highly decentralized. For data storing, it uses uniform key distribution through consistent hashing typical for DHTs. Scatter uses two policies for load balancing. In the first policy, the newly joined node in the system is directed to randomly sample k groups, and then it joins the one handling a large number of operations. In the second policy, based on load distribution, neighboring groups can trade-off their responsibility ranges.

MongoDB [9, 14] is schema-free document-oriented database written in C++. MongoDB uses replication to provide data availability and sharding to provide partition tolerance to manage data across the distributed environment. It stores data in the form of chunks. To manage even distribution of chunks across all the servers in the cluster, a balancer is used in this system. Whenever balancer detects an uneven chunk count event (i.e., chunk difference between minimal loaded and maximal loaded shards is greater than or equal to 8), it redistributes the chunks among shards until the load difference between any two shards is less than or equal to two [15].

3   Maintenance of Load in MongoDB

The basic concept of automatic load balancing of MongoDB is breaking up the larger collections into smaller chunks and distribute evenly over all available shards so that each subset of the data set belongs to one shard. The criteria of partitioning the collection in the database of MongoDB are that specify a shard key pattern for the chunk in two more parameters, *minkey* (minimum size of the chunk) and *maxkey* (maximum size of the chunk) [14]. We can say that chunks can have three attributes of the collection (i.e., *minkey, maxkey,* and *shardkey*). When chunk size reaches to a maximum size (i.e., 200 MB as configured for automatic balancing) then the *splitter* splits the chunk into two new equal chunks.

As already mentioned, the basic idea of automatic load balancing of MongoDB is that if the difference between the number of chunks of any two shards is greater than or equal to eight as detected by balancer of MongoDB, then balancer consider it as imbalanced shards and starts migrating chunks to other shards until the difference will decrease to two [15].

As discussed CAP theorem in Sect. 1, MongoDB embraces the properties of availability and partition tolerance. Hence, to ensure the availability, it uses replicated servers with automatic failover. In case of any failure in the system, partition tolerance ensures smooth functioning by allowing it to continue work as a whole. In the imbalance condition, the chunk migrations among the shards are managed according to the automatic load balancing algorithm of the MongoDB. To implement availability and partition tolerance in distributed systems, replication and sharding are commonly used which are briefly discussed below:

3.1   Replication

Replication is the process of synchronizing data across multiple servers connected in a distributed manner. It provides redundancy and increases data availability by making multiple copies of data on different database servers. In this way, data will be protected from the single point failure and loss of one server will not affect the availability of the data because the data can be recovered from the other copy of the replica set. The replica is $p_j^r \in S_i$ where, r represents the replica of a particular node $S_i = \{p_1^r, p_2^r, p_3^r\}$ where, $S_i \in S, S \in \mathbb{Z}^+$ and $1 \leq j \leq 3$. It should be noted that one node has only three replicas in which one must be a *primary* replica and others are *secondary* replicas.

Every node has replication group G of size n, so the quorum is a subset of nodes in a replication group G. Let view v is a tuple over G that defines important information for G and view id is denoted as $i_v \in \mathbb{N}$ [16].

In some cases, replication can be used to service more read operations on the database. To increase the availability of data for distributed applications, we can also use different data centers to store the database geographically. Replica sets have the same data in the replica group. In this group, one replica is *primary,* and rest are *secondary* [14]. The *primary* accepts all the read/write operations from the clients. In the case, if *primary* is unavailable, one of the *secondary* replicas is elected as *primary*. For the election purpose, Paxos algorithm is used [17].

3.2 Sharding

MongoDB scales the system, when it needs to store data more than the capacity of a single server (or shard) with the help of horizontal scaling. The principle of horizontal scaling is to partition data by *rows* rather than splitting data into *columns* (e.g., normalization and vertical partitioning do in the relational database) [14]. In MongoDB, horizontal scaling is done by automatic sharding architecture to distribute data across thousands of nodes. Moreover, sharding occurs on a per collection basis; it did not take into consideration of the whole database. MongoDB is configured in such a way that it automatically detects which collection is growing monotonically than the other. That collection has become the subject of sharding while others may still reside on the single server. Some components that need an explanation to understand the architecture of the MongoDB sharding is given in Fig. 1.

- **Shards** are the servers that store data (each run *mongod* process) and ensure availability and automatic failover, each shard comprising a replica set.
- **Config Servers** "store the cluster's metadata," which include the basic information of chunks and shards. These chunks are contiguous ranges of data from collections that are ordered by the shard key.
- **Routing Services** are run *mongos* processes performing read and write request on behalf of client applications.

Auto-sharding in MongoDB provides some necessary functionality without requiring large or powerful machines [15].

1. Automatic balancing if changes occur in load and data distribution.
2. Ease of adding new machines without downtime.
3. No solitary point of failure.
4. Ability to recover from failure automatically.

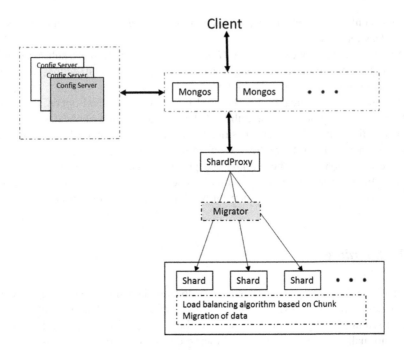

Fig. 1 Modified MongoDB distributed architecture [15]

In the system, S is the set of shards and each shard consists of S_i replica sets then we can state it as $S = \left\{ S_i : S_i \in S \, where \, p_j^{r_i} \in S_i, i \geq 2, 1 \leq j \leq 3 \right\}$, here $p_j^{r_i}$ is represent j replicas available in ith shards.

4 Proposed Method for Load Balancing

4.1 Basic Idea About Load Balancing and Preliminaries

In this section, we are going to introduce all the terms that we will use in this document. For every data item $d \in D$, where D is the set of all data items, we define all types of load here, that represented by Γ. The *load* $l_t : D \to \mathbb{R}$, $t \in \Gamma$ is a function that use for assigning the associated load value of load type t from set D. There exists an associated load value for every unit of replication $U \in D$, i.e., $l_t^U = \sum_{v \in U} l_t(v)$. And any node H in the distributed system, at a particular node U_H contain all units of replication, and an associated value $l_t^H = \sum_{U \in U_H} l_t^U$. Every node has capacity $c_t^H \in \mathbb{R}$ for each load type t. Thus, the inequality $l_t^H < c_t^H$ must be maintained as invariant, as the violation would result in failure of H. We also calculate the *utilization* [18] of a node $u_t^H = l_t^H / c_t^H$ at $t \in \Gamma$. If a system has utilization μ_t^S where S is a set of all nodes in the system and average utilization $\hat{\mu}_t^S$ of $t \in \Gamma$ [18], given as

$$\mu_t^S = \frac{\sum_{H \in S} l_t^H}{\sum_{H \in S} c_t^H}, \quad \hat{\mu}_t^S = \frac{1}{|S|} \sum_{H \in S} u_t^H \tag{i}$$

In addition to the above, we need to consider the third parameter that represents the *cost* of moving replication unit or data item U from one host to another host in S, i.e., $\rho U: S \times S \rightarrow \mathbb{R}$, this parameter is linearly depends on l_{size}^U. If the system is considered uniform, then $H, H', H'' \in S$ and $U \in H$ such that $\rho U(H, H') = \rho U(H, H'')$ is seems to be a constant where $\rho U \in \mathbb{R}$.

Let

$$L_S^H = \{l_t^H | t \in \Gamma, U \in H\} \tag{ii}$$

$$C_H = \{c_t^H | t \in \Gamma\} \tag{iii}$$

$$L_H = \{l_t^H | t \in \Gamma\} \tag{iv}$$

$$L_S = \{(C_H, L_H, L_S^H) | H \in S\} \tag{v}$$

where L_S is referred as the system statistics for S. The migration is done by the balancer, i.e., *MIGRATOR*(U, H) to *MIGRATOR*(U, H') where U for a unit of replication and H, H' are the hosts.

4.2 Modified Load Balancing Algorithm

In the algorithm, there are two methods one is *IsBalance*() that will return a Boolean value depending on whether the particular *shard* or *host* H is balanced or not. However, the condition of balance is as follows: if a shard has more data than its threshold value, then it will become imbalanced. The threshold value is *Const* $* c_t^H$ (e.g., *Const* = 0.7 or 0.8 or 0.9) where c_t^H the capacity of the *shard* H. If a shard shows that it is imbalanced, then it needs to migrate. The second method is *MIGRATOR*() which migrates data from imbalanced shard to a balanced shard until $\hat{l}_t^S$ data remains in the shard.

We are calculating the total data occupied in all shards that are l_t^S and then calculate average data occupied by all shards that is $\hat{l}_t^S$.

Furthermore, we check if the shard is balanced or not, and for each value of imbalance shard, we migrate chunks from imbalance shard to balance shard until the condition $\left(l_t^{H_i} \geq l_t^S \;\; \mathbf{OR} \;\; l_t^{H_j} \geq l_{t_{max}}^{H_t} \right)$ met and this process repeated until all shards become balance.

4.3 Experimental Results

To show the effectiveness of modified MongoDB, we have compared our approach with traditional MongoDB and compared the two on the basis of chunk migration rate and space utilization metrics.

To prove our claim, we have performed the experiments four times with a different number of chunks and noted the results. In the first experiment, we have considered shards with 100 chunk capacity. Whenever imbalance event occurs, balancer algorithm executes automatically and redistributes chunks among shards in order to maintain balance in the system. Furthermore, our approach performs less chunk migration which in turn reduces the overhead cost of migration over MongoDB load balancing algorithm, resulting into the efficient utilization of the shards.

For analytical purpose, the same experiment is performed with 1000, 10000, and 100000 chunk count capacity shards which is clear from the Fig. 2a.

It should be noted that the memory utilization of the shards in the process of load balancing, then automatic load balancing algorithm and modified MongoDB performs exactly the same as mentioned in Fig. 2b. Hence, our algorithm performs better by minimizing overhead cost due to chunk migrations which leads to improved load balancing computational complexity without compromising with space utilization. Thus, we are able to improve two factors of the balancing algorithm—computation cost of chunk migrations and memory utilization of the shards.

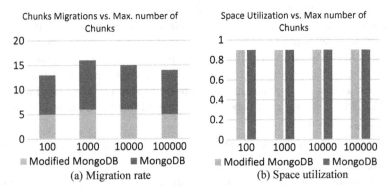

Fig. 2 Experimental evaluation of modified MongoDB and MongoDB based on migration rate and space utilization

5 Conclusion and Future Work

The large-scale applications and data processing require handling of issues like scalability, reliability, and performance of distributed storage systems. One of the prominent issues among them is to handle the skewness in the data distribution and accessing of data items. We have presented an improved algorithm of load balancing for NoSQL database MongoDB, which handles aforementioned issues by providing automatic load balancing. We have analyzed our algorithm and shown that our approach is better than many similar systems employed specifically in MongoDB database [14], in terms of chunk migration and memory utilization for the individual shard.

Our proposed method is for MongoDB based NoSQL database systems. We will try to incorporate this approach into existing different flavors of NoSQL.

References

1. Church, George M., Yuan Gao, and Sriram Kosuri, 2012, "Next-generation digital information storage in DNA." *Science* 337.6102: 1628–1628.
2. Dean, Jeffrey, and Sanjay Ghemawat, 2008, "MapReduce: simplified data processing on large clusters." *Communications of the ACM* 51.1: 107–113.
3. Lakshman, Avinash, and Prashant Malik, 2010, "Cassandra: a decentralized structured storage system." *ACM SIGOPS Operating Systems Review* 44.2: 35–40.
4. M. Ali-ud-din, et al., 2014, "Seven V's of Big Data understanding Big Data to extract value," *American Society for Engineering Education (ASEE Zone 1), 2014 Zone 1 Conference of the, Bridgeport, CT, USA.*
5. E. Dumbill, 2012, "What is big data?," O'Reilly Media, Inc., Available: https://beta.oreilly.com/ideas/what-is-big-data.
6. DeCandia, Giuseppe, et al., 2007, "Dynamo: amazon's highly available key-value store." *ACM SIGOPS operating systems review* 41.6: 205–220.
7. Cooper, Brian F., et al., 2008, "PNUTS: Yahoo!'s hosted data serving platform." *Proc. of the VLDB Endowment* 1: 1277–1288.
8. Chang, Fay, et al., 2008, "Bigtable: A distributed storage system for structured data." *ACM Trans. on Computer Systems (TOCS)* 26.2: 4.
9. "MongoDB," MongoDB Inc., 2015, Available: https://en.wikipedia.org/wiki/MongoDB.
10. E. A. Brewer, *Towards robust distributed systems. (Invited Talk),* Oregon, 2000.
11. Featherston, Dietrich, 2010, "cassandra: Principles and Application." *Department of Computer Science University of Illinois at Urbana-Champaign.*
12. Thusoo, Ashish, et al., 2010, "Data warehousing and analytics infrastructure at facebook." *Proc. of the 2010 ACM SIGMOD Inter. Conf. on Management of data.*
13. Glendenning, Lisa, et al. "Scalable consistency in Scatter, 2011," *Proc. of the Twenty-Third ACM Symposium on Operating Systems Principles.*
14. MongoDB Documentation," 25 June 2015. [Online].
15. Liu, Yimeng, Yizhi Wang, and Yi Jin., 2012, "Research on the improvement of MongoDB Auto-Sharding in cloud environment." *Computer Science & Education (ICCSE), 2012 7th Inter. Conf. on.* IEEE.
16. Gifford, David K, 1979, "Weighted voting for replicated data." *Proc. of the seventh ACM symposium on Operating systems principles.*

17. Lamport, Leslie, 1998, "The part-time parliament." *ACM Transactions on Computer Systems (TOCS)* 16.2: 133–169.
18. Godfrey, Brighten, et al., 2004, "Load balancing in dynamic structured P2P systems." *INFOCOM 2004. Twenty-third Annual Joint Conf. of the IEEE Computer and Communications Societies*. Vol. 4.

Classification of Diabetes Mellitus Disease (DMD): A Data Mining (DM) Approach

Himansu Das, Bighnaraj Naik and H. S. Behera

Abstract The diabetes mellitus disease (DMD) commonly referred as diabetes is a significant public health problem. Predicting the disease at the early stage can save the valuable human resource. Voluminous datasets are available in various medical data repositories in the form of clinical patient records and pathological test reports which can be used for real-world applications to disclose the hidden knowledge. Various data mining (DM) methods can be applied to these datasets, stored in data warehouses for predicting DMD. The aim of this research is to predict diabetes based on some of the DM techniques like classification and clustering. Out of which, classification is one of the most suitable methods for predicting diabetes. In this study, J48 and Naïve Bayesian techniques are used for the early detection of diabetes. This research will help to propose a quicker and more efficient technique for diagnosis of disease, leading to timely and proper treatment of patients. We have also proposed a model and elaborated it step-by-step, in order to make medical practitioner to explore and to understand the discovered rules better. The study also shows the algorithm generated on the dataset collected from college medical hospital as well as from online repository. In the end, an article also outlines how an intelligent diagnostic system works. A clinical trial of this proposed method involves local patients, which is still continuing and requires longer research and experimentation.

Keywords Diabetes mellitus disease (DMD) · Data mining (DM)
J48 · Naïve Bayesian

H. Das (✉) · H. S. Behera
Department of Information Technology, Veer Surendra Sai University of Technology,
Burla, Sambalpur 768018, Odisha, India
e-mail: das.himansu2007@gmail.com

H. S. Behera
e-mail: mailtohsbehera@gmail.com

B. Naik
Department of Computer Application, Veer Surendra Sai University of Technology,
Burla, Sambalpur 768018, Odisha, India
e-mail: mailtobnaik@gmail.com

© Springer Nature Singapore Pte Ltd. 2018
P. K. Pattnaik et al. (eds.), *Progress in Computing, Analytics and Networking*,
Advances in Intelligent Systems and Computing 710,
https://doi.org/10.1007/978-981-10-7871-2_52

1   Introduction

Out of many chronic diseases, diabetes is one of them. It occurs mainly when the pancreas is unable to produce the desired amount of insulin required for a human body or when the human body cannot effectively manage the produced insulin. When taken as a whole, the risk of dying among the people with diabetes is at least double the hazard of their peers without diabetes. As per the prediction of World Health Organization (WHO), diabetes will be one of the major leading causes of death in 2030 and death rate will double between 2005 and 2030. It could also be described as the situation in which the body is unable to process properly the food for utilization as energy. The majority of the food consumed by us is turned into glucose, which is further used as energy by us when required. The pancreas, an organ of our body which lies near the stomach of a human body, produces a special type of hormone called insulin helps glucose to get into the cells of our body. The persons affected by diabetes, the body of the affected persons are either do not produce enough insulin or unable to consume its own insulin as well. This leads to increase the sugar level in our blood. For this cause of increasing the sugar in the blood, people call diabetes as 'sugar'. Several symptoms are normally found in the persons affected by this disease. The main symptoms are frequent urination, feeling pain in the muscles, increased hunger, and thirst. It needs early detection of the disease. It can cause many severe complications if not treated at the early stage. Short-term complications include diabetic ketoacidosis, nonketotic hyperosmolar coma, or death. Major chronic complications may arise like dysfunction of heart which leads to stroke, foot ulcers, chronic kidney failure, damage to the retinas of the eyes, nerves, and teeth. The diabetes is mainly categorized in three types [1]. First, the Type 1 DMD occurs due to the failure of pancreas to produce enough insulin. The cause still remains unknown. Second, Type 2 DMD begins with insulin resistance, a situation in which cells will be unsuccessful to respond to insulin appropriately. With the progress of diabetes, be short of insulin may also develop. The common causes may be due to excessive body weight and insufficient exercise required in the changed lifestyle. And Third, gestational diabetes, which occurs at the time of pregnancy of a women without a prior history of diabetes suddenly increases high blood-sugar levels. Advancement in the field of computer science and high-performance computing has benefited almost all disciplines including medical science in finding better results over traditional practical solutions. Many tools have been developed for effective analysis of image processing and effective analyzing by applying data mining techniques in order to help clinicians in making better decisions for the diagnosis of the diseases of patients. Nowadays, data mining plays a vital role and becomes an essential methodology for medical diagnostics. Data mining helps in finding the hidden pattern lies in the pathological data, large-scale medical images and the daily records to understand more clearly about the hidden relationships between diagnostic features of different patient groups [2–4]. Nowadays, data mining has been used extensively in the areas of science and engineering, such as genetics, bioinformatics, medicine, and education [5–9]. The primary objective of our research is to find whether a patient is affected by diabetic or not. In order to accomplish this objective, very popular data mining algorithms like J48 and Naïve Bayesian are used. By using this algorithm, it becomes easy to understand the whole process [10–13]. These algorithms help to analyze the disease from all the aspects.

The organization of the remaining section of this paper is as follows. Section 2 discusses the basic concepts to understand our work. The related works are represented in Sect. 3. Section 4 introduces our proposed approach for detecting diabetes mellitus disease. Section 5 analyzes the experimental results of the collected dataset, and Sect. 6 describes the comparison of the techniques after applying proposed approach. Section 7 concludes the paper.

2 Basic Concepts

This section presents some of the basic algorithmic concepts which are required to understand the proposed approach.

2.1 Naive Bayesian Algorithm

It is a supervised learning optimal classifier algorithm that is based on the concept of Bayes' theorem. This model is easy to construct, with easy iterative parameter assessment which makes it mostly valuable for very huge datasets. This classifier is used to convert the prior probability into posterior probability by using likely used values. This Naive Bayes' theorem is also often used to carry out complex classification tasks.

This theorem provides a technique to calculate the posterior probability $P(X|Y)$, from $P(X)$, $P(Y)$, and $P(Y|X)$. This Naive Bayes classifier assumes that the outcome of the cost of a predictor (Y) on a given class (X) is independent of the costs of other predictors. This hypothesis is called class conditional independence. The Bayes' theorem is represented in Eq. 1.

$$P(X|Y) = (P(Y|X)P(X))/P(Y) \tag{1}$$

Here, $P(X|Y)$ is the posterior probability of X conditioned on Y, $P(X)$ is the prior probability or apriori probability of X, similarly $P(Y|X)$ is the probability of Y conditioned on X and $P(Y)$ is defined as the prior probability.

2.2   J48 Algorithm

The J48 decision tree algorithm is used for classification. It uses each and every phase of the data attribute which is divided into smaller subclasses to establish on a decision. The J48 algorithm inspects the normalized information gain that outcomes dividing the data by selecting an attribute. In generally, the higher the normalized information gain of attributes is used to build the decision then this algorithm recurs the lesser reduct of elements. The J48 algorithm selects the particular attributes, dissimilar element values, and lost feature values of the information. If all the instances of the subset are considered with the same set, then after splitting the instances fit into the identical set. All attributes in the sequence will be measured, and the expansion in information will be chosen for the confirm on the attribute. The suitable element will be recognized to resultant from the recent classification constraint.

3   Related Work

Not much work has been done in the field of diabetes mellitus disease (DMD). Here, some of the existing work is represented as follows. Sankaranarayanan and Pramananda Perumal [14] focused their study on two classification methods, i.e., rule classification and decision trees. The decision tree was based on the algorithm from the rule classifier. The attributes specified after the physical examination research were code, sex, and age. The concept of making an algorithm by considering all the attributes was taken from their study and rule classification method. They even gave the concept of data warehouse which could be used for further examination of patients and their classification which is a considerable point for our research. Further research of Iyer et al. [15] compared two of the major algorithms of data mining techniques J48 decision trees and Naive Bayesian algorithm. From the results obtained, both the methods have a comparatively small difference in error rate, though the percentage split of 70:30 for Naïve Bayes technique gives the least error rate as compared to other J48 implementations. According to their algorithms, Naive Bayes had a lesser error rate than J48 decision tree, and hence, it was considered better. These algorithms were more accurate and specific for classification. These algorithms gave faster results than those used in our paper hence could be used for future modification.

In some other research of Velu and Kashwan [16], they worked on Pima Indian Diabetes (PID) dataset. They used three techniques such as genetic algorithm (GA), EM algorithm, and h-means with clustering. The result stated that the double crossover genetics process and h-means + based techniques were superior on performance comparison. They performed simulation on WEKA software for three models to test the classification. For this simulation tests, they have taken seven attributes with 768 instances of diabetic patients gathered from the different hospitals. Their results showed that out of 768 instances, 500 patients were experienced with negative and 268 patients were experienced as positive. Correlation coefficient was determined to be 0.96 which specifies that there was a strong relationship between these two samples. They basically classified diabetic patients as positive and negative on the basis of seven attributes by using the above algorithms. This classification technique is used as a reference in our work.

Motka et al. [17] proposed four different approaches for classifying the disease into two main classes: diabetic and non-diabetic. They used the techniques PCA with ANFIS, ANFIS, neural detworks, and PCA with neural networks. They observed that after combining PCA with neural network for classification gives the better accuracy. They used soft computing techniques for classification and MATLAB GUI. Their classification was proper and simple. Rajesh and Sangeetha [18] applied many classification algorithms on diabetes dataset and analyzed the performance of those algorithms. A classification rate of 91% was obtained for the C4.5 algorithm. Future enhancement of this work includes modification of the C4.5 algorithms to advance the classification rate to achieve greater accuracy in classification. C4.5 is considered the best of all the algorithms for classification. Patil and Joshi [19] in their study gave a certain set of rules using association rule data mining algorithms, i.e., apriori algorithm which is further used in this study also. They implemented it in WEKA and generated those top ten powerful rules for diabetes = 'yes'. Whereas diabetes is equal = 'no'. These rules had their own support and confidence. In this paper, Apriori algorithm for classification of DMD is implemented and considered their rules also.

4 Proposed Model

In this section, proposed method for determining diabetes is presented. This system saves the time of the doctors as well as of patients by generating the report through its data repositories. This generator determines whether the patient is diabetic or not. Figure 1 represents the block diagram of the proposed framework.

The proposed work can be vitalized as presented below:

Patients: They are the main focus point of our system. They are responsible for providing all the data for the repository. With their help, the process of collecting data becomes very easy.

Data collection from patients: In order to collect data from patients, they are provided with the set of questions. Those questions include name, age, sex, blood sugar level, and plasma glucose concentration which is a 2 hours in an oral glucose tolerance test, etc.

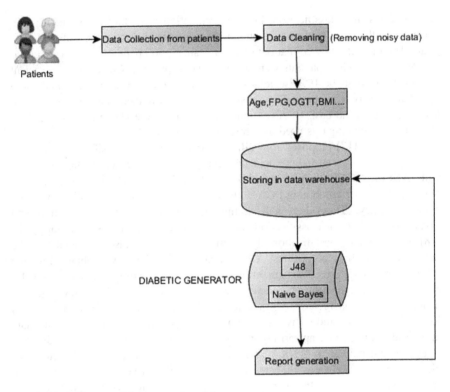

Fig. 1 Block diagram of the proposed model

Data cleaning step is very decisive. Here, unnecessary data are removed and only important data are sent for further implementation, for example, sex, age, oral glucose tolerance test (OGTT). Next step is storing in the data warehouse, where the data are stored in the data warehouse. This is done so to maintain all the records about patients which could be referred whenever required. Finally, in diabetes generator step which generates a report after processing all the data by specifying whether the patient is diabetic or non-diabetic.

5 Results and Discussion

We have collected 200 data by preparing a questionnaire given in Fig. 2, from a local medical college hospital out of which 60% is used to training purposes of the model and the rest 40% of the collected data is used to test in our model. The data are collected first and then preprocessed to fill the missing values. Some redundant data are also omitted. For the future use, the data are stored in the warehouse.

1. Name :

2. Age:

3. Gender : Male ☐ Female ☐ *(tick one)*

4. Occupancy : (WORKING/NOTWORKING)

Instructions:

This questionnaire will help us to find out the summary of occurrence of diabetes in people of various age groups. Each item in this questionnaire is describing a specific attribute of the diabetes disease. We want your opinion as how likely is the occurrence of diabetes with the given set of attributes. Given the actual choices that you face, tick the choice that you will prefer. There are six questions in all.

1. Age (Years)

      i. 21-35 ☐   ii. 36-50 ☐   iii. 51-65 ☐   iv. 66-71 ☐

2. Body Mass Index (kg/m^2) = *Weight:*   , *Height:*

      i. 22-24.9 ☐   ii. 25-30 ☐   iii. 31-40 ☐   iv. 41-68 ☐

3. Diastolic Blood Pressure (mm/Hg) *(Lower range pressure)*

      i. 50-70 ☐   ii. 71-85 ☐   iii. 86-100 ☐   iv. 101-114 ☐

4. Diabetes Pedigree Function *(Hereditary)*

      i. Yes ☐   ii. No ☐

5. Plasma Glucose Concentration (mg/dl)

      i. 78-108 (low) ☐   ii. 109-134 (intermediate) ☐

      iii. 135-170 (high) ☐   iv. 170-199 (Very High) ☐

6. Are you suffering from Diabetes?

      i. Yes ☐   ii. No ☐

7. Type of Diabetes :

Fig. 2 Questionnaire to collect the data from the patients

By using the diabetes generator, the data are classified. Results obtained from this model are as follows:

In this dataset, total eight numbers of attributes are used, namely age (years), plasma glucose concentration test, triceps skin fold thickness (mm), diastolic blood pressure (mm Hg), 2 hours serum insulin (mu u/ml), diabetes pedigree function, body mass index (weight in kg/(height in m)^2), and class variable.

Each attribute used has its own role in predicting whether the patient is diabetic or non-diabetic. Using WEKA software, the graph is generated in Fig. 3 which describes the possibility of having diabetes and not having. Red color shows the test is positive, i.e., a person is having diabetes and blue shows tested negative.

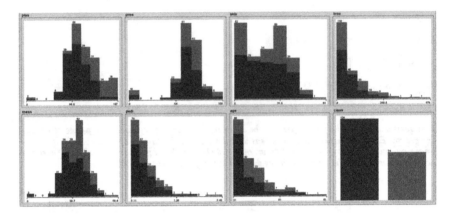

Fig. 3 Graphical representation of all the attributes of dataset

Table 1 Description of output after applying Naive Bayers theorem	Tested negative	Tested positive	
	107	19	Tested negative
	36	38	Tested positive

At first, Naive Bayes theorem is applied in WEKA software. In the output, we observed that 145 instances are correct and 55 instances are incorrect. Through this, we got the exact statistical measures; few of them are as follows (Table 1):

    i. The Mean absolute error—0.3142
   ii. Relative absolute error—67.3187%
  iii. Root relative squared error—92.2618%
  iv. Root mean squared error—0.4456
   v. Kappa statistics—0.3808.

Next, the J48 method is applied which shows 139 instances to be correct and 61 instances to be incorrect out of total 200 instances. The statistical measures are as follows (Table 2 and Fig. 4):

    i. Mean absolute error—0.3822
   ii. Relative absolute error—81.9009%
  iii. Root relative squared error—100.5779%
  iv. Root mean squared error—0.4857
   v. Kappa statistics—0.3051.

Table 2 Description of output after applying J48 theorem	Tested negative	Tested positive	
	106	20	Tested negative
	41	33	Tested positive

```
J48 pruned tree
------------------

plas <= 139
|   mass <= 26.2: tested_negative (44.0/1.0)
|   mass > 26.2
|   |   plas <= 94: tested_negative (23.0/1.0)
|   |   plas > 94
|   |   |   age <= 47
|   |   |   |   age <= 34: tested_negative (54.0/17.0)
|   |   |   |   age > 34
|   |   |   |   |   pres <= 70
|   |   |   |   |   |   plas <= 118: tested_negative (3.0)
|   |   |   |   |   |   plas > 118: tested_positive (3.0)
|   |   |   |   |   pres > 70: tested_positive (10.0)
|   |   |   age > 47: tested_negative (6.0)
plas > 139: tested_positive (57.0/15.0)

Number of Leaves  :     8

Size of the tree :      15
```

Fig. 4 J48 pruned tree that was generated by WEKA

6 Comparison

In this section, both the algorithms are used to test the diabetes dataset and the results are described. Table 3 compares both the methods and could easily conclude that Naive Bayes theorem is better than the J48 as the time to build the model is less.

Time to build the module and appropriately classified instances are higher when Naive Bayes algorithm is used, and classification accuracy is also higher in Naive Bayes algorithm than that of J48 algorithm. The above results also that on diabetes dataset Naïve Bayes performs much more better than of J48. Figure 5 makes it clearer to compare the performance of both the methods.

Table 3 Comparison between J48 and Naive Bayesian theorem

Evaluation criteria	J48	Naïve Bayesian
Time to build module (in seconds)	0.08	0
Correct classified instances	139	145
Incorrect classified instances	61	55
Prediction accuracy	69.5	72.5

Fig. 5 Performance of J48 with Naive Bayes

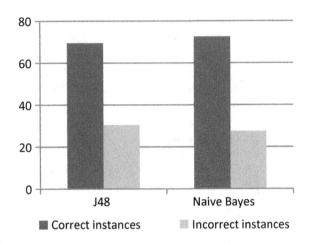

7　Conclusion

Data mining is an integrated field with the vast variety of techniques from several fields. It is a combination of machine learning, statistics, pattern recognition, and artificial intelligence systems for analysis of huge amount of data to discover the hidden patterns in the data. Nowadays data mining techniques are applied in medical sciences for decision making. It also plays an essential role in diabetes dataset to expose and uncover the hidden knowledge from a massive amount of unused diabetes data that will significantly assist to progress the quality treatment for the patients suffering from diabetes. In this research, the classification techniques used for predicting diabetes in patients are J48 and Naive Bayes theorem. Naive Bayesian theorem performs more efficiently and effectively as compared to J48. Whether it is time to build the model or identifying correct instances or accuracy, Naive Bayes always proved its productivity.

In future work are planned to propose more complex and integrated model by hybridizing machine learning techniques which will be able to predict all types of diabetes. Further, it will also include collecting data from different local areas of the country in order to get more précised and accurate data which will result in more précised and accurate outcome.

References

1. American Diabetes Association. "Diagnosis and classification of diabetes mellitus." Diabetes care 37, no. Supplement 1 (2014): S81–S90.
2. Thirumal, P. C., and N. Nagarajan. "Utilization of data mining techniques for diagnosis of diabetes mellitus-a case study." ARPN Journal of Engineering and Applied Science 10, no. 1 (2015).

3. Karegowda, Asha Gowda, M. A. Jayaram, and A. S. Manjunath. "Cascading k-means clustering and k-nearest neighbor classifier for categorization of diabetic patients." International Journal of Engineering and Advanced Technology 1, no. 3 (2012): 147–151.
4. Kaur, Gaganjot, and Amit Chhabra. "Improved J48 classification algorithm for the prediction of diabetes." International Journal of Computer Applications 98, no. 22 (2014).
5. Daghistani, Tahani, and Riyad Alshammari. "Diagnosis of Diabetes by Applying Data Mining Classification Techniques." International Journal of Advanced Computer Science and Applications (IJACSA) 7, no. 7 (2016): 329–332.
6. Marinov, Miroslav, Abu Saleh Mohammad Mosa, Illhoi Yoo, and Suzanne Austin Boren. "Data-mining technologies for diabetes: a systematic review." Journal of diabetes science and technology 5, no. 6 (2011): 1549–1556.
7. Shivakumar, B. L., and S. Alby. "A survey on data-mining technologies for prediction and diagnosis of diabetes." In Intelligent Computing Applications (ICICA), 2014 International Conference, pp. 167–173. IEEE, 2014.
8. Christobel, Y. Angeline, and P. Sivaprakasam. "A New Classwise k Nearest Neighbor (CKNN) method for the classification of diabetes dataset." International Journal of Engineering and Advanced Technology 2, no. 3 (2013): 396–200.
9. Das, Himansu, Ajay Kumar Jena, Janmenjoy Nayak, Bighnaraj Naik, and H. S. Behera. "A novel PSO based back propagation learning-MLP (PSO-BP-MLP) for classification." In Computational Intelligence in Data Mining-Volume 2, pp. 461–471. Springer, New Delhi, (2015).
10. Amit kumar Dewangan, Pragati Agrawal.: Classification of Diabetes Mellitus Using Machine Learning Techniques. Vol. 2, 5 (2015).
11. Srikanth, Panigrahi, and Dharmaiah Deverapalli. "A critical study of classification algorithms using diabetes diagnosis." In Advanced Computing (IACC), 2016 IEEE 6th International Conference on, pp. 245–249. IEEE, 2016.
12. Saravananathan, K., and T. Velmurugan. "Analyzing Diabetic Data using Classification Algorithms in Data Mining." Indian Journal of Science and Technology 9, no. 43 (2016).
13. Saxena, Krati, Zubair Khan, and Shefali Singh. "Diagnosis of Diabetes Mellitus using K Nearest Neighbor Algorithm." International Journal of Computer Science Trends and Technology (IJCST) (2014).
14. Sankaranarayanan, Sriram, and T. Pramananda Perumal. "A predictive approach for diabetes mellitus disease through data mining technologies." In Computing and Communication Technologies (WCCCT), 2014 World Congress on, pp. 231–233. IEEE, 2014.
15. Iyer, Aiswarya, S. Jeyalatha, and Ronak Sumbaly. "Diagnosis of diabetes using classification mining techniques." arXiv preprint arXiv:1502.03774 (2015).
16. Velu, C. M., and K. R. Kashwan. "Visual data mining techniques for classification of diabetic patients." In Advance Computing Conference (IACC), 2013 IEEE 3rd International, pp. 1070–1075. IEEE, 2013.
17. Motka, Rakesh, Viral Parmarl, Balbindra Kumar, and A. R. Verma. "Diabetes mellitus forecast using different data mining techniques." In Computer and Communication Technology (ICCCT), 4th International Conference on, pp. 99–103. IEEE, 2013.
18. Rajesh, K., and V. Sangeetha. "Application of data mining methods and techniques for diabetes diagnosis." International Journal of Engineering and Innovative Technology (IJEIT) 2, no. 3 (2012).
19. B. M. Patil, R. C. Joshi, Durga Toshniwal.: Association rule for classification of type-2 diabetic patients (2010).
20. Vijayan, Veena, and Aswathy Ravikumar. "Study of data mining algorithms for prediction and diagnosis of diabetes mellitus." International journal of computer applications 95, no. 17 (2014).

Improved Cost-Effective Technique for Resource Allocation in Mobile Cloud Computing

Enakshmi Nandi, Ranjan Kumar Mondal, Payel Ray,
Biswajit Biswas, Manas Kumar Sanyal and Debabrata Sarddar

Abstract Mobile cloud computing (MCC) is a big research topic in this modern technology-based era. This technology combines cloud computing with mobile computing in an innovative way to give better performance and cost-effective service to mobile users. MCC gives opportunities to execute different applications on the mobile devices by transferring the compute-intensive job to the cloud, but there are some problem arising in case of connectivity with mobile devices and cloud servers. To satisfy the user's demand and accessing cloud server to offload, the task from mobile device to cloud in mobile cloud computing is a difficult job. According to our knowledge we know that the cloud computing has been built upon the growth of distributing computing and virtualization concept. Thus, efficient mapping of tasks to available resource in cost-effective way in the mobile cloud environment is a challenging issue. Our main aim is to allocate nodes to their respective resource at cloud server by maintaining optimal response time and increase the quality of service by maintaining both resource cost and computation performances in mobile cloud environment.

Keywords Mobile cloud computing · Activity-based costing technique
Resource allocation · Processing time · Processing cost

E. Nandi (✉) · R. K. Mondal · P. Ray · B. Biswas · M. K. Sanyal · D. Sarddar
University of Kalyani, Kalyani, India
e-mail: enakshminanditechno14@gmail.com

R. K. Mondal
e-mail: ranjan@klyuniv.ac.in

P. Ray
e-mail: payelray009@gmail.com

B. Biswas
e-mail: biswajit.biswas0012@gmail.com

M. K. Sanyal
e-mail: manas_sanyal@rediffmail.com

D. Sarddar
e-mail: dsarddar1@gmail.com

© Springer Nature Singapore Pte Ltd. 2018   551
P. K. Pattnaik et al. (eds.), *Progress in Computing, Analytics and Networking*,
Advances in Intelligent Systems and Computing 710,
https://doi.org/10.1007/978-981-10-7871-2_53

1 Introduction

Modern era is based on technology-based application, where recent trends follow enhancement of mobile subscriptions due to the rapid advance in mobile computing and wireless technology. As per analysis of TechNavio analysts prediction, said that Enterprise Mobile Cloud Computing market in North America will produce at a CAGR of 18.12% in the year 2011–2015 [1]. Main reason for this success is the raising requirement enterprise mobility. According to progress in cloud computing field which gives substantial advantages to mobile subscribers as cloud infrastructures and platforms provide virtually large-scale computing power with elastic scalability and better resource sharing and utilization. This helps to defeat several traditional bounding in mobile computing. Mobile cloud computing has several benefits, such as it helps to enhance battery life and processing power in mobile devices. It helps to increase resource sharing and reuse of existing computing resources in Internet-based services and cloud infrastructure. It can be easy to cope up with advance services with applications required for mobile subscribers with low-end mobile devices [1]. General infrastructure of mobile cloud computing (MCC) is as shown in Fig. 1. Here, we see that mobile devices are linked with mobile networks via base stations or BTS; access point or satellite help to form and control connections and functional interfaces between networks and mobile devices. Respective requests and related information to mobile subscribers like user ID, location transfer to central processors which linked with servers rendering mobile network services. Mobile network operators supply services to mobile subscribers as AAA (for authentication, authorization, and accounting) which is based on home agent (HA) and subscribers' data saved in database system. When users' requests are supplied to a cloud with the help of Internet, cloud controllers terminate the requests to give mobile clients with the respective cloud services [2]. These services have generated the concepts of utility computing, service-oriented architecture, and virtualization. Resource allocation with their relevant task has been done in cloud environment and mobile cloud environment. But we have to maintain proper cost of utilization resources with maintain performance of resource scheduling technique is challenging issue.

Nithiapisary Muthuvelu et al. [3] proposed a scheduling technique to perform dynamic job allocation with the basis of grouping activity at runtime. This technique depends on processing necessity of each application on the available grid application according to their capability [4]. T.F. Ang et al. [5] was presented a scheduling process based on grouping independent of each task with higher processing requirements and reschedule them with incorporate network conditions. S. Selvarani et al. designed improved activity-based costing technique, where grouping of various tasks has been done with the available resources, where coarse-grained tasks should be processed with particular selected resources for maintaining lower computation–communication ratio [4].

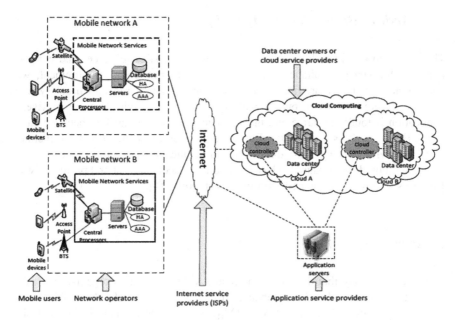

Fig. 1 Mobile cloud architecture

In our method, we represent cost-effective resource allocation technique for maintaining minimum cost as well as minimum completion time in mobile cloud environment to deliver better services and application of huge amount of mobile users simultaneously.

2 Problem Definitions

Assignment problem is a well-known method, where different types of tasks have to assign with dissimilar resources such a way that the assignment value should be minimum. In case where no. of tasks is not equal to the no. of resources, then it is called unbalanced assignment problem. Consider a situation where one resource should be allocated to execute all tasks, in that case Shortest Job First (SJF) and Fast Come First Serve (FCFS) methods should be used.

In such case where the required no. of resources is higher than the tasks, then TPL [6] and LB3M [7] methods are to be used. But for more optimized result we have to think better approach than these existing algorithms. Thus, we think about our new method in case of resource allocation in mobile cloud environment.

2.1 Activity-Based Costing Technique

This is an innovative technique for measuring both cost of resources and computation performance simultaneously. As we used mobile cloud environment, we know that in cloud environment different application will run on virtual system concept, where various resources will be distributed as virtual manner. Every application is totally separate and independent, and there is no link between each other. Here resources are sacrificed according to action executed by each distinct unit of service. To measure direct cost of applications, each personal use of resources should be measured. Thus, we find more accurate cost and profit analysis from this technique, compared with other techniques [4].

3 Proposed Method

In this case we say that determine the matrix value as well as organize the tasks versus the mobile nodes of an unbalanced matrix; thus, we take the problem that consist of set of 'm' resources $M = \{M_{i1}, M_{i2}, ..., M_{im}\}$ and set of 'n' tasks $T = \{T_{i1}, T_{i2}, ..., T_{in}\}$ has been taken for assigning completion time on the 'm' existing resources and the performance value C_{ij}, where $i = 1, 2, ..., m$ and $j = 1, 2, ..., n$ have been taken within the value of the matrix where $m > n$. First, we take summation of each row and column of the matrix, then save result in the array, known as row sum and column sum. Next, we select first n rows with row sum, such that starting with minimums to the next minimum value in the row sum array and remove rows equivalent to rest of tasks. Later, we want to save new array that should be the array for principal subproblem. Repeat this step until rest of tasks are minimum than resource nodes. In this case remaining tasks less than n, then remove columns by column sum, such that equivalent to those values to next most values declare as last subproblem. At last stage combine the finished results in the updated array which is declared as the array for the last subproblem.

3.1 Algorithm of Our Proposed Method

At starting phase of this algorithm with executing total tasks with respective distinct resources. It first classifies tasks with minimum completion time and the application developing it. So task with the minimum completion time is scheduled first. Next it considers lower completion time from the time when some applications are scheduled with some tasks. When min–min prefers the least tasks, it loads the fast executing application more which imparts other applications in idle stage. But this step is comfort for a splendid completion compared to other algorithms.

Table 1 Execution time for separate tasks with different mobile nodes

Task	Nodes			
	N_{i1}	N_{i2}	N_{i3}	N_{i4}
T_{i1}	14	16	20	30
T_{i2}	45	34	23	55
T_{i3}	76	71	69	73
T_{i4}	85	90	78	91

Algorithm:

Step I: At beginning stage add all tasks of each resource (column-wise) concurrently.

Step II: Next figure out maximum total task.

Step II.I: Then if we obtain two same maximum total tasks value, thus we choose the node which has minimum unassigned task value and allocate the selected task with respective resource.

Step II.I.I: For this case, if we find more than one minimum completion time of a definite resource then we choose that task which corresponding summation of the total task value should be maximum.

Step III: Later we have to choose the unassigned resource which has least completion time for that definite task selected in step II and then the task is carried out to the selected resource.

Step IV: For this respective field if we get more than one same value of the unassigned task once more time, and then choose that unassigned resource which corresponding resources have greater value than another one. In next step, this task will be forwarded to the particular resource for the purpose of execution.

Step V: Repeat step II to Step IV, until expectation will be fulfilled, that is assignment of all tasks with their corresponding resources completely.

Here in Table 1 we consider an example to understand our method. But due to page limitation we do not show each step separately. We just show first and final step. We have taken tasks T_{i1}, T_{i2}, T_{i3}, and T_{i4} as subtasks and N_{i1}, N_{i2}, N_{i3}, and N_{i4} are their respective mobile nodes required to perform all tasks allotted with separate resources concurrently. Table 2 shows the final optimal result.

4 Experimental Results

We used CloudSim to create simulation field. Here, we consider inputs which are total no. of tasks, average value of MI of all tasks, percentage of MI deviation, coarseness of size, and respective overhead time with tasks. At first we consider the value of MIPS with respective resources in Table 1.

Table 2 Optimal result for assignment of mobile nodes with their corresponding tasks

Task	Nodes			
	N_{i1}	N_{i2}	N_{i3}	N_{i4}
T_{i1}	14	16	20	**30**
T_{i2}	**45**	34	23	55
T_{i3}	76	71	**69**	73
T_{i4}	85	**90**	78	91

Table 3 MIPS for resources

Resource	MIPS
R1	130
R2	142
R3	154
R4	230

We simulated our method with four nodes; the granularity time is 5 s and average MI of tasks is 9. We have shown our result in table as follows (Table 3).

Figure 2 shows the comparison between improved ABC algorithms with our proposed method on the basis of time required to complete the tasks with respective values in Table 4. These results give lesser time value by utilizing our method compared to improved ABC method.

Figure 3 shows comparison between improved ABC and proposed method on the basis of expenditure spent on the purpose of processing various tasks for the values according to Table 5. These results also show that our method takes less cost to complete respective tasks compared with improved ABC method.

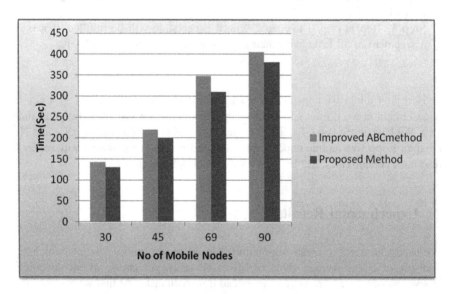

Fig. 2 Comparison of processing time between improved ABC and proposed method

Table 4 Simulation results of processing time for improved ABC and proposed method

No. of mobile nodes	Processing time measured in seconds	
	Improved ABC method	Proposed method
30	142.64	130.41
45	220.32	200.03
69	348.04	310.25
90	405.60	380.37

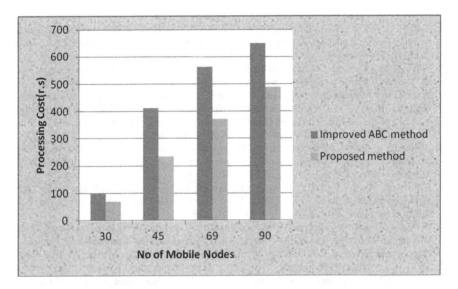

Fig. 3 Comparison of processing cost between improved ABC and proposed method

Table 5 Simulation results of processing cost for improved ABC and proposed method

No. of mobile nodes	Processing cost in rupees	
	Improved ABC method	Proposed method
30	100.21	70.02
45	412.62	235.09
69	563.38	372.05
90	648.91	487.59

5 Conclusion and Future Work

In this paper we first demonstrate new resource allocation technique. Then we compare our method with improved ABC algorithm with respective various parameters such as processing time and processing cost to complete various tasks. According to our experiments results analysis and from Figs. 2 and 3 we conclude that our approach gives better performance with respect to minimum completion time with minimum cost. But many issues stay open still now. So further improvement should be required to get better approach by utilizing more parameters in optimized way. In future we will plan to use Type-2 fuzzy logic system to get new way in mobile cloud computing field by using our method.

References

1. Gao, J., Gruhn, V., He, J., Roussos, G., & Tsai, W.T. (2013, March). Mobile cloud computing research-issues, challenges and needs. In *Service Oriented System Engineering (SOSE), 2013 IEEE 7th International Symposium on* (pp. 442–453). IEEE.
2. Dinh, Hoang T., et al. "A survey of mobile cloud computing: architecture, applications, and approaches." *Wireless communications and mobile computing* 13.18 (2013): 1587–1611.
3. Nithiapidary Muthuvelu, Junyang Liu, Nay Lin Soe, Srikumar Venugopal, Anthony Sulistio, Rajkumar Buyya, "A Dynamic Job Grouping-Based Scheduling for Deploying Applications with Fine-Grained Tasks on Global Grids", *This paper appeared at the Australasian Workshop on Grid Computing and e-research (Aus Grid2005)*, vol. 44.
4. Selvarani, S., and G. Sudha Sadhasivam. "Improved cost-based algorithm for task scheduling in cloud computing." *Computational Intelligence and Computing Research (ICCIC), 2010 IEEE International Conference on*. IEEE, 2010.
5. T.F. Ang, W.K. Ng, T.C. Ling, L.Y. Por, C.S. Liew, "A Bandwidth-Aware Job Grouping-Based Scheduling on Grid Environment," *The proceedings of Information Technology Journal*, vol. 8, no. 3, pp. 372–377, 2009.
6. S. Wang, K. Yan, W. Liao, and S. Wang, "Towards a Load Balancing in a Three-level Cloud Computing Network", Proceedings of the 3rd IEEE International Conference on Computer Science and Information Technology (ICCSIT), Chengdu, China, Sept. 2010, pp. 108–113.
7. Hung, C.L., Wang, H.H. and Hu, Y.C., 2012, April. Efficient load balancing algorithm for cloud computing network. In *International Conference on Information Science and Technology (IST 2012), April* (pp. 28–30).

Comparison of Statistical and Soft Computing Models for Predicting Hardness and Wear Rate of Cu-Ni-Sn Alloy

S. Ilangovan, R. Vaira Vignesh, R. Padmanaban
and J. Gokulachandran

Abstract Castings of Copper–Nickel–Tin alloy were produced by varying the composition of Ni and Sn. The cast specimens were subjected to homogenization and solution treatment. The specimens were characterized for microstructure, hardness and subjected to adhesive wear test. Statistical regression model, artificial neural network model and Sugeno fuzzy model were developed to predict the hardness and wear rate of the alloy based on %Ni, %Sn and ageing time of the specimens. As Sugeno Fuzzy logic model uses adaptive neuro-fuzzy inference system, an integration of neural networks and fuzzy logic principles, the prediction efficiency was higher than statistical regression and artificial neural network model. The interaction effect of %Ni, %Sn and ageing time on the hardness and wear rate of the specimens were analysed using the Sugeno Fuzzy model.

Keywords Spinodal alloy · Hardness · Wear · Ageing time
Regression · Fuzzy logic · Artificial neural network

1 Introduction

Copper–Nickel–Tin (Cu-Ni-Sn) alloy system is one of the candidate materials for load bearing applications in engineering [1]. Wear is a penalty in such motion-contact established applications. Hence, the tribological properties of

S. Ilangovan · R. Vaira Vignesh · R. Padmanaban (✉) · J. Gokulachandran
Department of Mechanical Engineering, Amrita School of Engineering,
Amrita Vishwa Vidyapeetham, Coimbatore, India
e-mail: dr_padmanaban@cb.amrita.edu

S. Ilangovan
e-mail: s_ilangovan@cb.amrita.edu

R. Vaira Vignesh
e-mail: r.vairavignesh@gmail.com

J. Gokulachandran
e-mail: j_gokul@cb.amrita.edu

© Springer Nature Singapore Pte Ltd. 2018
P. K. Pattnaik et al. (eds.), *Progress in Computing, Analytics and Networking*,
Advances in Intelligent Systems and Computing 710,
https://doi.org/10.1007/978-981-10-7871-2_54

559

Cu-Ni-Sn alloy system have to be improved. The tribological properties of Cu-Ni-Sn alloy system can be engineered by varying the chemical composition, processing route and heat treatment methods. The wear resistance of materials can be increased by increasing their hardness, which in turn can be improved by techniques such as dispersion hardening, surface modification and heat treatments. Cahn-Hilliard proposed a novel concept known as spinodal hardening, which is specific to Cu-Ni-Sn alloy system. The Cu-Ni-Sn alloy system has an unstable phase in the matrix. The decomposition of this unstable phase into solute-rich and solute lean regions, which do not mix at all proportions at all temperatures, is known as spinodal decomposition [2].

Schwartz et al. [3] aged Cu-9Ni-6Sn alloy system at different temperatures and improved its yield strength through spinodal decomposition. Baburaj et al. [4] reported the origination of discontinuous reaction, at the grain boundaries of prolonged aged specimens. Schwartz et al. [5] proposed that grain boundary precipitates in the spinodal decomposed Cu-9Ni-6Sn alloy reduced its yield strength. Kato and Schwartz [6] reported that yield strength of aged Cu-10Ni-6Sn alloy did not vary with variation in ageing temperature. Deyong et al. [7] studied the hardness of Cu-Ni-Sn alloy system by varying the composition of Sn, at a fixed composition of Ni (10%). Singh et al. [8] studied the worn debris characteristics of Cu-15Ni-8Sn alloy specimens subjected to wear test.

In this study, the hardness and wear rate of Cu-Ni-Sn alloy system were evaluated with respect to change in the composition of alloying elements and ageing time. Mathematical and soft computing models were developed to predict the hardness and wear rate based on statistical regression, artificial neural network (ANN) and Sugeno fuzzy logic. The efficiency of the developed models was determined based on the correlation coefficient (R), coefficient of determination (R^2) and root mean squared error value (RMSE). It was found that the Sugeno fuzzy model had the least error in prediction and was highly accurate in predicting the hardness and wear rate of the specimens. Hence, Sugeno fuzzy model was used to study the effect of alloy composition and ageing time on the hardness and wear rate of the specimens.

2 Materials and Methods

2.1 Materials and Casting Process

Copper, Nickel and Tin rods of purity 99.9% were used for casting the alloy. The metal rods were melted in a graphite crucible using electric furnace, as per the composition is given in Table 1. The melting was performed in an inert atmosphere using Argon gas to avoid contamination of the molten metal. The molten metal was poured at 1250 ± 10 °C into the moulds.

Table 1 Hardness of the specimens at different ageing time

Sl.	Composition of alloy (%)			Vicker's Hardness					
				Ageing time (h) @ 350 °C					
	Ni	Sn	Cu	0	1	2	3	4	5
1	4	6	90	130	174	190	196	202	175
2	5	6	89	138	205	223	233	248	235
3	8	6	86	163	291	308	321	335	320
4	9	6	85	171	313	330	360	344	333
5	11	6	83	235	368	402	385	368	352
6	15	6	79	260	400	450	435	415	400
7	6	4	90	125	142	162	201	239	205
8	6	6	88	154	167	222	266	230	207
9	6	8	86	182	234	300	259	227	171
10	5	5	90	130	174	218	247	266	258

Table 2 Wear rate of the specimens at different ageing time

Sl.	Composition of alloy (%)			Wear rate (10^{-4} mm^3/m)					
				Ageing time (h) @ 350 °C					
	Ni	Sn	Cu	0	1	2	3	4	5
1	4	6	90	9.5	7.42	7.07	6.15	2.83	5.22
2	5	6	89	7.02	6.81	6.54	6.35	5.08	6.26
3	8	6	86	3.53	3.28	2.06	1.74	1.63	2.12
4	9	6	85	6.89	5.54	2.34	1.51	2.18	3.88
5	11	6	83	4.79	1.51	0.99	0.99	1.57	2.24
6	15	6	79	1.12	1.09	0.86	0.92	1.06	1.11
7	6	4	90	20.06	17.98	13.27	7.95	7.12	11.8
8	6	6	88	16.41	12.15	7.52	4.36	7.89	11.56
9	6	8	86	11.07	6.36	4.63	5.26	8.51	13.82
10	5	5	90	9.47	6.74	6.48	5.09	4.85	4.94

2.2 Heat Treatment Process

The cast workpieces were subjected to the following heat treatment processes: homogenization, solution heat treatment and ageing heat treatment. Heat treatments were performed in a muffle-type furnace in Argon atmosphere. The specimens were homogenized at a temperature of 825 °C for 10 h, which is greater than the miscibility gap of Cu–Ni–Sn alloy system. The homogenized rods were quenched below 200 °C to avoid formation of γ phases and prevent premature spinodal hardening. The rods were aged at 350 °C for five different time intervals (1, 2, 3, 4 and 5 h) and then quenched in water.

2.3 Microstructure

The specimens for analysing the microstructure of the specimens were prepared as per standard ASTM E3 – 11 and were etched with an etchant made using 1.5 g $FeCl_3$, 100 ml of HCl and 100 ml of H_2O. The microstructure was analysed using an optical microscope (Make: Carl Zeiss Axiovert microscope).

2.4 Hardness and Wear Rate

Vicker's hardness measurements were performed as per the standard ASTM E384, with a diamond indenter under a load of 50 g, applied for a period of 20 s. The wear test was performed using a pin-on-disc tribometer, with the specimen as the pin and EN316 steel as counter disc, as per the standard ASTM G99. Specimens measuring $\phi 5$ mm and length 40 mm were machined from the as-cast and heat treated rods.

$$\text{Wear rate} = \frac{\Delta M}{\rho * L} (\text{mm}^3/\text{m}) \tag{1}$$

The parameters chosen for the wear study were a normal load of 20 N, track diameter of 90 mm, sliding velocity of 3 ms^{-1} and sliding distance of 1800 m. High precision weighing balance of readability 0.0001 g was used to weigh the specimen before and after the wear test. The wear rate of the specimens was calculated using Eq. (1), where ΔM is mass loss, ρ is density of the alloy and L is sliding distance.

2.5 Statistical and Soft Computing Models

Statistical regression. The response variable is well modelled by a higher order polynomial function of the predictor variables. The general mathematical equation (statistical regression equation) that describes a second-order model for predicting the response variable y using predictors x_i is given in Eq. (2).

$$y = \beta_0 + \sum_{i=1}^{n} \beta_i x_i + \sum_{i=1}^{n} \beta_{ii} x_i^2 + \sum \sum_{i<j} \beta_{ij} x_{ij} + \in \tag{2}$$

where y is the response variable, $\in$ is error value and $\beta_i, \beta_{ii}, \beta_{ij}$ are the coefficients of the predictor variables x_i, x_i^2, x_{ij}, respectively.

Artificial Neural Network model. Artificial intelligence (AI) is used for intelligent computation and developing complex decision analysis systems [9].

Cascade forward back propagation networks contain three layers of neurons. The primary layer of neurons is the input layer, the concluding layer of neurons is the output layer and the intermediate layer(s) of neurons is (are) the hidden layer(s). The artificial neurons weigh and sum the input forming an activation function [10, 11]. The activation function is transformed by artificial neuron using a hyperbolic tangent sigmoid (TanSig) transformation function to get the output, and it is given by Eq. (3).

$$f(x) = \frac{2}{1 + e^{-2x}} - 1 \tag{3}$$

where x is the input variable and $f(x)$ is the TanSig function. Levenberg-Marquardt (LM) algorithm is one of the efficient supervised learning algorithms for training the ANN.

The learning rate, ε, is set to unity in LM algorithm and an additional term e^λ is introduced in the second derivative error, which makes it efficient than any other learning algorithms.

Sugeno fuzzy model. Fuzzy logic is a mathematical tool that is used to identify the uncertainness in a system [12]. Gaussian membership function efficiently assigns the membership values to the element [12, 13]. Hence, Gaussian membership function given by Eq. (4) was used to assign the membership values to the elements (%Ni, %Sn, ageing time). This process of assigning a membership value for crisp quantity is known as fuzzification.

$$f(x; \sigma, c) = e^{\frac{-(x-c)^2}{2\sigma^2}} \tag{4}$$

Sugeno fuzzy system generates fuzzy rules from the input–output data set. Defuzzification is the process of converting fuzzy quantities into crisp quantity. The defuzzified value using weighted average method is given by Eq. (5).

$$y^* = \frac{\sum \mu_c(\bar{y})\bar{y}}{\sum \mu_c(\bar{y})} \tag{5}$$

where y^* is the defuzzified value, $\sum$ is used for algebraic sum, $\mu_c(\bar{y})$ is fuzzy relation and $\bar{y}$ is average.

3 Results and Discussion

3.1 Microstructure

The microstructure of the as-cast specimen exhibited dendritic structure, as observed from Fig. 1a. The homogenized and solution treated specimens were free from precipitates and dendritic structure.

(a)   (b)

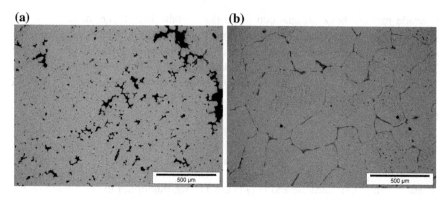

Fig. 1 Microstructure of the **a** as-cast specimen; **b** 2 h aged specimen Cu-11Ni-6Sn

The non-dendritic microstructure indicated the uniform dispersion of alloying elements in the matrix [14, 15]. The solution treated and 2 h aged Cu-9Ni-6Sn specimen had grain boundary precipitates as shown in Fig. 1b. The amount of α and γ (DO$_3$) phases in the matrix increased with increase in ageing time [14, 15]. The grain boundary was partially filled with equilibrium phases, as the ageing time is minimal [16].

3.2 Hardness and Wear Test

The experimentally measured hardness of the solution treated specimens and specimens aged for different ageing time are given in Table 1. The increase in hardness of the specimens with respect to change in composition and ageing time is credited to the formation of spinodal structure in early stages of ageing and subsequent ordering reaction to form meta-stable phase with DO$_{22}$. The decrease in the hardness beyond an ageing time of 4 h was attributed to the formation of equilibrium grain boundary precipitates—α and γ (DO$_3$) phases in the matrix [16]. The formation of meta-stable phase DO$_{22}$ with increase in ageing time hardened the matrix.

The increase in hardness of solution treated specimens is attributed to the solution hardening effect of Ni and Sn [17]. The spinodal decomposition and ordering reaction increased the hardness of the aged specimens [1, 6]. The contribution of Ni and Sn in increasing the hardness is attested by the fact that high Ni and Sn concentration produced peak hardness even at low ageing time.

3.3 Mathematical and Soft Computing Models

Statistical regression model. The technical computing environment MATLAB R2015 © was used to develop statistical regression model. Eighty percentage of the experimental data was used to develop the model, and the remaining data was used for testing the developed model.

The statistical regression model developed for predicting the hardness and wear rate of the specimens is given by Eq. (6) and Eq. (7), respectively.

$$
\begin{aligned}
Hardness =\ & 346.6239 + 117.7092 \times Ni + 230.1961 \times Sn \\
& + 36.97766 \times T - 27.15268 \times Ni^2 + 322.528 \\
& \times Ni \times Sn + 1.274217 \times Ni \times T - 28.28299 \\
& \times Sn^2 - 30.93539 \times Sn \times T - 65.40577 \times T^2
\end{aligned}
\tag{6}
$$

$$
\begin{aligned}
Wear =\ & 1.44123 - 2.90443 \times Ni - 17.8387 \times Sn - 1.01477 \times T \\
& + 1.58028 \times Ni^2 - 24.2938 \times Ni \times Sn \\
& + 0.288442 \times Ni \times T + 5.49673 \times Sn^2 + 3.43094 \\
& \times Sn \times T + 2.62791 \times T^2
\end{aligned}
\tag{7}
$$

Where Ni represents %Ni, Sn represents %Sn, and T represents the ageing time. A linear trend is observed between the experimental and predicted values of hardness and wear rate as shown in Fig. 2a and Fig. 2b, respectively. The R^2 values for statistical regression models for predicting the hardness and wear rate were found to be 0.935 and 0.869, respectively. The RMSE value of statistical regression model to predict hardness and wear rate was found to be 25.51 and 1.85, respectively.

Artificial Neural Network model. Cascade forward back propagation neural network was used to build the ANN model, and the model was developed using MATLAB R2015 ® as shown in Fig. 3. The model was built using a layer of input neurons, two hidden layers of neurons, and one output layer of neurons. Eighty percentage of the experimental data was used to train the network using LM algorithm. Twenty percentage of the data was used for testing and validating the trained network.

The regression analysis of the experimental and predicted results of the ANN model is shown in Fig. 4. The R for the training data, testing data, validation data and overall data was found to be 0.9378, 0.9283, 0.9449 and 0.9347, respectively. The RMSE value for the developed model was found to be 58.41, which is higher than the statistical regression model.

Sugeno fuzzy model. In this study, the elements of fuzzy set were %Sn, %Ni, ageing time, hardness and wear. As Gaussian membership functions ensure smooth boundaries [18], it was used in this study. Three levels (low, medium and high) were used to classify the composition and ageing time. The ANFIS architecture for both hardness and wear rate prediction models is given in Fig. 5. Eighty percentage

(a) **(b)**

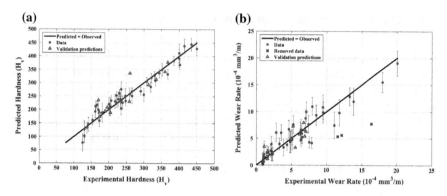

Fig. 2 Experimental versus predicted **a** hardness; **b** wear rate

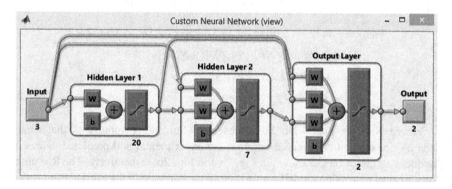

Fig. 3 Layout of artificial neural network model

of the experimental data was used for training the model, and the remaining data was used for testing and checking the trained model. The plot of experimental and predicted hardness/wear is shown in Fig. 6a/Fig. 6b, respectively.

RMSE value was found to be 17.17 for hardness model and 1.84 for wear rate model, respectively. As displayed in the figures Fig. 6a and Fig. 6b, a linear trend was observed between the experimental and predicted results of Sugeno fuzzy models.

3.4 Comparison of RMSE and Prediction Efficiency of the Models Developed

The closeness of R^2 and R to unity indicates that the difference between experimental and predicted values is minimum [19]. But the closeness of RMSE value to zero indicates that the model has high accuracy in prediction. Hence, the developed soft computing models were evaluated based on RMSE (Table 3).

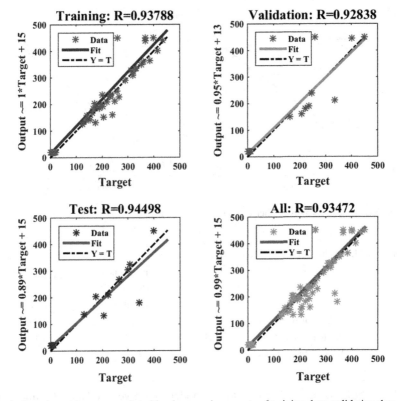

Fig. 4 Experimental versus predicted hardness and wear rate of training data, validation data, test data and overall data

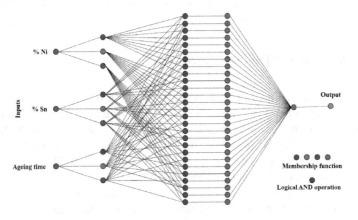

Fig. 5 ANFIS architecture for both hardness and wear rate Sugeno fuzzy model

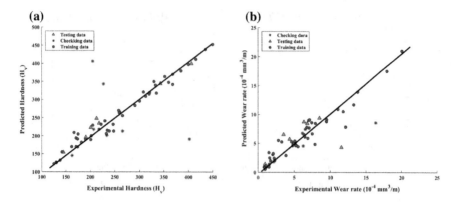

Fig. 6 Experimental versus predicted **a** hardness; **b** wear rate

Table 3 RMSE values of the developed models

Sl.	Model	Root Mean Squared Error (RMSE)	
		Hardness	Wear
1	Statistical regression model	25.5	1.85
2	Artificial neural network model	58.41	58.41
3	Sugeno fuzzy model	17.7	1.84

The RMSE values of the developed models are given in Table 3. Among the developed models, RMSE value of the Sugeno fuzzy model was found to be the least. So Sugeno fuzzy model was used to study the effects of Ni concentration, Sn concentration and ageing time on the hardness and wear rate of the specimens.

3.5 Interaction Effect of Ni, Sn and Ageing Time

It is observed from Fig. 7a that at 4% concentration of Sn, the hardness of the specimen is minimum at all concentrations of Ni. The hardness of the specimens increased with increase in concentration of Sn up to 7%, beyond which the hardness decreased. It is observed from Fig. 7b that the specimens aged for 1, 2 and 3 h exhibited higher hardness than the solution treated specimens. The hardness of the alloy decreased beyond an ageing time of 3 h.

Precipitation of equilibrium α and γ phases softened the matrix with increase in ageing time [17]. It decreased the hardness of the matrix. Non-induction of spinodal decomposition in the specimens with low concentration of Ni resulted in softer matrix. Figure 7c displays that the hardness of the specimen increased with increase in Sn content. Increase in Sn concentration beyond 6% decreased the hardness of

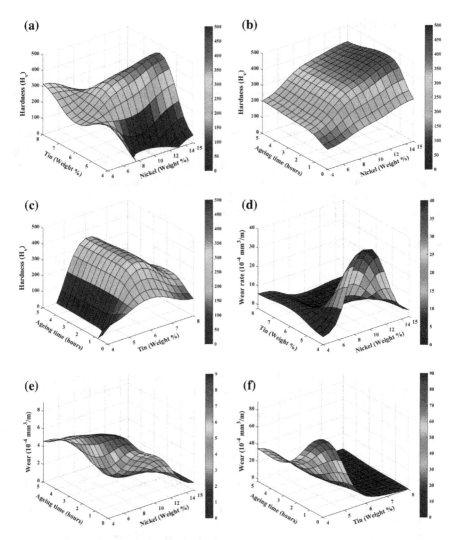

Fig. 7 Interaction effect of **a** %Ni and %Sn on hardness; **b** %Ni and ageing time on hardness; **c** % Sn and ageing time on hardness; **d** %Ni and %Sn on wear rate; **e** %Ni and ageing time on wear rate; **f** %Sn and ageing time on wear rate

the matrix. The primary contribution of Sn to hardness is by solution hardening rather than spinodal hardening.

As shown in Fig. 7d, wear rate of the specimens was high at low concentration of Sn and 10%–12% of Ni. Minimum wear rate is observed in the specimens that had high hardness, which is consistent with the Archard's adhesive theory of wear. As observed from Fig. 7e and Fig. 7f, the solution treated samples (ageing time = 0 h) had poor wear resistance. This is attributed to the soft nature of the matrix [20]. At high concentration of Sn, the wear resistance of the specimens was high at all ageing times.

4 Conclusion

The Cu-Ni-Sn spinodal alloys with varying compositions were cast successfully. Mathematical (RSM) and soft computing (ANN and Sugeno fuzzy) models relating the concentration of Ni, Sn and ageing time with the hardness and wear rate of the alloys were developed. The conclusions from the study are as follows:

- Among the developed models, Sugeno fuzzy model had high accuracy in prediction and hence used to study the interaction effect of %Ni, %Sn and ageing time on the hardness and the wear rate of the specimens. The integration of neural networks and fuzzy logic principles in ANFIS improved the prediction efficiency of the Sugeno fuzzy model.
- The hardness and wear resistance of the specimens improved with the increase in ageing time.
- High concentration of Ni and Sn increased the hardness and wear resistance of the specimens. Ni contributes to spinodal hardening and Sn contributes to hardness by solution hardening.

References

1. Ilangovan S, Sellamuthu R (2016) Measurement of the variation of mechanical properties with aging temperatures for sand cast Cu-5Ni-5Sn alloy. Journal of Engineering Science and Technology 11 (11):1609–1619
2. Ditchek B, Schwartz LH (1980) Diffraction study of spinodal decomposition in Cu-10 w/o Ni-6 w/o SN. Acta Metall 28 (6):807–822
3. Schwartz LH, Plewes JT (1974) Spinodal decomposition in Cu-9wt% Ni-6wt% Sn—II. A critical examination of mechanical strength of spinodal alloys. Acta Metallurgica 22 (7):911–921
4. Baburaj EG, Kulkarni UD, Menon ESK, Krishnan R (1979) Initial stages of decomposition in Cu-9Ni-6Sn. J Appl Crystallogr 12 (5):476–480
5. Schwartz LH, Mahajan S, Plewes JT (1974) Spinodal decomposition in a Cu-9 wt% Ni-6 wt% Sn alloy. Acta Metallurgica 22 (5):601–609
6. Kato M, Mori T, Schwartz LH (1980) Hardening by spinodal modulated structure. Acta Metall 28 (3):285–290
7. Deyong L, Tremblay R, Angers R (1990) Microstructural and mechanical properties of rapidly solidified Cu-Ni-Sn alloys. Mater Sci Eng, A 124 (2):223–231
8. Singh JB, Cai W, Bellon P (2007) Dry sliding of Cu–15 wt%Ni–8 wt%Sn bronze: Wear behaviour and microstructures. Wear 263 (1–6):830–841
9. Russell SJ, Norvig P, Canny JF, Malik JM, Edwards DD (2003) Artificial intelligence: a modern approach, vol 2. Prentice hall Upper Saddle River
10. Zurada JM (1992) Introduction to artificial neural systems, vol 8. West St. Paul
11. Yegnanarayana B (2009) Artificial neural networks. PHI Learning Pvt. Ltd.
12. Sivanandam SN, Sumathi S, Deepa SN (2006) Introduction to Fuzzy Logic using MATLAB. Springer Berlin Heidelberg
13. Nguyen HT, Prasad NR (1999) Fuzzy Modeling and Control: Selected Works of Sugeno. Taylor & Francis

14. Schwartz LH, Plewes JT (1974) Spinodal decomposition in Cu-9wt% Ni-6wt% Sn—II. A critical examination of mechanical strength of spinodal alloys. Acta Metall 22 (7):911–921
15. Schwartz LH, Mahajan S, Plewes JT (1974) Spinodal decomposition in a Cu-9 wt% Ni-6 wt% Sn alloy. Acta Metall 22 (5):601–609
16. Ilangovan S, Sellamuthu R (2012) An investigation of the effect of Ni content and hardness on the wear behaviour of sand cast Cu–Ni–Sn alloys. Int J Microstruct Mater Prop 7 (4):316–328
17. Zhao DM, Dong QM, Liu P, Kang BX, Huang JL, Jin ZH (2003) Structure and strength of the age hardened Cu–Ni–Si alloy. Mater Chem Phys 79 (1):81–86
18. Vignesh RV, Padmanaban R, Arivarasu M, Karthick KP, Sundar AA, Gokulachandran J (2016) Analysing the strength of friction stir spot welded joints of aluminium alloy by fuzzy logic. IOP Conference Series: Materials Science and Engineering 149 (1)
19. Ramalingam VV, Ramasamy P (2017) Modelling Corrosion Behavior of Friction Stir Processed Aluminium Alloy 5083 Using Polynomial: Radial Basis Function. Transactions of the Indian Institute of Metals 70 (10):2575–2589
20. Zhang S-Z, Jiang B-H, Ding W-J (2008) Wear of Cu–15Ni–8Sn spinodal alloy. Wear 264 (3–4):199–203

Development of Policy Designing Technique by Analyzing Customer Behavior Through Big Data Analytics

Puja Shrivastava, Laxman Sahoo, Manjusha Pandey
and Sandeep Agrawal

Abstract Technological developments and market trends are two leading affairs of the current era, posing customer as most important entity to be caught. Use of big data analytics to retain customers by offering them customer-oriented policies and making them feel important and precious for the service-providing company is the core thought behind this research paper. A framework to obtain process and analyze service usage data, with a new algorithm known as Altered Genetic K-Means clustering algorithm based on mapReduce is presented here. This paper implements mapReduce-based Altered Genetic K-Means Clustering (AGKM) algorithm on data acquired from BSS/OSS of telecom CRM and cleaned by R, to categorize customers having similar call activities. Results show that specific group of customers such as students, senior citizens, housewives, business people, and employees can be identified and according to their call timings, durations, call types, net usage, etc., policies (tariff plans in this case) can be designed. The novelty of this work is in its thought of capturing customers by knowing them well in place of first predicting churn and then taking action.

Keywords Big data analytics · K-means clustering · Genetic algorithm
MapReduce · Framework · Service usage · Customer behavior
Policy designing

P. Shrivastava (✉) · L. Sahoo · M. Pandey · S. Agrawal
School of Computer Engineering, KIIT University, Bhubaneswar, Odisha, India
e-mail: pujashri@gmail.com

L. Sahoo
e-mail: laxmansahoo@yahoo.com

M. Pandey
e-mail: manjushapandey82@gmail.com

S. Agrawal
e-mail: sandygarg65@gmail.com

© Springer Nature Singapore Pte Ltd. 2018
P. K. Pattnaik et al. (eds.), *Progress in Computing, Analytics and Networking*,
Advances in Intelligent Systems and Computing 710,
https://doi.org/10.1007/978-981-10-7871-2_55

573

1　Introduction

Policy designing is a crucial task due to its importance in deciding the survival and future success of business. Competitive scenario compels to take help of new technologies to know the market trends plus the customer needs. Evolution of big data technology has provided a good platform where structured, semi-structured, and unstructured data generated in one action or for one entity can be processed together. An overall framework under the big data environment starting from the study of data generation, collection, processing, and analyzing is presented in this paper, with the novel thought of capturing customers without giving them any chance to get agitated with the services of company. To achieve the goal of customer retention through big data analytics is not as easy as it seems due to the lack of any generalized architecture and algorithm. This paper discusses a generalized architecture in second part, customer behavior modeling in third section, AGKM in fourth segment, results and discussions in fifth part, and conclusion and future scope in sixth phase.

2　Framework for Customer-Oriented Policy Designing Technique

This section having two parts where the first part discusses state of the art and second part presents the architecture proposed by authors.

2.1　State of the Art

Very few academic works are available in the context of architectures for the big data environment and attached systems. Evolution of big data technology has changed the perception of computer scientists with the shift of technology toward the data-centric architecture and operational models. An architecture called as Big Data Architecture Framework (BDFA) is proposed in [1] to deal with all portions of big data environment such as infrastructure, analytics, data structures, models, life cycle of data, and data security. Real-time big data is the current and upcoming challenge, and an architecture is proposed in [2] for the real-time big data generated from the different sensors. The three main elements of this architecture include remote sensing big data acquisition unit (RSDU), data processing unit (DPU), and data analysis decision unit (DADU) where the first unit obtains data from the satellite and sends it to the base station, second unit compiles the data, and third unit provides decisions based on the results received from the DPU. Architectures for customer relationship management system in the context of big data technology are studied in [3] proposed by different service-based companies. It concludes in the three sections: collaborative technologies, operational technologies, and analytical technologies in the ecosystem of big data. Design of a new architecture for the customer relationship management system for the tourism industry in the context of big data environment is proposed in the [4]. Current architectures deal with data sources, data compilations, and conclusion making as subsections; internal functions of these subsections can be rearranged as per the data set.

2.2 Proposed Framework

A generalized framework under the big data environment is presented in Fig. 1 with five phases named as data generation system as first phase, study of system constraints and data types in second phase, third phase is data filtration in the form of customer details and service usage details, fourth phase is analytical engine with AKGM, and last phase is the customer-oriented data product (policy).

Phase 1 of this architecture is the data generation system since the availability of data is the root of further work. Customer relationship management (CRM) data of telecom sector is considered as a case here so the business support system (BSS) and operation support system (OSS) are data generation systems and provide all data including customer details and call detail records (CDR).

Phase 2 works on the types and structures of the generated data and the limitations of the existing system. Customer details are structured data sets, but CDRs are number of log files generated for each calls either it is a voice call, video call, SMS or MMS. Recognition of data types and structures is more important for the analysis. Limitations of physical infrastructure, software applications, monetary, strategic planning, skill development, and vision are studied in the second part of this phase.

Phase 3 this phase filters the obtained data in the form of customer details and the attributes of call activities in its one section; another section acquires available data analyzing algorithm for big data environment if possible.

Phase 4 is the analytical engine to analyze the cleaned and processed data and categorize it in clusters of customer having similar service usage activities. Here a

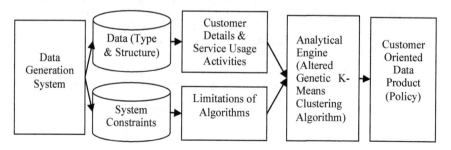

Fig. 1 Proposed architecture

new algorithm named as Altered Genetic K-Means (AGKM) clustering algorithm is projected to overcome existing problems of K-Means clustering algorithm in big data environment.

Phase 5 this phase is the customer-oriented data product; after the analysis of data, a recommender system can generate policies according to the service usage details provided to it.

3 Modeling of Customer Behavior

Traditionally, four types of customer behavior models are defined: economic, learning, psychoanalytic, and sociological models. Economic model is based on maximum utility and learning model is based on the change of customer behavior after the service use. Psychoanalytical model based on the personal interests and ideology of customer and sociological model based on the sociological condition of customer [5]. Author has canvassed the behavior of telecom customer in the form of calling activities, use of messaging services and data usage as shown in Table 1 named as details of customer behavior. Objective of this work is to study the call activities and net usage of customer as behavior to further generate tariff plans for the benefit of both customer and company. Customer behavior is defined here with the help of attributes according to the services such as calling, messaging, and net pack with additional value vouchers [6]. Table 2 describes attributes of customer behavior, and Table 3 shows the attributes required to represent customer details.

Table 1 Details of customer behavior

S.N.	Name of service	Kind of service	Count of use	Day of use	Time of use	Duration
1.	Calls	Local	No. of calls per day/ week	Working days/ weekends	Working hours/ non-working hours	Short (5 mnts)/ medium (5 mnts to10 mnts)/long (More than 10 Mnts)
		National				
		International				
2.	SMS/ MMS	Local	No. of SMS/ MMS per day/ week	Working days/ weekends	Working hours/ non-working hours	Short/long SMS/ MMS
		National				
		International				
3.	Internet pack	Net use	No. of Net begin	Working days/ weekends	Working hours/ non-working hours	Minutes or hours spent on Internet

Table 2 Attributes of customer behavior

Attribute Name	Description
$Call_{short}$	Call duration less than 10 min
$Call_{medium}$	10 min < Call duration <= 30 min
$Call_{long}$	30 min < Call duration
$Call_{local}$	Count of local calls per 24 h
$Call_{national}$	Count of long distance calls per 24 h
$Call_{international}$	Count of calls made out of country per 24 h
$Call_{workinghours}$	No. of calls in working hours
$Call_{non-workinghours}$	No. of calls in non working hours
$Call_{workingdays}$	No. of calls in working days
$Call_{non-workingdays}$	No. of calls in non-working days
SMS_{short}	160 characters
SMS_{long}	More than 160 characters
SMS_{local}	No. of local SMS per 24 h
$SMS_{national}$	No. of national SMS per 24 h
$SMS_{international}$	No. of international SMS per 24 h
$SMS_{workinghours}$	No. of SMS in working hours
$SMS_{non-workinghours}$	No. of SMS in non working hours
$SMS_{workingdays}$	No. of SMS in working days
$SMS_{non-workingdays}$	No. of SMS in non-working days
MMS_{short}	600 KB
MMS_{long}	More than 600 KB
MMS_{local}	No. of local MMS per 24 h
$MMS_{national}$	No. of national MMS per 24 h
$MMS_{international}$	No. of international MMS per 24 h
$MMS_{workinghours}$	No. of MMS in working hours
$MMS_{non-workinghours}$	No. of MMS in non working hours
$MMS_{workingdays}$	No. of MMS in working days
$MMS_{non-workingdays}$	No. of MMS in non-working days
Net_{loging}	No. of times net connected per 24 h
$Net_{workingdays}$	Net usage in working days
$Net_{non-workingdays}$	Net usage in non-working days
$Net_{workinghours}$	Net usage in working hours
$Net_{non-workinghours}$	Net usage in non-working hours
Net_{time}	No. of hours spent on Internet
VV_{call}	Value voucher for calling service
$VV_{message}$	Value voucher for messaging service

To analyze the customer behavior, two data sets are used: first is set of attributes for the description of calling/messaging/net usage activities, and another is a set of attributes describing customer details.

Table 3 Attributes of customer description

Attribute Name	Description
Cust_Id	Identification of customer
Gender	Female/male
$Age_{teenage}$	$13 = < Age < 18$
Age_{Adult}	$<= 18$
$Age_{seniorcitizen}$	$<= 65$
Profession	Type of work
Social-status	Annual income
Phone-service	Mobile, landline, Internet
Type-of-service	Prepaid, postpaid
Payment-method	Cash, e-payment, credit card
Paperless-bill	Yes/no
Bill-range	Money spent on phone recharge

Let $B = \{b_1, b_2, b_3,...b_n\}$, be the set of defined behavior that is call, messaging, and net usage activities. C is a subset of set B and |C| denotes the number of defined behaviors included in C. $CDR = \{set\ of\ call\ detail\ records\}$, obtained from operation support system (OSS), where each call detail is a kind of behavior. |CDR| denotes the total number of call detail records in a particular time period. Each behavior can be identified by behavior identification number (bid). Support of C is the proportion of behavior in *CDR* that contains C, i.e., $\phi(C) = |\{CDR|\ CDR \in CDR, C \subseteq CDR\}|/|CDR|$. The support count or frequency of C is the number of call detail records in *CDR* that contains C [7]. So, customer behaviors can be obtained as patterns and clustered for similar patterns.

4 Altered Genetic K-Means Clustering for MapReduce

Implementation of data mining techniques for big data analytics needs several modifications and enhancements in algorithms. Right now not a single algorithm is suitable for the big data analytics. Every algorithm suffers from the problem of high computing time and stability. Combining clustering algorithms and including distributive environment concept can provide better algorithms [8]. Implementation of k-means in mapReduce framework faces the problem of local optimum convergence; inclusion of evolutionary algorithm with k-means clustering algorithm in mapReduce framework improves the cluster quality but increases the time complexity [9].

A combination of genetic and k-means algorithms in MapReduce is implemented in [10] which shows improvement in the quality of clusters by providing globally optimized clusters but increases the time complexity. To overcome the problem of time complexity and obtaining globally optimize clusters, author has proposed an alteration of genetic k-means algorithm for big data clustering in MapReduce framework, by opting only first three steps of genetic algorithm.

4.1 Altered Genetic K-Means Algorithm (AGKM) for MapReduce

Step1:	Form chromosome—A string of length **k** * **d** where **k** = number of clusters expected and **d** = number of attributes.
Step2:	Initialize chromosome by randomly selecting data points from the data set.
Step3:	Create **p** number of chromosomes = population.
Step4:	Divide data set in **p** parts; each part with one chromosome is allocated by name node to **p** number of data nodes.
Step5:	Shape clusters as per the centroids encoded in chromosome at every data node by allocating data points x_i, i = 1, 2, ...n, to clusters C_j with center z_j where
Step6:	Here $\lVert x_i - z_j \rVert$ is Euclidean distance. Euclidean distance between two points x and y, calculated as $d = \sqrt{\sum_{i=1}^{n}(x_i - y_i)^2}$
Step7:	Update chromosome by substituting new centroid z_i^* which is the mean point of the respective cluster, computed as $z_i^* = \frac{1}{n_i}\sum_{x_j \in c_i} x_i, i = 1, 2 \ldots k.$
Step8:	Iterate for the till convergence or fix number of iteration.
Step9:	Final chromosomes from all data nodes are passed to the reducer, and reducer combines chromosomes according to their similarity.
Step10:	Obtain clusters according to newly combined chromosomes which will provide globally optimized clusters.

Selection of chromosomes on the basis of fitness, sending them to mating pool, crossover, and mutation—all these steps of genetic algorithms are not required for the proposed clustering algorithm; thus, it reduces the computation time that is the time complexity.

5 Results and Discussions

Presented algorithm implemented with R on Hadoop2.7.0 single node is installed on Ubuntu 14.0 with core i5 processor, 8 GB RAM, and 500 GB hard disk. Results show the call activity of particular age group, gender, profession, call timing, and call duration with month-wise net pack usage. Figure 2 clearly shows that literate people make more calls than illiterate people—the red cluster shows literate group, and group cluster shows group of illiterate people.

Figure 3 clearly shows the five distinct clusters of people with different profile with total number of calls made.

Figure 4 depicts the clusters of male and female making frequent SMS/MMS.

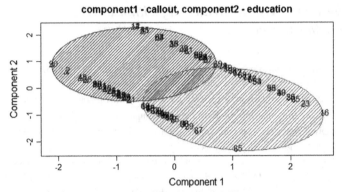

Fig. 2 Literate and illiterate people group

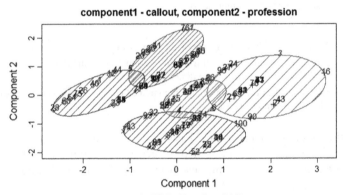

Fig. 3 Profession and total number of calls made

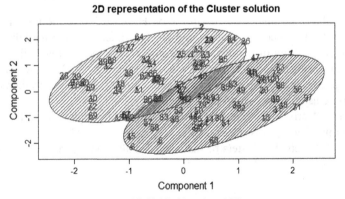

Fig. 4 Gender and SMS/MMS frequency

6 Conclusion and Future Scope

To develop a generalized policy design technique, we need an algorithm for the better categorization of data in big data environment. Big data clustering techniques are trending due to the inclusion of evolutionary techniques in it. Genetic K-Means clustering algorithm for big data analytics provides better clusters, but it faces the problem of increased time complexity. Presented AKGM clustering algorithm is an alteration of Genetic K-Means clustering algorithm and provides globally optimized clusters from the data set in less computing time.

AGKM clustering algorithm is framed for Hadoop/MapReduce, and it works smoothly as per the expectations by providing globally optimized clusters within less computing in comparison with others.

Further, we have planned to implement this algorithm on variety of data sets with multiple node implementation of Hadoop, to obtain global clusters of similar customer behavior.

References

1. Demchenko Y., et al. Defining Architecture Components of the Big Data Ecosystem. IEEE, 2014. pp. 104–112.
2. Rathore M.M.U., et al. Real-Time Big Data Analytical Architecture for Remote Sensing Applications. IEEE Journal of Selected Topics in Applied Earth Observations and Remote Sensing, Vol. 8, No. 10, Oct 2015. pp. 4610–4621.
3. Dair A. et al. Review Current CRM Architectures and Introducing New Adapted Architecture to Big Data. IEEE 2015.
4. Fardoie S.R., et al. A new design architecture for e-CRM systems (Case study: tour package choice in tourism industry). ICMIT, IEEE 2008. pp. 463–468.
5. https://www.tutorialspoint.com/consumer_behavior/consumer_behavior_models_types.htm.
6. Zhang Y., et al. Behavior-Based Telecom Tariff Service Design with Neural Network Approach. 2011 Crown.
7. http://glaros.dtc.umn.edu/gkhome/node/1121.
8. Adil, F., et al. A Survey of Clustering Algorithms for Big Data: Taxonomy and Empirical Analysis. IEEE Transactions on Emerging Topics in Computing, Vol. 2, Iss. 3, 2014. pp 267–279.
9. Pooja, B., Kulvinder, S. Big Data Mining: Analysis of Genetic K-Means Algorithm for Big Data Clustering. International Journal of Advanced Research in Computer Science and Software Engineering, Vol. 6, Iss. 7, July 2016. pp 223–228.
10. Ujjwal, M., Sanghamitra, B. Genetic algorithm-based clustering technique. Pattern Recognition 33, Elsevier, 2000. pp 1455–1465.

Analytical Model for OpenFlow-Based Software-Defined Network

Chiranjit Sarkar and S. K. Setua

Abstract Software-defined network (SDN) is an emerging network architecture that can be adapted as a building block for cloud-enabled data centers. SDN decouples the traditional network in Data Plane (collection of forwarding devices or OpenFlow-enabled switches) and Control Plane (collection of one or more controllers), which communicates with each other using OpenFlow protocol. Proper installation of SDN necessitates the performance test of OpenFlow-enabled switches and controllers. Efficiency, reliability, and scalability are few parameters that should be considered to calculate the efficiency of an OpenFlow-based SDN. An analytical model of the OpenFlow-based network is suggested in this paper. Our proposed model is based on queueing theory and exponential models. The average packet arrival rate of a controller and maximum waiting time for an OpenFlow-enabled switch to get a PACKET_OUT message are taken as parameters to define our approach.

Keywords OpenFlow · SDN · M/M/1 queueing model

1 Introduction

In traditional networks approach, the network architect faces many difficulties when different network vendors use their own protocols or different protocols to communicate with the global world. Moreover, each and every year network vendors introduce a variety of new products to the market that follows different or new protocol, resulting in much more complex scenarios for network architects to manage the entire network. To overcome this situation, SDN is considered as a

C. Sarkar (✉) · S. K. Setua
Department of Computer Science and Engineering, University of Calcutta,
Kolkata, India
e-mail: chiranjit.1992@hotmail.com

S. K. Setua
e-mail: sksetua@gmail.com

© Springer Nature Singapore Pte Ltd. 2018
P. K. Pattnaik et al. (eds.), *Progress in Computing, Analytics and Networking*,
Advances in Intelligent Systems and Computing 710,
https://doi.org/10.1007/978-981-10-7871-2_56

promising approach toward the future Internet [1], and OpenFlow is an outstanding implementation of SDNs. OpenFlow was initially introduced by Nick McKeown to empower the research experiments [2]. SDN decouples the traditional network into two major parts, *Data Plane*: collection of OpenFlow-enabled switches or routers that creates the physical fabric of the network, and *Control Plane*: one or more controller(s) that control the Data Plane, in other words the controller is the only device which has some policies to make a decision for new incoming flows or packets.

In OpenFlow networks, OpenFlow-enabled switches by their own cannot make any decisions; they can only forward packets following the instructions of a centralized controller. This offers a higher flexibility of packet flows in the routing and gives freedom to change the behavior of a segment of the network without influencing overall traffic. In SDN, only software changes are required to enable OpenFlow on a system (network) and hardware vendors need not open up their system to support OpenFlow. However, most work focuses on availability, scalability, and functionality. The performance of OpenFlow networks has not been investigated properly till date.

Understanding the performance and limitation is a key factor to enhance the productivity of SDN in production (cloud-enabled data center) or experimental environment with some new protocols and mechanism. Therefore, we aim to provide a performance model of an OpenFlow system in this paper. The model is based on the results of queueing theory and probability distribution function. The advantage of our analytical model is that it can provide results in a few unit of time whereas the simulation or real-time OpenFlow-based networks may require several units of time to complete, depending on the computing hardware. Additionally, the M/M/1-N feedback queue increases approximation of the actual controller performance.

The model analyzes the *packet waiting time* for an OpenFlow-enabled switch, as well as the *probability to drop packets* if the OpenFlow-enabled switch is under high load. The model also analyzes the packets arrival rate of a controller. Using the information stated above, the model can derive a conclusion when a controller is unable to handle a new OpenFlow-enabled switch and when an OpenFlow-enabled switch shifts from one controller to another.

The remaining sections of the paper are structured as follows. An overview of OpenFlow architecture is given in Sect. 2. In Sect. 3, we summarized the previous related works. Our proposed model is introduced in Sect. 4. We conclude the paper by summarizing the main contribution in Sect. 5.

2   Overview of OpenFlow

OpenFlow is one of the building blocks of a software-defined network (SDN). It was initially standardized by the Open Network Foundation (ONF) [3], as a standard communication interface between the Control Plane and Data Plane

(OpenFlow-enabled switches and routers, both physical and virtual or hypervisor-based). The ONF has publicly released their first OpenFlow protocol version (v1.0.0) on December 2009 [4].

In SDN, entire network decouples into two planes (i.e., *Control Plane* and *Data Plane*); these open two new interfaces for network managers, namely *Northbound Interface* and *Southbound Interface*. In *Northbound Interface*, APIs are used for deploying policies or rules in the controller(s) that eventually control the SDN. *Southbound Interface*, a type of open-source protocol known as OpenFlow protocol, is used to establish a secure communication channel between Control Plane (controller(s)) and Data Plane (OpenFlow-enabled switches or routers).

An OpenFlow-enabled switch in an OpenFlow network contains a set of queues for *ingress ports* [5] and a set of flow tables which contain flow entries to perform respective actions. Whenever any packet is received in any port of an OpenFlow-enabled switch, OpenFlow-enabled switch executes the procedures shown in Fig. 1. OpenFlow-enabled switch extracts the header field from the incoming packet and performs a pipeline-based searching operation to find a match, over a set of flow tables [5] associated with that particular OpenFlow-enabled switch. If a match is found in any of the flow tables, a corresponding set of instructions or actions are executed and update relative statistics (i.e., update counters) for that particular flow entry. If a packet header does not match any flow entry in the entire set of flow tables, this is referred as *table miss*, and the behavior of table miss depends on the table configuration. On first flow table miss, the instructions in the flow entry may explicitly direct the packet to another flow table, where the same process is repeated again. Whenever final table miss occurs, the associate OpenFlow-enabled switch either drops that particular packet or encapsulates it as a *PACKET_IN* message and forwards to the controller via a reserved

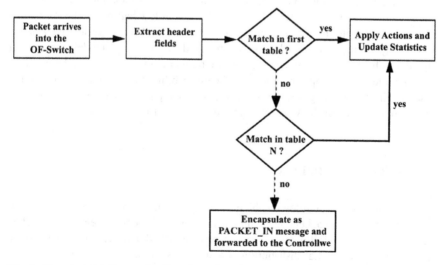

Fig. 1 Flowchart detailing packet flow through an OpenFlow-enabled switch

port. After receiving a *PACKET_IN* message, the controller processes it and acknowledges the OpenFlow-enabled switch with a *PACKET_OUT* message containing some encapsulated instructions.

3 Related Work

Different communication protocols are used in traditional network, but in SDN architecture a single type of protocol is deployed to build a communication channel between OpenFlow-enabled switches and controller(s), known as *OpenFlow* protocol. OpenFlow allows users to implement rules into the flow tables of an OpenFlow-enabled switch using Secure Shell (SSH). Using the OpenFlow protocol agents, flow tables built a communication channel by exchanging messages and configuration management with the controller(s). Nowadays, there are several controllers available which support OpenFlow protocols, for example, Floodlight [6], Beacon [7], Open Daylight [8], POX/NOX [9], Ryu [10]. Each of the mentioned controllers is discriminated with respect to the programming language, performance, and the application domain. As SDN is a new emerging technology, the controller performance is a very important issue which we are going to analyze in this paper.

In [11], Zhihao Shang and Katinka Wolter presented an OpenFlow queueing model that illustrates the influence of packet_in message's probability over the performance of OpenFlow networks by capturing the packets' sojourn time in both OpenFlow-enabled switches and controllers.

In [12], Michael Jarschel et al. derived a basic model that considers the forwarding speed and blocking probability of packets between an OpenFlow-enabled switch and an OpenFlow controller and validates using a simulation. Their model is based on measurements of switching time over OpenFlow hardware, and it can also be used to estimate the packet sojourn time and the probability of lost packets.

In [13], Samer Salah Al_Yassin proposed a queueing model that is an OpenFlow-based model of controller–switch interaction, which can be used to estimate the packet sojourn time and the probability of lost packets in such a system. The author suggested sojourn time, average packet executed time, waiting probability metrics of the Control Plane in his paper for evaluation.

4 Design and Analysis

In our model, each OpenFlow-enabled switch of the network is connected to more than one controller, packets are assumed to arrive to OpenFlow-enabled switches and controller(s) by following a Poisson process and those packets are served by following an exponential distribution. To analyze such scenario, we prefer to use M/M/1 queueing model.

Each ingress port of the OpenFlow-enabled switches and the controller has a *finite* amount of queue capacity of length M and N, so we use **M/M/1: M** queueing model and **M/M/1: N** queueing model, respectively. The behavior of the packet flow in our model is identical to SDN. When a packet is arrived in an OpenFlow-enabled switch for the first time, the controller installs a flow entry. The remaining packets of the same flow are forwarded directly.

Our queueing model for OpenFlow network is represented in Fig. 2a. The OpenFlow-enabled switches and controller are modeled as queueing nodes to analyze the time of our OpenFlow-based network. We assumed that a controller connects with *n* number of OpenFlow-enabled switches, each OpenFlow-enabled switch has *m* numbers of ingress port, and each port has a queue of finite length M to store incoming packets which is processed with respect to the arrival time, i.e., First Come First Serve (FCFS) order which is shown in Fig. 2b. Each port of the OpenFlow-enabled switch is either connected to an end user or an OpenFlow-enabled switch.

The packets arrival process to each port follows a Poisson process. The *average arrival rate* within *j*th port of *i*th OpenFlow-enabled switch is $\lambda_i^{(j)}$, and arrival rate in different ports is independent. The processing time of flows in the OpenFlow-enabled switch follows exponential distribution with the parameter μ_s, which represents the expectation of flow processing rate. All OpenFlow-enabled switches in our model have the same service rate (μ_s), and controller(s) have service rate of μ_c.

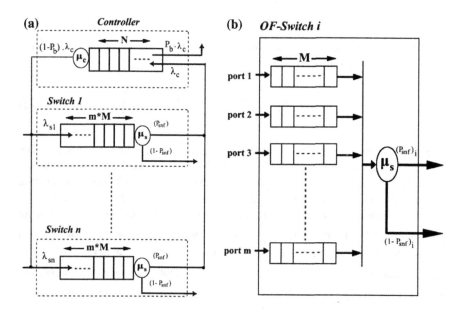

Fig. 2 **a** Queueing model of OpenFlow-based networks. **b** Queueing model of OpenFlow-enabled switch

In our model, we present two different scenarios that help us to decide whether a controller is capable to handle an OpenFlow-enabled switch or not.

Scenario I.

Adding a new OpenFlow-enabled switch to a controller already controlling n number of OpenFlow-enabled switches.

The service rate of the queue associated with jth port for ith OpenFlow-enabled switch (i.e., $\mu_{s_i}^{(j)}$) is expressed in (1) as follows:

$$\mu_{s_i}^{(j)} = \lambda_i^{(j)} \cdot \frac{\mu_s}{\sum_{j=1}^{m} \lambda_i^{(j)}} \tag{1}$$

The traffic intensity of jth port of ith OpenFlow-enabled switch (i.e., $\rho_i^{(j)}$) is expressed in (2) as follows:

$$\rho_i^{(j)} = \frac{\lambda_i^{(j)}}{\mu_{s_i}^{(j)}} \tag{2}$$

The probability of the queue in jth port of ith OpenFlow-enabled switch is full (i.e., $P_{M_i}^{(j)}$) is expressed in (3) as follows:

$$P_{M_i}^{(j)} = \rho_i^{(j)M} \cdot \left(\frac{1 - \rho_i^{(j)}}{1 - \rho_i^{(j)M+1}} \right) \tag{3}$$

The arrival rate in jth port is affected by the finite queue length (i.e., $\lambda_{i_e}^{(j)}$) is expressed in (4) as follows:

$$\lambda_{i_e}^{(j)} = \lambda_i^{(j)} \cdot \left(1 - P_{M_i}^{(j)} \right) = \lambda_i^{(j)} \cdot \left(\frac{1 - \rho_i^{(j)M}}{1 - \rho_i^{(j)M+1}} \right) \tag{4}$$

Packets arrive the OpenFlow-enabled switch following Poisson process. The packets that are matched with the flow table are forwarded accordingly to the instruction stated in the flow table following exponential distribution. Packets that suffer a table miss are forwarded to the controller as *PACKET_IN* message.

The probability of new flow rate (rate of issuing *PACKET_IN* message) in jth port of ith switch is denoted as $P_{nf_i}^{(j)}$. Packets are classified into two classes [14] leaving the OpenFlow-enabled switch in Poisson process: a *new flow* rate of $P_{nf_i}^{(j)} \cdot \lambda_{i_e}^{(j)}$ and *existing flow* rate of $\left(1 - P_{nf_i}^{(j)} \right) \cdot \lambda_{i_e}^{(j)}$. A total *arrival rate* of an *ingress port* for the ith OpenFlow-enabled switch (i.e., λ_i) is expressed in (5), and total *new flow rate* (i.e., $(P_{snf})_i$) is expressed in (6).

$$\lambda_i = \sum_{j=1}^{m} \lambda_{i_e}^{(j)} \tag{5}$$

$$\left(P_{snf}\right)_i = \sum_{j=1}^{m} P_{nf_i}^{(j)} \cdot \lambda_{i_e}^{(j)} \tag{6}$$

Now, we estimate the arrival rates of the controller before (λ_c) and after (λ_{CN}) adding a new OpenFlow-enabled switch to the controller which is already connected to n OpenFlow-enabled switches.

The controller arrival rate (λ_c) for n OpenFlow-enabled switches is expressed in (7).

$$\lambda_C = \sum_{i=1}^{n} \left(P_{snf}\right)_i \tag{7}$$

We assume that the controller system is stable in the scenario where $\lambda_c < \mu_c$.

Now, when we connect a new OpenFlow-enabled switch (s) to this controller, its arrival rate increases with rate $\left(P_{snf}\right)_s$. So the new arrival rate for this controller becomes λ_{CN} is expressed in (8) as follows:

$$\lambda_{CN} = \lambda_C + \left(P_{snf}\right)_s \tag{8}$$

The probability of the new OpenFlow-enabled switch finding new flows $\left(P_{snf}\right)_s$ can be calculated using (6).

If $[\lambda_{CN} > \mu_c]$, then the new switch is not suitable to be connected to the current controller and shifts to next available controller.

The blocking probability of jth port of ith OpenFlow-enabled switch (i.e., $P_{B_i}^{(j)}$) is expressed in (9) as follows:

$$P_{B_i}^{(j)} = \left(1 - P_{M_i}^{(j)}\right) \tag{9}$$

Hence, the number of packets lost in jth port of ith OpenFlow-enabled switch (i.e., $P_{loss_i}^{(j)}$) is expressed in (10) as follows:

$$P_{loss_i}^{(j)} = \lambda_i^{(j)} \cdot P_{Bi}^{(j)} \tag{10}$$

Scenario II.

An existing OpenFlow-enabled switch decides to shift from one controller to another when it has to wait for a limited amount of time. Although an OpenFlow-enabled switch is incapable of taking any decisions, but in this paper we are formulating a straightforward function based upon the acknowledgement time interval of *PACKET_OUT* message from the controller. As previously mentioned, we assume that the controller has the arrival rate of λ_C and the service rate of μ_c.

The traffic intensity of the controller(s) (i.e., ρ_c) is expressed in (11) as follows:

$$\rho_c = \frac{\lambda_c}{\mu_c} \tag{11}$$

P_k is denoted as the k number of new flow present in the controller system, and the normalized form of the probability distribution is as follows:

$$
\begin{aligned}
&\sum_{k=0}^{N} P_k = 1 \\
&P_0 + P_1 + P_2 + \cdots + P_N = 1 \\
&P_0 + \rho \cdot P_0 + \rho^2 \cdot P_0 + \cdots + \rho^N \cdot P_0 = 1 \\
&P_0 \left(1 + \rho + \rho^2 + \cdots + \rho^N \right) = 1 \\
&P_0 \left(\frac{1 - \rho^{N+1}}{1 - \rho} \right) = 1 \\
&P_0 = \frac{1 - \rho}{1 - \rho^{N+1}}
\end{aligned}
\tag{12}
$$

Here, P_0 (in (12)) denotes the probability when a controller is not dealing with any flow, i.e., controller system is empty.

$$P_1 = \rho \cdot P_0 = \rho \cdot \left(\frac{1 - \rho}{1 - \rho^{N+1}} \right) \tag{13}$$

P_1 (in (13)) denotes the probability when a controller is dealing with a single flow, i.e., controller system contains only one new flow.

Hence, the probability that a new flow comes to the controller and serves directly without any waiting is $(P_0 + P_1)$.

The probability of the controller queue is full (i.e., P_N) is expressed in (14) as follows:

$$P_N = \rho^N \cdot P_0 = \rho^N \cdot \left(\frac{1 - \rho}{1 - \rho^{N+1}} \right) \tag{14}$$

The number of expected flows in the controller system (i.e., L_c) is expressed in (15) as follows:

$$L_c = \sum_{n=0}^{N} n \cdot P_n = \sum_{n=0}^{N} n \cdot \rho^n \cdot P_0 = P_0 \cdot \rho \cdot \sum_{n=0}^{N} n \cdot \rho^{n-1} = P_0 \cdot \rho \cdot \sum_{n=0}^{N} \frac{d}{d\rho} \cdot \rho^n$$

$$= \frac{1-\rho}{1-\rho^{N+1}} \cdot \frac{\rho}{(1-\rho)^2} \cdot \left[1 + N \cdot \rho^{N+1} - (N+1) \cdot \rho^N\right] \qquad (15)$$

$$= \frac{\rho}{(1-\rho^{N+1}) \cdot (1-\rho)} \cdot \left[1 + N \cdot \rho^{N+1} - (N+1) \cdot \rho^N\right]$$

The arrival rate of the controller is effected by the finite queue length of N (i.e., λ_e) is expressed in (16) as follows:

$$\lambda_e = \lambda_c(1 - P_N) = \lambda_c \left[1 - \rho^N \cdot \left(\frac{1-\rho}{1-\rho^{N+1}}\right)\right] = \lambda_c \left(\frac{1-\rho^N}{1-\rho^{N+1}}\right) \qquad (16)$$

By applying Little's formula (17), we can get the expected time spent (sojourn time) in the controller system of a new flow (i.e., W_c) is expressed in (18).

$$L_c = \lambda_e \cdot W_c \qquad (17)$$

$$W_c = \frac{L_c}{\lambda_e} = \frac{1}{\lambda_e} \cdot \frac{\rho}{(1-\rho^{N+1}) \cdot (1-\rho)} \cdot \left[1 + N \cdot \rho^{N+1} - (N+1) \cdot \rho^N\right]$$

$$= \frac{1}{\lambda_c} \cdot \left(\frac{1-\rho^{N+1}}{1-\rho^N}\right) \cdot \frac{\rho}{(1-\rho^{N+1}) \cdot (1-\rho)} \cdot \left[1 + N \cdot \rho^{N+1} - (N+1) \cdot \rho^N\right] \qquad (18)$$

$$= \frac{1}{\lambda_c} \cdot \frac{\rho}{(1-\rho^N) \cdot (1-\rho)} \cdot \left[1 + N \cdot \rho^{N+1} - (N+1) \cdot \rho^N\right]$$

The mean service time for a *PACKET_IN* messages in the controller is denoted by $\left(\frac{1}{\mu_c}\right)$.

So, turn-around time (T) for a controller to produce *PACKET_OUT* message for respectable OpenFlow-enabled switch can be formulated as given in (19), which is as follows:

$$T = W_c + \frac{1}{\mu_c} \qquad (19)$$

If an OpenFlow-enabled switch waits for the *PACKET_OUT* message from the controller more than T amount of time, then the OpenFlow-enabled switch will assume that the controller is either idle or incapable to serve it. In this scenario, the OpenFlow-enabled switch shifts from one controller to next available controller.

5   Conclusion

In this paper, we have suggested an analytical model based on M/M/1 queueing model for an OpenFlow-enabled SDN to understand the performance and limitation. We have formulated two scenarios, one describing the limitation of a controller to control the number of OpenFlow-enabled switches based on the flow rate and another measuring the tolerance of an OpenFlow-enabled switch based on sojourn time to decide when to shift from one controller to another. These two expressions may help the researcher or the network engineer for a more reliable SDN-based network.

References

1. Rowshanrad S., Namvarasl S., Abdi V., Hajizadeh M., Keshtgary M.: A survey on sdn, the future of networking. Journal of Advanced Computer Science & Technology, Vol. 3, no. 2, pp. 232 (2014)
2. Casado M., Freedman M.J., Pettit J., Luo J., McKeown N.: Ethane: Taking Control of the Enterprise. SIGCOMM'07 (2007)
3. Open networking foundation, https://www.opennetworking.org/
4. OpenFlow switch Specification v1.0.0, http://archive.openflow.org/documents/openflow-spec-v1.0.0.pdf
5. OpenFlow switch Specification v1.5.0, https://www.opennetworking.org/images/stories/downloads/sdn-resources/onf-specifications/openflow/openflow-switch-v1.5.0.noipr.pdf
6. Floodlight OpenFlow controller, http://www.projectfloodlight.org/
7. Beacon Controller, https://openflow.stanford.edu/display/Beacon/Home
8. OpenDaylight, https://www.opendaylight.org/
9. NOX controller, https://github.com/noxrepo/nox
10. Ryu SDN Framework, https://osrg.github.io/ryu/
11. Shang Z., Wolter K.: Delay Evaluation of OpenFlow Network Based on Queueing Model. [cs.DC] (2016)
12. Jarschel M., Oechsner S., Schlosser D., Pries R., Goll S., Gia P.T.: Modeling and Performance Evaluation of an OpenFlow Architecture. ITC'11 (2011)
13. Al_Yassin S.S.: Modeling and Assessment Performance of OpenFlow-Based Network Control Plane. International Journal of Science and Research (IJSR), Vol. 4 Issue 9 (2015)
14. Papoulis A., Pillai S. U.: Probability, random variables, and stochastic processes. Tata McGraw-Hill Education (2002)

Enhanced Parallel Image Retrieval Technique Using Relevance Feedback

M. Sridevi, Vishnu Balakrishnan, Janardhan J. Kammath and Sherine Davis

Abstract The retrieval of relevant images to a given query is a challenging problem. Many researchers have proposed solutions to solve this problem. The idea of 'Human in Loop' adds more useful data to the existing data, which can help refine the output of content-based image retrieval (CBIR) system. In this paper, we extend on 'Human in Loop' by setting up a relevance feedback system. It helps the CBIR system to understand closer similarities between images which mere feature vectors and algorithms can't identify. This paper aims at improving the performance and efficiency of a CBIR system by using Bitmaps to show relevance among the vast number of images, for which feature vectors have already been extracted and stored, and parallel indexing and comparison process are performed to reduce computation time. Use of Bitmap helps learn the feedback obtained from multiple users regarding the relevance between various images until a saturation point is reached. The results show its superiority in comparison with existing models such as QBIC, MARS and VIPER techniques.

Keywords CBIR · Colour moments · Bitmaps · Parallelization
Image retrieval

M. Sridevi (✉) · V. Balakrishnan · J. J. Kammath · S. Davis
Department of Computer Science and Engineering, National Institute of Technology,
Tiruchirappalli, Tamil Nadu, India
e-mail: msridevi@nitt.edu

V. Balakrishnan
e-mail: vishnubalakrishnan95@gmail.com

J. J. Kammath
e-mail: iamjan95@gmail.com

S. Davis
e-mail: sherinedavis@outlook.com

© Springer Nature Singapore Pte Ltd. 2018
P. K. Pattnaik et al. (eds.), *Progress in Computing, Analytics and Networking*,
Advances in Intelligent Systems and Computing 710,
https://doi.org/10.1007/978-981-10-7871-2_57

1 Introduction

This generation has seen the rise of the various image capturing technologies, especially with advancement in portability, speed and simplicity of capturing images through devices like mobile phones, personal digital assistant (PDA), digital single-lens reflex (DSLR) camera and GoPros. The rapid growth in digital images, as seen on the Internet, is attributed to such developments. And this in turn raises the issue of how this vast collection of digital images can be managed, and much more importantly how relevant images can be retrieved with relative ease and accuracy. CBIR deals with this segment of issues in digital imaging. Most of the proposed solutions use properties like colour, texture and shape for comparison and retrieval. Hence, the choice of colour model, distance metric and colour features are critical to the success of the scheme. Once accuracy is achieved in the retrieval of images from huge databases, next objective would be to improve the response time. Large image database incurs large response time due to the factors like the number of features being queried and lack of proper structure in storing of feature vectors. This makes parallel processes for the CBIR framework. The choice of such process also becomes critical for the success of the image retrieval system.

2 Related Work

Many systems and methods have been proposed and studied in [1–4] both in commercial and academic domains. All of them have a basic framework with preprocessing of the image, which deals with extracting relevant features, creating a feature vector, comparing this against the many feature vectors stored in a database, for the corresponding set of images stored and then retrieving the most similar one. Emphasis must be given to fine-tuning each of these separate processing segments. Some studies that worked on improving this base framework include, [1] showing that better results can be achieved by using a combination of multiple features, like texture using grey-level distribution moments (GLDM) and spatial grey-level dependence matrix (SGLDM) methods and shape using Fourier descriptors and moment invariants. In [2], the effect on precision and recall of CBIR systems is computed for different colour models (RGB, I1I2I3, YIQ, HSV, HSI, YUV, LAB, XYZ, CMYK, YCbCr and HMMD), colour features (colour moments, colour histogram and colour coherence vector) and distance metrics (Euclidean distance and quadratic distance) and showed HSV fares well in comparison with the rest. The author in [5] emphasizes the impact of 'Human in Loop', technically referred to as relevance feedback system, also seen in multimedia analysis and retrieval system (MARS) [3, 6]. Davar Giveki et al. [4] discuss about the merits of using wavelet transforms and segmentation, where images are initially converted into various colour models and later broken down into multiple colour channels for the respective colour models, after which they are segmented, on which wavelet transform is done to obtain the necessary feature vectors.

3 Proposed Work

Efficiency in a CBIR system refers to the ability of the system to put out relevant images to what was requested from a vast collection of images present in data sets. Obtaining higher levels of efficiency is possible if more association can be made between images based on various attributes. But, this is limited by various technical issues, hindering the process of identifying similar images. Moving out from the realm of the system as software components working within themselves with material provided, they can be extended by considering the response given by a client, to the result which was shown, for the query that was made. This helps model a relationship between images beyond the scope of what was discerned by the feature extractors.

This paper works on a technique that makes use of the feedback given by clients, to model relationships between images based on similarity or relevance to a query. This model also matures, in terms of knowledge, over the period of usage (across multiple queries). Every query adds to knowledge base of the system, in turn building up on efficiency over time, ensuring that further queries display results with improved levels of relevance.

The paper implements a relevance feedback system and results to a query are displayed, the client is given options to provide feedback to the system, stating whether if the image displayed is relevant to the query image submitted or not. This helps realize relations between images outside the scope of the algorithms. All these feedbacks are recorded using a greyscale image, whose size depends on the number of images. With the use of such a structure, a 2-dimensional array, the relation between each image pair can be recorded and they can be easily extended across transitively relevant images. It also reduces space requirements and provides ease in accessing data stored.

The basic framework as shown in Fig. 1 consists of the following: colour-based feature extraction, edge-based feature extraction, comparison, result and relevance feedback. The blocks, colour-based feature extraction and edge-based feature extraction are expected to consume much time for large data sets. Hence, it is preferred to parallelize them over multiple smaller sets within the data set.

3.1 Feature Extraction

One of the most important steps of content-based image retrieval is feature extraction. By feature extraction, this paper only deals with the visual feature extraction and not any form of textual features. And, among the visual features, this

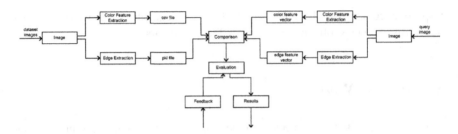

Fig. 1 Basic framework of the proposed system

paper deals with only the general features like colour and shape. As the viewpoint varies with the people, there is no single best method for any feature extraction. A widely chosen feature for comparison of images is colour histogram [7]. But, colour histogram doesn't provide a mechanism to uniquely differentiate images, and hence edge features are also taken into consideration.

3.1.1 Colour Feature Extraction

Colour is one of the most important features of an image, and thereby colour extraction is made as one of the most important parts of image retrieval. One of the most widely used colour-based feature extraction techniques is colour histogram [5, 7]. A histogram is a representation of a number of pixels in an image graphically. It is an easy technique, and it can be used to understand the distribution of colour in an image. The histogram remains the same with the small changes in camera position. The problem with this technique is that there is a possibility even for two different type of objects will have similar histograms. So, it is very important to have some other feature extraction technique along with it.

The colour feature extraction is done for all the images in the data set, and the results are stored in a *csv* file. For a large data set, serially extracting features from images will be time-consuming. Hence, this operation is carried out in parallel.

Similarly, the same colour histogram is done for the query image, and the result is stored as a colour feature vector which is forwarded to the next step (i.e. comparison block).

3.1.2 Edge Feature Extraction

An edge can be described as a sudden discontinuity in brightness in an image. This sudden change or discontinuity describes the shapes in an image. So, the edge detection would also mean understanding shapes in the image, which could be very useful in image retrieval.

There are different approaches for edge extraction, and this paper uses most widely used Canny edge detector [8]. Like the colour feature extraction, the edge extraction is also done in parallel for all the images in the data set, and then they are stored in a *pkl* [9] file. And the edge feature is extracted from the query image and stored in edge feature vector.

3.2 Relevance Feedback

Better understanding about the relation between images can be obtained using relevance feedback mechanism. This additional input obtained at a later stage is incorporated using 'Evaluation' phase. The most relevant images collected after the procedure of comparison, realized using ordering of images in terms of the degree of dissimilarity, is analysed using the feedback available from clients after previously executed queries. These feedbacks provide a simple prompt to the client asking whether if a given image is relevant to the image that was submitted by the client as a query, which can be answered as 'yes' or 'no'. The feedback, for a given pair of images, submitted is recorded using a greyscale image [10]. The feedback helps refine the degree of dissimilarity. The formulae used are mentioned in Eq. (1).

4 Comparison and Evaluation

The comparison function employed implements a naïve method of finding similarities among images using Euclidean distance metrics. The feature vectors recorded in these files are distributed across multiple threads to process them in parallel. The images are split equally across the number of threads available. This is crucial, as it ensures that the system doesn't end up spending majority of the time in managing the threads. Larger the number of cores, faster the system.

The computation done by each of the spawned thread results in a metric that defines the degree of dissimilarity (DoD) between a given pair of images [11]. Larger the value makes the images more dissimilar. DoD is computed using the formula as given in Eq. (1). All the results of the computation are gathered up in a list and sorted in descending order or decreasing order in terms of similarity between images. The most relevant ones are passed on to be evaluated by the next functional block named 'Evaluation'.

$$DoD = 0.6 \times A(x, y) + 10 \times B(img_x, img_y) \qquad (1)$$

where A = *chi-squared distance between two feature vectors of images x and y*
  $B(img_x, img_y)$ = *value returned by matchshapes(img_x img_y) for images x and y*
  Unlike the mentioned techniques in [1, 2, 4], here precision and recall rates improve with number of queries made, rather than staying static. Hence, relevance feedback makes the system dynamic and realistic and improves the overall performance as is shown in Fig. 2.

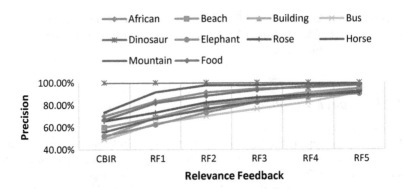

Fig. 2 Average precision of retrieval

4.1 Performance Analysis

For analysing the performance of the CBIR, two widely used metrics, namely precision and recall, are used [12]. Precision is defined as the CBIR system's ability in retrieving relevant images and is given by Eq. (2), while recall is defined as the CBIR system's ability in retrieving all the relevant images and is given by Eq. (3). They are defined as follows: (Table 1).

$$Recall(R) = \frac{No.of\ relevant\ images\ retrieved}{Total\ no.of\ relevant\ images} \tag{2}$$

$$Precision(P) = \frac{No.\ of\ relevant\ images\ retrieved}{Total\ no.\ of\ images\ retrieved} \tag{3}$$

Figure 2 shows the average precision obtained by the proposed solution. It can be seen that the precision of retrieval is a continuously increasing curve and all the

Table 1 Average precision (%) for 30% recall

Category	CBIR	RF1	RF2	RF3	RF4	RF5
African	70	83.31	91.14	94.43	95.55	97.73
Beach	60.04	68.84	80.15	84.25	91.13	94.66
Building	51.24	68.86	75.51	85.53	91.23	92.12
Bus	48.89	63.33	70.08	76.42	82.37	91.06
Dinosaur	100	100	100	100	100	100
Elephant	52.23	62.41	73.33	82.52	86.83	90
Rose	65.55	73.29	82.16	86.67	88.89	91.09
Horse	73.43	91.47	97.52	97.52	98.96	98.96
Mountain	55.84	67.93	76.48	82.61	88.46	92.35
Food	66.67	81.79	88.15	93.33	96.71	97.8

Table 2 Average precision (%) for 20% recall

Category	CBIR	RF1	RF2	RF3	RF4	RF5
African	66.5	78.51	81.34	85.28	88.33	90
Beach	51.67	66.99	76.06	81.66	85	90.65
Building	56.82	76.39	88.74	93.04	100	100
Bus	53.19	68.33	76.51	78.17	88.67	91.72
Dinosaur	100	100	100	100	100	100
Elephant	66.67	76.14	81.62	90.05	93.24	96.84
Rose	75	85.16	91.52	95	95	95
Horse	80.21	85.33	95.21	95.21	98.33	100
Mountain	41.67	63.44	75.03	81.79	88.31	95.11
Food	61.58	78.25	90	95.12	98.17	98.17

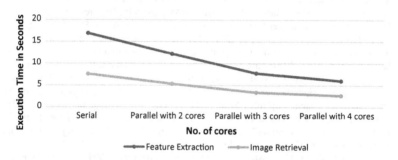

Fig. 3 Execution time for serial and parallel extraction

classes of images in the database reach approx. 100% precision towards the end. Thus, using the concept of 'Human in Loop', i.e. relevance feedback, in image retrieval enhances the performance of the system to achieve more relevant and precise results (Table 2).

Figure 3 shows the effect of parallel processing in image retrieval. It can be seen that as the number of cores available for processing increases, the execution time for feature extraction and image retrieval decreases. Thus, the uses of multiple cores for parallel processing improve the system performance significantly.

5 Conclusion

This paper implemented a CBIR system that made use of relevance feedback to obtain additional input, valuable information pertaining to the relevance between images, which is used to refine further query processing for similar images. The result shows that the first few iterations of queries on the same image provide precision and recall which is completely dependent on the success of underlying feature detection techniques. But at later stages, with enough number of client inputs obtained, the computation of relevant images has become faster and very high levels of precision and recall is obtained. This work can be extended further on huge databases for retrieving relevant images by making use of more efficient structures that can hold inter-image relational information, reducing computational cost and time.

References

1. Vadhri Suryanarayana, Dr. M. V.L.N. Raja Rao et al (2012) "Image retrieval system using hybrid feature extraction technique", IJCSIT Vol 04 No 1 Page No.:2–8
2. Swapnil Saurav, Prajakta Belsare et al (2015) "Holistic Correlation of colour models, colour features and distance metrics on CBIR", IRJET Vol 02 Issue 07
3. Amit Singla, Meenakshi Garg (2014) "QBIC, MARS and VIPER: A review on Content Based Image Retrieval Techniques", IJECS Vol 03, Issue 08 Page No.: 7680–7684, Page No.: 3
4. Davar Giveki, Hadis Tarrah et al (2015) "A New Content Based Image Retrieval Model Based on Wavelet Transform", Journal of Computer and Communications 3 Page No.: 66–73
5. Shih-Fu Chang et al (1999) "Image retrieval: Current Techniques, Promising Directions and Open Issues", Journal of Visual Communication and Image Representation, Page No.: 2, 9
6. Michael Ortega-Binderberger et al (2004) "Relevance Feedback Techniques in the MARS image retrieval system", Springer Multimedia Systems Vol 09 Issue 06 Page No.: 535–547
7. C.S. Gode, Apurva N. Ganar (2014) "Enhancement of Image Retrieval by Using Colour, Texture and Shape Features", Electronic Systems, Signal Processing and Computing Technologies (ICESC), International Conference
8. Lijun Ding, Ardeshir Goshtasby (2001) "Pattern Recognition", Vol 34 Issue 03 Page No.: 721–725
9. R Jain, R Kasturi and B G Schunck (1995) "Machine Vision", Binary Image Processing, McGraw–Hill, Page No.: 169–173
10. E Trucco and A Verri (1998) "Introductory Techniques for 3D Computer Vision", Prentice Hall Page No.: 71–79
11. Sunil Kopparapu and M Satish (2014) "Optimal Gaussian Filter for Effective Noise Filtering", TENCON 2014–2015 IEEE Region 10 Conference, Page No.: 3
12. https://en.wikipedia.org/wiki/Translation_lookaside_buffer

Extrapolation and Visualization of NPA Using Feature Based Random Forest Algorithm in Indian Banks

J. Arthi and B. Akoramurthy

Abstract The instigation of Non-Performing Assets (NPAs) in Indian banks was post 2009, when world was doing quantitative easing (QE) to save them off recession in 2008. The problem of NPA in India has witnessed the gross NPA rise to 79.7% and net NPA from 2.8% in September 2015 to 4.6% in March 2016. Banking has its NPA data increasing year by year which is a serious concern for the Indian banks. In this paper, an algorithm to determine and predict NPA is proposed. The proposed algorithm creates a pattern based on NPA data sets from various banks, and features are extracted to predict and eradicate financial debts. Also, a visual banking dashboard is developed exclusively for NPAs. The learning task in the proposed Feature based Random Forest algorithm is carried out by incorporating features extracted from the dataset considered and hence improves the prediction accuracy. The result of prediction is visualized using Tableau which, not only provides insights on the data but also aids in data-driven decision making.

Keywords NPA · Data visualization · Random forest algorithm
Prediction

1 Introduction

Banking is an important segment that contributes to the economic progress of a country. The contribution of technology to the banking industry has leveraged the reach of banking to a much greater extent. Banking channels have been highly benefited with the emergence of technology paving way to Internet banking, mobile banking, and even satellite banking. From business driver to an enabler, technology

J. Arthi (✉)
Kongu Engineering College, Perundurai, India
e-mail: arthighp@gmail.com

B. Akoramurthy
IFET College of Engineering, Villupuram, India
e-mail: akor.theanchor@gmail.com

© Springer Nature Singapore Pte Ltd. 2018
P. K. Pattnaik et al. (eds.), *Progress in Computing, Analytics and Networking*,
Advances in Intelligent Systems and Computing 710,
https://doi.org/10.1007/978-981-10-7871-2_58

has occupied a significant position to influence the banking industry through its various supporting tasks such as analytics, prediction, visualization. Right from service delivery to security, technology has empowered the banking domain. Banking industry has been facing a lot of issues in handling its customers. The changing demands and the need to handle a variety of customers have created a pressure to the bankers to indulge in the efficient use of technology. Among the several issues in banking, non-performing asset (NPA) has become one of the grave issues that affect the credit delivery of banks. With banks occupying a significant position in the economic growth, their performance plays a crucial role. Bank's performance is measured by several factors which include operating income and expenses, return on assets, return on equity, net interest margin, and as NPA reflects the performance of banks, it becomes very essential to identify and eliminate the occurrence of it. NPA arise primarily due to the credit defaults in banks.

Efforts have been taken to purge the factors that contribute to the occurrence of NPA in banks including the economic conditions, growing number of defaults, inappropriate lending policies, deprived credit appraisal systems, deviation of funds, mismanagement. Despite these efforts, the problems with NPA are on the rise and this can be brought down only if it is possible to predict the occurrence of NPA. This can be achieved by observing and analyzing the NPA-related data. Analyzing such data is quite difficult as the occurrence of NPA is different in different banks. Though researches and efforts have been carried out to predict NPA occurrence in banks, it is affected by various parameters such as interest rates and hence it is becoming quite difficult to accurately predict and communicate the occurrence of NPA to the bankers.

In this context, the need for a dedicated algorithm to predict NPA with the changing parameters is required. It can be observed that the prediction is not to be restricted to that of the NPA but also with respect to the factors influencing them. Hence, the analysis of such data needs to take a different approach when compared to that of the analysis of any other data set. Analytical reasoning is central to the analyst's task of applying human judgments to reach conclusions from a combination of evidence and assumptions. Financial data analysis is one of the most sensitive and challenging tasks to any data analyst as the task of analysis not just stops with the prediction about the data but also with respect to the communication of the result to aid financial expert's appropriate decisions. Data visualization is one of the most powerful means of communicating the information gained through data. Business analysts use data visualization as a powerful means of communication and at times use it for decision making. With the growing need for data visualization, the field of visual analytics has gained significant importance. The strength of financial data analytics can be further enhanced by making use of visual analytics. Visual analytics incorporates computational and theory-based tools with various interactive techniques and visual representations to enable human-information discourse. The design of the tools and techniques is based on cognitive, design, and perceptual principles. This science of analytical reasoning provides the reasoning framework upon which one can build both strategic and tactical visual analytics technologies for threat analysis, prevention, and response.

This paper proposes an algorithm that is exclusive for handling financial data to predict the occurrence of NPA. Also, the power of visual analytics is utilized to augment the decision-making task by creating a visual interaction with the data.

2 Theoretical Study

An asset is a resource with economic value that an individual, corporation or country owns or controls with the anticipation that it will provide future benefit. Assets contribute to the profitability of banks. Non-performing assets refer to a classification for loans that are in default or are in arrears on scheduled payments of principal or interest. Non-performing assets are classified based on the time taken for the overdue payment. The identification of risk is one of the major tasks of a banker in case of assets since it directly contributes to the bank performance. The following figure illustrates the various types of assets that are to be classified as non-performing assets (Fig. 1).

2.1 Concept of NPA

All the advances given by a bank are termed as assets. Assets in banks can be classified either a performing asset or a non-performing asset. An asset is performing when it generates the expected income (i.e., repayment) and does not pave way to any unusual risks. It becomes a non-performing asset if it fails to generate the expected income or may lead to some risks. In other words, non-performing assets include the assets in a bank that do not generate regular income. Asset in banks becomes non-performing when it stops generating income like interest fees, commission or dues for more than 90 days. NPA is confined to loans, advances,

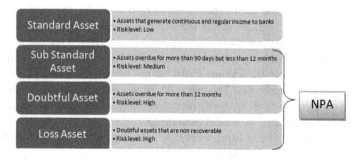

Fig. 1 Classification of NPA

and investments. Loans are assets for banks as the repayment of principal and interest payments is one of the primary sources of cash flows. Banks yield profit out of these loans. If the payments get delayed by a period of 30 days beyond the specified due date, then it is classified as past due and if it exceeds beyond a period of 90 days then it is termed to be a non-performing asset.

3 Literature Review

Several researches have aimed to study the causes for non-performing assets, its detection and elimination. Such studies have exemplified the negative impact that NPA causes not only on the stability of banks and its growth but also on its performance. The issue of NPA and its impact on the profitability of banks were not much considered in the Indian banking sector prior to 1991. The accounting treatment also failed to project the problem of NPA, as interest on loan accounts was accounted on accrual basis [1]. The major cause for the alarming increase of NPAs in public sector banks is mismanagement of the banks. Narasimham Committee identified the NPAs as one of the possible effects of malfunctioning of public sector banks [2]. It has been examined that the reason behind the falling revenues from traditional sources is 78% of the total NPAs accounted in public sector banks [3]. An evaluation of the Indian experience in Financial Sector Reforms published in the RBI Bulletin gives stress to the view that the sustained improvement of the economic activity and growth is greatly enhanced by the existence of a financial system developed in terms of both operational and allocation efficiency in mobilizing savings and in channelizing them among competing demands (2015). The application of visual analytics to financial stability monitoring was elaborated in the work of [4]. This paper analyzes the various means of visualizations such as fixed, interactive, and non-interactive visualizations and how they can be incorporated to illustrate the financial stability of an organization. This paper also describes and categorizes the analytical challenges faced by macroprudential supervisors and indicates where and how visual analytics can increase supervisors' comprehension of the data stream to support informed decision and policy making. The work in [5] proposes a random forest-based early warning system for banks to prevent bank failures. The key variable used here is the rate of interest that the bank is charging on its loans, average rate of interest the bank is paying for its deposits, and the average rate of interest the bank is charging for its loans. Based on this, the random forest algorithm was able to create a warning for the expected bank failure. The work in [6] briefs about the various statistical and intelligent techniques that were used in bankruptcy prediction. This paper illustrates various intelligent techniques such as data envelopment analysis, neural networks, and case-based reasoning techniques that were used to predict bankruptcy.

From the study of the existing works, it is evident that very few works have focused on the prediction of NPA.

4   Contributions of the Proposed System

Based on the theoretical study, it can be observed that the need for handling NPA is crucial. The study of the existing systems makes it evident that very few works have been proposed to predict the occurrence of NPA in Indian banks. The proposed system:

- Provides a methodology to handle NPA data for prediction
- Classifies features that contribute to the occurrence of NPA
- Proposes a novel feature-based random forest algorithm
- Utilizes the power of data visualization to illustrate the prediction of NPA-related data

5   Proposed System

The need for handling non-performing assets has found significant importance as it does not generate any income for banks and also the banks are required to make provisions for such NPA out of the current profit. The contribution of NPA to bankruptcy is also on the rise, and hence, the need for prediction has become crucial. The prediction on the occurrence of NPAs will be a boon to banks as this prediction may help them to forecast. Unlike traditional methods, the prediction for NPA requires additional parameters for consideration as several factors contribute to the occurrence of NPA. In this regard, feature-based random forest algorithm is proposed which constructs a large number of trees to achieve higher classification accuracy. The following section describes the proposed feature-based random forest algorithm and the classification of features that contribute to the occurrence of NPA in banks. The working of the proposed system is shown in Fig. 2.

The non-performing asset data is collected from various banks and is preprocessed. Preprocessing is one of the most common tasks in manipulating data sets. Though random forest algorithm is capable of handling tasks such as identifying outliers and handling missing values, the task of the proposed feature-based random forest algorithm can be simplified by executing the preprocessing task separately. For the preprocessing task, the proposed system makes use of the box plot analysis. Box plot analysis is employed not only to empathize the data that is considered but also to comprehend the distribution of data. This preprocessing task also enables the identification of the internal features (discussed in the next section) that contribute to the occurrence of NPA. Preprocessing yields an optimized data set by eliminating the outliers and also identifies valid internal features that contribute to the occurrence of NPA in banks. The term valid is used here as the utilization of box plot analysis for preprocessing enables the system to identify the valid range of values present in the data in which the values are distributed. Only if the values are significant they are considered for feature classification. Pattern creation is done

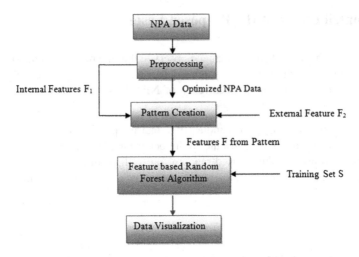

Fig. 2 Working of the proposed system

based on the internal features extracted (F_1) and the optimized data that is obtained as a result of the preprocessing task. The proposed system makes use of the pattern that has the best of the internal features denoted by f (significant features with a valid range of values among patterns) and the external features F_2 for creation of the pattern. The proposed feature-based random forest algorithm takes the optimized data set along with the features F (which includes f and F_1) and a training set S. The following section describes the feature-based random forest algorithm. The prediction results are visualized using data visualization techniques. In this work, data visualization tool Tableau is used for the visualization of the predicted results.

6 Feature-Based Random Forest Algorithm

Random forest algorithm is a notion of the general technique of random decision forests that are an ensemble learning method for classification, regression, and other tasks that operate by constructing a multitude of decision trees at training time and producing class i.e. the mode of the classes (classification) or mean prediction (regression) of the individual trees. Random forest algorithm is commonly utilized in several machine learning tasks and is not specific to any particular application. In this paper, feature-based random forest algorithm is proposed which is dedicated to the prediction of non-performing assets in Indian banks. The proposed algorithm works by creating a pattern which is obtained as a result of preprocessing. From this optimized data set, patterns are created to determine the features with which trees are to be built in the feature-based random forest algorithm.

6.1 Feature Classification

Internal features: The parameters that are considered for the credit risk analysis and those that are present in the NPA data set are considered as the internal features. This includes factors such as credit rating and customer portfolio. It is denoted by F_1 since they are the primary features based on which the pattern is to be created for the formation of trees. The best among the factors are chosen, and those factors are considered for improving the accuracy of classification. This is denoted by f.

External features: In this case, the varying interest rates are considered as the external feature. Interest rate is one of the prime factors that influence the customers in getting and repaying loans. Apart from this, rate of interest that the bank is charging on its loans, average rate of interest the bank is paying for its deposits, and the average rate of interest the bank is charging for its loans can also be considered as external factors. Since it is not fixed and is not a dependent variable with respect to the attributes in the data set, it is termed as external features. It is denoted by F_2. The following figure illustrates the proposed feature-based random forest algorithm.

```
Algorithm Feature based Random Forest
Algorithm
    Precondition: A training set S=(x₁,y₁),..,(xₙ,yₙ), features F
                from pattern P, number of    trees      in forest B
    function RandomForest(S,F)
        H←∅
        for i∈1,...,B do
                S⁽ᴵ⁾←A bootstrap sample from S
                pᵢ←PatternTreeLearn(S⁽ᴵ⁾,F₁,F₂,f)
                H←H U {pᵢ}
        end for
    return H
    end function
    function PatternTreeLearn(S,F₁,F₂,f)
            At each node:
                    f←pattern that best has F₁
                    Split based on best feature in f and F₂
        return the learned tree
    end function
                Feature based Random Forest Algorithm
```

The proposed algorithm takes a training set S as the input along with the features F that is obtained from the pattern created (P). The number of trees in the in the forest is taken as B. Here, H denotes the prediction result. Pattern based on which the learning is carried is implemented with the features that were mentioned. It can be observed the best of the internal features are considered for arriving at the decision of the split in the tree. The term best is utilized since the features that have the optimal value among the patterns are considered so that when the sample is

Fig. 3 Preprocessing using
box plot analysis

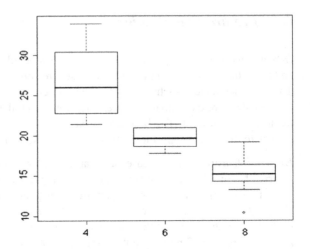

extracted with replacement, there will not be complexity in splitting the trees. This
is done in order to improve the accuracy of classification and in turn improve the
prediction results. Since the proposed algorithm is dedicated to handling NPA,
external factors such as interest rates are also considered. Thus, the split in the tree
is to be based on the best among the internal factors f and the external factors F_2.
This function yields the learned tree which is used for determining the prediction
result. This feature-based random forest algorithm enables the user to vary the
features, and hence, more number of features may be added or reduced. Based on
the nature of banks, the features may also be modified.

7   Experimental Results

The proposed system makes use of the data set collected from various public sector
and private sector banks in India. The data set consists of 15-year NPA data which
had been extracted from secondary source for 10 public and private sector banks
based on market capitalization. Implementation of the proposed system is carried
out using R language. SPSS is used to analyze the input data. Data visualization is
carried out with tableau. Figure 3 illustrates the application of box plot analysis to
the attributes in the data set. It can be observed that various statistical parameters
can be extracted from the preprocessing task. Outliers can be easily identified, and
the range of data can be determined. Moreover, the mean of the data can be
obtained which in turn contributes to the determination of variance. Variance is one
of the most important terms that have to be considered when implementing the
random forest algorithm as it is one of the prime factors for splitting the trees.
Hence, the application of the box plot analysis to the preprocessing task can be
found much suitable. Figure 4 illustrates the analysis of pattern using the decision
boundary. Data in blue line denotes the possibility of data can be predicted. Red

Fig. 4 Pattern analysis using decision boundary

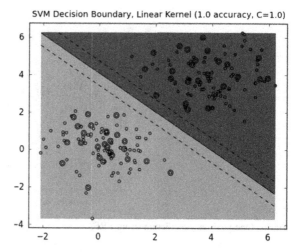

line denotes non-possibility of data prediction. Classifying a considerable portion of data as 'not viable' for prediction is the based on the features extracted from the dataset. The identified internal and external features optimize the dataset considered for prediction task. The following figures illustrate the classification accuracy of the proposed feature-based random forest algorithm.

F_1 score is used to determine the classification accuracy. The F_1 score is calculated using Eq. (1)

$$F_1 = 2 \cdot \frac{precision \cdot recall}{precision + recall} \tag{1}$$

Fig. 5 Six-month data prediction using FRFA

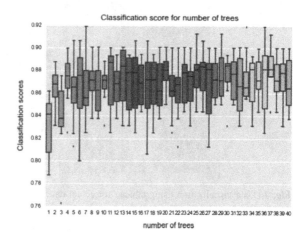

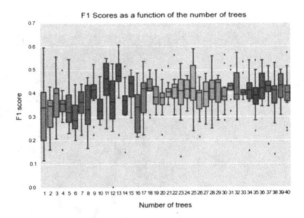

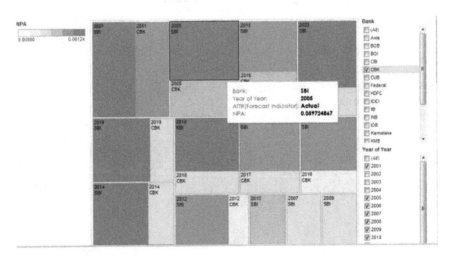

Fig. 6 One-year data prediction using FRFA

Figures 5 and 6 clearly show that the proposed feature-based random forest algorithm is able to achieve classification accuracy to a maximum of 0.89 which is quite high when compared to other methods that aim to predict NPA. Figures 7 and 8 illustrate the prediction of NPA using data visualization. The visualization is not only done for the actual data but also for the estimated data. Hence, the proposed system is not only able to achieve higher classification accuracy but also visualizes the data so as to facilitate understanding of data to the bankers in a simplified manner.

Fig. 7 Data visualization using tableau for actual data

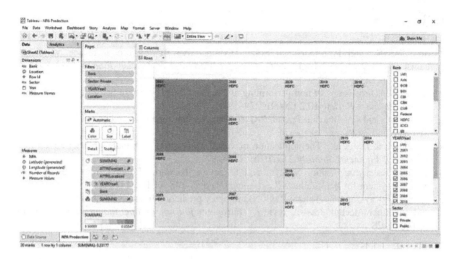

Fig. 8 Data visualization using tableau for estimated data

8 Conclusion

NPAs reflect the overall performance of the banks. The Indian banking sector faced a serious problem of NPAs. A high level of NPAs suggests high probability of a large number of credit defaults that affect the profitability and liquidity of banks. The extent of NPAs has comparatively higher in public sectors banks. To improve the efficiency and profitability, the NPAs have to be scheduled. Various steps have been taken by the government to reduce the NPAs. It is highly impossible to have zero percentage NPAs. With the influence of data analytics on the bank data, it is possible to predict the occurrence of NPA. In this paper, a system to predict and visualize NPA was proposed. A dedicated algorithm to handle NPA-related data, feature-based random forest algorithm is proposed. The proposed algorithm classifies the features considered for the NPA prediction and creates pattern based on those features. The main advantage of this algorithm is that the features can be varied based on the type of the bank considered. The proposed system is executed using the data collected from 10 public and private sector-based banks in India with nearly 15 years of data. The proposed algorithm was able to achieve a maximum of 0.89 as the classification accuracy which is quite high for NPA data prediction. The visualization of the prediction results using tableau will be a boon for the bankers and can be a ready to implement solution for the bankers to forecast NPA occurrence.

References

1. Siraj, K. K., and P. Sudarsanan Pillai. "Comparative study on performance of Islamic banks and conventional banks in GCC region." *Journal of Applied Finance and Banking* 2.3 (2012): 123.
2. Ramu, N. "Dimensions of non-performing assets in urban cooperative banks in Tamil Nadu." *Global Business Review* 10.2 (2009): 279–297.
3. Veena, D., and GV Bhavani Prasad. "Asset Quality Management in Indian Banks-A Study of SBI & ICICI." (2014).
4. Flood, Mark D., et al. "The application of visual analytics to financial stability monitoring." *Journal of Financial Stability* 27 (2016): 180–197.
5. Tanaka, Katsuyuki, Takuji Kinkyo, and Shigeyuki Hamori. "Random forests-based early warning system for bank failures." *Economics Letters* 148 (2016): 118–121.
6. Kumar, P. Ravi, and Vadlamani Ravi. "Bankruptcy prediction in banks and firms via statistical and intelligent techniques—A review." *European journal of operational research* 180.1 (2007): 1–28.

Discovering Significant Performing Variables of Athlete Students Through Data Mining Techniques

Parag Bhalchandra, Aniket Muley, Rahul Sarode,
Sinku Kumar Singh, Mahesh Joshi and Pawan Wasnik

Abstract Performance analysis of student-athletes has been a concern of many research studies. A number of factors including social, emotional, financial conditions are found to have adverse effect on academics and sport performances. Similarly, the academic stress and sports performance have been associated with various factors belonging to personality attributes, cognitive competencies, concentration level, socioeconomic background, locality, etc. However, these were hidden and no attempts were made to discover them. In the underlined research work, these aspects were discovered using data mining techniques. We have devised out our own dataset for the work from actual field data. Principal component analysis was implemented in SPSS platform for finding significant factors in our study.

Keywords Data mining · Stress patterns · Behavior patterns
Stress performance analysis

R. Sarode · S. K. Singh · M. Joshi
School of Educational Sciences, S.R.T.M. University, Nanded 431606, MS, India
e-mail: rahulsarode243@gmail.com

S. K. Singh
e-mail: drsinkukumarsingh@gmail.com

M. Joshi
e-mail: maheshmj25@gmail.com

A. Muley (✉)
School of Mathematical Sciences, S.R.T.M. University, Nanded 431606, MS, India
e-mail: aniket.muley@gmail.com

P. Bhalchandra (✉) · P. Wasnik
School of Computational Sciences, S.R.T.M. University, Nanded 431606, MS, India
e-mail: srtmun.parag@gmail.com

P. Wasnik
e-mail: pawan_wasnik@yahoo.com

© Springer Nature Singapore Pte Ltd. 2018
P. K. Pattnaik et al. (eds.), *Progress in Computing, Analytics and Networking*,
Advances in Intelligent Systems and Computing 710,
https://doi.org/10.1007/978-981-10-7871-2_59

1   Introduction

In recent years, there has been a tremendous scope for data mining techniques as it gives us abilities to discover hidden data from large datasets. Data mining helps us to look for association between variables and pattern matching in large data which otherwise is invisible to naked eye [1, 2]. The data mining application needs a data warehouse or a large dataset and typical data mining algorithms. Data mining is operative in many fields, viz., business management, sales analysis, customer prediction, scientific analysis; it has tremendous scope for educational data also. Nowadays, due to computerizations, ICT technology, Web portals, and the educational institutes are equipped with digital data. Such large digital data, accumulated over the years, resulted in educational data warehouse. These warehouses can be explored with data mining approaches, called Educational Data Mining (EDM) or Academic Analytics. The discovered association between variables or patterns through EDM can be used for proper resource management of academia and student-centric activities [3, 4].

The key objective of this study is to set up educational mining applications to collected datasets. The lesser research objective is to inspect association of variables related to physical fitness of students. A student's dataset was created with actual physical tests on grounds and using standard questionnaire method [2]. The secondary research objective, as stated above, comes in consideration mainly because the physical fitness and general health of student-athletes have been more and more alarming in recent days. The students are under significant training stress which can cause subjective stress and influence health outcomes. Student-athletes experience elevated stress at unsurprising level due to number of personal, financial, and managerial factors. Some of these factors have been discovered before [5]. However, other similar factors and their association with previously discovered factors are still hidden. This case is very promising for data mining applications. Today, college students have declined physical activities due to number of factors. College sports students have to perform academic assignments as well as physical activities demanding large part of their mental, physical energy. This creates imbalance between academics and sports performance which resulted in academic stress among student players. Academic has been studied widely as an important predictor of health, physical fitness, and performance of both player and non-player students. Stress is manifested as an alarm for physical fitness. It is in plural forms like unease, dejection, unwillingness, and different forms of negative thoughts. It is common phenomenon in student life which may affect his occupational life ahead.

On this backdrop of discussions, it is very necessary to examine associations among the research discovered variables with the stress and performance. Since these associations are invisible, we need to implement data mining algorithms for their discovery. Three schools of our university took this as an interdisciplinary challenge. These schools have collaboratively tried to establish data mining techniques to personally devise out dataset. A student's primary dataset was collected with actual physical tests on grounds and using standard structured questionnaire method. According to Bernstein et al. [6], stress is viewed as a negative psychophysical effect of situation that affects an individual's life and daily activities. It appears to be problem in occupational activities. The situations, occurrences that cause disruption, threat to daily work or desired assignments are defined as stressors. Stress does not have uniform effect on peoples rather it varies according to age, sex, emotional maturity, cognitive ability, personality attributes, etc. Every individual may find that there are some factors which would be stressors for him/her but not for others. Up to some extent, stress would not have any effect but when a person perceives it at high degree then it would affect his/her daily activities, occupation, etc. Thus, enhancing the ability of coping with stress is very important during college life.

On this background, many researchers have identified stress as an important predictor for performance of college students in academics and sports [7]. Academic stress and sports performance have been associated with various factors belonging to personality attributes, cognitive competencies, concentration level, socioeconomic background, locality, etc. [8]. The negative impact of stress is seen as anxiety, physical, and psychological weakness. The remedies for stress management includes several techniques like time management, good study habits, social support, positive thinking, enhancing hobbies, exercise. Students perceive that to manage the time for big volume of content, difficulty level of content and pressure of achieving higher grade create stress among them [9, 10]. It has further revealed that stressors alone are not only responsible for stress but also the mechanism of person to react the stress and his perception of stress is important factor in forming stress. The reviewed literature demonstrates that the stress can go ahead to academic decline, poor relationships with peers and family members, and overall frustration with life [11, 12]. Students frequently get fatigue, uncomfortable mind, restlessness due to decreased physical fitness. Fitness in physical form is very necessary to live a quality life. Our work is relied on scientific definition of fitness with six factors [5, 13]. Association of these six factors is already analyzed in Petrie and Stoever [14], Sandler [12]. However, no evidence was found to discover hidden association between these variables. In the light of the above discussions, there is compelling interest in all investigators in determining the health-related physical fitness and general health of student-athletes. The School of Educational Sciences has Department of Physical Education which has helped us to get concise data about fitness of students. The School of Computational Sciences and Statistical Sciences helped for introduction of data mining and other logics. A brief overview of collected information is given in next section.

2 Methodology

As the purpose of this study is to determine health-related physical fitness on general mental health of students, we did some prior work before actual experiments could start. In order to devise out our own dataset, we did assessment of students using fitness tests. These tests were actually performed on the ground. All the data was personally collected from the fieldwork.

The proper enactment of dataset took six months time. Some distinguished activities in data collection are elaborated as below:

1. In all, 200 urban and 200 rural student-athletes participated in the study and their age ranged between 18 and 28 years. This is taken as targeted population.
2. Personally tailored dataset for data mining purpose. The data source was primary. The data was collected through respondents in the form of physical fitness test and questionnaires during the intercollegiate games/sport event under the jurisdiction of Swami Ramanand Teerth Marathwada University, Nanded, MS, India.
3. There were considerations related to the sampling method and sample size. The purposive sampling method and nonrandom method of sampling were undertaken. The sample size was set to 200 for urban and rural. The sample is also categorized in biological maturity of student-athletes in two age groups including 18–22 years and 23–28 years. The collected data also included demographic information about age, height, weight, and rural or urban residential information.
4. For proper scientific analysis, the inclusion criteria were set as,

   a. An informed consent was taken from the student.
   b. Age group was fixed as 18–28 years.
   c. Locality was set as urban or rural depending upon post-Graduation College's location.
   d. During the time of study, the student was not part of any health treatment.
   e. No dependency on drugs, alcohol, and cigarette smoking during the experimental period.

5. Similarly, the exclusion criteria were decided to be,

   a. Should not have on the go physical illness or injuries within 2 weeks of study as well as should not have any chronic disease like cardiac, respiratory.
   b. Non-consent given students were ignored.

6. The assessment of physical fitness tests was done through the following means [6, 12, 14].

   a. Flexibility was assessed using the sit and reach test using *flexometer* foot stop.
   b. Cardiovascular strengths were measured using the *nine (9)-minute run test.*
   c. The *hand grip dynamometer* was used for measuring hand grip strength.

7. The General Health Questionnaire (GHQ-12) [6, 12, 14] was used to determine mental health. Responses were recorded using four-point *Likert scale* (0, 1, 2, 3). The correlation between inventories was determined using Pearson's product moment coefficients [1, 2].
8. After all the data collection, it was reviewed for three times to eliminate errors and unexpected readings.

3 Results and Observations

The SPSS 22.0v software's [2] descriptive statistical tool was used for all studied variables. Initially, we have performed chi-square test to see the significance of physical fitness of students with their habits, to test the significance of students with their age, and to test the independent of age from performance [7]. In this study, while computing exercising habits of student-athletes in terms of performing and non-performing, as well as rural and urban resident aspects, it is found that there is no significant difference in such point of view. It clearly shows that athlete's awareness about exercise is independent of location. Further, questionnaire was tested by SPSS 22.0v software and factor analysis is performed through Kaiser-Mayer-Olkain measure.

Figure 1 shows age group-wise frequency distribution of the athletes. Table 1 shows the significant difference among the rural and urban student-athletes with their types of exercises. Table 2 shows the significant difference about the frustration level of student-athletes in rural and urban student-athletes. It is also observed that rural resident student-athletes are found to be more frustrated than urban living student-athletes. It may be mainly due to the lack of awareness,

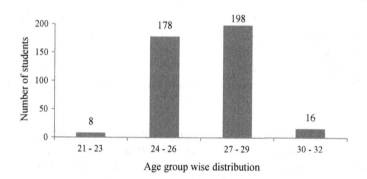

Fig. 1 Age group-wise frequency distribution of the athletes

Table 1 Locality versus exercise type chi-square tests

	Value	df	Asymp. sig. (two-sided)
Pearson chi-square	121.379[a]	20	0.000
Likelihood ratio	147.863	20	0.000
N of valid cases	400		

NB [a]20 cells (47.6%) have expected count less than 5. The minimum expected count is 0.50

Table 2 Locality versus frustrations chi-square tests

	Value	df	Asymp. sig. (2-sided)
Pearson chi-square	96.545[a]	16	0.000
Likelihood ratio	119.805	16	0.000
N of valid cases	400		

NB [a]6 cells (17.6%) have expected count less than 5. The minimum expected count is 1.00

Table 3 Locality versus conflicts chi-square tests

	Value	df	Asymp. sig. (2-sided)
Pearson chi-square	96.545[a]	16	0.000
Likelihood ratio	119.805	16	0.000
N of valid cases	400		

NB [a]6 cells (17.6%) have expected count less than 5. The minimum expected count is 1.00

Table 4 Locality versus pressures chi-square tests

	Value	df	Asymp. sig. (2-sided)
Pearson chi-square	31.752[a]	11	0.001
Likelihood ratio	34.583	11	0.000
N of valid cases	400		

NB [a]6 cells (25.0%) have expected count less than 5. The minimum expected count is 0.50

unavailability of advanced facilities, equipments, advanced technology, healthy food, and financial support. Table 3 shows significance difference among conflicts of rural and urban student-athletes. Further, it is observed that urban resident student-athletes are having conflict of interests. Table 4 represents the significant difference among pressure on rural and urban student-athletes. Through descriptive statistical tool it is also found that the rural background student-athletes are under more pressure than urban resident student-athletes. It may be due to unavailability of facilities and unawareness as compared to urban student-athletes.

From Table 5, it is observed that changes among rural and urban student-athletes are significant. These changes are found in urban resident student's more than rural student-athletes. From Table 6, it is observed that there is significance among different age group student-athletes with their pressure sustaining capacity of student-athletes. Based on cross-tabulation of our dataset it is observed that pressure sustaining student-athletes of 27–29 age group is found to be more as compared to other age group student-athletes.

Table 5 Locality versus changes chi-square tests

	Value	df	Asymp. Sig. (2-sided)
Pearson chi-square	35.968[a]	10	0.000
Likelihood ratio	43.216	10	0.000
N of valid cases	400		

NB [a]8 cells (36.4%) have expected count less than 5. The minimum expected count is 1.50

Table 6 Age group versus pressures chi-square tests

	Value	df	Asymp. Sig. (2-sided)
Pearson chi-square	58.487[a]	33	0.004
Likelihood ratio	45.672	33	0.070
Linear-by-linear association	0.382	1	0.537
N of valid cases	400		

NB [a]30 cells (62.5%) have expected count less than 5. The minimum expected count is 0.02

Table 7 represents total variation of 61.66% explained by the principal component analysis (PCA) performed for athlete students. Here, six-factor solution suggested by eigenvalues greater than one criterion explained 61.66% of the variance in the data. After being varimax rotated to obtain a simple structure, the six-factor solution gave a clear idea about the factor structure. The loading factors are greater than 0.50 was considered significant. It is observed that larger the absolute size of the factor loading, the more important the loading in factor matrix. When the original 12 items were analyzed by the PCA with varimax rotation, a six factor emerged. Table 8 represents the rotated component matrix for six factors. In the first factor, it is observed that physiological and behavioral aspects of the students are significant. The second factor explores significance of the parameters about conflicts and living arrangements of the students. The third factor suggests that self-imposed and frustration parameters are found to be significant. Further, it has been identified that changes, exercise timing, and age of the students are significant parameters in the fourth to sixth factors, respectively.

Below Fig. 2 represents scree plot from which we can easily identify a number of useful factors, wherein a sharp break in sizes of eigenvalues which results in a change in the slope of the plot. This suggests that a six-component solution could be the right choice which includes the total variance of 61.66%; about 33.23% of the total variance is represented in the first three loading factors. These loading factors are shown in Fig. 3.

Table 7 Total variance explained: extraction method: principal component analysis

Component	Initial eigenvalues			Extraction sums of squared loadings			Rotation sums of squared loadings		
	Total	% of variance	Cumulative (%)	Total	% of variance	Cumulative (%)	Total	% of variance	Cumulative (%)
Age	1.547	12.888	12.888	1.547	12.888	12.888	1.458	12.148	12.148
Living_arrangement	1.387	11.559	24.447	1.387	11.559	24.447	1.340	11.164	23.312
Exercise_time	1.277	10.641	35.088	1.277	10.641	35.088	1.191	9.925	33.237
No._of_cig_per_day	1.118	9.317	44.405	1.118	9.317	44.405	1.187	9.893	43.130
Frustrations	1.065	8.876	53.281	1.065	8.876	53.281	1.156	9.637	52.768
Conflicts	1.006	8.380	61.661	1.006	8.380	61.661	1.067	8.894	61.661
Pressures	0.964	8.036	69.697						
Changes	0.903	7.523	77.220						
Self_imposed	0.876	7.299	84.519						
Physiological	0.711	5.926	90.445						
Emotional	0.656	5.470	95.915						
Behavioral	0.490	4.085	100.000						

Table 8 Rotated component matrix

	Component					
	1	2	3	4	5	6
Age	−0.046	−0.019	0.026	−0.074	−0.012	0.825
Living_arrangement	0.105	0.718	−0.291	−0.129	0.115	0.020
Exercise_time	0.080	−0.025	−0.045	0.091	0.701	0.307
No._of_cigararte_per_day	−0.119	0.145	0.230	−0.332	0.061	0.187
Frustrations	−0.031	−0.230	0.590	−0.271	−0.080	−0.265
Conflicts	−0.059	0.829	0.191	0.032	−0.035	−0.032
Pressures	0.025	−0.097	−0.014	0.071	−0.768	0.303
Changes	0.041	−0.005	0.147	0.845	0.031	0.035
Self_imposed	0.034	0.079	0.754	0.168	0.016	0.156
Physiological	0.763	0.183	−0.140	0.149	−0.104	−0.154
Emotional	−0.549	−0.004	−0.236	0.448	0.092	−0.213
Behavioral	0.729	−0.116	0.026	0.044	0.176	0.002

Fig. 2 Scree plot

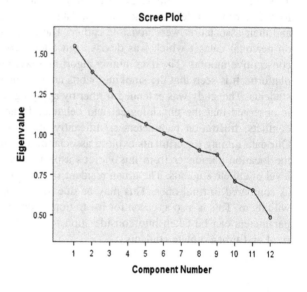

Fig. 3 Component loadings
plot

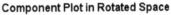

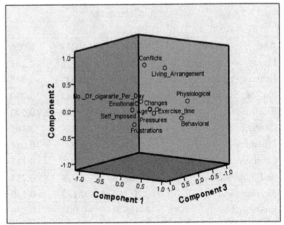

4 Conclusion

This study had given emphases on the most influencing parameters affecting performance of the athlete students through data mining techniques. These parameters and their association were invisible earlier. The experimentations were carried out on personal dataset which was devised out after recording field activities for six consecutive months. The data mining algorithms were implemented through SPSS platform. It is seen that the smoking habits are significant among the urban athlete students. The study was extended further by applying rotated factor analysis, and it is observed that the physiological and behavioral variables, living arrangements, conflicts, frustration parameters significantly affect the performance of students. Our data mining experiments explore association of stress level with age. Further, the location parameter from this various aspects is observed to affect confidence level of athlete students. The urban resident students are found to be more attentive as compared to rural ones. This may be due to availability of advanced amenities with them. This is also a reason for frustration among rural athletes. In future, these parameters can be taken into consideration for computing the performance of the rural and urban athlete students.

References

1. Margaret Dunham, Data Mining: Introductory and Advanced Topics, Pearson publications, 2002.
2. Han, J. and Kamber, M., (2006) "Data Mining: Concepts and Techniques", 2nd edition.
3. Jim Gray. Behrouz. et al., (2003) Predicting Student Performance: An Application of Data Mining Methods With The Educational Web-Based System Lon-CAPA © 2003 IEEE, Boulder.

4. Abouserie, R. (1994). Sources and levels of stress in relation to locus of control and selfesteem in university students. Educational Psychology, 14(3), 323–330.
5. Salmon, J., Owen, N., Crawford, D., Bauman, A., Sallis, J.F. (2003) Physical activity and sedentary behavior A population-based study of barriers, enjoyment and performance. Health Psychology.
6. Campbell R. L. & Jarvis G. K. (1992). Perceived level of stress among university undergraduate students in Edmonton, Canada. Perceptual and Motor Skills, 75, 552–554.
7. Parag Bhalchandra, Aniket Muley, et al, Prognostication of Student's Performance: An Hierarchical Clustering Strategy for Educational Dataset, Computational Intelligence in Data Mining—Volume 1, Advances in Intelligent Systems and Computing book series (AISC, volume 410), pp 149–157.
8. Petrie, Trent A.; Stoever, Shawn. (1997) Journal of College Student Development, v38.
9. Bernstein, D.A.; Penner, L.A.; Stewart, A.C. and Roy, E.J. (2008) Psychology (8th edition). Houghton Mifflin Company Boston New York.
10. Bruinings, A.L., Van Den Berg-Emons, H.J., Buffart, L.M., Van Den Heijden-Maessen, H.C., Roebroeck, M.E., Stam, H.J. (2007). Energy cost and physical strain of daily activities in adolescents and young adults with myelomeningocele. Dev. Med. Child. Neurol., 49: 672–677.
11. Fairbrother, K. & Warn, J. (2003). Workplace Dimensions, Stress and Job Satisfaction. Journal of Managerial Psychology, 18(1): 8–21.
12. Yitzhak, W. (2000). Physical activity and health. 6th Sport Sciences Congress, 3–5, Ankara.
13. Patil, R.B., Doddamani, B.R., Milind, Bhutkar., S.M., Awanti. A. (2012) Comparative Study of Physical Fitness among Rural Farmers…, AJMS Al Ameen J Med Sci 5(1).
14. Sandler, M. E. (2000). Career decision-making self-efficacy, perceived stress, and an integrated model of student performance: A structural model of finances, attitudes, behavior, and career development. Research in Higher Education 41(5): 537–578.

Newspaper Selection Analysis Technique

Gourab Das and S. K. Setua

Abstract Print agencies are fighting for their existence in current data-driven and digital era. Everyday they are coming up with some new approaches to attract the current generation. Going with the flow, they are now seeking the help of the data scientist to innovate new ideas by analyzing the future business. Standing on this approach, this paper predicts the reading habits of the common people. To create a good analogy on the dataset, we have segregated our thoughts into data preprocessing and machine learning. Training a machine learning model using raw data alone can never produce good solution in most of the cases. Efficient preprocessing techniques need to be embedded in order to have better result. It is utmost important to note that not all the machine learning models are quite useful. To get better accuracy in this classification problem, we have trained the dataset using ensemble classifier like gradient boosting and extreme gradient boosting. After training both the classifiers with train dataset, we have predicted the accuracy on unseen test dataset. Main aim of this paper is to show that these machine learning models generalize the test dataset quite well and do not overfit on the train dataset.

Keywords Data analysis · Newspaper · Preprocessing · Machine learning
Gradient boosting · Extreme gradient boosting

1 Introduction

Print industries are living dangerously with the advent of television, Internet, and social media. Their existence is getting threatened by the lack of reading habit of young generation in the current digital age. Print agencies are engaging in an intensive competition among themselves to capture this shallow market. So, they

G. Das (✉) · S. K. Setua
University of Calcutta, Kolkata, India
e-mail: gourab4gd@gmail.com

S. K. Setua
e-mail: sksetua@gmail.com

© Springer Nature Singapore Pte Ltd. 2018
P. K. Pattnaik et al. (eds.), *Progress in Computing, Analytics and Networking,*
Advances in Intelligent Systems and Computing 710,
https://doi.org/10.1007/978-981-10-7871-2_60

are looking for new ideas to earn high revenue. The profit of the print industry is coming from the advertisement and circulation of the newspapers and magazines. Simultaneously, they are also following the cost-cutting avenue. To capture maximum reader, the print media is now adopting various business ideas like creation of reports containing high values, excellence printing quality with lower cost, forming multimedia platform, proper selection of advertisement to capture the current generation. Most recently, they are seeking the help of data scientist such that they can take decisions to form a good business model after analyzing the data scientifically.

Currently, we have the abundance of data on various application domains which is also known as big data in the world of information and technology. Analysis of this huge data is gradually becoming an important aspect in corporate parlance. Data analysis technique can be segregated into two parts: data preprocessing and machine learning. Generally, machine learning model can never be trained directly with the raw dataset. Attributes related to the dataset which is also known as feature have the maximum importance. Data preprocessing technique performs various pre-training operations on those features. It is quite natural that machine requires numerical data such that they can be processed by well-known learning technique but it contains several non-numerical attribute values which is necessary to be substituted by suitable numerical value before being used for training purpose. Besides, many values of the datasets may not be available in both training and test dataset. These empty cells are required to be filled with some kind of numerical data such that maximum information can be extracted. Feature selection, feature extraction, and feature engineering are three of the most important techniques in data preprocessing. Feature selection techniques allow us to select the subset of important features among all. Another well-known technique, feature extraction combines all the features and generates a new set of features. Feature engineering is one of the most important aspects of the domain of data science. It is a technique to create additional features inferring from existing features such that prospect of learning can be enhanced.

After all requisite preprocessing, appropriate machine learning model is utilized for training with the data. In this paper, we have performed a supervised learning task where the models are trained on a training dataset in the presence of a variable which is known as target variable. After training the model, it is necessary to predict the values of target variable on the unseen test dataset. Our problem is modeled on a "Newspaper Reading" dataset. It is a binary classification problem where our aim is to correctly predict whether a person would read a particular newspaper or not. Scientific analysis and learning techniques need to be embedded to extract as much information as possible from the dataset such that accuracy in predicting unknown test dataset can be maximized. Ensemble learning algorithms like gradient boosting [1] and extreme gradient boosting [2] have been utilized in this paper. Both the models are evaluated on the basis of accuracy metrics of unseen test dataset.

Structure of the paper is as follows: Sect. 2 mentions brief description of the various data preprocessing technique. Ensemble machine learning techniques especially gradient boosting and extreme gradient boosting are specified in Sect. 3. Section 4 gives the detailing of the dataset we have worked on. Section 5 consists of all the experimental results. Finally, we conclude the paper with Sect. 6.

2 Data Preprocessing

Generally, machine learning model can never be trained directly with the raw dataset. These datasets consist plenty of non-numerical and categorical values, and it is essential to replace categorical values by suitable numerical data before being used for training. Preprocessing techniques must be embedded before the actual implementation of machine learning or deep learning. There are no hard and fast rules for preprocessing rather it is completely dependent on the application domain. Some of the general methods of doing these are given below.

- Substitution of categorical and non-numerical data with suitable numerical values.
- Filling the empty cells with some numbers.
- Feature selection.
- Feature extraction.
- Feature engineering.

2.1 Substitution of Categorical and Non-Numerical Data with Suitable Numerical Value

Many attributes of a dataset are provided in forms of non-numerical and categorical values. It is necessary to replace those values with suitable number before applying the learning algorithms. Various policies can be implemented and are described as follows:

i. Replacing each category by some sequential number 0, 1, 2, up to $N-1$, where N is the number of distinct categories assigned to a particular attribute.
ii. Substituting each category with some correlation value calculated from the target variable and the corresponding categorical variable.

There are various ways to replace the categorical and non-numerical data. But they are dataset dependent. All techniques are not quite useful to every dataset. Before applying a particular technique, the dataset should be analyzed rigorously.

2.2 Filling the Empty Cells with Some Numbers

Some attribute values of the dataset to be used for training purpose by the machine learning algorithm may not be available in most of the cases. It is essential to fix the problem by replacing these null values with some constant values. Selection of these constants is quite arbitrary; we may select some random number like 0.01, −999, 999 or define some fixed value after finding some kind of correlations between the null attribute values and the target variable. Sometimes, it is also useful to remove those features where most of the cells are empty.

2.3 Feature Selection

Feature selection technique guides us to select the most important features among all which has maximum impact on the target variables. Non-important features sometimes negatively affect the machine learning model. It reduces the accuracy of the classification problems and increases the mean-square error of the regression problem. Bad features overfit on training dataset and fail to generalize on the unseen test dataset. Scikit learn [3, 4] provides many inbuilt methods to deal with such problems and are described as follows:

   i. Select K Best feature selection model assigns score to the K best features in the dataset based on their importance.
   ii. Recursive feature elimination (RFE) technique removes a feature one by one in every iteration and trains the model with remaining features of the dataset recursively.
   iii. Stability selection [5] is based on subsampling in combination with selection algorithms. Scikit learn implements it using randomized lasso [6] and randomized logistic regression.
   iv. In Scikit learn, every regression and classification algorithm has an attribute known as "feature_importances_" which assigns scores to every features based on their importance after learning.

2.4 Feature Extraction

Feature extraction is a useful technique to build derived set of features by mapping the original one into new and reduced feature base. It reduces the complexity of the feature base and helps to train the model much quicker than using original feature set. If proper methods are followed, desired result can be extracted from this technique. Some of the feature extraction techniques are principal component analysis (PCA), supervised PCA, Kernel PCA, Isomap [7], locally linear embedding [8], t-SNE [9] etc.

2.5 Feature Engineering

Among the five techniques mentioned above to implement data preprocessing, Feature engineering has the maximum impact to adjudge the goodness of the model. Creation of additional features inferring from existing features is known as feature engineering. Real life problems may be specified using single dataset or spanned across multiple datasets. To enhance the accuracy of the learning model, it is utmost important to find the correlations among the various features in the datasets. Single dataset may be described using explicit or visible set of features and implicit or invisible set of features. Sometimes, it may be useful to discover and augment some implicit features by finding some relationship with the target variable. In multiple dataset problems using the same technique, we can generate some features by exploring the pattern between the external attribute values and the target variable. Time series analysis is an important tool in feature engineering process. The biggest down fall of this technique is that it varies across problem domain. Dataset belonging to different domain has different way to engineer the features. Domain knowledge always plays a key role in defining and discovering the impact factors of the hidden features.

3 Machine Learning Methods

Supervised machine learning methods are segregated into regression and classification problem. Regression problem is based on continuous target variable where we aim to predict data and to reduce the root-mean-square error with respect to values of the target variable. But, classification problem is based on discrete target variable; here, we train the model to increase the accuracy of predicting the target variable. The analysis we perform in this paper is a classification problem. In this paper, we implemented averaging or ensemble machine learning methods to solve the problem. Boosting methods are the most useful to enhance or boost the performance of ensemble model. Gradient boosting and extreme gradient boosting are the part of the boosting algorithm.

Boosting. The idea of boosting introduces the concept of weak learner. Weak learners are those whose performance is slightly better than random choice. Boosting algorithm attempts to convert the weak learner into strong learner. This conversion is made possible by ensembling or averaging all the weak learners using weighted average technique. Basic boosting algorithm can be described using following steps.

Step 1. Base learner assigns equal weight to all the sample points in the dataset.

Step 2. Higher weights are assigned to the points which have been misclassified by previous classifier and trained again by another weak learner.

Step 3. Iterate Step 2 until there is no change in accuracy in classification problem or no change in error in a regression problem.

Some of the boosting algorithms are Adaboost (Adaptive Boosting), gradient boosting, and extreme gradient boosting. We have considered the later two for this paper.

Gradient Boosting [1]. Decision tree is utilized as weak learner. Sequentially, many weak learners are added one by one to minimize the cost function using very well-known optimization technique called gradient descent. Gradient boosting creates a strong learner which is maximally correlated with negative gradient of cost function.

Extreme Gradient Boosting (XGBoost) [2]. Extreme gradient boosting is the regularized version of gradient boosting. It has both linear and tree learning model. Its computation speed is quite high and has great bias-variance trade-off. XGBoost objective function consists of both cost function and regularized function, and it is specified in (1) [10]:

$$\text{Obj}(\theta, f) = L(\theta) + \Omega(f). \tag{1}$$

Here, L is the loss function, Ω is the regularization term, θ are the parameters to be learned, and f is the learnable function containing the structure of tree and leaf score. For regression problems, loss function is mean-squared-error and for classification problem it is log-loss. Regularization part is expressed in (2) [10]:

$$\Omega(f) = \gamma T + \frac{1}{2} \lambda \left(\sum_{j=1}^{T} w_j^2 \right). \tag{2}$$

where T is the number of leaves, γ is the coefficient, and w is the vector of scores on leaves.

4 Datasets

The dataset utilized in this paper is specified as a binary classification problem. Our aim is to predict the newspaper reading habits of an individual person. Multiple newspapers are circulated in a particular zone. Among those we have to predict the readability of a particular newspaper based on some appropriate machine learning model like boosting. Two datasets have been provided to train the model. Those are customer data and family data. Customer data describes the background of the individual subscriber; target variable is also mentioned in this dataset and it is sized over 100 K. Family data table details the family of the individual belongs to the first dataset. Feature engineering process in this case generates new attribute values by discovering some kind of correlations between the features in the family data and the target variables in the customer data, and it has the size around 150 K. Pertaining on this information, we have to train a model to maximize the accuracy level on unseen test set.

5 Experimental Results

In this paper, we have trained gradient boosting and extreme gradient boosting model with the newspaper reading datasets. We have divided the whole datasets into training dataset and test dataset. Both the models are trained with the training set in a way such that prediction accuracy on unseen test set can be maximized. Attributes of this dataset are described in forms of A0, A1, A2 up to A37, A38. Target variable is A10. Family data contains feature like A0, B1, B2, B3, and B4. Two datasets are related by attribute A0. As part of feature engineering, we have created three new features A40, A41, and A42 in customer data to embed the information hidden in family data. Some of the features of both the datasets are filled with null values; we have replaced those null contents with −999. Visualization of the relationship between various attributes of the dataset with the target variables A10 helps us to extract the set of important features. Figure 1 plots the heat map to represent the correlation among various attributes.

From the Fig. 1, we can see that the features A28 and A37 are represented by a line which specifies that there exists no correlation of A28 and A37 with all other attributes.

Amount of correlationship for rest of the attributes with target variable A10 is described by bar chart in Fig. 2. After performing the preprocessing steps, we have used these data for training of gradient boosting and extreme gradient boosting classifier. We split this dataset into 60% training dataset and 40% test dataset and shuffle it randomly. Performance of these 2 models is determined by the accuracy on the unknown test dataset.

5.1 Gradient Boosting Classifier

We have trained the model using various parameters but the variances of accuracy on unknown test dataset are large for various models. Using Scikit-learn GridSearchCV, we have identified the best model with the highest accuracy.

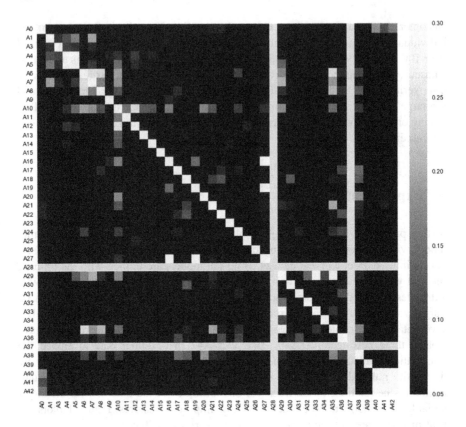

Fig. 1 Correlations among various features

The parameters for the above model are learning rate = 0.21, depth = 6, and number of estimate = 400. After training, the model accuracy is 92.75% for the target variable A10 on the training dataset. When we have tested this gradient boosting classifier on unseen test dataset, it has got the accuracy 88.3%. So, it can be specified that model does not overfit on training dataset and generalizes the test dataset fairly. We have plotted the important features in Fig. 3.

5.2 Extreme Gradient Boosting Classifier

Our second model is extreme gradient boosting classifier. Various parameters settings generate different accuracies on the unknown test dataset. GridSearchCV is utilized again to extract the best model. The parameters setting for the best model we have obtained are learning rate = 0.21, depth = 6, number of estimate = 600, and L2 regularization parameter = 0.3. Accuracy of the model on the training

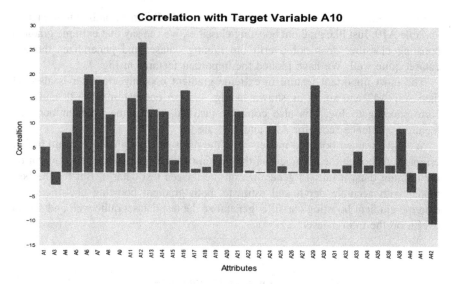

Fig. 2 Correlation with target variable A10 with all other attributes

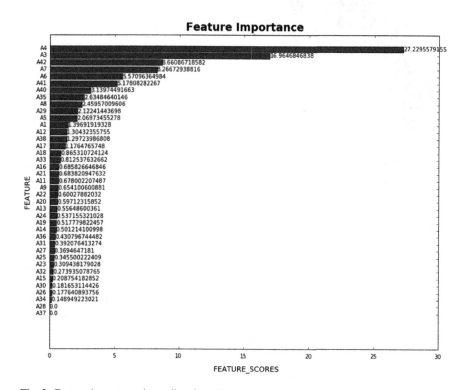

Fig. 3 Feature importance in gradient boosting

dataset is 93.2%, and on unseen test dataset, it is 88.28% corresponding to the target variable A10. Just like gradient boosting classifier, we can say that extreme gradient boosting classifier does not overfit on training dataset and generalizes the test dataset quite well. We have plotted the important features in Fig. 4.

The most important feature in extreme gradient boosting classifier is also A4 then A3, A42 and so on as shown in Fig. 4. Zero correlation of A28 and A37 corresponding to Fig. 1 is also correctly justified as extreme gradient boosting feature importance score for A28 and A37 are 0.

We have trained both the models with the datasets for higher depth and higher estimate. Although the accuracy on the training dataset increases due to overfit on the training data, it fails to generalize on the unseen test dataset. But for the best model with accurate depth and estimate, both gradient boosting classifiers and extreme gradient boosting classifier generalize the test dataset quite well and do not overfit on the train dataset.

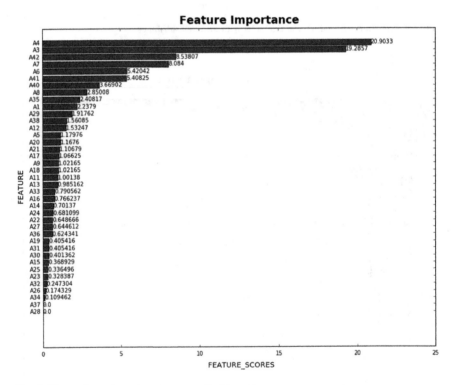

Fig. 4 Feature importance in extreme gradient boosting

6 Conclusion

Data preprocessing techniques are the utmost important thing before training a learning model. After generating three features in the customer data inferring from the family data, we have managed to increase the accuracy 3 and 4% at one lap. But there exists no state-of-the-art technique to preprocess data. This data preprocessing technique is completely dataset and application dependent. So understanding the dataset is quite important to preprocess data in terms of feature engineering, feature selection, and in many ways. In machine learning aspect, there is a scope of improvement in terms of model selection, parameter selection, and so on. In this paper, we have classified the accuracy of reading habits of particular newspaper using gradient boosting and extreme gradient boosting. From the results, it has been shown both the models generalize the test dataset very well and do not overfit on the training dataset.

References

1. Friedman, J.H.: Greedy Function Approximation: A Gradient Boosting Machine. The Annals of Statistics. 2001; 29:1189–1232
2. Chen, T., Guestrin, C.: XGBoost: A scalable Tree Boosting System. arXiv preprint arXiv:1603.02754v3, 2016
3. Pedregosa, F., Varoquaux, G., Gramfort, A., Michel, V., Thirion, B., Grisel, O., Blondel, M., Prettenhofer, P., Weiss, R., Dubourg, V., Vanderplas, J., Passos, A., Cournapeau, D., Brucher, M., Perrot, M., Duchesnay., E.: Scikit-learn: Machine learning in Python. JMLR, 12:2825–2830, 2011
4. Scikit Learn Framework http://scikit-learn.org/stable/
5. Meinshausen, N., Buhlmann, P.: Stability selection. Journal of the Royal Statistical Society Series B, 72 (2010), 417–473
6. Wang, S., Nan, B., Rosset, S., Zhu, J.: Random Lasso. arXiv preprint arXiv:1104.3398v1, 2011
7. Tenenbaum, J.B., de Silva, V., Langford, J.C. (2000): A global geometric framework for nonlinear dimensionality reduction. Science, 290, 2319–2323
8. Saul, L. K., Roweis, S. T. (2000): An introduction to locally linear embedding. Science, 290, 2323–2326
9. Van Dar Maaten, L., Hinton, G.: Visualizing Data Using t-SNE. JMLR, 1 (2008) 1–48
10. XGBOOST: http://xgboost.readthedocs.io/en/latest/model.html

Variants of Wormhole Attacks and Their Impact in Wireless Sensor Networks

Manish Patel, Akshai Aggarwal and Nirbhay Chaubey

Abstract In wireless sensor networks, nodes have limited battery, transmission power, and processing capabilities. For routing the packets, cooperation between nodes is needed. Wireless sensor network is vulnerable to wide range of attacks. A more dangerous attack is wormhole attack in which packets are received in one area and replied in another area of the network. For on-demand routing protocols, route discovery mechanism is affected by wormhole attack and routing is disturbed. In this paper, we have presented variants of wormhole attacks and their impact in wireless sensor networks.

Keywords Wireless sensor network · Attack · Vulnerable · Wormhole

1 Introduction

Wireless sensor networks consist of densely deployed sensor nodes. Sensor nodes are deployed in an area known as sensor fields. A sensor node consists of analog-to-digital converter, battery, processor, and radio transceiver [1, 2]. Sensor nodes are remotely managed. These nodes are vulnerable to many types of security attacks [3].

In wormhole attack, one malicious node records packets from one area of the network and through high-speed out-of-band channel tunnels to another malicious node in different part of the network [4, 5]. In on-demand routing protocols, route request packet is captured by one malicious node and tunnel to another malicious node which is far away located and replied to the destination. The destination node

M. Patel (✉) · A. Aggarwal · N. Chaubey
Gujarat Technological University, Ahmedabad, Gujarat, India
e-mail: it43manish@gmail.com

A. Aggarwal
e-mail: akshai.aggarwal@gmail.com

N. Chaubey
e-mail: nirbhay@ieee.org

© Springer Nature Singapore Pte Ltd. 2018
P. K. Pattnaik et al. (eds.), *Progress in Computing, Analytics and Networking*,
Advances in Intelligent Systems and Computing 710,
https://doi.org/10.1007/978-981-10-7871-2_61

believes that source node is just one or two hops away but actually it is many hops away. The destination node sends route reply packet, and a route is created between source and destination through malicious nodes. Wormhole attacks and damages many ad hoc routing protocols such as ad hoc on-demand distance vector routing (AODV) and dynamic source routing (DSR) [6]. To launch the attack, attacker does not need to know protocol used or services offered in the network or any secret material in the sensor node. Detecting wormhole attack is very hard, and it is a gateway to many more attacks such as sinkhole, denial of service, jellyfish, black hole, selective forwarding, Sybil.

Section 2 presents description of wormhole attack. In Sect. 3, we have described variants of wormhole attacks. Simulation result and analysis are presented in Sect. 4. Finally, conclusion is presented in Sect. 5.

2   Description of Wormhole Attack

As shown in Fig. 1, two malicious nodes M1 and M2 create a high-speed low-latency tunnel. M1 is located in one area of the network, and M2 is located in another area of the network. Malicious node M1 captures traffic from one area and tunnels it to another area. Due to this, the routing process is disturbed [7, 8]. Suppose W is a source node which broadcasts route request packet to establish path with node Y. The route request packet is captured by malicious node M1 and tunnel to malicious node M2. Malicious node M2 replies it to node Y. Node Y sends route reply packet to node W on the same path. After establishing the path, the data packets send by node W to node Y follow path through the tunnel. Malicious node can analyze the traffic, drop, delay, reorder, and modify the packets. Due to wormhole, many more attacks can be launched.

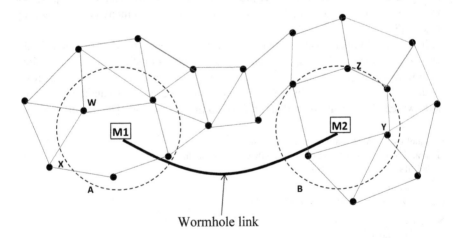

Wormhole link

Fig. 1 Wormhole attack with two malicious nodes

3 Variants of Wormhole Attack

In [9–11], authors have presented the simulation of attacks in wireless sensor network. In this section, we have discussed some of the variants of wormhole attacks.

3.1 Sinkhole-Based Wormhole Attack

In this type of attack, the goal of attacker is to attract the traffic and then selectively forward the packets. To launch this attack, two high-powered malicious nodes are needed. An attacker put one malicious node near to the destination node and another malicious node near to the source node. When the destination node sends route reply packets, it is captured by first malicious node and tunnels it to second malicious node. The tunneled RREP reaches faster to the source node compared to the normal route. Source node and all its neighbors use path to the destination through second malicious node. An attacker can selectively forward the packets while dropping the others.

3.2 Denial of Service-Based Wormhole Attack

In this type of attack, when second malicious node receives route request packet from first malicious node, it broadcasts to all its neighbors and the neighbor nodes send it to the destination. When the neighbor nodes receive the route request packet from the legitimate path, the packet will be dropped because it is a duplicate packet. The RREQ forwarded through the legitimate path cannot reach the destination. When the destination node sends route reply packet, the neighbor nodes will not have reverse route to forward the RREP packets. The route reply packet is not forwarded by the neighbor nodes of the destination.

3.3 Black hole-Based Wormhole Attack

When the source node broadcasts the RREQ packet, it is captured by malicious node and tunnels to another malicious node. Second malicious node replies it to the destination. When the destination node sends RREP packet, it is received by the source node via tunnel. In this way, path is created between source and destination via malicious nodes. When the source node sends data packets, the packets will be dropped by the malicious node. It creates a black hole attack.

In indirect black hole attack, a route reply packet is captured by the malicious node M and it is tunneled to the target node T. The target node T forwards it to the source node. The source node and all other neighbor nodes mark the target node T as the first hop neighbor. The target node T has incomplete route toward the destination. Due to this, all packets are dropped. It creates an indirect black hole attack.

3.4 Jellyfish-Based Wormhole Attack

During the route discovery process, two malicious nodes establish tunnel and all the traffic reaches to the destination via this tunnel. Malicious node can launch jellyfish attack in three different ways: (1) jellyfish attack by reordering the packets in which an attacker node reorders the data packets before the packets are forwarded, (2) jellyfish periodic dropping attack in which an attacker selectively drops the packets, and (3) jellyfish delay variance attack in which an attacker delays packets randomly.

4 Result and Analysis

We have simulated variants of wormhole attacks in NS2. We assumed that all sensor nodes are static. We have measured packet delivery ratio and throughput for two scenarios: without creating the attack and after creating the attack. Packet delivery ratio is used to measure the no. of packets delivered to the destination node to that of the packets delivered from the source node. Throughput is the no. of data packets delivered from source to the destination per unit of time. The results of sinkhole-based wormhole attack are given in Table 1, denial of service-based wormhole attack are given in Table 2, black hole-based wormhole attack are given in Table 3, and jellyfish-based wormhole attack are given in Table 4.

Table 1 Result of sinkhole-based wormhole attack

No. of nodes	Without attack PDF (%)	With attack PDF (%)	Without attack throughput (KBPS)	With attack throughput (KBPS)
60	99.70	85.14	84	72.15
80	99.76	85.90	84.75	72.90
100	99.78	86.20	85.10	73.20

Table 2 Result of denial of service-based wormhole attack

No. of nodes	Without attack PDF (%)	With attack PDF (%)	Without attack throughput (KBPS)	With attack throughput (KBPS)
60	99.70	46.10	84	57.10
80	99.76	46.85	84.75	58.05
100	99.78	47.05	85.10	58.30

Table 3 Result of black hole-based wormhole attack

No. of nodes	Without attack PDF (%)	With attack PDF (%)	Without attack throughput (KBPS)	With attack throughput (KBPS)
60	99.70	59.40	84	62.30
80	99.76	59.85	84.75	62.65
100	99.78	60.10	85.10	62.75

Table 4 Result of jellyfish-based wormhole attack

No. of nodes	Without attack PDF (%)	With attack PDF (%)	Without attack throughput (KBPS)	With attack throughput (KBPS)
60	99.70	82.10	84	70.15
80	99.76	82.70	84.75	70.60
100	99.78	83.10	85.10	70.90

5   Conclusion

To launch the wormhole attack, attacker does not need to break any cryptography mechanism. Wormhole is very dangerous for wireless sensor network as it is the gateway for many attacks. We have presented the impact of all these attacks in wireless sensor network. During the attack, packet delivery ratio and throughput decrease sharply. Impact of multiple wormhole attackers in wireless sensor network is a future research issue.

Acknowledgements   The authors are highly thankful to the Gujarat Technological University (Smt. S R Patel Engineering College, Unjha) for providing the opportunity to conduct this research work.

References

1. Y. C. Hu, A. Perrig and D. B. Johnson; "Packet leashes: a defense against wormhole attacks in wireless networks" IEEE Computer and Communications Societies, IEEE, vol. 3, pp. 1976–1986, 2003.
2. Jennifer Yick, Biswanath Mukherjee, Dipak Ghosal; "Wireless sensor network survey" International Journal of Computer and Telecommunications Networking, volume 52, Issue 12, August 2008, pp 2292–2330.

3. Padmavathi, G., Shanmugapriya, D.; "A survey of attacks, security mechanisms and challenges in wireless sensor networks" International Journal of Computer Science and Information Security (IJCSIS) 2009, 4, 117–125.
4. Ayaz Hassan Moon, N.A. Shah, Ummer Iqbal, Adil Ayub; "Simulating and Analysing Basic Security Attacks in Wireless Sensor Networks using QualNet" IEEE International Conference on Machine Intelligence Research and Advancement 2013.
5. Li Lu, Muhammad Jawad Hussain, Guoxing Luo and Zhigang Han; "Pworm: passive and Real-Time Wormhole Detection Scheme for WSNs", International Journal of Distributed Sensor networks, Volume 2015, Article ID 356382, 16 pages.
6. Muhammad Imran, Farrukh Aslam Khan, Tauseef Jamal, Muhammad Hanif Durad, "Analysis of Detection Features for Wormhole Attacks in MANETs" International Workshop on Cyber Security and Digital Investigation, Procedia Computer Science 56 (2015) Elsevier, pp 384–390.
7. Saswati Mukherjee, Matangini Chattopadhyay, Samiran Chattopadhyay, Pragma Kar; "Wormhole Detection Based on Ordinal MDS Using RTT in Wireless Sensor Network", Journal of Computer Networks and Communications, Volume 2016, Article ID 3405264, 15 pages.
8. Rupin Singh, Jatinder Singh, Ravinder Singh, "WRHT: a Hybrid Technique for Detection of Wormhole Attack in Wireless Sensor Networks", Hindawi Publishing Corporation, Mobile Information Systems, Volume 2016, Article ID 8354930, 13 pages.
9. Karlof C, Wagner D; "Secure routing in wireless sensor networks: attacks and countermeasures", Ad Hoc Networks Journal, Special Issue on Sensor Network Applications and Protocols, 2003; 113–127.
10. Alvaro Diaz, Pablo Sanchez; "Simulation of Attacks for Security in Wireless Sensor Network" Journal of Sensors 2016, 16, 1932.
11. Christiana Ioannou, Vasos Vassiliou; "The Impact of Network Layer Attacks in Wireless Sensor Networks" IEEE International Workshop on Secure Internet of Things 2016.

Optimal Choice Between Chemotherapy and Immunotherapy for Leukemia Treatment Depends on Individual Patients' Patho-physiological State

Probir Kumar Dhar, Tarun Kanti Naskar and Durjoy Majumder

Abstract Chemotherapy is the firsthand choice of any cancer therapy including leukemia. However, immunosuppression is commonly seen in leukemic patients. So for the management of leukemia, cytokine-based immunotherapy is also suggested as either a combination therapy along with the conventional chemotherapy or alone. However, therapy is applied on individual patients on the basis of evidence-based medicine, i.e., population-based statistical analysis and/or on the basis of clinicians' personal experience. Here, we propose an analytical rationality for therapeutic selection among these two options. Our simulation runs suggest that choice would be based on individual patients' patho-physiological state like immunity profile or another hematological status. Simulation runs also suggest that in some cases chemotherapy may bring detrimental effect and direct immunotherapy would be beneficial for long-term successful therapeutic outcome. Further, this model helps in the optimization of cytokine-based immunotherapy protocol.

Keywords Delay ordinary differential equation · Feedback · Optimization
Immunotherapy · Leukemia

P. K. Dhar
ECE Department, BCET, SSB Sarani, Durgapur, Burdwan 713212, West Bengal, India
e-mail: probir@rocketmail.com

P. K. Dhar · T. K. Naskar
Department of Mechanical Engineering, Jadavpur University, Kolkata 700032, India
e-mail: tknaskar@gmail.com

D. Majumder (✉)
Department of Physiology, West Bengal State University, Kolkata 700126, India
e-mail: durjoy@rocketmail.com

P. K. Dhar · T. K. Naskar · D. Majumder
Society for Systems Biology & Translational Research, 103, Block – C,
Bangur Avenue, Kolkata 700055, India

© Springer Nature Singapore Pte Ltd. 2018
P. K. Pattnaik et al. (eds.), *Progress in Computing, Analytics and Networking*,
Advances in Intelligent Systems and Computing 710,
https://doi.org/10.1007/978-981-10-7871-2_62

643

1 Introduction

Considering immunity, several models of solid tumors are available. These models were designed with competition between tumor and immunocytes which are basically the representation of predator–prey systems in ecology [1–5]. Later, host immunity and tumor interaction within tumor microenvironment are considered in model [6]. Role of antibody in the efficiency of cellular immunity is also considered in model [7].

However, very few models have considered immunotherapeutic strategy under the condition of leukemia. Considering chronic myeloid leukemia (CML), it is postulated that in application of lower dose chemotherapy, outcome will depend on individual patients' T cell population [8]. Immune-boosting mechanism may facilitate the possibility of therapeutic outcome [9]. However, further analytical work negates the therapeutic strategy of combined application of lower dose chemotherapy with G-CSF in CML [10].

So far, majority of the immunity-based leukemia models do not consider the other lineages of the hematopoietic system (like RBC and platelets) and hence ignore the effects of toxicity imposed by leukemic cells or drug-related toxicity on the normal counterpart of the hematopoietic system. These limitations have been overcome in a delay ordinary differential equation (**DODE**)-based model of leukemia [11, 12]. Inclusion of toxicity effect makes the system move toward the physiological collapse and represents immune suppression and pancytopenic feature that are commonly observed in leukemia condition [11]. Flexibility of this model offers a special feature to test the efficacy of different therapeutic strategies or their combinations like chemotherapy and/or immunotherapy (cytokine-based or adoptive immunotherapy).

Conventionally, immunotherapy is applied synergistically with chemotherapy, and in clinic, it is generally applied after the completion of chemotherapy. This is practiced with the assumption that chemotherapy reduces the tumor (leukemic) load, and thereby, immune system can overrule within the physiological system. However, drug toxicity and toxicity imposed by malignant (leukemic) cells are the realistic limitations in clinic toward the outcome of chemo-/immunotherapy application. Application of myeloablative chemotherapeutic drug simultaneously eliminates the immune population to such a lower level that application of immune-boosting agent fails to generate immune population to counter leukemic load as well as other normal (cellular) counterpart of the hematopoietic system. Through this analytical model, here we propose an analytical framework to optimize not only the patient-specific treatment selection but also the dose, duration, and time of application.

2   Modeling Methods

A DODE model was developed to test the efficacies of different therapeutic strategies, namely low-dose chemotherapy (**CHEMO**), high-dose myeloablative chemotherapy (**MYL**) along with RBC (T_{RBC}) and platelet ($T_{PLATELET}$) transfusion, and immune-boosting agent as cytokine (CYT) [11, 12]. The developed model cells with three states, i.e., normal cell (g), drug-sensitive cell (s), and dug-resistive cell (r), have been considered. Each cellular state belongs to three lineages—erythrocytic, leukocytic, and megakaryocyte lineage. According to the cell maturity level in each lineage, three types of cell, i.e., stem cell (S), precursor cell (erythroblast, $P1$; leukoblast, $P2$; megakaryoblast, $P3$); and mature cell (RBC, $B1$; WBC, $B2$, and platelet, $B3$), population are considered (Table 1). Different considered variables and their parametric values (along with their unit) that are used in model are already described in ref. [12]. Algorithmic steps for model development are represented stepwise in Fig. 1. The model is represented by the following DODE.

$$N(k) = AN(k-1) + \sum_{m=1}^{4} A_m N(k-dk_m) + RBC_{tf} T_{RBC}(k)$$
$$+ PLATELET_{tf} T_{PLATLET}(k) \tag{1}$$

where $N(k) = [N_1(k);\ N_2(k);\ \ldots;\ N_{21}(k)]$, $N(k\text{-}1) = [N_1(k-1);\ N_2(k-1);\ \ldots;\ N_{21}(k-1)]$, $N(k-dk_1) = [N_1(k-dk_1);\ N_2(k-dk_1);\ \ldots;\ N_{21}(k-dk_1)]$, $N(k-dk_2) = [N_1(k-dk_2);\ N_2(k-dk_2);\ \ldots;N_{21}(k-dk_2)]$, $N(k-dk_3) = [N_1(k-dk_3);\ N_2(k-dk_3);\ \ldots;\ N_{21}(k-dk_3)]$, $N(k-dk_4) = [N_1(k-dk_4);\ N_2(k-dk_4);\ \ldots;\ N_{21}(k-dk_4)]$.

In Eq. 1, matrix A is a [21 × 21] matrix whose diagonal elements $a_{i,j}$ are represented by $(1 + m_{Nx} - c1 \times Nxdr - a_{Nx} - CN_{xy} - CN_{xz} - C_{myl} \times Myl_{Nx} d_{myl}(k) + C_{CYT} \times m_{DCYT} \times d_{CYT}(k))$ where $(i, j) \equiv (1,1), (2,2), (3,3), \ldots (21,21)$. In Nx, x denotes the cellular state (i.e., normal (g), drug-sensitive (s), and drug-resistive (r)) of concerned cell type (N). For example, $P2s$ represents drug-sensitive (s) leukoblast ($P2$) cell type. Again the multiplication rate, apoptosis rate, and differentiation rate of the concerned cell type (Nx) are denoted by m_{Nx}, a_{Nx}, $Nxdr$. $c1$ works as an ON/OFF switch for cell differentiation. It will become ON on the day of differentiation of the concerned progenitor cell. CN_{xy} and CN_{xz} are representing the conversion rate (C) from concerned cellular state (represented by first subscript) to another cellular state (represented by second subscript). For example, $CP2_{rs}$ represents conversation rate of leukocyte cell type from drug-resistive to drug-sensitive state. The matrix elements $a(i, j) = CN_{yx} + CN_{zx}$ are representing the conversion rates from other cell types where $(i, j) \equiv (i\text{-}2, j\text{-}1)$, $(i\text{-}2, j)$, $(i\text{-}1, j\text{-}2)$, $(i\text{-}1, j)$, $(i, j\text{-}2)$, $(i, j\text{-}1)$) with $i = j = 3, 6, 9, 12, 15, 18, 21$.

In Eq. 1, in matrix A_1, $a_1(i, j) = Sgdr/3$ is represented by $(i, j) = (4,1), (7,1), (10,1)$. Again, $a_1(i, j) \equiv Ssdr/3$ where $(i, j) \equiv (5,2), (8,2), (11,2)$. Again,

Table 1 Considered variables in model: number of cells (Nx), multiplication rate (m_{Nx}), apoptosis rate (a_{Nx}), differentiation rate ($Nxdr$), differentiation delay ($Nxdt$), and conversion rate (CN_{xy} and CN_{xz}). In Table 1, rows marked green, blue, and gray indicate the considered variables for normal, dug-sensitive, and drug-resistive cell, respectively

	Cell type	Nx^{a} (Cells /μL)	m_{Nx}^{a} (Cells /day)	a_{Nx}^{a} (Cells /day)	$Nxdr^{a}$ (Cells /day)	$Nxdt^{a}$ (Days)	CN_{xy} & CN_{xz}^{a} (Cells/day)
Stem	Stem cell	Sg	m_{Sg}	a_{Sg}	$Sgdr$	$Sgdt$	CS_{gz}, CS_{gr}
		Ss	m_{Ss}	a_{Ss}	$Ssdr$	$Ssdt$	CS_{sz}, CS_{sr}
		Sr	m_{Sr}	a_{Sr}	$Srdr$	$Srdt$	CS_{rg}, CS_{rs}
Progenitor cell	Erythroblast	$P1g$	m_{P1g}	a_{P1g}	$P1gdr$	$P1gdt$	$CP1_{gz}, CP1_{gr}$
		$P1s$	m_{P1s}	a_{P1s}	$P1sdr$	$P1sdt$	$CP1_{sg}, CP1_{sr}$
		$P1r$	m_{P1r}	a_{P1r}	$P1rdr$	$P1rdt$	$CP1_{rg}, CP1_{rs}$
	Leukoblast	$P2g$	m_{P2g}	a_{P2g}	$P2gdr$	$P2gdt$	$CP2_{gz}, CP2_{gr}$
		$P2s$	m_{P2s}	a_{P2s}	$P2sdr$	$P2sdt$	$CP2_{sg}, CP2_{sr}$
		$P2r$	m_{P2r}	a_{P2r}	$P2rdr$	$P2rdt$	$CP2_{rg}, CP2_{rs}$
	Megakaryoblast	$P3g$	m_{P3g}	a_{P3g}	$P3gdr$	$P3gdt$	$CP3_{gz}, CP3_{gr}$
		$P3s$	m_{P3s}	a_{P3s}	$P3sdr$	$P3sdt$	$CP3_{sg}, CP3_{sr}$
		$P3r$	m_{P3r}	a_{P3r}	$P3rdr$	$P3rdt$	$CP3_{rg}, CP3_{rs}$
Matured cell	RBC	$B1g$	m_{B1g}	a_{B1g}	$B1gdr$	$B1gdt$	$CB1_{gz}, CB1_{gr}$
		$B1s$	m_{B1s}	a_{B1s}	$B1sdr$	$B1sdt$	$CB1_{sg}, CB1_{sr}$
		$B1r$	m_{B1r}	a_{B1r}	$B1rdr$	$B1rdt$	$CB1_{rg}, CB1_{rs}$
	WBC	$B2g$	m_{B2g}	a_{B2g}	$B2gdr$	$B2gdt$	$CB2_{gz}, CB2_{gr}$
		$B2s$	m_{B2s}	a_{B2s}	$B2sdr$	$B2sdt$	$CB2_{sg}, CB2_{sr}$
		$B2r$	m_{B2r}	a_{B2r}	$B2rdr$	$B2rdt$	$CB2_{rg}, CB2_{rs}$
	Platelet	$B3g$	m_{B3g}	a_{B3g}	$B3gdr$	$B3gdt$	$CB3_{gz}, CB3_{gr}$
		$B3s$	m_{B3s}	a_{B3s}	$B3sdr$	$B3sdt$	$CB3_{sg}, CB3_{sr}$
		$B3r$	m_{B3r}	a_{B3r}	$B3rdr$	$B3rdt$	$CB3_{rg}, CB3_{rs}$

[a]For all parametric values, we have followed Dhar and Majumder 2015 [12]

$a_1(i, j) = Srdr/3$ where $(i, j) \equiv (6,3), (9,3), (12,3)$. In matrix A_2, $a_2(i, j) = P1gdr/3$ where $(i, j) \equiv (13,4)$, for $a_2(i, j) = P1sdr/3$ where $(i, j) \equiv (14,5)$ and $a_2(i, j) = P1rdr/3$ where $(i, j) \equiv (15,6)$. For the other elements of A_2 matrix, $a_2(i, j) = 0$. In matrix A_3, $a_3(i, j) = P2gdr/3$ where $(i, j) \equiv (16,7)$, for $a_3(i, j) = P2sdr/3$ where $(i, j) \equiv (17,8)$, and for $a_3(i, j) = P2rdr/3$ where $(i, j) \equiv (18, 9)$. For the other elements of A_3 matrix, $a_3(i, j) = 0$. In matrix A_4, $a_4(i, j) = P3gdr/3$ where $(i, j) \equiv (19,10)$, for $a_4(i, j) = P3sdr/3$ where $(i, j) \equiv (20,11)$, and for $a_4(i, j) = P3rdr/3$ where $(i, j) \equiv (21,12)$. For the other elements of A_4 matrix, $a_4(i, j) = 0$.

2.1 Inclusion of Toxicity Effect

Genotypic toxicity effect due to malignancy is represented by the matrix element $a(i, j) = -Tox$, where $(i, j) \equiv (1,2), (1,3), (4,5), (4,6), (10,11), (10,12)$. Tox is a

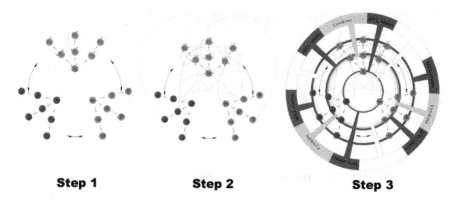

Step 1 **Step 2** **Step 3**

Fig. 1 Stepwise development of algorithm. Step1, heterogeneous cell population of the hematopoietic system (green, blue, and gray circles representing g-type, s-type, and r-type cell populations, respectively. The dashed black arrows indicating the feedback signals, solid black straight arrows representing the cell differentiation, and curved solid black both side arrows representing the conversions of cells); Step 2 includes the effect of cachexia (it is the detrimental effect produced by the leukemic blast cells on the normal cell population that result in complex symptoms like loss of weight) on g-type cells by the s- and r-type cells (green, blue, and black solid arrows represent phenotypic effect of low, medium, and high cachexia, respectively, whereas solid magenta arrows represent genotypic toxicity effect); Step 3 design of MYL and cytokine (represented by the red part and yellow part, respectively) within the TCU (therapeutic control unit represented by concentric circular block)

fractional number representing the malignancy-related toxicity effect on the normal cell population. The high phenotypic cachexia effect due to $P2r$ is represented by the matrix element $a(i, j) = - M_{Tox1}$, where $(i, j) \equiv (1,9)$, $(4,9)$, $(7,9)$, $(10,9)$, $(13,9)$, $(16,9)$, $(19,9)$. The medium phenotypic cachexia effect due to $P2s$ is represented by the matrix element $a(i, j) = - M_{Tox2}$, where $(i, j) \equiv (1,8)$, $(4,8)$, $(7,8)$, $(10,8)$, $(13,8)$, $(16,8)$, $(19,8)$. The low phenotypic cachexia effect due to $B2s$ is represented by the matrix element $a(i, j) = - M_{Tox3}$, where $(i, j) \equiv (1,17)$, $(4,17)$, $(7,17)$, $(10,17)$, $(13,17)$, $(16,17)$, $(19,17)$. The low phenotypic cachexia effect due to $B2r$ is represented by the matrix element $a(i, j) = - M_{Tox3}$, where $(i, j) \equiv (1,18)$, $(4,18)$, $(7,18)$, $(10,18)$, $(13,18)$, $(16,18)$, $(19,18)$. For the other elements of A matrix, $a(i, j) = 0$. M_{Tox1}, M_{Tox2}, and M_{Tox3} all are fractional numbers representing the cachexia effects by $P2r$, $P2s$, $B2r$, and $B2s$ on the normal cell population.

2.2 Inclusion of Immunity-Related Killing

Again, the immunity-related killing effect is represented by the matrix elements $a(i, j) = kill_{im} \times kill_{eff} \times CF(k - 1)$ where $i = 2, 3, 8, 9, 17, 18, 20, 21$ and for all $i, j = 16$.

2.3 Inclusion of Drug Application in Model

Again, d_{myl} represents the MYL drug profile in the system. Myl_{Nx} denotes the MYL drug sensitivity of the concerned cell type. C_{myl} represents the ON/OFF switch for MYL drug application. Again, d_{CYT} represents the CYT drug profile in the system. C_{CYT} represents the ON/OFF switch for CYT drug application. m_{DCYT} denotes the cytokine drug sensitivity.

2.4 Inclusion of Supportive Therapy

In RBC_{tf} matrix, $RBC_{tf}(13,1) = 1$ on the day of RBC transfusion, else $= 0$ for $RBC_{tf}(i, j) = 0$ where $i \neq 13$ and $j = 1$. In $PLATELET_{tf}$ matrix, $PLATELET_{tf}(19,1) = 1$ on the day of platelet transfusion, else $= 0$ for $PLATELET_{tf}(i, j) = 0$ where $i \neq 19$ and $j = 1$.

3 Simulation Results

Simulation exercises have been carried out with the developed algorithm considering the parameter setting for a vigorously grown leukemia as presented in Dhar and Majumder 2015 in the presence of high-dose MYL or low-dose CHEMO and cytokine therapy either in single or in combination [12]. MATLAB 6.5 platform has been used for simulation run. Simulation observations are depicted as follows.

3.1 Application of MYL and Cytokine Therapy

In case of (high-dose) MYL application either in single or in combination with cytokine shows no positive outcome in terms of long-term leukemia-free survival [12]. With MYL regimen, leukemic cell population was found to remain in lower quantity as long as drug level in system is above a certain threshold level without significant level of toxicity. As time progresses, with the accumulation of toxicity, there is a delay in subsequent MYL application. As a result, with the completion of MYL regimen, the leukemic cells are found to regain its growth in an exponential manner.

Simulation studies indicate that at the starting point of the therapy, cytokine application (for immune boosting) alone would be successful, provided there is a minimum level of functional immunocytes (i.e., leukocytes that are capable of killing leukemic cells) and this becomes the most important for long-term therapeutic benefit.

Furthermore, simulation exercises suggest that though MYL can reduce leukemic cells rapidly; however, prior MYL application simultaneously reduces the leukocytic lineage to such a lower level that later cytokine application failed to boost immunity to minimum threshold level (required to counter leukemic population). At that time, number of leukemic cells is another determining factor that prevents immune boosting, as at that moment leukemic cell count was enough to produce considerable toxicity that prevents development of new leukocyte.

3.2 Application of CHEMO with Cytokine Therapy

For the above leukemic condition, rigorous simulation study has been carried out by varying dose, application cycle, and interval for the following therapeutic strategies: CHEMO in single, CHEMO followed by cytokine therapy, and cytokine in single. Simulation indicates that only CHEMO application shows no positive outcome in terms of long-term leukemia-free survival; However, an optimal choice between CHEMO followed by cytokine therapy or cytokine in single for a successful treatment outcome in terms of recovery of normal cell populations with the constraint that the simultaneous elimination of malignant counterpart from system will depend on patients' patho-physiological condition. It has been found that here a judicious dosing strategy (i.e., drug dose, cycle, and interval between two successive drug applications) is needed for the strategy of CHEMO followed by cytokine therapy and/or cytokine in single and this plays an important role in therapeutic success.

When chemotherapeutic drug dose was varied in steps, it was found that above a certain higher dose (upper bound), later application of cytokine becomes unable to ensure leukemia-free survival. This indicates chemotherapy over dose completely removed the normal leukocytic lineage from the system (Fig. 2a). Again, variation in chemotherapeutic drug application cycle shows similar result due to same reason (Fig. 2b). Variation in CHEMO application interval (gap period is varied from 14 days to 16 days) while keeping the cytokine application starting day remains fixed; i.e., on day 160, it was observed that change in interval modulates the need of supportive therapy (number and types of transfusion). Hence, this, in turn, either favors or inhibits the growth and development of leukemic cell population as well as leukocytic cell population (Fig. 2c). Moreover, time gap between last CHEMO and first application of cytokine dose and CHEMO-cytokine schedule plays an important role in therapeutic outcome.

Thus, in the present parametric settings, for CHEMO strategy the optimized dose, cycle number, and interval are determined (through simulation) to be 0.35, 8, and 15 days, respectively. In the present parametric settings, leukocyte number is in optimum level to dominate over the malignant cell in long run, and as a result, long-term leukemia-free survival is possible.

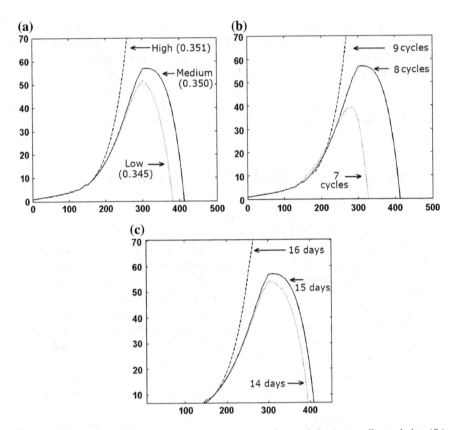

Fig. 2 Effect of chemotherapeutic drug ($drug_{myldose}$) on drug-resistive stem cell population (Sr) with the variation in dose (in A), drug application cycle (in B), and drug application interval (in C). In **a**, the continuous line, dotted line and dashed line correspond to drug dose ($drug_{myldose}$) 0.35, 0.345, and 0.351, respectively. In **b**, the continuous line, dotted line, and dashed line correspond to cycle (n_{myl}) 8, 7, and 9, respectively. In **c**, the continuous line, dotted line, and dashed line correspond to interval (t_{myld}) 14, 15, and 16 days, respectively. In all the cases, minimum WBC number requirement to start leukemic cell killing is considered as 224. In all the plots, x-axis represents 'Days' and y-axis represents 'Counts'

With 14-day interval (between two successive CHEMO doses), the gap period between last CHEMO dose application and first CYT dose would be 10 days and chemo schedule manages to keep the malignant cells to remain within a level (on day 160, Sr cell count is 8.8027 against $B2g$ as 231) so that it could be dominated by the functional immunocytes (WBC population), whereas in case of 16-day interval, gap period between last CHEMO and first CYT dose becomes shorten to 6 days and this chemoschedule was unable to maintain $B2g$ to a requisite amount (on day 160, $B2g$ cell count is 235 against Sr as 8.84) to compete against leukemic

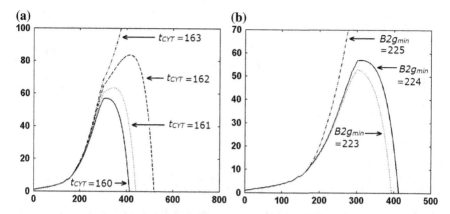

Fig. 3 a Effect of delay in CYT drug application starting day (t_{CYT}) on drug-resistive stem cell population. In the 2D graph, the continuous line corresponds to t_{CYT} = day 160, the dotted line to t_{CYT} = 161, the dashed line to t_{CYT} = 162, and the dot dashed line to t_{CYT} = day 163. In all the cases, minimum WBC requirement to start leukemic cell killing is considering as 224. **b** Variation in minimum immunity cell population ($B2g_{min}$) to start malignant cell killing. In the 2D graph, continuous line corresponds to $B2g_{min}$ = 223, the dotted line to $B2g_{min}$ = 224, and the dashed line to $B2g_{min}$ = 225. In all the plots, x-axis represents 'Days' and y-axis represents 'Counts'

population. Hence, application of cytokine drug could not get enough target cells (i.e., normal leukoblast cells) to boost. Hence, in this case, no positive outcome is possible.

Simulation studies show that with the present parametric settings, delay in first CYT drug application is also failed to control leukemic growth (Fig. 3a). From overall simulation studies, it is noted that there should be a minimum number of functional immunocytes ($B2g_{min}$) to start immunity-related killing of leukemic cells and it is determined to be 224 (Fig. 3b).

3.3 Application of Cytokine Therapy Alone

With the application of cytokine drug ($drug_{CYTdose}$) alone, it is assumed that minimum required number of WBC ($B2g_{min}$) would be 3065 to start leukemic cell killing. With this setting, dose of cytokine ($drug_{CYTdose}$) was varied in steps and it was found that higher dose completely removes the leukemic population, whereas below a threshold value ($drug_{CYTdose}$ = 0.8) cytokine therapeutic schedule was unsuccessful to control leukemia-free survival (Fig. 4).

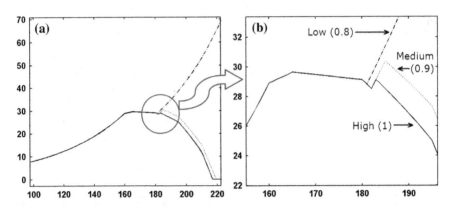

Fig. 4 **a** Effect of cytokine dose ($drug_{CYTdose}$) on drug-resistive stem cell population. In the 2D graph, the continuous line corresponds to $drug_{CYTdose} = 1$, the dotted line to $drug_{CYTdose} = 0.9$, and the dashed line to $drug_{CYTdose} = 0.8$. **b** The figure on the right is a zoomed version of the figure in the center. Here, minimum WBC requirement to start leukemic cell killing is considered as 3065. In all the plots, x-axis represents 'Days' and y-axis represents 'Counts'

4 Discussion

Through this model, the conventional competitive approach of tumor immune system dynamics can be represented. This model shows therapeutic success will depend on immune potentiation. This corroborates the earlier model [8]. Moreover, this observation adds the finding that this can be true for acute leukemic cases, as all simulations are carried out with vigorously growing leukemia.

Our developed model also confirmed the previous finding of Michor et al. 2005 that combination of low-dose chemotherapy and cytokine has no extra therapeutic benefit [13]. However, here we have identified the condition and mechanism. Prior applications of MYL have a deteriorating effect on immunocytes of system, and hence, later application of cytokine is unable to provide immune-potentiating effect due to unavailability of cytokine target cells (immunocytes). Moreover, our simulation study shows that a minimal level of functional immunocytes, if present in the system then, there is no need of prior MYL application.

Through this analytical model, cytokine-dosing strategy can be optimized depending on the patients' patho-physiological state, i.e., leukemic burden, number of functional immunocytes, and sensitized immunocytes. In the model, immune potentiation is considered in terms of functional immunocytes. Therefore, through this model, efficacy of adoptive immune therapy can also be assessed. We hope this analytical model not only helps in choosing the right therapeutic regimen but also provides a way out in designing therapy in leukemia patients.

Acknowledgements PKD is pursuing Ph.D. from Jadavpur University. All authors acknowledge the logistic support provided by Society for Systems Biology & Translational Research.

References

1. DeLsi, C., Rescigno, A.: Immnue surveillance and neoplasia 1 a minimal mathematical model. Bulletin of Mathematical Biology. 39 (1977) 201–221.
2. Grossman, B.G.: Tumour escape from immune elimination J Theor Biol 83 (1980) 267–296.
3. Kustnetsov, V.A., Malakin, A.M., Taylor, M.A., Perelson, A.S.: Nonlinear dynamics of immunogenic tumors: Parameter estimation and global bifurcation analysis, Bull. Math. Bio. 56 (1994) 295–321.
4. Preziosi, L.: From population dynamics to modeling the competition between tumors and immune system Mathl. Comput. Modelling. 23 (1996) 135–152.
5. Michor, F., Beal, K.: Improving cancer treatment via mathematical modeling of population dynamics. Cell. 163 (2015) 1059–1063.
6. Bellomo, N., Forni, G.: Dynamics of tumor interaction with the host immune system, Mathl. Comput. Modelling 20 (1994) 107–122.
7. Kolev, M.: Mathematical modeling of the competition between tumors and immune system considering the role of the antibodies. Mathl. Comput. Modelling. 37 (2003) 1143–1152.
8. Kim, P.S., Lee, P.P., Levy, D.: Dynamics and potential impact of the immune response to chronic myelogenous leukemia, PLoS Comp Biol. 4 (2008):e1000095.
9. Kim, P.S., Lee, P.P., Levy, D.: A PDE model for imatinib-treated chronic myelogenous leukemia. Bull. Math. Biol. 70 (2008) 1994–2016.
10. Foo, J., Drummond, M.W., Clarkson, B., Holyoke, T., Michor, F.: Eradication of chronic myeloid leukemia stem cells: a novel mathematical model predicts no therapeutic benefit of adding G-CSF to imatinib. PLoS Computational Biology. 5 (2009), e10000503.
11. Dhar, P.K., Mukherjee, A., Majumder, D.: Difference delay equation-based analytical model of hematopoiesis. Aut. Contrl. Physiol. State. Func. 1 (2012) 1–11.
12. Dhar, P.K., Majumder, D.: Development of the analytical model for the assessment of the efficiencies of different therapeutic modalities in leukaemia. J. Comp. Syst. Biol. 1 (2015) 1–45.
13. Michor, F., Hughes, T.P., Iwasa, Y., Branford, S., Shah, N.P., Sawyers, C.L., Nowak, M.A.: Dynamics of chronic myeloid leukemia. Nature 435 (2005) 1267–1270.

Trusted Model for Virtual Machine Security in Cloud Computing

K. Sathya Narayana and Syam Kumar Pasupuleti

Abstract With growing of cloud computing, security of virtual machines also increases due to malicious insiders and external attackers. Virtual machines (VMs) in cloud computing need to be protected, since they are hosting critical data. In this paper, we propose trusted model for VM security in cloud computing. In our model, we encrypt the VM image and store in cloud, and it stops inside attackers from violating the confidentiality. Then, trusted third party (TTP) keeps on monitoring the VMs in cloud for integrity of VMs. Further, we are improving the availability of virtual machines using snapshot technique. Snapshot is very useful when VM is lost. Through security analysis, we prove confidentiality, integrity, and availability of VM. We evaluate the performance of our scheme in performance analysis.

Keywords Cloud computing · Virtual machine (VM) · Confidentiality
Integrity and availability · Hypervisor

1 Introduction

Cloud computing is rapidly increasing due to its benefits such as low cost and scalability. In cloud computing model, physical resources are virtualized and delivered to end users. These virtualized resources are created using virtualization software. This is called hypervisor or virtual machine monitor (VMM). Hypervisor is a platform; it allows multiple OSs run on single physical machine. There are two

K. Sathya Narayana (✉)
School of Computer Science and Information Science (SCIS),
University of Hyderabad (UoH), Hyderabad, India
e-mail: satyak2679@gmail.com

S. K. Pasupuleti
Institute for Development and Research in Banking Technology (IDRBT),
Hyderabad, India
e-mail: psyamkumar@idrbt.ac.in

P. K. Pattnaik et al. (eds.), *Progress in Computing, Analytics and Networking*,
Advances in Intelligent Systems and Computing 710,
https://doi.org/10.1007/978-981-10-7871-2_63

Fig. 1 Type 1

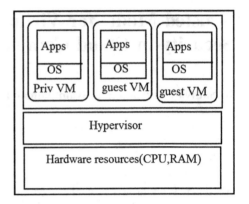

types of hypervisors: type 1 hypervisor (bare metal hypervisor) and type 2 hypervisor (hosted hypervisor).

In type 1 (Fig. 1), hypervisor is directly run on physical hardware and communicates with hardware directly. There is a privilege domain which manages the guest virtual machines and controls the resource sharing between the virtual machines. In type 2 (Fig. 2), hypervisor is run above the host operating system and communicates with hardware though OS. Host operating system is managing and controlling the virtual machines. In the security point of view, type 1 environment is far better than type 2 environment. In type 2 environment, attackers easily compromise the hypervisors because vulnerabilities are more in the type 2 environment because host operating system has larger code. But in type 1 environment, privileged domain has lesser code and less vulnerability. Even though privileged domain (Management VM) is also untrusted because it has whole operating system, device drivers, and also software components of VM management.

However, VMs in cloud computing are insecure due to following reasons: (1) Virtual machine configuration can be modified during virtual machine load time

Fig. 2 Type 2

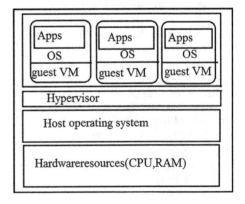

or run time. (2) Since multiple users share the same physical hardware, malicious users can attack the other VMs by injecting malicious code. (3) When virtual machine migrates, the information of VM may leak. (4) External attackers may attack the software components of a cloud environment.

To secure the VMs in cloud computing, recently Jinho Seol et al. [1] proposed cloud architecture, which isolates VM owner's data from malicious management VMs or cloud administrators using hardware security module. Such restriction protects the VM owner's data from malicious cloud administrators. But in performance point of view, it has minimal penalties. Similarly, Chunxiao Li et al. [2] proposed a secure execution environment on virtualized computing platform under assumption of an untrusted management operating system. This is a secured virtualization architecture, even under an untrusted management operating system. But it creates high computation overhead on server.

In this paper, we propose a trusted model for VM security in cloud computing. In our model, first data owner generates key pair and encrypts the virtual machines using key. Key generation module has cryptographic keys. These keys are delivering to encryption/decryption module for encrypt or decrypt the virtual images. Then, our model uses trusted third party to verify the integrity information of virtual machines. The trusted third party is separated from the cloud because these attacks on the virtual machines will be reduced. For availability of virtual machine, we are using snapshot. Through the security and performance analysis, we prove security and efficiency of our model.

The main contributions of our paper as follows:

- We propose trusted model for securing VMs in cloud, and this encrypts the VM image and stores it in cloud for confidentiality.
- Then, we use trusted third party to verify the integrity of VMs in cloud.
- We ensure availability of VM by using snapshot technique in cloud.
- We analyze the security and performance of our scheme through security and performance analysis.

Rest of the paper is organized as follows: Problem statement is described in Sect. 2, proposed method is described in Sect. 3, security and performance analysis are discussed in Sects. 4 and 5, respectively, and finally, conclusion is described in Sect. 7.

2 Problem Statement

2.1 System Architecture

The system architecture consists of three entities: data owner, cloud server, and trusted party (Fig. 3).

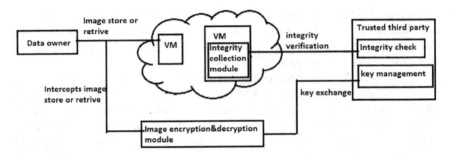

Fig. 3 System architecture

Data owner: The data owner creates VM and stores it in cloud.
Cloud server: The cloud server provides platform for creating VMs.
Trusted third party: The TTP verifies the integrity of VMs.

2.2 System Model

Securing the virtual machines from malicious insiders and hypervisor level, attacks are difficult task. In untrusted cloud computing environment, an attacker can easily compromise the VM and access data from VMs. Thus, confidentiality, integrity, and availability of VMs in cloud need to be protected. In traditional methods, guest user encrypting the virtual machines and storing these keys in the cloud, it would be chance for steeling the cryptographic keys by cloud service provider and access the VM. To address these issues, we propose a trusted model to secure VM in cloud computing, and it ensures the confidentially, integrity, and availability of VM image in cloud.

2.3 Threat Model

In threat model, we consider following attacks, which are occurred in virtual environment.

- **Untrusted cryptographic environment**: Cryptographic operations are occurred in privileged VM. Decrypted VM is stored in memory of privileged VM. So plaintext of the VMs is stored in memory of privileged VM. Cloud administrator easily accesses the plaintext of VM by using root access on privileged VM.
- **Violating the integrity of virtual machines**: Cloud providers can easily change the virtual machines by accessing on storage devices.

- **Man-in-middle attack**: When guest users are accessing the virtual machines, cloud administrator sends the access of corrupted VM than allocated VM.
- **Unauthorized login**: Many cloud service providers are storing the cryptographic keys of virtual machines in their servers. Because of this, cloud malicious insiders access VMs and login the VMs without user concern.
- **Untrusted management**: The guest user sends a request (shutdown the VM) to cloud administrators to shutdown the VM. They ignore to shutdown the VM. But guest user thinks that VM is stopped. By this, VM is running without user concern. Zero-day attacks are easily happened in these VMs.

2.4 Design Goals

We propose a trusted model to ensure the following goals:

- **Confidentiality**: protect data of VM from illegal access by unauthorized users.
- **Integrity**: protect the correctness of data from attackers.
- **Availability**: make virtual machines in cloud which should be available to the users.

3 Proposed Method

We propose cloud architecture; it protects the security of guest VMs by providing confidentiality, integrity, and availability. Our proposed method consists of five phases: (1) key generation module, (2) encryption module, (3) integrity module, (4) decryption module, and (5) availability module.

3.1 Key Generation Module

Key generation is responsible to generate the keys used for encryption. Generate using random bit generator. Key generation module is presented in key management. In the key generation module, generate the two pair keys (U_k, V_k). U_k is public key generated in trusted authority. $U_k \in (g, Z_p)$—here p is prime, g is random bits generated by random bit generator. U_k is a public key for all the VMs, and V_k is sent to the decryption module by secure channel.

3.2 Encryption Module

When a user stops the running virtual machine, then VM data stores in cloud. The encryption module encrypts the VM data before it stores in cloud. Encryption module interacts with key generation module to get encryption keys to encrypt the image. For encrypt the VM images, we are using asymmetric key like RSA. After encryption process, encryption module sends the VM image to cloud. These encrypted VM images are protected from the attacks and illegal access by attackers. The procedure for encryption is as follows:

Plain VM images (VM_p): This is original VM images.
Encrypted VM images (VM_c): This is encrypted VM images. This is created after processing of encryption module using Eq. (1).

$$VM_c = E_f\left(VM_{p,}\ U_k\right) \tag{1}$$

where U_k is a public key, and E_f is the encryption function.

3.3 Integrity Verification Module

The main idea of integrity verification is to improve and protect the correctness of data. Initially, the data owner generates hash values for encrypted image using Eq. (2) and sends to the trusted third party. The TTP collects the hash values of every running process by Eq. (3) and compares the present hash value with initial value which is shown in Eq. (4), if both are identical send the message, integrity is protected. Otherwise, integrity of the VM lost.

  (i) Initial virtual machine hash values are

$$h_1 = H(VM_c) \tag{2}$$

 (ii) TTP collected VM hash values are

$$h_2 = H(VM_c) \tag{3}$$

(iii) Compare the both hash values and send the results to the data owner.

$$VM_h = (h_1 \equiv h_2) \tag{4}$$

After integrity verification, the results send to data owner.

3.4 Decryption Module

If integrity of VM is protected, then data owner decrypts the VM image in cloud for accessing it. The major functionality of image decryption module is to decrypt the VM image. It intercepts a request to stored image from the disk. After getting VM image from disk, data owner decrypts VM image using private key as shown in Eq. (5).

Stored VM image $= VM_c$
Data owner key or private key $= V_k$
Decrypt the virtual image obtained from storage

$$VM_d = D_f(VM_c, V_k) \tag{5}$$

D_f is a decryption function.

3.5 Availability Module

To obtain availability of the VMs, we are using snapshot technique, which is a default property of hypervisor.

Snapshot: Snapshot in virtualization is file-based snapshot, and snapshots save the state of the virtual machine, VM image, and configuration of the virtual machine certain point of time. We can make several snapshots during the virtual machines running. It provides the user to come previous state of the virtual machine by using snapshot. When user wants to reproduces the same virtual machine environment in different situations, snapshot provides such environments.

Live migration [9] is also used for providing availability of the virtual machines. Live migration is transfer the virtual machines from one physical system to another physical system with low downtime when current physical system lack of resources. Hybrid approach [10] technique is used for better live migration with low downtime. This technique was using both pre-copy and post-copy of traditional live migration methods.

4 Security Analysis

In this section, we analyze our proposed method on security terms. In this, we consider three aspects of VM security: confidentiality, integrity, and availability.

4.1 Confidentiality

In the encryption module, after user shutdown the VMs, these VMs are encrypted before stored in the cloud. The encrypted keys of these VMs are stored in the trusted third party not in the cloud. This will provide protection to the VMs from the inside attacks. To protect confidentiality of the virtual machine, we built secure connection between guest user and VM images. By this, we can stop man-in-middle attacks on virtual machines. Hence, virtual machine image encryption protects the confidentiality of VM data from any unauthorized copying of virtual machines.

4.2 Integrity

The integrity of the virtual machines is protected securely by verifying the integrity in trusted third party. It is effective way to verify the integrity of the VM. Hash values of VMs are collected and those hash values are sent to the trusted third party. VMs encrypted and stored in the cloud after shutdown of the VMs. Our integrity verification method detects the any intrusions in the virtual machine (data, configurations, and applications) to stop affecting the virtual environment.

4.3 Availability

For the availability of the virtual machine, we are using snapshot, which is the basic property of hypervisor. Applications running in the VMs are accidently stopped or corrupted. In this time, snapshots are working as recovery points. It will avoid the VM delete and work as backup data.

5 Performance Analysis

In this section, we evaluate the performance of our proposed method in terms of computation overhead and communication overhead.

In our experiment, we set up the cloud platform using open stack. This platform consists of two servers: controller and compute. The controller node system requirements of our scheme Intel i7-6500U with 16 GB RAM and for computing node Intel i5-2450U with 4 GB RAM. The TTP machine set ups with 4 GB RAM, 2 core. We used pairing cryptography library in our experiment.

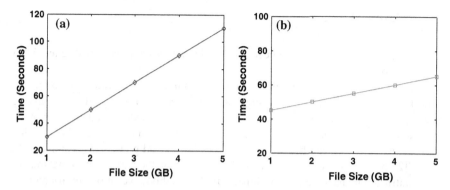

Fig. 4 **a** Computation overhead of encryption module. **b** Computation overhead of decryption module

5.1 Computation Overhead

Computation power of our scheme would be calculated in three modules. These are encryption, decryption, and integrity check module.

In encryption and decryption modules, we measure the performances of guest images using cryptographic operations. In our method, we used RSA 256-bit algorithm for encryption and decryption. Figure 4a, b shows the computation overhead of encryption and decryption modules, respectively. From Fig. 4a, b, we can observe that as soon as the size of VM is increasing, computation cost is also increasing linearly.

In integrity phase, we use SHA-1 hashing algorithm to generate the hash value of VMs, and it has more rounds to mix the information; so it is unable to break the hashing of VMs. It is a fastest hashing function for short strings. From Fig. 5, we can see the computation cost for integrity verification.

Fig. 5 Computation cost of integrity check module

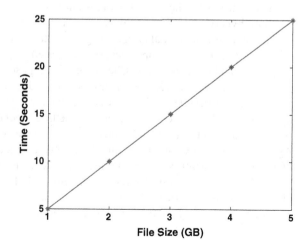

6 Related Work

Recently, several methods have been proposed to address the security of guest VMs in cloud computing.

Jinho Seol et al. [1] proposed a cloud architecture, which protects guest users' data from cloud administrators using hardware security module. They are giving priority to provide protection from internal attacks than external attacks. They are providing restricted interfaces for privileged domain, and it would be creating communication overhead between privileged domain and guest VMs. Chunxiao Li et al. [2] proposed security architecture for securing the virtual machine images from untrusted management environment. In this method, execution environment is protected from inside attacks by modifying hypervisor. For securing the storage of guest VMs, a guest user should encrypt the VM images or should provide master key for cryptographic operations. However, these actions are burden for guest users.

WANG Chunlu et al. [3] present an integrity validation framework that provides integrity verification for virtual images on real time. In this method, they are concentrating on providing a correctness of data by integrity verification. However, this scheme lacks in providing confidentiality of virtual machines. Seongwook et al. [4] proposed an H-SVM; it is a hardware-based approach for protecting the virtual machines from untrusted hypervisor. In this method, hypervisor has low access to memory pages in hardware. But hypervisor is still participating to allocate the memory pages to the virtual machine for better resource management. However, in this scheme, dynamic page mapping and unmapping of memory pages slow down the performance of virtual machines. Muhamamad Kazim et al. [5] proposed a security method that providing protection for virtual disk images in cloud by encryption. Their proposed method is used to protect disk images from data leakage and malware attacks. However, this scheme lacks in correctness of VM disk images. C. Ram et al. [6] proposed a method that gets maximum security by using a cryptographic coprocessor. However, these approaches are focused on protecting specific operations rather than protecting entire execution environment. F. Zhang et al. [7] proposed the nested virtualization method that is cloud-visor adding addition hypervisor layer. If hypervisor was compromised, nested hypervisor should provide confidentiality and integrity of the virtual machine. However, performance degradation occurs because the nested hypervisor intercedes between guest VMs and hypervisors. X. Chen et al. [8] proposed a method overshadow that creates a multishadowing; this method shows a different view of memory pages according to access level. It gives additional layer of protection for application under vulnerable guest OS. However, this method is concentrating only on memory pages of data. But our method protects the entire execution environment. Ashima Agarwal et al. [9] explain a live migration; this technique is providing availability of the virtual machines. Live migration transfers the virtual machines from one physical system to another physical system with low downtime when current physical system lack of resources. Shashank Sahni et al. [10] proposed a hybrid approach for live migration; this technique is used for better live migration with low downtime. This technique is using both pre-copy and post-copy of traditional live migration methods. However, we are using snapshot technique for availability of the VMs instead of live migration.

7 Conclusion

In this paper, we proposed a trusted third party for protecting VMs in cloud computing. In our model, we encrypt the VM image and store in cloud for confidentiality of VM. Later, we verified the integrity of VM by trusted party using cryptographic hash functions. For availability of VM, we used snapshot method to backup the VM data. Through the security analysis, we proved the confidentiality, integrity, and availability of VM in cloud. We analyzed the performance of our scheme in performance analysis. Hence, this trusted model will protect the VMs in cloud.

References

1. J. Seol, S. Jin, D. Lee, J. Huh, and S. Maeng "A Trusted IaaS Environment with Hardware Security Module" *IEEE Transactions on service computing,* Vol. 9, No. 3 2016
2. Chunxiao Li, A. Raghunathan, Niraj K. Jha, "A Trusted Virtual Machine in an Untrusted Management Environment" *IEEE Transactions on service computing,* Vol. 5, No. 4 2012
3. WANG Chunlu, LIU Chuanyi, LIU bin, DONG Yingfei, "DIV: Dynamic integrity validation framework for Detecting compromises on Virtual machine Based Cloud Services in Real timed", *china communications,* august 2014
4. Seongwook Jin, Jeongseob Ahn, Jinho Seol, Sanghoon Cha, Jaehyuk Huh, and Seungryoul Maeng "H-SVM: Hardware-Assisted Secure Virtual Machines under a Vulnerable Hypervisor" *IEEE Transactions on service computers,* Vol. 64, No.10 2015
5. Muhammad kazim, rahat masood, Muhammad Awais shilbi "Securing the virtual machine images in cloud computing" in 'SIN'13 November 26–28, 2013
6. C. Ram and G. Sreenivaasan, "Security as a service (SasS): Securing user data by coprocessor and distributing the data," in Proc. Trendz Inf. Sci. Comput., 2010, pp. 152–155
7. F. Zhang, J. Chen, H. Chen, and B. Zang, "Cloud Visor: Retrofitting protection of virtual machines in multi-tenant cloud with nested virtualization," in Proc. 23rd ACM Symp. Oper. Syst. Principles, 2011, pp. 203–216
8. X. Chen, T. Garfinkel, E.C. Lewis, P. Subrahmanyam, C.A. Waldspurger, D. Boneh, J. Dwoskin, and D.R. Ports, "Over-Shadow: A Virtualization-Based Approach to Retrofitting Protection in Commodity Operating Systems," Proc. Int'l Conf. Architectural Support for Programming
9. Ashima Agarwal, Shangruff Raina "live migration of virtual machines in cloud," International Journal of Scientific and Research Publications, Volume 2, Issue 6, June 2012
10. Shashank Sahni, Vasudeva Varma A "Hybrid Approach to Live Migration of Virtual Machines," Cloud Computing in Emerging Markets (CCEM), 2012 IEEE International Conference

An Efficient Technique for Medical Image Enhancement Based on Interval Type-2 Fuzzy Set Logic

Dibya Jyoti Bora and R. S. Thakur

Abstract Medical images are generally of poor contrast and hence needs a special enhancement technique to improve the visibility before further analysis on those images can be done. The membership function in a Type-1 fuzzy set is not properly defined and hence there lie uncertainties in the result. But, type-2 fuzzy set considers uncertainty in the type-1 membership function itself. Hence, a type-2 fuzzy set based enhancement technique is introduced in this paper. A new membership function is defined. Through the new membership function, the fuzziness of the image is reduced to a great level which automatically enhances its contrast. The results obtained are found better than the traditional state of the art algorithms.

Keywords Image enhancement · Contrast improvement · Entropy
Fuzzy image processing · Medical image · Type-2 fuzzy set

1 Introduction

Medical images are poorly illuminated and often suffer from low contrast [1]. These poor contrast images may hamper in the process of proper diagnosis of patients. Since the poor quality of images leads to information loss in the image and hence results in inaccurate analysis. So, there arises the need of a proper enhancement technique to increase the visibility of poor contrast images. The crisp based technique is not sufficient enough to deal with the vagueness present in a medical image. So, fuzzy set-based techniques are suggested for medical image enhancement [1]. Zadeh [2] first introduced the concept of the fuzzy set where a membership function

D. J. Bora (✉)
Department of Computer Science and Applications, Barkatullah University,
Bhopal, India
e-mail: research4dibya@gmail.com

R. S. Thakur
Department of Computer Applications, MANIT, Bhopal, India
e-mail: ramthakur2000@yahoo.com

© Springer Nature Singapore Pte Ltd. 2018
P. K. Pattnaik et al. (eds.), *Progress in Computing, Analytics and Networking*,
Advances in Intelligent Systems and Computing 710,
https://doi.org/10.1007/978-981-10-7871-2_64

is used for finding out the degree of contribution of every pixel towards the fuzzy set. The values of the membership degree lie in [0, 1]. But, the membership function defined is not definite and results may vary from researcher to researcher depending on the type of the membership function like Gaussian, triangular etc. So, Zadeh [3] again brought the concept of type-2 fuzzy set concept in [3]. In the type-2 fuzzy set, the membership function of the type-1 fuzzy set is also considered fuzzy and it is again refined by a new membership function which is an interval based on proper lower and upper bound. The enhancing power of type-2 fuzzy set based enhancement technique is totally dependent on how efficient the new membership function is. So, in this paper, we have defined a new efficient membership function. On deriving this membership function, we have gone through the different membership functions presented by the authors in [4–6]. Although the current enhancement technique is employed on gray medical images, the same can be easily extended to color medical images by choosing a suitable color space for color based computations [7].

The rest of the paper is organized as follows: in Sect. 2, previous work done in the field and motivation towards proposed work are presented. In Sect. 3, the definition of the image in fuzzy logic is illustrated. In Sect. 4, an in-depth discussion on type-2 fuzzy set is carried out. In Sect. 5, the methodology of the proposed approach is described by properly illustrating the involved techniques. Section 6 is the experiment and result discussion section. Finally, the conclusion is drawn at Sect. 7.

2   Related Works and Motivation Towards Proposed Work

Ensafi et al. [6] showed that type-2 fuzzy logic system is performing better contrast enhancement than the type-1 fuzzy counterpart. For the type-2 fuzzy enhancement, they have introduced a new membership function. The proposed technique is actually extended type-2 version of the type-1 adaptive fuzzy histogram hyperbolization.

Lin et al. [8] proposed a novel method FACE (Fuzzy Automatic Contrast Enhancement) which first performs fuzzy clustering of the input image where the pixels with same colors in the CIELAB color space are classified into analogous clusters with smaller characteristics. In each cluster, pixels are spread out from the center to enhance the contrast. The authors introduced a universal contrast enhancement variable and optimize its value to maximize entropy value.

In [9, 10], Chaira introduced a type-2 fuzzy set based medical image contrast enhancement technique where she used Hamacher T co-norm as an aggregation operator to form a new membership function. The new membership function produces the enhanced version of the original image. The type-2 fuzzy set has the benefit that it considers fuzziness in the membership function itself.

Tizhoosh et al. [11] introduced the concept of image enhancement through fuzzy histogram hyperbolization. They then brought the concept of local adaptive feature to two previous fuzzy enhancement techniques: minimization of fuzziness and fuzzy histogram hyperbolization and obtained results far better than their global version [12].

In [13], Tizhoosh used type-2 fuzzy set-based technique for thresholding images through a new measure of ultrafuzziness. The author demonstrated the efficiency of the proposed technique by thresholding laser cladding images.

Bansal et al. [14] introduced a fingerprint image enhancement technique where they first pre-process the image with Hong's algorithm after that apply type-2 fuzzy logic to produce the final enhancement. The efficiency of the proposed technique is proved through experiments in several images.

From the literature, it is observed that medical images contain a very high level of vagueness which is not possible to be removed using type-1 fuzzy set-based techniques because of the crisp nature of the membership function. So, type-2 fuzzy set-based techniques are developed to deal with the fuzziness of the type-1 membership function. The capability of the type-2 fuzzy set is fully dependent on the new membership function. So, specifically from the works of Ensafi et al. [6] and Chaira [9, 10], we have been motivated to design a new membership function whose value ultimately offers the enhancement version of the input low contrast medical image.

3 Definition of Image in Fuzzy Logic

Fuzzy set for the first time is introduced by Zadeh [2] in 1965. A fuzzy set F can be defined as a pair (X, μ) where X is a class of objects $\{x_1, x_2, \ldots\ldots, x_n\}$ with continuous grades of membership in X measured with a membership function μ, such that $\mu: X \rightarrow [0, 1]$. The fuzzy set F can also be represented as $\{\mu(x_1)/x_1, \mu(x_2)/x_2, \ldots\ldots, \mu(x_n)/x_n\}$. If $\mu(x) = 0$, then x not considered as an object of class X, while if, then x is regarded as fully belong to X. If, then x is considered as a fuzzy object. The support of (X, μ) is the set $\{x \in X | \mu(x) > 0\}$ and the core or kernel is $\{x | \mu(x) = 1\}$ [15].

A formal fuzzy image processing step can be depicted through the following Fig. 1:

More formally, a definition of image processing in fuzzy logic can be put forward [16, 17] in the following way:

Consider, $I(x, y)$ is our original image. F is the set of mappings which map $I(x, y)$ into the fuzzy domain $(0, 1)$ (perception domain). Here perception refers to any subjective characteristic of the concerned image. In the fuzzy domain, the image is represented by $I_f(x, y)$. A set of fuzzy operators ξ, say, changes this fuzzy

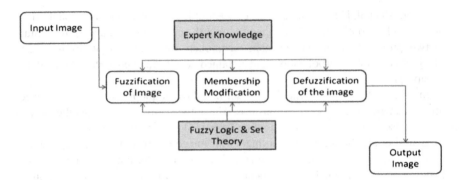

Fig. 1 Fuzzy image processing

image $I_f(x, y)$ into $I_f(x, y)'$. Finally, a defuzzification function D transfers it back to the original domain.

In fuzzy logic [16], an image I_f of size $M \times N$ and L gray levels is considered as an array of fuzzy singletons where every singleton has a value of membership which denotes its degree of brightness level from 0 to L-1. A fuzzy singleton represents a fuzzy set with one supporting point. So, mathematically we can write the equation of the image I_f in the fuzzy set as follows:

$$I_f = \bigcup_m \bigcup_n \frac{\mu(g_{mn})}{g_{mn}} \tag{1}$$

where g_{mn} is the gray value associated with the (m, n)th pixel and $\mu(g_{mn})$ is its membership value. Different subjective properties of the image like sharpness, brightness, edginess etc. can be characterized by the membership function either globally or locally [17].

4 Type-2 Fuzzy Set

In 1975, Zadeh introduced the concept of the type-2 fuzzy set [3]. The uncertainty exists in the membership function of Type-1 membership function leads to the invention of the type-2 fuzzy set. The type-2 fuzzy set is an extension of the type-1 fuzzy set and found very useful in cases when there arises difficulty in agreeing on the accuracy of the type-1 membership function due to vagueness in its shape, location or other such parameters [6, 18]. Mainly four such reasons are identified which fuels the uncertainty [6, 18] which are: (i) uncertainty in the meaning of the words, (ii) penalty associated with a histogram of values, (iii) uncertainty in the measurements, and (iv) noise present in the data.

Fig. 2 **a** Type-1 membership function; **b** Blurriness invokes the type-2 membership function

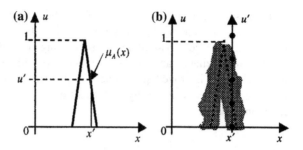

Now, in Zadeh's type-2 fuzzy set, the membership function is bound under interval based values with proper upper and lower bound. It implies that type-1 membership function is blurred to obtain the type-2 membership function. Mendel et al. showed this in their paper [18] and the following diagram (Fig. 2) from the same paper illustrates this fact.

Say A be a type-2 fuzzy set. It can be represented as follows [9, 10, 12]:

$$A_{TYPEII} = \left\{ x, \widehat{\mu}_A(x,u) | \forall x \in X, \forall u \in J_x \subseteq [0,1] \right\} \tag{2}$$

where $\widehat{\mu}_A(x,\mu)$ is the Type II membership function, J_x is the primary membership function of x and the upper and lower limits (shown clearly in Fig. 3) are defined as:

$$\mu^{upper} = [J_x]^\alpha$$
$$\mu^{lower} = [J_x]^{1/\alpha} \tag{3}$$

where $0 < \alpha \leq 1$.

The FOOTPRINT OF UNCERTAINTY (FOU) is used to show the uncertainty in the primary membership of a type-2 fuzzy set. The following equation expresses the FOU in terms of the primary membership function J_x:

$$FOU(A_{TYPEII}) = \bigcup_{x \in X} J_x \tag{4}$$

Fig. 3 Type-1 and Type-2 fuzzy set membership area with respect to upper and lower limit

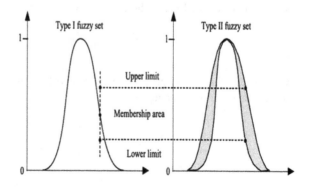

Because of its capability to deal with uncertainty in a much better way than its counterparts like the type-1 fuzzy set, intuitionistic fuzzy set, type-2 fuzzy set has been used in major areas of image processing like edge detection, thresholding, image enhancement and image segmentation [4, 9, 10, 13, 19]. In image enhancement, it is proved quite beneficial [9, 10]. The efficiency of type-2 fuzzy set on image enhancement is fully dependent on how cleverly the type-2 membership function is defined.

5 Methodology of the Proposed Approach

The proposed technique is mainly based on the works presented in [6, 9, 10].

First, the image I of size $M \times N$ is fuzzified using the following primary membership function J_x as:

$$J_x = \frac{I - I_{\min}}{I_{\max} - I_{\min}}$$ (5)

where I is the gray level of the image (say A) of the range 0 to L-1, $I_{\min}$ is the minimum gray value and $I_{\max}$ is the maximum gray value.

Now, next thing we need to define upper and lower bounds so that an interval based type-2 fuzzy set can be constructed. These upper and lower bounds can be easily calculated with the Eqs. (3) described in Sect. 4. Here, we need to find an optimal value of α through trial and error strategy.

Now, for designing the new membership function, we focus on the fact that a darker region should look brighter. This is possible if we somehow make a higher value of μ^{upper} for dark portion as it will lead to having higher gray values for them. Based on this idea, we have introduced following Eq. (6) for calculating the new membership function:

$$\widehat{\mu}_A = \frac{\mu_{low} \cdot \lambda + \mu_{high} \cdot (1 - \lambda)}{1 - (1 - \lambda) \cdot \mu_{low} \cdot \mu_{high}}$$ (6)

where λ is calculated using the equation below:

$$\lambda = \frac{I_{mean}}{L}$$ (7)

where I_{mean} is the mean gray value calculated from the image and L is the number of gray levels in the image.

In the Eq. (6), a greater portion of μ_{high} is allocated in the numerator section and finally, a normalized output is obtained through the division with the defined denominator in the equation.

6 Experiment and Results Discussion

In this section, the efficiency of the proposed technique is verified through proper experiments conducted on some poor contrast medical images collected from MedPix imaging database [20]. Matlab is used for implementing the proposed technique. Experiments are conducted on a system with i-5 processor and 64-bit Windows 10 operating system. We have compared our results with some state of the art algorithms CLAHE [21] (where clip limits are determined with a binary search based technique described in [22]) and an intuitionistic fuzzy image enhancement technique introduced in [1].

Now, first, we try to find the value of α which will give a better enhancement result. For that, we adopted trial and error strategy. We begin with $\alpha = 0.3$ and ends with $\alpha = 0.8$.

From the results (shown in the above Fig. 4), it is clearly visible that enhancement result is better for $\alpha \geq 0.7$. So, we have fixed our α value as 0.7 for the rest of the experiments.

The experiments are conducted on more than 30 different medical images. The results and comparative study are provided below for four such images in Fig. 5.

To compare the results both subjective and objective evaluations are carried out. They are demonstrated below:

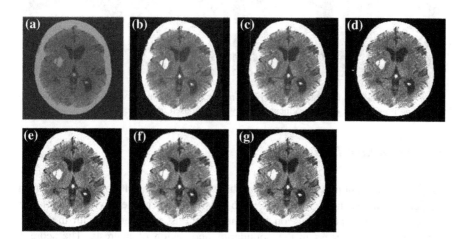

Fig. 4 **a** Original Image; **b** Result for $\alpha = 0.3$; **c** Result for $\alpha = 0.4$; **d** Result for $\alpha = 0.5$; **e** Result for $\alpha = 0.6$; **f** Result for $\alpha = 0.7$; **g** Result for $\alpha = 0.8$

Image 1:

Image 2:

Image 3:

Image 4:

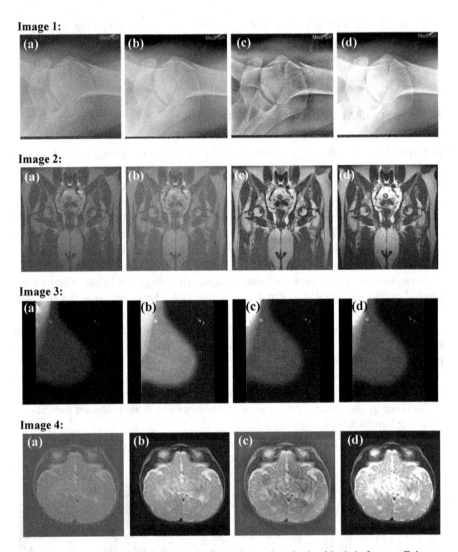

Fig. 5 **a** Original Low Contrast Image; **b** Enhancement done by intuitionistic fuzzy; **c** Enhancement done by CLAHE; **d** Enhancement done by the proposed technique

6.1 Subjective Evaluations

Subjective evaluation is carried out on the experimental results by 5 experts from the field. Mean Opinion Score (MOS) [6] has been determined by the experts for the proposed approach based on how much contrast is enhanced with the lesser appearance of vagueness in the boundaries and region of interests. The score 1

Table 1 Subjective evaluation

Expert	Is visual improvement done after enhancement: Yes/No	Visual improvement rating (Value Ranges from 1 to 6)
1	Yes	2
2	Yes	2
3	Yes	1
4	Yes	1
5	Yes	1
Average	*Yes*	*1.4*

signifies excellence performance, 2 indicates very good, 3 for good, 4 means average, 5 is for bad and 6 represents worst performance.

The following Table 1 gives the overall evaluation:

So, the average rating is 1.4 which is in between excellent and very good. So, the results can be considered as very good and proposed method can be recommended for contrast improvement of poor contrast medical images.

6.2 Objective Evaluations

To conduct the objective evaluation, we have adopted two metrics: Entropy and PSNR (Peak Signal to Noise Ratio). The entropy of an image can be calculated using the following Eq. 8:

$$E = -sum(p \cdot {}^* \log_2(p)) \tag{8}$$

where p is the histogram counts obtained from the histogram of the concerned image.

The PSNR value of an image is calculated using the following Eq. 9:

$$PSNR = 10 \log_{10}(MAXi^2/MSE) \tag{9}$$

where MAX_i the maximum possible pixel value of the image and MSE is the Mean Squared Error obtained with the following equation no. (10):

$$MSE = \sum_{(y=1)}^{M} \sum_{(x=1)}^{N} [I(x,y) - I'(x,y)]^2 \tag{10}$$

where, M, N are the dimensions of the image and $I(x,y)$ is the original image, $I'(x,y)$ is the enhanced version of the image.

Table 2 Objective evaluation

Image no.	Objective evaluation	Intuitionistic fuzzy	CLAHE	Proposed approach
Image 1	Entropy	6.1954	6.0712	*6.7869*
	PSNR	24.7129	24.1331	*24.8607*
Image 2	Entropy	6.0101	5.9712	*6.1994*
	PSNR	29.7169	26.5197	*31.4253*
Image 3	Entropy	7.1041	6.9017	*6.7357*
	PSNR	12.2485	11.0866	**11.2091**
Image 4	Entropy	4.98245	4.4811	*5.34275*
	PSNR	13.7620	13.1866	*15.2806*
Average	Entropy	6.0730125	5.8563	*6.2661875*
	PSNR	20.110075	18.7315	*20.693925*

We have selected entropy and PSNR for the objective evaluation as both of these two metrics include not only the enhancement impact and but also consider the noise sensitivity issue. For a better enhancement, the entropy value should be high. And, for a better suppression of noises, the PSNR value should be high. So, higher the values of entropy and PSNR, the better are the enhancement achieved by an enhancement technique.

From the Table 2, it is clear that on average, the proposed approach is showing higher values of entropy and PSNR than the other state of the art techniques in comparison, this means the proposed approach succeeds to produce better enhancement results.

7   Conclusion and Future Work

We have introduced an interval type-2 fuzzy set based enhancement technique for poor contrast medical images in this paper. A new type-2 fuzzy membership function is proposed. The vagueness in the boundaries and region of interests are removed to a satisfactory level. The experimental results prove the superiority of the proposed approach through both subjective and objective evaluations. So, the proposed technique can be considered as an efficient one to be used as a pre-processing step in every area of medical imaging where critical analysis of the input image is utmost required for an accurate result. The future work for further improvement of the proposed technique is possible if local region based enhancements on predefined sized tiles of the input image are adopted than globally considering the entire image at a time. Also, the proposed work may be extended to medical color image enhancement if a proper color space other than RGB is considered for color based arrangement and computations involved.

References

1. Chaira T (2012) Medical image enhancement using intuitionistic fuzzy set. 2012 1st International Conference on Recent Advances in Information Technology (RAIT). https://doi.org/10.1109/rait.2012.6194479.
2. Zadeh L A (1965) Fuzzy Sets. Inf. and Cont., 1965, 8, pp. 338–353.
3. Zadeh L A (1975) The concept of a linguistic variable and its application to approximate reasoning-1. Inf. Sci. 8, 199–249, https://doi.org/10.1016/0020-0255(75)90036-5.
4. Chaira T (2015) Rank-ordered filter for edge enhancement of cellular images using interval type II fuzzy set. Journal of Medical Imaging 2:044005. https://doi.org/10.1117/1.jmi.2.4.044005.
5. Hamacher H (1978) Uber Logische Aggregationen nicht-binar explizierterntscheidungs-Kriterion, R.G. Fisher Verlag, Frankfurt.
6. Ensafi P, Tizhoosh H (2005) Type-2 Fuzzy Image Enhancement. Lecture Notes in Computer Science 159–166. https://doi.org/10.1007/11559573_20.
7. Bora D (2017) Importance of Image Enhancement Techniques in Color Image Segmentation: A Comprehensive and Comparative Study. Indian J.Sci.Res. 15(1): 115–131, https://arxiv.org/abs/1708.05081.
8. Lin P, Lin B (2016) Fuzzy automatic contrast enhancement based on fuzzy C-means clustering in CIELAB color space. 2016 12th IEEE/ASME International Conference on Mechatronic and Embedded Systems and Applications (MESA). https://doi.org/10.1109/mesa.2016.7587156.
9. Chaira T (2013) Contrast enhancement of medical images using type II fuzzy set. 2013 National Conference on Communications (NCC). https://doi.org/10.1109/ncc.2013.6488016.
10. Chaira T (2014) An improved medical image enhancement scheme using Type II fuzzy set. Applied Soft Computing 25:293–308. https://doi.org/10.1016/j.asoc.2014.09.004.
11. Tizhoosh, H. R., Fochem, M., (1995) Image Enhancement with Fuzzy Histogram Hyperbolization, proceedings of EUFIT'95, vol. 3, pp. 1695 – 1698, Aachen, Germany.
12. Tizhoosh H.R., Krell G., Michaelis B. (1997) Locally adaptive fuzzy image enhancement. In: Reusch B. (eds) Computational Intelligence Theory and Applications. Fuzzy Days 1997. Lecture Notes in Computer Science, vol 1226. Springer, Berlin, Heidelberg.
13. Tizhoosh H (2005) Image thresholding using type II fuzzy sets. Pattern Recognition 38:2363–2372. https://doi.org/10.1016/j.patcog.2005.02.014.
14. Bansal R, Arora P, Gaur M, Sehgal P, Bedi P (2009) Fingerprint Image Enhancement Using Type-2 Fuzzy Sets. 2009 Sixth International Conference on Fuzzy Systems and Knowledge Discovery. https://doi.org/10.1109/fskd.2009.396.
15. (2017) Fuzzy set. In: En.wikipedia.org. https://en.wikipedia.org/wiki/Fuzzy_set. Accessed 5 Mar 2017.
16. Chacón M M Fuzzy Logic for Image Processing: Definition and Applications of a Fuzzy Image Processing Scheme. Advances in Industrial Control 101–113. https://doi.org/10.1007/978-1-84628-469-4_7.
17. Krell G, Tizhoosh H, Lilienblum T, Moore C, Michaelis B Fuzzy image enhancement and associative feature matching in radiotherapy. Proceedings of International Conference on Neural Networks (ICNN'97). https://doi.org/10.1109/icnn.1997.614017.
18. Mendel J, John R (2002) Type-2 fuzzy sets made simple. IEEE Transactions on Fuzzy Systems 10:117–127. https://doi.org/10.1109/91.995115.
19. Bora DJ (2017) An Optimal Color Image Edge Detection Approach. IEEE International Conference on Trends in Electronics and Informatics ICEI 2017.
20. (2017) MedPix. In: Medpix.nlm.nih.gov. https://medpix.nlm.nih.gov/home. Accessed 4 Mar 2017.

21. Pisano E, Zong S, Hemminger B, DeLuca M, Johnston R, Muller K, Braeuning M, Pizer S (1998) Contrast Limited Adaptive Histogram Equalization image processing to improve the detection of simulated spiculations in dense mammograms. Journal of Digital Imaging 11:193–200. https://doi.org/10.1007/bf03178082.
22. Bora D (2017) AERSCIEA: An Efficient and Robust Satellite Color Image Enhancement Approach. Proceedings of the Second International Conference on Research in Intelligent and Computing in Engineering. https://doi.org/10.15439/2017r53.

Employing Kaze Features for the Purpose of Emotion Recognition

Ashutosh Vaish and Sagar Gupta

Abstract In this research, a novel approach for emotion detection is exploited by taking the Accelerated Kaze (A-Kaze) features for emotion recognition. The Kaze Features work in a way such that object boundaries can be preserved by making blurring locally adaptive to the image data without severely affecting the noise-reducing capability of the Gaussian blurring, thereby increasing the accuracy of the system. After extracting the Kaze features, GMM is constructed and thus a Fisher Vector representation is made. The extracted features are passed through an SVM detector. An efficiency of 87.5% has been shown thus proving that Kaze can also be used effectively in the field of facial image processing.

Keywords Real time · Emotion recognition · Kaze features
State of mind · Accelerated Kaze · Facial expressions

1 Introduction

The face of a human is a site for majority of sensory inputs and outputs and is thus capable of understanding and communicating someone's effective state of mind. A number of researchers have been working on detection of emotions, through facial cues [1, 2]. Facial expressions give a way to the machine for understanding human emotions. The application of the system includes the purpose of pain detection in people who are unable to communicate effectively verbally, such as children [3], and also for detecting mental disorders, such as depression and anxiety [4]. Although a number of systems are available for the purpose, our approach ensures that a system with high accuracy and low computation cost can be

A. Vaish · S. Gupta (✉)
Bachelors of Technology, Maharaja Surajmal Institute of Technology,
Janak Puri, New Delhi 110058, India
e-mail: absagargupta@gmail.com

A. Vaish
e-mail: ashuvaish1@gmail.com

© Springer Nature Singapore Pte Ltd. 2018
P. K. Pattnaik et al. (eds.), *Progress in Computing, Analytics and Networking*,
Advances in Intelligent Systems and Computing 710,
https://doi.org/10.1007/978-981-10-7871-2_65

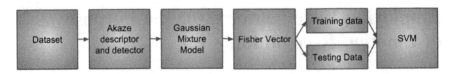

Fig. 1 Working of the proposed approach

constructed. It is shown by [5] that emotions are experienced similarly in people regardless of their culture.

The emotion detection is accomplished in three steps, namely preprocessing, feature extraction followed by training the classifier. The preprocessing ensures that all the images being given to the system are uniform in nature (color, size, etc.) and of high quality. A feature descriptor converts the image into a machine-usable form, which is then fed into the classifier. An N-class classifier is used for detecting the emotions into n different classes.

Since the Extended Cohn–Kanade Dataset [6] used is free from illumination variance, occlusion, and head poses, it is used in the approach. The approach is novel in detecting and computing the emotions through Accelerated Kaze (A-Kaze) features, which makes the blurring locally adaptive without severely affecting the noise reduction capability of Gaussian blurring, thus preserving the boundary lines of the image. In the presented approach, from preprocessed images, the A-Kaze features are taken. With the application of Gaussian mixture model (GMM), Fisher Vector (FV) is constructed. These are used for training the SVM for recognition of emotion. The N emotions can be classified by using N classifiers in the approach of *one-against-all* technique that we have used. The block diagram has been presented in Fig. 1.

The presented system results in 87.5% accuracy when trained and tested on CK+ dataset.

2 Literature Review

This section describes the overall literature review of the developments in the field of emotion detection and the usage of Kaze features in other areas.

2.1 Emotion Recognition Systems

Face localization is the primary step in emotion detection. The facial images taken in the dataset for emotion recognition are free from occlusion and are taken in an ambient environment. Viola-Jones [7] developed an effective approach for facial recognition using Haar-like features. The next step of feature description extracts information from the image, thus representing them in digital form based on various algorithms. Rathee et al. [8] utilizes LBP features and finds the emotion.

SVM is trained with the descriptors of various emotions and tested on test data to find the efficacy of the system. Some researchers utilize k-nearest neighbor, linear discriminative analysis, etc., for classification. In [8, 6], the authors have utilized multiclass SVM for expression classification.

2.2 Feature Descriptors

Previously Speeded-Up Robust Transform [9] (SURF) and Scale-Invariant Feature Transform [10] (SIFT) features have been used for the purpose of feature representation. The A-Kaze features used in this paper were first introduced by [11] as Kaze and then revised as A-Kaze in [12]. These features have been proven better than the other two descriptors as the blurring in the image is made locally adaptive, thus the natural boundaries of the image are preserved, only eliminating the noise. The Kaze features have been successfully used in [13] and in [14]. Kaze features have been successfully employed for classification of echocardiography videos in [15].

3 Kaze

Kaze features overcome the difficulty of preserving the natural boundary of images. The previous feature descriptors depicted the features at various scale levels by constructing or rounding off the Gaussian scale-space of an image. But the borderline of the objects is smoothened to the same extent as that of both details and noise, thereby severely affecting localization accuracy and distinctiveness.

From the previous research [16], it is duly known that nonlinear diffusion approaches yield better results than linear ones and astonishing results have been obtained in the applications such as image segmentation [17] and denoising [18]. Therefore, 2D features are detected in a nonlinear scale-space by the means of nonlinear diffusion filtering. The expansive computations and high number of iterations because of small step size limited the usage of the nonlinear diffusion filtering from practical computer vision components, such as feature detection and description.

This limitation is overcome by the use of additive operator splitting (AOS) technique [19]. The classic nonlinear diffusion formulation is depicted in the following equation number (1):

$$\frac{\partial K}{\partial t} = div(o(x,y,t) \cdot \nabla K) \tag{1}$$

where div represents divergence and ∇ represents gradient operators. The diffusion is made adaptive to the local image structure due to conductivity function (o) in the diffusion equation. The function c is dependent on the local image differential structure. The scale parameter is represented by t.

The scale-space in logarithmic steps that are arranged in a series of C octaves and L sub-levels is discretized. Down sampling is not performed at every new octave as was the case with SIFT, thus the original image resolution is maintained. The sub-level indexes are usually identified by a discrete index c and a sub-level l and are mapped to their corresponding scale f according to Eq. (2).

$$f_j(c,l) = f_0 2^{c+l/L}, \ c \in [0 \ldots C-1], \ l \in [0 \ldots L-1], \ j \in [0 \ldots M]. \tag{2}$$

where f_0 represents the base scale level and N gives the total number of the filtered images. Convolving an image with Gaussian of standard deviation, f is similar to filtering the image for time $f^2/2$. This has been depicted in Eq. (3).

$$t_j = \frac{1}{2}f_j^2, \ j = \{0 \ldots M\}. \tag{3}$$

The maxima are searched in all images except where j = 0 and j = M. The response is checked over a window of 3 × 3. We have used A-Kaze features as presented by [12].

4 Experimental Results

The proposed method is evaluated on Extended Cohn–Kanade Database [5] for emotion detection. The algorithm has been explained below:

4.1 Algorithm

1. Images from the dataset are lifted and preprocessed.
2. Images are cropped, grayscaled, and registered to remove any movements or rotation of head.
3. A-Kaze features are extracted from the images.
4. With the application of Gaussian mixture model, Fisher Vector (FV) is constructed.
5. The FV generated is used for training SVM.

Table 1 Confusion matrix of the proposed approach

	Anger	Disgust	Fear	Happy	Sad	Surprise
Anger	20	1	0	0	0	0
Disgust	2	38	0	2	1	2
Fear	0	0	14	1	0	0
Happy	0	0	0	28	1	4
Sad	3	1	0	0	19	1
Surprise	0	5	0	0	0	37

4.2 Results

The features are extracted using the facial feature descriptor mentioned above. The A-Kaze features are then used for making the Fisher Vector (FV) representation by the application of Gaussian mixture models. The FV representation is then used for training the classifier.

Eighty percent of the images are used for constructing the classifier, while the other 20% is used for testing the system. Confusion matrix of the proposed approach is shown in Table 1. As per our knowledge, this is the first time that the Kaze features are being used for the purpose of emotion detection.

We utilized 100 Gaussians and created Fisher Vectors having a dimension of 12200 of the whole dataset for training the classifier. The reduction algorithms, such as PCA and LDA, were used, but observed to be lowering the efficiency of the approach and thus neglected due to minimal computation speed difference when using A-Kaze. Setting the number of Gaussians as 150, 200 yielded nearly same results. The respective accuracies of each emotion are given in Table 2.

The Fisher Vectors were used to train the linear kernel SVM classifier. We have used one-against-all technique. LIBSVM [20] toolkit was used for classification of images into various emotions. An overall accuracy of 87.5% was achieved.

Table 2 Respective accuracies of the emotions

Emotions	Accuracy (in %)
Anger	95.23
Disgust	84.44
Fear	93.33
Happy	84.85
Sad	79.17
Surprise	88.09

5   Conclusion and Future Scope

A-Kaze features were used for the very first time for detection of emotion. The Fisher Vectors were constructed using GMM. The number of Gaussians was kept fixed at 100. An accuracy of 87.5% was achieved. The Kaze features have turned out to be having huge potential for application into similar fields such as micro-expression analysis, depression detection, and pain recognition.

References

1. L. S. Chen. *Joint processing of audio-visual information for the recognition of emotional expressions in human-computer interaction.* PhD thesis, University of Illinois at Urbana-Champaign, Dept. of Electrical Engineering, 2000.
2. L. S. Chen, H. Tao, T. S. Huang, T. Miyasato, and R. Nakatsu. Emotion recognition from audiovisual information. In Proc. IEEE Workshop on Multimedia Signal Processing, pages 83–88, Los Angeles, CA, USA, Dec. 7–9, 1998. s.
3. Kaltwang, S., Rudovic, O., & Pantic, M. (2012). Continuous pain intensity estimation from facial expressions. *Advances in visual computing,* 368–377.
4. Cohn, Jeffrey F., et al. "Detecting depression from facial actions and vocal prosody." *Affective Computing and Intelligent Interaction and Workshops, 2009. ACII 2009. 3rd International Conference on.* IEEE, 2009.
5. Ekman, P., & Friesen, W. V. (1971). Constants across cultures in the face and emotion. *Journal of personality and social psychology, 17*(2), 124.
6. Lucey, P., Cohn, J. F., Kanade, T., Saragih, J., Ambadar, Z., & Matthews, I. (2010, June). The Extended Cohn-Kanade Dataset (CK+): A complete dataset for action unit and emotion-specified expression. In *Computer Vision and Pattern Recognition Workshops (CVPRW), 2010 IEEE Computer Society Conference on* (pp. 94–101). IEEE.
7. Viola, Paul, and Michael Jones. "Rapid object detection using a boosted cascade of simple features." *Computer Vision and Pattern Recognition, 2001. CVPR 2001. Proceedings of the 2001 IEEE Computer Society Conference on.* Vol. 1. IEEE, 2001.
8. Rathee, N., Vaish, A., & Gupta, S. (2016, April). Adaptive system to learn and recognize emotional state of mind. In *Computing, Communication and Automation (ICCCA), 2016 International Conference on* (pp. 32–36). IEEE.
9. Bay, H., Tuytelaars, T., & Van Gool, L. (2006). Surf: Speeded up robust features. *Computer vision–ECCV 2006,* 404–417.
10. Lowe, D. G. (2004). Distinctive image features from scale-invariant keypoints. *International journal of computer vision, 60*(2), 91–110.
11. Alcantarilla, P., Bartoli, A., & Davison, A. (2012). KAZE features. *Computer Vision–ECCV 2012,* 214–227.
12. Alcantarilla, P. F., & Solutions, T. (2011). Fast explicit diffusion for accelerated features in nonlinear scale spaces. *IEEE Trans. Patt. Anal. Mach. Intell, 34*(7), 1281–1298.
13. Alcantarilla, P. F., Bergasa, L. M., Jiménez, P., Sotelo, M. A., Parra, I., Fernandez, D., & Mayoral, S. S. (2008, June). Night time vehicle detection for driving assistance lightbeam controller. *In Intelligent Vehicles Symposium, 2008 IEEE* (pp. 291–296). IEEE.
14. Alcantarilla, P. F., Oh, S. M., Mariottini, G. L., Bergasa, L. M., & Dellaert, F. (2010, May). Learning visibility of landmarks for vision-based localization. *In Robotics and Automation (ICRA), 2010 IEEE International Conference on* (pp. 4881–4888). IEEE.

15. Li, Wei, et al. "The application of KAZE features to the classification echocardiogram videos." Multimodal Retrieval in the Medical Domain. *Springer International Publishing,* 2015. 61–72.
16. Weickert, Joachim, BM Ter Haar Romeny, and Max A. Viergever. "Efficient and reliable schemes for nonlinear diffusion filtering." *IEEE transactions on image processing* 7.3 (1998): 398–410.
17. Weickert, Joachim. "Efficient image segmentation using partial differential equations and morphology." *Pattern Recognition 34.9* (2001): 1813–1824.
18. Qiu, Zhen, Lei Yang, and Weiping Lu. "A New Feature-preserving Nonlinear Anisotropic Diffusion Method for Image Denoising." *BMVC. 2011.*
19. Yacoob, Y., and Davis, L., "Recognizing human facial expressions from long image sequences using optical flow," *IEEE Transactions on Pattern Analysis and Machine Intelligence,* vol. 18, pp. 636–642, June 1996.
20. Chang, C. C., & Lin, C. J. (2011). LIBSVM: A library for support vector machines. *ACM Transactions on Intelligent Systems and Technology* (TIST), 2(3), 27.

Application of Artificial Immune System Algorithms in Anomaly Detection

Rama Krushna Das, Manisha Panda, Sanghamitra Dash
and Sweta Shree Dash

Abstract Anomaly detection is a concept which is widely applied to a number of domains. Anomaly-based intrusion detection system (ABIDS) has the ability to detect previously unknown attacks which are important since new vulnerabilities and attacks are constantly appearing. There are several techniques of anomaly detection techniques which are developed over the years, practically and in research area to observe new attacks on the network systems. This paper proposes the better artificial immune system (AIS) algorithm for anomaly detection. We have taken two datasets; one is the NSL-KDD dataset which purely focuses on intrusion detection (ID) and another Adult dataset which is not meant for ID. Here, we have performed our assessment by using the NSL-KDD dataset which is an altered version of the broadly utilized KDDcup99 dataset. The evaluation for selection of better AIS algorithm is done by several parameters such as accuracy, specificity, False Negative Rate, False discovery Rate, and Negative Predicted Value.

Keywords Anomaly detection · Artificial immune system · Intrusion detection system · Accuracy · Specificity · False Negative Rate (FNR)
False Discovery Rate (FDR) and Negative Predicted Value (NPV)

R. K. Das (✉)
National Informatics Centre, Berhampur, India
e-mail: ramdash@yahoo.com

M. Panda
Parala Maharaja Engineering College, Berhampur, India
e-mail: manishapanda2013sai@gmail.com

S. Dash
Department of Electronic Science, Berhampur University, Berhampur, India
e-mail: smdash71@gmail.com

S. S. Dash
Department of CSE, Institute of Technical Education and Research,
Bhubaneswar, India
e-mail: sweta.soa@gmail.com

© Springer Nature Singapore Pte Ltd. 2018   687
P. K. Pattnaik et al. (eds.), *Progress in Computing, Analytics and Networking*,
Advances in Intelligent Systems and Computing 710,
https://doi.org/10.1007/978-981-10-7871-2_66

1 Introduction

Anomaly detection is the main security issue that has been studied in different research areas and application fields [1]. The two main advantages of ABIDS compared to signature-based intrusion detection systems are as follows: first, the power of detecting unknown attacks and "zero day" vulnerabilities. This occurs due to the facility of anomaly detection systems for modeling the common process of the system and for the detection of deviations against them. The second benefit is for each and every system, the profiles of the normal activity are already personalized, so building or creating the same is very problematic for an attacker to know with certainty what are the steps it should carry out, in order not to get detected [2]. In this paper, a brief study of anomaly detection is made on the clean KDD-Cup 99 dataset of NSL-KDD [3, 4] and Adult dataset [5]. The artificial immune system-based classifiers are used for the evaluation on the above two datasets. The AIS classifier algorithms AIRS1, AIRS2, AIRS2Parallel, CLONALG, CSCA, Immunos1, Immunos2, and Immunos99 are used to evaluate different parameters from the above two datasets. The results of parameters are compared for both the above datasets to justify the best classifier. The test option *percentage split* is used for training and testing the AIS classifiers. Several parameters such as accuracy, specificity, False Negative Rate (FNR), False Discovery Rate (FDR), and Negative Predicted Value (NPV) are also used for the selection of the best classifier.

2 Anomaly Detection Techniques

Anomaly detection techniques may be divided into knowledge, statistical, and machine learning-based ABIDS, which further have principal subtypes of each. Other than the above possibilities, the question of how much efficient it should be a prime consideration in selecting and implementing ABIDS. In the statistical-based techniques, it captures the network traffic results and creates a profile which represents its problematic behavior. This created profile is centered on metrics such as the traffic rate, the number of packets for each protocol, the rate of connections, the number of different IP addresses [6–8]. One of the most extensively used knowledge-based IDS schemes is the expert system approach, and it mainly comprises of three steps. This system is mostly planned for the classification of the audit data based on a set of rules. In the first rule, the identification of different attributes and classes from the training data occurs. In the second rule, a set of classification rules, parameters, or procedures are deduced. In the third rule, classification of the audit data occurs [9, 10]. The machine learning techniques are based on the establishment of an explicit or implicit model which permits the patterns examined to be classified.

3 Application of Anomaly Detection

Anomaly detection is used in a variety of domains such as fault detection, bank fraud, credit card fraud detection, mobile phone fraud detection, health problems, insurance claim fraud detection, image processing, video surveillance, context error, insider trade detection, intrusion detection, event detection in sensor networks, and detecting of ecosystem turbulence. It uses preprocessing to remove anomalous data from the dataset.

4 Experiment

This experiment is carried out, using a PC with Intel Core i5 Processor, @ 2.30 GHz, 16 GB RAM, Windows 10 Professional (64 bit) OS, and Weka [11] data mining tool. Weka contains tools for data preprocessing, classification, regression, clustering, association rules, and visualization. It is also widely used for developing new machine learning schemes [12]. Here, we have taken two types of datasets for the evaluation process, and those are the NSL-KDD dataset and the Adult dataset. NSL-KDD dataset [13] consists of 41 attributes and one target attribute (types of attacks). The target attribute consists of five subclasses namely Normal, DoS, R2L, Probes, and U2R. It consists of 125973 total number of instances. The other dataset used is Adult dataset [14] which consists of two sets, one for learning purpose and other for testing. The dataset has 14 attributes and a target attribute consisting of 2 subclasses. One class is less than equal to 50 k and another is greater than 50 k, which is based on income. It consists of 48842 total number of instances. Both the datasets were evaluated using different AIS algorithms, and the results were found out using Weka tool and compared against each other.

Below are two tables, Tables 1 and 2, giving values for accuracy, specificity, FNR, NPV, and FDR for the two dataset used. Some of the artificial immune system algorithms are used for the evaluation process, based on several evaluation criteria.

Table 1 Results of the AIS algorithms taking NSL-KDD dataset

Algorithm	Accuracy	Specificity	FNR	NPV	FDR
AIRS1	0.9405	0.9423	0.6137	0.9623	0.2879
AIRS2	0.9366	0.9396	0.5896	0.9647	0.3876
AIRS2PARALLEL	0.9287	0.9494	0.3296	0.9436	0.4265
IMMUNOS1	0.9188	0.9512	0.2810	0.9352	0.4613
IMMUNOS2	0.9207	0.9154	0.2355	0.9512	0.2747
IMMUNOS99	0.9060	0.9470	0.2925	0.9292	0.4637
CLONALG	0.9263	0.9392	0.6056	0.9456	0.2020
CSCA	0.9775	0.9812	0.3658	0.9824	0.1013

Table 2 Results of the AIS algorithms taking Adult dataset

Algorithm	Accuracy	Specificity	FNR	NPV	FDR
AIRS1	0.7816	0.7045	0.2954	0.6971	0.3028
AIRS2	Could not find any result after running it for 45 days				
AIRS2PARALLEL					
IMMUNOS1	0.7003	0.769	0.2309	0.6927	0.3072
IMMUNOS2	0.7665	0.5	0.5	0.3832	0.1167
IMMUNOS99	0.7071	0.7671	0.2328	0.6919	0.308
CLONALG	0.7665	0.5	0.5	0.3832	0.1167
CSCA	0.7762	0.6058	0.3941	0.6743	0.3256

Table 1 shows different values of accuracy, specificity, FNR, NPV, and FDR values against the NSL-KDD dataset for different AIS-based classifiers.

Table 2 shows different values of accuracy, specificity, FNR, NPV, and FDR values against the Adult dataset for different AIS-based classifiers. We can see that in this case the Adult dataset is not compatible with the AIRS2 and AIRS2Parallel algorithms. Here, we can draw a point that if the proper dataset is not chosen, then the classifiers are unable to process it irrespective of days we run it.

5 Discussion

From the above experiment, we came across different results such as accuracy, specificity, FNR, NPV, and FDR for NSL-KDD dataset as well as for the Adult dataset. The attributes of NSL-KDD dataset are compatible with each AIS classifiers taken but the attributes of Adult dataset are incompatible with AIRS2 and AIRS2Parallel algorithms. Due to the incompatibility of the Adult dataset, we were not able to get results for those two mentioned algorithms in spite of running it for 45 days. In other cases, we can see that both the dataset show better results for CSCA classifier. It is observed from the above experiment that the CSCA classifier gives highest accuracy rate of **0.9775** and lowest False Negative Rate (FNR) of **0.3658** for NSL-KDD dataset. It is also observed that the CSCA classifier gives second highest accuracy rate after AIRS1 of **0.7762** and second lowest FNR rate of **0.3941** for Adult dataset. Hence, it can be concluded that, for both the datasets, CSCA classifier shows high value of accuracy with respect to low values of FNR.

Different figures are shown below representing the graphs with accuracy, specificity, FNR, NPV, and FDR for the NSL-KDD dataset and Adult dataset.

Figure 1a, b shows the classification accuracy for NSL-KDD and Adult dataset for different AIS algorithms representing graphically.

Figure 2a, b shows the graphical representation of specificity of NSL-KDD and Adult dataset for different AIS algorithms.

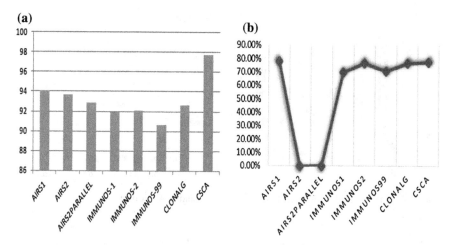

Fig. 1 Classification accuracy for **a** NSL-KDD dataset and **b** Adult dataset

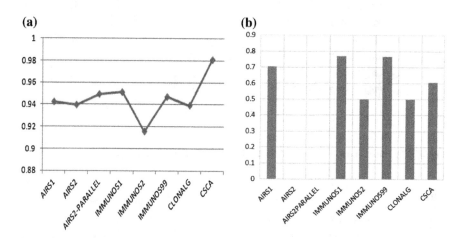

Fig. 2 Specificity for **a** NSL-KDD dataset and **b** Adult dataset

Figure 3a, b shows the graphical representation of classification of FNR of NSL-KDD and Adult dataset for different AIS algorithms.

Figure 4a, b shows the graphical representation of classification of NPV of NSL-KDD and Adult dataset for different AIS algorithms.

Figure 5a, b shows the graphical representation of classification of FDR of NSL-KDD and Adult dataset for different AIS algorithms.

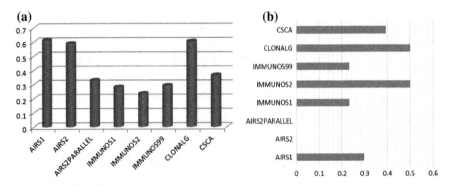

Fig. 3 Classification of FNR for **a** NSL-KDD dataset and **b** Adult dataset

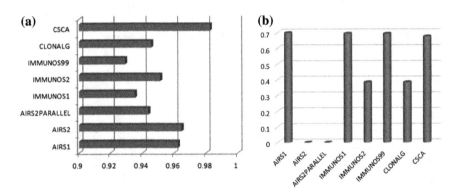

Fig. 4 Classification of NPV for **a** NSL-KDD dataset and **b** Adult dataset

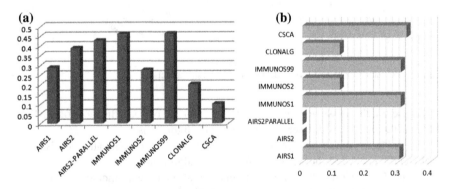

Fig. 5 Classification of FDR for **a** NSL-KDD dataset and **b** Adult dataset

6 Conclusion

Anomaly-based intrusion detection system is attracting many of the researchers due to the increasing vulnerabilities and attacks in the network system. In this paper, we represented a detailed application of the AIS algorithms in the field of anomaly detection. From the rigorous experiment and discussion, we can conclude that the CSCA algorithm is a better AIS algorithm for the anomaly detection system. The result is based on several parameters like accuracy, specificity, FNR, NPV, and FDR. We can see that the NSL-KDD dataset shows better results in case of CSCA classifier. The Adult dataset also showed comparatively better results in case of CSCA classifier. So, we can conclude that CSCA classifier is better suited for anomaly detection. It can also be concluded that, for getting better results through Weka tool using different AIS classifiers, it is advisable to select compatible datasets for the best result.

References

1. Philippe Esling and Carlos Agon, Time-Series Data Mining, ACM Computing Surveys, Volume 45, No. 1, Article 12 (2012): 1–34.
2. Animesh Patcha, Jung-Min Park, "An overview of anomaly detection techniques: Existing solutions and latest technological trends", Elsevier, Science Direct, Computer Networks, 51, pp. 3448–3470, 2007.
3. Mahbod Tavallaee, Ebrahim Bagheri, Wei Lu, and Ali A. Ghorbani: A Detailed Analysis of the KDD CUP 99 Data Set-CISDA 2009.
4. KDD Cup 1999 data (https://kdd.ics.uci.edu/databases/kddcup99/kddcup99.html) last visited-05/12/2016.
5. UCI Machine Learning Repository – Adult Data Set (https://archive.ics.uci.edu/ml/datasets/Adult).
6. Denning DE, Neumann PG. Requirements and model for IDES – a real-time intrusion detection system. Computer Science Laboratory, SRI International; 1985. Technical Report #83F83-01-00.
7. Ye N, Emran SM, Chen Q, Vilbert S. Multivariate statistical analysis of audit trails for host-based intrusion detection. IEEE Transactions on Computers 2002; 51(7).
8. Detecting hackers (analyzing network traffic) by Poisson model measure. Available from: (http://www.ensc.sfu.ca/people/grad/pwangf/IPSW_report.pdf).
9. Estévez-Tapiador JM, García-Teodoro P, Díaz-Verdejo JE. Stochastic protocol modeling for anomaly based network intrusion detection. In: Proceedings of IWIA 2003. IEEE Press, ISBN 0-7695-1886-9; 2003. pp. 3–12.
10. Sekar R., Gupta A., Frullo J., Shanbhag T., Tiwari A., Yang H., et al. Specification-based anomaly detection: a new approach for detecting network intrusions. In: Proceedings of the Ninth ACM Conference on Computer and Communications Security; 2002. pp. 265–74.
11. Weka: Data Mining Software in Java, (http://www.cs.waikato.ac.nz/~ml/weka/) last visited 02/02/2016.

12. Ian H. Witten, Eibe Frank, Mark A. Hall (2011). "Data Mining: Practical machine learning tools and techniques, 3rd Edition". Morgan Kaufmann, San Francisco. Retrieved 2011-01-19.
13. "Antigen". US National Library of Medicine. Retrieved 2015-07-30.
14. Kephart, J. O. (1994). "A biologically inspired immune system for computers". Proceedings of Artificial Life IV: The Fourth International Workshop on the Synthesis and Simulation of Living Systems. MIT Press. pp. 130–139.

Higher Order Neural Network and Its Applications: A Comprehensive Survey

Radha Mohan Pattanayak and H. S. Behera

Abstract Over the years, neural networks have shown its strength in various fields of research. There is a vast improvement in the efficiency and effectiveness of various classification techniques mainly with the introduction of higher order neural networks. Due to great learning and storage capacity with grater computational ability than the existing traditional neural networks, nowadays, researchers are very much attracted toward the higher order neural network due to their nonlinear mapping ability with less number of input units. In this paper, a comprehensive survey on Pi-Sigma higher order neural network and its different applications to various domains over more than a decade has been reviewed. These techniques are vastly used in classification and regression in several domains including medical, time series forecasting, image processing, and engineering. The extensive survey provides a recent development in higher order neural network and its applications in several application domains.

Keywords Pi-Sigma neural network (PSNN) · Jordan Pi-Sigma neural network (JPSNN) · Ridge polynomial neural network (RPNN) · Dynamic ridge polynomial neural network (DRPNN) · Recurrent Pi-Sigma neural network (RPSNN)

R. M. Pattanayak (✉)
Department of Computer Science and Engineering, Godavari Institute
of Technology (Auto.), East Godavari, Rajahmundry 533296, Andhra Pradesh, India
e-mail: radhamohan.pattanayak@gmail.com

H. S. Behera
Department of Computer Science and Engineering & Information Technology,
Veer Surendra Sai University of Technology, Burla 768018, Odisha, India
e-mail: hsbehera_india@yahoo.com

© Springer Nature Singapore Pte Ltd. 2018
P. K. Pattnaik et al. (eds.), *Progress in Computing, Analytics and Networking*,
Advances in Intelligent Systems and Computing 710,
https://doi.org/10.1007/978-981-10-7871-2_67

1 Introduction

Data analysis is the process of examining data to find useful patterns and draw conclusions that assist in decision-making process [1]. It integrates various techniques under statics, engineering, and science to perform pattern recognition, rotation distortions, etc. [2]. Since 1990, the data mining tools and techniques have been used extensively, in various areas of engineering, design, business management, e-commerce, microarrays gene expression, stocks, production control, etc. A neural network architecture is suitable for approximating higher order functions such as polynomial equations, but modeling high-frequency nonlinear discontinuous data is very difficult. In early days, different types of feed forward and recurrent neural networks have been used by the researchers, but these networks suffer from some limitation such as more training time, inefficiency, and high implementation cost. Due to these limitations, researchers are attracted toward higher order neural network (HONN).

In late 1980s, the HONN models were introduced with the addition of some higher order logical processing units with the earlier version of the feed forward neural network. Basically, the HONNs are good in solving the nonlinear problems. The first HONN model is developed by Ivakhnenko [3]. Learning, invariance, and generalization in higher order neural networks have been developed by Giles and Maxwell [4] and Mats B. [5] in 1987 and 1990.

This paper mainly focuses on extensive survey of four higher order neural networks like PSNN, JPSNN, RPNN, and DRPNN. Section 2 describes different variants of higher order neural networks. Section 3 briefly describes different real-life applications of these networks. Section 4 describes analytical discussion about these networks, and finally the conclusion and future work are discussed in Sect. 5.

2 Higher Order Neural Network (HONN)

Over the year, the traditional NNs [6] have been used in various diversified areas, but in recent time the HONNs are playing the major role with some unique features such as stronger approximation with faster convergence property, high storage capacity, and higher fault tolerance capacity in classification. Table 1 shows PSNN with its different variants used in various diversified applications.

2.1 Pi-Sigma Neural Network (PSNN)

To overcome the increased weight problem in single layer network, Shin Y. et al. [8, 10] have developed Pi-Sigma neural network (PSNN) as a feed forward network

Table 1 Different types of PSNN in various application areas

Variants of PSNN	Author	Year	Application domain	Reference
BPSN	Shin et al.	1991	Realization of Boolean function	[7]
PSNN	Shin et al.	1991	Classification	[8]
RPNN	Shin et al.	1992	Function approximation	[9]
PSNN	Shin et al.	1992	Classification	[10]
PSNN	Ghosh et al.	1992	Classification	[11]
PSNN	Shin et al.	1992	Pattern recognition	[12]
PSNN	Shin et al.	1992	Pattern classification	[13]
RPNN	Shin et al.	1995	Classification	[14]
CPSNN	Shin et al.	1997	Classification	[15]
RNN	Medsker et al.	1999	Classification	[16]
RPSN	Hussain et al.	2002	Image compression	[17]
RPNN	Voutriaridis C. et al.	2003	Pattern recognition	[18]
RPNN	Ghazali et al.	2006	Prediction of financial time series	[19]
PSNN	Xiu et al.	2007	Model for switch reluctance motor	[20]
VCS-PSNN	Song et al.	2008	Visual cryptography	[21]
PSNN	Nie et al.	2008	To train Pi-Sigma	[22]
PSNN	Husssain et al.	2009	Prediction of speech signal	[23]
DRPNN	Ghazali et al.	2007	Time series forecasting	[24]
DRPNN	Ghazali et al.	2009	Prediction of time series	[25]
DRPNN	Ghazali et al.	2009	Prediction of financial time series	[26]
RPNN	Ghazali et al.	2009	Prediction of financial time series	[27]
DRPNN	Ghazali et al.	2010	Classification	[28]
JPSNN	Husaini et al.	2011	Temperature prediction	[29]
PSNN	Husaini et al.	2011	Temperature forecasting	[30]
JPSNN	Ghazali et al.	2012	Prediction of temperature	[31]
RPNN	Yu et al.	2012	Train to RPNN	[32]
RNN	Cao et al.	2012	Wind speed forecasting	[33]
CRO-PSNN	Panigrahi et al.	2013	Pattern classification	[34]
DE-PSNN	Karali et al.	2013	Train HONN	[35]
CRO-PSNN	Sahu K. et al.	2013	Training to PSNN	[36]
PSNN	Panigrahi et al.	2013	Time series forecasting	[37]
PSO-GA-PSNN	Nayak et al.	2014	Classification	[38]
RPNN	Behera et al.	2014	Classification	[39]
JPSNN	Nayak et al.	2014	Classification	[40]

(continued)

Table 1 (continued)

Variants of PSNN	Author	Year	Application domain	Reference
PSNN	Nayak et al.	2015	Stock market forecasting	[41]
FFA-PSNN	Nayak et al.	2016	Classification	[42]
PSNN-TLBO	Nayak et al.	2016	Classification	[43]
BHO-JPSNN	Nayak et al.	2016	Nonlinear classification	[44]
DE-CRO-PSNN	Panigrahi	2017	Pattern classification	[45]
RPNN	Waheeb et al.	2017	Time series forecasting	[46]

Black hole optimization (BHO), teaching learning-based optimization (TLBO), genetic algorithm (GA), firefly algorithm (FFA), visual cryptography schema-Pi-Sigma neural network (VCS-PSNN), complex Pi-Sigma neural network (CPSNN), practical swarm optimization (PSO), chemical reaction optimization (CRO)

(FFN), which finds the product of sum of the inputs units and feeds it into a nonlinear function. The model has a single hidden layer of tunable weights and product units in the output layer [47]. As shown in Fig. 1, the input layers are connected to the summing layer and the outcome result of this layer is inputted to the product unit. In between input and summing layer, the weights are trainable and in between summing and product unit, it is non-trainable, i.e., set to unity. Though the network structure has used only one trainable hidden layer, the trainable weights drastically reduce the training time. The activation function used by summing unit is linear activation function, whereas it is nonlinear for product unit, which is used to calculate the output of the network. The output of the network and the output of jth hidden unit, i.e., h_j, can be calculated in Eqs. (1) and (2), respectively.

Fig. 1 Pi-Sigma neural network (PSNN)

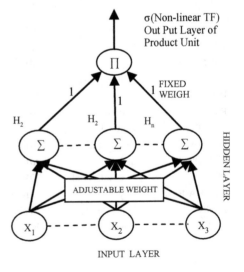

$$Y = f\left(\prod_{j=1}^{k} h_j\right) \qquad (1)$$

$$h_j = \theta_j + \sum_{i=1}^{k} W_{ij}X_i \qquad (2)$$

where θ_j is the bias, W_{ij} is weight between ith input and jth hidden unit.

2.2 Jordan Pi-Sigma Neural Network (JPSNN)

By reducing the increase of no of weight vectors along with the processing unit [8], Jordan [48] has been developed a new recurrent HONN as JPSNN. It is very similar with the feed forward PSNN structure. The JPSNN has a recurrent connection between output and input which is not in PSNN. The JPSNN network structure has three layers such as input, product, and summing. The weight vector $X_k(t)$ between input and hidden layers is trained, while the weights from the hidden layer to output layer are fixed to 1, as shown in Fig. 2. The newly generated data can be tested with trained weight vector, and the time delay will be represented by Z^{-1}. The output of the JPSNN is feed forward until it reaches to h_k, then there will be an error which occurs and this will be passed to the input unit in a backward pass. By incrementing the weights in iterative way, all the weights in the network will be updated. The output of the network can be calculated by in Eq. (3). Let X_k is the input vector to the network at time t for kth external inputs, and W_{ij} are the trained weight for

Fig. 2 Jordan Pi-Sigma neural network (JPSNN)

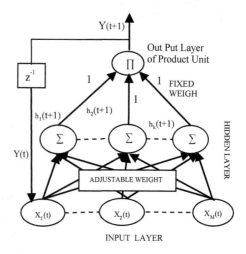

external inputs, $h_k(t+1)$ is the hidden layer summing unit, $Y(t+1)$ is the output at time $t+1$, and $f(.)$ is activation function used as sigmoid function.

$$Y(t) = \begin{cases} X_k(t) & \text{if } 1 \leq k \leq N \\ 1 & \text{if } k = N+1 \\ O_k(t) & \text{if } k = N+2 \end{cases} \qquad (3)$$

2.3 Ridge Polynomial Neural Network (RPNN)

By combining more than one PSNNs, Shin et al. [14] have developed the RPNN as a feed forward neural network (FFNN). As shown in Fig. 3, in RPNN structure, all PSNN consists of input layer, summation unit vectors in one hidden layer, and a product unit vector in output layer. RPNN network architecture is of two types, such as static and dynamic. In static structure, the number of units and weights of a network remains constant as its first construction but in dynamic network structure during the learning time the network size may be changed [14].

The output of the each PSNN network, the jth summing unit of each PSNN, and the output of the RPNN can be calculated by in Eqs. (4), (5), and (6), respectively, where $X_1, X_2, X_3, \ldots X_i$ are the input signals, the weight between each input unit X_i and hidden units Y_{ki} is W_{kij} for the kth output unit.

$$P_i(n) = \prod_{i=1}^{j} h_j(n) \qquad (4)$$

Fig. 3 Ridge polynomial
neural network (RPNN)

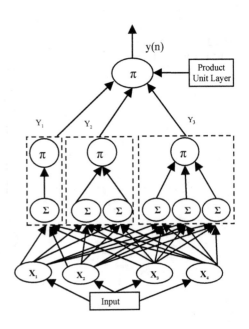

$$h_j(n) = \sum_{j=1}^{i} W_{kij} \times X_i(n) + \theta_{kj} \tag{5}$$

$$Y(n) = f\left(\sum_{i=1}^{k} P_i(n)\right) \tag{6}$$

2.4 Dynamic Ridge Polynomial Neural Network (DRPNN)

By considering a recurrent link into the RPNN structure, a new NN, i.e., dynamic ridge polynomial neural network (DRPNN) has been proposed by Ghazali R. et al. [24], where it combines the properties of HONN and RNN. As shown in Fig. 4, the DRPNN structure has been constructed by collecting several numbers of PSNNs with different degree. The structure has a feedback link in between the output and input layers, where the activation of the output unit will be feed to the summing unit in each PSN unit and allowing to each PSN to see the output of the previous pattern. DRPNN structures have memories which help the network for retaining the information which can be used later. In the network, all the weight vectors are learnable in between input and the first summing layers, but the rest are set to unity value. Let $U_1(n)$, $U_2(n)$, ... $U_m(n)$ are the external inputs and $y(n-1)$ is the output of the network at previous time. So the total inputs to the network will be the combination of all external inputs $U(n)$ and $y(n-1)$. The total inputs to the network, i.e., $Z_i(n)$, the output of the DRPNN, i.e., $y(n)$, the output produced by each PSN structure, i.e., $P_i(n)$ and the summation unit in each PSN, i.e., $h_i(n)$ can be calculated in Eqs. (7), (8), (9), and (10), respectively, where k is the total number of PSN used, $h_j(n)$ is the summation unit in each PSN structure, and W_{jo} and σ are bias and sigmoid function, respectively.

$$Z_i(n) = \begin{cases} U_i(n), & \text{if } 1 \leq i \leq M \\ y(n-1), & i = M+1 \end{cases} \tag{7}$$

$$y(n) = \sigma \sum_{i=1}^{k} P_i(n) \tag{8}$$

$$P_i(n) = \prod_{j=1}^{i} \left(h_j(n)\right) \tag{9}$$

$$h_i(n) = \sum_{i=1}^{M+1} W_{ij}(n) + W_{jo} \tag{10}$$

Fig. 4 Dynamic ridge
polynomial neural network
(DRPNN)

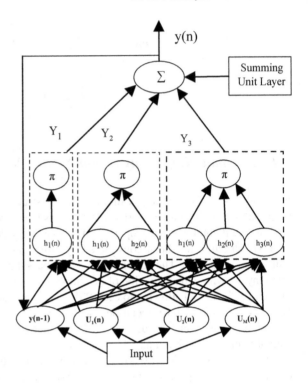

3 Literature Survey

A higher order PSNNs have been developed by Ghosh and Shin [11]. It has one layer of weight vector which reduced the training time drastically. Shin and Ghosh [7] developed a higher order PSNN which will reduce the weight vectors along with the processing units. To solve classification problem, Nayak et al. have developed BHO-JPSN [44] and GA-JPSN [40]. They compared the proposed model with various algorithms and found that in both cases, the proposed model has shown better accuracy upon the classification problem. Nayak et al. [42] proposed the PSNN with firefly algorithm to optimize the weights of PSNN. Nayak et al. have developed a hybrid PSO-GA-PSNN model [38] and TLBO-PSNN [43], to increase accuracy for the classification problem. Nie and Deng [22] used a hybrid genetic learning algorithm to train the PSNNs which overcome the speed problem of PSNN. Shin et al. [15] proposed complex Pi-Sigma network (CPSN) to reduce the weights in the PSN structure. They measured the performance of the CPSN and found that the proposed network is having very fast learning and less computational complexity. To train the dataset, Behera and Behera [39], has proposed RPNN with firefly algorithm (FFA) and compared the result of FFA-RPNN with FFA-MLP, and finally found that FFA-RPNN has shown better result in all different datasets.

Panigrahi et al. [34] and Sahu et al. [36] proposed CRO-PSNN algorithm and compared the result with two differential evolution (DE) algorithms. The comparison result showed that the proposed method has better accuracy over other two methods. To train the PSNN, Karali et al. [35] have proposed DE algorithm, and Panigrahi [45] proposed DE-CRO. The result of the algorithm has been tested with CRO, CRO-HONN, DE/rand/1/bin, and DE/best/1/bin and found that the proposed model has shown better result over others.

Husaini et al. [29, 49] proposed JPSN for prediction of temperature for next day. The prediction result is compared with MLP and PSNN and found that the mean absolute error of JPSN was lowest from PSNN and MLP. Nayak et al. [41] proposed gradient descent (GD) and GA-PSNN for prediction in stock markets. The experimental result showed the GA-PSNN model performs better result in terms of average percentage of errors (APE). Hussain et al. [23] proposed PSNN for the prediction of speech signal. They compared the result of PSNN with fundamental link network and MLP and found that the FLN showed higher signal-to-noise ratio over PSNN. Ghazali et al. have proposed RPNN [19] for forecasting the financial time series data. By comparing RPNN model with MLP, FLNN, PSN, they found that RPNN showed better result with more learning speed. Ghazali et al. [50, 24] proposed DRPNN for the prediction of the exchange rate time series. They compared the result with MLP and RPNN and found that DRPNN showed good prediction result. Husaini et al. [30] have proposed PSNN for forecasting temperature. They compared PSNN with MLP based on two parameters, i.e., (a) minimum error and (b) CPU time and found that PSNN has performed better prediction compared to MLP.

Song et al. [21] have proposed visual cryptography schema with PSNN (VCS-PSNN), to encode a secret image into n different participants. Though PSNN has smaller numbers of weight and less training time, VCS-PSN model reduces the communication rate and differentiate the information in an encrypted image. Hussain and Liatsis [17] have proposed a new RPSN which utilizes both the formation of dynamic image and predictive image coding. In this work, they used the RPSN as predictor structure in differential pulse code modulation (DPCM) system. They tested RPSN with PSN and HONN and found that the peak signal-to-noise ratio (PSNR) value of RPSN has shown more accuracy and performance for both 1-D and 2-D images. Xiu et al. [20] have developed a switched reluctance motor (SRM) by implementing Pi-Sigma neural network. They have also used Takagi-Surgeon (T-S)-type fuzzy inference system (FIS) [51] and found that the proposed model has shown high accuracy, fast computational speed, and robustness characteristic. Panigrahi and Behera [37] have implemented five normalization techniques such as Min-Max, decimal scaling, z-score, vector, median to normalize the univariate time series data. The experimental result has represented that decimal scaling and vector process have shown better accuracy compared to others.

To predict the stationary and non-stationary financial time series, Ghazali et al. [26, 52, 53] have developed DRPNN as a HONN. They compared the simulation of

DRPNN with other HONN models and found that DRPNN has better performance to capture the chaotic movement of the signal with more profit. To improve efficiency of RPNN, Yu et al. [32] have developed the RPNN by adding a penalty term to train the network. In this model, they have used monotonicity theorem and two convergence theorem and they proved that the corresponding algorithm has monotonicity properties as well as weak and strong convergence. Barbounis T. et al. [54] and Cao Q. et al. [33] have developed RNN for forecasting the wind speed. They compared this model with ARIMA and found that the recurrent model performs better over ARIMA model and also found that the multivariate model is shows better result over univariate model. Rao R. V. et al. [55] have developed TLBO method to find the solution for large-scale nonlinear problem. They compared this optimization model with some recent model in different benchmark problems such as multimodality, regularity, and dimensionality and found that in all aspects, TLBO shows better performance over other techniques. By applying regional connectivity strategies on third-order HONN, L. Spirkovska et al. [56] used the network structure to attain the rotation and translation invariant recognition in pattern recognition application. Hara Y. [57] has defined an unsupervised method, Learning Vector Quantization (LVQ) and Maximum Likelihood (ML) to classify the synthetic aperture radar (SAR) image and found that the ML has shown better accuracy over LVQ method. Voutriaridis C. et al. [18] have proposed to RPNN for function approximation then in pattern recognition task in the network and found a good result. Hsieh T.J. et al. [58] have proposed artificial bee colony (ABC) algorithm with RNN network, i.e., ABC-RNN for forecasting the stock price. They compared the result of ABC-RNN with various methods and found that ABC-RNN has shown better accuracy over all methods.

4 Analytical Discussion

Many of the HONNs have exponential increase in weights which makes to increase the order of the network, but in contrary the PSN structure has less number of weights and capable of solving the classification problem with more accuracy and high speed manner. The PSN structure has forwarded many difficult problems such as zeroing polynomials [59] and polynomial factorization [60], more effectively over other HONNs.

The HONNs are using multivariate polynomials, so it is causing explosion of weights, but in contrary RPNN [9, 16] uses univariate polynomial, so it is very easy to handle. Though RPNN has capacity to increase the information, it helps to solve more complex problems with fast learning [61, 62].

By considering the past inputs and target values, the RPNN can contain dynamic systems [52] but this type of dynamic representation will not accomplish to a network of internal feedback. But in contrary, DRPNN has a recurrent feedback

Fig. 5 Research work in various fields over the year

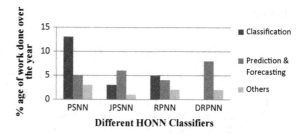

[27] so the network outputs depend on external inputs along with entire history of the system inputs. DRPNN has memories which have capacity to solve the above limitation and demonstrate a strong dynamic performance.

Figure 5 shows different research works performed in various diversified areas such as classification, prediction, and forecasting, others, i.e., image coding, cryptography, pattern recognition, and many more in various HONNs, i.e., PSNN, JPSNN, RPNN, DRPNN over the years.

5 Conclusion

In this study, we provide a comprehensive overview of procedures, functionalities, and applications of PSNN and its different variants such as JPSNN, RPNN, and DRPNN. Mainly the survey has focused with its different generalizations in various diversified fields such as temperature forecasting, stock market prediction, image processing, cryptography for image compression, nonlinear classification with different datasets from 1991 to 2017. PSNN is a very popular feed forward network, and it has been implemented widely in various application domains. During the above-mentioned period, we found that many of the researchers have trained to all the four network modules by using different optimization algorithms such as differential evolution (DE), PSO, GA, CRO, TLBO for reducing the approximation error and optimizing the weight vector.

With the above-explained models and their algorithms, our future research will include testing these models with more numbers of nonlinear boundary classification problems, evolution of these models by using some optimization techniques, training the network models by using some hybrid optimization models which will increase the efficiency of model and classification accuracy, and in addition with, the performance of the HONN can be improved by optimizing the architecture using any evolutionary algorithm.

References

1. Lippmann R.P. (1989) Pattern Classification using Neural Networks, IEEE Communications Magazine, 47–50.
2. Reid M.B. (1989) Rapid Training of Higher-order Neural Networks for Invariant Pattern Recognition, Processing of IJCNN Washington D.C, 1:689–692.
3. Ivakhnenko A.G. (1971) Polynomial theory of complex systems, IEEE transactions on Systems, Man, and Cybernetics, 1(4):364–378.
4. Giles C.L., Maxwell T. (1987) Learning, invariance, and generalization in high-order neural networks, 26:4972–4978.
5. Mats B. (1990) Higher order artificial neural networks. DIANE Publishing Company, Darby PA, USA, ISBN 0941375927.
6. Lippmann. R. P (1987) An introduction to computing with neural nets. IEEE ASSP Magazine, 4–22.
7. Shin Y., Ghosh, J. (1991) Realization of boolean functions using binary pi-sigma networks. In: Dagli, C.H., Kumara, S.R.T., Shin, Y.C. (eds.) Intelligent engineering systems through artificial neural networks, ASME Press, New York, 205–210.
8. Shin Y., Ghosh J. (1991) The Pi-Sigma Networks: An Efficient Higher-Order Neural Network for Pattern Classification and Function Approximation, In: Proceedings of International Joint Conference on Neural Networks, Seattle, WA, USA, 13–18.
9. Shin Y., Ghosh J. (1992) Approximation of multivariate functions using ridge polynomial networks, In Neural Networks, IJCNN., International Joint Conference on, 380–385.
10. Shin Y. (1992) Efficient higher-order feed forward networks for function approximation and classification (Doctoral dissertation, University of Texas at Austin).
11. Ghosh J., Shin Y. (1992) Efficient higher-order neural networks for classification and function approximation, Int J Neural Syst, 4(3):323–350.
12. Shin Y., Ghosh J., Samani D. (1992) Computationally efficient invariant pattern recognition with higher order Pi-Sigma Networks, The University of Texas at Austin.
13. Shin Y., Ghosh J., Samani D. (1992) computationally efficient invariant pattern classification with higher order pi-sigma networks, in Intelligent Engineering Systems through Artificial Neural Networks, C. H. Dagli, L. I. Burke, and Y. C. Shin, Eds. New York: ASME Press, 2: 379–384.
14. Shin Y., Ghosh I. (1995) Ridge Polynomial Networks, IEEE Transactions on Neural Networks, 6(3): 610–622.
15. Shin Y., Jin K-S. Yoon Byung-Moon. (1997) A complex pi-sigma network and its application to equalization of nonlinear satellite channels Neural Networks, International Conference on, 1:148–152.
16. Medsker L., Jain L.C. (1999) Recurrent neural networks: design and applications. CRC press.
17. Hussain A.J., Liatsis P. (2002) Recurrent pi-sigma networks for DPCM image coding, Neurocomputing, 55:363–382.
18. Voutriaridis C., Boutalis Y.S., Mertzios G. (2003) Ridge Polynomial Networks in pattern recognition, EC-VIP-MC 2003, 4th EURASIP Conference focused on Video/Image Processing and Multimedia Communications, Croatia, 519–524.
19. Ghazali R., Hussain A., El-Dereby W. (2006) Application of Ridge Polynomial Neural Networks to Financial Time Series Prediction, International Joint Conference on Neural Networks (IJCNN), 913–920.
20. Xiu J., Chang-Liang Xia. (2007) Modeling of Switched Reluctance Motor Based on Pi-sigma Neural Network, IEEE International Symposium on Industrial Electronics, 1258–1263.
21. Ge S., Peng C., Miao X. (2008) Visual Cryptography Scheme Using Pi-sigma Neural Networks, International Symposium on Information Science and Engineering, 2: 679–682.
22. Nie Y., Deng W. (2008) A Hybrid Genetic Learning Algorithm for Pi-Sigma Neural Network and the Analysis of Its Convergence, Fourth International Conference on Natural Computation, 3:19–23.

23. Husssain A.J., Jameel A.J., Al-Jumeily D., Ghazali R. (2009) Speech prediction using higher order neural networks, International Conference on Innovations in Information Technology (IIT), 294–298.

24. Ghazali R., Hussain A. J., Al-Jumeily D., & Merabti M. (2007, April) Dynamic ridge polynomial neural networks in exchange rates time series forecasting. In International Conference on Adaptive and Natural Computing Algorithms, Springer, Berlin, Heidelberg, 123–132.

25. Ghazali R., Hussain A.J., Al-Jumeily D., Lisboa P. (2009)Time series prediction using dynamic ridge polynomial neural networks, In Developments in eSystems Engineering (DESE), Second International Conference on, 354–363.

26. Ghazali R., Hussain A.J., Nawi N.M., Mohamad B. (2009) Non-stationary and stationary prediction of financial time series using dynamic ridge polynomial neural network, Neurocomputing, 72(10): 2359–2367.

27. Ghazali R., Jumeily D. (2009) Application of Pi-Sigma Neural Networks and Ridge Polynomial Neural networks to Financial Time Series Prediction, In: Zhang, M. (ed.) Artificial Higher order Neural Networks for Economics and Business, Information Science Reference, 271–293.

28. Ghazali R., Hussain A., Nawi N.M. (2010) Dynamic ridge polynomial higher order neural network, Artificial Higher Order Neural Networks for Computer Science and Engineering, 255–268.

29. Husaini N.A., Ghazali R., Nawi N.M. and Ismail L.H. (2011) Jordan Pi-sigma neural network for temperature prediction, in Ubiquitous Computing and Multimedia Applications. Springer, Berlin, Heidelberg, 547–558.

30. Husaini N.A., Ghazali R., Nawi N.M., Ismail L.H. (2011) Pi-Sigma Neural Network for Temperature Forecasting in Batu Pahat, In: Zain, J.M., Wan Mohd, W.M.b., El-Qawasmeh, E. (eds.) ICSECS, Part II. CCIS Springer, Heidelberg, 180: 530–541.

31. Ghazali R., Husaini N.A., Ismail L.H., Samsuddin N.A. (2012) An application of Jordan Pi-sigma neural network for the prediction of temperature time series signal, Recurrent Neural Networks and Soft Computing, 13(4):275–290.

32. Yu X., FengChen Q. (2012) Convergence of gradient method with penalty for Ridge Polynomial neural network, Neurocomputing, (97): 405–409.

33. Cao Q., Ewing B.T., Thompson M.A. (2012) Forecasting wind speed with recurrent neural networks. Eur. J. Oper. Res, 221(1): 148–154.

34. Panigrahi S., Pandey S., Singh R. (2013) A Novel Evolutionary Higher Order Neural Network for Pattern Classification, International Journal of Engineering Research and Technology, 2 (9).

35. Karali Y., Panigrahi S., Behera H.S. (2013) A novel Differential evolution based algorithm for higher order neural network training, Journal of Theoretical & Applied Information Technology, 56(3).

36. Sahu K.K., Panigrahi S., Behera H.S. (2013) A Novel Chemical Reaction Optimization Algorithm For Higher Order Neural Network Training, Journal of Theoretical & Applied Information Technology, 53(3).

37. Panigrahi S., Behera H.S. (2013) Effect of Normalization Techniques on Univariate Time Series Forecasting using Evolutionary Higher Order Neural Network, Int. J. Eng. Adv. Technol 3(2): 280–285.

38. Nayak J., Naik B., Behera H.S. (2014) A hybrid PSO-GA based Pi sigma neural network (PSNN) with standard back propagation gradient descent learning for classification. Control, Instrumentation, Communication and Computational Technologies (ICCICCT), International Conference on. IEEE (2014).

39. Behera N.K.S., Behera H.S. (2014) Firefly based ridge polynomial neural network for classification, IEEE International Conference on Advanced Communications, Control and Computing Technologies, 1110–1113.
40. Nayak J., Kanungo D.P., Naik B., Behera H.S. (2014) A higher order evolutionary Jordan Pi-Sigma Neural Network with gradient descent learning for classification, International Conference on High Performance Computing and Applications (ICHPCA), 1–6.
41. Nayak S. C., Misra B.B., Behera H.S. (2015) A Pi-Sigma Higher Order Neural Network for Stock Index Forecasting. Computational Intelligence in Data Mining, Springer India, 2: 311–319.
42. Nayak J., Naik B., Behera H.S. (2016) A novel nature inspired firefly algorithm with higher order neural network: Performance analysis, Engineering Science and Technology, an International Journal, 19(1):197–211.
43. Nayak J., Naik B., Behera H.S. (2016) Optimizing a higher order neural network through teaching learning based optimization algorithm, Computational Intelligence in Data Mining, Springer India, (1):57–71.
44. Nayak J., Naik B., Behera H.S. (2016) Solving nonlinear Classification problems with black hole optimization and higher order Jordan Pi-Sigma neural network: a novel approach, 2(4): 236–251.
45. Panigrahi S. (2017) A Novel Hybrid Chemical Reaction Optimization Algorithm with Adaptive Differential Evolution Mutation Strategies for Higher Order Neural Network Training, International Arab Journal of Information Technology (IAJIT), 14(1).
46. Waheeb W., Ghazali R., Herawan T. (2017) Time Series Forecasting Using Ridge Polynomial Neural Network with Error Feedback, In: Herawan T., Ghazali R., Nawi N., Deris M. (eds) Recent Advances on Soft Computing and Data Mining. SCDM 2016. Advances in Intelligent Systems and Computing Springer, Cham, 549.
47. Schmitt M. (2002) On the complexity of computing and learning with multiplicative neurons, Neural Computation, 14(2):241–301.
48. Jordan M.I. (1986) Attractor Dynamics and Parallelism in a Connectionist Sequential Machine, Proceedings of the Eighth Conference of the Cognitive Science Society, New Jersey, USA.
49. Husaini N.A., Ghazali R., Ismail L.H., Herawan T. (2014) A Jordan Pi-Sigma Neural Network for Temperature Forecasting in Batu Pahat Region. In: Herawan T., Ghazali R., Deris M. (eds) Recent Advances on Soft Computing and Data Mining, Advances in Intelligent Systems and Computing Springer, Cham, 287.
50. Ghazali R. (2007) Higher order neural networks for financial time series prediction, PhD diss., Liverpool John Moores University.
51. Liu Y., Yang J., Yang D., Wu W. (2014) A modified gradient-based neuro-fuzzy learning algorithm for pi-sigma network based on first-order takagi-sugeno system. J Math Res Appl, 34(1): 114–126.
52. Ghazali R., Nazri M.N., Mohd N.M.S. (2011) Dynamic Ridge Polynomial Neural Network with a Real Time Recurrent Learning Algorithm: Forecasting the S&P 500 (<Special Issue> SOFT COMPUTING METHODOLOGIES AND ITS APPLICATIONS), Biomedical fuzzy and human sciences: the official journal of the Biomedical Fuzzy Systems Association, 16(2): 97–103.
53. Ghazali R., Hussain A.J., Liatsis P. (2011) Dynamic Ridge Polynomial Neural Network: Forecasting the univariate non-stationary and stationary trading signals, Expert Systems with Applications, 38(4): 3765–3776.
54. Barbounis T., Theocharis J. (2007) A locally recurrent fuzzy neural network with application to the wind speed prediction using spatial correlation. Neurocomputing 70: 1525–1452.
55. Rao R.V., Savsani V.J., Vakharia D.P. (2012) Teaching–learning-based optimization: an optimization method for continuous non-linear large scale problems, Information sciences 183(1):1–15.

56. L. Spirkovska and M.B. Reid, (1990) Connectivity Strategies for Higher-order Neural Networks applied to Pattern Recognition, Proceedings of IJCNN, San Diego, 1:21–26.

57. Hara Y. (1994) Application of neural networks to radar image classification, IEEE Transactions on Geoscience and Remote Sensing, 32(1): 100–109.

58. Hsieh T.J., Hsiao H.F., Yeh W.C. (2011) Forecasting stock markets using wavelet transforms and recurrent neural networks: an integrated system based on artificial bee colony algorithm. Appl. Soft. Comput, 11(2): 2510–2525.

59. D.S. Huang, H.H.S. lp, K.C.K. Law and Z. Chi (2005) Zeroing polynomials using modified constrained neural network approach. IEEE Transactions on neural networks, 16(3):721–732.

60. S. Perantonis, N. Ampazis, S. Varoufakis and G. Antoniou (1998) Constrained learning in neural networks, Application to factorization of 2-d polynomials, Neural Processing Letter, 7 (1):5–14.

61. Tawfik H., Liatsis P. (1997) Prediction of Non-linear Time series using Higher Order Neural Network, Proceeding IWSSIP'97 Conference, Poznan, Poland.

62. Voutriaridis C., Boutalis Y.S, Mertzios G. (2003) Ridge Polynomial Networks in Pattern Recognition.EC-VIP-MC 2003, 4th EURASIP Conference focused on Video/Image Processing and Multimedia Communications, Croatia, 519–524.

Application of Genetic Algorithm to Derive an Optimal Cropping Pattern, in Part of Hirakud Command

Ashutosh Rath, Sandeep Samantaray, Sudarsan Biswal
and Prakash Chandra Swain

Abstract Proper management with available limited water resources is to be given top priority to meet the threat of food security due to increase in population. Establishment of a new major irrigation project is a challenging task due to social, environmental and other multiple causes. The present study is conducted on Senhapali Canal, a distributary of Hirakud system in Sambalpur District of Odisha State, India, which is very close to Hirakud Dam over River Mahanadi. In the present work, experiments are conducted to develop a suitable cropping pattern through optimization techniques like LINDO and Genetic Algorithm. The developed cropping pattern gives net returns of Rs. 585 lakhs while using LINDO and Rs. 590.07 lakhs if GA is used. Hence, the cropping pattern obtained by using Genetic Algorithm may be adopted by the farmer to get more net returns than the existing one adopted by farmers.

Keywords Genetic Algorithm · Hirakud command area · Optimization
CROPWAT · ADV Flow Tracker

A. Rath (✉) · S. Biswal · P. C. Swain
Department of Civil Engineering, Veer Surendra Sai University of Technology, Burla, India
e-mail: erashutoshrath@gmail.com

S. Biswal
e-mail: sudarsanbiswal92@gmail.com

P. C. Swain
e-mail: pcswain.vssut@hotmail.com

S. Samantaray
Department of Civil Engineering, College of Engineering and Technology, Bhubaneswar, India
e-mail: samantaraysandeep963@gmail.com

© Springer Nature Singapore Pte Ltd. 2018
P. K. Pattnaik et al. (eds.), *Progress in Computing, Analytics and Networking*,
Advances in Intelligent Systems and Computing 710,
https://doi.org/10.1007/978-981-10-7871-2_68

711

1   Introduction

There is a great necessity of irrigation in Indian tropical climate. Agriculture plays an important role in economical performance of the country. It contributes about 15 to 20% of the total GDP. More than 60% of population of the country depend directly or indirectly on agriculture. Due to rapid increase in population and stagnation in agricultural production there is an increase in food scarcity in Odisha. Hence an integrated planning of available land and water resources in the state is required to maximize the economic returns. Optimization techniques are used to find the best feasible solution and operating policy which can provide improvement in the system performance. Genetic Algorithm (GA) based on the concept of natural selection and process of evolution utilized largely for solving all types of optimization problems considering all the boundary conditions. The aim of this study is to develop a method to get maximum yield from a particular crop land and also by managing the irrigation water in that particular area. Frizzone et al. developed a separable linear programming model, considering a set of technical factors which might influence the profit of an irrigation project. Srivastava et al. [7] proposed an integrated Genetic Algorithm (GA) for development of watershed and NPS pollution model. Kumar et al. [4] described the application of Genetic Algorithm (GA) in water distribution to various crops from an irrigation reservoir. Azamathulla et al. [1] made a comparative study between the Genetic Algorithm and linear programming for high efficiency of reservoir operating system. Yang et al. [8] used Genetic Algorithm for multi-objective planning of both surface and subsurface water. Mehdipour et al. [5] described rule curve for reservoir operation. Singh [6] developed a optimization model to increase farm income. Banik et al. derived a comparative crop water assessment using CROPWAT. CROPWAT is used to develop a model for water assessment of using field data. The aim of the present work is to formulate a feasible and acceptable cropping pattern in the proposed study area for deriving optimal benefits.

2   Study Area

The Senhapali Distributary, given in Fig. 1, emerges out of the power channel of the Hirakud system to provide irrigation to villages Chaunrpur, Senhapali, Berhampura, Baguria, Bakbira, Jharpali, Tihikipali. The CCA of Senhapali Distributary is 871 ha. There are two cropping seasons, namely kharif from June to December and Rabi from January to May. The study area produces a large portion of food crops of the Odisha State. So this area is also known as the food bowls of the state of Odisha. At the present scenario, the farmers of the area are showing their disinterest in cultivation, because of huge financial loss they are facing for last few years due to uncertainty of rainfall and decrease in the water availability.

Fig. 1 Command area map
of the Senhapali Distributary

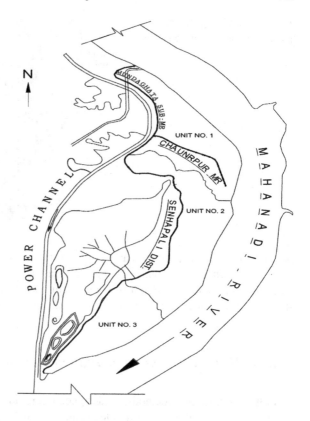

3   Materials and Method

3.1   CROPWAT 8.0

The CROPWAT software which was developed by FAO, in the year 2006, applied to find the water needed for various crops. The software requires the data such as climate/ETo, rain, soil, types of crops.

3.2   Flow Monitoring with Flow Tracker

The Flow Tracker is described in Fig. 2. As per the specification, it can be operated with a frequency of magnitude 10 MHz. It is found that acoustic velocimeters can be applied for measuring both mean and turbulent velocities accurately and report estimates of the error based on velocity range settings. The Flow Tracker ADV measures the phase change caused by the Doppler shift in acoustic frequency that occurs when a transmitted acoustic signal reflects off the particles in the flow.

Fig. 2 Flow Tracker with 2D
probe principle of operation

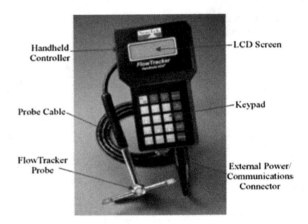

Handheld Controller — LCD Screen

Probe Cable — Keypad

FlowTracker Probe — External Power/Communications Connector

The magnitude of the phase change is proportional to the flow velocity. The flow velocity determines the phase change. It can measure the velocities of various sections even in shallow depth of about 3 cm with a velocity ranging from 0.1 to 450 cm/s. The various parts of the instruments are shown in the figure.

3.3 LINDO: Classical Optimization Techniques

LINDO: Optimization methods are designed to provide the 'best' values of system design and operating policy variables values that will lead to the highest levels of system performance.

3.4 Genetic Algorithm

3.4.1 Methods of Operation of GA

It is one of the popular methods used for optimization, which was put forth by John Holland (1960). But it became more popular in the 1980s. Its concept was based on biology. Darwin's principle: survival of the fittest. It is based on the bio-inspired operators like mutation, crossover and selection. In engineering, first the model was transformed to a function and solution is found and then the parameters are found which are to be optimized. Genetic Algorithm optimization tool always provides a potential solution. The Genetic Algorithm is expressed by encoding of the search space, represented by a chromosome. 1. It starts with a set of population. 2. Solution for each one is found and new population was found on the basis of data in which new population is better than the old one. 3. Then the Solution is done on the basis of more fitness value which will help for reproduction of next generation. 4. Process was continued till the termination criteria were satisfied GA.

3.4.2 Steps of Genetic Algorithm

1. Population initialization using random generation. 2. Fitness function evaluation for each individual. 3. Following steps are updated until the stopping criteria are reached. i. For reproduction best fit individual is selected. ii. Crossover and mutation processes are done to generate new offspring. iii. Again fitness of individual member is calculated. iv. Less fit individual is replaced with new one. 4. Best solution was found. 5. Process will be continued until reach the stopping criteria

4 Derivation of Optimized Crop Pattern

The objective function is determined by considering the net benefits that the farmers are expected to get after deducting all the expenditures given in Eq. (1). While (2), (3) and (4) present the cost of fertilizers, seeds and labour, the constraints are the available land and the water flow in the canals which is ascertained with the help of the Flow Tracker given by Eqs. (6), (7) and (8).

Objective function:

$$\text{MAXP} = \sum_{i}^{n} \begin{bmatrix} (P_i * Y_i * A_i) - A_i[(\text{Cost of Fertilizers})_i + (\text{Cost of Seed})_i \\ + (\text{Cost of Labour})_i + (\text{Cost of water requirements})_i] \end{bmatrix} \quad (1)$$

where

P   Profit,
P_i Price of each crop in market (Rs/qntl),
Y_i Yield of each crop (qntl/ha),
A_i Area of each crop (ha).

$$\text{Cost of Fertilizer} = [(U_i * U_c) + (D_i * D_c) + (M_i * M_c)] * A_i \quad (2)$$

where

U_i Urea required for each crop (kg/ha),
U_c Cost of urea (Rs/kg),
D_i DAP required for each crop (kg/ha),
D_c Cost of DAP (Rs/kg),
M_i MOP required for each crop (kg/ha),
M_c Cost of MOP (Rs/kg).

$$\text{Cost of Seed} = [(S_i * S_c)] * A_i, \tag{3}$$

where S_i = Seed required for each crop (kg/ha),

S_c = Cost of seed (Rs/kg).
$$\text{Cost of Labour} = [(L_i * L_c)] * A_i, \tag{4}$$

where L_i = Labour required for each crop (person/ha),

L_c= Cost of labour (Rs/person).
$$\text{Cost of Water} = [(W_{ri} * W_c)] * A_i, \tag{5}$$

where W_{ri} = Water requirement for each crop (m),

W_c = Cost of water (Rs/ha * m), ha = hectare, m = Metre.
Water availability constraints:

$$\sum (W_{ri} * A_i) \leq W_t \tag{6}$$

where W_t = Total water available from canal.
Land area constraints in different seasons:

$$\sum A_i \leq A_t, A_t = \text{The Cultivation area in different Season (Kharif and Rabi)} \tag{7}$$

Crop area constraints:

$$L_{bi} \leq A_i \leq U_{bi},$$

where L_{bi} = Lower bound of each crop, U_{bi} = Upper bound of crop nonnegative constraints:

$$A_i \geq 0 \tag{8}$$

4.1 Crop Yield of the Study Area

In this study, the crop yield for the kharif season only for the study area is taken into consideration. The data are verified by comparing with the report collected from Irrigation Department, Government of Odisha. Then the Solution is done on the basis of more fitness value which will help for reproduction of next generation. The detail of which is described in Table 1.

4.2 Water Requirement of Crops Using CROPWAT

CROPWAT is applied to find out the crop water requirements of the crops of the study area by considering local climatic conditions, soil data and rainfall data, as given in Table 2.

4.3 Discharge Measurement

The canal is divided into various cross sections for the velocity measurement. The instrument is placed at various width and heights to calculate the velocity. The calculated discharge at various sections is given in Table 3.

5 Results and Discussions

With the present cropping pattern, the farmers are getting a net benefit of 0.6705 million USD. The LINDO optimization suggests a net benefit of 0.8775 million USD by adopting the cropping pattern proposed by the software. By using the maximization technique and putting that equation in the main function and taking

Table 1 Crops and yields data of the study area

Crop	Yield (quintal/ha)	Crop	Yield (quintal/ha)
Paddy	33	Til	5.5
Maize	22	Potato	110
Arhar	10	Vegetables	125
Green Gram	6	Chilly	15
Black gram	5	Ginger	160
Other pulses	5	Turmeric	40
Groundnut	13		

Table 2 Crop water requirement (CWR) value for each crop in study area

Types of crops	CWR (m)	Cost of crop (Rs/qntl)	Types of crops	CWR (m)	Cost of crop (Rs/qntl)
Paddy	0.7901	1900	Potato	0.3042	1100
Maize	0.322	4000	Vegetables	0.2892	1500
Green gram	0.308	7250	Chilly	0.2338	10000
Black gram	0.308	8500	Ginger	0.2338	8000
Other pulses	0.244	8000	Turmeric	0.2338	11000
Groundnut	0.1931	4900	Arhar	0.308	10950
Til	0.2088	14000	Potato	0.3042	1100

Table 3 Measured discharge data

Number	Mean velocity (m/s)	Area of section (m^2)	Discharge (m^3/s)
1	0.359	2.311	0.830
2	0.426	1.938	0.826
3	0.482	1.675	0.807
4.1	0.332	2.395	0.795
4.2	0.369	2.141	0.790
5.1	0.354	2.173	0.769
5.2	0.435	1.705	0.741
6.1	0.280	2.625	0.735
6.2	0.300	2.43	0.729
7	0.380	1.905	0.724
8	0.344	1.978	0.680
9	0.251	2.504	0.629
10	0.287	2.175	0.624
11	0.732	0.840	0.615
12.1	0.545	1.106	0.602
12.2	0.441	1.204	0.531
13.1	0.504	1.045	0.527
13.2	0.596	0.827	0.493
14	0.199	2.015	0.401
15	0.147	2.048	0.301
16	0.275	0.660	0.181

the fitness function and constraint function into consideration, the values are calculated in GA. The crossover value and population values are changed, and after various iterations, the best cropping pattern for kharif season is found out. The benefits suggested by GA are more as compared to the LINDO. The optimal cropping pattern suggested by the Genetic Algorithm is given in Table 4.

It gave the different area of crops which should be adopted to arrive at the maximum profit. The cropping pattern is shown below.

GA gave the best fitness value and mean fitness value at generation value indicated by Fig. 3. The figure clearly shows the best and mean fitness values. The area of allocation by GA for various crops is shown in the graphical form in Fig. 4.

6 Conclusions

In this study, a total of 13 different types of crops for kharif season have been taken into consideration for investigation. The total cultivable area considered for calculation is equal to the total cultivable area adopted by farmers for kharif.

Table 4 Proposed crop areas by GA

Crop	Notation	Area of crop (ha)
Paddy	P	460.21
Maize	M	34.61
Arhar	A	24.49
Green gram	O	34.94
Black gram	B	43.54
Other pulses	S	76.44
Groundnut	G	9.85
Til	T	19.74
Potato	U	18.00
Chilly	C	29.49
Ginger	I	9.97
Turmeric	W	9.91
Vegetables	V	99.76

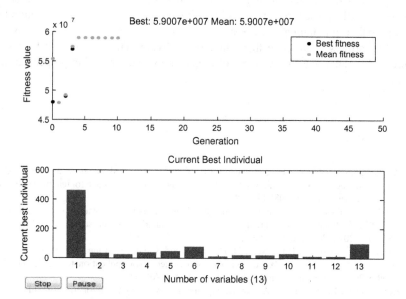

Fig. 3 Profit obtained and area of crop for maximum profit using GA for kharif season

Area Proposed for various Crops in Kharif Season

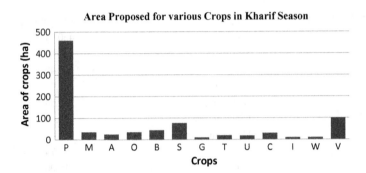

Fig. 4 Cropping pattern for kharif season obtained using GA

The major crop in the study area is paddy. The present benefits the farmers are getting are amount to 0.6705 million USD. The cropping pattern suggested by LINDO, the profit suggests a net benefit of 0.8775 million USD in kharif season. This is about 46% more as compared to the present habit. A net benefit of 0.885 million USD using Genetic Algorithm is obtained. This is about 48% more as compared to the present one. Hence GA is found to be an effective optimization tool for optimal crop planning and can be used for other command area. The study will help the farmers to improve their standard of living. The benefits can be further increased by adopting the principle of crop rotation and providing proper marking facilities.

References

1. Azamathulla, H. Md., Wu, Fu-C., Ghani, A.Ab., Narulkar, S.M.: Zakaria, N.A., and Chang, C.K.: Comparison between genetic algorithm and linear programming approach for real time operation. J. Hydro-environ. Res. (2008) 172–181.
2. Banik, P., Tiwari, N.K., and Ranjan, S.: Comparative crop water assessment using CROPWAT. International Journal of Sustainable Materials, Processes & ECO-Efficient – IJSMPE. (2014) Volume 1: Issue 3.
3. Frizzone, J.A., Coelho, R.D., Neto, D. Dourado., and Soliani, R.: Linear programming model to optimize the water resource use in irrigation projects: an application to the Senator Nilo Coelho Project. Sci.agric. (Piracicaba, Braz.). (1997) Vol. 54.
4. Kumar, D.N., Raju, K.S. and Ashok, B.: Optimal reservoir operation for Irrigation of Multiple Crops Using Genetic Algorithm. Journals of Irrigation and Drainage Engineering. (2006) Vol. 132, No. 2, April 1, 2006, ASCE, ISSN 0733-9437/2006/2-123-129.
5. Mehdipour, E. Fallah., Haddad, O. Bozorg., and Mariño, M.A.: Extraction of Multi-crop planning rules in a reservoir System: Application of Evolutionary Algorithms. Journal of Irrigation and Drainage Engineering. (2013) Vol. 139, No. 6.
6. Singh, A.: Optimizing the Use of Land and Water Resources for Maximizing Farm Income by Mitigating the Hydrological Imbalances. Journal of Hydrologic Engineering. (2014) Vol. 19, No. 7, July 1, 2014. © ASCE, ISSN 1084-0699/2014/7-1447-1451013. ASCE, ISSN 0733-9437/2013/6-490-498.

7. Srivastava, P., Hamlet, J.M., Robillard, P.D., and Day, R.L.: Watershed optimization of best management using AnnAGNPS and a genetic algorithm. Water Resour. Res. (2002) 38(3), https://doi.org/10.1029/2001wr000365.
8. Yang, C.-C., Chang, L.C., Chen, C.-S., and Yeh, M.-S.: Multi-objective planning for conjunctive use of surface and subsurface water using genetic algorithm and dynamics programming. Water Resour. Man. (2009).

Collaborative Filtering Using Restricted Boltzmann Machine and Fuzzy C-means

Dayal Kumar Behera, Madhabananda Das, Subhra Swetanisha
and Bighnaraj Naik

Abstract Recommender system is valuable to find items as per users' taste from a large volume of items. Various popular techniques to perform personalized recommendations are content based, collaborative, and hybrid recommender. Collaborative filtering is widely used in this domain which can be of memory based or model based. The datasets used in recommender systems are very often sparse. Hence, accurate prediction can be made by grouping users/items into cluster. In this paper, an attempt is made to cluster the users using FCM clustering algorithm, and then, RBM is used to predict the user's preferences. Experiment is carried out on MovieLens benchmark dataset. The results depict the performance of using both FCM and RBM to build the model for recommendation.

Keywords Collaborative filtering · Restricted Boltzmann Machine
User-based filtering · Movie recommendation

1 Introduction

In the age of Web 3.0, the exponential growth of data and number of users of the Internet results information overload problem. It is very challenging to efficiently extract the constructive information from all the available online information

D. K. Behera (✉) · M. Das
Department of CSE, KIIT University, Bhubaneswar, India
e-mail: dayalbehera@gmail.com

M. Das
e-mail: mndas_prof@kiit.ac.in

D. K. Behera · S. Swetanisha
Department of CSE, Trident Academy of Technology, Bhubaneswar, India
e-mail: sswetanisha@gmail.com

B. Naik
Department of Computer Application, VSSUT, Burla, Odisha, India
e-mail: mailtobnaik@gmail.com

© Springer Nature Singapore Pte Ltd. 2018
P. K. Pattnaik et al. (eds.), *Progress in Computing, Analytics and Networking*,
Advances in Intelligent Systems and Computing 710,
https://doi.org/10.1007/978-981-10-7871-2_69

(structured and unstructured) as the growth of the Internet is increasing rapidly day by day. Recommender system (RS) is collection of software tools and techniques that direct users in a personalized way to appealing/required items from a huge space of option. This personalized RS aims to discover new item to the user from a large collection of data based on the past preferences and tastes. Systems using recommendation can use different recommendation techniques like collaborative filtering-based [1, 2], content-based [3], knowledge-based [4], and hybrid recommendations [5, 6]. Content-based system recommends items that are similar to the items that the users liked in the past. However, collaborative filtering-based recommendation is simple and recommends items that other users with similar tastes of the active user liked in the past.

However, recommendation system is considered to be a bigdata problem as the number of items and preferences of users are huge and unstructured. Most of the collaborative filtering algorithms are not suitable for very large datasets. In the paper [7], R. Salakhutdinov et al. proposed how RBM, i.e., Restricted Boltzmann Machine, can be applied on large dataset and compare the result with SVD model. In this paper, we have used Fuzzy C-means to cluster, upon which Restricted Boltzmann Machine is implemented to predict the rating of the user for which they have not given the rating, and based on the predicted rating, the system recommends movies to the user. We have used the MovieLens dataset for experiment and compare the result of RBM with FCM and K-means.

2 Related Works

Collaborative filtering (CF) [8] is considered as the most popular technique implemented in recommender system. Goldberg et al. [9] introduced CF to deal with information Tapestry. In the literature, different methods are proposed in view of predicted ratings accuracy.

To devise recommendations for a group of users, the popular method is k-nearest neighbors-based CF. Fernando Ortega et al. [10] explained how group recommendations are performed using Matrix Factorization (MF), where proposed method is considering different size of the datasets. Hamidreza Koohi et al. [11] proposed a FCM approach and compared the result with K-means & SOM for the MovieLens dataset. Edjalma Queiroz da Silva et al. [1] proposed genetic algorithm-based recommendation for combining various feasible techniques on MovieLens dataset.

Collaborative filtering is also widely used in the field of movie recommendation. María N. Moreno et al. [12] proposed a structure to deal with some of issues like: scalability and sparsity associated with movies' recommendation. Shouxian Wei et al. come up with an approach using tags and ratings [5]. The main objective is to improve the fusion ability considering various aspects. Meng-Hui Chen et al. [13] proposed an AI-based immune network for collaborative filtering in movie recommendation. In the paper [14], a hybrid model using improved K-means and genetic algorithms (GAs) for movie's recommendation system is proposed by Zan Wang et al. to deal with the information overload problem.

3 Collaborative Filtering

CF approaches are divided into two categories: User based and item based.

3.1 User-Based CF

User-based collaborative approaches [11] measure the similarities between users. Table 1 depicts the rating matrix of users for different movies. To find the similarity among users, one popular method used in RS is Pearson's correlation coefficient.

$$sim(A, B) = \frac{\sum_{m \in M} (r_{A,m} - \bar{r}_A) (r_{B,m} - \bar{r}_B)}{\sqrt{\sum_{m \in M} (r_{A,m} - \bar{r}_A)^2} \sqrt{\sum_{m \in M} (r_{B,m} - \bar{r}_B)^2}} \tag{1}$$

The $sim(A, B)$ in Eq. 1 [11] calculates similarity between two users A & B. The symbol $\bar{r}$ represents average ratings of the user, and $r_{A,m}$ represents preference or rating of user A for movie m.

3.2 Fuzzy C-means Clustering (FCM)

Fuzzy logic can be applied to those problems where multi-valued logic is expected instead of crisp logic. Therefore, Fuzzy logic can be used for clustering because the idea behind the clustering is to group similar objects based on some degree of membership. Fuzzy C-means is a popular approach for Fuzzy classification.

In Fuzzy C-means, a data element is allowed to present in every cluster with membership grade from 0 to 1. Let the sample set be $X = \{x_1; x_2; ...; x_n\}$ divided

Table 1 Rating database for user-item matrix

	Movie 1	Movie 2	Movie 3	Movie 4
User 1	5	–	–	5
User 2	–	5	3	–
User 3	5	–	4	3

into C groups with centers as c_j ($j = \{1; 2; ...; C\}$) using FCM and the aim is to minimize the objective function [15], which is represented in Eq. 2.

$$J_a = \sum_{j=1}^{c} \sum_{i=1}^{n} u_{ij}^a \|x_i - c_j\|^2, 1 \leq a \leq \infty \tag{2}$$

where $u_{ij} \in [0,1]$ signifies the membership of ith data element to jth cluster center.

3.3 Restricted Boltzmann Machines (RBM)

RBM consists of two layers, a layer of visible units and a layer of hidden units with no connections in the same layer. RBM model [7] can slightly outperform Matrix Factorization and can be used as a deep model to learn.

Training RBM has two phases: (1) forward pass and (2) backward pass or reconstruction. In the forward pass, input data from all visible nodes are being passed to all hidden nodes. At the hidden layer's nodes, X (input data) is multiplied by a W (weight between the neurons) and added to hidden layer bias "h_bias." The resultant value is fed into the sigmoid function, which produces the node's output/ state. In the reconstruction phase, the samples from the hidden layer play the role of input. Contrastive divergence (CD) is actually a matrix of values that is computed and used to adjust values of the W matrix. Changing W incrementally leads to training of W values. Then, on each step (epoch), W is updated to a new value W' as shown in Eq. 3 where $\propto$ is the learning rate. Figure 1 represents RBM layers in movie recommendation.

$$W' = W + \propto * CD \tag{3}$$

Fig. 1 RBM for movie recommendation

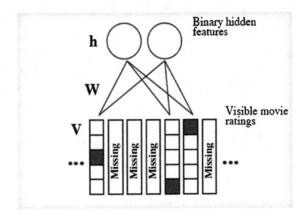

4 Experimental Design

The aim of this paper is to apply FCM [16] and RBM to user-based CF. The users' rating dataset is generally sparse and large in size. In order to predict rating of the missing entry in the dataset, RBM is used. To begin with, the dataset is divided into tenfold cross-validation subsets. In each case, 80% of the dataset is taken as training set and rest 20% is taken as test set for recommendation prediction. Firstly, clustering technique is applied to find the nearest group, and then on the resulting cluster, RBM is used to predict the missing ratings. The proposed experimental model is depicted in Fig. 2.

In the clustering process, Fuzzy C-means [16] clustering method is taken because it handles continuous rating between 0 and 1. Also, it deals with nonlinearities and uncertainties as compared to K-means and SOM [11]. FCM provides degree of belongingness of every user that belongs to different clusters. In order to find user group, centroid method is considered for defuzzification.

Once the RBM model is trained, it can be used to predict movies that an arbitrarily selected user from the testing set might like. This can be accomplished by feeding in the user's watched movie preferences (rating) into the RBM and then reconstructing the input. The values that the RBM produced are the estimated value of the user's preferences for movies that the user has not watched based on the preferences of the users that the RBM was trained on. Finally, top K best movies are chosen for recommendation.

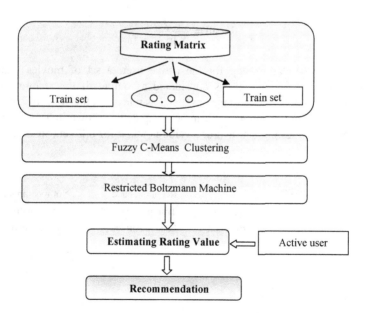

Fig. 2 Experimented model

5   Experimental Results

5.1   Dataset

In this study, MovieLens dataset from "grouplens.org" Web site is taken for experiments. It is considered as the benchmarked dataset for evaluating recommender system. The dataset used here contains one million real ratings from 6000 users on 4000 movies. It is so sparse: about 7% of ratings are available and rest 93% of ratings are missing.

5.2   Evaluation Metrics

In this work, precision, recall, and recommendation accuracy [11] are calculated for evaluating the results of the experimented method using Equations 4, 5, and 6 where tp is true positive, tn is true negative, fp represents false positive, and fn represents false negative.

$$\text{Accuracy} = \frac{\sum tp + \sum tn}{|Population|} \qquad (4)$$

$$\text{Precision} = \frac{\sum tp}{\sum tp + \sum fp} \qquad (5)$$

$$\text{Recall} = \frac{\sum tp}{\sum tp + \sum fn} \qquad (6)$$

In the recommendation step for the active user, a set of movies with their resultant recommendation score is considered as output. If the recommendation score is more than 50%, the item is considered as relevant, otherwise irrelevant. The confusion matrix for the active user can be computed as shown in Table 2, and for all the users in the testing set, average value is taken for different matrices.

Table 2 Recommendation confusion matrix

	Recommended	Not recommended
Relevant	True positive (tp)	False negative (fn)
Irrelevant	False positive(fp)	True negative (tn)

5.3 Implementation

5.3.1 Importing Necessary Libraries

After downloading the dataset, necessary libraries are imported to the projects workspace. Libraries like "Tensorflow" and "Numpy" are taken to model and to initialize the RBM, "Pandas" to easily manipulate the datasets, and "matplotlib" to plot the graph.

5.3.2 Loading and Formatting the Data

The input to the model contains X neurons, where X is the number of movies in the dataset. Each neuron contains a normalized rating value as 0 to 1. If user has not watched the movie, the value is 0 and for high rating, the value is closer to 1. After loading the dataset, the rating is normalized as per the requirement. Unnecessary columns are deleted from the dataset.

5.3.3 Setting the Model Parameters

To evaluate the proposed method, 80% of the data taken as training and 20% for testing for each tenfold cross-validated dataset. To minimize the dataset, first, clustering technique is used to cluster the dataset, and on different clusters, RBM is used. Sigmoid and Relu functions are taken as activation function. Mean Absolute Error is taken as error function. Each epoch uses certain batches with some size (e.g., each epoch uses ten batches with size 100).

5.3.4 Recommendation

Once the model is trained, it is used to predict movies that an active user might like. This is implemented by feeding the preferences of user's watched movie into RBM and then reconstructing the input. The output given by the RBM estimates the item's recommendation score for the active user. Based on the score, categories of relevant and irrelevant items are found, and then, the evaluation metrics are calculated from the confusion matrix.

5.4 Results

Table 3 shows the performance of RBM + K-means for different number of clusters.

Table 3 Recommendation with RBM + K-means

No of cluster	Accuracy (%)	Precision (%)	Recall (%)
3	79.6	59.4	13.8
5	78.3	57.2	11.7
7	79.1	56.4	13.6

Table 4 Recommendation with RBM + FCM

No of cluster	Accuracy (%)	Precision (%)	Recall (%)
3	82.8	64.5	18.1
5	81.5	63.3	16.6
7	80.2	60.7	17.2

Table 4 shows the results of FCM with RBM for different number of clusters. In case of three clusters, RBM with FCM algorithm results 82.8 accuracy, whereas with K-means results 79.6% accuracy.

6 Conclusion

Recommender system helps the end users to save time in finding relevant items out of large collections as per their tastes. But users' preferences on the items are very less as compared to number of items available. So finding the most suitable similar users and estimating the missing ratings is a major challenge in a sparse dataset. In this work, a recommendation model is designed by using Restricted Boltzmann Machine with different clustering techniques to predict the users' preferences for movie ratings. The model is implemented in python language, and some of the libraries used are tensorflow, numpy, and pandas. As per the achieved outcomes on the MovieLens dataset shown in Tables 3 and 4, it is observed that RBM with FCM clustering algorithm performs better as compared to RBM with K-means algorithm.

Acknowledgements The authors would like to express thanks to all the reviewers for valuable comments and suggestions.

References

1. Silva, E., Camilo-Junior, C., Pascoal, L., Rosa, T.: An evolutionary approach for combining results of recommender systems techniques based on collaborative filtering. Science Direct. Expert Systems With Applications 53 (2016) 204–218.
2. Bu, J., Shen, X., Xu, B., Chen, C., He, X., Cai, D.: Improving Collaborative Recommendation via User-Item Subgroups. IEEE Transactions on Knowledge and Data Engineering. vol. 28. no. 9, (2016).

3. Salehi, M., Kamalabadi, I., Ghoushchi, M.: An Effective Recommendation Framework for Personal Learning Environments Using a Learner Preference Tree and a GA. IEEE Transactions on Learning Technologies. vol. 6. no. 4. (2013).
4. Mendoza, L., García, R., González, A., Hernández, G., Zapater, J., RecomMetz: A context-aware knowledge-based mobile recommender system for movie showtimes. Science Direct. Expert Systems with Applications 42 (2015) 1202–1222.
5. Wei, S., Zheng, X., Chen, D., Chen, C.: A hybrid approach for movie recommendation via tags and ratings. Science Direct. Electronic Commerce Research and Applications 18 (2016) 83–94.
6. Nilashi, M., Ibrahim, O., Ithnin, N.: Hybrid recommendation approaches for multi-criteria collaborative filtering. Science Direct. Expert Systems with Applications 41 (2014) 3879–3900.
7. Salakhutdinov, R., Mnih, A., Hinton, G: Restricted Boltzmann Machines for collaborative filtering. In Proceedings of the 24th International Conference on Machine Learning. (2007).
8. Salah, A., Rogovschi, N., Nadif, M.: A dynamic collaborative filtering system via a weighted clustering approach. Science Direct. Neurocomputing 175 (2016) 206–215.
9. Goldberg. D., Nichols. D., Oki B. M., Terry. D., Using collaborative filtering to weave an Information tapestry. Commun. ACM 35 (1992) 61–70.
10. Ortega, F., Hernando, A., Bobadilla, J., Hyung Kang, J.: Recommending items to group of users using Matrix Factorization based Collaborative Filtering. Science Direct. Information Sciences 345 (2016) 313–324.
11. Koohi, H., Kiani, K.: User based Collaborative Filtering using fuzzy C-means. Science Direct. Measurement 91 (2016) 134–139.
12. Moreno, M., Segrera, S., López,V., Muñoz, M.: Web mining based framework for solving usual problems in recommender systems. A case study for movies' recommendation. Science Direct. Neurocomputing 176 (2016) 72–80.
13. Chen, M., Teng, C., Chang, P.: Applying artificial immune systems to collaborative filtering for movie recommendation. Science Direct. Advanced Engineering Informatics 29 (2015) 830–839.
14. Wang, Z., Yu, X., Feng, N., Wang, Z.: An improved collaborative movie recommendation system using computational intelligence. Science Direct. Journal of Visual Languages and Computing 25 (2014) 667–675.
15. Zahra, S., Ghazanfar, M., Khalid, A., Azam, A., Naeem, U., Prugel-Bennett, A.: Novel centroid selection approaches for KMeans-clustering based recommender systems. Science-Direct. Information Sciences 320 (2015) 156–189.
16. Zenebe, A., Zhou, L., Norcio, A.: User preferences discovery using fuzzy models. ScienceDirect. Fuzzy Sets and Systems 161 (2010) 3044–3063.

MistGIS: Optimizing Geospatial Data Analysis Using Mist Computing

Rabindra K. Barik, Ankita Tripathi, Harishchandra Dubey, Rakesh
K. Lenka, Tanjappa Pratik, Suraj Sharma, Kunal Mankodiya,
Vinay Kumar and Himansu Das

Abstract Geospatial data analysis with the help of cloud and fog computing is one of the emerging areas for processing, storing, and analysis of geospatial data. Mist computing is also one of the paradigms where fog devices help to reduce the latency period and increase throughput for assisting at the near of edge device of the client. It discusses the emergence of mist computing for mining analytics in geospatial big

R. K. Barik (✉)
School of Computer Applications, Kalinga Institute of Industrial Technology,
Bhubaneswar, India
e-mail: rabindra.mnnit@gmail.com

A. Tripathi
John Deere India Private Limited, Chennai, India
e-mail: ankita.tripathi8026@gmail.com

H. Dubey
Electrical Engineering, The University of Texas at Dallas, Dallas, TX, USA
e-mail: harishchandra.dubey@utdallas.edu

R. K. Lenka · T. Pratik · S. Sharma
Department of Computer Science & Engineering, IIIT Bhubaneswar, Bhubaneswar, India
e-mail: rakeshkumar@iiit-bh.ac.in

T. Pratik
e-mail: pk00095@gmail.com

S. Sharma
e-mail: suraj@iiit-bh.ac.in

K. Mankodiya
University of Rhode Island, Kingston, NY 02881, USA
e-mail: kunalm@uri.edu

V. Kumar
Department of ECE, Visvesvaraya National Institute of Technology, Nagpur, India
e-mail: vk@ece.vnit.ac.in

H. Das
School of Computer Engineering, Kalinga Institute of Industrial Technology,
Bhubaneswar, India
e-mail: das.himansu2007@gmail.com

© Springer Nature Singapore Pte Ltd. 2018
P. K. Pattnaik et al. (eds.), *Progress in Computing, Analytics and Networking*,
Advances in Intelligent Systems and Computing 710,
https://doi.org/10.1007/978-981-10-7871-2_70

733

data from geospatial application. This paper developed a mist computing-based framework for mining analytics from geospatial big data. We developed *MistGIS* framework for Ganga River Management System using mist computing. It built a prototype using Raspberry Pi, an embedded microprocessor. The developed *MistGIS* framework has validated by doing preliminary analysis including K-means clustering and overlay analysis. The results showed that mist computing can assist the fog and cloud computing hold an immense promise for analysis of big data in geospatial application particularly in the management of Ganga River Basin.

Keywords River · Cloud computing · Open-source GIS · Geospatial big data · Fog computing · Mist · Edge · Overlay analysis · K-means

1   Introduction

Cloud computing-based GIS framework has the unique capability to share and exchange of various formats of geospatial big data belonging to the different stakeholders. Cloud-based framework has also created an interface which used by different types of users to access geospatial big data along with associated metadata in a secured manner [1]. This cloud computing-based GIS framework has leveraged for many application fields, that is, land use, urban planning, marine, health, coastal and watershed management.

There are numerous emerging applications of cloud computing-based GIS framework. It has the ability to integrate and analyze heterogeneous thematic layers along with their attribute information to create and visualize alternative planning scenarios [2]. It has been integrating common geospatial data for various operations such as statistical computing, overlay analysis, data visualization, and query formation. These features differentiate cloud-based framework from other geospatial decision support systems [3].

Geospatial data contains geospatial distributions and informative temporal data. In traditional setup of cloud computing-based GIS framework, it inputs the geospatial data to the cloud server where it processed and analyzed [4]. This scheme has taken large processing time and required high Internet bandwidth. Fog computing overcomes this problem by providing local computation near the edge of the clients. With the concept of Mist computing, it enhances the cloud and fog computing for geospatial data processing by reducing latency at increased throughput. Fog devices such as Intel Edition and Raspberry Pi provide low-power gateway that can be able to enlarge throughput and reduce latency near the client's edge layer [5]. In addition, it reduces the cloud storage for geospatial big data. Also, the required transmission power needed to send the data to cloud is reduced, and now we send the analysis results to cloud rather than data. This leads to improvement in overall efficiency. Fog devices can act as a gateway between clients such as mobile phones and wearable sensor devices. The increasing use of smart devices led to generation of huge geospatial big data. Cloud, fog, and mist services leverage these data for assisting different analysis. It suggests that the use of low-resource machine learning on fog devices which kept close to smart devices. This research paper presents a *MistGIS* framework that relied on geospatial big data analysis on Ganga River Basin, India. So geospatial big data have been processed at the mist and edge using fog devices and finally have been stored in the cloud layer. In the present research paper, it has presented the following contributions:

- It gives the detailed concepts and architectural framework about the edge, cloud, fog, and mist computing;
- It discusses about proposed architecture of *MistGIS* framework that leads to process the various geospatial data analysis at the edge computing environment;
- It performs a unique case study of Ganga River Basin Management System has been elaborated with the use of mist assisted cloud architecture by doing overlay analysis and K-means clustering.

2 Related Works

2.1 Edge Computing

Data are gradually produced and processed at the edge of the network. Same works have been done before in microdata center, and cloudlet as cloud computing is not constantly capable enough for data processing when the volumetric data are produced at the edge of the network devices. Edge computing allows for more edge devices or sensors to interface with the cloud. However, the cloud computing environments are not set up for the volume, variety, and velocity of data. It has changed in the systems before the cloud must be adapted to improve make use of the cloud services accessible [6].

In the concept of edge computing, both data producers and consumer come into play for data processing and analytics. At the edge nodes, the processing are performed the different computing tasks from the cloud as well as request service and content from the cloud layer. Edge computing can perform various task such as data storage, distribute request, computing, processing, and delivery service from the cloud computing layer to client tier layer [7]. With the verity of jobs in the edge network, the edge nodes need to be well calculated to meet the requirement efficiently in privacy protection, security, and reliable service.

2.2 Cloud Computing

Cloud computing is a computation model that provides shared resources and on-demand facilities over the Web. It possesses computational infrastructure and adequate storage for data visualization and analysis. Cloud computing can provide an evolution from the desktop/laptop to different cloud data servers. Various Internet-based processing architectures have created in an open environment with shared assets. It was facilitated by four distinct types of service model, that is, Platform as a Service (PaaS), Infrastructure as a Service (IaaS), Software as a Service (SaaS), and Database as a Service (DaaS). It has deployed multitenant design and instance of services which has permitted various types of clients to contribute smooth services. Another characteristic in cloud computing environment is to rely on geospatial Web services in geospatial applications [8]. Various cloud platforms have provided different functionalities and applications statistics through geospatial Web services [9, 10].

2.3 Fog Computing

Fog computing was first coined by Cisco in 2012. It is a computing paradigm that decentralizes the resources in data centers for improving the quality of experience and service. Fog computing does not require computational resources from cloud data centers. In this way, data storage and computation are brought closer to the users leading to reduced latencies as compared to communication overheads with remote cloud servers. It refers to a computing paradigm that uses interface kept close to the devices that acquire data. It introduces the facility of local processing leading to reduction in data size, lower latency, high throughput, and power-efficient systems. Fog computing has successfully applied in smart cities and health care [5, 6, 11]. Fog computing solves the problem by keeping data closer to local computers and devices, rather than routing everything through a central data center in the cloud. Fog devices are embedded computers such as Intel Edison and Raspberry Pi that act a gateway between cloud and mobile clients. From the above discussions, we can see that it requires an efficient, reliable, and scalable fog computing-based GIS framework for sharing and analysis of geospatial [12] and medical big data across the Web. Fog computing is a novel idea that helps to reduce latency and increase throughput at the edge of the client with respect to cloud computing environment [13].

3 Proposed Model

3.1 Mist Computing

Mist computing has taken edge and fog computing concepts further by pushing some of the computation to the edge of the network, actuator devices and to the sensor which build the entire network for cloud data center. With the help of mist computing, the computation has performed at the edge of the network in the microcontrollers of the embedded nodes. The mist computing paradigm decreases latency and increases the autonomy of a solution [14]. Cloud, fog, and mist computing are complementary to each other w.r.t. the application tasks, which are more computationally intensive, and can be executed in the gateway of the fog layer while the less computationally intensive tasks can be executed in the edge devices. The processing and the collecting of data are still stored in the cloud data center for the availability to the user. The important application of mist computing is a collection of different services which has been distributed among the computing nodes [15–17]. Both, fog computing and mist computing, are derived by Cisco and positioned between the edge and the fog, which has extended the client–server architecture, similar or equal to edge [18, 19]. By considering this mist computing, the proposed framework, that is, *MistGIS* has sketched for processing of geospatial data analysis.

3.2 MistGIS *Framework*

Figure 1 shows the proposed architecture *MistGIS* framework. The *MistGIS* framework has categorized into four layers as cloud layer, fog layer, mist layer, and edge layer. In *MistGIS* framework, we used Raspberry Pi in every fog node for better efficiency in time analysis. In this framework, Raspberry Pi Model B Platform has employed. Raspberry Pi consists of a 900 MHz 32-bit quad-core ARM Cortex-A7 CPU with 1 GB RAM. For Wi-Fi connectivity in Raspberry Pi, it used Wi-Fi dongle of Realtek RTL8188CUS chipset.

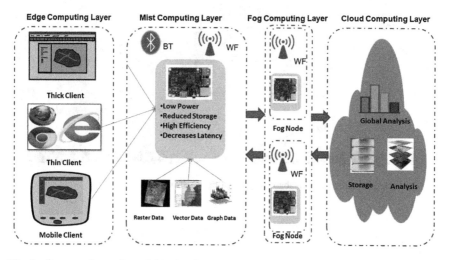

Fig. 1 Conceptual overview of *MistGIS* framework

4 Case Study: River Ganga Basin Management

4.1 Geospatial Database for Ganga River Basin

Ganga River alongside her voluminous streams being the foundation of divine and physical edibles of Indian evolution. Accordingly, her opulence is one of the major nationwide trepidations. The physical surroundings of the Ganga Basin being ruled by gigantic multifaceted amalgamation of man-made and natural practices that lead to ecological filth. For regulatory of these filths, Ganga River Basin Environment Management Plan (GRBEMP) pursues, customs & resources to fortify the basin atmosphere against distinguishable hostile impressions. For growth of GRBEMP, Ministry of Environment and Forests of India in consortium with seven IITs of India has come to build a robust system for suitable management of Ganga Basin. In GRBEMP framework, it has given temporal and geospatial information of administrative boundaries, soil, DEM, land use, dam, and well location data related to basin of Ganga [20, 21]. Figure 2 shows the various layer of Ganga River geospatial database in Quantum GIS environment.

The shape files related to dam and well locations have used in *MistGIS* framework. Basically, geospatial database of well location of Ganga has been utilized for K-means clustering and overlay analysis.

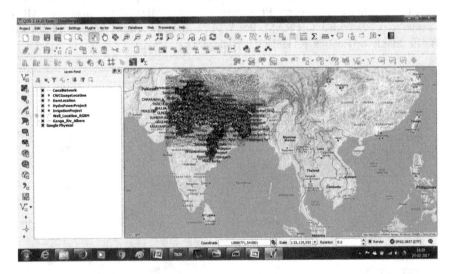

Fig. 2 Integrated geospatial database for Ganga River Basin

4.2 *Machine Learning Approaches in* MistGIS *Framework*

In this section, it has used K-means unsupervised machine learning for doing clustering to group similar items together [22]. In the present study, we are using R tools for K-means clustering implementation. It has taken well location shape files for operation. For implementation in R, it has required to convert shape files into. csv file format. The converted.csv files are used for clustering. In these techniques, we used longitude, latitude, wellcode, district, and well-type parameters from that. csv files. Figure 3a shows the clustering on longitude and latitude where it has divided into five number of clusters. Figure 3b has illustrated the clustering on

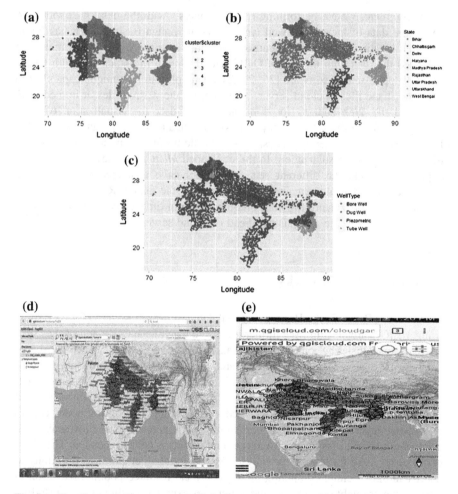

Fig. 3 **a** Five clusters in K-means approach; **b** Cluster in state-wise of India; **c** Cluster in well type related to the Ganga Basin; **d** Overlay analysis has performed in thin client layer [23]; **e** Overlay analysis has performed on mobile client layer in *MistGIS* framework [24]

longitude and latitude where it visualized as per state-wise. From Fig. 3b, it has clearly visualized that there are eight numbers of states and one union territory lies with Ganga. Figure 3c described the location of well and categorized according to the types of well type. From the above clustering analysis, it experimented that there is required to add additional fog nodes in between fog computing layer and cloud computing layer. So, it requires to illustrating the idea of Fog-to-Fog interface for better and efficient management of geospatial data.

4.3   Performing Overlay Analysis in MistGIS Framework

In this segment, we are performing overlay analysis with the help of downloaded geospatial data of location of well type related to Ganga Basin [25]. It has found that well location geospatial data are saved/stored in shape (.shp) file formats. We uploaded the data with the use of QGIS Cloud plug-in in association with Quantum GIS open-source software [26, 27, 21]. This plug-in has unique capability to store the shape files in cloud server. After storing the desired files, it immediately generated the Web address for thin and mobile user for visualization of data. Figures 3d and 3e show the overlay analysis on thin and mobile client, respectively. It has observed that overlay analysis is one of the useful and important techniques for geospatial data visualization. In the developed MistGIS framework, it has also experimented that the different sets of clusters have generated with well-type geospatial data that are remained on the lines of the Ganga River Basin. It has concluded that how many fog nodes required for run time analysis of various data sets which reduced the analysis overhead on cloud server.

5   Concluding Remarks

In this paper, River Ganga Basin geospatial database was considered for case study using MistGIS architecture. We further leveraged machine learning approaches such as K-means clustering on well-type data from River Ganga Basin geospatial database. We also validated MistGIS architectures for application-specific case studies. Raspberry Pi used as processors in mist computing layers. Mist nodes not only reduce storage requirements but also result in efficient transmission at improved throughput and latency. The edge computing done on fog nodes creates an assistive layer in scalable cloud computing. With increasing use of wearable and Internet-connected sensors, enormous amount of data is being generated. The cloud could be reserved for long-term analysis. Mist computing emphasizes proximity to end users unlike cloud computing along with local resource pooling, reduction in latency, better quality of service, and better user experiences. In our future studies, we will add various intelligent tasks with the help of the developed MistGIS architecture. This paper relied on fog computer for low-resource machine learning.

As a use case, we employed K-means clustering on Ganga River Basin data. Fog computing reduced the onus of dependence on cloud services with availability of big data. We can expect mist architecture to be crucial in shaping the way big data handling and processing happens in near future. It would be interesting to study the feasibility aspects of *MistGIS* implementation in health sector.

References

1. Chen, Z., Chen, N., Yang, C., Di, L.: Cloud computing enabled web processing service for earth observation data processing, IEEE journal of selected topics in applied earth observations and remote sensing, Vol. 5, No. 6, (2012)1637–1649
2. Brovelli, M.A., Minghini, M., Moreno-Sanchez, R. and Oliveira, R.: Free and open source software for geospatial applications (FOSS4G) to support Future Earth, International Journal of Digital Earth, (2016) 1–19
3. Huang, Q., Yang, C., Liu, K., Xia, J., Xu, C., Li, J., Gui, Z., Sun, M. and Li, Z.: Evaluating open-source cloud computing solutions for geosciences, Computers & Geosciences, (2013) 5941–52
4. Yang, C., Michael G., Qunying H., Doug N., Robert R., Yan X., Myra B. & Daniel F.: Spatial cloud computing: how can the geospatial sciences use & help shape cloud computing?, International Journal of Digital Earth, Vol. 4, No.4, (2011) 305–329
5. Barik, R. K., Dubey, H., Samaddar, A. B., Gupta, R. D. & Ray, P. K.: FogGIS: Fog Computing for geospatial big data analytics, IEEE International Conference on Electrical, Computer & Electronics Engineering, (2016) 613–618
6. Dubey, H., Constant, N., Monteiro, A., Abtahi, M., Borthakur, D., Mahler, L., Sun, Y., Yang, Q., Mankodiya, K.: Fog computing in medical internet-of-things: Architecture, implementation, and applications, Handbook of Large-Scale Distributed Computing in Smart Health-care, Springer International Publishing AG (2017)
7. Chiang, M., Zhang, T.: Fog and iot: An overview of research opportunities, IEEE Internet of Things Journal, Vol. 3, No.6, (2016) 854–864
8. Evangelidis, Konstantinos, Konstantinos, Ntouros, Stathis, Makridis, Constantine, Papatheodorou.: Geospatial services in the Cloud, Computers & Geosciences, Vol. 63, (2014) 116–122
9. Barik, R. K., & Samaddar, A. B.: Service Oriented Architecture Based SDI Model for Education Sector in India, International Conference on Frontiers of Intelligent Computing: Theory and Applications, (2014) 555–562
10. Patra, S.S. and Barik, R.K.: Dynamic Dedicated Server Allocation for Service Oriented Multi-Agent Data Intensive Architecture in Biomedical and Geospatial Cloud, In Cloud Technology: Concepts, Methodologies, Tools, and Applications, IGI Global, (2015) 2262–2273
11. Dubey, H., Yang, J., Constant, N., Amiri, A.M., Yang, Q., Makodiya, K.: Fog data: Enhancing telehealth big data through fog computing. In: ACM Proceedings of the ASE BigData & Social Informatics, (2015) 14
12. Ma, Y., Wu, H., Wang, L., Huang, B., Ranjan, R., Zomaya, A. and Jie, W.: Remote sensing big data computing: challenges and opportunities, Future Generation Computer Systems, Vol. 51, (2015) 47–60
13. Barik, R., Dubey, H., Sasane, S., Misra, C., Constant, N. and Mankodiya, K.: Fog2Fog: Augmenting Scalability in Fog Computing for Health GIS Systems. In Connected Health: Applications. In: 2017 IEEE/ACM International Conference on Systems and Engineering Technologies (CHASE), (2017) 241–242
14. http://www.thinnect.com/mist-computing/ [accessed on 17th July 2017]

15. http://rethinkresearch.biz/articles/cisco-pushes-iot-analytics-extreme-edge-mist-computing [accessed on 17th July 2017]
16. Orsini G, Bade D, Lamersdorf W.: Computing at the mobile edge: designing elastic android applications for computation offloading, In IEEE IFIP Wireless and Mobile Networking Conference (WMNC), (2015) 112–119
17. Barik, R.K., Dubey, A.C., Tripathi, A., Pratik, T., Sasane, S., Lenka, R.K., Dubey, H., Mankodiya, K. & Kumar, V.: Mist Data: Leveraging Mist Computing for Secure and Scalable Architecture for Smart and Connected Health, Procedia Computer Science, Vol. 125, (2018) 647–653
18. Preden JS, Tammemäe K, Jantsch A, Leier M, Riid A, Calis E.: The benefits of self-awareness and attention in fog and mist computing, Computer, Vol. 48, No.7, (2015) 37–45
19. Uehara M.: Mist Computing: Linking Cloudlet to Fogs, In International Conference on Computational Science/Intelligence & Applied Informatics, Springer, Cham, (2017) 201–213
20. Internet-2:http://gisserver.civil.iitd.ac.in/grbmp/downloaddataset [Accessed on: 27th January 2017]
21. Barik, R.K.: CloudGanga: Cloud Computing Based SDI Model for Ganga River Basin Management in India, International Journal of Agricultural and Environmental Information Systems (IJAEIS), Vol. 8, No. 4 (2017) 54–71
22. Gupta, A. and Merchant, P.S.: Automated Lane Detection by K-means Clustering: A Machine Learning Approach, Electronic Imaging, Vol. 14, (2016) 1–6
23. Internet-3:http://qgiscloud.com/cloudganga/FogSDI [Accessed on: 6th February 2017]
24. Internet-4:http://m.qgiscloud.com/cloudganga/FogSDI [Accessed on: 6th February 2017]
25. Internet-1: Ganga River Basin, Management Plan – 2015, Link: http://pib.nic.in/newsite/PrintRelease.aspx?relid=133450 [Accessed on 23th January, 2017]
26. Barik, R.K., Samaddar, Arun B. and Gupta, R.D.: Investigations into the Efficacy of Open Source GIS Software, International Conference, Map World Forum, on Geospatial Technology for Sustainable Planet Earth, Feb 10–13 (2009)
27. Lenka, R.K., Barik, R.K., Gupta, N., Ali, S.M., Rath, A. and Dubey, H.: Comparative analysis of SpatialHadoop and GeoSpark for geospatial big data analytics, In Contemporary Computing and Informatics, IEEE International Conference on, (2016) 484–488

Unsupervised Morphological Approach for Retinal Vessel Segmentation

B. V. Santhosh Krishna, T. Gnanasekaran and S. Aswini

Abstract Glaucoma, diabetic retinopathy, atherosclerosis, hypertensive retinopathy, age-related macular degeneration (AMD), retinopathy of prematurity (ROP) are some of the retinal diseases which may lead to blindness manifest as artifacts in the retinal images. For the early diagnosis of these systemic diseases, retinal vessel segmentation of retinal is initial assignment. In present scenario, retinal blood vessel segmentation automatically and accurately remains as a challenging task in computer-aided analysis of fundus images. In this paper, we put forward an unsupervised morphological approach for automatically extracting blood vessels from retinal fundus images that can be used in the computer-based analysis. Proposed method uses mathematical morphology with modified top-hat transform for preprocessing and hysteresis thresholding for the segmentation of blood vessels. The proposed approach was evaluated on the DRIVE database and is compared with the recent approaches. Proposed method achieved an average accuracy of 95.95% and best accuracy of 97.01% shows that the approach is efficient.

Keywords Morphology · Retinal diseases · Vessel segmentation
Top-hat transform

B. V. Santhosh Krishna (✉)
Velammal Institute of Technology, Chennai, Tamil Nadu, India
e-mail: santhoshkrishna1987@gmail.com

T. Gnanasekaran
RMK Engineering College, Chennai, Tamil Nadu, India
e-mail: t.gnanasekaran@gmail.com

S. Aswini
S A Engineering College, Chennai, Tamil Nadu, India
e-mail: aswinisriramulu@gmail.com

© Springer Nature Singapore Pte Ltd. 2018
P. K. Pattnaik et al. (eds.), *Progress in Computing, Analytics and Networking*,
Advances in Intelligent Systems and Computing 710,
https://doi.org/10.1007/978-981-10-7871-2_71

1 Introduction

Ophthalmologists make use of human retina for the analysis and diagnosis of various systemic diseases. In general, retinal image called as fundus is used for diagnosing and treating ophthalmologic and cardiovascular diseases like age-related macular degeneration (AMD), diabetic retinopathy (DR), glaucoma, retinopathy of prematurity (ROP), hypertension, arteriosclerosis, and choroidal neovascularization [1]. Some of these diseases are more dangerous. The above diseases may cause blindness when they are not diagnosed accurately and perform early intervention [2]. Accurate retinal vessel segmentation plays a significant role in enumerating these features for medical diagnosis. Retinal vessels are the only part of blood circulation system which will be non-invasive when it is observed directly [3]. For quantitative analysis of retinal images, vessel segmentation is the initial step [4]. Morphological features of blood vessels, such as length, width, branching angles can be extracted using segmented vascular tree. Manual segmentation is very lengthy and tiresome task since it needs more training as well as skill set. It is universally acknowledged by the physicians that automatic quantification is the fundamental step for building a computer assisted diagnosis for systemic disorders in retinal images. In the clinical study of various retinopathic pathologies, two-dimensional (2D) color fundus and three-dimensional (3D) optic coherence tomography (OCT) images are generally agreed and in use [5]. Due to the difficulty in procuring OCT images, fundus images are utilized by majority of physicians. Furthermore, the high price of getting OCT images makes it unsuitable for large scale diagnosis. Hence in this work, we mainly focus on vessel segmentation automatically from fundus images that helps physicians to identify the pathologies in retinal images. Here for testing the proposed approach, fundus images, field of view (FOV) mask, ground truth images were taken from globally accepted dataset—Digital Retinal Images for Vessel Extraction (DRIVE). The input to the segmentation approach is the color fundus image. First, the input RGB image is converted to the green channel image, and then preprocessing is carried out using CLAHE and modified top-hat transform. Then Gaussian hysteresis thresholding is applied for vessel extraction, and smoothing is done using kernel filter. Comparison is done between the ground truth image and the segmented image for the measurement of accuracy.

The organization of the rest of the paper is as follows: Related works are discussed in Sect. 2. Proposed approach is presented in Sect. 3. The experimental results are discussed in Sect. 4. Conclusion and future work is given in Sect. 5.

2 Related Works

Several works on retinal vessel segmentation on fundus images are found in the literature which can be classified as follows: machine learning-based implementations, matched filtering mechanism, morphological image processing, model-based and vessel tracking methods [1]. Further, machine learning-based algorithms are classified into supervised and unsupervised approaches. Lupascu et al. suggested a segmentation approach by means of unsupervised clustering. They used features of pixels extricated from the output of various filters and transforming them to self organizing maps. In this approach, DRIVE dataset is used and obtained accuracy rate of 94.59% [6]. Fraz et al. suggested a method based on dual Gaussian where a collection of Gabor filter and second-order derivative, where a feature vector is generated using mathematical morphological transform. In this method, an accuracy rate of 94.56% is achieved [7]. Yin et al. introduced a method where it deals with vessel edge detection. Maximum a posteriori (MAP) method is utilized to detect vessel edge points and achieved 92.67% accuracy [8]. Nguyen et al. used a multiscale line detection approach with different lengths for enhancement. In this approach, accuracy rate of 94.07% is obtained [9]. Roychowdhury et al. proposed a supervised approach where mathematical morphological processing is applied for binary imaging and achieved accuracy of 95.2% [10]. Sohini Roychowdhury et al. offered an unsupervised iterative blood vessel segmentation approach with an average accuracy, sensitivity, and specificity of 0.9595, 0.7281, and 0.9684, correspondingly [11]. Azzopardi et al. suggested a combination of shifted filter responses for detecting blood vessels, and achieved average accuracy, sensitivity, and specificity are 0.9442, 0.7655, and 0.9704, respectively [4]. Bao et al. suggested a cake filter-based segmentation method in which they used real component fusion for separating vessel pixels from the background pixels. Later, a simple thresholding method is used for getting final vessel map [12]. Another method proposed by Mapayi et al. uses adaptive thresholding method on gray-level concurrence matrix and achieved a accuracy rate of 95.11% [13]. Recently, Zafer Yavuz et al. proposed a novel method which uses Gabor, Frangi Gauss filters along with top-hat transform for preprocessing and K-means and fuzzy means for vessel segmentation. They reported 95.71% accuracy with DRIVE dataset [14].

3 Proposed Method

An outline of the proposed approach is as follows: First, green channel image is extracted from the original color (RGB) fundus image. Contrast Limited Adaptive Histogram Equalization (CLAHE) is employed on the green channel image for enrichment of disparity in blood vessels and as a result, normalized green channel image is obtained. Image smoothing is done using Gaussian Kernel mean filtering. Then vessel contrast enhancement is done by applying morphological modified top-hat transform. As a result of morphological operations, white bright retina structures are eliminated and blood vessels are enhanced. Extraction of blood vessels is made using hysteresis thresholding technique. Finally, comparison is made between the segmented image and the ground truth image from the DRIVE dataset for measuring accuracy, sensitivity, and specificity. This process is explained using a flow diagram in Fig. 1.

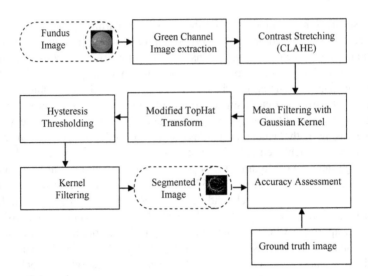

Fig. 1 Block diagram of proposed method

3.1 RGB to Green Channel Image

Preprocessing is carried out as the initial step in image segmentation since training of images is not required. Preprocessing will dilute the non-uniform illumination of images during image acquisition and remove the noise present. In this stage, the extraction of green channel image is done from the original fundus color image. Further processing is done on green channel image. The green component image shows the higher disparity with blood vessels and surroundings over the remaining two color component images (red and blue) as shown in Fig. 2. Hence, retinal features are clearer in the green channel image.

3.2 Contrast Stretching

For enriching the disparity of blood vessels, Contrast Limited Adaptive Histogram Equalization (CLAHE) is employed. This method improves vessel structure by

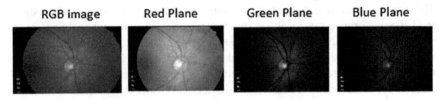

Fig. 2 Red, green, blue planes generated from fundus image

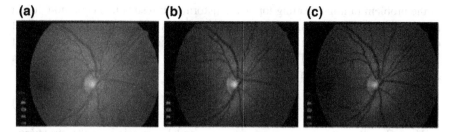

Fig. 3 **a** Original image. **b** Gray image. **c** CLAHE image

cutting the histogram at some threshold and equalizing by avoiding amplification of noise. The clipping level with clip limit is set from 0 to 0.01 which is used to determine the noise level for smoothening and improving the contrast level in histogram. In our approach, clip limit is set from 0 to 0.02. To keep the consistency with other modalities, image intensities are inverted in a way that the intensity of the vessels is better than the background as shown in Fig. 3.

3.3 Mean Filtering with Gaussian Kernel

Smoothing of image is carried out using a mean filter of size 3*3 followed by a Gaussian Kernel of size 3*3 with a standard deviation of 1.5. The overall performance is improved due to reduction of noise while using this filter. We assume that the kernel is unimodal and isotropic. Here a background image is generated and subtracted from the former image which results in homogenization of the background.

3.4 Vessel Enhancement

Enhancement of vessels in artery is done using a combination of morphological connected (dilation, erosion, top hat) set of operations. Morphology deals with shapes. Morphological image processing is performed by sliding a structuring element over an image. In the output image, every pixel's value is obtained by comparing the corresponding pixel in the input image. On binary image, the fundamental operations of mathematical morphology such as dilation (dilating the boundary), erosion (eroding the boundary), opening (erosion followed by dilation), and closing (dilation followed by erosion) are performed. On a gray-level image, dilation brightens small dark areas. Darkening of small bright areas like noise is done by erosion, and removal of small bright spots is made by opening. Closing will brighten small dark area and remove small dark holes. Noise sensitivity is one of the problem in implementing top-hat transform that results in a condition that in an image that is opened pixels values are always fewer than or equal to the input ones. In such conditions, the subtracted image holds modest intensity variations that can be set up in the data. To circumvent these issues, a modified top-hat transform (1), which is adopted from [19], is given by

$$MT_{hat} = G - (G \bullet E_C) \circ E_O \tag{1}$$

Here G is the input green channel image, and E_C and E_O are the structuring elements of disk shaped for both closing ($\bullet$) and opening ($\circ$) operators with a radius of 8 pixels.

3.5 Hysteresis Thresholding

Vessel segmentation is performed using hysteresis thresholding method. This method uses a twofold operation in such a way that thresholding is done for two limits of gray values in the intensity of the image. Twofold threshold procedure performs better than single thresholding, as in some cases where the intensity of the objects at some places is maximum, but in certain places the contrast between object and background falls less than noise level. Threshold computation is made quicker by using a percentile-based threshold rule [20]. To build up this rule, factors considered are (i) high confidence vessels are separated by strong threshold, (ii) high confident background pixels are separated by weak threshold, and (iii) the vessels in the map are classified by gray levels thicker than the background pixels as illustrated in Fig. 4.

Depending upon the percentile of the image surface that is charged positively, the two threshold limits are calculated. The thick area under the histogram correlates to the image surface positively enclosed with vessels. The strong threshold (T_s) is given by the percentile enclosing it. The scrambled portion covered under the histogram correlates to the image surface covered by background. Hence, the weak threshold (T_w) is calculated by deducting the portion of the image surface positively covered by background from 100%. Later, T_s selects only vessels pixels and T_w selects all vessel pixels practically. As a final step, post-processing is done using a

Fig. 4 Histogram of vessel map

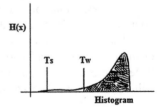

small kernel (morphological closing operator) of 3*3 size is used for smoothing the boundaries and object size to remove small undesired objects

4 Experimental Results and Discussion

4.1 Evaluation Methodology

The proposed technique is examined both qualitatively and quantitatively with 20 images from DRIVE dataset [15]. The qualitative assessment is performed based on visual observations. Visual inspections of segmentation approach of the proposed framework are shown in Fig. 5 with major processing steps. Quantitative assessment is made by examining the error images, which are acquired by subtracting the segmented image by the proposed method in relative to the one which is manually segmented image available as ground truth in the dataset. The quantitative assessment of the image segmentation is done in the form of sensitivity (S_n), specificity (S_p), accuracy (Acc), and precision (PPV). Accuracy depicts the overall segmentation performance. The ground truth databases are utilized to calculate accuracy. Sensitivity also known as true positive rate shows effectiveness in detecting the pixels with positive rates. Specificity also called true negative rate measures the detection of pixels with negative rates. Specificity is associated with the false-positive rate (FPR). Precision (PPV) describes random errors which is a measure of statistical variability. These metrics are defined in Table 1.

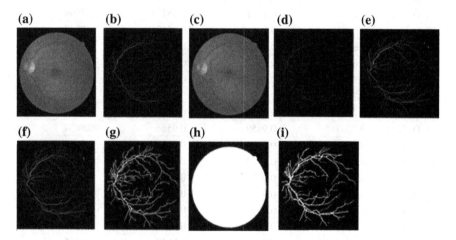

Fig. 5 **a** Original fundus image, **b** gray image, **c** enhanced gray image (green channel image), **d** smooth cross section, **e** reconstruction by dilation, **f** reconstruction by erosion, **g** output after thresholding, **h** FOV mask, **i** segmented output

Table 1 Performance metrics

Performance metric	Formula
Accuracy (Acc)	(TP + TN)/(TP + FP + TN + FN)
Sensitivity (S_n)	TP/(TP + FN)
Specificity (S_p)	TN/(TN + FP)
Precision (PPV)	TP/(TP + FP)

where TP—true positive, TN—true negative, FP—false positive, and FN—false negative

4.2 Experimental Results

The proposed method uses 20 fundus images, FOV masks, and ground truth images from the dedicated test set of DRIVE dataset. All simulations are carried out in MATLAB tool on a laptop with Intel core i3 processor with 2.4 GHz with 2 GB RAM. Results of the proposed method are shown in Table 2. The average accuracy, sensitivity, specificity, and precision of our method are 0.9595 (95.95%), 0.7281, 0.9684, and 0.7813, correspondingly (Table 3).

Table 2 Results obtained by proposed method on DRIVE dataset

Image no	Sensitivity (S_n)	Specificity (S_P)	Accuracy (Acc)	Precision (PPV)
01_D_Test	0.8041	0.9780	0.9626	0.7821
02_D_Test	0.7638	0.9856	0.9629	0.8581
03_D_Test	0.6696	0.9836	0.9523	0.8185
04_D_Test	0.7327	0.9846	0.9614	0.828
05_D_Test	0.7189	0.9803	0.9558	0.7903
06_D_Test	0.6647	0.9821	0.9512	0.7999
07_D_Test	0.6849	0.9811	0.9542	0.7845
08_D_Test	0.6319	0.8460	0.9643	0.7947
09_D_Test	0.6948	0.9837	0.9643	0.7901
10_D_Test	0.7172	0.9792	0.9576	0.7555
11_D_Test	0.7011	0.9801	0.9551	0.7757
12_D_Test	0.7082	0.9734	0.9505	0.7153
13_D_Test	0.7007	0.9859	0.9586	0.8434
14_D_Test	0.7811	0.9795	0.9635	0.7703
15_D_Test	0.7709	0.9764	0.9617	0.7155
16_D_Test	0.7279	0.9780	0.9554	0.7663
17_D_Test	0.7105	0.9793	0.9656	0.7595
18_D_Test	0.7368	0.9778	0.9587	0.7404
19_D_Test	0.8343	0.9824	0.9701	0.8108
20_D_Test	0.7984	0.9749	0.9619	0.7165
Maximum	0.8343	0.9859	0.9701	0.8581
Minimum	0.6319	0.8460	0.9505	0.7153
Average	**0.7281**	**0.9684**	**0.9595**	**0.7813**

Table 3 Comparison with other methods

Year	Method	Sn	Sp	Accu
Supervised methods				
2006	Soars et al. [16]	0.7332	0.9782	0.9461
2010	Lupacasu et al. [17]	0.7200	–	0.9597
2012	Fraz et al. [1]	0.7406	0.9807	0.9480
2014	Cheng et al. [18]	0.7252	0.9798	0.9474
Unsupervised methods				
2012	Fraz et al. [1]	0.7152	0.9759	0.9430
2015	Azzoapardi et al. [4]	0.7655	0.9704	0.9442
2016	Roychowdhury et al. [11]	0.7390	0.9780	0.9490
	Proposed method	**0.7281**	**0.9684**	**0.9595**

5 Conclusion and Future Work

In this paper, we have given an unsupervised morphological approach for segmentation of retinal vessels. DRIVE dataset is used for examining the performance and observed that the proposed method achieved average accuracy, sensitivity, specificity, and precision of 0.9595, 0.7281, 0.9684, and 0.7813, respectively. As a concluding remark, we strongly believe that our method can be extended for efficient automated diagnosis and disease screening with fundus images. In the future work, we aim to study the measurements of segmented retinal vessels and adapt them into the proposed vessel segmentation method for screening of various retinal diseases.

References

1. Fraz, M.M., Remagnino, P., Hopper, A., Uyyanonavara, B., Rudnicka, C., Owen,G.: Blood Vessel Segmentation Methodologies in Retinal images- A survey. Computer Methods and Programs in Biomedicine, Vol. 108 (2012) 407–433
2. Abramoff, M.D., Folk, J.C., Han, D.P., Walker, J.D., Willliams, D.F., Russell, S.R.: Automated Analysis for Detection Referable Diabetic Retinopathy. Jama Opthalmology, Vol 131 (2013) 351–357
3. Yusup, M., Chen, X.Y.: Epidemiology survey of visual loss. International Journal of opthalmology Vol. 10, No. 2 (2012) 304–307
4. Azzopardi, G., Strisciuglio, N., Vento, M., Perkov.: Trainable COSFIRE filters for vessel delination with application to retinal images. Medical Image Analysis, Vol 19 (2015) 46–57
5. Abramoff, M.D., Garvin, M.K., Sonaka, M.: Retinal Imaging and Analysis. IEEE Reviews in Biomedical Engineering, Vol. 3 (2010) 169–208
6. Lupascu, C., Tegolo, D.: Automatic unsupervised segmentation of retinal vessels using self-organizing maps and K-means clustering. Computational Intelligence Methods for Bioinformatics and Biostatistics (2011) 263–274
7. Moazam Fraz, M., Alicja, R., Rudnicka, C., Owen, G., Sarah.: Delineation of Blood Vessels in Pediatric retinal images using decision trees-based ensemble classification, International journal of computer assisted radiology and surgery (2013) 1–17

8. Yin, Y., Adel, M., Bourennane, S.: Automatic Segmentation and Measurement of Vasculature in Retinal Fundus Images Using Probabilistic Formulation Computational and Mathematical Methods in Medicine Vol. 2013 (2013)
9. Nguyen, U.T.V., Bhuiyan, A., Park, L.A.F., Ramamohanrao, K.: An effective retinal blood vessel segmentation method using multi-scale line detection. Pattern Recognition, Vol. 46 (2013) 703–715
10. Roychowdhury, S., Koozekanani, D., Keshab, K., Parhi.: Blood Vessel Segmentation of Fundus images by Major Vessel Extraction and Sub-Image Classification. Biomedical and Health Informatics, IEEE Journal (2014) 2168–2194
11. Sohini Roychowdhury., Koozekani, D., Keshab, K, Parhi.: Iterative Vessel Segmentation of Fundus Images. IEEE Transactions on Biomedical Engineering, Vol. 62 (2015) 1738–1749
12. Bao, X.R., Zhang, S.: Segmentation of retinal blood vessels based on cake filter. Biomed Research International, Vol. 2015 (2015)
13. Mapayi, T., Viriri, S.,Tapamo, J.R.: Adaptive Thresholding Technique for Retinal Vessel se gmentation based on GLCM energy information. Computational and Mathematical Methods in Medicine, Vol. 2015 (2015)
14. Zafer Yavuz., Cemal Kose.: Blood Vessel Extraction in Color Retinal Fundus Images with enhancement filtering and Unsupervised Classification. Hindawi Journal of Healthcare Engineering, Vol. 2017 (2017)
15. Staal, J.J., Abramoff, M.D., Niemeijer, M., Viergever, M, A. Vaan Ginnekan.: Ridge based vessel segmentation in color images of the retina, IEEE Transactions on Medical Imaging, Vol. 23 (2004) 501–509
16. Soares, J.V.B., Leandro, J.J.G., Cesar, R.M.: Ridge based vessel segmentation in color images of the retina, IEEE Transactions on Medical Imaging, Vol. 23 (2006) 1214–1222
17. Lupascu, A., Tegolo, D., Trucco, E.: Retinal vessel segmentation using AdaBoost, IEEE Transactions on Information Technology Biomedicine, Vol.14, No.5 (2010) 1267–1274
18. Cheng, E.K., Du, L., Wu, Y., Zhu, Y.J., Megalooikonomou., Ling, H.B.: Discriminative vessel segmentation in retinal images by fusing context-aware hybrid features, Machine Vision and Applications, Vol. 25, (2014) 1779–1792
19. Mendonca, A., Campilho, A.C.: Segmentation of retinal blood vessels by combining the detection of centerlines and morphological reconstruction. IEEE Transactions of Medical Imaging, (2007) 1200–1213
20. Alexandru Paul Condurache, Til Aach.: Vessel Segmentation in Angiograms using Hysteresis Thresholding. Proceedings of the IAPR Conference on Machine Vision Applications (2005) Tsukuba Science City, Japan

Classification of Intrusion Detection Using Data Mining Techniques

Roma Sahani, Shatabdinalini, Chinmayee Rout,
J. Chandrakanta Badajena, Ajay Kumar Jena and Himansu Das

Abstract Nowadays, Internet became a common way for communication as well as a key path for business. Due to the rapid use of Internet, its security aspect is turn more important day by day for which various network intrusion detection systems (NIDSs) are used to protect network data as well as protect the overall network from various attacks. Various intrusion detection systems (IDSs) are placed in different positions of network to protect it. There are various ways by which intrusion detection system can be implemented from which decision tree approach is most commonly used. It provides the easiest way to identify the most corrected field to select, manage, and make proper decision about their identification from a large dataset. This paper focuses to identify normal and attack data present in the network with the help of C4.5 algorithm which is one of the decisions tree techniques, and also it helps to improve the IDS system to identify the type of attacks present in a network. Experimentation is performed on KDD-99 dataset having number of features and different class of normal and attack type data.

R. Sahani · Shatabdinalini · J. Chandrakanta Badajena (✉)
Department of Information Technology, College of Engineering & Technology,
Bhubaneswar, Odisha, India
e-mail: j.chandrakantbadajena@gmail.com

R. Sahani
e-mail: romasahani5@gmail.com

Shatabdinalini
e-mail: shatabdikisd@gmail.com

C. Rout
Department of Computer Science and Engineering, Ajay Binay Institute of Technology,
Cuttack, Odisha, India
e-mail: chinu123.abit@gmail.com

A. K. Jena · H. Das
School of Computer Engineering, KIIT Deemed to be University,
Bhubaneswar, Odisha, India
e-mail: ajay.bbs.in@gmail.com

H. Das
e-mail: das.himansu2007@gmail.com

© Springer Nature Singapore Pte Ltd. 2018
P. K. Pattnaik et al. (eds.), *Progress in Computing, Analytics and Networking*,
Advances in Intelligent Systems and Computing 710,
https://doi.org/10.1007/978-981-10-7871-2_72

Keywords NIDS · Decision tree · C4.5 · KDD-99

1 Introduction

Nowadays, every organization and institution use Internet for their communication as well as one of the business medium to reach to the customer. As much as the use of Internet increased, the growth of network attacks also increased accordingly [1] for which high confidence on network systems connectivity and their resources has generally increased the potential damage due to the presence of attacks which are launched against the systems from remote resources. It is quite very difficult to prevent all the type of attacks by using firewalls because every time different attacks contain unknown weaknesses or bugs [2]. Therefore, real-time intrusion detection systems are used to detect attacks and also used to stop an attack in progress; it gives an alarm signal to the authorized user or network administrator about the presence of malicious activity or the presence of attacks.

Intrusion detection includes a lot of tools and techniques such as machine learning, statistics, data mining, and so on for the identification of an attack [1, 3]. In recent years, data mining method for network intrusion detection system has been giving high accuracy and good detection on different types of attacks [4]. Decision tree technique is one of the intuitionist and frank classification methods in data mining which can be used for this purpose. It has a great advantage in extracting features and rules. So, the decision tree gives a greater significance to intrusion detection. The tree is constructed by identifying attributes and their connected values which will be used to examine the input data at each intermediary node of the tree. After the tree is formed, it can advise newly coming data by traversing, initial from a root node to the leaf node by visiting all the internal nodes in the path depending upon the test environment of the attributes at each node. The main issue in constructing decision tree is which value is chosen for splitting the node of the tree.

In this paper, an improved version of C4.5 algorithm is proposed from the basic concept of C4.5. The detection of intrusion components undergoes two stages. In the first stage, the algorithm evaluates the KDD-99 dataset [5] and constructs the decision tree for detecting the class type as 'Normal' or 'Attack' type of data in the leaf node in the tree. In the second stage, the classification of attack type is done which will show the attack type. We have considered four types of attacks such as DOS, R2L, U2R, and PROBE [6].

The rest of the paper is organized as follows. Section 2 provides the basic concepts about intrusion detection system with their attack types and also an idea about the decision tree. Section 3 provides some related work for IDS using DT. The proposed model for intrusion detection with respect to attack classification is presented in Sect. 4. In Sect. 5, we illustrated the results and experimental analysis of the proposed model with result comparisons. Finally, Sect. 6 concludes the work.

2 Basic Concepts

In this section, we discussed about IDS with its classification methods and about various attack classes. It also focuses how decision tree is constructed and various techniques in decision tree for making proper decision.

2.1 Intrusion Detection System

Intrusion detection system is the software systems which are basically designed to identify and helps to prevent the malicious activities and security strategy violations. Intrusion detection systems (IDSs) were first introduced by James P. Anderson [7]. These systems are placed at the choke point such as organization's connection to a stem line or can be placed on each of the hosts that are being monitored to defend from intrusion which is classified as analysis approach and placement of IDS [8].

Based on analysis approach, it can be either misuse detection or anomaly detection. Misuse detection approach is also known as signature-based approach which is basically used for detecting known type of attacks. In case of anomaly detection monitors the network traffic and compares it with established normal traffic profile. It makes decisions on the basis of network behaviors with the help of some statistical techniques. This approach is able to identify unknown attacks.

According to placement approach of IDS, it can be classified as host-based and network-based systems [9]. In host-based IDS, it is present on each host that needs for monitoring. It is able to determine if an attempted attack is successful and can detect local attacks. In Network Based Systems is monitored the network traffic from unauthorized access by which the hosts are makes secure connection with host systems. This mechanism takes less cost for deployment, and it is also promising for identifying attacks to and from multiple hosts.

Many researchers have proposed and implemented IDS according to which network attacks are having four major categories. Every attack on a network can be one of these attack type [6, 10].

Denial-of-Service Attack (DoS): Attacker makes the systems as busy as possible and also makes system or network resource unavailable to its actual users.

Remote to Local Attack (R2L): Attacker targets to access one or no of network systems which main purpose is to view or steal data illegally and introduce different type malicious software to network system.

User to Root Attack (U2R): This attack type starts working out with access to a normal user account on the system and is able to exploit some vulnerability to gain root access to the system.

Probing Attack: Probing is an attack in which the attackers scan the network systems in order to find out the weaknesses of the network system that may later be exploited so as to compromise the system.

2.2 Decision Tree

Data mining is the procedure for discovering knowledge from huge datasets with the help of statistics and artificial intelligence technique to solve complex real life problems [11–19]. The decision tree (DT) is an important classification method in data mining classification. A decision tree is defined as a flowchart-like or tree-like structure from different verities of data. In DT, each inner node represents a test on an attribute, whereas each stem represents the outcome of the test and each leaf node represent a class label. The path from root node to leaf node represents the classification rules [20]. From an intrusion detection perspective, classification algorithms can distinguish network data as attacks, benign, scanning, or any other category of interest using information like source/destination ports, IP addresses, and the number of bytes sent during a connection [21].

A decision tree classifier has a simple form which can be compactly stored and that efficiently classifies new data. This classifier consists of various algorithms like CART, ID3, C4.5 [22–24].

CART: Classification and regression tree (CART) was proposed by Leo et al. [25] as an umbrella term. It constructs a binary tree model which means a node in a dataset can only be divided into two groups. CART can handle any type of data like both categorical and numerical data. CART uses Gini index for selecting attribute. The attribute with the largest reduction in impurity is used for splitting the nodes of the dataset. It uses cost-complexity pruning and also generates regression trees [26].

ID3: In 1980, a machine researcher named J. Ross Quinlan developed a predictive modeling tool at the University of Sydney which is known as Iterative Dichotomiser 3 (ID3) [26]. This algorithm was designed based on the principles of Occam's razor, with the idea of creating the smallest, most efficient decision tree. ID3 uses information gain of each attribute for construction decision tree. The features having the highest gain can select for the splitting of data records. ID3 algorithm has some drawbacks, such as for a while, data may be over-classified, only one attribute at a time is considered for making decision tree. Only one attribute at a time is tested for making a decision, and it does not handle continuous attribute as well as missing value for making tree.

C4.5: C4.5 is the extension of ID3 algorithm and an arithmetical classifier. It overcomes the problems associated with ID3 algorithm like handling continuous data and missing values. It follows the same procedure as ID3 for categorical data and uses split ratio technique for numerical type of data. This approach is better classifier in comparison with ID3. It can easily handle the missing values of the dataset.

3   Related Work

Many researchers proposed various anomaly detection mechanisms for IDS with the help of decision tree of which some are discussed below.

Rai et al. [27] used C4.5 decision tree for making taking decision. They have taken into consideration the two important issues, feature selection and split value for constructing the decision tree. In this paper, the algorithm was designed to address these two issues. This paper implements its algorithm by selecting the attributes from different levels of decision tree nodes, and then, it calculates the gain ratio for every attribute. Then select the attribute with the largest gain ratio to decide the root node of the decision tree. This paper used a novel approach for selecting the best attribute to split the dataset on each iteration. This work gets good accuracy with even less number of features selected using information gain.

Swamy and Vijaya Lakshmi [4] used two techniques like voting criteria and attribute selection method for selecting best attribute for splitting attribute for reaching in the leaf node or class node. In this work, firstly, all the attributes ware was selected and then attributes ware was shorted according to min-max principle. If all attributes ware belongs to the same class, then mark it as leaf node otherwise by using attribute selection method a best splitting attribute was taken. According to splitting criteria, the classification is carried out until it does not reach the leaf node. If all attribute does not belong to the same class then make a major voting for selecting the leaf level. It detects different types of attacks with high accuracy and less error-prone.

Phutane et al. [28] used data mining algorithms as improved C4.5 in order to detect the different types of attacks with high accuracy and less error-prone as well as it helps to increase performance of the system. In this approach, every time the input which is coming from the client system is stored in a database. If incoming data is similar to older one, then no need to go through the apriori algorithm, simply test the type of data which is already defined. If not, then apriori algorithm is applied which consists of associate rules in which all the data are collected. After that, all the frequent item set should be found by applying minimum support mechanism. Then, find the subsets which are common to at least a minimum number constant of the item sets. This would continue until there is no further extension or comparison is found. Then test the leaf data to the defined data type like attack types or normal data. It uses apriori algorithm for making decision tree, and minimum support mechanism gives the way for splitting of attributes or data. This proposed work overcomes the limitations of ID3 algorithm and also increases the system performance and better result in case of large database.

Shon Nadiammai and Hemalatha [29] gives four solutions for different IDS problems, they included the problem of data categorization, high level of personal effort, unlabeled data, and circulated denial-of-service attack efficacy. They solved the first problem (classification of data) using efficient data adapted decision tree (EDADT). The aim of this method was to reduce the dimensionality of model by feature extraction of significant features to every type of attack. The authors compared the proposed algorithm to other methods like C4.5, SVM, and others. The results they obtained show that their algorithm achieved the highest accuracy rate.

By studying various aforesaid algorithms, it is obtained that for making decision tree selecting correct attribute and way of selection is more important and classifying attack is much more important factor in IDS. For these reasons, our main objective is to select the best attribute which has the highest gain ratio for constructing the decision tree which will give the result whether the data are a normal data or an attack data. And our work also focuses to classify the data which are attack type corresponding to its class type (DoS, R2L, U2R, and Probing).

4   Proposed Model

This system is the process of identifying the normal and attack data in the network.

For our work, we have used KDD99 dataset which was used in the third International Knowledge Discovery and Data Mining Tools for building a network intrusion detector [30]. It consists of 42 features including class column having normal and attack type data. The proposed model undergoes two stages. In the first stage, the network dataset is preprocessed in which dataset having discrete type of data is converted to numeric data and then decision tree is constructed with the help of preprocessed dataset which is capable of distinguishing the record of normal data or attack data in the leaf node of the tree. The second stage is the detection phase which identifies the attacks corresponding to its class type with their number of occurrences and identifies the noisy data or missing-valued data named as unknown attack. Figure 1 represents the proposed model of our approach.

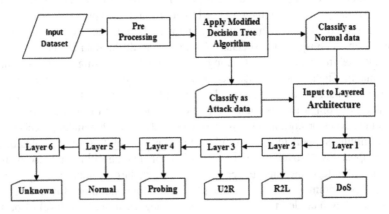

Fig. 1 Flow of proposed model

4.1 Proposed Modeling Framework

This proposed model is an improved version of C4.5 algorithm which handles both continuous and categorical data simultaneously for classifying dataset as normal and attack at leaf level. In basic C4.5, the dataset requires a shorted format, and it handles categorical and continuous data separately which is a time-consuming process and also selecting split value is an important factor for making decision tree. By focusing such scenarios, we have modified some cases in our proposed model, like instead of handling both categorical and continuous data separately, we simply convert the categorical data to continuous data in preprocessing and without any shoring the dataset we directly apply the algorithm for classification. For splitting purpose, we have applied geometric mean which helps to give a better decision tree result. This model makes the decision tree for identification of attack and normal data present in the dataset. The steps of the algorithm are as follows:

Algorithm

Input: Any Dataset with
Number of samples in dataset (RW), Number of unique elements in class column (UC), Column in Dataset (D), Number of distinct values presents in D column (V), D_j: Number of each element in that D column (D_j), Number of unique element in column (T_i)
Output: Classified data

Begin
1. If input dataset having same class type, then
   Leaf ← class name.
2. If single class is present in input data
   Leaf ← Histogram (class column)
3. Entropy of dataset(Entp(RW)) $= \sum_{i=1}^{UC} \frac{freq\ (Ti,RW)}{|RW|} * \log \frac{freq\ (Ti,RW)}{|RW|}$
4. Information of each attributes (INFO$_{Att}$ (D)) $= \sum_{j=1}^{V} |\frac{D_j}{RW}| * Entp(D_j)$
5. Information Gain (IG (D)) = Entp (RW) - INFOAtt (D)
6. Split information (Split_info(D)) $= \sum_{j=1}^{V} |\frac{D_j}{RW}| * \log |\frac{D_j}{RW}|$
7. Gain Ratio $(Gain_{Ratio\ (D)}) = \frac{IG(D)}{Split\_info\ (D)}$
8. Decision node (a_best) ← highest gain ratio attribute
9. Split value ← means (a_best attribute's values)
   Left subset ← (dataset < split value)
   Right subset ← (dataset > split value)
10. Repeat steps from 1 to 9 on each subsets produced by dividing the set on attribute 'a_best' and insert those nodes as descendant of parent node.
End

After successfully construction of decision tree, we have to classify the attacks according to its classification, such as either DoS or U2R, R2L or PROB type. For

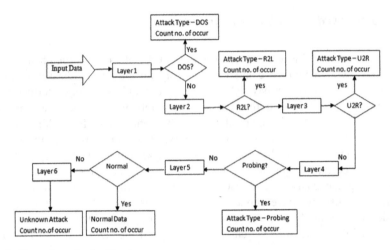

Fig. 2 Flow of attack classification

this reason, the dataset goes to the layered architecture to finding attack type with its number of occurrences.

The input dataset samples undergo six stages in which at each stage the samples are compared against the attack class type. Each attack class consists of its attack name which belongs to that category. In each layer, the test result shows the number of samples that belong to its category. Suppose a sample goes to the layered architecture, then first it checks whether it is a DoS type if yes the simple discard that sample and make DoS type as one, if no then it checked with R2L type if yes then increase the no of occurrence of R2L type if no then check whether it is U2R type and then Probing type. If the sample does not belong to these four attack types then check whether it is a normal type data or not, if yes then increase the number of occurrence of normal type, and if it does not belong to any one of these categories, then make it as unknown attack type and note the number of occurrences. Finally, the result shows the number of samples presents in each class type. In every layer, the data are filtered to its appropriate class type. The classification of the flow of attack is shown in Fig. 2.

5   Results and Experimental Analysis

In order to evaluate the performance of proposed algorithm for network intrusion detection, we work on five different class classifications with the help of KDD-99 dataset for both training and testing purpose. For the training purpose, 21606 number of random samples is taken which consists of 20 number of class types as one normal and 19 attack types. These 19 attacks belong to four major attack categories with some undefined attack category mark it as unknown attack type.

Table 1 Result of proposed model for data classification

Number of samples		Number of samples
Normal		10221
Attack	DoS	9083
	R2L	1877
	U2R	12
	Probing	300
	Unknown	113

Fig. 3 Result of types of attacks and non-attack

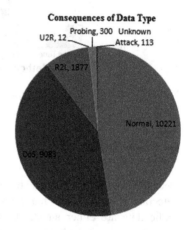

Consequences of Data Type

The purposed model successfully builds DT with proper identification of attack type. From the total 21606 number of samples, verities of data which are identified from the proposed model are given in Table 1.

The graphical representation of the result table is represented in Fig. 3.

The output scenario of proposed model is compared with other decision tree algorithm like CART, existing C4.5 which is an extension of ID3 algorithm with respect to performance time, accuracy, and error percentage which gives an idea that proposed model gives better result when compared to other two presented in Table 2 and graphically represented in Fig. 4.

Table 2 Result comparison with other classifiers

Classification techniques	Performance time (min)	Accuracy rate (%)	Error rate (%)
CART	1.3	86.42	13.58
ID3 extension (C4.5)	16.26	99.079	0.91
Proposed model	4.5	99.79	0.51

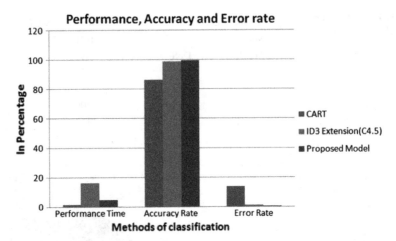

Fig. 4 Comparison of performance, accuracy, and error rate in different techniques with proposed model

6 Conclusion

Decision tree is one of the most effective and popular technique for intrusion detection system. It can make proper decision of whether the incoming network traffic data are either an attack or normal data. The proposed model builds the decision tree with the help of gain ratio and geometric mean for splitting the dataset. It also successfully identifies different type of attacks present in the dataset with identification of unknown data. The result of the proposed model is compared with other DT techniques like CART and ID3 extension (C4.5) with the help of KDDCUP-99 dataset, and proposed model gives 99% accuracy for attack identification with lesser time. The advantages of proposed model over C4.5 are the probability to achieve high detection rate over dissimilar types of attacks with less error rate and time. The future work is to test the performance of this model over a large dataset and also to handle the classification of unknown attack in an automatic control system.

References

1. Barbara, Daniel, et al.: ADAM: Detecting intrusions by data mining. In Proceedings of the IEEE Workshop on Information Assurance and Security. (2001): 11–16.
2. Swamy, K.V.R., and K.S. Vijaya Lakshmi: Network intrusion detection using improved decision tree algorithm. International Journal of Computer Science and Information Security 10.8 (2012): 4971–4975.
3. Farid, Dewan Md, et al.: "Attacks classification in adaptive intrusion detection using decision tree." World Academy of Science, Engineering and Technology 63 (2010): 86–90.

4. IDS over Firewall, https://www.scribd.com/document/45263670/Limitations-Of-Firewall. January 2017.

5. Sarkar, Sutapa: High Performance Network Security Using NIDS Approach. International Journal of Information Technology and Computer Science (IJITCS) 6.7 (2014): 47–55.

6. Das, Niva, and Tanmoy Sarkar: Survey on host and network based intrusion Detection System. Int. Journal of Advanced Networking and Applications 6.2 (2014): 2266–2269.

7. KDD99 dataset, http://kdd.ics.uci.edu/databases/kddcup99/kddcup99.html, 2017.

8. Paliwal, Swati, and Ravindra Gupta: Denial-of-service, probing & remote to user (R2L) attack detection using genetic algorithm. International Journal of Computer Applications 60.19 (2012): 57–62.

9. Kumar, Sandeep, and Satbir Jain: "Intrusion detection and classification using Improved ID3 algorithm of data mining." International Journal of Advanced Research in Computer Engineering & Technology (IJARCET) 1.5 (2012): 352–356.

10. Moon, Daesung, et al.: DTB-IDS: An intrusion detection system based on decision Tree using behavior analysis for preventing APT attacks. The Journal of supercomputing (2015): 1–15.

11. P Sarkhel, Himansu Das, and L K Vashishtha, "Task Scheduling Algorithms in Cloud Environment", In 3rd International Conference on Computational Intelligence in Data Mining, Springer India, 2017.

12. I Kar, RNR Parida, Himansu Das, "Energy Aware Scheduling using Genetic Algorithm in Cloud Data Centers" in International Conference on Electrical, Electronics, and Optimization Techniques, IEEE, 2016.

13. Himansu Das, A K Jena, P K Rath, B Muduli, S R Das, "Grid Computing Based Performance Analysis of Power System: A Graph Theoretic Approach", in International Conference on Intelligent Computing, Communication & Devices, Springer India, 2015, pp. 259–266.

14. Himansu Das, G S Panda, B Muduli, and P K Rath. "The Complex Network Analysis of Power Grid: A Case Study of the West Bengal Power Network." In International Conference on Advanced Computing, Springer India, 2014, pp. 17–29.

15. KHK Reddy, Himansu Das, D S Roy, "A Data Aware Scheme for Scheduling Big-Data Applications with SAVANNA Hadoop", in Futures of Network, CRC Press, 2017.

16. Panigrahi, C R, M Tiwary, B Pati, and Himansu Das., "Big Data and Cyber Foraging: Future Scope and Challenges." In Techniques and Environments for Big Data Analysis, Springer India, 2016, pp. 75–100.

17. Himansu Das, D.S.Roy, "A Grid Computing Service for Power System Monitoring," International Journal of Computer Applications (IJCA), 2013, Vol. 62 No. 20, pp 1–7

18. Himansu Das, Bighnaraj Naik, Bibudendu Pati, and Chhabi Rani Panigrahi, "A Survey on Virtual Sensor Networks Framework," International Journal of Grid & Distributed Computing (IJGDC), 2014, Vol. 7 no. 5, pp 121–130

19. Himansu Das, D.S.Roy, "The Topological Structure of the Odisha Power Grid: A Complex Network Analysis", in International Journal of Mechanical Engineering and Computer Applications (IJMCA), 2013, Vol.1 Issue 1, pp 12–18

20. Rathee, Anju, and Robin Prakash Mathur: Survey on decision tree classification algorithms for the evaluation of student performance. International Journal of Computers & Technology 4.2a1 (2013): 244–247.

21. Patel, B.R. and Kushik K.R.: A survey on decision tree algorithm for classification. Int. Journal of Engineering Development and Research 2.1 (2014): 1–5.

22. IDS History, http://csrc.nist.gov/publications/history/ande80.pdf. May 2017.

23. Das, Himansu, Ajay Kumar Jena, Janmenjoy Nayak, Bighnaraj Naik, and H. S. Behera. "A novel PSO based back propagation learning-MLP (PSO-BP-MLP) for classification." In Computational Intelligence in Data Mining-Volume 2, pp. 461–471. Springer, New Delhi, (2015).

24. DARPA Intrusion Detection Evaluation KDD dataset, http://kdd.ics.uci.edu//databases/ kddcup98/kddcup98.html. December 2016.

25. CART model, http://www.datasciencecentral.com/profiles/blogs/introduction-to-classification-regression-trees-cart. February 2017.

26. Quinlan, J. Ross: Induction of decision trees. Machine learning 1.1 (1986): 81–106.
27. Recent attack Presents over internet, http://www.internetworldstats.com/stats.htm. May 2017.
28. Rai, Kajal, M. Syamala Devi, and Ajay Guleria: Decision Tree Based Algorithm for Intrusion Detection, Int. Journal of Advanced Networking and Applications 7.4 (2016): 2828–2834.
29. Phutane, Ms Trupti, and Apashabi Pathan: Intrusion detection system using decision tree and apriori algorithm. Journal of Computer Engineering and Technology 6.7 (2015): 09–18.
30. Shon Nadiammai, G.V., and M. Hemalatha: Effective approach toward Intrusion Detection System using data mining techniques. Egyptian Informatics Journal 15.1(2014): 37–50.

Rare Correlated High Utility Itemsets Mining: An Experimental Approach

P. Lalitha Kumari, S. G. Sanjeevi and T. V. Madhusudhana Rao

Abstract High utility itemsets are having utility more than user-specified minimum utility. These itemsets provide high profit but do not exhibit correlation between them. High utility itemsets mining generate huge number of itemsets considering only single interesting criteria. Existing algorithm mines correlated high utility itemsets mining extracts itemsets that provide high utility with correlation between them. The limitation of this algorithm is that it does not consider the rarity of itemsets. To overcome this limitation, this proposed algorithm mines rare correlated high utility itemsets. Firstly, it mines correlated high utility itemsets. Secondly, it determines whether the itemsets support is no greater than minsup specified by the user. It can be shown by experimental results that the proposed algorithm reduces considerably runtime and number of candidate itemsets.

Keywords Correlated itemsets · Rare itemsets · Correlated high utility itemsets
Frequent itemsets

1 Introduction

Frequent itemsets mining methods generate a large number of itemsets that may not be necessarily applicable for decision-making applications. Rare itemsets mining generate important itemsets for some special applications such as inventory

P. Lalitha Kumari (✉) · S. G. Sanjeevi
Department of CSE, National Institute of Technology, Warangal 506004, Telangana, India
e-mail: lalitharam.p@gmail.com

S. G. Sanjeevi
e-mail: sgs@nitw.ac.in

T. V. Madhusudhana Rao
Department of CSE, Sri Sivani College of Engineering, Srikakulam 532402,
Andhra Pradesh, India
e-mail: madhu11211@gmail.com

© Springer Nature Singapore Pte Ltd. 2018
P. K. Pattnaik et al. (eds.), *Progress in Computing, Analytics and Networking*,
Advances in Intelligent Systems and Computing 710,
https://doi.org/10.1007/978-981-10-7871-2_73

systems, biomedical systems, marketing analysis. Rare itemsets mining result in itemsets with less minimum support threshold. High utility itemset mining approaches were solely considering only the utility, but not considering the correlation between them. Some research works have proposed effective algorithms for mining correlated high utility itemsets that generate the high utility itemsets with correlation. Those algorithms still generate more number of itemsets which do not consider the frequency or rarity of itemsets. High utility itemsets with rarity are the itemsets that are having utilities no less than user-given minimum utility and considers itemsets rarity.

Many algorithms [1, 7–10, 12, 13, 22, 23] have been proposed for mining the frequent itemsets in transactional databases. Apriori [1] is a well-known algorithm which works on the basis of candidate generation and test approach for mining frequent itemsets [1, 9, 12, 22, 23]. Apriori algorithm level-wise compares itemsets that support with user-specified minimum threshold. It returns all itemsets which satisfy minimum support threshold. Apriori-based approach algorithms need many scans for mining frequent itemsets. FP-growth algorithm [7, 8] as proposed to mine frequent itemsets efficiently than Apriori that considerably reduces number of scans. This approach needs two scans to find frequent itemsets using FP-tree.

Rare itemsets mining [11, 19, 21] has been experimented in recent years to generate all rare items that have low frequencies. Correlated itemsets mining is proposed in [4–6, 18]. For instance, let us consider medical database which consists the various symptoms as items: high temperature, headache, muscle pain, fatigue. If we consider the symptoms for fever and compare with the symptoms of dengue fever, there are several itemsets that appear to be the same as the symptoms for dengue fever. It is very hard to differentiate normal fever from dengue fever. In this case, identification of rare symptoms is necessary which causes the dengue fever. To determine the rare itemsets, that are more valuable, rare itemsets must consider with different values. This rare itemset must exhibit inherently the correlation with other. Consider two itemsets such as:

A: (high temperature, headache, muscle pain), B: (high temperature, headache, fatigue) are rare itemsets those are extracted from medical database. From these, itemsets (high temperature, headache) are common in more number of transactions and are correlated with each other. The itemsets (high temperature, headache, muscle pain) should be considered as more important than (high temperature, headache, fatigue). These itemsets are having low frequencies. These itemsets are treated as more serious symptoms for determining dengue fever. Itemsets (high temperature, headache, muscle pain, fatigue) can be considered as important rare correlated high utility itemsets. Traditional rare itemsets mining algorithms are thus not suitable to apply to mine useful rare itemsets in these circumstances. This leads to motivate for proposing algorithm for mining rare correlated high utility itemsets.

The main contribution of this work is (a) a new algorithm called RCHUI miner has been proposed for mining rare correlated HUIs. (b) This algorithm efficiently mines all rare correlated itemsets with high utilities in two phases. First, it generates correlated high utility itemsets. Second, it checks whether itemsets are rare itemsets or not. Third, experimental results reveal that the RCHUI miner approach generates less number of itemsets with more interestingness.

The rest of paper is narrated as follows. Background knowledge has been described in Sect. 2. RCHUI miner algorithm along with working principle has been detailed in Sect. 3. Description of the experimental results of the RCHUI miner has been discussed in Sect. 4. Finally, conclusion with future work has been elucidated in Sect. 5.

2 Related Work

Many efficient algorithms to mine high utility itemsets have been proposed. For mining high utility itemset, two-phase algorithm was proposed by Liu et al. [15]. In this, transaction-weighted utility (TWU) has been introduced as upper bound to utility to maintain the downward closure property and to prune search space. Mengchi Liu and Junfeng Qu [16] have proposed an approach to mine high utility itemset without generating candidates. They proposed a novel list called utility-list structures to maintain information about each itemset to mine all high utility itemsets effectively. However, two-phase algorithm follows the generate-and-test approach for generating candidates, for which it consumes heavy computational resources. Moreover, if more number of candidates is generated, time required to determine utilities of them is increased. To overcome limitations mentioned above, IHUP [15] and UP-growth [20] were proposed which are based on FP-growth approach.

UP-growth was proposed by Tseng et al. [20] for mining high utility itemset. In their work, they proposed pattern growth-based technique within two scans of database. By using various strategies, i.e., DLU, DGU, DGN, and DLN candidate itemsets are pruned during mining process efficiently. HUI miner was proposed by Liu et al. [15] with tight overestimated utility strategy for pruning the search space. Many other studies have also been proposed to extend high utility itemsets mining. To mine different concise representations of HUIs, such as maximal HUIs [3], closed HUIs [17], and generators of HUIs, various efficient algorithms have been proposed. HUIM on incremental, dynamic database and on data streams has been proposed by Ahmed et al. in [2]. Itemsets with negative profits are also considered in mining HUIs with negative unit profits using FHN algorithm proposed by Philippe-Fournier et al. FHN discovered HUIs without generating candidates and introduced several strategies to handle items with negative unit profits efficiently. To avoid difficulties in setting a proper utility threshold in [14–17], attempts have been done to mine a set of top k-itemsets with the highest utility.

Mining rare correlated high utility itemsets mining: The problem of rare correlated high utility itemset mining can be stated as to extract all correlated high utility itemsets with rarity. An itemset 'X' is a rare correlated high utility itemset if it is a high utility itemset whose bond, bond(X) is no less than a user-specified minimum bond threshold minbond, specified by the user and its support is no greater than user-specified minimum support.

3 Basic Preliminaries

3.1 Utility Mining

Let $I = \{i_1, i_2, i_3, ..., i_n\}$ be a set of items and a database called DB comprised of tables having utilities and transactions. Utility table (Table 2) consists of itemsets and their associated utilities. In the transaction table (Table 1), each transaction 'T' is assigned with individual identifier (Tid) and is a subset of 'I,' where every item has been assigned with count value. The itemset containing 'α' items is called α-itemset. Basic definitions are detailed in [15].

For a given database and minutil, high utility itemset is an itemset if its utility is no less than given user-specified minimal utility threshold denoted as minutil, or the product of a minutil and the total utility of a mined database, if the minutil is expressed as percentage. It must be observed that maintaining downward closure property of HUIs is difficult as it does not hold for high utility itemsets (HUIs).

For instance, consider a transaction database having only one transaction, $\{m, 1; n, 1\}$ and external utility of m = 1 and external utility of n = 2. And if minutil is 6, then for $u(\{m\}) = 5$, $u(\{n\}) = 10$ and $u(\{m, n\}) = 15$, $\{n\}$ and $\{m, n\}$ are high utility itemsets and $\{m\}$ is not. It indicates that the downward closure property does not valid for high utility itemsets. This shows that high utility itemsets mining is challenging compared to frequent itemset mining.

If the TWU of each item is not satisfied with minutil, then items are deleted from transactions. If TWU of each item $\geq$ minutil, then transactions are rearranged according to the ascending order of the TWU of every item. If the minutil is set as 30, then all items are having their TWU greater than minutil, i.e., 30 so no item is deleted. If we set minutil is 40, then items 'f' and 'g' are deleted, and then transactions are revised according to the ascending order of their TWUs. The TWU of each item is presented in Table 3. The arrangement of each item according to their TWU is as follows:

Table 1 Transactional database

Tid	Transaction	Count
1	{c, e, a, b, d, f}	{1, 3, 5, 5, 3, 1}
2	{c, e, b, d}	{3, 3, 4, 3}
3	{c, a, d}	{1, 5, 1}
4	{c, e, a, g}	{6, 6, 10, 5}
5	{c, e, b, g}	{1, 1, 2, 2}

Table 2 Utility table

a	b	c	d	e	f	g
1	2	1	2	1	1	1

Table 3 Transaction-weighted utility (TWU) of each item

Item	a	b	c	d	e	f	g
TWU	65	61	96	58	88	30	38

$$f > g > d > b > a > e > c$$

Current HUIM algorithms are having key problem that some large number of itemsets are generated those have weak correlation between them. In this paper, integration of utility and correlation is done with rarity as another constraint. Researchers have already described different correlation measures [4–6, 14] in their researches. Correlated itemsets can be found by using bond measure. Conjunctive support of an itemsets X in database D is denoted as conj|X|, where conj|X| is the number of transactions in conj(X).

The disjunctive support of an itemset X in a database D is denoted as disjsup(X) and defined as |{Tc ∈ D/X ∩ Tc ≠ Φ}|. The bond of itemset X is defined as bond (X) = conj(X)/disjsup(X). An itemset X is said to be correlated if bond(X) is greater than minbond, for a given user-specified minbond threshold (0 ≥ min-bond ≥ 1). Anti-monotonic property is maintained for bond measure.

Property 1 *Anti-monotonicity of the bond measure can be defined as follows: Let S and T be two itemsets such that S ⊆ R. It follows that* bond(S) ≥ bond(R) *[5]. By using the above property, it can be stated that the problem of mining rare correlated high utility itemsets as follows.*

Definition 1 (*Rare correlated high utility itemset mining*) An itemset X is a rare correlated high utility itemset if it is a high utility itemset and its bond(X) is no less than a user-defined minimum bond threshold minbond, and its support should be less than minsup specified by the user.

To mine rare correlated HUIs, the proposed algorithm behaves as follows: firstly, our proposed algorithm extracts all correlated HUIs by using structures called as EUCS. The structure of the EUCS is described in [6]. Fournier-Viger P. et al. developed the approach to mine correlated high utility itemsets using EUCS structure. This structure can be used to determine conjunctive and disjunctive support of an itemset without scan database. This algorithm does not consider the rarity of itemsets. Secondly, proposed algorithm extracts rare correlated itemsets that provide high utility. Algorithm 1 returns all high utility itemsets with correlation-based EUCS structure. It will check whether TWU is more than minutil to maintain downward closure property. Later, correlated high utility itemsets are checked with their support. The itemsets that have support less than minsup are extracted from EUCS structure. Itemset's information is maintained in utility-list structure. This algorithm has been explained in [16].

Proposed RCHUI miner Algorithm

Input: D: a transaction database, minutil: a user-specified utility threshold, minsup: user-specified support threshold, minbond: user-specified bond threshold

Output: the set of rare correlated high utility itemsets

1. Determine TWU of every item by scan database D;

2. Let K* contain the set of items and each item TWU $\geq$ minutil;

3. Define '>' on the ascending order of TWU values on K*;

4. Construct utility-list of every item k $\in$ K* by scan D again and create EUCS;

5. Calculate the conjunctive support and disjunctive support of each itemset from EUCS structure;

6. Determine the bond for each itemset;

7. Check if SUM({k}.utilitylist.iutils) $\geq$ minutil and bond(k) $\geq$ minbond. k.support < minsup;

8. Then output each item k $\in$ K* such that k.support < minsup;

9. Search (Θ, K*, minutil, EUCS);

4 Experimental Results and Analysis

The experimental results of the RCHUI miner have been illustrated in this section. The RCHUI miner algorithm adopts basic framework from HUI miner. We assessed our algorithms by performing experiments on computer with a 2.10 GHz, Intel Core i3 CPU with 4 GB of RAM, and run on Windows 7. Implementation of our proposed algorithm is done in Java. The performance of our proposed algorithm can be evaluated with three datasets. We have considered absolute values for maximum periods. For foodmart dataset, less number of candidates are generated when minutil is set to 3k, 4k, 5k. For foodmart dataset (Fig. 1a), candidate itemsets are generated more for all variations of minutil, i.e., for 3k, 3.5k, 4k, 5k. As a second observation in mushroom dataset (Fig. 1b), we have noticed that the number

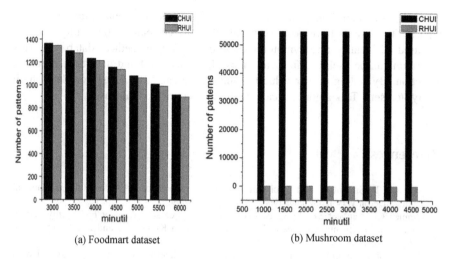

(a) Foodmart dataset   (b) Mushroom dataset

Fig. 1 **a, b** Results of RCHUI for different datasets

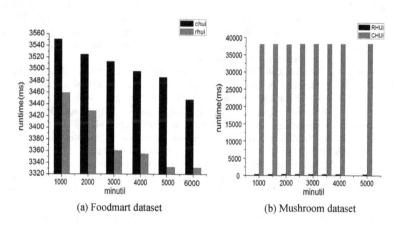

(a) Foodmart dataset   (b) Mushroom dataset

Fig. 2 **a, b** Comparison of runtime for different datasets

of RCHUIs is quite less as compared to correlated HUIs. Figure 2 shows the runtime comparison of mushroom dataset and foodmart dataset. Runtime has been considerably reduced when compared to correlated HUIs with RCHUI miner.

5 Conclusion

In this work, a novel approach called RCHUI miner has been proposed for efficient discovery of rare correlated high utility itemsets through bond measure. This algorithm works in two phases; first, we find correlated high utility itemsets satisfying the minutil and minbond measures. In the second phase, rare correlated high utility itemsets have been extracted. The rare correlated high utility itemsets are used to identify rare symptoms of rare diseases in medical databases. This algorithm can be useful to find various applications like fraud detection, intrusion detection. By setting proper value to minsup, we can extract rare correlated high utility itemsets. This algorithm can extend to incremental databases.

References

1. Agrawal R, Srikant R, Fast algorithms for mining association rules. In: 20th international conference on very large databases, (1994) pp. 487–499.
2. Ahmed CF, Tanbeer SK, Jeong B, Lee Y, Efficient tree structures for high utility pattern mining in incremental databases. IEEE Transactions on Knowledge and Data Engineering. (2009). pp. 1708–1721.
3. Bai-En Shie, Philip.S.Yu, Vincent.S.Tseng, Efficient algorithms for mining maximal high utility itemsets from data streams with different models, Expert Systems with Applications (2012), pp. 12947–12960.
4. Barsky, M., Kim, S., Weninger, T., Han, J., Mining Flipping correlations from large datasets with taxonomies. In: Proc. 38th Int. Conf. on Very Large Databases. (2012). pp. 370–381.
5. Ben Younes, N., Hamrouni, T., Ben Yahia, S.: Bridging conjunctive and disjunctive search spaces for mining a new concise and exact representation of correlated patterns. In: Proc. 13th Int. Conf. Discovery Science. (2010). pp. 189–204.
6. Fournier-Viger P., Lin J.CW., Dinh T., Le H.B. Mining Correlated High-Utility Itemsets Using the Bond Measure. In: Martínez-Álvarez F., Troncoso A., Quintián H., Corchado E. (eds) Hybrid Artificial Intelligent Systems. HAIS 2016. Springer. (2016).
7. Grahne G, Zhu J, Fast algorithms for frequent itemset mining using FP-Trees. IEEE Transactions on Knowledge and Data Engineering. (2005). pp. 1347–1362.
8. Han J, Pei J, Yin Y, Mining frequent itemsets without candidate generation. In: Proc. of the 2000 ACM SIGMOD int'l conf. on management of data. (2000). pp. 1–12.
9. Hu Y, Chen Y, Mining association rules with multiple minimum supports: a new mining algorithm and a support tuning mechanism. Decision Support Systems. (2006). pp. 1–24.
10. Huynh-Thi-Le Q, Le T, Vo B, Le HBAn efficient and effective algorithm for mining top-rank-k frequent itemsets. Expert Systems Applications. (2015). pp. 156–164.
11. Kiran RU, Reddy PK, An improved multiple minimum support based approach to mine rare association rules. CIDM 2009. (2009). pp. 340–347.
12. Lee G, Yun U, Ryu K, Sliding window based weighted maximal frequent itemsets mining over data streams. Expert Systems Applications. (2014). pp. 694–708.
13. Lee G, Yun U, Ryang H, An Uncertainty-based Approach: Frequent Itemset Mining from Uncertain Data with Different Item Importance. Knowledge-Based Systems. (2015). pp. 239–256.
14. Lin, J. C.-W., Gan, W., Fournier-Viger, P., Hong, T.-P, Mining Discriminative High Utility Patterns. Proc. 8th Asian Conference on Intelligent Information and Database Systems. Springer. (2016).
15. Liu Y, Liao W, Choudhary A, A two-phase algorithm for fast discovery of high utility itemsets. Advanced Knowledge Discovery in Data Mining. (2005). pp. 689–695.
16. Mengchi Liu, Junfeng Qu, Mining High Utility Itemsets without Candidate Generation, Proceedings of the 21st ACM international conference on Information and knowledge management, (2012), pp. 55–64.

17. Sahoo, J., Das, A.K. & Goswami, A. An efficient fast algorithm for discovering closed+ high utility itemsets, Applied Intelligence (2016), pp. 44–74.
18. Soulet, A., Raissi, C., Plantevit, M., Cremilleux, B.: Mining dominant patterns in the sky. In: Proc. 11th IEEE International Conference on Data Mining. (2011). pp. 655–664.
19. Tempaiboolkul J, Mining rare association rules in a distributed environment using multiple minimum supports. ICIS 2013. (2013). pp. 295–299.
20. Tseng VS, Wu CW, Shie BE, Yu PS, UP-Growth: an efficient algorithm for high utility itemset mining. In: Proc. of the 16th ACM SIGKDD int'l conf. on knowledge discovery and data mining (KDD 2010). (2010). pp. 253–262.
21. Weng CH, Mining fuzzy specific rare itemsets for education data. Knowledge-Based Systems. (2011). pp. 697–708.
22. Xu T, Dong X, Mining frequent itemsets with multiple minimum supports using basic Apriori. ICNC 2013. (2013). pp. 957–961.
23. Yun U, Yoon E, An efficient approach for mining weighted approximate closed frequent patterns considering noise constraints, International Journal of Uncertainty Fuzziness Knowledge Based Systems. (2014). pp. 879–912.

Crow Search Optimization-Based Hybrid Meta-heuristic for Classification: A Novel Approach

Bighnaraj Naik and Janmenjoy Nayak

Abstract This paper proposed a novel crow search optimization-based hybrid approach to solve classification problem of data mining. Being a recently developed population-based algorithm, crow search algorithm (CSA) has been strived the attention of all range researchers to solve wide range of complex engineering and optimization problems. In this paper, CSA is used with functional link neural network to solve classification problem. The results of the proposed method have been compared with other swarm-based approaches, and the experimental results reveal that the proposed method is superior to others.

Keywords Crow search optimization · FLANN · Classification

1 Introduction

The original evolvement of the term "meta-heuristic" is quite interesting and intends to solve different wide range of problems through heuristic methods. The algorithmic framework of meta-heuristic approaches is quite simple as general algorithms which help to apply them for solving the real-life problems with a few modifications. The broad classification of meta-heuristic-based algorithms can be of

B. Naik
Department of Computer Application, Veer Surendra Sai University of Technology,
Burla, Sambalpur 768018, Odisha, India
e-mail: mailtobnaik@gmail.com

J. Nayak (✉)
Department of Computer Science and Engineering, Sri Sivani College of Engineering,
Srikakulam 532410, Andhra Pradesh, India
e-mail: mailforjnayak@gmail.com

© Springer Nature Singapore Pte Ltd. 2018
P. K. Pattnaik et al. (eds.), *Progress in Computing, Analytics and Networking*,
Advances in Intelligent Systems and Computing 710,
https://doi.org/10.1007/978-981-10-7871-2_74

evolutionary-based, swarm-based, physical-based, chemical-based, population-based and nature-based approaches etc. Although these approaches are quite successful, but sometimes a single meta-heuristic may not be able to completely obtain the true aspects of exploration and exploitation. Prior to the early days of research on the use of a single meta-heuristic algorithm, last decade has seen some advance hybrid methods by combining two or more algorithms for solving some real complex real-life problems. The main advantage of using the hybrid methods is to explore the strengths of each of the individual algorithms or procedures for some synergetic performances in combination to both the algorithms. In such cases, if one will be limited to exploration capabilities, then the other may lead towards exploitation and the outcome of such meta-heuristic is quite promising one. Moreover, hybrid approaches result more efficiently in terms of high accuracy or good computational speed. Meta-heuristic algorithms involve the stochastic components which make them suitable for global optimization and may not stuck at local optima. While solving some complex optimization problems, quality solutions may be obtained in a realistic span of time by using meta-heuristic algorithms. The main advantage of using meta-heuristic algorithm is that it tends to global optimal solution for complex problems [1].

Moreover, for solving multimodal and nonlinear problems, meta-heuristics have shown promising potential in wide variety of diversified problems. With random solutions and local search procedures, some meta-heuristics may able to solve some complex problems, but they may not ensure for optimal solutions. As per Glover's convention, all optimization algorithms based on nature or simply called, nature-inspired algorithms are called meta-heuristics [2]. Based on the literature of the current research of the nature-inspired algorithms, it can be predicted that surprisingly those are effective for solving complex real-world problems. The main reason behind the success rate of nature-inspired and swarm-based algorithms is having the capability to solve the NP-hard problems. To resolve the real-life problems, some of the earlier developed optimization techniques fail and the solutions of many real-life problems have been obtained by hit and trail methods. So, this is the basis for the researchers to focus towards the development of some competitive optimization algorithms, which are efficient to resolve the complex problems. In this paper, a newly developed crow search optimization is considered with functional link ANN for solving classification problems [19–28]. The reason for choosing this algorithm is simple to understand and easy implementation of computing steps. Further, the paper is divided into following parts: Sect. 2 describes the preliminaries, i.e., working procedures and principles of CSA. Section 3 elucidates some latest literature of crow search optimization, which helps to analyse its popularity. The proposed method has been described in Sect. 4. In Sect. 5, the details about experiment such as experimental set-up and result analysis have been elaborated. Section 6 concludes the work with some future research directions.

2 Preliminaries

2.1 Crow Search Optimization

This optimization is developed based on the behaviour of crows and is proposed by Askarzadeh [3]. Normally, we may find the crows in almost all part of the universe, and they are assumed to be the most intelligent bird among other birds in the birds' community [4]. They have hefty brain as compared to the size of their body. Moreover, the level of intelligence of their brain is considered to be just lower than human brain. Because of this, they are able to remember their food storage locations even after some months. They burgle food of other birds in their absence and always try to be in safe and hiding place, where no one can reach. Also, it is true that they behave intelligently, when they are in a group as compared to a single crow. In any unfriendly situation, they may warn each other for better safety. During seasonal time, they collect food, keep food for future in a safe place and also able to intelligently hide the food from others [5]. They are able to remember faces, and they can use tools with sophisticated communication skills.

By considering the above facts, the crow search algorithm is developed and it simulates the optimization process in following ways. Crow can conceal their food in a safe place, and at the time of need, they may use it. They are greedy in nature as always a competition is there among them for searching better food locations. During the search of safe location, at a certain moment, if any crow is finding that some other one is following it, then suddenly the first crow is able to make fool the other one by simply changing its destination. So, in the algorithm, the environment where the crow finds its safe location and travels around is considered to be the search space. The crow is considered to be as one member in the population, and the whole group of crows is the population. Every position covered by crow/crows is said to be one feasible solution, and the quality of food location searched by the crow is considered to be the fitness function. Among all the food locations, the best one is known to be the global solution to solve the problem.

3 Related Works

Since the development of CSA, it has been successfully applied in various problem domains of engineering and other diversified areas. Literature of some of the important applications is narrated below. Oliva et al. [6] have used CSA for segmenting the magnetic resonance image in an effective way. They found the results obtained by their proposed method are superior and CSA is able to tackle some

Table 1 Applications of CSA

Sl. No	Method	Area of application	Reference
1	CSA	Optimization problems	[11]
2	CSA	Cloud computing	[12]
3	CSA	Power system	[13]
4	CSA	Radial distribution networks	[14]
5	Multi-objective CSA	Optimization problems	[15]
6	CSA	Distribution system	[16]
7	CSA	Power generation	[17]
8	CSA	Document classification	[18]

critical issues like early convergence, maintaining balance in between diversification and exploration. With the help of population diversity information and Gaussian distribution, Coelho et al. [7] have enhanced the performance of original CSA and found some better results for their developed method for the application in electromagnetic optimization. Sayed et al. [8] have introduced a new chaotic-based CSA for solving feature selection problem with consideration of twenty benchmark data sets. They found improved classifier performance with the proposed method as compared to some other standard methods. For solving the problem of optimal placement of static synchronous compensators, Choudhary et al. [9] have implemented a novel technique with CSA to find the best location. With the proposed method, they able to minimize the total line losses in the power system through the placement of static synchronous compensators. Liu et al. [10] have proposed an extreme learning-based model with CSA for resolving the fuzziness of the water quality and incompatibility of water parameters. From the training and testing results, they concluded that the ELM-CSA-based model can be used to evaluate the quality of groundwater. Apart from these applications, some other applications have been mentioned in Table 1. By inspiring from all these successful applications and the popularity of CSA algorithm, in this paper, a novel attempt has been made for solving the data mining problem with higher order neural network.

4 Proposed Model

In this proposed work, we have used CSA for obtaining an optimal functional link ANN model (FLANN) for nonlinear data classification. In this section, the step by step process to obtain the optimal weight set for the FLANN model from population of weight sets (crow memory) by using crow search algorithm is illustrated. Here, the objective is to find out the optimal weight set for FLANN model for faster convergence during training and testing phases.

4.1 PseudoCode of Proposed CSA-Based Method

Step – 1

Set iter = 1. Initialize the crow memory $CM^{iter} = \left(C_1^{iter}, C_2^{iter} ... C_N^{iter} \right)$ with N no. of weight set (crows), where C_1^{iter} represents 1st weight set (crow) at iteration 'iter' among N number of weight sets. Here the dimension of CM^{iter} and C_N^{iter} depends on the dimension of the data set (D) used to train the FLANN model.

Step – 2

Compute fitness of all the weight set C_i^{iter} for i=1 to N as follow:

for i=1:1:N

Compute $S_i = \varphi(D) \times C_i^{iter} = \left(s^1, s^2 ... s^L \right)$, where L is the no. of instances in D, $\varphi(D)$ is the functionally expanded data sets, S and s^i is the intermediate result vector and i^{th} intermediate result value of ith input instance from D respectively.

Compute $O = \tanh(S) = \left(o^1, o^2 ... o^L \right)$, where O is the output vector, $\tanh(.)$ is the higher order activation function and o^i is the ith output value of ith input instance from D.

Compute $e = o_i - t_i = \left(o^1 - t^1, o^2 - t^2 ... o^L - t^L \right) = \left(e^1, e^2 ... e^L \right)$, where e is the error vector, o^i and t_i is the ith output value and target value of ith input instance from D respectively.

Compute the total error of the network $e_i = \sum_{i=1}^{L} e^i$

Compute the fitness of the weight set C_i^{iter} is calculated as $f_i = \frac{1}{e_i}$

End_for

Step – 3

Select best weight set C_h^{iter} (best crow hiding point in iteration 'iter') in CM^{iter} based on the best fitness f_i.

Step – 4

while iter < Max_iter

    for i=1:1:N

    Randomly select one crow C_i^{iter}

Set Awareness Probability (AP).
If rand(1) >= AP

$$C_i^{iter+1} = C_i^{iter} + rand(1) \times fl^{iter} \times \left(C_h^{iter} - C_i^{iter} \right);$$

Else $C_i^{iter+1} = C_i^{iter} \pm rand(1);$

End_if
End_for

Evaluate all the weight sets (crows) in CM^{iter} *and* CM^{iter+1}

If C_i^{iter} *in* $CM^{iter} > C_i^{iter+1}$ *in* CM^{iter+1}

Then replace C_i^{iter+1} *in* CM^{iter+1} *with* C_i^{iter} *in* CM^{iter}.

End_if

Set weight set with best fitness among all weight sets in CM^{iter+1} *as in Step - 2.*

Update crow memory $CM^{iter} = CM^{iter+1}$.

Find out best weight set C_h^{iter+1} *from* CM^{iter+1} *with best fitness value.*

Update hiding position $C_h^{iter} = C_h^{iter+1}$.

End_while

Step – 5

Find out best C_{best}^{iter} *form* CM^{Max_iter} *with best fitness value.*

Step – 6

Set C_{best}^{iter} *weight set in FLANN network for faster convergence while training and testing phase.*

Step – 7

Exit

In the above pseudocode, the recent literature on FLANN and its implementation details may be obtained in [19–28]. In this study, the gradient descent learning has been adopted to train the FLANN.

5 Simulation Result

The proposed scheme has been implemented in MATLAB and tested on data sets from UCI repository [29]. Optimal fitness value of all the considered schemes is carefully observed (Table 2).

Figure 1 represents the changes in fitness observed in considered schemes in various iterations on Monk 2 data set. It has been noticed that fitness of PSO-based FLANN model is found to be better than GA-based FLANN and CSA-based FLANN. Similarly, the proposed model is found to be better in almost all the data sets except Ionosphere data set (Table 2). During simulation, the crow search algorithmic parameters of the proposed method are set as in Table 3. The FLANN's set-up and its parameters have adopted from previous literature [20–29].

Table 2 Comparison of fitness among GA-based trained FLANN, PSO-based trained FLANN and CSA-based trained FLANN

Data sets	Fitness obtained by various hybrid models		
	GA-based trained FLANN	PSO-based trained FLANN	CSA-based trained FLANN
Wine	2.462398	2.462398	2.729584
Iris	5.972679	5.97268	6.38756
Hayesroth	1.888252	1.869618	1.947664
Monk 2	2.024735	2.033361	3.057657
Ionosphere	1.677268	1.696773	1.689465
Hepatitis	2.58331	2.813839	2.947563
Pima	2.216361	2.216474	2.219834
Dermatology	1.888967	1.981951	2.877354

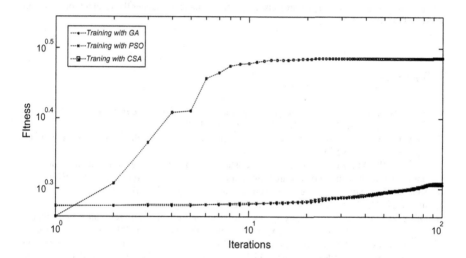

Fig. 1 Performance comparison on Monk 2 data set

Table 3 Parameter setting used for simulation

Parameters	Suggested value
N: No. of crows	50
fl: flight length	2
AP: Awareness Probability	0.1
Max_iter	100

6 Conclusion and Future Work

In this paper, a novel crow search optimization-based functional link neural network model is developed to solve the classification problem of data mining. The proposed method is compared with some other evolutionary- and swarm-based methods like GA-based trained FLANN and PSO-based trained FLANN. The performance is compared in terms of fitness of all the models. On testing eight no. of data sets, the results divulge that the proposed method has obtained superior results than others with less iteration. In future, the performance of the proposed model may be tested on some other high-dimensional data sets to analyse the nature of the algorithm and further, some more other swarm-based algorithms may be taken into considerations for comparison purpose.

Acknowledgements This work is supported by Technical Education Quality Improvement Programme, National Project Implementation Unit (A unit of MHRD, Govt. of India, for implementation of World Bank assisted projects in technical education), under the research project grant (VSSUT/TEQIP/37/2016).

References

1. S. Voss, *Meta-heuristics: the state of the art, in: Local Search for Planning and Scheduling*, Ed. A. Nareyek, LNAI 2148, pp. 1–23, 2001.
2. Glover F. Future paths for integer programming and links to artificial intelligence. Comput Oper Res 1986; 13:533–49.
3. Askarzadeh, Alireza. "A novel metaheuristic method for solving constrained engineering optimization problems: crow search algorithm." Computers & Structures 169 (2016): 1–12.
4. Rincon, Paul, Science/nature|crows and jays top bird IQ scale, BBC News.
5. https://en.wikipedia.org/wiki/Corvus_%28genus%29.
6. Oliva, Diego, et al. "Cross entropy based thresholding for magnetic resonance brain images using Crow Search Algorithm." Expert Systems with Applications 79 (2017): 164–180.
7. dos Santos Coelho, Leandro, et al. "Modified crow search approach applied to electromagnetic optimization." Electromagnetic Field Computation (CEFC), 2016 IEEE Conference on. IEEE, 2016.
8. Sayed, Gehad Ismail, Aboul Ella Hassanien, and Ahmad Taher Azar. "Feature selection via a novel chaotic crow search algorithm." Neural Computing and Applications (2017): 1–18.
9. Choudhary, Garima, Niraj Singhal, and K. S. Sajan. "Optimal placement of STATCOM for improving voltage profile and reducing losses using crow search algorithm." Control, Computing, Communication and Materials (ICCCCM), 2016 International Conference on. IEEE, 2016.
10. Liu, Dong, et al. "ELM evaluation model of regional groundwater quality based on the crow search algorithm." Ecological Indicators 81 (2017): 302–314.
11. Rajput, Swati, et al. "Optimization of benchmark functions and practical problems using Crow Search Algorithm." Eco-friendly Computing and Communication Systems (ICECCS), 2016 Fifth International Conference on. IEEE, 2016.
12. Satpathy, Anurag, et al. "A Resource Aware VM Placement Strategy in Cloud Data Centers Based on Crow Search Algorithm." (2017).

13. Aleem, Shady HE Abdel, Ahmed F. Zobaa, and Murat E. Balci. "Optimal resonance-free third-order high-pass filters based on minimization of the total cost of the filters using Crow Search Algorithm." Electric Power Systems Research 151 (2017): 381–394.

14. Abdelaziz, Almoataz Y., and Ahmed Fathy. "A novel approach based on crow search algorithm for optimal selection of conductor size in radial distribution networks." Engineering Science and Technology, an International Journal 20.2 (2017): 391–402.

15. Nobahari, Hadi, and Ariyan Bighashdel. "MOCSA: A Multi-Objective Crow Search Algorithm for Multi-Objective optimization." Swarm Intelligence and Evolutionary Computation (CSIEC), 2017 2nd Conference on. IEEE, 2017.

16. Askarzadeh, Alireza. "Capacitor placement in distribution systems for power loss reduction and voltage improvement: a new methodology." IET Generation, Transmission & Distribution 10.14 (2016): 3631–3638.

17. Askarzadeh, Alireza. "Electrical power generation by an optimised autonomous PV/wind/tidal/battery system." IET Renewable Power Generation 11.1 (2016): 152–164.

18. Allahverdipour, Ali, and Farhad Soleimanian Gharehchopogh. "An Improved K-Nearest Neighbor with Crow Search Algorithm for Feature Selection in Text Documents Classification." Journal of Advances in Computer Research (2016).

19. Naik, Bighnaraj, Janmenjoy Nayak, and Himansu Sekhar Behera. "A global-best harmony search based gradient descent learning FLANN (GbHS-GDL-FLANN) for data classification." Egyptian Informatics Journal 17.1 (2016): 57–87.

20. Naik, Bighnaraj, Janmenjoy Nayak, and H. S. Behera. "A TLBO based gradient descent learning-functional link higher order ANN: An efficient model for learning from non-linear data." Journal of King Saud University-Computer and Information Sciences (2016).

21. Naik, Bighnaraj, et al. "A self adaptive harmony search based functional link higher order ANN for non-linear data classification." Neurocomputing 179 (2016): 69–87.

22. Naik, Bighnaraj, Janmenjoy Nayak, and H. S. Behera. "A FLANN based non-linear system identification for classification and parameter optimization using tournament selective harmony search." Computational Intelligence in Data Mining—Volume 2. Springer, New Delhi, 2016. 267–283.

23. Naik, Bighnaraj, Janmenjoy Nayak, and H. S. Behera. "A Hybrid Model of FLANN and Firefly Algorithm for Classification." Handbook of Research on Natural Computing for Optimization Problems. IGI Global, 2016. 491–522.

24. Naik, Bighnaraj, Janmenjoy Nayak, and H. S. Behera. "A FLANN based non-linear system identification for classification and parameter optimization using tournament selective harmony search." Computational Intelligence in Data Mining—Volume 2. Springer, New Delhi, 2016. 267–283.

25. Naik, Bighnaraj, Janmenjoy Nayak, and Himansu Sekhar Behera. "An efficient FLANN model with CRO-based gradient descent learning for classification." International Journal of Business Information Systems 21.1 (2016): 73–116.

26. Naik, Bighnaraj, et al. "A harmony search based gradient descent learning-FLANN (HS-GDL-FLANN) for classification." Computational Intelligence in Data Mining-Volume 2. Springer, New Delhi, 2015. 525–539.

27. Naik, Bighnaraj, Janmenjoy Nayak, and H. S. Behera. "A honey bee mating optimization based gradient descent learning–FLANN (HBMO-GDL-FLANN) for Classification." Emerging ICT for Bridging the Future-Proceedings of the 49th Annual Convention of the Computer Society of India CSI Volume 2. Springer International Publishing, 2015.

28. Naik, Bighnaraj, Janmenjoy Nayak, and Himansu Sekhar Behera. "A novel FLANN with a hybrid PSO and GA based gradient descent learning for classification." Proceedings of the 3rd International Conference on Frontiers of Intelligent Computing: Theory and Applications (FICTA) 2014. Springer, Cham, 2015.

29. Bache, K., and M. Lichman. "UCI machine learning repository. University of California, School of Information and Computer Science, Irvine, CA." Retrieved from the World Wide Web October 27 (2013): 2014.

A Survey of Feature Selection Techniques in Intrusion Detection System: A Soft Computing Perspective

P. Ravi Kiran Varma, V. Valli Kumari and S. Srinivas Kumar

Abstract In the process of detecting different kinds of attacks in anomaly-based intrusion detection system (IDS), both normal and attack data are profiled with the help of selected attributes. Various types of attributes are collected to create the attack and normal traffic patterns. Some of the attributes are derived from protocol header fields, and some of them represent continuous information profiled over a period. *"Curse of Dimensionality"* is one of the major issues in IDS. The computational complexity of the model generation and classification time of IDS is directly proportional to the number of attributes of the profile. In a typical IDS preprocessing stage, more significant features among the available features are selected. This paper presents a brief taxonomy of several feature selection methods with emphasis on soft computing techniques, viz., rough sets, fuzzy rough sets, and ant colony optimization.

Keywords Intrusion detection system · IDS · Feature selection
Soft computing · Survey

1 Introduction

Intrusion detection system (IDS) and Firewall [1, 2] stand in the front line of defending the network perimeter. Anderson [3] proposed one of the earliest works in the area of IDS that tried to monitor security violations through audit records.

P. Ravi Kiran Varma (✉)
MVGR College of Engineering, Vizianagaram, Andhra Pradesh, India
e-mail: ravikiranvarmap@gmail.com

V. Valli Kumari
Andhra University College of Engineering, Visakhapatnam, Andhra Pradesh, India
e-mail: vallikumari@gmail.com

S. Srinivas Kumar
University College of Engineering Kakinada, JNT University, Kakinada,
Andhra Pradesh, India
e-mail: samay_ssk2@yahoo.com

© Springer Nature Singapore Pte Ltd. 2018
P. K. Pattnaik et al. (eds.), *Progress in Computing, Analytics and Networking*,
Advances in Intelligent Systems and Computing 710,
https://doi.org/10.1007/978-981-10-7871-2_75

Denning [4] is one of the early researchers who provided a strong motivational background for researchers in the area of IDS. He has demonstrated that, by profiling the regular activity, any deviations from normal can be identified. The audit records of several activities like the login and session activity, commands and execution sequence of programs, file access activity are collected. These audit records are used to detect the intrusions. Lunt [5] has done a survey of off-line and on-line IDS and identified several audit trail attributes employed in the data set. John et al. [6] reiterated the importance and the role of IDS in an organization's security posture. Dataset dimensionality is sometimes a bottleneck for computational intelligent and data analysis tasks. There exist many methods, algorithms, and tools in order to minimize data size. Optimization often involves attribute selection or reduction, and it is the objective of many researchers. Andreas et al. [7] demonstrated the importance of feature selection and also presented the relation between the selected features and accuracy. This paper presents a comprehensive survey of feature selection methods with an emphasis on soft computing techniques, viz., rough sets and ACO.

2 Soft Computing Techniques for Feature Selection

A remarkable contribution made by Pawlak [8, 9] to the research community is one of the earlier works on rough sets. Rough sets (RSs) are very efficient mathematical methods which can be used for attribute reduction. RS has an advantage that they do not require any additional information other than the data set itself. RS deals with the concept called vagueness. rough sets are based on calculating the similarity between the values of attributes of the data set objects. This concept is called indiscernibility. The application of rough set in the field of mobile communications for "churn prediction" is demonstrated by Pawlak. RS is found to be useful at several stages of knowledge discovery in databases (KDDs), [10] feature selection, feature extraction, reducing of data, generating decision rules, and also for extraction of patterns. Rough set-based dynamic reducts are used to create decision rules for classification problem [11]. Chouchoulas and Shen [12] have contributed to rough set-based dimensionality reduction and applied it to text categorization for e-mail classification, where there is vagueness or incompleteness in the data. Their work has proved the ability of rough set to considerably reduce data set sizes that in turn reduces the storage size. Quick reduct, a greedy based, fast reduction algorithm is used for reduction.

Discernibility matrix-based approach is one form of reduction processes using rough sets proposed by Skowron and Rouszer [13]. The discernibility-based reduction takes long computational time compared to quick reduct for large data sizes. Let $\breve{A}_C$ be a set of conditional attributes and $\breve{A}_D$ be a set of decision attributes; a decision-making table is defined as $Ð = (\bar{U}, \breve{A}_{all}, V, f)$, $\breve{A}_{all} = \breve{A}_C \cup \breve{A}_D$. Each element of a discernibility matrix, e_{ij}, as shown in Eq. 1, consists of set of all conditional attributes $\breve{A}_C$, that categorize the given objects, O_i and O_j into different classes.

$$
e_{ij} = \begin{cases} \hat{a}_C \in \breve{A}_C \colon \hat{a}_C(O_i) \neq \hat{a}_C(O_j) & \text{if } \exists\, \hat{a}_D \in \breve{A}_D, \hat{a}_D(O_i) \neq \hat{a}_D(O_j) \\ \varnothing & \text{if } \forall\, \hat{a}_D \in \breve{A}_D, \hat{a}_D(O_i) = \hat{a}_D(O_j) \end{cases} \tag{1}
$$

Jensen has worked on rough set applications in several domains. One such early work by Jensen and Shen [14] is done in the area of World Wide Web (WWW) bookmark data, where incompleteness and uncertainty of data can be found. The authors have investigated the suitability of rough sets for data reduction of bookmarks and found to be useful. Feature selection for face mammogram is achieved with the help of rough sets and PCA [15]. Duntsch and Gediga [16] explained the role of rough sets for the purpose of attribute minimization, rule generation, and prediction. Thangavel and Pethalakshmi [17] have presented a comprehensive review of various applications of rough sand also hybridized rough sets for attribute reduction. However, all these works are based on greedy hill climbing-based reduction. The drawback of greedy-based quick reduct algorithm is that the solution may not be the global best solution at all times. Metaheuristic search techniques along with rough sets found to produce best results compared to greedy-based techniques.

3 Research Contributions in Feature Selection for IDS

KDD Cup 1999 dataset [18] is used as a benchmark dataset by the majority of researchers in the area of IDS. This data set consists of 41 features and five major classes of attacks including normal traffic. The goal of feature selection in IDS is to select the most appropriate and important features from these 41, that results in a reduction of data size. IDS will take lesser time to classify attacks with lesser attributes, but the challenge is to maintain or improve the classification accuracy and reduce the false alarm rate. Therefore, there is a never ending research in the area of feature selection for IDS. Ganapathy et al. [19] surveyed the existing literature on feature selection and classification techniques in the area of IDS. Along with the survey, they also proposed intelligent rule-based feature selection along with an intelligent rule-based enhanced multiclass support vector machine (IREMSVM) classifier. This algorithm is based on the Minkowski distance. They have reported 19 selected attributes and an average accuracy of around 90%. However, only three classes of attacks are considered.

Fries [20] proposed a genetic algorithm (GA)-based feature selection where each bit location of the chromosome is treated as one feature. They employed a wrapper-based feature selection with a fuzzy inference system as the classifier, 99.6% accuracy with 0.2% false positives (FPS) is reported after reducing the features to eight. All the five classes are addressed here; however, since the approach is wrapper based, it consumes a lot of time. Li et al. [21] have employed chi-square feature ranking method and used the top six features for classification using transductive confidence machine for K-nearest neighbor. They have attained an accuracy of 99.32% post the feature reduction phase with an FP rate of 2.81%. They have used Euclidian distance for KNN clustering. The detection rates of User to Root (U2R) and Remote to Local (R2L) attacks are lesser in this method. The distance calculations have high computational complexity.

Sung and Mukkamala [22] utilized three types of feature ranking systems, viz., wrapper based, SVM, linear genetic programming, and multivariate adaptive regression splines. Rufai et al. [23] proposed a membrane computing and bee algorithm hybrid for selecting prominent features of IDS data set. They have reported an accuracy of 95.60%. Again, since they are wrapper-based methods, the time consumption for solution construction is large compared to filter-based methods.

Barot et al. [24] used correlation-based feature selection along with a decision table majority classifier. After selecting the top five features, they have reported 90.9% average classification accuracy. Correlation-based feature selection depends on the merit of a feature subset F that contains n number of features; the merit is given by Eq. 2. Their approach suffered from low classification accuracy and in particular lower rates for U2R and R2L attacks. In Eq. 2, $\overline{r_{cf}}$ is the average of all the feature–classification correlations, and $\overline{r_{ff}}$ is the average of all the feature–feature correlations.

$$Merit_{F_n} = \frac{n\overline{r_{cf}}}{\sqrt{n+n(n-1)\overline{r_{ff}}}} \tag{2}$$

Ahmed [25] has proposed a combination of statistical and optimization problem-solving approaches for feature selection. He has compared the performance of GA and particle swarm optimization (PSO) in selecting best particles of principal component analysis (PCA). The PCA–GA method has produced an accuracy of 98.2% for ten selected features, while the PCA–PSO method has produced an accuracy of 99.4% for eight selected features. However, in their paper, the fitness functions for both PSO and GA are not mentioned. An improvement of accuracy was obtained by employing PCA feature reduction and neural network classifier by Varma and Kumari in [26]. Few works that addressed the feature selection problem in IDS are [27–32].

3.1 Rough Set-Based Feature Selection for IDS

Muthurajkumar et al. [33] applied rough sets for feature selection and fuzzy SVM for classification; they have reported an average attack detection accuracy of 98.27%. Chimphlee et al. [34] have worked on rough sets for reducing the IDS data features. They have reduced the data set to 11 features and later evaluated with a fuzzy C-means clustering algorithm. An accuracy of 93.45% is reported. RS lower and upper approximations are used to find the important features of IDS data. Even though good detection rates are reported for probe attacks, the detection rates of other attacks are not promising. Rung-Ching et al. [35] identified 29 features; SVM classifier is used to evaluate the identified features, and an accuracy of 89.13% is reported. This work also suffers from lower detection rates.

Greedy search-based rough set quick reduct is used by Liu [36] for reducing intrusion detection data attributes; they have obtained improved detection accuracies. Their algorithm produced 15 attributes and reported an accuracy of 99.19% with decision tree as a classifier. However, the detection rates of all the classes of attacks are not mentioned. Chunhua et al. [37] proposed elicitation-based rough set attribute selection by employing different types of discretization techniques. An accuracy of 92.46% is reported after the attribute reduction process. However, there are no details about the major classes of attacks in this work, and it also suffers from lower detection accuracy. Li-Zhong et al. [38] also tried to reduce the IDS data features by using rough sets and evaluated the performance using neural network classifier. They have obtained an accuracy of 88.5%. However, the works mentioned above are not heuristic search based, and hence, the solution set obtained may not be the global best reduct.

Anazida et al. [39] have employed rough sets as a primary phase of attribute selection. They have proposed a PSO–SVM combined wrapper based global best attribute selection in the second phase. With their Rough-PSO approach, they have identified six prime attributes and reported an accuracy of 93.408%. Sengupta et al. [40] demonstrated the application of rough set-based reduct calculation in intrusion detection data set. They have used a Q-learning algorithm to select the best reduct out of different possible reducts produced by the discernibility matrix-based rough set reducts. An accuracy of 98% is achieved with this approach.

3.2 Limitations of Rough Set-Based Feature Selection for IDS

Most of the existing literature employing rough sets for IDS is greedy hill climbing based, which produces a local minimal reduct. There is a need to apply global search strategies and optimization techniques for IDS data set. Even though there are few works employing heuristic search techniques, most of them are wrapper based, and the algorithms take a long time for execution. Till now, no one has applied rough set-based mutual information to find the *core* attributes of IDS data set. Further, there is a need to study and find the feasibility and applicability of ACO search with rough set feature significance as a heuristic factor. Varma et al. [41, 42] have addressed these issues and applied a novel rough set and ACO-based algorithms for IDS and obtained comparable results.

There is a need to identify an essential network traffic features that are to be monitored to detect most popular real-time intrusive attacks like DoS, DDoS, probing, account hijacking. Varma et al. [43] proposed fuzzy entropy-based heuristic in ant colony optimization (ACO) to search for a global best smallest set of network traffic features for real-time intrusion detection dataset. The advantage of fuzzy-rough techniques over rough sets based attribute selection is that fuzzy-based methods do not require an additional phase of data discretization for real-valued data. Rough set-based attribute selection requires the real-valued data to be discretized as a preprocessing stage. The proposed feature reduction algorithm is tested on the University of California, Irvine (UCI), standard benchmark datasets and found to be efficient. Further, the algorithm is applied to Real-Time IDS data set and found to produce promising results.

4 Conclusion

While evaluating IDS, the terms True Positives (TP), True Negatives (TN), False Positives (FP), and False Negatives (FN) are used. True Positives mean a number of attacks correctly detected as attacks. True Negatives mean normal data correctly detected as normal. False Positives mean a number of normal activity instances wrongly detected as an attack by IDS. False Negatives mean a number of attacks wrongly detected as normal. Intrusion detection literature uses several performance parameters, which includes classification accuracy and number of features selected.

Classification accuracy is one of the performance measures of IDS. The main goal or objective of feature selection or attribute reduction in IDS design is to see that it maintains high classification accuracy, even after reduction. It tells how good the classification model is, the higher is, the better. It specifies the percentage of samples being correctly identified with their respective classes. The formula for classification accuracy is given in Eq. 3.

$$Classification\ accuracy = \frac{TP + TN}{TP + TN + FP + FN} \tag{3}$$

Figures 1 and 2 show the comparative graphs of the evaluation parameters classification accuracy and number of features selected. By comparing similar feature selection algorithms for IDS, it can be observed that the soft computing-based algorithms, the rough set theory, and ACO [42] proved to be much promising. Researchers may explore several hybrid soft computing algorithms for feature selection of IDS data sets.

Fig. 1 Comparison of performance measure, classification accuracy

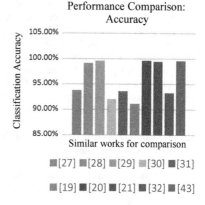

Fig. 2 Comparison of performance measure, number of attributes

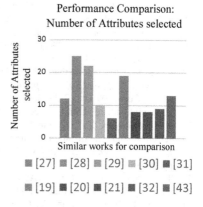

References

1. P Ravi Kiran Varma, V Valli Kumari and S Srinivas Kumar, "Packet Filter Firewall Rule Anomalies and Mitigation Techniques: A Technical Review," *CiiT International Journal of Networking and Communication Engineering,* vol. 9, no. 4, pp. 101–108, 2017.
2. Ravi Kiran Varma P, Valli Kumari V and Srinivas Kumar S, "Ant colony optimization-based firewall anomaly mitigation engine," *Springerplus,* vol. 5, no. 1, pp. 1–32, 2016.
3. J. P. Anderson, "Computer Security Threat Monitoring and Surveillance," NIST, USA, Fort Washington, PA, 1980.
4. E. D. Dorothy, "An Intrusion-Detection Model," *IEEE Transactions on software engineering,* vol. 13, no. 2, pp. 222–232, 1987.
5. F. T. Lunt, "A survey of intrusion detection techniques," *Computers and Security,* vol. 12, pp. 405–418, 1993.
6. M. John, C. Alan and A. Julia, "Defending Yourself: The role of Intrusion Detection Systems," *IEEE Software,* vol. 17, no. 5, pp. 42–51, 2000.
7. G K J Andreas, N G Wilfried, A D Michael and F E Gerhard, "On the Relationship between feature selection and classification accuracy," *JMLR Workshop and Conference Proceedings,* vol. 4, pp. 90–105, 2008.

8. Z. Pawlak, "Rough Set Theory and its Applications," *Journal of Telecommunications and Information Technology,* vol. 3, no. 2, pp. 7–10, 2002.
9. Z. Pawlak, "Rough Sets," *International Journal of Computer and Information Sciences,* vol. 11, no. 5, pp. 341–356, 1982.
10. S. Rissino and G. Lambert-Torres, "Rough Set Theory – Fundamental Concepts, Principals, Data Extraction, and Applications," in *Data Mining and Knowledge Discovery in Real Life Applications, Julio Ponce and Adem Karahoca (Ed.),* InTech, 2009.
11. J. G. Bazan, H. S. Nguyen, S. N. Hoa, S. Piotr and W. Jakub, "Rough Set Algorithms in Classification Problem," in *Rough Set Methods and Applications,* Physica-Verlag, 2000, pp. 49–88.
12. A. Chouchoulas and Q. Shen, "Rough Set-Aided Keyword Reduction for Text Categorisation," Center for Intelligent Systems and their Applications, The University of Edingurgh, Edinburgh, UK, 2001.
13. A. Skowron and C. Rauszer, "The discernibility matrices and functions in information systems," in *Intelligent Decision Support,* Dordrecht, Kluwer Academic Publishers, 1992, pp. 331–362.
14. R Jensen and Q Shen, "A Rough Set Aided System for Sorting WWW Bookmarks," *Web Intelligence: Research and Development,* pp. 95–105, 2001.
15. R. W. Swiniarski and A. Skowron, "Rough set methods in feature selection and recognition," *Pattern Recognition Letters,* pp. 833–849, 2003.
16. I. Duntsch and G Gediga, "Rough Set Data Analysis," *Encyclopedia of Computer Science and Technology,* vol. 43, no. 28, pp. 281–301, 2000.
17. K. Thangavel and A. Pethalakshmi, "Dimensionality Reduction Based on Rough Set Theory: A Review," *Applied Soft Computing,* pp. 1–12, 2009.
18. "KDD Cup 1999 Data," 28 Oct 1999. [Online]. Available: http://kdd.ics.uci.edu/databases/kddcup99/kddcup99.html. [Accessed 25 May 2015].
19. S. Ganapathy, K. Kulothungan, S. Muthurajkumar and M. Vijayalakshmi, "Intelligent feature selection and classification techniques for intrusion detection in networks: a survey," *EURASIP Journal on Wireless Communications and Networking,* vol. 2013, no. 271, pp. 1–16, 2013.
20. T. P. Fries, "A Fuzzy-Genetic Approach to Network Intrusion Detection," in *Proceedings of the ACM GECCO'08,* Atlanta, 2008.
21. Y. Li, B. Fang, G. Li and Y. Chen, "Network Anomaly Detection Based on TCM-KNN Algorithm," in *Proceedings of the ACM ASIA CCS'07,* Singapore, 2007.
22. A. H. Sung and S. Mukkamala, "The Feature Selection and Intrusion Detection Problems," in *Advances in Computer Science -ASIAN 2004, LNCS Series,* Springer Berlin Heidelberg, 2004, pp. 468–482.
23. K. I. Rufai, R. C. Muniyandi and Z. A. Othman, "Improving Bee Algorithm Based Feature Selection in Intrusion Detection System Using Membrane Computing," *Journal of Networks,* vol. 9, no. 3, pp. 523–529, 2014.
24. V. Barot, S. S. Chauhan and B. Patel, "Feature Selection for Modeling Intrusion Detection," *I.J. Computer Network and Information Security,* vol. 2014, no. 7, pp. 56–62, 2014.
25. I. Ahmed, "Feature Selection Using Particle Swarm Optimization in Intrusion Detection," *International Journal of Distributed Sensor Networks,* vol. 2015, pp. 1–8, 2015.
26. Ravi Kiran Varma P and Valli Kumari V, "Feature Optimization and Performance Improvement of a Multiclass Intrusion Detection System Using PCA and ANN," *International Journal of Computer Applications,* vol. 44, no. 13, pp. 4–9, 2012.
27. J. A. N. Feng, S. B. Yuefei and Z. A. Lin, "A relative decision entropy-based feature selection approach," *Pattern Recognition,* vol. 48, no. 2015, pp. 2151–2163, 2015.
28. Emiro de la Hoz, Eduardo de la Hoz, Andres Ortiz, Julio Ortega and Atonio Martenez-Alvarez, "Feature selection by multi-objective optimisation: Application to network anomaly detection by hierarchical self-organizing maps," *Knowledge-Based Systems,* vol. 71, no. 2014, pp. 322–338, 2014.

29. Ifthikar Ahmed, Azween Abdullah, Abdullah Alghamdi and Muhammad Hussain, "Optimized intrusion detection mechanism using soft computing techniques," *Telecommunication Systems,* vol. 52, no. 4, pp. 2187–2195, 2013.

30. A. Adel Sabry Eesa, B. Zeynep Orman and C. Adnan Mohsin Abdulazeez Brifcani, "A novel feature-selection approach based on the cuttlefish optimization algorithm for intrusion detection systems," *Expert Systems with Applications,* vol. 42, no. 2015, pp. 2670–2679, 2015.

31. Y. Y. Chunga and N. Wahidb, "A hybrid network intrusion detection system using simplified swarm optimization (SSO)," *Applied Soft Computing,* vol. 12, no. 2012, pp. 3014–3022, 2012.

32. W. Xingzhu, "ACO and SVM Selection Feature Weighting of Network Intrusion Detection Method," *International Journal of Security and its Applications,* vol. 9, no. 4, pp. 129–270, 2015.

33. S. Muthurajkumar, K. Kulothungan, M. Vijayalakshmi, N. Jaisankar and A. Kannan, "A Rough Set based Feature Selection Algorithm for Effective Intrusion Detection in Cloud Model," in *Elsevier Science and Technology,* Elsevier, 2013, pp. 8–13.

34. W. Chimphlee, A. H. Abdullah, M. N. M. Sap, S. Chimphlee and S. Srinoy, "A Rough-Fuzzy Hybrid Algorithm for Computer Intrusion Detection," *The International Arab Journal of Information Technology,* vol. 4, no. 3, pp. 247–254, 2007.

35. Rung-Ching, C. Kai-Fan and H. Chai-Fen, "Using Rough Set and Support Vector Machine for network intrusion detection," *International Journal of Network Security & its Applications,* vol. 1, no. 1, pp. 1–13, 2009.

36. C.-J. Liu, "The Application of Rough Sets on Network Intrusion Detection," in *Proceedings of the Sixth International Conference on Machine Learning and Cybernetics,* Hong Kong, 2007.

37. C. Gu and X. Zhang, "A Rough Set and SVM Based Intrusion Detection Classifier," in *IEEE Second International Workshop on Computer Science and Engineering,* Qingdao, 2009.

38. L.-z. Lin, Z.-g. Liu and X.-h. Duan, "Network Intrusion Detection by a Hybrid Method of Rough Set and RBF Neural Network," in *IEEE Proceddings of the 2nd International Conference on Education Technology and Computer,* Shangai, 2010.

39. Z. Anazida, M. Mohd Aizani and S. Siti Marijam, "Features Selection Using Rough-DPSO in Anomaly Intrusion Detecttion," in *Springer LNCS: Computational Science and Its Applications-ICCSA,* Kuala Lumpur, Malaysia, 2007.

40. N. Sengupta and J. Sen, "Designing of online intrusion detection system using rough set theory and Q-learning algorithm," *Neurocomputing,* vol. 111, pp. 161–168, 2013.

41. Ravi Kiran Varma P, Valli Kumari V and Srinivas Kumar S, "A Novel Rough Set Attribute Reduction based on Rough Sets and Ant Colony Optimization," *International Journal Intelligent Systems Technologies and Applications,* vol. 14, no. 3/4, pp. 330–353, 2015.

42. P. R. K. Varma, V. V. Kumari and S. S. Kumar, "Application of Rough Sets and Ant Colony Optimization in feature selection for Network Intrusion Detection," *International Journal of Applied Engineering Research,* vol. 10, no. 22, pp. 43156–43163, 2015.

43. Ravi Kiran Varma P, Valli Kumari V and Srinivas Kumar S, "Feature selection using relative fuzzy entropy and ant colony optimization applied to real-time intrusion detection system," *Procedia Computer Science,* vol. 85, no. 2016, pp. 503–510, 2016.

Feed Forward Neural Network-Based Sensor Node Localization in Internet of Things

Ajay Kumar and V. K. Jain

Abstract Internet of Things and wireless sensor networks have attracted worldwide researchers because of their various applications in different fields. Specifically, in IoT, knowledge of location is a very critical issue which deals with identifying the position of deployed node in the sensor network. It is extremely advantageous to propose scalable, cost efficient, and proficient localization procedure for IoT. This paper provides a sensor positioning algorithm named centroid algorithm which is a range-free position identifying scheme. The centroid of the polygon is used to compute the coordinates of estimate position to get better node location precision and further neural networks such as feed forward have been implemented to improve the accuracy. A comparison of centroid algorithm and feed forward neural network-based localization has been done and found that the neural network promises better results for higher localization accuracy.

Keywords Centroid algorithm · Global positioning system · Neural networks
Internet of Things · Wireless sensor networks

1 Introduction

Wireless sensor networks (WSNs) are the key components of Internet of Things (IoT) that is comprised of hundreds or thousands of nodes. The nodes can nous the environment, perform computation, and can communicate with other nodes in the same environment. Nodes are deployed by scattering them in some area of interest and are capable of communicating wirelessly. These networks are implemented for performing a number of applications such as environmental monitoring, forest

A. Kumar (✉) · V. K. Jain
Department of CSE, College of Engineering and Technology, Mody University
of Science and Technology, Lakshmangarh, India
e-mail: ajaykr0088@gmail.com

V. K. Jain
e-mail: drvkjain72@gmail.com

© Springer Nature Singapore Pte Ltd. 2018
P. K. Pattnaik et al. (eds.), *Progress in Computing, Analytics and Networking*,
Advances in Intelligent Systems and Computing 710,
https://doi.org/10.1007/978-981-10-7871-2_76

monitoring, industrial monitoring, agriculture monitoring, disaster prevention. The network has source node to transmit their data to the destination node through intermediate or relay nodes. The destination node is associated to a central sink, also known as the Base Station (BS), which provide connection to the wired world [1].

One of the easiest ways to identify the location is the physical configuration, but it is not practically possible in big networks or when sensors are positioned in unreachable areas like volcanoes and underwater [2]. The alternate way is to add Global Positioning System (GPS) to every sensor node. But, GPS does not work efficiently as the line of sight is not available due to high buildings and dense tree areas, needed between satellite and receiver. The poor signal reception may decrease the accuracy. Moreover, using GPS in the large-scale area is not cost efficient. Therefore, many location estimating methods have been anticipated to estimate the location of nodes in WSNs [3]. Newly proposed localization methods [4] identify the location of various sensor nodes with the help of location of anchor nodes, which can localize themselves using GPS or by nodes placed at known position, in the network. Localization methods can be classified as *range-based methods* and *range-free methods* [5], according to the mechanisms used for estimating location.

Range-based position identifying methods first accurately determine the distance or angle information between the nodes and then with the help of trilateration or triangulation techniques they estimate the desired position of the nodes [6]. Range-free localization algorithms establish the communication using radio connectivity to identify their location. Range-free algorithms are simple and low cost in comparison to range-based techniques as in these schemes, distance measurement, angle of arrival and special hardware are not used [7]. Range-free schemes are widely used due to large observable advantages such as conservation in power consumption and low cost [8].

Neural networks are the interconnections of neurons with activation functions. Neural networks are trained so that a particular input yields a specific output [9]. Implementing neural networks in wireless sensor networks is a promising area for more accurate and faster localization [10]. Various classes of neural networks whose performance has been compared in this paper are feed forward networks, radial basis networks, and recurrent networks.

J. Blumenthal et al. in [11] proposed a centroid algorithm which is a range-free localization scheme. In this algorithm, all un-localized nodes locate themselves as the centroid of all the received beacon's positions. Centroid algorithm is simple and easy to implement. C. Alippi et al. in [12] also proposed enhanced centroid algorithms using certain weighted methods. Identifying node position using received signal strength of RF signals has been considered broadly [13]. Two centroid localization algorithms, the linear weighting centroid (LWC) and neighbor weighting centroid (NWC), have been also proposed to improve the accuracy of centroid algorithm. Yu Liu et al. [14] proposed an improved centroid localization algorithm (ICLA) approach uses additional topological knowledge and RSS for considerably improvement in accuracy.

2 Proposed Methodology

2.1 Centroid Algorithm-Based Approach

In this technique, an unknown node finds its location using the well-known positions of the anchor nodes. Anchor nodes are the nodes which already know their location as they are equipped with GPS. Centroid algorithm uses the location information of all the beacons and calculates the position of unknown node as the centroid of all the received beacon positions. Implementation of centroid scheme contains the following actions:

- All anchor or beacon nodes transmit their position and uniqueness to all unknown sensor nodes available in their communication scope. A node is in the transmission range or not can be decided using the distance between anchor node and unknown node. This distance can be estimated by measuring received signal strength (RSS) at the unknown node. As we know, distance is inversely proportional to RSS value using the formula given in Eq. (1).

$$P_r = \frac{P_t\, G_t\, G_r\, \lambda^2}{(4\pi)^2\, d^2} \tag{1}$$

where

P_r Power (Received),
P_t Power (Transmitted),
G_t Antenna gain (Transmitter),
G_r Antenna gain (Receiver),
λ Transmitter signal wavelength (meters),
d Separation among anchor node and unknown node

- The nodes receive the signal information for a time T and collect the position information from various fix (beacon) nodes.

- All un-localized nodes obtain their location by forming a polygon and measure the centroid (*Xest, Yest*) from the known location of anchor nodes in their scope by using the procedure mentioned in Eq. (2).

$$(X_{est}, Y_{est}) = \left(\frac{X_i + \cdots + X_n}{N}, \frac{Y_i + \cdots + Y_n}{N} \right) \tag{2}$$

where (X_i, Y_i) and (X_n, Y_n) are anchor nodes coordinates, (X_{est}, Y_{est}) is the calculated location of the node, and N is the number of beacon nodes.

2.2 Neural Network-Based Approach

Another technique to obtain the accurate localization is neural network-based localization [9]. The neural network in the interconnection neurons with their activation functions.

Using the recorded values of unknown nodes, a neural network can be trained. Real positions of unknown nodes are provided to the input layer of neural network. Hidden layer transforms input, which will be used by the output layer. Output layer produces output as the estimated positions of unknown nodes. The accuracy of the localization between the real and the estimated (calculated) values is measured using mean square error (MSE) formula.

The neural network is trained by initializing the various layers and number of neurons to each layer and transfer function to each layer is initialized. The output generated from neural network is the estimated position of unknown nodes. From real and estimated positions, mean square error can be measured. The process is repeated with updated weights and biases till mean square error is less than that of mean square error of centroid method.

3   Results

3.1 Centroid Algorithm-Based Approaches

Centroid algorithm is implemented and executed using the MATLAB R2013a simulator. In this algorithm, we have taken 100 anchor nodes and performance has been done by firstly taking 10 unknown nodes and then 50 unknown nodes. We have deployed these nodes in the network area of 100×100 m with the communication range of 30 m between them. The network was generated by using the parameters given in Table 1.

In Fig. 1, dots represent the anchor node's positions, stars represent the real location of un-localized nodes, and circles represent the location of un-localized

Parameters	Values
Number of anchor nodes	100
Number of unknown nodes	10 and 50
Communication range	30 m
Deployment area	100 * 100 m

Table 1 Recreation parameters for centroid algorithm

Fig. 1 Location estimation using centroid algorithm for 10 nodes

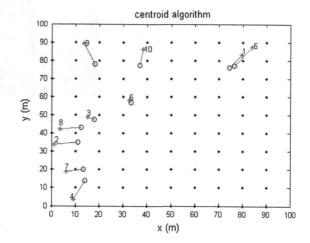

centroid algorithm

nodes estimated by centroid algorithm. The red lines represent the displacement of unknown nodes from their real positions to positions estimated using centroid algorithm. In Fig. 2, bars represent the estimated error of individual 10 unknown nodes. Error has been defined as the variation between real and estimated positions of unknown nodes. We observed that node 5 gives the maximum error as it is displaced maximum from its real position after implementing centroid algorithm. Similarly, node 6 gives the minimum error as it is displaced minimum. The average error of all 10 unknown nodes comes out to be 0.2807 m.

In Fig. 3, dots represent the anchor node's positions, stars represent the real positions of un-localized sensor nodes, and circles represent the positions of un-localized sensor nodes estimated by centroid algorithm. The red lines represent the displacement of unknown nodes from their real positions to positions estimated using centroid algorithm.

In Fig. 4, bars represent the estimated error of individual 50 unknown nodes. An error has been defined as the variation between real and estimated positions of unknown nodes. In Fig. 4, node 24 represents the maximum error as it is displaced maximum from its real position to estimated position. Similarly, node 5 represents the minimum error. The average error of all 50 unknown nodes comes out to be 0.1703 m.

Fig. 2 Error distribution for 10 unknown nodes using centroid algorithm

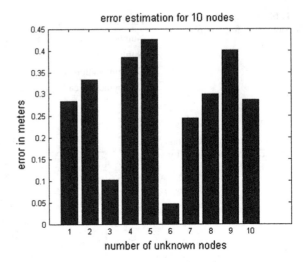

Fig. 3 Location estimation using centroid algorithm for 50 nodes

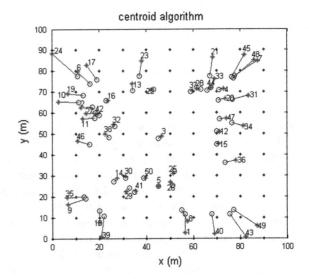

3.2 Neural Network-Based Approach

In case of neural networks, real coordinates of unknown nodes have been taken as the key to the network, and with the help of neural networks, output data is achieved. This output is the estimated coordinate location of unknown nodes achieved by neural networks. Now, the output data is compared with the target data and the variation between output data and target data becomes the error. Feed forward neural network is trained and generated by using the parameters given in Table 2.

Fig. 4 Error distribution for 50 unknown nodes using centroid algorithm

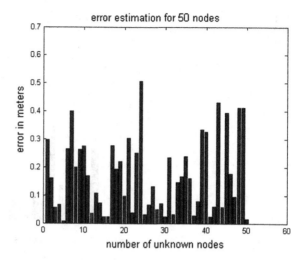

Table 2 Simulation parameters for feed forward neural network

Parameters	Values
Number of neurons	10
Number of epochs	50
Performance function	MSE
Training function	TRAINLM
Adaption learning function	LEARNGDM

Fig. 5 Error estimation for 10 nodes using feed forward networks

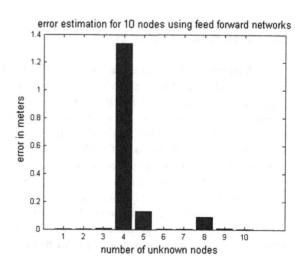

Fig. 6 Error estimation for 50 nodes using feed forward networks

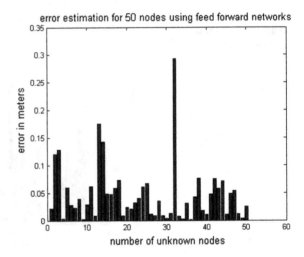

error estimation for 50 nodes using feed forward networks

Table 3 Performance comparison for 10 unknown nodes

Method	Error in meters
Centroid algorithm	0.2228
Feed forward networks	0.1574

Table 4 Performance comparison for 50 unknown nodes

Method	Error in meters
Centroid algorithm	0.1701
Feed forward networks	0.0459

3.2.1 Feed Forward Networks

Figure 5 represents the estimated error for 10 individual unknown nodes using feed forward neural networks. Here, node 4 shows the maximum error which means it is displaced maximum from its real position.

Similarly, Fig. 6 represents the estimated error for 50 individual unknown nodes in which node 32 shows the maximum error. The average estimated error for 10 unknown nodes comes out to be 0.1574 m and for 50 nodes it is 0.0459 m.

Tables 3 and 4 show the performance comparison of the experimental results. Average localization error for all unknown sensor nodes is used to evaluate the performance of different localization schemes. After comparing the values, we can say that feed forward neural networks have best performance than the other networks on the basis of estimated error. Therefore, implementing feed forward neural network in localization is a better choice for higher localization accuracy.

4 Conclusion

In this paper, centroid algorithm and feed forward neural networks have been discussed and their performances are evaluated on the basis of error estimation. Accurate localization of wireless devices is a crucial requirement for many applications. Therefore, neural network-based approaches have been used to obtain better accuracy. It can be seen that radial basis neural networks give better results than the other networks when error is taken into consideration. Therefore, neural network implementation is a better option to obtain higher accuracy for localization in wireless sensor networks required for Internet of Things.

References

1. Ian F. Akyildiz, Weilian Su, Yogesh Sankarasubramaniam and Erdal Cayirci, "A Survey on Sensor Networks," *IEEE Communications Magazine,* Vol. 40, No. 8, pp. 102–114, 2002.
2. Carlos F. García-Hernández, Pablo H. Ibargüengoytia-González, Joaquín García and Hernández, "Wireless Sensor Networks and Applications: a Survey," *International Journal of Computer Science and Network Security (IJCSNS),* Vol. 7, No. 3, pp. 264–273, 2007.
3. Y. Shang, W. Rumi, Y. Zhang, and M. Fromherz, "Localization from connectivity in sensor networks," *IEEE Transactions on Parallel and Distributed Systems,* Vol. 15, No. 11, pp. 961–974, 2004.
4. Shweta Singh, R. Shakya and Y. Singh, "Localization Techniques in Wireless Sensor Networks," *International Journal of Computer Science and Information Technologies (IJCSIT),* Vol. 6, No. 1, pp. 844–850, 2015.
5. P. K. Singh, B. Tripathi and N. P. Singh, "Node Localization in Wireless Sensor Networks," *International Journal of Computer Science and Information Technologies (IJCSIT),* Vol. 2, No. 6, pp. 2568–2572, 2011.
6. Nabil Ali Alrajeh, Maryam Bashir and Bilal Shams, "Localization Techniques in Wireless Sensor Networks," *International Journal of Distributed Sensor Networks,* vol. 2013, Article ID 304628, 9 pages, 2013.
7. N. Patwari, A. Hero, M. Perkins, N. Correal, and R. O'Dea, "Relative location estimation in wireless sensor networks," *IEEE Transactions on Signal Processing,* Vol. 51, No. 8, pp. 2137–2148, 2003.
8. N. Bulusu, J. Heidemann, and D. Estri n, "GPS-less low-cost outdoor localization for very small devices," *Personal Communications, IEEE,* Vol. 7, No. 5, pp. 28–34, 2000.
9. Chen, Chien-Sheng, "Artificial neural network for location estimation in wireless communication systems," *Sensors,* Vol. 12, No. 3, pp. 2798–2817, 2012.
10. Ali Shareef, Yifeng Zhu, and Mohamad Musavi, "Localization using neural networks in wireless sensor networks," Proceedings of the 1st international conference on MOBILe Wireless MiddleWARE, Operating Systems, and Applications. ICST (Institute for Computer Sciences, Social-Informatics and Telecommunications Engineering), ACM, 2008.
11. J. Blumenthal, R. Grossmann, F. Golatowski, and D. Timmermann, "Weighted Centroid Localization in Zigbee-based Sensor Networks," *Intelligent Signal Processing, IEEE,* pp. 1–6, 2007.
12. C. Alippi, A. Mottarella, and G. Vanini. "A RF map-based localization algorithm for indoor environments," *IEEE International Symposium on Circuits and Systems, (ISCAS),* pp. 652–655, 2005.

13. G.-A. Lusilao Zodi, Gerhard P. Hancke, and Antoine B. Bagula, "Enhanced Centroid Localization of Wireless Sensor Nodes using Linear and Neighbor Weighting Mechanisms," *Proceedings of the 9th International Conference on Ubiquitous Information Management and Communication*, ACM, 2015.
14. Liu, Yu, Xiao Yi, and You He, "A novel centroid localization for wireless sensor networks," *International Journal of Distributed Sensor Networks,* vol. 2012, Article ID 829253, 8 pages, 2012.

Recognition of Various Handwritten Indian Numerals Using Artificial Neural Network

Geetika Mathur and Suneetha Rikhari

Abstract In current years, extracting documents written by hand is extensively studied topic in image analysis and optical character recognition. These extractions of document images find their applications in document analysis, content analysis, document retrieval, and much more. Many complex text extracting processes such as maximization likelihood ratio (MLR), neural networks, edge point detection technique, corner point edge detection are generally employed for extraction of text documents from images. This article uses feed-forward propagation model of neural network for recognition of various Indian handwritten numerals like Punjabi, Hindi, Bengali, Telugu, and Marathi. Recognition is achieved by initially acquiring the image, then preprocessing it and then feature extraction. Preprocessing is performed by binarizing the image and segmenting the preprocessed image by cropping it to its edges. Feature extraction involves the normalizing the numeral matrix into 12×10 matrixes. Feature recognition applies artificial neural network for detection of numerals. The network is constructed with 120 input nodes, 10 hidden layer nodes, and 10 output nodes. The network has one input, single output, and a hidden layer. The numbers used for training are divided using a morphological method, and the network is trained for various Indian numerals. The proposed system has 98% recognition accuracy with respect to training data.

Keywords Neural network · OCR · Multilingual documents
Handwritten documents

G. Mathur (✉) · S. Rikhari
Department of E.C.E., College of Engineering and Technology, Mody University,
Lakshmangarh (Sikar) 332311, India
e-mail: geetika.mathur123@gmail.com

S. Rikhari
e-mail: suneetha.rikhari@gmail.com

© Springer Nature Singapore Pte Ltd. 2018
P. K. Pattnaik et al. (eds.), *Progress in Computing, Analytics and Networking*,
Advances in Intelligent Systems and Computing 710,
https://doi.org/10.1007/978-981-10-7871-2_77

1 Introduction

Character recognition can be defined as the technique of sorting the given input characters as per a predefined class of characters. Numerous researches have been done in the field of handwritten number recognition schemes for Indian languages in the past few years. Handwritten number recognition schemes for Guajarati numerals using neural network [1], Bengali digits using multistage classifiers [2], Devanagari numbers using support vector machines [3] are some of the examples for the research being done on the handwritten numerals detection. Some challenges with recognition of handwritten data are that the style of writing of character may be non-uniform, there are different styles of writing same character, the curves in the character are uneven, and two or more characters can be similar looking [4]. This may increase the complication in the recognition system.

Table 1 Indian numbers and its equivalents in English

Punjabi Number	Hindi Numbers	Telugu Numbers	Bengali Numbers	Marathi Numbers	Corresponding English number
੧	१	౧	১	१	1
੨	२	౨	২	२	2
੩	३	౩	৩	३	3
੪	४	౪	৪	४	4
੫	५	౫	৫	५	5
੬	६	౬	৬	६	6
੭	७	౭	৭	७	7
੮	८	౮	৮	८	8
੯	९	౯	৯	९	9
੦	०	౦	০	०	0

In accordance with the record of Indian census, In India, 122 main languages in addition to 1599 additional languages are spoken. It becomes a difficult task for recognizing any Indian character and digits. In the proposed recognition method, artificial feed-forward neural network is employed to recognize various Indian digits from 0 to 9. Table 1 shows the basic numbers. The accuracy rate for detection of various numerals in this case is 98% which in previous works the recognition rate for various languages was around 89%.

2 Optical Character Recognition

OCR for handwritten numerals contains five phases that are scanning of the text image, preprocessing, segmentation along the sharp edges, extracting features, and then post-processing. In scanning step, the digital image is acquired. The optical scanner used can change the quality of image obtained, so it is critical to use a good quality scanner. In practical applications, the images that are scanned are never perfect as there is some unwanted noise in the acquired image which causes disruption in the recognition of the characters. Preprocessing stage provides appropriate transformation of image like from colored image into binary image for feature extraction and then segmenting the image by cropping it to its sharp edges. Feature extraction involves normalizing the numeral matrix into 12 × 10 matrices. The neural network is the constructed with 120 input nodes and 10 output nodes for feature recognition. The network has one input, single output, and a hidden layer. The numbers used for training are divided using a morphological method, and the system is trained for various Indian numerals. Figures 1, 2, 3, 4, and 5 show examples for some of the Indian numerals [5].

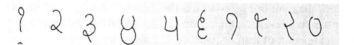

Fig. 1 Samples of Punjabi number series

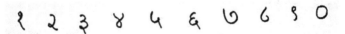

Fig. 2 Samples of Hindi number series

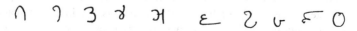

Fig. 3 Samples of Telugu number series

Fig. 4 Samples of Marathi number series

Fig. 5 Samples of Bengali number series

Fig. 6 Flowchart for the algorithm

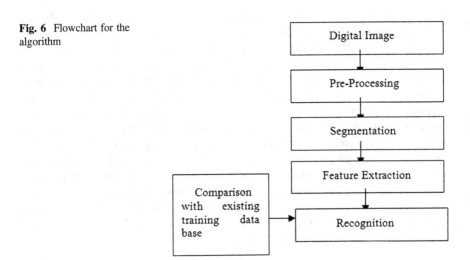

The block diagram in Fig. 6 depicts the flowchart for the proposed recognition system. It has five levels: scanning the image, preprocessing, segmentation along the edges, extraction of features, and digit recognition.

2.1 Optical Scanning

In the scanning process, digitalization of the document is done. The quality of the digitalized document depends greatly on the scanner used. So, a scanner with high speed and good color quality is necessary for proper acquisition of the digital image. The training as well as the test images are digitalized using a high-quality scanner. The training data set had each character written ten times to improve the recognition rate. An example of handwritten numerals obtained and scanned by computer is depicted in Fig. 7a. The scanner we are using here is camera of a cell phone.

Fig. 7 **a** Scanned image,
b segmented regions,
c extracted features

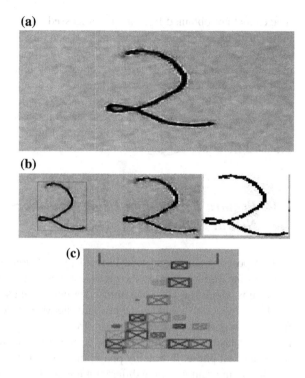

2.2 Preprocessing and Segmentation

The digitalized image is then preprocessed. Preprocessing involves binarization of RGB image, detection of edge, and dilation of images present in image. In binarization, using thresholding the gray image is transformed into binary image [6]. The first step is conversion of image into binary. Using this binary image, connected regions of the text in the image are found and then the 8 neighbors-based segmentation is computed. For the given pixel P with given coordinates (a, b) in the given binary image B, all neighbors (a + 1, b), (a − 1, b), (a, b + 1), (a, b − 1), (a + 1, b + 1), (a − 1, b − 1), (a − 1, b + 1), (a + 1, b − 1) are connected if the values on neighbors are 1 in binary image, and for all those neighbors whose values are 1, their connected neighbors are computed until no new connected neighbors are found. Figure 7b shows the segmented regions obtained from binary image [7].

2.3 Feature Extraction

In character recognition, the most critical stage is extraction of required features. Intensity distribution, pattern, shape, and texture of the isolated object of the segmented objects could be examples of features of the object obtained [8]. The digit images that are obtained from the preprocessed stage are then fed to the next stage that is feature extraction. Each image is resized by 120 × 100 pixels.

The resized images must be standardized by cropping them sharp along the edge of the numeral. This process is then followed by feature extraction stage in which the image is resized again to meet the network's input requirement, i.e., matrix of size 12 × 10. In this matrix, pixel of value 1 will be assigned to the extracted features. The 12 × 10 matrix is concatenated into a stream of data which then acts as input to the network of 120 input neurons. Figure 7c shows the 12 × 10 matrix extracted from the image.

2.4 Feature Recognition Using Feed-Forward Neural Network

The proposed system uses feed-forward propagation neural network for identification of the digits present in the given test image. Artificial networks are computer algorithms which learn just like human learning. The used network has single input, single output, and a hidden layer. This network is called feed forward as the information is always fed forward, i.e., from input layer to hidden layer and then to the output layer. The neural network is implemented in two phases,' viz. training phase and test phase. In training phase, the neural network is trained using different sets of training samples (here different numerals from 0 to 9). The training numerals are distributed using morphological technique. The database created contains 500 sample images (10 samples for a numeral × 10 numeral for each language × 5 languages). To train the network, the feed-forward neural network is created using the following parameters:

1. Transfer function used for hidden layer: logsig
2. Transfer function used for output layer: logsig
3. Training function: traingdx
4. Total number of iterations: 9000
5. Performance function: Mean square error
6. Number of times the network is trained: 4
7. Number of times the network is tested: 6.

Training of the network stops when any one of the conditions is reached:

1. The maximum numbers of epochs are finally reached.
2. Performance is minimized with respect to the objective.
3. Mu surpasses the maximum value.
4. Amount of validation tests surpasses the max. value. [4].

Once the training is completed, a matrix which gives the data about the actual and the expected classifications is computed by the classification system. This matrix is named as confusion matrix In general terms "the confusion matrix depicts

Fig. 8 Sample testing data used to test the network for Punjabi language

the number of ways the classification system got confused while making the prediction." Hence, the classification process is well determined using this matrix. This classification performance is hence determined using a matrix. Each column represents the outcomes in the predicted class, whereas each row signifies the occurrences in the actual class of pattern recognition (or vice versa may also be true) [9].

The testing phase can be also referred as the recognition process. The extracted features from the images are given to the trained network which then classifies the digit according to the trained class. Figure 8 depicts the example of the test numbers that can be utilized to check if the classification is done properly [10].

3 Result

The database of the numbers is created, and the test image set of ten images per digit is employed for testing the system developed using the network. The results are tabularized and displayed in Table 2.

The rate of recognition for the detected numerals is 98%.

Figures 9, 10, 11, 12, and 13 plot the confusion matrices for each given languages.

4 Conclusion

The proposed method is able to train and recognize 100 numerals of the selected Indian language efficiently. For the selected Indian input vector of 12 × 10, 98% recognition rate is attained. If some unwanted noise is added in the image because of unique writing styles, the network has to be trained for a longer duration of time or be retained by increasing the hidden layer neurons. The advantage of this system is its flexibility. The proposed algorithm can be implemented to recognize almost any numerals of any language.

Table 2 Tabulated result

Applied input	No. of times the input numerals are recognized properly (N)					Percentage recognition (N/10) × 100%				
	Punjabi	Bengali	Hindi	Telugu	Marathi	Punjabi	Bengali	Hindi	Telugu	Marathi
0	10	10	10	10	10	100	100	100	100	100
1	10	9	10	10	10	100	90	100	100	100
2	10	10	10	10	10	100	100	100	100	100
3	10	10	10	10	10	100	100	100	100	100
4	10	10	10	10	10	100	100	100	100	100
5	10	10	10	10	10	100	100	100	100	100
6	10	10	10	10	10	100	100	100	100	100
7	10	10	10	10	10	100	100	100	100	100
8	9	10	10	10	10	90	100	100	100	100
9	10	10	10	10	10	100	100	100	100	100

Note: Where 10 is the number of times the applied input digits are appearing in the test image

Fig. 9 Confusion matrix for
Punjabi numerals

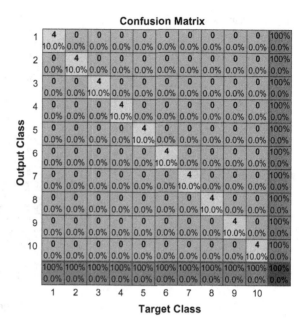

Fig. 10 Confusion matrix for
Hindi numerals

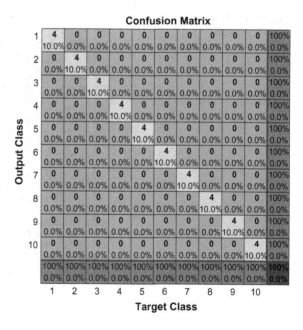

Fig. 11 Confusion matrix for
Telugu numbers

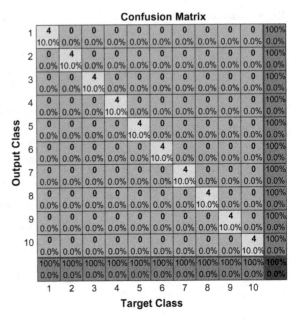

Fig. 12 Confusion matrix for
Marathi numbers

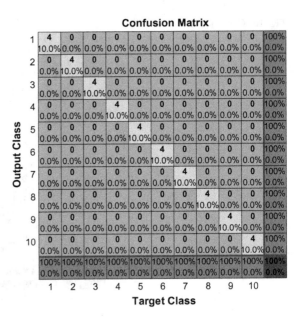

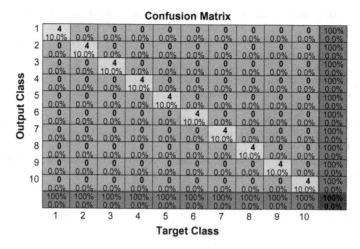

Fig. 13 Confusion matrix for Bengali numerals

5 Future Scope

This developed algorithm can be used for recognizing digits in old document. This designed system can be further extended for identification of handwritten characters of various Indian languages.

References

1. Desai, Apurva A. "Gujarati handwritten numeral optical character reorganization through neural network", Pattern recognition 43, no. 7, pp. 2582–2589, 2010.
2. Bhattacharya, Ujjwal, and Bidyut B. Chaudhuri. "Handwritten numeral databases of Indian scripts and multistage recognition of mixed numerals." IEEE Transactions on Pattern Analysis and Machine Intelligence, no. 3, pp: 444–457, 2009.
3. Leo Pauly, Rahul D Raj, Dr. Binu paul, "Hand written Digit Recognition System for South Indian Languages using Artificial Neural Networks", Contemporary Computing (IC3), 2015 Eighth International Conference on, pp. 122–126, 2015.
4. Gunjan Singh, Sushma Lehri, "Recognition of Handwritten Hindi Characters using Backpropagation Neural Network", (IJCSIT) International Journal of Computer Science and Information Technologies, Vol. 3 (4), pp. 4892–4895, 2012.
5. Sukhpreet Singh, "Optical Character Recognition Techniques: A Survey", *Journal of Emerging Trends in Computing and Information Sciences,* Vol. 4, No. 6 June 2013, pp. 545–550, ISSN 2079-8407.
6. Neeraj Kumar and Sheifali Gupta, "Offline Handwritten Gurmukhi Character Recognition: A Review", International Journal of Software Engineering and Its Applications, Vol. 10, No. 5 (2016), pp. 77–86.

7. Anwar Ali Sanjrani, Junaid Baber, Maheen Bakhtyar, Waheed Noor, Muhammad Khalid, "Handwritten Optical Character Recognition System for Sindhi Numerals", 2016 International Conference on Computing, Electronic and Electrical Engineering (ICE Cube), https://doi.org/10.1109/icecube.2016.7495235.
8. Shalin A. Chopra, Amit A. Ghadge, Onkar A. Padwal, Karan S. Punjabi, Prof. Gandhali S. Gurjar, "Optical Character Recognition", *International Journal of Advanced Research in Computer and Communication Engineering*, Vol. 3, Issue 1, January 2014, pp. 4956–4958, ISSN (Online): 2278-1021, ISSN (Print): 2319-5940.
9. Powers, David M W (2011), "Evaluation: From Precision, Recall and F-Measure to ROC, Informedness, Markedness & Correlation", Journal of Machine Learning Technologies. 2 (1): 37–63.
10. Guriqbal Singh, Vikas Mongia, "Recognition Of Punjabi Script Character And Number For Multiple Fonts", International Journal Of Engineering And Computer Science, ISSN: 2319–7242, Volume 4 Issue 10 Oct 2015, pp. 14594–14598.

A Collaborative Location-Based Personalized Recommender System

Madhusree Kuanr and Sachi Nandan Mohanty

Abstract With the rapid development of information and communication technology, numbers of tourists are increasing all over the world due to the easy way to plan for the tour. Location-based recommender system considers both user's behavior and preference for recommendation process. In this paper, we have proposed a location-based personalized recommender system which offers a set of spots to the tourist by considering the place, food, and product preference of the tourists. The proposed system uses collaborative filtering technique to recommend the best spots along with food availability and product availability to the tourist according to the opinions of the local users who already visited those spots. Cosine similarity measure is used to find the local users who are similar to the given query user. The results revealed that collaborative filtering is the more reliable technique for personalized recommender systems. The proposed system is evaluated in terms of precision, recall, and f-measure values.

Keywords Recommender systems · Collaborative filtering · Location-based
Cosine similarity

1 Introduction

In the age of information overload, nowadays people go for a variety of choices to make decision about what to buy from market, where to visit for sparing time and even to find the person to date. A recommendation system (RS) is a personalization tool that recommends products to the taste of the individual users. Recommender

M. Kuanr (✉)
Department of Computer Science, Utkal University, Bhubaneswar, Odisha, India
e-mail: madhu.kuanr@gmail.com

S. N. Mohanty
Deaprtment of Computer Science & Engg., Gandhi Institute for Technology,
Bhubaneswar, Odisha, India
e-mail: dr.sachinandan@gift.edu.in

© Springer Nature Singapore Pte Ltd. 2018
P. K. Pattnaik et al. (eds.), *Progress in Computing, Analytics and Networking*,
Advances in Intelligent Systems and Computing 710,
https://doi.org/10.1007/978-981-10-7871-2_78

system uses some data of the user from its click and other options and produces a list of recommendations to the individual users. RS produces listing of recommendations by using different approaches like collaborative recommendation approach, content-based recommendation approach, and hybrid approach [1]. In information retrieval, RS is tool whose objective is to assist users in their information search processes, helping them to filter the retrieved products, using the proposed product by information available on the internet to support users in their search and information retrieval processes [2]. Collaborative recommender system (CRS) is to exploit information about the past activities or the opinions of an existing user community for predicting which items the current user of the system will most possibly like or be interested in. Content-based recommender system recommends items based on a comparison between the content of the items and a user profile. It works with data that provided by the user either explicitly through the ratings or implicitly through clicking on a link. Knowledge-based system filters smartly a set of targets, in order to satisfy the preferences of user. This processing extends knowledge, where the recommendation system has to interpret and then use it. Recent research has established that a hybrid recommender system by combining the techniques of collaborative and content-based recommender system could be more effective than the pure approaches.

The rest of the paper is organized as follows. The next section contains the related work. In Sect. 3, we have described the proposed model. Section 4 has illustrated results and discussion. Finally in Sect. 5, we have explained conclusion and future work.

2   Related Work

In modern research, recommender system is used in different domains for filtering the information, which has been widely exploited in e-commerce, suggesting products and services to users [3]. A recommender system is a personalization tool that provides users with a list of items that best fit their individual flavor [4]. The tourists themselves will be one of the main contributors to their current context. Recent research evidence suggests that personalized and location-based recommender systems discourse the design and execution issues for delivering location-based tourism related content services [5]. Universal tourist support system is built upon multi-agent and Semantic Web technologies for providing personalized assistance and automation to the tourists with different preferences and often changing requirements during their tours [6]. A collaborative recommender system utilizes the knowledge implicit in a community of users with their preferences on offered items to discover the relevance of these items to other users within the community that have not conveyed any preference on the proposed items [7]. Collaborative filtering methods work on the gathering and analysis of a large amount of information on user behavior, activities, or preferences, in order to predict what they would like based on their similarity with other users. A personalized location-aware recommendation system has been designed to infer user's preferences and thus to recommend nearby locations such as hospitals, food courts, shopping, and so on [8].

The main perseverance of this research is the development of a recommender system in tourism sector of India. These user profiles will be composed by functionality levels regarding accessibility issues like country, state, place, location, local foods, and local products in addition to basic socio-demography information. This research presumes a vital importance in tourism sector in India and any other area where individual user knowledge is a key factor. The output of the recommender system will be recommendations of suitable places as per expectation of the users.

3 Proposed Model

The proposed method uses collaborative filtering technique for recommendation where it employs the cosine-based similarity to find the similar users to a particular querying user which is a tourist. The steps involved in the proposed model are shown in Fig. 1. It uses the opinions of the local people about the different spots present in that place who have already visited those places. It measures their opinions about a spot in terms of a rating value which is also defined through certain parameters like crowd management, security, cleanness of the spot according to the type of the place. The type of the spot the tourist wants to visit may be spiritual, historical, and adventurous or place of fun. The local users also provide information about the special localized food items and products available in that spot through the rating values. The local user's rates the food items according to the criteria. The products are rated by the local users through the criteria like taste and hygienic. It recognizes similar users based on the cosine similarity value. The cosine similarity value is determined for all the local users with respect to the querying user. The users who are having cosine similarity value as 1 are assumed as the similar users because their place, food, and product parameters are matching with the querying user. If a tourist, for example, wants to visit places in Bhubaneswar and his preference for place type is spiritual, food type is vegetarian, and product type is ladies product then the similar users can be identified using cosine similarity as shown in Table 1 and Fig. 2.

Out of those similar users, the users having rating value greater than 6 for place, greater than 5 for food, and greater than 4 for product will be considered for the recommendation. Then the average rating is calculated which is the average value of the three rating values for place, food, and product for those users. These users again will be sorted in the decreasing order of their average rating value. If two similar users are having same rating values, then the user with latest rating value

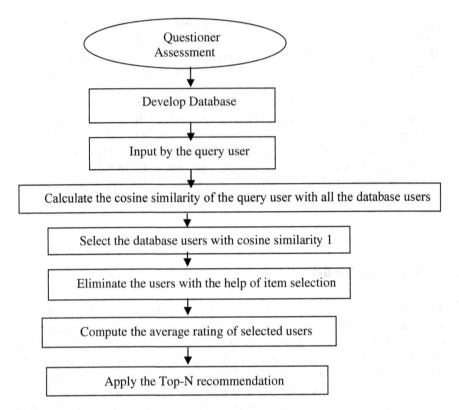

Fig. 1 Proposed model

Table 1 Cosine similarity of the querying user with some local users

User Id	Country name	State name	Place name	Place type	Food type	Product type	Cosine similarity
1	1	11	120	10	60	80	1
2	1	12	121	20	60	80	0.998
3	1	12	124	20	70	90	0.9973
4	1	12	121	30	70	100	0.9895
5	1	11	120	40	60	80	0.9827
6	1	11	120	10	60	80	1
7	1	13	131	40	70	80	0.9847

will be considered for recommendation. Then the system takes the top n users for the recommendation. The places visited, food taken, and product purchased by those users will appear in the recommendation list in that order.

Fig. 2 Cosine similarity

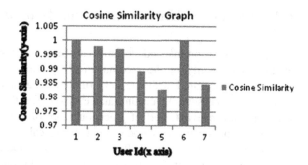

4 Results and Discussion

4.1 Dataset Description

Two hundred (Male = 110, Female = 90) married individuals from Bhubaneswar, Odisha, India, participated in the study. They were given the questionnaire, and they took about 40 min to complete the questionnaire.

The socio-demographic profiles of male and female students were compared using F test when the data were in interval scale and chi-square test when the data were in nominal scale. More number of male individuals participated in the study compared to the female individuals. Because of high male participants participated in the experiment having enrollment ratio (>0.80). Most of the male individuals were the natives from urban areas and the female individuals from semi-urban areas. Very few male as well as female individuals were from rural areas. The both male and female individuals were predominantly from nuclear family having minimum 1 to maximum 5 members and few were from joint/extended families. The average annual income of parents and family members of male and female individuals did not differ. On the average, the annual income varied from as low as 5,000 to as high as 65 lakh Indian rupees (Table 2).

Table 2 Participants sample profile

Characteristic	Descriptive statistics	Male	Female	χ^2	F
Gender	N (%)	112(77.50)	88(22.50)	121.00***	
Birthplace Urban Semi-urban Rural	N (%)	69(54.20) 28(27.70) 12(18.10)	46(42.2) 34(47.80) 11(10.00)	13.42***	
Age	M (SD)	20.81(4.50)	23.61(3.97)		28.34***
Years studied		15.99(3.06)	16.73(3.52)		52.11***
Family size		5.67(1.85)	5.69(1.34)		0.01
Income (in INR)		466399 (771448)	530888 (988621)		0.42

INR Indian rupees, $^{*}p < 0.05$. $^{**}p < 0.01$. $^{***}p < 0.001$

4.2   *Evaluation Metrics and Result Analysis*

Researches on recommended systems have been using several types of measures to evaluate the quality of the recommended system. The power of the presented approach is measured with the help of three evaluation metrics, i.e., precision, recall, and f-measure. Precision can be defined as the fraction of recommended items that are relevant. Perfect precision score of 1.0 means that every item recommended in the list was good. Another typical evaluation metric used by the information retrieval is recall. It is defined as the fraction of relevant recommendations that are presented to the user. Perfect recall score of 1.0 means that all good recommended items were suggested in the list. F-measure is a single value obtained by combining both precision and recall. It indicates an overall utility of the recommended list.

$$\text{Precision} = \frac{\textit{Number of products liked and recommended}}{\textit{Number of products recommended}} \tag{5}$$

$$\text{Recall} = \frac{\textit{Number of products liked and recommended}}{\textit{Number of products liked}} \tag{6}$$

$$F - \text{measure} = \frac{2 * \textit{precision} * \textit{recall}}{\textit{precision} + \textit{recall}} \tag{7}$$

To evaluate the performance of the proposed system, initially 10 tourist places are selected. Opinions of 20 users for each tourist places who are local to that tourist place are collected in the database. The opinions contain information of the spots with local food court and local market present in each tourist place. When a user is booking a ticket online, then the system identifies its location of staying and also takes some preference for food and shopping products as input. Then the system computes the cosine similarity of the querying user with all the users present in the database by using the following formula.

$$\cos(d1, d2) = \frac{(d1 \cdot d2)}{\|d1\| \, \|d2\|} \tag{8}$$

where $(\cdot)$ indicates vector dot product, and $\|d1\|$ and $\|d2\|$ are the length of vectors d1 and d2, respectively.

Table 1 shows the result of finding cosine similarity of a query user with all the local users available in the database. Figure 2 shows the cosine similarity calculated for different users with respect to one querying user. The user having the cosine similarity value exactly 1 is considered as the similar user to the querying user.

Precision and recall are calculated for different users for top N recommendations, where N = 5. F-measure has been taken for test accuracy for five different users, and the results are shown in Fig. 3.

Fig. 3 Graph for precision, recall, and f-measure

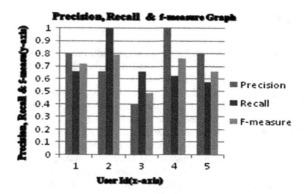

Fig. 4 Precision and recall graph

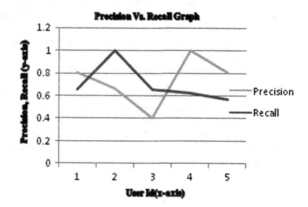

A graph is plotted showing the relation between precision and recall value which is shown in Fig. 4.

5 Conclusion and Future Work

The proposed system will store the opinions of the local users about the spots and the foods and products for purchase available in those spots. It uses collaborative filtering technique to find the similar users to a given querying user. The system recommends the best spots along with good foods and products. This system may be helpful for tourists who wish to explore the best spots and avail the good foods and products available in those spots. The proposed approach will only recommend the spots available in Bhubaneswar. In the future work, we can apply the same technique to tourists of all the states of India for accuracy of our proposed system. In future, we will also try to recommend a itinerary plan to the tourists which will recommend the order of visiting the spots along with food and product recommendation by considering the shortest distance.

References

1. García-Cumbreras, M. Á., Montejo-Ráez, A., & Díaz-Galiano, M. C. (2013). Pessimists and optimists: Improving collaborative filtering through sentiment analysis. *Expert Systems with Applications, 40*(17), 6758–6765.
2. Herrera-Viedma, E., Herrera, F., Martínez, L., Herrera, J., & López (2004), A. Incorporating filtering techniques in a fuzzy linguistic multi-agent model for information gathering on the web. Fuzzy Sets and Systems, 148, 61–83.
3. Schafer, J., Konstan, J., & Riedl, J. (2002): Meta-recommendation system: user-controlled integration of diverse recommendations. In Proceedings of the eleventh international conference on information and knowledge management, 43–51.
4. Inma Garcia, Laura Sebastia, Sergio Pajares, & Eva Onaindia. (2011): The Generalist recommender System GRSK and Its Extension to Groups. Web Information Systems and Technologies, 215–229.
5. Kakaletris, G., Varoutas, D., Katsianis, D., Sphicopoulos, T., & Kouvas. (2004): Designing & Implementing an open infrastructure for location-based tourism related content delivery. Wireless Personal Communications, 30, (2), 153–165.
6. Dickson K. W. Chiu & Ho-fung Leung. (2005): Towards ubiquitous tourists service coordination and integration: a multi-agent and semantic web approach. In Proceedings of the 7th international conference on Electronic commerce (IECE '05). ACM, New York, NY, USA, 574–581.
7. Miguel Á. García-Cumbreras, Arturo Montejo-Ráez & Manuel C. Díaz-Galiano. (2013): Pessimists and optimists: Improving collaborative filtering through sentiment analysis. Expert Systems with Applications. 40 (17), 6758–6765.
8. Veningston. K, R. Shanmugalakshmi. (2015): Personalized Location aware Recommendation System, International Conference on Advanced Computing and Communication Systems (*ICACCS* -2015), Jan. 05–07, 2015, Coimbatore, INDIA.

Resource Allocation in Cooperative Cloud Environments

Himansu Das, Ajay Kumar Jena, J. Chandrakant Badajena,
Chittaranjan Pradhan and R. K. Barik

Abstract In cloud computing environment, cloud application services and resources belong to different virtual organizations with different objectives. Each component of cloud environment is self-governing and self-interested. They share their resources and services to achieve their objectives. The cloud computing environment provides infinite number of computing resources such as CPU, memory and storage to the users in such a way that they can dynamically increase or decrease their resources and its use according to their demands. In resource allocation model having two basic objectives as cloud provider wants to maximize their revenue by achieving high resource utilization while cloud users want to minimize their expenses while meeting their requirements. However, it is essential to allocate resources in an optimized way between two parties. In some situations, single cloud may not satisfy all the requirements of the users. To achieve this objective, two or more cloud providers cooperatively work together to satisfy the user's requirements. These cooperative cloud providers should share and optimize the computational resources in a reasonable technique to make sure that no users get much resource than any other users and also improve the resource utilization.

H. Das (✉) · A. K. Jena · C. Pradhan
School of Computer Engineering, KIIT Deemed to be University,
Bhubaneswar, Odisha, India
e-mail: das.himansu2007@gmail.com

A. K. Jena
e-mail: ajay.bbs.in@gmail.com

C. Pradhan
e-mail: chitaprakash@gmail.com

J. Chandrakant Badajena
Department of Information Technology, College of Engineering & Technology,
Bhubaneswar, Odisha, India
e-mail: j.chandrakantbadajena@gmail.com

R. K. Barik
School of Computer Application, KIIT Deemed to be University,
Bhubaneswar, Odisha, India
e-mail: rabindra.mnnit@gmail.com

© Springer Nature Singapore Pte Ltd. 2018
P. K. Pattnaik et al. (eds.), *Progress in Computing, Analytics and Networking*,
Advances in Intelligent Systems and Computing 710,
https://doi.org/10.1007/978-981-10-7871-2_79

Keywords Cloud computing · Resource allocation · Cooperative
Utilization bound

1 Introduction

In recent few years, the concept of cloud computing [1, 2] plays a vital role in both
the industry and academic people. In cloud computing environment, the software
and hardware are provided to the customers in the form of virtualization technology. We can virtualize many resources such as computing resources, software,
hardware, operating system and network storage to manage them in the cloud
computing environment, and every virtualized environment has nothing to do with
the physical platform. It is an intelligence computing technique where service
providers are dynamically scalable their resources that are supplied to customer as a
service over the Internet. Cloud computing is particularly useful to small- and
medium-size businesses; those are completely outsourcing their data centre
resources from the cloud service providers. Due to the quick advancement of the
cloud computing technology, several service providers such as Amazon, Yahoo,
Microsoft, Google and IBM are deploying their data centres in different locations
around the globe to distribute the cloud services.

Resource allocation [3] is the core concept of the virtualized cloud environment,
which manages the computing resources in the cloud environment to facilitate the
execution of large number of tasks that entail significant computation. Resource
allocation [4] addresses several factors such as scheduling [5] and energy consumption [6]. Identifying and selecting a favourable resource type dynamically to
execute a task in cloud environments must be analysed, and they have to be suitably
selected as per the task [7] properties. The computing resources must be allocated
dynamically to satisfy the quality of service (QoS) requirements as required by
users via service level agreements (SLAs) and also reduce energy consumptions [8].

The main objective of this work is resource allocation [9] in a cooperative cloud
environment [10] to allocate VM resources among the cloud users on demand basis
without exceeding their resource capabilities and expense in prices. When a cloud
provider allocates resource to multiple users, they proportionally occupy cloud
provider capacity and increase the expense. The objective is to allocate each user to
a required number of resources in order to maximize the resource utilization [11]
and minimize the total expense.

The remainder of this chapter is organized as follows. Section 2 provides the
related work of resource allocation, Sect. 3 describes the resource allocation
strategy in cooperative cloud environment, Sect. 4 discusses on analysis of result in
cooperative cloud environment, and finally Sect. 5 concludes the chapter with
future direction of this work.

2 Literature Survey

Most of the complex computing environments like grid, cluster and cloud need high-performance architectural design to solve the real-world complex problem [12–17]. Cloud computing is one of the most emerging areas in the last decade where computing resources are distributed geographically throughout the globe with the help of virtualization technology. In cloud computing environment, one of the most challenging issues is resource allocation [3, 10] where the resources are distributed dynamically among the cloud users to reduce the expenses without exceeding its resource capacity. Dynamic resource allocation and re-allocation [4] of computing resources are the key components that accommodate unpredictable demands which ultimately return profit for both cloud user and service providers. But in very few situations, these resources may not be able to fulfil all the requests of all the users simultaneously. So, some cloud providers cooperatively work together to share their resources among themselves to satisfy all the request of the users. It also provides on-demand resource management that shares the resources in a reasonable way such that no other users get much better chance than other users. Resource allocation using game theory is one of the most challenging areas proposed in [3] to consider the fairness allocation of resources among the users and also increase the resource utilization. They also propose how to reduce the wastage of resources and better utilization of resources. The coalition and uncertainty-based game theoretic principle also provides better resource utilization and user satisfaction. Prediction mechanism [6] is designed by using support vector machine (SVM) to estimate the resource utilization based on SLA. Optimization of resource allocation problem using improved differential evolution algorithm is proposed in [7]. An economic resource allocation strategy [9] focuses on minimum wastage of resources using coalition formation and uncertainty principle of game theory. In the recent work, Hassan et al. [10] proposed a cooperative game theoretic solution which is jointly valuable to the cloud providers and to the cloud users also. In dynamic horizontal cloud federation environment, they studied in the cooperative resource allocation model by using game theory in which they used price-based strategy to allocate the resources. They proposed two different utility maximizing cooperative games such as maximizing the total profit of the primary cloud provider and maximizing the social welfare for cooperative cloud provider. Some work also emphasizes on quality of services [11] of resource allocation mechanism by using game theory approach.

Finally, an efficient resource allocation mechanism is one of the fundamental requirements in cloud computing environment. Many works have been done on development and design resource allocation mechanism by using different architectures, algorithms and services. But there is need for development of cooperative cloud environment where the resources are shared among the cooperative clouds. By keeping view to this problem, one resource allocation model is designed and experimented in cooperative cloud environment to provide the optimum resource utilization.

3 Resource Allocation Model

In cloud computing environment, resource allocation is one of the major challenges in which resources are dynamically allocated among the end-users on demand basis without exceeding their resource capabilities and costs. This resource allocation model allocates the computing resources among the cloud users based on the users demand in cooperative cloud environment. This resource allocation model is similar to the model of [3] where resources are allocated based on the resource request and allocation. Here, authors try to use the same resource allocation model as proposed in [3] but in different environment, i.e. cooperative cloud environment where one cloud has not enough resources to satisfy the request of the cloud users. In this situation, two or more clouds cooperatively work together to satisfy the end-users requirements and maximizes their resource utilization efficiently to get benefited out of it.

3.1 System Model

Let us consider there are 'n' number of physical servers accessible in this cloud environment. Each computing server has m kinds of resources. The total capacity of all the servers can be represented in a capacity vector $C = (C_1^{(m)}, C_2^{(m)}, \ldots, C_j^{(m)}, \ldots, C_n^{(m)})$. There are several set of virtual machines that are used for computational work. Each virtual machine has three number of computing resources such as CPU, memory and storage. The detail configuration of each kind of virtual machine is denoted in Table 1 which is used as data set for our computation in resource allocation model. Each virtual machine incurred his certain prices as per its use which is specified in Table 1.

Cloud providers are categorized based on four types of VMs, and each type is denoted by the vector $\vec{v} = (\vec{v}1, \vec{v}2, \vec{v}3, \vec{v}4)$. The jobs submitted by the ith user are denoted as J_i which consists of several virtual machines with specific configuration as per the requirements of the user. These specific requirements may not be available for a single cloud. In this case, two or more cloud providers cooperatively work together to satisfy the user's requirements by sharing their resources among themselves to maximize their profit. The performance and satisfaction of the users will be enhanced when the required numbers of VMs are assigned to the jobs as per

Table 1 Types of virtual machines

VM type	CPU	Memory	Storage	Price
Small	1 × 1.6	1.75	0.22	1
Medium	2 × 1.6	3.5	0.48	1.3
Large	3 × 1.6	7	0.98	1.8
X Large	4 × 1.6	14	1.99	2

the requirements. On the other hand, the cloud providers cost will raise to create more number of VMs dynamically by cooperating among different cloud providers along with their service level agreements. So, cloud providers should dynamically take decision on the number of VMs assigned to each job when one cloud is not enough to provide it in the same time they will cooperatively share the resources among themselves by satisfying the service level agreements. Here, two basic definitions of resource request matrix and resource allocation matrix that are used in this paper are represented as follows.

Definition 1 (*Request Matrix*) The resources request by user can be defined by a resource request matrix denoted by R. Let R be a resource request matrix with $p \times q$ dimensions in which the rows indicate the VM types such as small, medium, large and extra large that each user needs for their computation, and column indicates the quantity of each resource types. This resource request matrix can be represented by Eq. 1.

$$R = \begin{pmatrix} \vec{r1} \\ \vec{r2} \\ \vdots \\ \vec{rp} \end{pmatrix} = \begin{pmatrix} r_{11} & \cdots & r_{1q} \\ \vdots & \ddots & \vdots \\ r_{p1} & \cdots & r_{pq} \end{pmatrix} \tag{1}$$

Definition 2 (*Allocation Matrix*) The resource allocation matrix denoted by $A^{(n)}$ of the p physical servers having n number of resources each can be described in Eq. 2. Let A be resource allocation matrix with $p \times q$ dimensions which indicate number of resources allocated to each server. Where $a_{ij}^{(n)}$ specifies the number of virtual machines allocated to each physical server depending upon the user's requirement. The resource allocation matrix can be represented by Eq. 2.

$$A^{(n)} = \begin{pmatrix} \vec{a}_1^n \\ \vec{a}_2^n \\ \vdots \\ \vec{a}_p^n \end{pmatrix} = \begin{pmatrix} a_{11}^{(n)} & \cdots & a_{1q}^{(n)} \\ \vdots & \ddots & \vdots \\ a_{p1}^{(n)} & \cdots & a_{pq}^{n} \end{pmatrix} \tag{2}$$

A resource allocation matrix A which specifies the collection of all possible resource allocation status of each cloud provider of the virtual machines based on the resource request matrix is represented in Eq. 3.

$$A = \left\{ A^{(CP1)}, A^{(CP2)}, \ldots, A^{(CPm)}, \ldots, A^{(CPp)} \right\} \tag{3}$$

In Fig. 1, the resource allocation model implementation along with the example is specified in which the resources are allocated to each physical server in cloud environment. Let us consider there are two cloud providers available in this cloud environment with certain capacity of each resource type such as number of CPUs available, amount of memory available, amount of storage available and the amount

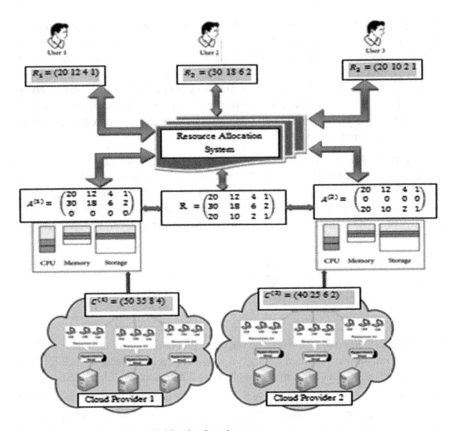

Fig. 1 Resource allocation model in cloud environment

of cost incurred as per uses. These two cloud providers' resource capacity vectors are represented as (50, 35, 8, 4) and (40, 25, 6, 2), respectively.

The resource request matrix of each user are represented in the R1, R2, ..., Rn individual vectors in which the resources like small VMs, medium VMs, large VMs and extra large VMs will be requested when VMs are created on the physical server. Suppose there are three cloud users' requests for three different types of VMs which can be represented as (20, 12, 4, 1), (30, 18, 6, 2) and (20, 10, 2, 1), respectively. Now in this decision-making process, resource allocation model will check the capacity of all cloud providers in data centre and analyse all the requests of the cloud user to produce the resource requirement matrix which is represented in Eq. 4.

$$R = \begin{pmatrix} 20 & 12 & 4 & 1 \\ 30 & 18 & 4 & 2 \\ 20 & 10 & 2 & 1 \end{pmatrix} \tag{4}$$

All these three requests of three users are neither served by the cloud provider 1 nor cloud provider 2. Cloud provider 1 can allocate resource for only user 1 and user 2 because resource requirement of all three users is greater than the capacity of cloud provider 1. So, allocation matrix of cloud provider 1 will be represented in Eq. 5. In this allocation matrix, it is clearly seen that cloud provider 1 is unable to satisfy the user 3 requirements.

$$
A^{(CP1)} = \begin{pmatrix} 20 & 12 & 4 & 1 \\ 30 & 18 & 4 & 2 \\ 0 & 0 & 0 & 0 \end{pmatrix}
\tag{5}
$$

Similarly, cloud provider 2 can allocate resource for only user 1 and user 3 because resource requirement of all three users is greater than the capacity of cloud provider 2. So, allocation matrix of cloud provider 2 will be represented in Eq. 6. In this allocation matrix, it is clearly seen that cloud provider 2 is unable to satisfy the user 2 requirements.

$$
A^{(CP2)} = \begin{pmatrix} 20 & 12 & 4 & 1 \\ 0 & 0 & 0 & 0 \\ 20 & 10 & 2 & 1 \end{pmatrix}
\tag{6}
$$

As a result, neither cloud provider 1 or cloud provider 2 can satisfy the requirements of three users which are specified in the resource request matrix in Eq. 4. This may be the situation in which the requirements of the cloud users may not be fulfilled by the single cloud only. In this case, two or more clouds cooperatively work together to satisfy all users requirement.

To address the aforesaid problem, now resource allocation model in cooperative cloud environment [10] is used. Here, we consider two types of cloud providers called primary cloud provider (PCP) having enough number of resources which provide its resources to the other cloud providers, and another cloud provider called secondary cloud provider (SCP) who borrowed resources from the primary cloud providers due to its deficiency of resources due to high demand in case of certain scenarios. A cloud provider can be at the same time both PCP and SCP. A PCP initiates a cooperative environment when it realizes that at a certain situation in the future it may not be able to provide services to its users due to its high requirements. As a result, PCP dynamically increases its own infrastructure capabilities by asking for additional VM resources from other SCPs for a certain amount of time. At the same time, each PCP needs to ensure its quality of service requirements precise in the service level agreement (SLA) contracts with the users. The main objective is to maximize the PCP as well as SCP revenues and maximize their resource utilization while minimizing the utilization cost of the VM resources provided by the SCPs. As a result, it is essential to design a model for the resource allocation of VMs by supplying among CPs. Such a mechanism needs to be eventually designed for dynamic allocation and also ensure mutual benefits so that the cloud providers are also encouraged to join or form cooperative platform.

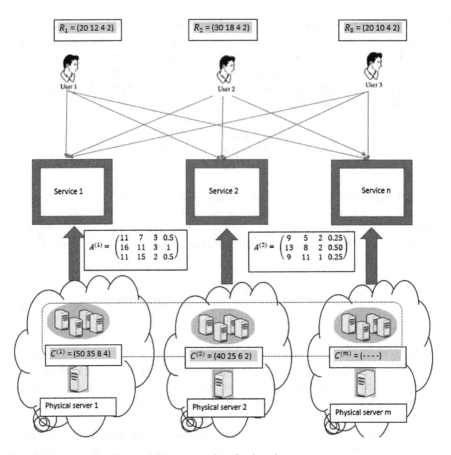

Fig. 2 Resource allocation model in cooperative cloud environments

In Fig. 2, the resource allocation model implementation along with example is specified in which the resources are allocated to each physical server in cooperative cloud environment to address the aforesaid problem. This cooperative cloud concept plays into role when one cloud may not have enough resources to satisfy all the requirements of the users, then two or more cloud providers cooperatively work together to satisfy the requirements of the users and in the same time they also maximize their resource utilization based on the SLA.

In Fig. 2, the cooperative cloud environment is established between three cloud providers based on certain SLA. Every user requests for certain type of VMs to run its task as per their requirements. Multidimensional resources are required for execution of a task or job, and these requirements differ from job to job.

To achieve the efficient resource utilization in cooperative cloud environment, the resources should be distributed normally among the cloud providers in which it makes an optimal allocation system between the providers which satisfy the fairness and efficiency. In cooperative cloud environment, cloud users may have mixed requests for different resource types as per their need. The resources are assigned to the cloud users in as per their needs and accessibility. Each cloud user has highest portion share of the total capacity among different resources which is called leading share. The main objective of this resource allocation system is considered to be equalizing the leading share of each cloud users.

Let us assume that the required resource matrix 'R'. The total number of virtual machines required for all the physical servers are $C = \left(\sum_n C_1^{(n)}, \sum_n C_2^{(n)}, \ldots, \right.$ $\left. \sum_n C_j^{(n)} \sum_n C_k^{(n)} \right)$. It is the first requirement to normalize the requirement matrix. The normalized matrix can be defined as N, which is represented in Eq. 7.

$$N = \begin{pmatrix} N_{11} & \cdots & N_{1k} \\ \vdots & \ddots & \vdots \\ N_{s1} & \cdots & N_{sk} \end{pmatrix} = \begin{pmatrix} \frac{r_{11}}{C_1} & \cdots & \frac{r_{12}}{C_2} \\ \vdots & \ddots & \vdots \\ \frac{r_{s1}}{C_1} & \cdots & \frac{r_{sk}}{C_k} \end{pmatrix} \tag{7}$$

The major portion of any kind of resources allocated to the user is known as dominant share of a user. Let us consider the scenario in Fig. 2, the total amount of resources available on these two cloud providers are $C = C_1^{(1)} + C_2^{(2)} = (90, 60, 14, 8)$ and the resource request matrix is presented in Eq. 4. The normalized matrix [3] can be represented in Eq. 8.

$$N = \begin{pmatrix} \frac{2}{9} & \frac{1}{5} & \frac{2}{7} & \frac{1}{8} \\ \frac{1}{3} & \frac{3}{10} & \frac{3}{7} & \frac{1}{4} \\ \frac{2}{9} & \frac{1}{6} & \frac{1}{7} & \frac{1}{8} \end{pmatrix} \tag{8}$$

Now according to normalized resource matrix, we get new allocation matrix for each cloud providers. In this allocation matrix, cloud provider 1 can allocate the resources to all users. The optimal allocation matrix for cloud provider 1 is represented in Eq. 9.

$$A^{*(CP1)} = \begin{pmatrix} 11 & 7 & 3 & 0.5 \\ 16 & 11 & 3 & 1 \\ 11 & 15 & 2 & 0.5 \end{pmatrix} \tag{9}$$

Similarly, the allocation matrix for cloud provider 2 is represented in Eq. 10.

$$A^{*(CP2)} = \begin{pmatrix} 9 & 5 & 2 & 0.25 \\ 13 & 8 & 2 & 0.50 \\ 9 & 11 & 1 & 0.25 \end{pmatrix} \tag{10}$$

Now, all three users get resources from cloud providers and they can get leftover resources from same physical server without changing cloud provider using cooperative model of allocation.

4 Resource Utilization

In this resource allocation model, the main objective is to maximize the resource utilization [11] and minimize the expenses. Suppose, in this allocation model, n users want to share m number of computational resources. Each resource type R_j has a fixed price p_j as per their execution time and its type of VMs used is given in Table 2.

Let A the allocation matrix be a $s \times k$ dimensional matrix where rows state the VM type that each user needs and columns explain the amount of different types of resources.

$$A^{(CP1)} = \begin{pmatrix} 20 & 12 & 4 & 1 \\ 30 & 18 & 4 & 2 \\ 0 & 0 & 0 & 0 \end{pmatrix}$$

From allocation matrix, another two $n \times m$ matrixes are obtained called total execution time (TET) matrix and expense matrix (E). The entry t_{ij} of TET is the turnaround time it takes for resource R_j to complete the task. The TET matrix will be calculated as

$$TET(A^{(CP1)}) = \begin{pmatrix} 20 \times 0.8 & 12 \times 0.4 & 4 \times 0.2 & 1 \times 0.1 \\ 30 \times 0.8 & 18 \times 0.4 & 4 \times 0.2 & 2 \times 0.1 \\ 0 & 0 & 0 & 0 \end{pmatrix}$$

$$TET(A^{(CP1)}) = \begin{pmatrix} 16 & 4.8 & 0.8 & 0.1 \\ 24 & 7.2 & 0.8 & 0.2 \\ 0 & 0 & 0 & 0 \end{pmatrix} \tag{11}$$

The entry e_{ij} of E is the expense the user pays for resource R_j to complete the task. The expense matrix E will be calculated as

Table 2 Price and execution time in virtual machine

Type	Execution time	Price in $
Small	0.8	1
Medium	0.4	1.3
Large	0.2	1.8
X Large	0.1	2

$$E = \begin{pmatrix} 16 \times 1 & 4.8 \times 1.3 & 8 \times 1.8 & 0.1 \times 2 \\ 24 \times 1 & 7.2 \times 1.3 & 8 \times 1.8 & 0.2 \times 2 \\ 0 & 0 & 0 & 0 \end{pmatrix}$$

$$E = \begin{pmatrix} 16 & 6.24 & 1.44 & 0.2 \\ 24 & 9.36 & 1.44 & 0.4 \\ 0 & 0 & 0 & 0 \end{pmatrix}$$

(12)

Let w_t and w_e denote the weights of total execution time and expense, then the utilization can be computed by Eq. 13.

$$u_i(a)_i = \frac{1}{w_t \circ \max_{t_{ij}} \{t_{ij}\} + w_e \; w_t \circ \sum_j e_{ij}}$$

(13)

To simplify the computation, let us assume $w_t = w_e = 0.5$; then the utilization is

$$u_1(a)_1 = \frac{1}{0.5 \times (16 + (16 + 6.24 + 1.44 + 0.2))} \approx 0.05015$$

$$u_2(a)_2 = \frac{1}{0.5 \times (24 + (24 + 9.36 + 1.44 + 0.4))} \approx 0.0337$$

$$u_3(a)_3 = 0$$

Similarly for $A^{(CP2)} = \begin{pmatrix} 20 & 12 & 4 & 1 \\ 0 & 0 & 0 & 0 \\ 20 & 10 & 2 & 1 \end{pmatrix}$, the utilization is as follows

$$u_1(a)_1 = \frac{1}{0.5 \times (16 + (16 + 6.24 + 1.44 + 0.2))} \approx 0.05015$$

$$u_2(a)_2 = 0$$

$$u_3(a)_3 = \frac{1}{0.5 \times (16 + (16 + 5.20 + 0.72 + 0.2))} \approx 0.0524$$

Similarly for cooperative cloud environment and as per optimal resource allocation matrix of the cloud provider 1 is $A^{*(CP1)} = \begin{pmatrix} 11 & 7 & 3 & 0.5 \\ 16 & 11 & 3 & 1 \\ 11 & 15 & 2 & 0.5 \end{pmatrix}$, the utilization of cloud provider 1 is as follows.

$$u_1(a)_1 = \frac{1}{0.5 \times (8.8 + (8.8 + 3.64 + 1.08 + 0.1))} \approx 0.0892$$

$$u_2(a)_2 = \frac{1}{0.5 \times (12.8 + (12.8 + 5.72 + 1.08 + 0.2))} \approx 0.0613$$

$$u_3(a)_3 = \frac{1}{0.5 \times (8.8 + (8.8 + 7.80 + 0.72 + 0.1))} \approx 0.0762$$

Similarly for cooperative cloud environment and as per optimal resource allocation matrix of the cloud provider 2 is $A^{*(CP2)} = \begin{pmatrix} 9 & 5 & 2 & 0.25 \\ 13 & 8 & 2 & 0.50 \\ 9 & 11 & 1 & 0.25 \end{pmatrix}$, the utilization of cloud provider 1 is as follows.

$$u_1(a)_1 = \frac{1}{0.5 \times (7.2 + (7.2 + 2.6 + 0.72 + 0.05))} \approx 0.0706$$

$$u_2(a)_2 = \frac{1}{0.5 \times (10.4 + (10.4 + 4.2 + 0.72 + 0.05))} \approx 0.0776$$

$$u_3(a)_3 = \frac{1}{0.5 \times (7.2 + (7.2 + 5.7 + 0.36 + 0.1))} \approx 0.0587$$

So now we can see the difference in utilization between normal resource allocation and cooperative resource allocation. In normal resource allocation, two user requests are satisfied, whereas in cooperative cloud resource allocation model, all the three users' requests are satisfied. So, it clearly proved that the cooperative resource allocation model provides the better user satisfaction and resource utilization than normal resource allocation model.

5 Results and Analysis

This section represents an evaluation of the resource allocation model in the cooperative cloud environment and focuses on how resource utilization is enhanced in cooperative cloud environment than normal cloud environment. The assessment of this model is made by implementation of this model, and simulation shows that the utilization in cooperative cloud environment is better and perfectly distributed among all the cloud users than the normal cloud environment.

5.1 Experimental Set-up

The experimental set-up to evaluate the performance of resource allocation model consists of following specifications. There are three types of resources considered in this experimental set-up that includes CPU, memory and disk storage. We consider cloud provider offering four types of VM instances. Here, we consider four types of VM instances VM = {VM1, VM2, VM3, VM4} which represents the small, medium, large and extra large VM instances, respectively. These four types of VMs that are used in this model are specified in Table 1, and its each VM types along with its pricing model is specified in Table 2.

5.2 Results

In our experiment, we take four different types of resource requests from the user side which are specified as (20, 12, 4, 1), (30, 18, 6, 2) and (20,10, 2, 1), with the first number in each request indicates the number of small VMs required, the second number indicates the number of medium VMs required, and so on. This model also considers two cloud providers with capacity (50, 35, 8, 4) and (40, 25, 6, 2) which are presented. The capacity vector is represented as $C^1 = (50, 35, 8, 4)$ and $C^2 = (40, 25, 6, 2)$ in resource allocation model.

When three users request for four different types of resource to cloud provider 1, resource allocation system checks the capacity states of cloud provider 1 in data centre and analyses that resource requirement of all three users is greater than the capacity of cloud provider 1. So, this allocation model allocates the VMs to the user 1 and user 2 but user 3 does not get the resource due to insufficient resource. Figure 3 represents the cloud provider 1 unable to provide the required number of resources to the user 3.

Similarly when three users request for four different types of resource to the cloud provider 2, resource allocation system checks the capacity states of the cloud provider 2 in data centre and analyses that resource requirement of all three users is greater than the capacity of the cloud provider 2. So, this allocation model allocates the VMs to the user 1 and user 3 but user 2 does not get any resource due to resource deficiency. Figure 4 represents the cloud provider 2 unable to provide the required number of resources to the user 2.

In this resource allocation model, cloud provider 1 or cloud provider 2 cannot allocate the resources simultaneously to all users at a time. So, to overcome this problem, we use cooperative resource allocation model in cloud environment. In this cooperative resource allocation model, cloud provider 1 dynamically and transparently enlarges its own virtualization technologies by asking for further VM resources with the cloud provider 2 for a specific period of time based on the SLA.

In previous existing model, capacity of cloud provider 1 and cloud provider 2 was $C^1 = (50, 35, 8, 4)$ and $C^2 = (40, 25, 6, 2)$, respectively, but by using

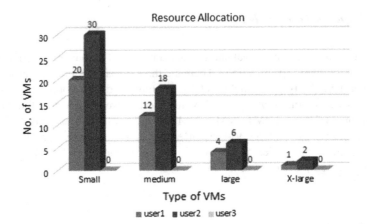

Fig. 3 Resource allocation for cloud provider 1 in cloud environment

Fig. 4 Resource allocation for cloud provider 2 in cloud environment

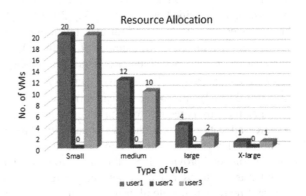

cooperative model for resource allocation, the capacity vector of service provider becomes the summation of both cloud providers. It is represented as $C = C_1^{(1)} + C_2^{(2)} = (90, 60, 14, 8)$.

Now cloud provider can allocate the resources to all three users using normalized matrix given in Fig. 5. In cooperative model, cloud provider can provide the resource to all users without enlarging its own physical infrastructure and all users can get resources from same cloud provider without swapping to other cloud providers.

5.3 Resource Utilization

This model considers that three users share four different types of computational resources for their computation. Each resource has their fixed price for usages and

Fig. 5 Resource allocation in cooperative cloud environment

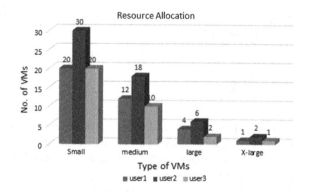

execution time according to its capacity in given Table 2. The execution time and pricing model are similar to the ones used by Microsoft Azure. The total execution time (TET) matrix and expense matrix (E) are obtained from allocation matrix of cloud provider 1, cloud provider 2 and cooperative cloud provider. The entry of TET is the turnaround time it takes for resource R_j to complete its task. Similarly, the entry of E is the expense of the user that pays for resource R_j to complete the task.

In resource allocation model, we saw that cloud provider 1 allocates the resources to the user 1 and user 2 but user 3 does not get the resource for its execution. The TET and E of user 1 and user 2 get some values but user 3 gets null values. So, utilization will be 0.05012, 0.0337 and 0 for cloud provider 1. Similarly for cloud provider 2, resource allocation model allocates the resources to the user 1 and user 3 but user 2 does not get the resource. The TET and E of user 1 and user 3 get some values but user 2 gets null values. So, utilization will be 0.05012, 0 and 0.0524 for cloud provider 2.

In cooperative cloud environment, this allocation model allocates the resources to the user 1, user 2 and user 3. The TET and E for user 1, user 2 and user 3 are assigned with some values. So, utilization will be 0.05012, 0.0337 and 0.0524 for cooperative cloud service provider which is represented in Fig. 6. So, we can

Fig. 6 Resource utilization in cooperative cloud environment

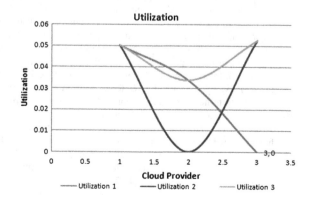

analyse that cooperative resource allocation model gives better result compared to previous existing model.

6 Conclusion

In this work, the resource allocation problem in cloud computing using cooperative resource allocation model with normalized matrix was investigated. This model is compared with resource allocation model of normal cloud environment. This work not only supports resource allocation problems in cooperative cloud environment for users, but also optimizes the resources in most efficient manner for each physical server. In future work, this work can be modelled by using some optimization techniques to maximize the resource utilization and minimize the expenses.

References

1. R Buyya, CS Yeo, S Venugopal, J Broberg, I Brandic, "Cloud computing and emerging IT platforms: vision, hype, and reality for delivering computing as the 5th utility" Futur. Gener. Comput. Syst. 25(6), 599–616 (2009).
2. I. Foster, Y. Zhao, I. Raicu, and S. Lu. Cloud computing and grid computing 360-degree compared, In Proceedings of Grid Computing Environments Workshop, pages 1–10, 2008.
3. Xu, Xin, and Huiqun Yu. "A game theory approach to fair and efficient resource allocation in cloud computing." Mathematical Problems in Engineering 2014 (2014).
4. Endo, Patricia Takako, Andre Vitor de Almeida Palhares, Nadilma Nunes Pereira, Glauco Estacio Goncalves, Djamel Sadok, Judith Kelner, Bob Melander, and Jan-Erik Mangs. "Resource allocation for distributed cloud: concepts and research challenges." IEEE network 25, no. 4 (2011).
5. Sarkhel, Preeta, Himansu Das, and Lalit K. Vashishtha. "Task-Scheduling Algorithms in Cloud Environment." In Computational Intelligence in Data Mining, pp. 553–562. Springer, Singapore, 2017.
6. Huang, Chenn-Jung, Chih-Tai Guan, Heng-Ming Chen, Yu-Wu Wang, Shun-Chih Chang, Ching-Yu Li, and Chuan-Hsiang Weng. "An adaptive resource management scheme in cloud computing." Engineering Applications of Artificial Intelligence 26, no. 1 (2013): 382–389.
7. Tsai, Jinn-Tsong, Jia-Cen Fang, and Jyh-Horng Chou. "Optimized task scheduling and resource allocation on cloud computing environment using improved differential evolution algorithm." Computers & Operations Research 40, no. 12 (2013): 3045–3055.
8. Kar, Ipsita, RN Ramakant Parida, and Himansu Das. "Energy aware scheduling using genetic algorithm in cloud data centers." In Electrical, Electronics, and Optimization Techniques (ICEEOT), International Conference on, pp. 3545–3550. IEEE, 2016.
9. Pillai, Parvathy S., and Shrisha Rao. "Resource allocation in cloud computing using the uncertainty principle of game theory." IEEE Systems Journal 10, no. 2 (2016): 637–648.
10. Hassan, Mohammad Mehedi, M. Shamim Hossain, AM Jehad Sarkar, and Eui-Nam Huh. "Cooperative game-based distributed resource allocation in horizontal dynamic cloud federation platform." Information Systems Frontiers 16, no. 4 (2014): 523–542.
11. Wei, Guiyi, Athanasios V. Vasilakos, Yao Zheng, and Naixue Xiong. "A game-theoretic method of fair resource allocation for cloud computing services." The journal of supercomputing 54, no. 2 (2010): 252–269.

12. Das, Himansu, Gouri Sankar Panda, Bhagaban Muduli, and Pradeep Kumar Rath. "The complex network analysis of power grid: a case study of the West Bengal power network." In Intelligent Computing, Networking, and Informatics, pp. 17–29. Springer, New Delhi, 2014.
13. Das, Himansu, Sanjay Kumar Mishra, and Diptendu Sinha Roy. "The topological structure of the Odisha power grid: a complex network analysis." IJMCA 1, no. 1 (2013): 012–016.
14. Das, Himansu, and D. S. Roy. "A grid computing service for power system monitoring." International Journal of Computer Applications 62, no. 20 (2013).
15. Das, Himansu, A. K. Jena, P. K. Rath, B. Muduli, and S. R. Das. "Grid computing-based performance analysis of power system: a graph theoretic approach." In Intelligent Computing, Communication and Devices, pp. 259–266. Springer, New Delhi, 2015.
16. Panigrahi, Chhabi Rani, Mayank Tiwary, Bibudhendu Pati, and Himansu Das. "Big Data and Cyber Foraging: Future Scope and Challenges." In Techniques and Environments for Big Data Analysis, pp. 75–100. Springer International Publishing, 2016.
17. KHK Reddy, Himansu Das, D S Roy, "A Data Aware Scheme for Scheduling Big-Data Applications with SAVANNA Hadoop", in Futures of Network, CRC Press, 2017.

Author Index

© Springer Nature Singapore Pte Ltd. 2018
P. K. Pattnaik et al. (eds.), *Progress in Computing, Analytics and Networking*,
Advances in Intelligent Systems and Computing 710,
https://doi.org/10.1007/978-981-10-7871-2

Printed in the United States
By Bookmasters